TEACHING
ENGLISH AS A
SECOND
LANGUAGE
*A Book
of
Readings*

Teaching English as a Second Language

A Book of Readings

Harold B. Allen
UNIVERSITY OF MINNESOTA

Russell N. Campbell
UNIVERSITY OF CALIFORNIA, LOS ANGELES

Second Edition

McGRAW-HILL INTERNATIONAL BOOK COMPANY

		MONTREAL
		NEW DELHI
		PANAMA
NEW YORK	JOHANNESBURG	RIO DE JANEIRO
ST. LOUIS	KUALA LUMPUR	SINGAPORE
SAN FRANCISCO	LONDON	SYDNEY
DÜSSELDORF	MEXICO	TORONTO

TEACHING ENGLISH AS A SECOND LANGUAGE:
A BOOK OF READINGS

Library of Congress Cataloging in Publication Data

Allen, Harold Byron, date ed.
    Teaching English as a Second Language.

    Includes bibliographical references.
    1. English language—Study and teaching—Foreign
students—Addresses, essays, lectures.
I. Campbell, Russell N., joint ed. II. Title.
PE1128.A2A38 1972 420'.7   71-38733
ISBN 0-07-001071-4

1234567890 DODO 798765432

This book was set in Theme by Allen-Wayne,
and printed and bound by R. R. Donnelley and Sons, Inc.
The designer was Allen-Wayne.
The editor was Winifred M. Davis.
Alice Cohen supervised production.

Contents

Foreword

For this second edition the *raison d'être* is like that of the first. It appears in these excerpts from the first foreword:

"This collection has one ultimate purpose: to help everyone now teaching or preparing to teach English to those for whom English is not the first language.

"Today such a teacher may be tutoring one foreign student in a comfortable living room, drilling twenty adults in a language laboratory, attempting to have repetition practice in a classroom filled with seventy secondary school pupils, or working on single sounds with a group of fifteen elementary school children. He may be in a university classroom in Ann Arbor, an elementary school in Texas or Florida, a lecture hall in Liverpool, a secondary school in Cairo, or a one-room village school in Ghana—indeed, he may be in some kind of school in almost any country in the world.

"But few such teachers, or even those preparing to become such teachers, have ready access to the rich information and insights to be found in the writings of the many distinguished leaders who have drawn upon their own thinking and experience to provide help for their present and future colleagues. . . .

"I believe that help can be found in such articles as this book contains. This help is not often in the form of lesson plans and practical suggestions that can be turned to account when the next class meets. Rather, it is to be found in the widening and the deepening of the base of theory and knowledge upon which the teacher must stand. Such widening may result from applying to one's own teaching the principles underlying a specific description of practice or technique. . . . This collection, then, can supplement a textbook by making it possible for a teacher to take advantage of the experience of others by applying them to his own situation. . . .

"Certainly it is not to be desired that any one theory, any one approach, or any one system be prescribed throughout the world, if indeed that were possible. But it may be hoped that the sharing of divergent points of view and the dissemination of information about varying methods and techniques will accelerate rather than hinder the general improvement that the world situation so urgently needs. To that end this book is dedicated."

What was said then is still true, and the need for help still exists throughout the world.

Abroad the demand for English and for English teachers, particularly for nationals trained to teach English in their own countries, has increased rather than decreased. Two recent conferences are representative of many developments. In May, 1969, a conference in Cairo brought together fifty representatives from ten Arabic-speaking nations to consider the preparation of teachers of English in the Arab world and the need for research in teaching English to Arab speakers. In June, a month later, a conference in Singapore, locally sponsored but supported by the British Council and the U.S. government, brought together English-teaching specialists for a similar purpose but with respect to the situation in southeast Asia and the south Pacific nations. In the developing countries of Africa the call for English teachers is urgent, and in Latin America the demand has been sustained.

At home, the rapid expansion of concern with the teaching of English to the Spanish-speaking population and to Indian children has likewise brought into high relief the need for teachers professionally trained in the discipline of second-language teaching. Hence since the first edition of this book there have sprung up several new teacher-training programs as well as supplementary in-service projects and workshops supported under the recent Bilingual Education Act (1967) or under other federal authorization.

A powerful impetus toward professionalization of this young discipline came from the creation of professional organizations. In the United States, Teachers of English to Speakers of Other Languages was formed in 1966. Acronymed as TESOL, it now has its own excellent journal, the *TESOL Quarterly;* its annual conventions and the journal are fruitful media for interchange and communication. In England a sister organization, the National Association of Teachers of English as a Foreign Language, was formed in 1967.

All these and related developments make more important the help that such an anthology as this can provide to teachers and prospective teachers. To increase the usefulness of this volume the senior editor, who alone had been responsible for the first edition, sought and fortunately obtained the collaboration of Russell N. Campbell as one much more immediately in touch with the actual classroom full of prospective teachers of English as a second language. He is almost entirely responsible for the many changes that appear in this edition.

More than half of the original articles, excellent as many of them still are, have been replaced by other articles in order to update the thinking on a given topic or to make the collection better balanced. The sectional arrangement has been altered, so that relationships within the TESL field are now more clearly shown. One Part has been devoted entirely to current controversial issues.

An innovation proposed by Campbell is the inclusion of brief study questions and their inclusion before an article instead of after it. So placed, he has found, they are much more likely to stimulate attention to the salient points of an article than if they are relegated to the easily-ignored final position.

The question of appending a comprehensive bibliography was reopened but the decision again was to omit it. Many of the articles themselves have relevant bibliographies and it seems redundant to duplicate, for the sake of comprehensiveness, the current bibliographies available from the Center for Applied Linguistics and the American Council on the Teaching of Foreign Languages, to say nothing of the extraordinarily useful *English Teaching Abstracts*.

Customary, and for us by no means perfunctory, is the recognition of the courtesy extended by both writers and publishers in granting the right to reprint these articles. We are most grateful, and certainly our colleagues in the profession must also feel deep appreciation for their generosity. Specific acknowledgement appears with each article.

HAROLD B. ALLEN
RUSSELL N. CAMPBELL

*Part
One*

*Theories
and
Approaches*

Overview

*A*lthough some of the articles in Part 1 look ahead to the classroom applications of Part 2, all have a primary concern with a substratum of theory. Anthony's opening article may serve as an introduction to both parts because of his definitions of terms common to both theories and methods. Anthony's assumptions, it should be noted, are derived from the structuralist school, with its insistence upon the uniqueness of the structure of any given language and upon the behavioral view of language as a set of habits. He nevertheless anticipates an important characteristic of transformational generative theory in recognizing that descriptions of the same language may vary according to the level of structure being described.

Wardhaugh, using Anthony's earlier paper as an original point of reference but referring discreetly to subsequent innovations in linguistic thinking and in psychology, describes more precisely the adhesive relationship that should exist between consistent ESL (English as a Second Language) theory and actual classroom techniques and practice. But both approach and practice, he declares in light of current cognitive psychology, should be more firmly oriented toward the student as a learner in a communicative situation rather than toward the teacher.

Bolinger, a linguist and also a foreign-language teacher, draws upon his experience and his orientation in viewing rather coolly the current linguistic ferment. He believes that contemporary generative linguists who are not polemic have genuine contributions to make to foreign language teaching. Similarly, the foreign language teacher who is not stubbornly doctrinaire in adherence to a given "method" can find much in linguistic theory to be incorporated into his own practice. Bolinger, in other words, is a pragmatist who declines to throw out all structural values simply because a new linguistic theory offers other values and different insights. John B. Carroll, a psychologist, espoused a somewhat similar position more recently, when in a still unpublished paper presented at the 1971 TESOL convention, he foresaw for the future a higher synthesis of structural and generative linguistics. "I believe," he said, "that the opposition between rule-governed behavior and habits is false and specious." Despite Bolinger's disclaimer of the need for an underlying theory for foreign language teaching, such a synthesis might well offer a basis for more productive educational research in TESL.

Like Wardhaugh, Newmark wants to see ESL theory and practice oriented toward the learner rather than toward the teacher. Without defining or providing an example, he argues for the learning of "chunks" of language, instead of what he finds to be only repeating and modifying pattern practice sentences divorced from actual communication. Some ESL teachers may feel that Newmark has set up straw men by exaggerating the weaknesses he decries, but his proposal itself is consistent with the trend toward motivated communication almost at the outset in a beginning course.

An article by Gatenby, a long-time professional British ESL teacher, is deliberately brought in at this point. Writing without taking account of American structuralism (in which he does not take much stock) and prior to generative grammar (which probably would also have failed to enchant him), Gatenby usefully observes that sound theoretical principles and practices of second-language learning are not recent innovations. Although it is now held to be related to current linguistic or psychological theory, some of the thinking offered in articles in this section and elsewhere was obviously anticipated—on purely empirical grounds—many years ago by earlier teachers. A full awareness of how much present-day ideas about learning a foreign language have their roots in the past can be gained from the recent comprehensive overview, *25 Centuries of Language Teaching* by Louis G. Kelly (Rowley, Mass.: Newbury House Publishers, 1969). As Gatenby suggests, it would appear that some ESL specialists have busied themselves in re-inventing the wheel.

Just as the ESL teacher concerned with basic linguistic theory finds that at least two schools of thought, the structural and the transformational generativist, relate now to his professional discipline, he also finds correspondingly that two schools of thought in psychology, the behavioral and the cognitive, compete for his professional acceptance. Like Bolinger with linguistic theory, Chastain believes that at present the teacher should not unreservedly accept the teachings of either school but, rather, should be eclectic in choosing from each what is best for particular students and specific purposes.

Mrs. Lakoff, however, as a transformationalist linguist, finds in transformational theory and its applications in ESL so much of value that she is convinced that even in its present tentative state it enables the teacher to do a great deal that he cannot do through use of only structural grammatical theory. She does not reject the use of pattern drill for certain purposes, but she insists that transformational grammar has much more to offer. In taking this position she also accepts an earlier pedagogical view that the learner has the right and the need to receive rational explanations about the second language while he is learning it; however, she does not warn that a teacher may easily be tempted to substitute explanation for actual teaching. Like other generativists Mrs. Lakoff, positing rules upon her intuitive control of her idiolect, can asterisk as ungrammatical a sentence which presumably does not occur in that idiolect but actually could occur elsewhere. Sentence 21, for example, may well strike a native speaker as much more plausible than Sentence 20, yet she holds the former ungrammatical. English-as-a-second-language teachers will need care in working with this concept of grammaticality lest their students become seriously confused. Mrs. Lakoff does, however, provide some help by averring that both the personal and the situational context must often be taken into account in determining what is grammatical and what is ungrammatical.

1

APPROACH, METHOD, AND TECHNIQUE

EDWARD M. ANTHONY

Given Anthony's definition of "approach," do you hold, or do you know of, assumptions about (a) the nature of language, and (b) the nature of language teaching and learning that differ from those listed in his sample set of assumptions characteristic of the audio-lingual approach?

Given the assumptions of the aural-oral approach, or your modification of it, what would be an example of *non-contradictory methodological decision* for some group of ESL students known to you?

Of what import is Anthony's three-way distinction in teacher evaluation?

Over the years, teachers of language have adopted, adapted, invented, and developed a bewildering variety of terms which describe the activities in which they engage and the beliefs which they hold. As one who has been concerned with the teaching of English as a foreign language for almost twenty years, I have sometimes found it taxing to beat my way through the undergrowth of overlapping terminology that surrounds this field. We talk and write of the aural approach and the audio-lingual method; the translation approach; the direct method and the mimic-and-memorize method; pattern practice techniques; grammar method; and even the natural or "nature" method of language pedagogy. For my own work, I have found it necessary and fruitful to impose system on three terms in the language-teaching lexicon. Perhaps it will be useful for the readers of *E.L.T.* to consider three new definitions.

It would seem a worthwhile endeavour to attempt to limit the use of some of the more common terms when we talk professionally about the concepts of language teaching. If, disagreeing about ways to teach language, we can refer to a framework about which we *do* agree, and focus clearly on the distinctions between views, we may be able to determine in what areas advocates of various language-teaching systems employ the same terms differently, and where we use differing terminology in what are essentially the same situations. We might well find out that language teachers do not differ among themselves as much as has

Reprinted by permission from *English Language Teaching*, 17 (January, 1963), 63–67. Professor Anthony is chairman of the Department of Linguistics at the University of Pittsburgh.

been heretofore supposed. The definitions below are therefore presented as a pedagogical filing system within which many ideas, opposing or compatible, may be filed.

The trio of terms which I am attempting to re-locate in the scheme of definitions are *approach, method,* and *technique.* The arrangement is hierarchical. The organizational key is that *techniques* carry out a *method* which is consistent with an *approach.* The definitions are offered with some diffidence—there are many roads to Nirvana, and this is certainly not the only route. Not every aspect of language teaching has been referred to this framework. It is quite possible that modifications and refinements are desirable.

First, let us take up the term *approach.* I view an approach—any approach—as a set of correlative assumptions dealing with the nature of language and the nature of language teaching and learning. An approach is axiomatic. It describes the nature of the subject matter to be taught. It states a point of view, a philosophy, an article of faith—something which one believes but cannot necessarily prove. It is often unarguable except in terms of the effectiveness of the methods which grow out of it.

Let me illustrate by citing the essentials of the aural-oral approach as I see them, not to advocate them particularly at this time, but only to exemplify what is meant by *approach.* First, here is a list of linguistic assumptions:

1. Language is human, aural-oral, and symbolically meaningful.

2. Any given language is structured uniquely. This can also be stated negatively: no two languages are structured alike.

3. The structure of a language can be discovered, and usefully and systematically described, although such descriptions may differ at various levels and for various purposes.

If language is accepted as aural-oral, an obvious corollary to these assumptions is that writing is a secondary manifestation and ultimately speech-based. I must, however, immediately add that this is not necessarily a statement of the relative importance of speech and writing. One can, of course, argue that writing, often more deliberate and thoughtful, and always more permanent than speech, is therefore more important.

The second type of assumptions—those that relate to language teaching and learning—take the form of three priority statements, one procedural statement, and a comparison statement, all arising out of the linguistic assumptions.

1. Primary manifestations (the aural-oral aspects) should be taught before secondary (reading and writing). Understanding the spoken language is taught more efficiently before oral production, and is indeed a first step toward production.[1]

2. The secondary manifestations (the reading and writing aspects) should be

---

[1] Note that no statement is made concerning the size of the portion of the spoken language which should be presented before oral production commences.

taught in the stated order, since graphic symbols must be seen before they are produced, and thus reading, in a sense, is actually a first step in learning to write.

3. Other uses of language—tertiary in this scheme—such as literary and artistic manifestations, pedagogically also follow reception/production order. It is perhaps doubtful if foreign students of English should be instructed in the production of literary English.

4. Our procedural assumption states that (a) languages are habits, (b) habits are established by repetition, and (c) languages must be taught through repetition of some sort.

5. An assumption that is not always accepted, and about which there is currently much discussion, revolves around the usefulness of bilingual comparison: each language is uniquely structured, as we have said. It is therefore beneficial to compare the learner's language with the target language in order to isolate those features of the target language which can be predicted, with a fair degree of accuracy, to cause trouble for the learner.

Let us move on to our second definition—of *method*. *Method* is an overall plan for the orderly presentation of language material, no part of which contradicts, and all of which is based upon, the selected *approach*. An *approach* is axiomatic, a *method* is procedural.

Within one approach, there can be many methods. Several factors influence the orderly presentation of language to students. The order will be influenced by the nature of the student's language as compared to English. Teaching English to Hindi speakers and teaching English to speakers of Chinese differ methodologically. The age of the student, his cultural background, and his previous experience with English modify the method employed. The experience of the teacher and his level of English mastery are significant. The goal of a course must be considered—whether it is aimed at reading, fluency in speech, inculcating translation skill—all these shape methodology. The place of English in the curriculum and the time available during a given course are not unimportant.

As can be seen from the above, textbooks ought to be written within methodological limitations.

It may be of value to compare briefly two methods which share an approach. The approach, again, is the aural-oral. The methods are frequently called *mim-mem* (mimic-memorize), and *pattern practice*. Both share the factor of goal—they aim at automatic oral production coupled with skill in understanding the stream of speech. They each function best under intensive course conditions. Each is primarily for adults, and neither *per se* assumes previous language learning experience. The order of presentation differs.

The mim-mem method begins with a situation—greetings perhaps, or food and meals, or getting a room at a hotel. The student must mimic a native speaker, real or recorded, and remember a rather large number of useful sentences within the situation. From the memorized sentences are drawn certain structures, phonological and grammatical, for particular emphasis and drill. The choice of these structures ideally depends on the result of a bilingual analysis and description. There is nothing in the mim-mem method which contradicts the assumptions which make up the aural-oral approach.

On the other hand, the pattern practice method ideally uses bilingual comparison at the very beginning, and starts with grammatical and phonological structures chosen with the results of a bilingual comparison in mind. These structures are drilled and built up into a situation through the addition of lexical items. Again, there is nothing here which contradicts the aural-oral approach. Both methods have been used with success. Both lie within the same approach, yet each has distinctive features.

The last term which will be discussed is *technique*. A technique is implementational—that which actually takes place in a classroom. It is a particular trick, stratagem, or contrivance used to accomplish an immediate objective. Techniques must be consistent with a *method*, and therefore in harmony with an *approach* as well.

Techniques depend on the teacher, his individual artistry, and on the composition of the class. Particular problems can be tackled equally successfully by the use of different techniques. For example, in teaching the difference between the pronounciation of English /l/ and /r/ to some Oriental students, teachers sometimes get results by requiring only imitation. If imitation fails, another technique requires the use of a pencil in the mouth to prevent the student's tongue from touching the alveolar ridge, hence inhibiting the pronounciation of /l/. Another teacher or the same teacher at another time might depend upon a drawing or chart of the human vocal apparatus.

When visitors view a class, they see mostly techniques. Teachers often feel uneasy in the presence of visitors, fearing a misinterpretation of their classes. This, in my view, arises largely out of a confusion of techniques with method. The effectiveness of a particular technique must be taken in relation to a method. A particular technique might at one time in the progress of a course be used quite wrongly because it is out of the order required by the method. Later on it might be quite correct.

Laboratory tape-recorders and phonographs are techniques. The recently-popular teaching machines are techniques. The closed-circuit television of the English Language Institute at the University of Michigan is a technique. And even the airplane which slowly circles over the American midwest transmitting educational TV signals is, under this classification, a four-engined technique.

Machines have enjoyed great favour recently. Great claims have been made for their effectiveness in language teaching. In truth, they have great value. But their value depends on *method* and *approach*. The operative factor in the use of language laboratories is not the number of booths or the modernity of the electronic equipment, but what kind of approach is adopted, and what method the equipment carries out. A teaching machine, however complex, is a *technique*,

the principles of step-increment learning are factors of *approach*, the actual programme employed displays *method*.

It is to be hoped that the use of the three terms *technique*, *method*, and *approach*, redefined and employed in the telescoping definitions outlined above,
will serve to lessen a little the terminological confusion in the language-teaching
field. The author would welcome comments and criticisms relating to their use.

2
TESOL: CURRENT
PROBLEMS AND
CLASSROOM
PRACTICES
RONALD WARDHAUGH

How could Wardhaugh's statement that *a learner always knows certain things about another language
before he learns it* be substantiated?

If the quotation above is true, what implications does
it have for the design and preparation of language
programs?

To what extent do you agree with Wardhaugh's assertion that it is in *techniques* that much of the interest of the classroom teacher lies? Where else could it
lie?

What is Wardhaugh's stand on *explanation* versus *drill*
in the presentation of new language material?

This paper is devoted to a discussion of some of the current theoretical problems
that we face in teaching English to speakers of other languages in order to relate
the theory of teaching English as a second language to some current practices in
teaching English as a second language. It attempts to bridge the gap between the
practical orientation of teachers and the theoretical concerns that should underlie
practice. We can never ignore theory in talking about classroom practices, because good practices must necessarily be built on good theory. Every classroom
practice that we have derives from an underlying theory of some kind: every
good practice derives from an adequate or good knowledge of language, psychology, and pedagogical philosophy; every bad practice gives evidence of some

Reprinted by permission from the *TESOL Quarterly*, 3 (June, 1969), 105–116. The author
is director of the English Language Institute at the University of Michigan.

or other weakness in our understanding of language, or of psychology, or of pedagogy.

In building, or at least attempting to build, a bridge between practice and theory, *linguistics, psychology,* and *pedagogy* will be discussed in turn. I intend to ask what some of the problems are in each of these three disciplines and show how these problems have certain consequences for classroom practice. In the conclusion, reference will be made to an interesting paper written several years ago by a former president of the TESOL organization, Professor Anthony of the University of Pittsburgh, in which he discussed the differences between *approach, method,* and *technique* in second language teaching.[1] This paper will present further arguments for keeping such important distinctions in mind in planning our teaching. Like Anthony, I too will insist on the priority of approach over method, and in turn, of method over technique.

First of all, what are some of the current problems in the discipline of linguistics as that discipline bears on problems of language teaching and language learning? One of the very first problems is that of coming to an understanding of the nature of language itself. While all linguists will acknowledge that a language is a system of some kind, they will tend to disagree among themselves as to how that system should be characterized and what its total scope should be. Is it, for example, a system which may be expressed in a set of rules, or a set of patterns, or in some other special kinds of grammatical category? Should the system merely describe or characterize a set of sentences which the linguist has happened to observe, possibly a very large set, or should it characterize the set of all possible sentences, a set he has no possible hope of ever observing because it is an infinite set? Even if linguists agree that a language is a system which may be expressed in the form of rules, there may well be disagreement about the "reality" of the rules a particular linguist writes. Are the rules he writes in his grammar psychologically real; that is, do they somehow also exist in a speaker's and a listener's minds, or are they merely an artifact, a peculiar view of what a linguistic description should be and should encompass? It is certainly true to say that in many cases there is a great deal of confusion about the terms *rule* and *rule of grammar* and it is well to be on the alert for potential confusion in the use of these terms.

Linguists will also tend not to be in complete agreement about what the discipline of linguistics is all about. Some will say that linguistics is really a search for language universals, that it is for linguistic characteristics which may be found in all languages; others will say that linguistics is a search for methods of analysis; still others will be concerned with making language descriptions, particularly descriptions of exotic languages, on a largely *ad hoc* basis. The results of such different emphases, of course, are very different kinds of linguistic interests, varying according to the particular linguist one reads or listens to, and very different kinds of understandings about the discipline of linguistics itself. It is not

---

[1] Edward M. Anthony, "Approach, Method, and Technique," *English Language Teaching,* 17 (1963), 63–67. [Article no. 1 in this collection. Eds.]

surprising, therefore, that there is a variety of views as to what a grammar is. Is a grammar a theory both about language in general and one language in particular, or is a grammar no more than a description of one language, or is a grammar simply some kind of demonstration that a particular linguistic analysis is workable? Then, even given some measure of agreement about what language is, what linguistics is about, what a grammar is or should be, there may well still be disagreement about whether actual language use is a *skill* which is largely *habitual* or an *ability* which is largely *creative*. Is language use a skill which can be learned much as one learns to type, or is it an ability, an ability like walking, which is acquired in an entirely different way from typing skill? Everyone learns to walk but not everyone learns to type. And everyone learns to talk, too. There do appear to be some critically important differences which must be recognized.

When attention is turned to second language learning and we examine it in the light of what linguists believe a language and grammar to be, we must ask ourselves what must be learned. Is it some kind of system of abstract rules, or some kind of system of habits, or some set of general principles? Or is it a collection of specific items, for example, "sentences" or "patterns," which are then manipulated by the second language learner in a way that we do not well understand today? Most linguists will admit that they really do not know much at all about exactly what must be learned in second language learning.

This overview of the discipline of linguistics suggests that there are all kinds of unanswered questions. In fact, one could say that linguists are currently more concerned with formulating questions than with proposing answers. A healthy attitude towards this state of affairs would be to accept it as a sign of the good health of the discipline, for it indicates the likelihood of major new advances, not of decay and dissolution. It is possible to see some of the results of this kind of concern for formulating interesting questions if one looks at certain very specific linguistic concepts which have been around for many years. For example, the concept of the phoneme has been with us for several decades. This concept has always been a controversial one in linguistics and it is just as controversial today as it was a decade or two ago. However, today the controversies relate to an entirely different set of problems: they now relate to the connection between meaning and sound within an overall language system rather than to such problems as neutralization and overall system, which plagued linguistics for so long. Then again the distinction between a class of words called *verbs* and another called *adjectives*, which seems to many of us to be such a simple and obvious distinction, has been called into question by some linguists who believe that verbs and adjectives are really the same kind of word. They claim that adjectives behave very much like verbs and that there are really only basically three types of words: noun-like words, verb-like words, of which adjectives are a sub-group, and a set of relational words, which do not have any propositional or referential content and function therefore quite differently from the other two types. There are many such problems one could discuss: the current concern with the place of meaning in linguistic analysis and linguistic description; the concern with various kinds of abstract syntactic processes; and the concern with the relationship of meaning to syntax, and of meaning and syntax together to phonology. In all of these areas the student of linguistics will see many questions asked, for linguistics is in a state of rapid development, of quick changes, and of great excitement. However, he will find few answers.

It is well to ask at this point how such facts as these influence what we do in our TESOL classrooms. How do current concerns in linguistic theory bear on classroom practices? First of all, we must say that our students still have to learn certain things if they are to speak the second language, regardless of the state that theoretical linguistics finds itself in. For example, students who are learning English must still learn to distinguish *beet* from *bit*, *bait* from *bet*, and *bet* from *bat*. They must learn that in English those words which we may still want to refer to as *adjectives* go in front of nouns, and that subjects usually precede predicates. They must still learn that adjectives do not agree in number with nouns. They must still learn that an animal which barks is called a *dog*, not a *Hund*, nor a *chien*, nor a *perro*. They must still learn what the acceptable sentence patterns of English are, even though these sentence patterns might be called *surface structures* and be somehow of less interest to theoretically-minded linguists than something called *deep structures*. Our students must still learn that there are basic building blocks which they must be able to put together to make sense in the new language. They must still learn to speak by being required to do some speaking, for they cannot possibly learn to speak only by thinking about speaking. Therefore, they need drill and they need practice. We cannot hope to inject them with some kind of abstract underlying structure in the hope that they will come out speaking English, several recent claims apparently to the contrary notwithstanding.

Certainly the discipline of linguistics is in a state of flux and the questions being asked are extremely theoretical. However, we cannot teach English as a second language by teaching our students to understand the questions or the theoretical formulations of some of the proposed answers. The students still need to hear dialogues; they still need to have expansion drills in which, given one part of a sentence, they add on another part, add then another part, and finally build up the complete sentence, as it were, from the back to the front. Students need substitution drills in which they learn to deal with problems such as anaphora, that is, the problems of the substitution of words like *it*, *one* and other pronominals, those very difficult words in English. They also need transformational exercises to practice changing one structure into another. It should be emphasized that *transformation* in this sense is not the transformation beloved of the generative-transformationalist grammarian. The generative-transformationalist uses the term transformation in an entirely different way, so that again it is necessary to be on the alert for confusion.

Now it is quite legitimate to ask, as many linguists do, what exactly a child is learning about language when he mimics dialogues, when he expands sentences, when he makes substitutions, when he changes one sentence into another. We are surely not just teaching the child rote habits which are completely unproductive, as sometimes we are accused. We are sometimes also accused of stifling his creativity, or, less severely, of not recognizing the fact that language use is a creative activity, and that creativity cannot be encouraged or even initiated by the kinds of exercises we employ. However, those who have criticized such practices have not yet demonstrated how a learner can create a second language *without* stimuli, and they have not been afraid to use language stimuli in their own teaching which look rather like those so many of us have been using for quite a long time. There is obviously need for good stimuli in language teaching, and the kinds of exercises just mentioned (mimicry, expansion, substitution and transformation) seem to be necessary in any kind of systematic second language teaching. It would be entirely foolish for us to throw these overboard in order to sail the completely uncharted sea of creativity!

The last statements should not be interpreted as presenting a case for mindless pattern drill, blind mim-mem methods, and pattern practice *ad nauseam*. The learner does make a large contribution in language learning and linguists have very rightly stressed that contribution in any kind of language learning. However, it must in all fairness be pointed out that linguists are uncertain what the contribution is, even though they are quite certain that it does exist. A learner always knows certain things about another language before he learns it. For example, he knows that certain kinds of phonological contrasts will occur, that there will be naming and action words, and he can be absolutely sure that there will be sentences which have definite structures to enable him to make statements, give commands, and ask questions. Of course, children cannot verbalize such understandings, but it is fair to assume that they do have them nevertheless. Our linguistic knowledge would suggest that when he learns a second language he is aware that both meaning and structure are involved in the learning and that there is a critical relationship between the context in which the language is used and the structure of the language which is used in that context. It is quite obvious that no one can learn a language in a vacuum in which the sounds he hears are unconnected to events in the real world, just as it is quite obvious that no one can learn a language without having actual linguistic data presented to him. What linguistic theory would seem to tell us is that we should not forget the *context* of language learning. Linguistic theory would suggest that we cannot rely exclusively on mimicry, dialogues, mim-mem methods and pattern practice drill, ignoring actual language use and the contexts in which language is used. Nor should we go to the opposite extreme of following a method, like the Direct Method, in which linguistic structure is almost totally ignored. Our classroom practices should follow some kind of middle road, some kind of strategy in which we use the natural contexts of language to prompt language use, together with an awareness of the language structures which must be mastered.

When we turn our attention to psychology, we discover many of the same problems that arose in considering the relevance of linguistic knowledge. Indeed linguistics itself has been called a branch of cognitive psychology, because many of the same questions interest both linguists and psychologists. For example, both linguists and psychologists are interested in the basic question of what the human mind is like, and particularly, what the human mind must be like, given the kind of structures that languages have. Linguists ask what kinds of structures all languages have and what the universal characteristics of language are. Then they tend to speculate on what human minds must be like to be able to use such languages. Or they may speculate that human languages must be as they are as a result of the structure of human minds. While we can observe human languages in action, we cannot directly observe human minds in action, because of a lack of sufficiently sophisticated equipment. Therefore, the study of language turns out to be one very interesting way of making hypotheses about the structure of human minds, and it is largely for this reason that linguistics has been referred to as a branch of cognitive psychology.

However, when we look at psychology in second language teaching and learning, we are really less concerned with speculation about what human minds are like than with the problems of language learning. Note the deliberate emphasis on language *learning* rather than on language teaching. It has been said, with some justification, that first languages are not taught; they are learned, for they are just too complicated to be taught. How can a parent, or a teacher for that matter, possibly teach something that even very sophisticated linguists hardly even begin to understand? In second language learning and teaching the same problem exists. How can anyone teach a second language when so little is known about any one language, never mind two, and also so little is known about almost every aspect of the learning process? It is necessary to assume that the learner makes a tremendous contribution in the process.

Given that so little is known about the structure of language, it therefore seems difficult to explain how a second language can be learned through some of the simplistic psychological learning models that are available, through, for example, any kind of stimulus-response theory, that is, through a theory in which a language is said to be a simple habit system. Nor can that variation of behavioristic learning theory called reinforcement theory adequately describe or account for how a second language can be learned in its totality. Learning a second language means acquiring a system of rules, but just as very little is known about these rules, even less is known about how such rule systems are acquired. Certainly it is possible to speculate about the effectiveness of deductive learning and inductive learning. But most of what is said on this topic is speculative and has not been proved out in any rigorous manner. We can also make hypotheses about the influence of motivation on learning, of both extrinsic and intrinsic motivation. We can investigate different types of learning as these vary, for example, with the age or the sense preferences of the learner. We can inquire into various halo effects associated with learning, those halo effects associated with the equipment we use, our materials, the time of day our class is held, the teacher's personality, and particular mixes of students. There are numerous psychological factors in any learning situation, and we really know very little about them.

There are certain data available on the learning process, of course, that do have special interest for us. One of the most interesting collections of such data is the evidence that linguistic interference provides. We know that students from certain linguistic backgrounds have difficulty in learning various aspects of English and that they do make predictable mistakes while learning. The Spanish student fails to distinguish *beat* and *bit* and *bait* and *bet*, and he does not pronounce *school* as *school* but as *eschool*. The Japanese student comes to study at the *Engrish Ranguage Institute*. Such mistakes, or deviations from an expected response, can tell us a lot, but not possibly as much as some people have claimed they can tell us. There was a time when contrastive analysis, as it is called, the analysis of the two languages involved in second language learning and a statement of their contrasts, promised to work us miracles. The miracles never came. We should not abandon such analyses but rather we should look at the unexpected responses in more fruitful ways than we have done in the past.

There are many problems then in psychology and we are just beginning to ask answerable and interesting questions about them. From what we do know already we can suggest ways in which classroom practices might be modified and improved. There seems to be one very obvious way in which there could be some rather immediate improvement in the classroom and that is through a change of emphasis from teaching to learning. Too often the classroom is regarded as a place in which the teacher is at the center of interest, a place in which everything flows from the teacher, who knows what is to be taught and exactly how he is going to teach it, and in which the learner is merely the end point of some kind of process. A change of direction seems called for, particularly if language is something that we understand but a little of and if any particular language is a system of which we have merely fragmentary knowledge. If our goal is somehow to help our students to acquire an adequate control of that second language, then the focus must be changed from the teacher to the *student*. Somehow we have to realize that the student must do the job for himself, that we can help him, that we can struggle with him in *his* task of learning the second language, but that since we know so little about that second language, we can provide little more than encouragement and a certain, but not unimportant, amount of help.

The emphasis, therefore, should be less on the teacher and the course or text and more on the student himself. We should attempt to stimulate him to use the language and encourage him to use the innate processes of language acquisition that he has. This means, of course, that in our methods it will be necessary to be eclectic rather than single-minded and monolithic. It means that we cannot rely on any one single narrow pedagogical approach. It means too that we must respond to the different needs of students, the different learning patterns they exhibit, and the different inclinations and motives that they have in learning. Obviously, in such a setting the teacher's role is less one of providing something absolutely sure, certain and definitive, for such certainty does not exist, and more one of trying to create an atmosphere in which learning is encouraged, in which the teacher's enthusiasm for learning, desire for his students' success, and overall commitment to his task somehow rub off on his students. Consequently, I see a need for lots of examples, lots of variety, and lots of context-oriented work.

All of this may seem rather paradoxical, particularly if some of the preceding statements have been interpreted as meaning that we know nothing about language. We certainly do know many things about language, but not a few of these are superficial. For example, many of the phonological contrasts that we know about exist as phonetic contrasts, that is, as actual contrasts in the stream of sound that comes out of the speakers' mouths, but not necessarily as contrasts at a more abstract level of language function. Many of the grammatical contrasts may be only surface contrasts existing in the sentences which are produced and may not be as significant as certain deep contrasts which interest linguists. These surface contrasts are still important in language use and fortunately we do know something about them. We must try to make sure that our students systematically acquire these same contrasts and some systematic approach to this task is possible. However, we should be more concerned with the student's gradual development as a person who controls a second language than with his apparent mastery of this pattern or that one. *We should attempt continually to find out what the student is doing with the language we are trying to teach him.* We should find out what the student is doing, not what the teacher is doing. We should find out what the student can do, because, after all, he is the one who is at the center of our task. Our task is to help him to learn.

It is at this point that interference phenomena are so important. When a student does say something incorrectly, does not control a certain contrast, produces an ungrammatical sentence, does not know the right word, we should, in Newmark and Reibel's terms, take this as evidence of his ignorance and incomplete learning.[2] Linguistic interference is therefore linguistic ignorance. We should assume that the student is trying to use the second language and, because he does not know enough, he is failing. The problem so far as pedagogy is concerned is that, having recognized this as ignorance, how do we deal with it? Do we treat it through more drill or through explanation? The answer again is not a particularly simple one, because different people learn in different ways and there are also variables like age and motivation. It is quite possible that drill activities will work better with younger students, but in similar circumstances

---

[2] Leonard Newmark and David A. Reibel, "Necessity and Sufficiency in Language Learning," *IRAL*, 6 (1969), 145-161.

older students may prefer explanation. However, it is doubtful that one can explain the differences between the vowels in *beat* and *bit*: the tenseness of one vowel versus the laxness of the other; the off-glide of one versus the lack of glide of the other; and the height of one versus that of the other. The student must learn to feel the difference in the vowels and it is hard, if not impossible, to explain a feeling of this kind. A grammatical point, however, may be explained, but explanation will not guarantee learning. Many of us know foreign students who know a lot *about* English but whose English is atrocious. Many of us know foreign students who speak beautiful English but do not know anything *about* English. In language teaching we must be prepared to mix drill *and* explanation because we can never be sure which technique works with which student.

Pedagogy has been kept to the last in this discussion because it is true to say that even less is known about pedagogy than is known about linguistics and psychology. Some people would even say that there is nothing to know, but I am not one of them. There is also the classic question: "Is teaching an art or is it a science?" And also the question: "Can we examine the teaching process in any scientific manner?" This paper does not propose to try to answer either question, except by saying that there is evidence that teaching is an art but that it can also be studied scientifically. Indirectly, comments have been made on teaching in the discussions of language and psychology. In second language teaching much of what is discussed under teaching actually turns out to be discussion of linguistics or of psychology. For example, it has long been fashionable to import into teaching certain techniques which linguists use in analyzing languages or in making language descriptions. Consider, if you will, the use of minimal pairs such as *beat-bit, bait-bet, bet-bat* in language teaching. Such use seems to be the importing of a linguistic technique into the classroom. The same use may be seen of ideas from psychology: one way of explaining certain psychological phenomena is to set up S-R bonds. Consequently the teacher attempts to import into the classroom a technique in which students are taught to associate certain stimuli with certain responses in a rather mechanical way. This again seems to be a direct extension into the classroom of a technique from another discipline.

To many of us, though, pedagogy involves such matters as the equipment we use rather than the content we teach, so that we become fascinated by the "hardware" of education, things like audio-visual aids, language laboratories, overhead projectors, tape recorders, reading kits, and so on. Many of the pedagogical issues we become concerned about turn out to be about such matters as whether or not we should install a language laboratory, or buy an overhead projector, or requisition one particular set of audio-visual aids. It is just such hardware that we show visitors to our school, that we insist on being provided with when we move into a new building, and that we fight the principal, curriculum supervisor, and school board for. And, rather tragically, it is just such hardware we nearly always end up by completely underusing when we do acquire it. We install a beautiful language laboratory and then find we do not have suitable tapes to play at the master console. We equip our new school with a closed-circuit television system and then find that we either cannot maintain it or do not know how to use it. We buy some elaborate equipment to use with programmed materials and then we find there are no programmed materials at all, or that the programmed materials which are available are completely inadequate. We should not get too caught up with bigger and better hardware at the expense of the "software" of education, the actual content of teaching. There is some reason to believe that the best hardware is chalk, a blackboard, and books, and the most valuable teaching aid in the classroom is a well-prepared teacher. We cannot solve our problems in the classroom by importing more and more equipment into it, nor is the language laboratory the answer to all our needs in second language teaching.

In pedagogy, if we escape being hung up on hardware, we generally get hung up with techniques. For example, we may always insist that sounds and structures must be taught in contrast to each other. We may always insist on contrasting *l*'s with *r*'s, *e*'s with *i*'s and one grammatical structure with another. Or we may insist that we must have a particular kind of textbook for a particular kind of student; for example, specially oriented texts for various ethnic groups. Or we may insist that every new item must be repeated *n* times, the particular value of *n* itself varying from three to five or more, but always some magical prime number! Or we may insist that whenever we present a new point the presentation has to follow a certain order: preparation, presentation, consolidation, evaluation, review, and so on. Or we may have notions about simple and complex sounds and structures, notions which are often intuitively based but present nevertheless. Or we may insist on programming a certain grammatical sequence in a certain series of steps, again largely on an intuitive basis. Or we may believe in the effects of spiraling or cycling of our materials rather than in straight line programming.

Publishers cater to these preferences and advertise their offerings as much for the particular techniques they exemplify as for any intrinsic content. They sell us English through pictures, or English through Basic English, or English through pattern drill, or English through generative-transformational grammar, or English through portable transistorized transmitters that can be plugged gently into the ear so that the learner can acquire English quite painlessly as he goes about his daily living and even daily sleeping. Teachers tend to accept such things as these, for they do appear to make our jobs easier. Having been a teacher and having been faced with the relentless succession of classes throughout the school day, I can understand why. We think our jobs will be easier if we have just the right texts, or if there is a language laboratory, or if we control a little teaching formula that will do the trick time and time again. Given the kinds of pressures that we work under in our classrooms, it is not surprising that it should be like this, nor am I saying that we should abandon techniques which succeed for us. However, we should ask ourselves why the techniques which succeed do succeed. The answer is likely to be that they work because they really involve our students in worthwhile activity and have a good theoretical justification.

It is impossible to teach language to children, especially, in a sterile, inactive environment. Language is a vehicle for dealing with reality. All linguistic activity must be associated with meaningful activity so any techniques designed to encourage meaningful activity are obviously important in language learning. Consequently, movement, involvement, and situation, and the concomitants of these – – – laughter, games, and stories – – – are important in teaching. Our teaching techniques should be focused on trying to encourage as much of this as possible. Good pedagogy then will be less concerned with gimmickry, the pat solution, the utterly predictable lesson plan, and the rather dull teacher-centered activities of classrooms than with involving students and the teacher in some kind of joint meaningful activity in which the focus is on language learning rather than on language teaching. But we should not forget the teacher. We should remember that he is extremely important, if only for the fact that he teaches not only the course that is prescribed, but also what *he himself is,* and what he is is usually learned much better by the students than any content he ever tries to get across!

It would be useful to sum up this discussion of linguistics, psychology, and pedagogy, the three aspects of second language teaching that we have to take into consideration, by referring to the article that Professor Anthony wrote several years ago, an article in which Anthony discussed the differences between what he called *approach, method,* and *technique.*

By *approach* Anthony referred to the assumptions that underlie our language teaching, that is, the assumptions we have about language and about psychology. He rightly said that such assumptions are generally matters of belief and that they are the axioms from which we derive the theorems, or the methods, and then the derivative techniques that we use. As classroom teachers we should concern ourselves with the underlying axioms of our profession, because everything that we do in our classrooms derives from the assumptions that we make. It does not matter whether or not we can articulate these assumptions; they are still there, articulated or not.

To Anthony *method* meant the plans for curriculum and teaching which derive from approaches, the plans by which we ultimately present the data. They are plans for the curriculum of a particular kindergarten room in which there are Mexican-American children, of a particular ghetto school, or of a small number of foreign students on a Midwest college campus, or of a special class for non-English-speaking students in a suburban school system. Method then is the particular kind of strategy that derives from an approach; it is the overall plan that we have in mind for teaching the language in a particular set of circumstances.

Technique, for Anthony, meant exactly how to do what you decide to do, the specific kinds of practices and techniques that one chooses to employ in a specific classroom. It is quite apparent to me that this is just where much of the interest of classroom teachers lies. We are all interested in becoming better classroom teachers. We all like to find something good and immediately useful in book displays at conventions. We all like to go away from professional meetings with at least one new practical idea that will work. But we would be doing a disservice to ourselves if all we do is hunt for gimmickry and new wrinkles, say a tape recorder with some new kind of switch, or a book which has appeared in a new cover, possibly even in a new edition, but really only the same old wine again. We should try instead, on occasion, to stand back from such concerns in order to achieve a perspective on our task and to evaluate our methods and our general approach. Periodically it is good to rephrase the basic questions that must be asked in a growing and vital discipline like teaching English to speakers of other languages.

Classroom teachers must be prepared to find out as much as they can about what the issues and questions are in linguistics and psychology, in order to gain some idea of where the answers might lie. In the years ahead it will be more vital to understand what the basic questions are in the discipline than it will be to understand what a certain switch does on the latest tape recorder, or how to use a particular set of flash cards, or what a very specific teaching technique will do in a rather limited set of circumstances. A teacher cannot get through a lifetime of teaching by throwing a succession of switches, or by using a collection of charts, or by inventing a new teaching wrinkle every day. Inevitably the result will be boredom or learning of the wrong things. However, he can take inspiration from a new idea about language teaching, from new sources of information, from new insights into the language-learning process, and from new ideas about what a total teaching strategy could be like. A good teacher probably should know how to use a tape recorder, an overhead projector, and some of the other media effectively, but a good teacher is not just a technician. A good teacher is someone who continually examines what he does, continually strives to arrive at new understandings of his discipline, and continually tries to steer a course between doubt and dogma. Good teaching practice is based on good theoretical understanding. *There is indeed nothing so practical as a good theory.* Teachers should focus from time to time not on techniques, not on methods, but on approach, that is, on theory, and should try in those moments to capture some of the excitement of the many challenges that confront us in teaching English to speakers of other languages.

3

THE THEORIST   DWIGHT BOLINGER
AND THE
LANGUAGE
TEACHER

Do you agree with Bolinger's comparison: linguistics is to language teaching as chemistry is to medicine?

To what degree do Wardhaugh (Art. 2) and Bolinger agree on the place of *drills* and *explanation* in the teaching of second languages?

According to the references made in this article, how closely do the tenets of the audio-lingual approach (cf. Anthony, Art. 1) correspond to the understanding that Palmer had of the teaching and learning of second languages?

An interesting assignment would be to draw from this article brief summary statements of the respective positions held by structuralists and transformationalists on the relationship of their disciplines to the teaching and learning of foreign languages.

If an applied linguist of the mid-1950s had gone to sleep in his cave, say around 1956, and awakened yesterday, the sight that greeted him would have sent him hurrying back to his dreams. Virtually every tenet that he had proclaimed in his heyday would have been returned to him upside down: writing once again beginning to assert itself over speech; grammar not learned inductively nor extended by analogy; language learning not a matter of habit-formation; the goal of language study to learn something about the human mind and not about linguistic behavior. And to cap this heap of insults, the poor fellow's descriptions of language were not very good and his claims to have anything to say to language teachers were not very well-founded either.

For those of us who could not enjoy the luxury of sleep while this clashing and reversing of gears was going on, the changes have meant some painful adjustments. For the teachers and the other people in the schools, who could not directly participate but were only aware that what they had been led to regard as the anchor of their faith and works, its scientific basis, was beginning to give

Reprinted by permission from *Foreign Language Annals*, 2 (October, 1968), 30–41. This is a slightly revised form of a talk given February 22, 1968, at Pennsylvania State University. The author is professor of Romance Languages and Literatures at Harvard University.

way, the effect was pure bewilderment. Recently an administrator at the Harvard Graduate School of Education, a man responsible for training teachers in cooperation with the public schools, asked me if it did not seem that a lot of hankypanky was going on among linguists—not in the sense of anything underhanded, he wanted to make clear, but a spate of dissension and name-calling that no respectable science ought to tolerate and that was bringing consternation to language teachers. I could not deny this dissension, and as for the consternation, it was apparent from their concern about it that more and more linguists were aware of its existence and were trying to resolve it, or at least to reassure the victims that everything would come out all right in the end.

It has been a decade now since the issue of the journal *Language* was published in which the article by Zellig Harris on transformations appeared, and Robert Lees masterminded a review of Chomsky's *Syntactic Structures*.[1] Within three or four years it became clear that the altered views of the nature of language to which these studies led would sooner or later affect the teaching of languages, and at first blush one wonders why it did not happen sooner. Perhaps a reason is to be found in our top-heavy bureaucracy with its control of money and propaganda. Government funds had become available to linguists, and those holding the prevailing views were the ones best situated to dig in, enjoy the largess, and win a following. On the propagandistic side, linguistics was sold to language teachers as their champion against the forces that had for years been pushing language-teaching closer and closer to the wall. Naturally this linguistics came in the popular brands and sizes because there was no other. The result was an entrenched position, extrication from which required a good deal of time and persuasion, not to mention bare knuckles. The conflict raged as a more or less internal one among linguists all through the first half of the sixties, but something of an understanding or at least a truce was reached by 1964 when the president of the Linguistic Society, one of the leaders of the older group, in his presidential address acknowledged the new movement as a "major breakthrough."[2] This peacemaking has been slower to come to the applied fields. Almost two years later, at the meeting of the Northeast Conference, a paper by Chomsky on linguistic theory in its relation to language learning was criticized by W. Freeman Twaddell as merely leading to further misunderstanding and frustration on the part of language teachers.[3]

I do not know whether by coincidence or by design the new organization calling itself the American Council on the Teaching of Foreign Languages chose

---

[1] July-Sept. 1957.

[2] Charles F. Hockett, "Sound Change," *Language*, 12 (1956), 196.

[3] Noam Chomsky, "Linguistic Theory," Northeast Conference on the *Teaching of Foreign Languages, Reports of the Working Committees*, 1966, pp. 43-44. Unless otherwise stated, later parenthetical references to Chomsky in the text will be to this article. Twaddell's rebuttal has not been published.

this moment to spring from the brain and body of the Modern Language Association, and with the perspicacity of the young it quickly recognized the dangers of the controversy both to linguistics and to language teaching and put it on the agenda for its first national meeting. Victor Hanzeli of the University of Washington was asked to give a paper on linguistics and language teaching, which he did with a combination of tact and reassurance that renews one's faith in what linguistics has already contributed and one's hope for what it may yet contribute, in spite of the overwrought claims of the old school, which pretends to be everything to everybody, and the overdrawn modesty of the new, which pretends to be nothing to nobody.[4]

I will not try to predict what the nature of the synthesis will be. That has to be worked out in conjunction with psychologists and educationists, and in part by simple trial and error in the classroom. But I am going to try to show why a synthesis is inevitable, given the nature of the medium. Language teaching is not linguistics, any more than medicine is chemistry. Medicine takes what it needs from chemistry and leaves the rest alone. Whether the source of a new cure is the result of some application of high-level chemical theory, or of the accidental observation of something happening in a test tube when microorganisms are exposed to a certain variety of mold, it makes no difference, and it should make no difference to the language teacher whether what he takes from linguistics is based on one theory or another or on no theory at all, provided it helps him to achieve the goals he is aiming at in his classes. If in addition to this the differences have been exaggerated, and the arguments pro and con are really not quite touching each other because of relativity in the frames of reference and deviations in the meanings of the terms, then he may with all the more confidence pick what he chooses without worrying about inconsistency.

What about this relativity and these deviations? It will pay us to examine the criticisms that the newer linguists have leveled at the older ones, to see whether the older school was really responsible for the views attributed to it, and, if so, whether these views have been fairly interpreted.

First I must make clear what I mean when I refer to an old school and a newer school. Time passes and children age quickly in the nuclear age. It has been only a short while since the adjective *new* was the prize of the school that now begins to seem quaint. Then it was the structuralists who personified the truth in its immemorial battle with error. American structuralism made its bow early in the twenties of this century. It leaned heavily on a native American pragmatism which in turn nourished and was nourished by the behaviorist tendency in psychology (of which more later); and it was in the mainstream of the major linguistic effort being carried forward at the time—field work in aboriginal languages. It was too busy collecting and classifying these languages to penetrate very

[4]Victor E. Hanzeli, "Linguistics and the Language Teacher," *Foreign Language Annals*, 2 (1968), 42–50.

deeply into any of them, and accordingly was prone to be satisfied with a sketch of the distinctive sounds and an outline of the morphology, with little attention paid to syntax or lexicon. Naturally such influence as it had on teaching tended to affect the areas that it was most interested in. The challenge that faces it today comes from linguists who have tried to pick up where structuralism left off, and have found that the neglected areas cannot be dealt with by using the old techniques. They advocate a formalized model of language with almost no ties to fieldwork but with very close ties to formal logic. They are rationalists rather than empiricists. Instead of collecting data and bringing order to it, they first bring order to their intuitions about language and then test the resulting theories against the data, of which they believe more than enough is lying around to serve any rational purpose.[5] In this country we identify them with the group known as transformationalists or generativists, or some combination of the two names. We can confine our observations to the local scene not only because it concerns us more deeply but also because in America the conflict has become more clearly polarized and threatens us with more drastic effects.

To get back to the views of the older school and their impact on language teaching, it is easy to prove that structuralism did not invent the principles that have become practically the trademark of the current audiolingual approach in language teaching. One has only to consult the writers on language pedagogy who were on the scene before structural linguistics began to be used as a source of pedagogical argument. The best authority is probably Harold Palmer, whose *Principles of Language Study* was published in 1921.[6] What is without a doubt the most familiar of the stereotypes associated with audiolingual teaching—the four-skill sequence of understanding, speaking, reading, and writing—was listed by Palmer in that order (p. 38). Palmer defined language-learning as "a habit-forming process" (p. 54). He urged repetitive drill and argued against the educationists who condemned learning by rote. His paragraph on the value of grammatical explanations is worth quoting: "Nearly all the time spent by the teacher in explaining why such and such a form is used and why a certain sentence is constructed in a certain way is time lost, for such explanations merely appease curiosity; they do not help us to form new habits, they do not develop automatism. Those who have learnt to use the foreign language and who do use it successfully have long since forgotten the why and the wherefore; they can no longer quote to you the theory which was supposed to have procured them their command of the language." (p. 57).

---

[5] "To plod laboriously through texts looking for sentences that one can easily think up in one's study strikes the transformationalist as a peculiar way to go about the job." Garland Cannon, rev. of Paul Roberts, *English Syntax* (alternate ed., New York, 1964), *Word*, **21** (1965), 466, quoting Roberts, p. 410. One can think them up, but will one?

[6] Harold Palmer, *Principles of Language Study*. Page references in parentheses are to the 1964 ed. (London: Oxford Univ. Press, 1964.)

Whatever was wrong with this point of view, we obviously cannot blame it on the structural linguists. Palmer was not primarily a linguistic theorist. He was a practical teacher and administrator, one who in today's bureaucracy would be at the top of the teaching-English-as-a-second-language hierarchy. His principles were elaborated from his experience. He had ample opportunity to listen to the barren rule giving in the typical classroom of his day—a classroom which alas still survives in too many places—and the improvements he advocated were the results of his own experiments.

So how do we explain the stubborn identification of these audiolingual practices with the school of American structural linguistics? The reasons are partly theoretical and partly historical. As we have all been reminded over and over, the New Key in language teaching got its first real foothold in the Intensive Language Program and shortly afterward in the Army Specialized Training Program during the Second World War. Most of the linguists who produced significant work in the late 1940s and all through the 1950s were men who had been conscripted between 1942 and 1945 and instead of being given marching orders were set to work preparing teaching materials for languages never before taught in American schools, or for languages that had been taught for generations but with materials that did not suit the objective of the military services, which was to get *speakers* in as short a time as possible. There was no leisure to spin theories or debate alternatives. The erstwhile scholars converted to language teachers took the best they could find and made it do. They did not invent their audiolingual methods but took them over from Palmer and earlier linguists such as Sweet and Jespersen. And the methods got results.

Nevertheless, it must be admitted that the teaching ideas adopted by the structuralists were not uncongenial to their theoretical slant. The man who had been the teacher of many of them and who did most to guide their thinking, Leonard Bloomfield, had borrowed a great deal from behaviorist psychology which in turn supported the audiolingual style of teaching. If language is a set of habits and learning is essentially a process of conditioning, then the apparatus of drill and reinforcement becomes the logical way to teach. In their teaching and in their descriptions of language, the structuralists moved in the realm of behavior; in their research they were interested in collected samples of speech, which they analyzed and classified. The aim of their teaching was to have students imitate those same specimens, trusting that somehow if enough of them were learned the student would have a stock from which to make analogies as the occasion demanded.

Even so, there were structuralists who were uneasy about embracing a linguistic justification for audiolingualism, and another historical event was needed to shackle them to it. After the war, in spite of the demonstrated need for more competent users of foreign languages, the enrollments in language classes were still going down. The Modern Language Association took alarm and started its well-known campaign to reverse the trend. The structuralists were using audiolingual methods and the structuralists were scientists, which offered an unbeatable combination: a new way of teaching plus scientific authority. They were the logical choice to serve as figureheads. From then on it was impossible to divorce audiolingualism and structural linguistics. Serious linguists winced when they heard a set of pedagogical principles referred to as a "linguistic method," but nothing could stop their being used as scientific front men for an educational cause, much like the list of respectable sponsors on the letterhead of a radical reform movement.

Since the pedagogical fame of the structuralists was not of their choosing but was thrust upon them, one may reasonably ask whether, if they had been asked as linguists to formulate their position, it would have come out quite the same as it did under the pressure of too much application and too little thinking. Does the audiolingual confession in the crude form in which it has been propagated fairly represent the theoretical views they might have advanced if they had had time and had really involved themselves in the movement instead of merely decorating it?

I will not try to restate audiolingual principles in more acceptable terms. This is no place to organize a theory which, unhappily, never was. Instead, I believe that the best way to answer the question is to look one by one at the criticisms that transformational grammarians have leveled at audiolingualism and try to see whether with a little more charity the audiolingual position may seem to be somewhat less false than the picture that has been painted of it. As part of this assignment, the theoretical grounds on which the transformationalists base their criticisms are also fair game.

To be correct with the transformationalists we must make clear first what it is that they are not criticizing. When Chomsky said at the Northeast Conference in 1966 that he was "rather skeptical about the significance, for the teaching of languages, of such insights as have been attained in linguistics and psychology" (p. 43) he neglected to explain that the insights he was talking about are those having more to do with how one gets a linguistic system into a student's head, and less with offering some workable description of the system. In his view the most important task of linguistics is to discover the nature of the language-learning mechanism that we are supposed to be born with; if linguistics could tell us about that, it would undoubtedly give a great boost to efforts to teach a foreign language. When he uses a term such as "linguistic insights" he means this kind of penetration, on the borders of psychology. It is his right, naturally, to define his terms to suit his purposes, but it is a bit unjust to define them in such a way as to depreciate the significance of other linguistic insights for language teaching. To take one example: until two wartime linguists, Raven McDavid and William Cornyn, reviewed the existing grammars of Burmese, found them wanting, and gathered and edited their own materials, Burmese was scarcely teachable in this country. If linguistics includes the humdrum, unpretentious work of sitting down with Latin documents and working out the structure of

Latin as a preliminary to making Latin grammars to teach Latin to Latin scholars, or sitting down with live informants who speak Navaho so as to teach Navaho to Vista volunteers in the Southwest, then linguistics provides language teaching with undeniable insights.

This raises a second question. Granted that structuralists produced descriptions of individual languages that were useful in their time, how good were they, really? The transformationalist is ready with his answer: "Even the small fragments of generative grammars that now exist," Chomsky declared, "are incomparably greater in explicit coverage than traditional or structuralist descriptions" (p. 47). Perhaps most of them are, but having spent some time struggling with two of the most frequently cited generative descriptions, I can testify that some of them are too easily satisfied with spur-of-the-moment evidence and make too many wrong assumptions about what is and what is not grammatical. Here is one example. Generativists started writing about the *some-any* contrast in English at least as early as 1960, but as of 1967 it was still being described as if the sentence *Anybody would be a fool to say that* or *Anything like that rarely appeals to me* were ungrammatical.[7] Generative descriptions are models of precision, but teachers are bound to worry if they fail to meet the condition laid down by the generativists themselves, of generating "all and only" grammatical sentences. No linguistic approach per se guarantees quality. That is the product of the imagination, skill, and dedication of the investigator. I do not mean to diminish in any way the potential of the generative approach: its very framework is one that places the greatest demands on explicitness; but we must also not lose sight of the importance of what one is explicit about.

But, as if to head off any defense of structuralism from this direction, the transformationalists claim that it may not make much difference whether we have good descriptions anyway. One of them, Peter Rosenbaum, after seconding Chomsky's claim about the superiority of transformational descriptions, makes the reasonable statement that "The constructs themselves do not and cannot provide any new educational insights. Rather, the ultimate value of valid linguistic descriptions. . .seems to depend entirely on the ingenuity and imagination of linguists, teachers, and educators competent in both areas."[8] This reasoning is advanced a step farther by Sol Saporta: after saying that "It is incongruous to argue that some less adequate formulation can be successfully applied where a more adequate one cannot," he goes on to admit "the possibility. . .that the difference between teaching based on a correct formulation and teaching based

---

[7] For the first analysis see R. B. Lees, rev. of my *Interrogative Structures of American English* (University, Ala., 1957), in *Word*, 16 (1960), 119-125. For the second see Charles J. Fillmore, "On the Syntax of Preverbs," *Glossa*, (1967), 91-125, esp. pp. 94 and 124.

[8] Rosenbaum, "On the Role of Linguistics in the Teaching of English," *Harvard Educational Review*, 35 (1964), 340.

on no formulation is minimal.[9] Certain realities of the classroom seem to have been overlooked here. It is entirely possible for a less adequate formulation to be more successful than a more adequate one, if the educational goals themselves are foreshortened. The writers of textbooks must always face the problem of how explicit their rules are to be. A partial formulation (which is inadequate by definition) is as often as not a requirement in a beginning text, to launch the student into the production of sentences of limited range, in order to have him produce anything at all. The burden of proof is on those who insist that a teacher or a textbook must offer (or even merely utilize at any given point) a fully adequate formulation, to show that such a method would be teachable. The attempt has yet to be made, and meanwhile it is not incongruous to argue that a formulation is more workable for being less adequate, grammatically speaking. There is no guarantee that pedagogical adequacy and grammatical adequacy always go hand in hand, though one would like to harmonize them as much as possible. Again, when the generativist argues that a good formulation is never sufficient in itself to teach the point in question—Rosenbaum compares it to the mechanics of a forward pass, which shows how something works but not how to make it work—he exaggerates in the opposite direction. A good description may not need anything to make it work, beyond our human capacity to follow instructions. If the description says, "Put the object pronoun on the end of the infinitive," and everything has been mastered up to that point, including knowing what pronouns are and what the infinitive is, the student hardly needs to be anointed with any mystical pedagogical essence in order to put it there. On the score of linguistic descriptions, it is wrong to claim either that a description is never enough in its own right, or that the best description from one standpoint is always the best description from another.

Now what about those insights of which Chomsky and Rosenbaum speak and about which I have said that they are as much psychological as they are linguistic? From the answer to this question are forged most of the weapons with which generative grammar attacks the prophets of audiolingualism. We must take a moment to visit the psychological beachhead on which the transformationalists have established themselves and from which they have launched their campaign against the theory, or lack of theory, of the opposition.

I avail myself of another quote from Chomsky: "There is no more reason," he says, "for assuming that the basic principles of grammar are learned than there is for making a comparable assumption about, let us say, visual perception" (p. 48). This is to say that, for all we know, children are born with a kind of linguistic endowment out of which develops whatever it is that represents the particular system of their native language. Sometimes this inborn capacity seems to be viewed as a capacity for acquiring a language: then it is referred to as a

---

[9]Saporta, "Applied Linguistics and Generative Grammar," *Trends in Language Teaching*, ed. Albert Valdman (New York, 1966), p. 88.

"language-learning device." At other times it appears to be viewed as the most fundamental level of the structure of language itself, from which it follows that all languages have the same internal grammar to begin with. In either case, one pictures a kind of static design, which is somehow "there," in the organism, and which is elaborated not by shaping but by discovery: "the child's discovery of. . . a generative grammar of his language."[10] It is as if all potential grammars were present to begin with, and the learner proceeded from discovery to discovery, guided we know not how but ending up with a complete grammar of his native language.

This view, which seems to me about as replete with mysticism as any, leads to the well-known distinction that transformationalists make between "competence" and "performance." The competence is what the speaker carries around with him. It is his internal grammar, the machine that enables him to grind out a sentence that nobody has ever heard before, in accordance with certain internal semantic commands that are part, presumably, of some auxiliary machine; it also enables him to tell when a sentence he is about to produce or hear someone else produce is well-formed, no matter whether he corrects it in case it turns out malformed. The performance on the other hand is the machine in action, producing sentences that are highly predictable in form but not always perfect—where the process is interfered with by other mechanisms or by accidents, the product may show defects, but these can always be recognized. One might use the analogy of a human face. The genetic design is responsible for what makes a face a face, and blemishes such as harelips or a misaligned septum clearly do not belong to those normal features. The linguistic competence is what makes a well-formed sentence a well-formed sentence, and it includes a sentence-recognizer which tells us when one is not well-formed.

Where the structuralist goes wrong, says the transformationalist, is in his unwillingness to posit this underlying reality. And this in turn stems from his anti-mentalism, his insistence on the evidence of his senses, on staying in the realm of performance and working only with the specimens of language that he finds around him. Since the grammar of a language must embrace everything that a speaker might say as well as what he says, to study just his productions is not enough. The correct procedure is an indirect one. You assume a grammar of a certain type, make sentences according to it, and then test them by comparing them with those which the internal grammars of live speakers produce. Then you modify the rules until the two products come out the same. By this process you eventually arrive at the facsimile of a real internal human grammar—which is the best that one can do, short of being able to peer into the head and watch the wheels spin.

It would take too long to go into all the implications of this fascinating

[10]Noam Chomsky, *Aspects of the Theory of Syntax* (Cambridge, Massachusetts, 1965), p. 58. The theme of discovery is recurrent. See Cannon (fn. 5, above), p. 465.

metaphor, but one of them is the key to most of the ideas about language teaching. It is the concept of inwardness and outwardness, which characterizes not only the separation of competence from performance but also the structure of the internal grammar itself. There are degrees of inwardness and outwardness in the grammar such that a deep grammar, which somewhere along the line gets identified with that endowment we are all born with, is distinguished from a surface grammar, which specifies the syntactic shape of the sentences that are actually uttered in a given language. Still more outward is the specification of the rules of expression by which the syntactic shape with all its little light bulbs in the form of words and morphemes screwed in place gets its shot of electricity and lights up. That illuminated display is the sentence that you hear or read. One effect of this inward-outward progression is the setting up of an apparently impenetrable barrier to any effective grammaticizing in the opposite direction. If you start with the production, with the sentence that you hear, about the most you can do is write some superficial rules to deal with the surface syntax; the deep grammar is too far in to reach.

When we take up the picture that behaviorism paints for us, we find it rather drab by comparison. Yet in some important respects it is not so very different. The same division between inwardness and outwardness is made, but the direction is reversed. The child's initial equipment is assumed to be much more formless. He is born with certain capacities, but these do not include an internal grammar. I. A. Richards points out that "all species of mental activity deeply resemble one another."[11] The mind needs no more than this to start with. If the behaviorist had used such a term as a "learning device" at all, it would have meant something more general, actually more versatile in not assuming anything about language or its structure. The nature of environment and experience is uniform enough across the world for the very real near-identity of humanity in its non-linguistic aspects to shape those formless capacities in ways that create the illusion of universals among languages; and in addition there is the strong possibility of a single origin, and hence a related tradition, in the languages themselves, which become self-perpetuating cultural artifacts analogous to rituals. The child does not come equipped with language but is apprenticed to it. As John B. Watson says, "Our view is that overt language develops under social training."[12] Overt babbling and associated vocal behavior is modified into socialized speech, and then, little by little, is internalized as implicit speech. But at this point in inwardness, behaviorism bogs down. It recognizes an inward activity when someone is actually thinking a thought, but says nothing about an inward capacity except in terms of conditioned reflexes. Its vulnerability may be, as the mentalists say, due to the incapability of a theory of conditioning to account for linguistic competence, or it may be due to the failure of behaviorists ever to get around

[11] "The Secret of Feedforward," *Saturday Review*, 3 Feb. 1968, p. 16.

[12] *Psychology from the Standpoint of a Behaviorist* (Philadelphia, 1919), p. 323.

to formulating a theory of grammar in accordance with their general position. All that Watson was interested in demonstrating was that language "is not different in essence from tennis playing, swimming, or any other overt activity except that it is hidden from ordinary observation and is more complex and at the same time more abbreviated so far as its parts are concerned than even the bravest of us could dream of" (p. 325). The behaviorist view is thus admittedly incomplete, but it has not been proved false. I am certainly not going to try to pick up the pieces, but I can see the plausibility of a view in which whatever it is that we call thought presents itself at the door of language with a complete set of specifications including the creation of new ideas that contemporary linguists insist on making their own, and getting back from language, by some very subtle form of conditioning, precisely the responses that correspond to each of the components of the thought. In short, if structuralists had worked a little harder, the new school might not be able now to embarrass them by encroaching on what perhaps does not belong as a part of language at all, the imaging level of psychology.

This is enough by way of confronting the two rival psychologies of language. It is time to turn to what they imply for the teaching of a second language. The trail has been blazed already by a number of linguists and applied linguists who have mostly used the implications to criticize the teaching now going on. By following their trail we can pick up where we left off some time back, when we were enumerating the criticisms against the audiolingual approach and trying to weigh the justifications for them.

The most alarming implication for foreign-language teaching is the question that the mentalist theory raises about whether it is possible to teach a language at all. For those who insist that a second language must be learned in the same way as the first, it comes as a shock to be told, in Saporta's words, that probably "children are not taught their language but. . .rather one could not prevent a normal child from acquiring the language of his environment."[13] But even the mentalist will not go this far—he may grant that what teaching we do leans very little on linguistic formulations, but for learning a second language he would not deny that a pedagogy can exist. It may be pointed out in passing that even where the first language is concerned, the notion of a child's not being taught is no better than a psychological half-truth. Child psychologists have noted ways in which mothers unconsciously simplify their speech in trying to communicate with very young children—for all we know this may be an instinctive way of giving easy models to follow. As you see, one can fight instinct with instinct:

[13]Saporta, p. 85. "Applying this rationalist view to the special case of language learning, Humboldt (1836) concludes that one cannot really teach language but can only present the conditions under which it will develop spontaneously in the mind in its own way." Chomsky, *Aspects of the Theory* . . .p. 51. But does "presenting the conditions" mean doing the same things that teachers have been doing all along, only calling it "teaching"? If so, the shift in theory has no pedagogical implications.

against the view that children have an instinct to speak or learn to speak and don't need to be taught, one can oppose the view that mothers have an instinct to teach and therefore children must need to be taught.

A second implication arises from the almost mathematically precise organization of the internalized grammar that the generativist conceptualizes. If one discovers a grammar, that grammar must exist in much the same form as a tightly integrated logical system, although it may be only as complete at any given time as the process of discovery has progressed. On the other hand, if one learns it, the imperfections of incomplete or haphazard learning would have to be built in, and the system might well be partially inconsistent as well as incomplete. The teacher who takes the discovery position would therefore have to know the system as a whole, or run the risk of ineffectual teaching. He might attempt to give his pupils a particular point without being aware that it is in conflict with some other point. Rosenbaum gives the example of the English teacher who insists that pupils drop the word *for* in sentences like *I'd hate for John to do it* without knowing whether this is somehow tied in with the use of the possessive in the phrase *John's doing it*, or with other supporting deep-seated structures—to be effective, the teaching must deal with the whole network at once. Until more is known about the grammar, he says, "it would be wildly presumptuous to speculate on the possibility of improving teaching techniques."[14] But his reasoning actually cancels itself out. Until we know more about the grammar it is presumptuous to speculate on whether the assumption that it displays more the earmarks of a discovered system than of a learned system is true, and meanwhile we have to teach, and must simply disregard counsels of perfection.

It is all the more wise to take this cautious position in view of some recent psycholinguistic experiments whose results seem to favor the learning model rather than the discovery model. The discovery model implies that once all the discoveries have been made (and a normal individual would naturally make all of them), the resulting population should be equal in competence. Lila R. Gleitman and her co-workers have turned up striking differences among speakers of different social groups in their ability to paraphrase, or bring out transformational relationships. She suspects that "grammars written by linguists may lack descriptive adequacy for normal populations: the linguists' informants are A-group members (that is latent grammar-writers). The linguist has succeeded in setting up a mirror and has described himself." She concludes that "Until we account for the fact that secretaries seem to be different in their linguistic competence from graduate students, we must reserve judgment on the hypothesis of equal competence—as well as on the nativist ramifications and neurophysiological suppositions that hang on it."[15]

[14] Rosenbaum, p. 348.

[15] Lila R. Gleitman, *Compound Nouns and English Speakers.* Preprint, issued by Eastern Pennsylvania Psychiatric Inst., Philadelphia, 10 Nov. 1967, of book to be published by Holden-Day, pp. 178–179.

The inwardness-outwardness rankings produce a third implication. If what is most fundamental is the deep grammar and the farther out one goes the more transient and superficial the phenomena become, the proportionately less attention ought to be given to what is farthest out. It follows that generativists do not care particularly whether the outward manifestation is carried by sounds or by letters. This echoes the feeling of the unreconstructed traditionalists during the early days of audiolingualism, who could be heard to say, "What difference does it make whether a sentence is spoken or written?" For some followers of generative grammar, this spells not merely an equalization of the two but a revival of the elevation of writing over speech. William Ritchie reasons that since "the nature of internalized linguistic knowledge is similar to visual, temporally constant representation of external events. . ., the type of task best suited to knowledge-formation is visual."[16] In other words, since the competence that we talked about is carried around in static form, and writing is also static, writing makes a better medium for teaching. Sympathetic as one may feel to the desire to get writing back on some kind of equality of footing, there are just too many flaws in this ratiocination to entitle it to be taken seriously. In the first place, in regarding speech phenomena as transitory it ignores the existence—and the prime need to cultivate—an auditory memory: it is precisely the presence of the written crutch that makes it difficult to acquire an unwritten retentiveness. In the second place, it leaves unexamined the precise sense in which writing is static: a book can be put on a shelf, but until it is being read by someone, until the written signs begin to undergo some kind of processing, the content has no existence as language. The author is right in the sense that for any form of factual learning a medium that can be arrested and held stationary is useful, but not in the sense that language is necessarily stationary. Nevertheless, one net effect of generative grammar is a renewed support for writing, which will be a good thing if it is not overdone.

Inwardness and outwardness are responsible for yet a fourth implication, which is that since the surface manifestations are of secondary importance, proportionately more attention should be given to deep structure. This is probably again a good recommendation for a bad reason. More attention should be paid to deep structure because too little attention was paid to it in the past, not because it is more important in foreign language teaching. In fact, if generativists argue in this fashion they seem to be contradicting themselves. They say that all languages are the same at the deepest layer of their grammar. In this sense I already know Chinese. It is as we move closer to the surface that languages become less alike, and more energy needs to be spent in teaching them.

The emphasis on competence and on understanding the how of language and not just its surface output gives a fifth implication: the requirement that the

[16]"Some Implications of Generative Grammar for the Construction of Courses in English as a Foreign Language," *Language Learning,* 17 (1967), 47.

rules of grammar be presented and taught forthright, not left in the care of induction on the part of bashful students. There is no question that the feasibility of induction has been exaggerated out of all proportion to students' ability to conduct it. I make a practice annually of mortifying my graduate class in applied linguistics with some simple problem in induction, basing it on a clearly delimited set of data in English or their major language; invariably some of them miss, and if the point is at all subtle, the majority do. If the future teacher cannot be relied upon to make a correct generalization, what can one expect of an undergraduate beginner? Yet we insist, and the reason must reside in our folklore. A generation of language teachers has emerged so scarred by the identification of grammar teaching with the teaching of normative and puristic rules that it has shied away from teaching grammar directly and deductively; sentences are given to repeat and practice usually grouped in certain ways to help the process along, but with the student expected to make his own guesses about the rules. At most, these might be explained later in a kind of embarrassed, offhand way as "summaries of behavior." The generativist position not only fosters a greater attention to grammar but is opposed to the very concept of induction, which assumes the possibility of discovering the nature of the machine by inspecting its products. Of all the effects of generative grammar on language teaching, this is probably one of the most beneficial, though again it is a conclusion that is more directly related to history than to generative theory. The structuralists were not to blame for the phobia about grammar; they merely lacked the means to combat it because their attention was so riveted on one narrow part of grammar, the phonological side, that the noxious effects of purism on the other parts of grammar, with which teachers had to be mainly concerned, were never counteracted. They also were in no position to diminish the teacher's vulnerability on another count—the need to correct students' *mistakes*. This had become another taboo concept, likewise wrongly identified with the puristic concern about mistakes in English. The audiolingual approach displays an almost pathological fear of ever pointing out anything wrong; this is one reason for the popularity of methods that left no room for error, the clearest example being the repetition drill. The structuralist was in no position to help because his doctrine permitted him to work only with actual samples of speech produced by native speakers, who by definition could do no wrong. The generativist has saved the day because he is as much interested in ungrammatical as in grammatical sentences—both are needed for him to test the adequacy of his formulations. But notice that there is nothing here inconsistent with induction as such. Induction merely needs objective evidence to work from; the teacher had this evidence all along, in the form of student mistakes. The structuralist chose to disregard it, and also to disregard the wrong sentences produced by children, and the errors made by foreigners and the mentally ill, and the lapses committed by normal speakers. So the anti-induction of the generativist contains a measure of sloganeering. He cannot do without induction himself, for he uses it to make the guesses which he blends into the formulations of his inner grammar. He has yet to prove that any of his rules emerge from his consciousness, directly from his "knowledge of his grammar," without the mediation of actually produced sentences over which observations are made and other sentences invented and tried out. Nevertheless, despite the sloganeering and the irrelevant darts and arrows in the direction of those perennial culprits, the structuralists, we can be grateful that teachers no longer need to be ashamed to call themselves grammarians and can make induction keep its place without throwing it away.

The mention of drill brings us of course to this most inviting target of all and the sixth implication which is that drill may be useless if not pernicious. The rationale of the pattern drill is behavioristic. It assumes that by using a construction over and over in a specially devised frame, a student will internalize the features of the construction. A generativist argues that for at least some types of construction this is false, again because one cannot go from surface grammar to deep grammar by way of induction. Saporta gives the English sentence *I like entertaining guests* as an example. It might be drilled for its two senses by inserting the word *the* in the proper place: *I like the entertaining guests* vs. *I like entertaining the guests*. But a drill that does this cannot be performed unless the student already knows where to put *the*—in other words, already knows the underlying grammar. And if the direction is reversed, and the student is drilled by being given *He entertains guests and likes it* and told to derive from it the sentence *He likes entertaining guests* and also given *He likes guests who are entertaining*, from which again to derive *He likes entertaining guests*, the result is no better because since the output is the same the drill can be performed automatically and "does not insure learning." The key word here is "insure." There are no guarantees in teaching. The generativists are right in planting suspicion as to the power of drills alone to yield control over points of grammar, but wrong to claim that "by definition, drills cannot teach rules."[17] "Teaching" something involves more than the initial grasp of a rule. That may of course be taught by a deductive presentation. But being given a rule is like being introduced to a stranger; we may be able to recognize him on later encounters, but cannot be said to know him. Teaching a rule involves not just the phase of grasping but the phase of familiarizing. To imagine that drills are to be displaced by rule-giving is to imagine that digestion can be displaced by swallowing. We have to return to the lowly origin of drills, which was in the humble setting of the classroom, before anybody thought of dressing them up in behaviorist philosophy. We have pragmatic reasons for retaining them, and retain them we should. This says nothing of the limitless need for improving them.

We can hurry over a couple of remaining implications. One, which is a point of only imagined controversy, is the avoidance of translation, vaguely imputed to structuralism in a process of guilt by association. The real reason why we avoid

[17] Hanzeli, p. 50.

it is probably the strong influence of the direct method on audiolingualism. A lot of direct-methodists climbed on the audiolingual bandwagon and brought their anti-translation music with them. It was they who insisted that all communication—even explanation of grammar—should be in the target language, a position that was scoffed at by Palmer, who pointed out that one does not learn shorthand from books written in shorthand (p. 115). The structuralists were not opposed to translation—one of the best audiolingual teaching manuals, that of Dacanay, gives several pages to justification of translation drills (pp. 145-146, 150-151).[18] And the usefulness of translation has been underscored on the generative side by Saporta, who points out that some way of incorporating meaning into teaching has to be found, and the easiest shortcut is by way of the learner's native language (pp. 83-84). There are good reasons for being cautious with translation, but Hanzeli describes them in terms that are appropriate for most of the things that teachers do and don't do: reasons, he says, "which may be good or bad, probably good, though; reasons which are psychological, pedagogical, pragmatic, commonsensical—but hardly linguistic" (p. 45).

I end my list of implications with one which the appliers of generative grammar have overlooked, but which follows both from the concept of the inborn language-learning device and from the abandonment of the phobia toward making mistakes. We have already heard the claim that children learn their first language but are not taught it. One pedagogical conclusion is that if acquiring a second language can be modeled at all on the first-language learning, part of the method ought to be arranging the conditions for learning in ways that will enable that inborn device to work. Since children learn by communicating with native speakers, and learn by their successes and their mistakes, we can infer that one set of conditions ought to be more face-to-face communicating, even in the early stages, with native speakers of the target language. This implies the supplementing of not just the audiolingual classroom but of any classroom at all—putting students into situations that will provide the strongest motivation for calling their innate abilities into play, and the strongest exercise of that ability. Oddly enough, this very obvious implication has been blocked by a belief which is scarcely more than a superstition: that by a certain age, the inborn mechanism ceases to operate.[19] All that we know is that most adults do not learn as rapidly as children do just by exposure. But in actual fact we do not know that the process in the child is one of simple exposure either, nor can we be sure that the real reason for an adult's failure to learn that way is not the many external interferences that cause him to shun the opportunities. In any case, it would be a shame not to experiment with this premise.

This ends my catalog of implications. I have tried to show that many if not

[18] Fe R. Dacanay, *Techniques and Procedures in Second Language Teaching* (Quezon City, Philippines, 1963).

[19] Cf. Saporta, p. 85.

most of the supposed weaknesses of audiolingual teaching have not been weaknesses of theory but of practice and proportion. I am not sure that language teaching needs a theory. If I were required to identify one benefit conferred by audiolingualism that surpasses all others, I would say that it is the insistence that teachers teach with all their might. How much we teach is certainly as important as how we teach. The continual tinkering with methods may be missing the main point. Intensity of teaching has little to do with theory. I appeal again to my analogy with medicine. Since the battle between the allopaths and the homeopaths subsided more than half a century ago, the notices of "medical theory" contain a hint of quackery—like the electronic medicine that was all the rage in the early twenties of this century. There are medical *theories*, such as the germ theory and the virus theory. Similarly there can be theories about particular aspects of teaching foreign languages, conceived in the light of classroom problems and tested pragmatically. Some of these theories can even be linguistic on a small scale, cut to the measure of the classroom needs. Within the limits of his discipline the language teacher can be his own theorist if he has eyes in his head and has the instinct to theorize that he was born with—as surely as he was born with an instinct for language.

If the language teacher is to follow Chomsky and be skeptical about the pronouncements of linguists on language teaching, let him not fall from one misguided faith into another but also be skeptical of the pronouncements of other linguists on the shortcomings of the pronouncements. Along with the foundation of his own professional organization, the American Council on the Teaching of Foreign Languages, let him acquire the pride of it. A professional is entitled to a mind of his own. He can be grateful for linguistic controversy precisely *because* it gives him a choice. As William Shipley, Paul Garvin, and Joseph Grimes point out in an article on the same subject that occupies us here, "From the teaching standpoint both positions have advantages: the first (the behaviorist one), in viewing language as basically stimulus and response, turns out to be highly useful for making oral exercises; the mentalist position on the other hand, is enormously helpful for the explanations that students may need to be given."[20] This attitude is not likely to appeal to the intellectual esthete for whom eclecticism is a disgustingly uncommitted philosophy. But teaching, like life, has its own criteria by which it integrates for its needs, and it should not bother language teachers whether they are clean enough to draw straight theoretical lines around.

[20] "Linguistica Descriptiva y la Ensenanza de Idiomas," *El Simposio de cartagena, Agosto de 1963, Informes y Communicaciones* (Bogotá, 1965), p. 301.

4

HOW NOT TO INTERFERE WITH LANGUAGE LEARNING

LEONARD NEWMARK

What dangers for the development of language courses does Newmark see that might be the result of an over-explicit knowledge of the languages we teach?

Try to specify what *complex bits of language* might be learned a *whole chunk at a time* in contrast to language that is learned in an *additive and linear* fashion.

Identify a *chunk* of language that you feel would be amenable to the kind of structured drill that Newmark would find acceptable.

Compare the overall recommendations made by Newmark with those made by Hornby (Art. 8). What are their areas of agreement and disagreement?

How would you compare Newmark's notions of teaching by *chunks* with the four-stage progression recommended by Prator (Art. 15)?

In the applied linguistics of the past twenty years much has been made of the notion of first-language interference with second-language learning. Our dominant conception of languages as structures and our growing sophistication in the complex analysis of these structures have made it increasingly attractive to linguists to consider the task of learning a new language as if it were essentially a task of fighting off an old set of structures in order to clear the way for a new set. The focal emphasis of language teaching by applied linguists has more and more been placed on structural drills based on the linguist's contrastive analysis of the structures of the learner's language and his target language: the weight given to teaching various things is determined not by their importance to the user of the language, but by their degree of difference from what the analyst takes to be corresponding features of the native language.

A different analysis of verbal behavior has been motivated in psychology by reinforcement theory; the application of this analysis has led, of course, to

Reprinted by permission from the *International Journal of American Linguistics*, 32 (January, 1966), 77–83. Professor Newmark is a member of the Department of Linguistics at the University of California, San Diego.

programmed instruction, step-by-step instruction based in practice on the identification of what are taken to be the components of the terminal verbal behavior. What could be more natural than the marriage of linguistics and psychology in the programmed instruction of foreign languages, with linguistics providing the "systematic specification of terminal behaviors" and psychology providing "the techniques of the laboratory analysis and control" of those behaviors.[1]

If the task of learning to speak English were additive and linear, as present linguistic and psychological discussions suggest it is, it is difficult to see how anyone could learn English. If each phonological and syntactic rule, each complex of lexical features, each semantic value and stylistic nuance—in short, if each item which the linguist's analysis leads him to identify had to be acquired one at a time, proceeding from simplest to most complex, and then each had to be connected to specified stimuli or stimulus sets, the child learner would be old before he could say a single appropriate thing and the adult learner would be dead. If each frame of a self-instructional program could teach only one item (or even two or three) at a time, programmed language instruction would never enable the students to use the language significantly. The item-by-item contrastive drills proposed by most modern applied linguists and the requirement by programmers that the behaviors to be taught must be specified seem to rest on this essentially hopeless notion of the language learning process.

When linguists and programmers talk about planning their textbooks, they approach the problem as if they had to decide what structural features each lesson should be trying to teach. The whole program will teach the sum of its parts: the student will know this structure and that one and another and another. . . .If the question is put to him directly, the linguist will undoubtedly admit that the sum of the structures he can describe is not equal to the capability a person needs in order to use the language, but the question is rarely put to him directly. If it is, he may evade the uncomfortable answer by appealing to the intelligence of the user to apply the structures he knows to an endless variety of situations. But the evasion fails, I think, against the inescapable fact that a person, even an intelligent one, who knows perfectly the structures that the linguist teaches, cannot know that the way to get his cigarette lit by a stranger when he has no matches is to walk up to him and say one of the utterances "Do you have a light?" or "Got a match?" (Not one of the equally well-formed questions, "Do you have fire?" or "Do you have illumination?" or "Are you a match's owner?").

In natural foreign language learning—the kind used, for example, by children to become native speakers in a foreign country within a length of time that amazes their parents—acquisition cannot be simply additive; complex bits of language are learned a whole chunk at a time. Perhaps by some process of stimulus sampling[2] the parts of the chunks are compared and become available

[1] Harlan Lane, "Programmed Learning of a Second Language," *IRAL* 2. 250 (1964).

[2] I take the term and notion from W. K. Estes, "Learning Theory," *Annual Review of Psychology* 13. 110 (1962).

for use in new chunks. The possible number of "things known" in the language exponentiates as the number of chunks increases additively, since every complex chunk makes available a further analysis of old chunks into new elements, each still attached to the original context upon which its appropriateness depends.

It is not that linguists and psychologists are unaware of the possibility of learning language in complex chunks or of the importance of learning items in contexts. Indeed it would be difficult to find a serious discussion of new language teaching methods that did not claim to reform old language teaching methods in part through the use of "natural" contexts. It is rather that consideration of the details supplied by linguistic and psychological analysis has taken attention away from the exponential power available in learning in natural chunks. In present psychologically oriented programs the requirement that one specify the individual behaviors to be reinforced leads (apparently inevitably) to an artificial isolation of parts from wholes; in structurally oriented textbooks and courses, contrastive analysis leads to structural drills designed to teach a set of specific "habits" for the well-formation of utterances, abstracted from normal social context.

Our very knowledge of the fine structure of language constitutes a threat to our ability to maintain perspective in teaching languages. Inspection of language textbooks designed by linguists reveals an increasing emphasis in recent years on structural drills in which pieces of language are isolated from the linguistic and social contexts which make them meaningful and useful to the learner. The more we know about a language, the more such drills we have been tempted to make. If one compares, say, the Spoken Language textbooks devised by linguists during the Second World War with some of the recent textbooks devised by linguists,[3] he is struck by the shift in emphasis from connected situational dialogue to disconnected structural exercise.

The argument of this paper is that such isolation and abstraction of the learner from the contexts in which that language is used constitutes serious interference with the language learning process. Because it requires the learner to attach new responses to old stimuli, this kind of interference may in fact increase the interference that applied linguists like to talk about—the kind in which a learner's previous language structures are said to exert deleterious force on the structures being acquired.

Consider the problem of teaching someone to say something. What is it we are most concerned that he learns? Certainly not the mere mouthing of the utterance, the mere ability to pronounce the words. Certainly not the mere demonstration of ability to understand the utterance by, say, translation into the learner's own language. Even the combination of the two goals is not what we are

---

[3] For example, see Dwight L. Bolinger et al., *Modern Spanish*, Harcourt, Brace & Co., 1960; L. B. Swift et al., *Igbo: Basic Course*, Foreign Service Institute, 1962; John J. Gumperz and June Rumery, *Conversational Hindi-Urdu*, n.p., 1962.

after: it is not saying *and* understanding that we want but saying *with* understanding. That is, we want the learner to be able to use the language we teach him, and we want him to be able to extend his ability to new cases, to create new utterances that are appropriate to his needs as a language user.

Recent linguistic theory has offered a detailed abstract characterization of language competence; learning a finite set of rules and a finite lexicon enables the learner to produce and interpret an infinite number of new well-formed sentences. Plausible detailed accounts also abound in the psychological and philosophical literature to explain how formal repertoires might be linked referentially to the real world. But the kinds of linguistic rules that have been characterized so far (syntactic, phonological, and semantic) bear on the question of well-formedness of sentences, not on the question of appropriateness of utterances. And the stimulus-response or associational- or operant-conditioning accounts that help explain how *milk* comes to mean "milk" are of little help in explaining my ability to make up a particular something appropriate to say about milk—such as *I prefer milk*—in a discussion of what one likes in his coffee, and even less my ability to ignore the mention of milk when it is staring me in the face. An important test of our success as language teachers, it seems reasonable to assert, is the ability of our students to choose to say what they want. It has been difficult for linguists and psychologists to attach any significance to the expression "saying what you want to say"; our inability to be precise about the matter may well have been an important reason for our neglect of it in language teaching. But importance of a matter is not measured by our ability at a given moment to give a precise description of it; we can be precise about the allophones of voiceless stops in English after initial /s/, but it seems absurd to claim that it is basically as important—some textbooks imply *more* important—to teach students to make these allophones properly as it is to teach them, for example, how to get someone to repeat something he has just said.

The odd thing is that despite our ignorance as experts, as human beings we have always known how to teach other human beings to use a language: use it ourselves and let them imitate us as best they can at the time. Of course, this method has had more obvious success with children than with adult learners, but we have no compelling reason to believe with either children or adults that the method is not both necessary and sufficient to teach a language.

If we adopt the position I have been maintaining—that language is learned a whole act at a time rather than learned as an assemblage of constituent skills— what would a program for teaching students to speak a foreign language look like?[4]

---

[4] I shall restrict myself here to the question of teaching a spoken language. How one teaches people to read and write a foreign language depends on their literacy in another language and on their mastery of the spoken language in which they are learning to be literate. The problems involved would take me too far afield of the subject I am discussing here.

For the classroom, the simple formulation that the students learn by imitating someone else using the language needs careful development. Since the actual classroom is only one small piece of the world in which we expect the learner to use the language, artificial means must be used to transform it into a variety of other pieces: the obvious means for performing this transformation is drama—imaginative play has always been a powerful educational device both for children and adults. By creating a dramatic situation in a classroom—in part simply by acting out dialogues, but also in part by relabeling objects and people in the room (supplemented by realia if desired) to prepare for imaginative role-playing—the teacher can expand the classroom indefinitely and provide imaginatively natural contexts for the language being used.

The idea of using models as teachers is hardly new in applied linguistics; and nothing could be more commonplace than the admonition that the model be encouraged to dramatize and the student to imitate the dramatization of the situation appropriate to the particular bit of language being taught. The sad fact is, however, that the drill material the model has been given to model has intrinsic features that draw the attention of the student away from the situation and focus it on the form of the utterance. Instead of devising techniques that induce the model to act out roles for the student to imitate, the applied linguist has devised techniques of structural drill that put barriers in the way of dramatic behavior and a premium on the personality-less manipulation of a formal repertoire of verbal behavior.

If what the learner observes is such that he cannot absorb it completely within his short-term memory, he will make up for his deficiency if he is called on to perform before he has learned the new behavior by padding with material from what he already knows, that is, his own language. This padding—supplying what is known to make up for what is not known—is the major source of "interference," the major reason for "foreign accents." Seen in this light, the cure for interference is simply the cure for ignorance: learning. There is no particular need to combat the intrusion of the learner's native language—the explicit or implicit justification for the contrastive analysis that applied linguists have been claiming to be necessary for planning language-teaching courses. But there is need for controlling the size of the chunks displayed for imitation. In general if you want the learner's imitation to be more accurate, make the chunks smaller; increase the size of the chunks as the learner progresses in his skill in imitation. We do not need to impose arbitrary, artificial criteria for successful behavior on the part of the learner. If we limit our demand for immediate high quality of production, we may well find that his behavior is adequately shaped by the same *ad hoc* forces that lead a child from being a clumsy performer capable of using his language only with a terribly inaccurate accent, and in a limited number of social situations, to becoming a skillful native speaker capable of playing a wide variety of social roles with the appropriate language for each.

To satisfy our requirement that the student learn to extend to new cases the ability he gains in acting out one role, a limited kind of structural drill can be used: keeping in mind that the learning must be embedded in a meaningful context, the drill may be constructed by introducing small variations into the situation being acted out (e.g., ordering orange juice instead of tomato juice, being a dissatisfied customer rather than a satisfied one, changing the time at which the action takes place) which call for partial innovation in the previously learned role. In each case the situation should be restaged, reenacted, played as meaning something to the student.

The student's craving for explicit formulization of generalizations can usually be met better by textbooks and grammars that he reads outside class than by discussion in class. If discussion of grammar is made into a kind of dramatic event, however, such discussion might be used as the situation being learned—with the students learning to play the role of students in a class on grammar. The important point is that the study of grammar as such is neither necessary nor sufficient for learning to use a language.

So far, I have been talking about the use of live models in language classrooms. How can such techniques be adapted for self-instruction? The cheapness and simplicity of operation of the new videotape recorders already make possible a large portion of the acquisition of a language without the presence of a model; it has been shown convincingly that under the proper conditions it is possible for human students to learn—in the sense of acquiring competence—certain very complex behaviors by mere observation of that behavior in use.[5] Acquiring the willingness to perform—learning in a second sense—seems to depend to a greater extent on reinforcement of the student's own behavior and is thus not quite so amenable to instruction without human feedback at the present time. However, extension of techniques (originally developed to establish phonological competence in step-by-step programmed instruction)[6] for self-monitoring to cover whole utterances with their appropriate kinetic accompaniment may suffice in the future to make the second kind of learning as independent of live teachers as the first and thus make complete self-instruction in the use of a language possible.

[5] For an excellent discussion of the roles of imitation and reinforcement in the acquisition and performance of complex behavior, see Albert Bandura and Richard H. Walters, *Social Learning and Personality Development*, Holt, Rinehart and Winston, 1963.

[6] For example, the techniques used in Stanley Sapon's *Spanish A*, in the TEMAC series for Encyclopedia Britannica Films, 1961.

5

CONDITIONS FOR   E. V. GATENBY
SUCCESS IN
LANGUAGE
LEARNING

If you were to combine the notions of Montaigne, Comenius, Locke, Ticknor, Marcel, and Gouin into a list of Do's and Don't's for language teachers, what would each category include? (It will be of interest to compare your resulting lists with suggestions found in other articles written by language experts in recent years.)

Gatenby speaks of a *natural process* in second language learning. From this article, what do you deduce to be the characteristics of the *natural process*?

With which of Gatenby's *seven governing factors of achievement* do you agree? Which do you doubt? With which do you disagree? What modifications would you make, if any, to his list of *governing factors*? Compare these factors with the four mentioned by Spolsky (Art. 42).

If there were as much failure in the secondary schools of the world in the teaching of mathematics, history or science as there is in the teaching of living foreign languages, education as a whole might be said to have broken down. There is certainly no other school subject in which more has been abandoned through despair of success. One cannot imagine an arithmetic teacher deciding to avoid multiplication and division on account of their difficulty, and to devote his attention to perfecting his pupils in addition and subtraction; yet a very similar procedure is adopted by the linguistic teacher who, exasperated by the inability of his pupils to learn, or of himself to teach, a foreign language as used by native speakers of it, cuts out hearing, speaking and writing and concentrates on reading only.

Admittedly there are difficulties, some real, some imaginary, some artificially created, in the learning and teaching of a second instrument of thought; and it may be accepted that the failure to overcome these or evade them is responsible for the enormous amount of time that is wasted in unsuccessful efforts to master

Reprinted by permission from *English Language Teaching*, 6 (1950), 143–150. The late Professor Gatenby had held the Chair of English at Sendai University in Japan and, later, that at the University, Ankara, Turkey.

a new idiom. Every generation of teachers and pupils learns what the obstacles are, and large numbers, like their predecessors, give up the struggle after a few half-hearted attempts to get beyond the early stages.

The strange thing is that though the problems connected with language learning were all known and solved more than a hundred years ago the solutions have never been given widespread acceptance or application. There is reluctance everywhere to sacrifice tradition. Languages have been a school subject for so long that educators refuse to abandon the text-book and writing materials. It is as though a patient, offered a remedy, insisted on clinging to the conditions responsible for his disease.

Montaigne (1533-1592), in his essay *"De l'institution des enfants,"* tells how he learnt Latin by the natural process:

> My late father, having by all the meanes and industrie, that it is possible for man, sought amongst the wisest, and men of best understanding to find a most exquisite and readie way of teaching, being advised of the inconveniences then in use, was given to understand, that the lingring while, and the best part of our youth, that we imploy in learning the tongues, which cost them nothing, is the onely cause we can never attaine to that absolute perfection of skill and knowledge, of the Greekes, and Romanes. I doe not beleeve that to be the onely cause. But so it is, the expedient my father found out was this; that being yet at nurse, and before the first loosing of my tongue, I was delivered to a Germane . . . he being then altogether ignorant of the French tongue, but exquisitely readie and skilfull in the Latine. This man, whom my father had sent for of purpose . . . had me continually in his armes, and was mine onely overseer. There were also joyned unto him two of his countrimen, but not so learned; whose charge was to attend, and now and then, to play with me; and all these together did never entertaine me with other than the Latine tongue. As for others of his household, it was an inviolable rule, that neither himselfe, nor my mother, nor man, nor maid-servant, were suffered to speake one word in my companie, except such Latine words, as every one had learned to chat and prattle with me. . . . And as for my selfe, I was about six yeares old, and could understand no more French or Perigordine, than Arabike, and that without art, without bookes, rules, or grammer, without whipping or whining, I had gotten as pure a Latine tongue as my Master could speake; the rather because I could neither mingle or confound the same with other tongues. (Florio's translation)

Comenius (1591-1670), in his *Janua Linguarum Reserata*, taught us the use of limited and selected vocabulary, the necessity for learning sentences rather than disconnected words, and in *Orbis Pictus* the use of pictures.

John Locke (1632-1704) knew the virtues of the oral approach, and in *Some Thoughts Concerning Education* recommended that French should be "talked into" an English child in a perfectly natural way. "Languages," he says, "were not made by rules or art, but by accident and the common use of the people. And he that will speak them well has no other rule but that, nor anything to trust to but his memory and the habit of speaking after the fashion learned from those that are allowed to speak by rote."

George Ticknor (1791-1871) delivered a lecture at Harvard on "The Best Methods of Teaching the Living Languages" (1832), and here, in addition to insistence on language as speech, we have perhaps for the first time recognition of the fact that there is no *one* method of teaching languages, but that the teacher must vary his method according to the age and attainments of his class, and further, select and arrange his materials to suit the individual needs and capacities of his pupils. He emphasized especially the three age-groups—little children, adolescents, and adults—for which method and material must be appropriately varied.

Claude Marcel, in *The Study of Languages Brought Back to its True Principles* (1867), warned against formal training in grammar or translation, and advocated the order hearing, reading, speaking, writing.

Francois Gouin, in his *L'Art d'enseigner et d'étudier les langues,* translated into English in 1892, invented the Sequential Series and a system of learning through action. Since Gouin, it is doubtful whether any new principle has been discovered. Later reforms have been based less on original theories than on the putting into practice of sound methods described or adumbrated many years earlier. West, for example, learned much from Marcel—or independently gave pre-eminence to reading; and Palmer developed and popularized items of technique which had formed part of Gouin's system.

The refusal of generations of teachers and educational administrators to benefit from the successful experiments and proved theories of the past is an example partly of human perversity: men will not choose the right or the best or what is good for them when it is pointed out. But the neglect of salvation is also partly due to sheer ignorance of the record of discovery: questionnaires are still sent out seeking evidence already available, and heated discussions take place on points of methodology which to a trained language-teacher should be axiomatic. This flogging of dead horses remains a pastime of educational conferences.

Two other hindrances to the spread of the latest information concerning foreign-language study are (*a*) the habit of neglecting movements outside one's own national borders, and (*b*) isolating every foreign language for special treatment. From the contents of a recent large volume of more than seven hundred pages entitled *Twentieth Century Modern Language Teaching*, published by The Philosophical Library, New York, a reader might easily be misled into concluding that French, Spanish and German were taught only in the schools of the U.S.A., and that each language presented problems entirely distinct from those of other languages. Yet second-language teaching as an art or as a science is in its main principles universal, like every other art or science, however great the variety may be in materials and conditions. Until the theory and practice of language study can be codified and become as widely known as the successful experiments of Froebel or Montessori or Dewey, there will be the same dismal record of failure in the language classrooms of secondary schools throughout the world.

An examination of particular examples of success in learning to speak a second language and to understand it when spoken will reveal what the basic principles are. As such examples we may consider:

(*a*) A small child who is taken abroad and rapidly becomes bilingual, or one who becomes bilingual through having experience of two linguistic environments in his own country.

(*b*) Kindergartens for foreign children.

(*c*) A small class of secondary school children with the right type of teacher.

(*d*) Intensive courses for adults similar to those formed according to the Army Specialized Training scheme in America or those at the School of Oriental and African Studies, University of London, during the last war.

(*e*) Specially selected students who are sent abroad by the Army, Navy or Foreign Office.

This does not exhaust the number of examples of successful learning that might be given. I have deliberately excluded the exceptionally gifted type of man, whose perception of any group of human sounds is perfect, who can imitate them and remember them, and identify them when he hears them again; and, on a lower plane, the dragoman type, with somewhat similar natural gifts but without the intelligence or education to make the best use of them.

It will be profitable before pointing out the common grounds of success in the five groups to glance at the conditions. The language itself—French, Arabic, or Chinese—and the country where the study goes on (except in (*e*)) have little or no bearing on the results.

In (*a*) the child finds itself in a new or different environment where, to satisfy its needs, it must learn to understand certain sounds and to make them. It cannot play with other children, it cannot make its wishes known to them or its nurse or the servant, unless it uses sound symbols different from those it uses and hears in the presence of father and mother. Nobody teaches it language in the conventional sense of the term. It may have a group of sounds repeated to it, or be occasionally corrected or laughed at for a mispronunciation. It learns to speak and hear only. More often than not it is unaware—as unaware as a speaker of dialect and standard—that it uses two languages, for a child learns not *a* language, but language. If the new or different contacts occupy some hours of every day, in from six to nine months the child will be speaking the second language as proficiently as native speakers of its own age.

In (*b*) we have an infants' department in a school in which language x is used throughout; or the school itself may be nothing more than a kindergarten where the teacher or teachers use x only. The pupils may, some of them, be native speakers of x, in which case they themselves are unconsciously teaching the other children. There may be amongst the children almost as many languages as pupils; or there may be one only in addition to x. But for all school activities, indoor or outdoor, x is not so much taught as used. The pupils follow the normal occupations of a kindergarten, all of them interesting—painting, drawing, games, making things, looking at pictures, listening to stories, especially stories where they can imitate actions—and all the time they hear x. After a short period of incubation they begin to remember and imitate, learning as bilinguals do from their playmates without conscious effort. They absorb the language by a natural process, and again the time required for proficiency in using the language as a native speaker of that age uses it is nine months.

(*c*) A small class of older children with a competent teacher is merely an extension of the kindergarten conditions, but instead of a whole morning or afternoon every day rarely more than five or six hours a week can be devoted to the use of *x*. In addition, educational authorities usually insist that reading and writing shall go *pari passu* with hearing and speaking; and outside the hours assigned to *x* the pupils have to be intellectually active with other subjects taught in the vernacular. Consequently it takes about three years to bring them to the level reached by kindergarten children in nine months. If they had equal hours, and could almost wholly neglect reading and writing—as all children do when learning the elements of their own language—the extra years would not be necessary.

In such classes almost everything depends upon the teacher, who should be a woman of a motherly type with a genuine affection for her pupils, able to bring a home atmosphere into the classroom. She will use *x* and allow it to be absorbed as much as possible through pleasurable activities. An official textbook is a hindrance, but must often be used for the teaching of reading. Children's storybooks, with attractive illustrations, are more helpful. There is plenty of evidence to show that the teacher need not be a native speaker of *x*, but she must be able to use it fluently and correctly.

(*d*) These intensive courses for soldiers and civilians for whom it was necessary to learn the speech of their allies or enemies were organized during the war of 1939-1945. No particular methodology was enforced on the teachers: they were judged, as all teachers should be, by their success or failure. The outstanding features of the courses in England and America were small groups of learners; trained teachers with a thorough knowledge of the language being studied, and preferably native speakers of it; concentration on the colloquial; several hours a day of application. Proficiency was achieved, and demonstrated in fairly severe tests, in from six to nine months.

(*e*) The "student-interpreters" who were sent to a foreign country for two years to learn its language were picked men, mentally disposed to their task, and they usually spent a year in mastering the elements of the language before going abroad. The common practice, where the standards of civilization permitted, was for the student to live with his teacher, a native of the country, and to dedicate the whole of his time to his work. In the two years he was expected to acquire proficiency not only in the colloquial but the written forms of the language, and in addition to make himself familiar with the culture of the people. That the majority of such students were successful in the stiff tests they had to undergo shows that two years, in addition to the preliminary year at home, was sufficient. With only the spoken language to master, they might well have achieved their aim in one year or less. This is borne out by the experience of ordinary citizens who go abroad and, determined or compelled to acquire the speech of their new environment, usually succeed in less than a year.

We may now, with these five different examples before us of children and adults able to become proficient in not more than a year in at least the elementary speech of a foreign language—and the speech is the foundation of all other linguistic skills—infer what the governing factors of the achievement are.

1. Necessity comes first. The child in a home environment or in a kindergarten is driven to adopt the prevailing forms of communication in order to share in the activities around it and thus be happy and contented rather than lonely and miserable. Other children in a Middle School are likewise impelled to follow the practice of the little society in which they find themselves or be wretchedly excluded from it. The adults, full of purpose, with either army discipline to "encourage" them when they flag or the threat of economic disaster at their heels, must prevail or perish.

2. There must be concentration on speech, and hearing and speaking must precede reading and writing, though where older children or adults are to some extent learning intellectually as well as imitatively the interval between the oral and visual forms may be short.

3. Translation and the study of grammar have no place in the process by which children learn a second language, though they are helpful to adults.

4. The particular physical environment is not of supreme importance. Japanese as speech can be learnt well and quickly in London or New York. What is essential is that the language being studied should be as far as possible the sole medium of communication in any given environment.

5. The rate of progress depends obviously upon the amount of time that can be allotted to the language. With three or four hours a day both children and adults may become proficient in speech in less than a year.

6. Classes and groups must be kept small. The pace slows down if there are more than ten adults or twenty children to one teacher.

7. In order to be learnt the language must be used.

These seven governing factors underlying success in the learning of second languages stand out prominently as part of the natural process of learning one's mother tongue.

1. Nature compels a child to acquire the speech that is used around it.

2. Nature does not teach the artificial process of reading and writing.

3. Translation and grammar are outside the natural process.

4. Every child learns to speak the language it hears irrespective of physical environment.

5. Nature supplies a full-time course.

6. Under natural conditions groups of learners are rare, but there are a number of teachers for each child.

7. Language is a natural activity.

BEHAVIORISTIC AND COGNITIVE APPROACHES IN PROGRAMMED INSTRUCTION

KENNETH CHASTAIN

Do you agree with Chastain's opening sentence as to what constitutes the language teacher's *central problem*?

In Markle's illustration are the two responses actually the same? Consider the stress patterns. What would be the short answers?

According to Chastain, is there a place for both *behavioristic* and *cognitive* approaches to language teaching? Explain.

Analyze one or more ESL textbooks to determine the author's reliance on either the behavioristic or cognitive approach.

INTRODUCTION

Modern language teachers are faced with one central problem: developing the language learner's ability in the second language to the point at which his language usage is characterized by the unconscious application of the rules of the language as conscious attention is paid to the ideas to be communicated. In other words, language, to be functional, must become a habit. The second-language learner is successful to the extent that he can create, almost instantaneously, language appropriate to any given communicative context.

The problem then becomes one of habit formation. How are habits acquired? How does one arrive at a level of proficiency which makes conscious attention to the act unnecessary, or even impossible? In general, two quite divergent answers have been given to the question of habit formation, one based on a behavioristic interpretation of learning and the other based on a cognitive interpretation.

Reprinted by permission from *Language Learning*, 20 (1970), 223-235. The writer is assistant professor of modern language education in the Department of Modern Languages, Purdue University.

THE BEHAVIORISTIC VIEWPOINT

The behaviorists feel that learning is basically a process of conditioning. The learner is led through a series of stimulus-response situations which take him closer and closer to the desired goal. Learning takes place as the bond between the stimulus and its associated response is being formed. When the learner can give the desired response to the specific stimulus, he has learned that connection. A person's learned behaviors, then, consist of a myriad of conditioned responses.

The conception of learning outlined in the preceding paragraph is considered to be a mechanistic interpretation of learning since the mind is not assigned a role in the conditioning process. The following illustration from Markle (1969: 5) serves as an excellent example of this mechanistic approach. She says that the student who can respond, "Paris is the capital of France." to the question, "What is the capital of France?" cannot be expected to answer the question, "What country is Paris the capital of?" Although the response is the same, the stimulus in each case is different. Since the stimuli are different, the appropriate response to the new stimulus cannot be expected prior to the necessary antecedent conditioning process.

The behaviorists conceive of language as conditioned verbal behavior consisting of a complex collection of stimulus-response bonds. Therefore, their view of the language learning process is one of providing the student with sufficient practice to acquire the appropriate language responses. The student is to spend the major part of his time responding actively to selected stimuli. Analysis of the language structures is not necessary and may even be detrimental to the conditioning process. The plan is to practice the language patterns to a saturation point. The goal is automatic, non-thoughtful responses to the stimuli. Language is a mechanical, not a mental, process and should be learned mechanically.

The basic tenets outlined in the preceding paragraph are, in general, based on experiments performed with animals by behaviorist psychologists. By presenting a series of stimuli and reinforcing selected behavior, these experiments have been able to condition desired responses. The conclusions based on the results of these studies have been extended to include learning in other contexts and with other species as well, specifically the human one.

Language teaching as a whole has been greatly influenced by behavioristic theories of learning. The descriptive linguists who played such an important role in developing new language teaching techniques were oriented toward mechanistic interpretations of learning. Politzer (1964) has stated that behaviorism was one of the basic contributions of linguistics to the teaching of modern foreign languages in the 1940s. Valette (1966) has pointed out that new textual materials in modern languages are based on the assumption that language learning is chiefly a mechanical process of habit formation. Morton and Lane (1961) have asserted that the tasks associated with second language learning are "indistinguishable" from those involved in conditioning learning in the animal laboratory. In fact, Lane (1964: 250) has stated that "there is nothing extrapolative in the application of laboratory techniques and nothing metaphorical in the use of concepts gained from a functional analysis of behavior in the laboratory."

In the past most programmed materials (with the exception of Crowder's branching programs) have reflected this mechanistic approach to learning. Almost without exception the published programs have been linear, and linear programs are applications, basically, of Skinner's behavioristic theories of learning. These Skinnerian materials conform to three basic principles. As the student progresses through the stimulus-response frames, he 1) is expected to make an active response to all stimuli, 2) is led through small step sequences which minimize the possibility of error, and 3) is given immediate feedback as to the correctness of his response (Markle 1969: 3-12).

Frames based on these principles exemplify the behavioristic approach to language learning. The objective is conditioned responses, and the learning technique is one of conditioning these responses. Frames such as the following (Burroughs 1964: 18) are based on the assumption that learning is a mechanical, not a mental process.

Joseph est le frère de Marie.

Joseph et Pierre *sont* les frères de Marie.

le frère < le_   frère_

le frère < les   _____

le frère est < les frères _____

The first frame in the introduction to Sapon's (1961: 1) programmed materials in Spanish indicates a similar approach.

You are looking at frame number 1. It contains some instructions, and an underlined space to write your *answers*.

The underlined space is used to write down your

a_____s.

The author then provides an additional instruction which explains to the student what to do and the procedure for finding the correct answer. Applied to teaching language the frames embody identical principles (Sapon 1964: 8):

> 1036. Here is the statement you just chorused:
> *Sí, mis lecciones son interesantes.*
>
> Read the statement aloud. - - - - - - - - -
>
> 1037. The word *lección* has an accent mark.
>
> Does the plural form *lecciones* have an accent mark? _____

THE COGNITIVE VIEWPOINT

In recent years cognitive psychologists have begun to challenge the basic tenets of behavioristic theories of learning. Their theories rest upon neuro-psychological bases of thought and language, and as such are said to be mentalistic. Learning is not viewed as an array of conditioned responses to previously met stimuli, but as the acquisition and storage of knowledge. Behaviorist psychologists focus on the individual's response while cognitive psychologists emphasize the mental processes underlying that response.

Ausubel (1936: 65) rejects the conditioning theory of learning saying, ". . . it is evident that the use of the conditioning paradigm to explain the process whereby representational meaning is acquired constitutes an unwarranted extension of principles that are valid for certain simple kinds of learning to a more complex task and qualitatively different kind of learning." Behavioristic theories, then, may explain simple levels of learning. However, they are not sufficiently encompassing to explain such complex processes as representational learning, i.e., the ability to symbolize the world through words.

In fact, the model for learning which Ausubel (1968: 38) postulates is quite different from behavioristic techniques. He feels that the learning process must be one of "meaningful learning." Information acquired in a rote fashion, i.e., "arbitrarily and verbatim" is of little use to the learner and is quickly forgotten. The important criterion is whether the new knowledge can be incorporated, or "subsumed," into the learner's existing cognitive structure, i.e., what he already knows. In order for the learner to relate new material to what he has learned previously this material must be "relatable to his structure of knowledge on a nonarbitrary and nonverbatim basis." The implication here is that the instructional materials should assist the student to understand all that he is to learn and to relate all new material to prior knowledge. This newly acquired knowledge must not be learned in an arbitrary or verbatim fashion. In other words, the student must be able, after learning, to state what he knows in his own terms. A word for word regurgitation is rote learning and as such not truly meaningful nor valuable to the student's cognitive processes. Information acquired by rote does not assist the learner in acquiring additional knowledge, and it is highly unlikely to transfer to new contexts. Ausubel (1968: 61) states that "the acquisition of large bodies of knowledge is simply impossible in the absence of meaningful learning."

The assumption based on behavioristic theories, has been that language is conditioned verbal behavior. However, many writers in language, psychology, and linguistics are now saying that language is much more complex than had been previously supposed. Spolsky (1966: 120) draws an important distinction when he states, "Knowing a language involves not just the performance of language-like behaviors, but an underlying competence that makes such performance possible. By ignoring this, it has been easy to make exaggerated claims for the effectiveness of operant conditioning in second-language teaching." Chomsky (1966: 43) questions the behavioristic interpretation of language learning saying, ". . . it seems to me impossible to accept the view that linguistic behavior is a matter of habit, that it is slowly acquired by reinforcement, association, and generalization. . . ." It now appears that the infinite variety of possible communicative utterances in the native speaker's repertoire cannot be accounted for on the basis of stimulus-response learning. Miller et al. (1960: 146) say that if the conditioning of stimulus-response connections were the means of language acquisition, a childhood 100 years long with no interruptions for sleeping, eating, etc., and a perfect retention of every string of twenty words after one presentation would be necessary to account for the language skill. McNeill (1965: 3) seconds this notion and emphasizes the creative aspects of language when he explains, "The use of language resembles more writing a play than performing in one."

Ohmann (1969: 31-2) points out that the native speaker is so familiar with his own language that he is unlikely to be aware of the complexity of the skill he possesses. He has the ability to comprehend and to use an infinite variety of sentences, many of them completely novel. To emphasize the complexity of language Ohmann uses as an example a situation in which twenty-five native speakers are asked to describe a scene in which a tourist is waiting outside a telephone booth while a bear talks on the phone. A computer analysis of the twenty-five descriptions showed that they contain enough linguistic data for "19.8 billion sentences, all describing just one situation." He goes on to say that, "When one reflects that the number of seconds in a century is only 3.2 billion, it is clear that no speaker has heard, read, or spoken more than a tiny fraction of the sentences he *could* speak or understand, and that no one learns English by learning any particular sentences of English."

Although programmed materials in the past have primarily been applications of Skinnerian theories of learning, it is not necessarily true that programmed instruction must limit itself to theories of conditioning. Programmed instruction is also evolving. As changes have occurred, the tendency has been to move away from the short, small-step frames of Skinner. In fact, Markle (1969: 12) says that they are 'out' at present. As programmers have abandoned the traditional linear programs the direction has been from conditioning to cognition. Markle and Tieman (1969: 10), discussing student learning, say that, "the test that he really understands the concept is always his ability, not to tell us what we have told him, but to go beyond our teaching to new examples and non-examples." Although the attempt in their presentation is to accomplish this understanding of concepts within the limits of conditioning theory, the end result seems to be very little different from the objectives of Ausubel.

Programmed materials in agreement with cognitive principles place initial emphasis upon understanding. After comprehending the concept, whether it be some aspect of phonology, semantics or syntax, the student continues practicing the language form to be learned. In Mueller and Niedzielski's (1968: 186–7) programmed French materials, for example, the lessons dealing with forms and sentence patterns begin with a complete explanation of the structure to be learned. In the first frame the student is asked to discriminate between correct and incorrect responses. Frames of drill exercises follow, and the oral sequence ends with application exercises in which the student is expected to expand upon what he has been practicing. The application exercises ask the student to pose questions as well as supply the answers. For example:

joue—Demandez-leur ce qu'ils font dans le jardin.
A. Qu'est-ce que vous faites?
B. Nous jouons.

A. Où est-ce que vous jouez?
B. Nous jouons dans le jardin.

In the intermediate course there is an increased emphasis on understanding prior to practice, and the focus of the exercises is placed on transformations. After studying an introductory explanation of the adjective function in prepositional phrases, prepositional infinitive phrases, and clauses, for example, the student proceeds through a series of frames in which he practices transformations of these forms. In the first frame he changes phrases such as "l'enseignement français" to "l'enseignement du français." A few frames later he is changing "La France a enseigné la liberté aux nations africaines. Elle en avait le devoir." to "La France avait le devoir d'enseigner la liberté aux nations africaines." Finally, he has progressed to the point of asking and answering questions similar to the following example:

On y a pris ce vote.

A. C'est ça la scène.
B. Quelle scène?
A. La scène où on a pris le vote.

Mueller and Niedzielski incorporate cognitive procedures into their materials and at the same time eliminate the traditional blanks found in linear programs. The following examples from Bull (1970) also include a great deal of stress on cognition, but retain the blanks. The following two frames exemplify the stress placed on the understanding and organization of knowledge:

Homework Program 167

Part 1:   *The Future*

1. What you are going to learn in the next paragraph will probably be something of a surprise to you.
   From the point of view of the first suffix of the Spanish verb forms there are only two tense forms in Spanish: those that have a present tense suffix and those that have a past tense suffix. Let's prove this. How many morphemes are there in either the present indicative *vendemos* or the present subjunctive *vendamos*? _____

Homework Program 181

HOW TO GET MEANING FROM STEMS AND FROM CONTEXT

1. One way of distinguishing between a well-trained and poorly trained foreign-language student is to measure how much time he spends looking up new words in the dictionary. The poorly trained student exhibits two main characteristics: first, he does not have the courage to trust his own linguistic detective ability; and second, he is too afraid of making a mistake. He may know, for example, *caer* and its perfect participle *caído*, but he will look up two words in translating *Miguel montaba a caballo cuando sufrió una caída penosa*.
   Does the *una* in front of *caída* tell you that this is the noun form of *caído*? _____

DISCUSSION

In some respects the instructor's task was much easier, at least psychologically, in the late fifties and early sixties than it is today. The general feeling pervading the profession at that time was one of general excitement and enthusiasm for a new approach, i.e., conditioning techniques in language instruction, whether in the classroom or in programmed materials. There was no hesitation, no self-doubt, no concern with choosing between opposing philosophies of language teaching. Today the situation is different. The instructor is confronted with two basic philosophies. How does he choose?

The answer seems to be that at present he cannot, or should not. Above all, he should avoid the temptation to say, "This is the right way." If anything has been learned to date, it is that there is no single best way. Students are different, and they learn in different ways. In a study at Purdue University, for example, the results of a statistical analysis of student data indicated with quite a high degree of certainty which students would be more successful in a cognitive class and which would be more successful in an audio-lingual habit class (Chastain 1969). The implication is clear. An effort must be made to provide as many different learning experiences as possible.

Other studies have dealt with low ability students. Pimsleur's (1963) research at the high school level led him to conclude that 10 to 20 percent of the beginning language students have a disability which causes them to be under-achievers in language classes. Studies reported by Mueller (1968) and by Mueller and Harris (1966) indicated that it is the student with average aptitude or below who profits most from programmed learning materials. Chastain (1970) found that audio-lingual students with low verbal ability achieve higher scores in the four language skills than students with high verbal ability. The opposite is true in cognitive classes.

If there is "no one way," what generalizations may be formulated at present? First, teachers and programmers need to realize that individualization consists of more than pace. One possibility is to move in the direction of providing programs which maximize the effectiveness of the student's capabilities as he proceeds through the course. There seems to be sufficient evidence to assume that some students prefer the Skinnerian approach while others learn better in materials which are based on cognitive theories of learning. The alternative is to include both types of instruction within any given program. Both possibilities should be explored.

Given the fact that materials based on both theories seem to be successful with certain groups of students the next question to be asked concerns the subject matter itself, "What aspect of language teaching can each do best?" Speaking as a language teacher, not as a programmer, this author suggests that phonology can best be taught according to conditioning techniques. Perhaps conditioning drills could be supplemented with drawings of tongue and lip positions and explanations in order to enhance cognitive understanding of each sound, but the basic objective and method in the acquisition of sounds early in the course sequence would seem to be primarily one of conditioning. Teaching vocabulary could be achieved by using both types of frames. With respect to simple connections between native language words and their foreign language equivalents, it would seem that conditioning should be stressed more than cognition. However, it seems logical at this stage to begin separating the students into two groups, one which needs to be drilled more and one which prefers, and has the ability, to learn by assimilating larger chunks of material. Teaching syntax would seem to require the programmer to provide both types of learning. For the slower student the frames would be designed to drill certain responses while the brighter students would be provided materials which have fewer drill frames, but which assist him in organizing the content of a higher conceptual level.

The preceding paragraph seemingly indicates that programmed materials can teach all three aspects of language. That is true. It is not a logical conclusion, however, to assume that programmed instruction is synonymous with self-instruction. Various writers have stated that in language learning programmed instruction by itself is not enough (Ornstein 1968, Spolsky 1966, Sweet 1968). If, then, programmed materials cannot produce the ideal bilingual student, what can they do? Again, from the viewpoint of a language teacher, this author feels that they can become a most important adjunct to the classroom teacher. Language acquisition, in this author's opinion occurs in three stages: 1) understanding, 2) drill, and 3) application. Seemingly, programmed materials can lead the student through the first two stages, but not the third. From a different perspective, that of the four language skills, one would expect students to be able to acquire the passive skills through the use of programmed materials. These same materials can drill speaking and writing, but at that point their possibilities become quite limited. Only the teacher can help the student take the step beyond to "real" language practice (Jarvis 1968).

It is appropriate at this point to digress from the discussion to describe a study conducted last semester at Purdue University (Jarvis 1970), which offered a theoretical distinction between drill language and "real" language. According to Jarvis, the important distinction is that "real" language activity provides the student with a "referent" for what he says. For example, as the student substitutes various colors for the word "white" in the sentence, "The house is white," he has no referent. Nor does he have a referent in a cued response drill in which he is told to answer *white* before being asked what color the house is. However, if the student is asked what color *his* house is, then he has a referent, i.e., his answer is a verbalization of a mental picture in his mind. Drills are mere manipulations of structural forms, and as such are qualitatively different from "real" language activity.

Jarvis' definition, coupled with the fact that past research has indicated above all else that students learn to do what they do, mandates that the student be given the opportunity for "real" language practice. Otherwise, he cannot be expected to acquire that native-like ability which is ostensibly the goal of language learning.

The necessity of providing language activity as outlined in the two preceding paragraphs is the ultimate objective of language teaching: yet it is the type of practice which programmed materials are least able to supply. Speaking the language involves a sequence of speeches in which two or more people interact with each other as they express their own ideas and opinions. Programmed materials, simulated tutoring and simulated conversation can provide this type of activity only in the most minuscule fashion.

CONCLUSION

The search for teaching techniques and procedures with which to achieve native-like ability in second-language learning continues. The fact that the profession is now willing to consider various approaches offers hope for a combination of theories and techniques which will be superior to the exclusive use of any single approach. Certainly the evidence at present lends little support to a continued search for the *one* way to teach. Teachers, students, and the many components of language itself are too varied to justify an insistence upon one particular method. The better question would be to ask which approach should be used with which students by which teachers and for which aspects of the language.

The indications are that these questions are now being asked. Recent changes in both audio-lingual and programmed materials toward including more elements of cognition reflect an increasing awareness of the complexity of language, language learning and the language learner. New terms such as "guided learning" by Valdman and "designed learning" by Carroll reflect an emerging awareness of the need to include as many different types of learning situations as possible in any instructional program if maximum efficiency and achievement are to be attained. The fact that previous attempts have failed should not deter additional efforts toward the goal. It is time for the profession to continue its search for new solutions to old problems. Past failures have little value as bases for arguments, but they can serve as valuable guideposts toward future progress. Experience *can* be the best teacher.

REFERENCES

Ausubel, David P. 1968. Educational psychology: a cognitive view. New York: Holt, Rinehart and Winston.

Bull, William E. 1970. Spanish for communication. (Mimeographed pre-publication edition).

Burroughs, Elaine. 1964. Programmed French: reading and writing. New York: McGraw-Hill.

Chastain, Kenneth. 1969. Prediction of success in audio-lingual and cognitive classes. Language Learning. 19. 27-39.

Chastain, Kenneth. 1970. A methodological study comparing the audio-lingual habit theory and the cognitive code-learning theory: continued. The Modern Language Journal. 54. 257-66.

Chomsky, Noam. 1966. Linguistic theory. Language teaching: broader contexts, ed. by Robert G. Mead, Jr., 43–49. Menasha, Wisconsin.

Jarvis, Gilbert. 1968. A behavioral observation system for foreign language skill acquisition. The Modern Language Journal. 52. 335–41.

Jarvis, Gilbert. 1970. A comparison of contextualized practice with particularized referents vs. practice with generic meaning in the teaching of beginning college French. Ph.D. dissertation, Purdue University.

Lane, Harlan. 1964. Programmed learning of a second language. International Review of Applied Linguistics. 2. 249–301.

Markle, Susan M. 1969. Good frames and bad: a grammar of frame writing. 2nd ed. New York: Wiley.

Markle, Susan M. and Philip W. Tieman. 1969. Really understanding concepts: or in frumious pursuit of the jabberwock, 2nd ed. Champaign, Illinois: Stipes Publishing Company.

McNeill, David. 1965. Some thoughts on first and second language acquisition. (Mimeographed) Cambridge, Massachusetts: Center for Cognitive Studies.

Miller, G. A., et al. 1960. Plans and the structure of behavior. New York: Holt, Rinehart and Winston.

Morton, F. Rand and Harlan L. Lane. 1961. Techniques of operant conditioning applied to second language learning. (An address to the International Congress of Applied Psychology) Copenhagen.

Mueller, Theodore H. 1968. Programmed language instruction—help for the linguistically underprivileged. The Modern Language Journal. 52. 79–84.

Mueller, Theodore and Robert Harris. 1966. First year college French through an audio-lingual program. International Review of Applied Linguistics. 4. 19–38.

Mueller, Theodore H. and Henri Niedzielski. 1968. Basic French: a programmed course. New York: Appleton-Century-Crofts.

Ohmann, Richard. 1969. Grammar and meaning. The American heritage dictionary of the English language, ed. by William Morris. Boston: Houghton Mifflin Company.

Ornstein, Jacob. 1968. Programmed instruction and educational technology in the language field: boon or failure? The Modern Language Journal. 52. 401–10.

Pimsleur, Paul, et. al. 1963. Under-achievement in foreign language learning. Washington: U.S. Department of Health, Education, and Welfare.

Politzer, Robert L. 1964. The impact of linguistics on language teaching: past, present and future. The Modern Language Journal. 48. 146–51.

Sapon, Stanley M. 1961. A programmed course in Spanish. Level A. Chicago: Encyclopaedia Britannica, Inc.

Sapon, Stanley M. 1964. Programmed Spanish. Level B. Rochester, New York: Mono Press.

Spolsky, Bernard. 1966. A psycholinguistic critique of programmed foreign language instruction. International Review of Applied Linguistics. 4. 119–29.

Sweet, Waldo E. 1968. Integrating other media with programmed instruction. The Modern Language Journal. 52. 420–03.

Valette, Rebecca M. 1966. Evaluating the objectives in foreign-language teaching. International Review of Applied Linguistics. 4. 131–9.

7

TRANSFORMA- ROBIN LAKOFF
TIONAL GRAMMAR AND LANGUAGE TEACHING[1]

What contribution, according to Lakoff, has transformational theory made to the work of the *intuitive* rationalist school of grammar?

Confirm that translations of sentences (2)-(7) are ungrammatical in languages other than English known to you. Try to explain why they are ungrammatical in both English and other languages.

What convincing arguments are there that "one could not expect to learn a language . . . by merely memorizing a list of sentences, however long?"

Under what conditions does Lakoff accept the usefulness of *pattern practice drills*?

What are some determiners of grammaticality that cannot be covered by rules? Summarize the role of *presupposition* in determining grammaticality.

Summarize Lakoff's views on the contributions of transformational grammar to language teaching.

As language teachers we have behind us two powerful traditions in language teaching. The first we can call rote-memorization, either the nineteenth-century and earlier variety which entailed memorizing lists of words and statements of rules, or the later behaviorist-psychology and structuralist linguistics pattern-practice variety that is common still today. The second is the intuitive-generalizing style of teaching. This tradition has been less popular: first, because it is harder to understand and needs a good teacher and good presentation to work, and second, because until recently it was considered heretical to suggest that people

Reprinted by permission from *Language Learning*, 19 (1969), 117–140. Mrs. Lakoff is assistant professor of linguistics at the University of Michigan.

[1]This is the revised version of a paper read at the Michigan Conference on Applied Linguistics: "Aspects of Language," held in Ann Arbor on January 18, 1969. I would like to express my gratitude to Ronald Wardhaugh, whose comments and advice have improved this paper in every way.

were in any interesting way different from rats. It was assumed that people learned languages, both native and second, as they and rats learned everything else: by repetition, by exercise, and by fitting new things into an old pattern already learned. The more you repeated something the better it was learned. [2] It was also assumed to be dangerous to let people think about sentences they were learning because they would not form a pattern correctly, since they would not establish a direct stimulus (heard sentence of situation) -response relationship. It was assumed that language was just another kind of stimulus-response; the speaker heard a sentence or felt some sensation, and this triggered, without the intervention of any kind of reflection, a response, also verbal. He was just like the rat pushing a switch for food. However, if the speaker thought about a sentence, or wondered why it was grammatical before he said it, or were concerned about its relationship to other sentences, he would break this stimulus-response link and would not be using language as a native speaker does. The same learning model was assumed for first-language learning too: the child learned the pattern by repeating the sentences he heard from his parents.[3] When he had repeated all the sentences that had been said in the first five years, and had memorized those, he had acquired the grammar of his parents and was a native speaker. Second-language learning was viewed as the same sort of process as first-language learning. It was important, too, to present to the second-language learner only correct sentences. Otherwise, like a rat presented with contradictory stimuli, he might not know which response was correct.

The second type of teaching was found, for example, in the *Nouvelles*

[2] A particularly clear exposition of the behavioral-structural position can be found in Morton (1966) which takes the point of view that it is not only possible but desirable to teach second-language learners to respond automatically to stimuli they are not supposed to understand. Thus, he says (p. 178) that the frames of his audio-lingual program for Spanish permit the student-subject:

1. to 'answer,' with 95 percent accuracy, all questions asked within Task III *without the aid of lexical meaning.*

2. to formulate 'questions,' with 90 percent accuracy, in response to the hearing of 'statements,' . . . *without the aid of lexical meaning.*

3. to manipulate . . . a finite and pre-specified number of syntactical and morphological structures *without the aid of lexical meaning.* (All italics are mine.)

It is not clear just what it is the students trained by this project have been taught to do: certainly they have not learned to use a language in anything like the way a language is naturally used, by native or non-native speakers.

[3] That such a notion of first-language learning is untenable is evident to anyone reading a book like Weir (1963). In this book, the author presents and discusses tapes of her infant's speech in its crib, where there was no stimulus to provoke the child's response, yet it spoke a great deal to itself. Much of this speech involves experimenting with words, 'practicing' vocabulary, rehearsing grammatical paradigms, and the like—anything but an imitation of adult's sentences!

Méthodes of the Port-Royal school in France in the seventeenth century,[4] and here and there since that time in 'rational' grammars. Never as popular as the other type and recently held in great disrepute, this type of teaching was based on the notion that human beings were quite different from rats and other animals in that they could reason. This distinguishing attribute was what allowed men to speak in the first place. Speech was the product of man's rationality: for someone to learn to speak a language correctly, he had to make use of his reasoning ability. Therefore, the teacher had to tell him why one said the things one said in the way one said them—and, therefore, he also had to explain that some things could not be said, and give the reasons for that: he had to provide the learner with both grammatical and ungrammatical sentences. There was an assumption that all men reasoned in the same way. However, there were also rules that took this basic universal logical structure and changed it into language-particular, illogical structures, in which things were "understood"—that is, not overtly present—and word-order, sometimes, was changed.

If the writer explained the universal logic, said the rational grammarians, and provided the rules that related it to the superficial illogical structures in which people spoke, learners would work out the relationships between their own language and the one they were learning. They would thus do a quicker and more thorough job of learning the second language, learning it less artificially and more idiomatically. They would, in fact, learn it as a native speaker does. The teacher's job, however, was harder because he had to discover what the underlying logic was, and this was not invariably obvious—in fact, it generally was not obvious at all. The behaviorists criticized this theory as mentalistic and unscientific, and ignored it along with all other theories that said that language was any more than a system of automatic responses to stimuli.

In the last ten years a new linguistic theory, transformational grammar, has arisen, in direct opposition to the behavioral-structuralist theories within which so many language texts have been written. As far as language and language learning are concerned, it has much in common with the beliefs of the rational grammarians. One very significant added element in the modern theory, of course, is the existence of transformational rules, the form of which and the sphere of applicability of which are strictly controlled by the theory itself, avoiding the fuzziness, arbitrariness and the *ad hoc* treatments of data that characterize the work of the "intuitive" rationalist school. In non-transformational intuitive grammar,[5] sentences are related to one another on no grounds except the intuition of the writer. Sometimes the relationship postulated would be considered

---

[4] The Port Royal grammars, written principally by Claude Lancelot (who collaborated with Antoine Arnauld to produce the recently much-discussed *Grammaire Générale et Raisonnée*) employed the linguistic theory of medieval grammarians like Sanctus, who held that language was a product of man's reasoning faculty, to produce grammars of various European languages, namely Greek, Latin, Spanish, Italian, and Portuguese.

[5] The works of Otto Jespersen are good examples of grammars of this type.

correct by modern analyses; sometimes they were absurd. The theory provided no automatic way of distinguishing truth from fiction: there was no formal definition of a possible underlying structure or a possible rule. Moreover, though the theory assumed an underlying universal logical structure, there were no constraints on the form of this structure, or on the permissible types of rules changing it to the superficial structure. Virtually anything could be treated as an underlying structure, and—in theory at least—virtually any operation could be performed on it. One sentence might have many possible analyses, with no means of discriminating among them as to which was right, and with no assumption made that there must be only one underlying structure for a non-ambiguous superficial sentence. Transformational theory, as exemplified most fully perhaps in Chomsky's *Aspects of the Theory of Syntax*, formalized these intuitive concepts so that they could be checked, constrained, and tested.

In this work, Chomsky assumed two levels of grammar and a set of transformational rules mediating between them. At the level of deep structure, everything is present that enables one to know what the sentence means: identical words, later deleted, abstract elements of various sorts that leave syntactic markings elsewhere in the sentence, and so forth. Transformational rules delete these under various conditions, producing surface structures. Therefore, the transformational analysis of a sentence like (1):

(1) I saw a boy that hates ice cream.

assumes a deep structure in which the noun phrase *a boy* occurs twice: once where it will occur in the surface structure, as the object of the main clause, and once where *that* occurs in the superficial structure. These two nouns are co-referential; both refer to the same boy necessarily or else the sentence would be meaningless, or rather, nonsensical, because infinitely ambiguous: without a principle of recoverability of deletion—allowing only identical elements to be deleted—one would never know what *that* referred to, and the sentence could be interpreted in infinite ways. But since all languages contain this principle, it is inconceivable that *that* could have replaced any noun but *a boy*, identical in reference to the subject, which is still present superficially. It is evident that *that* refers to *boy*, an animate human masculine singular noun, because of constraints on what can occur in the relative clause. If *that* were really just an infinitely ambiguous form not going back to a deep-structure noun *boy*, the ungrammaticality of (2)-(4) would be unrelated to that of sentences like (5)-(7) below—a patently absurd situation, since the speaker of English knows the same thing is wrong with both sets of sentences:

(2) *I saw a boy that elapsed yesterday.
(3) *I saw a boy that was pregnant.
(4) *I saw a boy that laughed at themselves.

But if we assume that the noun *boy* underlies *that* at some level of the grammar, we can immediately tell why all these sentences are ungrammatical, without having new special rules in the grammar to explain them: (2)-(4) are ungrammatical for the same reasons as (5)-(7) are (and the translations of both sets, in any natural language, also are):

(5) *The boy elapsed yesterday.
(6) *The boy was pregnant.
(7) *The boy laughed at themselves.

These are some of the reasons for proposing a theory with deep structures and transformational rules to change them into the superficial structures.

In addition, transformational grammar assumes that most sentences in a language are formed by combining two or more smaller sentences: sentence (1) is produced by combining (8) and (9):

(8) I saw a boy.
(9) A boy hates ice cream.

There will be constraints on what kinds of sentences can be combined if the transformational rule yielding relative sentences is to apply properly. Another obvious fact these sentences illustrate is that it is not possible to construct "the longest sentence" of any language: one could always, for instance, add a new relative clause, or a conjunction, or a complement sentence as in (10), where *that . . . stupid* is a complement embedded in the larger sentence:

(10) I told the boy *that he was stupid*.

The result is that there is no "longest sentence" of any language. Moreover, it follows that one could not expect to learn a language, native or foreign, by merely memorizing a list of sentences, however long. So the behaviorist theory of language learning is incompatible with this evidence. Moreover, a child at age five is already able to tell whether a given sentence of his language is grammatical or not—though he has never heard that sentence before. As Chomsky points out, on the basis of facts such as these, language-learning must be viewed as a process depending on reasoning rather than on memorization.

I should perhaps not have made such a categorical statement. Some linguistic phenomena are, of course, not based on logic: they are accidental. If we watch a child learning to speak his own language, or—even more clearly—an adult successfully learning a second language, we note that he often has recourse to his memory. The child learns vocabulary by memorization: though he quickly learns how to generalize—to find the rules—for constructing new sentences, he soon learns that if he constructs new words by a rule he devises, he will often not be understood, logical as his formulations may be. He learns a set of endings on words—plurals, tenses, diminutives, etc.—as a list that he must memorize. There are no 'reasons' why the plural has an ending and the singular has not. (He does, of course, learn that this is a rule—if he learns ten cases where the plural is formed with -s, he will try out an eleventh case he has never heard before, and generally be correct.) He also must learn that sentence (10) is good, but sentence (11) which has roughly the same 'logical' structure is not, nor is (12). These facts—which 'complementizers,' as they are called, go with which verbs—must be memorized, just as vocabulary items are.

(11) *I ordered the boy that he gives me his book.
(12) *I said the boy to be stupid.

And similarly, there are in every language exceptions to rules, and these must be memorized. There is no conceivable 'rule' to tell one why (13) is a good sentence of English, and (14) not. There are languages where the translations of both are good. If there is a difference of that sort in languages, it is generally the case that we are dealing with something 'illogical'—something that requires some amount of rote memorization: it is not universal.

(13) John is likely to leave.
(14) *John is probable to leave.

There are also cases where rules can be given to the learner, where all he will need to know to tell whether to apply the rule in a given case is what other words are present in the sentence, and what they mean: these are purely superficial phenomena. So, for instance, in sentence (1), a restrictive relative clause, the pronoun *that* is grammatical. But in sentence (15), *who* cannot be replaced with *that*: (15) is a non-restrictive relative sentence.

(15) I saw the boy, who was running fast.

Facts like these can be stated in rules, and generalizations learned. In this way they are different from the sorts of facts given earlier, which are idiosyncratic and must be memorized individually. But in both cases, rote learning is possible either of the list of forms or of the rule that generates a set of possible forms. The teacher can give a rule like "*That* is never used in non-restrictive relative clauses" and have the students memorize it; and, assuming that the teacher has fully and accurately explained the distinction between restrictive and non-restrictive relative clauses, there will be no mistakes. Pattern-practice drills are of value in these cases. There is nothing wrong with constructing drills to facilitate the memorization of facts about pluralization, complementizer-selection (as in (13)), subject-raising (as in (14)), or restrictive vs. non-restrictive relative pronouns.

In all these cases, the speaker or learner or teacher need only know the superficial form of the sentence in question. He need not worry about contextual factors outside the scope of rules: what has been said earlier, what the speaker knows about the topic of conversation, what is common knowledge, or knowledge of the world. But there are cases where such factors are irrelevant. Sometimes—more frequently than has been assumed—to judge whether a sentence is correct in its context, one must know something about the speaker's unstated belief about the world. In these cases, often, any of several variants of a sentence, out of context, will be completely grammatical—but in the specific context only one is correct. No rule can be given to the learner to enable him to make the correct distinctions; in these situations, a rule, to be of use, must provide the environment in which it applies—and in these cases, the relevant environment generally is implicit, rather than overtly present in another part of the sentence. Nor, of course, will memorization be of use here. Distinctions of this sort—I will discuss some examples below—are probably the hardest things to learn in the syntax of another language. Misusing them does not really create chaos, as failure to learn the memorizable rules may; it merely creates in the mind of the native speaker hearing the sentence a certain confusion, a sense that the other speaker is not using the language right or does not know something everyone else in the world knows, or something the speaker has already said he knows.

Numerous cases can be cited where rote learning and the listing of rules to memorize will be of little avail. In English, there are, for example, the articles, the past tense/perfect distinction, and the distinction between *some* and *any*. In Japanese there is the example of the use of honorific prefixes and suffixes and in Spanish, there are certain types of subjunctives. Of course, there are countless other examples too.

Consider the use of the articles in English. In any given sentence, either a definite or indefinite is generally possible. (I overlook special cases, like that of proper or mass nouns.) So, judging merely from the immediate environment, both (16) and (17) are grammatical:

(16) The boy is over there.
(17) A boy is over there.

That is, it is impossible to state a rule using as the environment the superficial form of the sentence alone to predict whether (16) or (17) will be correct in a given sentence. The problem is even worse in complex sentences. Sentence (18) is good, but (19), with only an adjective changed, is not:

(18) John spoke with a warmth that was surprising.
(19) *John spoke with a warmth that was usual.

and in (20) and (21), only a definite article is good if the adjective is one of the same class as *usual* in (19):

(20) John spoke with the enthusiasm that was expected.
(21) *John spoke with an enthusiasm that was expected.

To return to the earlier examples, in ordinary conversation, a speaker may say, "I'm looking for a boy who was asking for money yesterday." The conversation may then take a completely different turn, and deal for some time with different topics entirely. But if after a while, the second speaker in the conversation wants to refer again to the boy in question, he can use sentence (16), but not (17) to call attention to that fact, even though the boy may not have been the topic of conversation for some time and even though the first speaker himself used the indefinite article. In the sentences of (18)–(21), it is the meaning of the adjective that conditions the choice of article. The meaning has to do with how likely the speaker feels the warmth, or enthusiasm, was: whether he anticipated it or not. This fact, too, cannot be expressed as an invariable rule, or learned by memorizing sentences that follow the pattern. One must know what is in the speaker's mind, the hearer's mind, and in the previous conversation before one can judge the grammaticality of such sentences. Consider too sentences like (22) and (23):

(22) Albert is a doctor in my neighborhood.
(23) Albert is the doctor in my neighborhood.

The difference between these sentences cannot be found in any context that can be located by a rule. Either could perfectly well begin a conversation between two people one of whom didn't know Albert. The distinction lies in whether the speaker feels that it is normal, or necessary, for every neighborhood to have a doctor, or whether this is merely incidental, and Albert is a doctor who happens to live or work in the speaker's neighborhood. The choice of article thus depends on the speaker's feelings or beliefs about the world and how he sees its organization. No rule can give the learner this information. One can give general rules for article choice: use the definite article for something that is already known, or mentioned; otherwise use the indefinite. But that will not be of much help in a case like this, without additional information such as what presuppositions the speaker is making about the topics of the sentence. A native speaker can always match up his presupposition with the correct choice of article. The non-native speaker, unless he has learned the language extremely well, or has as his native language one in which there is an article system similar to that of English, will make mistakes, some more frequently than others. The task of the serious teacher, then, is to teach the non-native speaker what presuppositions go with what use of the articles. He must do this by identifying, in the learner's native language, where similar presuppositions have overt counterparts, and matching these language-specific superficial structures with those of the learned language. In practice, of course, it is extremely difficult to do this; frequently, as seems to be the case with Japanese, the presuppositions underlying the use of the English articles do not show up overtly at all in the Japanese nominal system. Then the teacher must simply give various situations in which one article would be used rather than another, or none, and explain as well as possible *why* the choice must be this way: the teacher must give the learner a boost to making his own generalizations, to learning how the native speaker understands and intuitively uses these sentences. This necessarily implies that it is essential to give the learner ungrammatical sentences, so that he can study these along with the grammatical ones to decide for himself what the difference is, so that when he is on his own and has to make a decision for himself, he can rely on his own new generalizing ability in this sphere to make the right generalization. With rote pattern practice alone, he would either be helpless presented with a situation that fell outside of the patterns he had studied (which would, of course, be extremely frequent) or he would overgeneralize, applying a pattern where it did not fit, since he would not know the reason why that pattern took that form. This is often true, as anyone who has taught English to speakers of Japanese know. Either the article is omitted entirely where it should appear, or the wrong one is used, since the speaker has no idea which, if any, article is correct in the given environment.

A second case from English involves the distinction between the past and perfect tenses. This distinction is very difficult for anyone whose tense-system is not as complex as that of English, or where the meanings of the tenses are differently divided. Compare, for example, sentences (24) and (25) pointed out by Jespersen.[6] Both are grammatical, but they are used in different situations:

(24) The patient has gradually grown weaker.
(25) The patient gradually grew weaker.

or (26) and (27):

(26) I saw John every day for twenty years.
(27) I have seen John every day for twenty years.

If (24) is used, the assumption must be that the patient is still alive. If (25) is used, there is no such assumption. That is, to tell which of two tenses to use in referring to something that happened in the past, the speaker must have access to information about what is true in the present, information that is nowhere overtly stated. No list could be used to predict accurately which of these sentences could be used in a given conversation. The use of (24) instead of (25), though not overtly carrying information that the patient was alive, could mislead a hearer. Similarly in (26) and (27) if there is a gap in time between the years in which the speaker saw John every day, and the time at which he is speaking, only (26) is possible. The use of (27) for (26) creates confusion if the speaker has not seen John for some time. The sentence is not ungrammatical, as *I saw the boy that elapsed*, or *I said John to be a fool*, are; but its use in the wrong context stamps one as a non-native speaker of English, just as certainly as the others would. But no rule can be given for the learner to follow in any situation.

Consider one last case from English. It is frequently stated that if in a positive sentence *some* can occur, in the corresponding negative, interrogative, or conditional sentence *any* is found instead. As that statement stands, it sounds as though the *some-any* distinction would be a very good candidate for rote learning and pattern practice. But the following sentences are not amenable to any imaginable form of pattern-practice drill:

[6] *A Modern English Grammar,* IV, p. 67.

(28) Does someone want these beans?
(29) Does anyone want these beans?
(30) If he eats some candy, let me know.
(31) If he eats any candy, let me know.

All these sentences are grammatical. Each pair is identical superficially except for the presence of *some* or *any*. If the rule above is correct, the pair of sentences should be synonymous. But it is clear that there are situations where (28) is appropriate, but not (29), and (30) but not (31), or vice versa. For example, (28) might be used if the speaker expected someone to ask for the beans and (29) if he really didn't think anyone would want them. The speaker might use (30) if he secretly hoped the person addressed would eat the candy but (31) if he hoped he wouldn't. Thus, we can explain the strangeness of (32) and (33), where these presuppositions are combined with overt statements that directly contradict them:

(32) ?If he eats some candy, I'll punish him severely.
(33) ?If he eats any candy, I'll give him ten dollars as a reward.

(In all these cases, the *any* is unstressed, not the stressed *any (at all)*). The oddness of these sentences cannot be ascribed to anything present overtly in the sentences themselves, not even necessarily to anything in the speaker's or the hearer's knowledge of the world. The presence of *some* or *any* can be predicted only if you know what is going on in the speaker's mind—that is, if you are the speaker. Hence, one cannot give a rule for the distribution of *some* and *any* in sentences of this type: rather, the learner must be informed as to which to use according to his state of mind, or his beliefs about things.

These presuppositions that I have been discussing are not confined exclusively to English. Far from it: no doubt if we analyze many of the constructions speakers of English find it difficult to master in other languages, we shall find they involve unstated presuppositions; the teacher's task is to help the student match up presupposition with superficial form. The Japanese use of honorifics is one such example. An honorific such as *o-* or *-san* carries with it the notion that the person or thing to which it is applied is in some sense important to the speaker—that it is necessary for his comfort or existence. Once one makes this assumption, it is easy to see, for instance, why food-names like those for rice, tea, or soy sauce, but not for less basic foods, commonly receive the honorific. One can also understand how this is related to the use of honorifics for people or toilets. Unless the learner understands that the use is based on a presupposition, he will try to find a rule the applicability of which is decided within the sentence itself. He will, of course, fail and he will think the whole system is ridiculous. That is why it is customary for westerners to giggle when they see, for instance, *o-shoyu* translated as "honorable soy sauce," and *o-teárai* as "honorable toilet." And well they may, for these translations are ludicrous. The essential point to understand is that if a person is important or essential to someone else, he is held in honor and is exalted. But if a thing is important, a different kind of importance is involved, for example being essential for life. Thus, a better translation of *o-shoyu* might be something like "useful, beneficial soy sauce," as opposed to *John-san*, "the exalted John." One must know the feelings of the speaker toward the person or thing. These attitudes may be conventional in a culture or may be universal. Here, then, too, presupposition is a factor in grammaticality, and misinterpretation of presupposition will result in ludicrous—even if intelligible— sentences.

Finally, I should like to take a case from Spanish to illustrate this point once more. In Spanish, one finds sentences like (34) and (35). (34) contains *vive* in the indicative and (35) contains *viva*, a subjunctive:

(34) Busco a un hombre que vive en Madrid.
(35) Busco a un hombre que viva en Madrid.

These sentences assume different things about the relationship between speaker and *hombre*. In (34) we can attempt to paraphrase the thoughts unconsciously present in the speaker's mind (I say *"unconsciously"* because these presuppositions are very seldom conscious, that is why these distinctions are so hard to teach) in this way: "I know that this man exists and lives in Madrid. You know who I mean. It's a specific person I have in mind—though I may not know his name."

(35) is quite different in the presuppositions it assumes: "For some reason, I need a man who lives in Madrid. Maybe no person of that description exists, but that is the sort of thing I am looking for."

For instance, if someone has asked, *"Qué busca Ud?"* "What are you looking for?" the answer can only be (35). And, normally, *"A quién busca Ud?"* "Who are you looking for?" will be answerable only by (34). (34) can also be followed by a sentence identifying the *hombre: Se llama Juan Valdez*. But it would be absurd to follow (35) with such a statement: the speaker doesn't even know whether someone answering that description exists, let alone what his name is. No conceivable rule could clarify these facts for the non-native speaker, no pattern practice would enable him to memorize the correct uses of subjunctive and indicative. He must know what the presuppositions are.

These examples provide ample evidence that there are many important facts about English and other languages that cannot be taught by behaviorist-structuralist methods. Then do I advocate the use of the techniques of transformational-rationalist grammar? Obviously I do; but I want to make very clear that I am not a partisan of much that has, faddishly, been produced recently as applications of transformational grammar.[7] While many things about these treatments are

---

[7] For example, cf. a number of recent works dealing with the teaching of English as a first or second language: Jacobs and Rosenbaum (1968), Roberts (1966), and Thomas (1966).

admirable, and the attempt to bring rationalism to the teaching of language should of course be applauded and encouraged, I do not feel that these attempts have succeeded. These authors are not really using transformational grammar; they are using only its hollow shell of formalism; they are not employing rationalism at all, but resorting to new forms of the same old mumbo-jumbo; they have substituted one kind of rote learning for another, and the new kind is harder than the old. Their treatments do not allow scope for presenting the sorts of facts I have been talking about any more than did the structuralists' treatments allow them to do so, and for much the same reasons. Rather than teaching students to reason, they seem to me to be teaching students to use new formulas. Instead of filling in patterns of sentences—surface structures—students now have to learn patterns of abstractions—the rules themselves. And these rules are, without exception, fakes. Little is known about the exact form of most transformational rules. Among the most mysterious are the favorites of writers of textbooks, like passivization and relativization, about which practically nothing positive is known. Hence the formulations are either wrong or grossly oversimplified, to the extent that the relevant generalizations—the point of introducing transformational concepts in the first place—cannot be stated. The result is that the student does not get any idea why people have gone to so much trouble to make learning the language so much harder. The writer fails to bring home the essential points: that sentences are related to other sentences both within a language and across languages; that sentences often are related that do not look anything like each other; and that often sentences that look alike are not related at all at a deep level. They have no reasons for their rules. Where Rosenbaum and Jacobs, for example, give motivations, they tend to be false and hard to understand as well. And, since they do not talk about deep structures and universal facts about language, they must omit the very sorts of facts I have mentioned above that cannot be treated in the kinds of transformational rules that are known at present. These facts can be dealt with only very informally. In the work that we are doing we try to do this,[8] and though it may not look as impressive, we feel that it will teach more. Previous writers have failed to utilize one of the most crucial assumptions of transformational theory—the logical nature of man and language—because they do not make use of the student's ability to generalize and form intuitions about the sentences he hears and says. They merely teach another language at the same time as they teach the one the student is trying to learn. They teach both badly: the transformational grammar

[8] "We" refers, here as elsewhere, to the Language Research Foundation of Cambridge, Mass. The grammar to which I am specifically referring is a teacher's manual now being written by myself as an aid in the teaching of English to speakers of Japanese; though, since it is based on universal principles, it would also be of use as a reference in the teaching of English to speakers of other languages. A text for the student's use is being written concurrently under the direction of Bruce Fraser, based on the teacher's manual. These materials will be published by the TEC Company of Tokyo, Japan.

because it is oversimplified and misunderstood; the language itself because it is lost in the tangles of formal statements.

As an illustration of the way we are trying to use transformational grammar, as opposed to the way others have, I would like to look at the treatment of passives in English. Passivization is a rather touchy subject now among most transformational grammarians who are aware of recent thought in the field. It is embarassing because, until a few years ago, it was one of the best-understood rules in the grammar. Everyone who had read *Aspects* knew that the passive transformation took an active sentence, that met the structural description of (36):

$$(36) \quad NP_1 - Aux - V - X - NP_2 - Y - by + passive - Z \Rightarrow$$
$$ \quad \, 1 \qquad 2 \quad 3 \quad 4 \quad \, 5 \qquad 6 \qquad \quad 7$$

and transformed it into (37):

$$(37) \quad 5 - 2 + be + en - 3 - 4 - 7 + 1 - 6 - \phi - 8$$

Now it is fairly evident that this rule is not very convincing: it has many more terms than a normal transformational rule; the assignment of constituents is quite *ad hoc*; item 7, *by+passive* is a strange constituent; and the fact that it is a re-writing of the node *Manner Adverb* is even stranger. It can be shown that this transformation will wrongly predict the assignment of constituent structure in the surface structure. Besides, it doesn't tell anything that we know about the relation between active and passive sentences. So, for instance, it gives no reason, in itself, why reflexive sentences can't passivize: that is, why (38) is not a good sentence.

(38) *John was washed by himself.

But no formulation that has yet been proposed has given either a satisfactory deep structure underlying passive sentences or the transformational rule that produces the superficial forms. Thus it is oversimplification, to present, as is done in some of these books, a rule like (39) and call it 'passivization': note that it is an oversimplification of the already ludicrously oversimplified (36)-(37):

$$(39) \quad NP_1 - Aux - V - NP_2 \Rightarrow NP_2 - Aux - Be + en - V - NP_1$$

Partisans of this approach may object that, after all, this formulation describes accurately what is going on, insofar as that it shows the learner how, given an active sentence, it can form the corresponding passive. After all, what does it matter to him that theorists rack their minds over this rule?

In fact, it doesn't really matter that the theorists have problems. What does matter is that the reason theorists have troubles with the passive, and have discarded this formulation of passivization, is, simply, that it doesn't express the generalizations about the passive that the correct rule, coupled with the right deep structure, would. Therefore, it is of no use as a pedagogical device: it does not enable students to reason better, nor does it make clearer generalizations that they need to know to use the passive as a native speaker does. This rule does not tell the student that verbs like *want, have,* and *suit* are exceptions to passivization: no formulation can tell them this; the list simply must be learned. It does not enable them to recognize environments in which passivization is not found—which would be the only justification for this transformational treatment. In short, it does not do any more than the classical statement in English: "To form the passive, exchange the subject and direct-object noun phrases of a transitive verb, insert the verb *to be* after the auxiliary if there is one, and put any verb following *be* in its past participle form." This is simple and concise, it avoids the difficulty of first explaining the terminology $NP_1, \rightarrow, +,$ and so on, and makes things much less mysterious. If you like you can give rule (39), treating it as a formula, but I think it is wrong to call it a transformation: it isn't a transformation in any modern sense. It is just a mnemonic device, and I'm not so sure it's all that mnemonic.

There must be a better way to talk about the formation of passives in English. Transformational grammar has enabled researchers who do work in the field to precisely and accurately make observations about passive sentences, and their relationship to actives, with respect to form and meaning. These observations remain valid and useful regardless of whether we know what the deep structure or the transformational rule looks like. The job of the textbook writer is to take these observations, including the presuppositions that one needs to be aware of in order to use the English passive correctly, and put them into understandable form. So, dealing with speakers of Japanese, we must also bear in mind that Japanese contains a construction which, in some of its uses, approximates that of the English passive. It exchanges the functions of subject and object and adds an ending on the verb, and serves to create a new focus, or topic, of the sentence. But one of the big pitfalls for speakers of Japanese is that it does other things as well: it seems to carry with it, sometimes at least, the presupposition: "the act affects the subject in a bad way." (Compare, in English, the construction *something happened to someone*, which involves a similar presupposition.) The Japanese passive therefore can be used with intransitive verbs if their action affects the subject unfavorably. But the English construction called the passive does not have the same deep structure as this use of the Japanese passive: the meaning is different. Apparently, in Japanese, two deep structures have merged transformationally so that they share the same surface structure and only one of the Japanese 'passives' is really the equivalent of the English. Whatever the theoretical interpretation of the non-overlapping of Japanese and English passives, the fact is that the speaker of Japanese must be taught not to say, "The accident was occurred on June 29," or "Bill was died last night." These mistakes are frequent, because the Japanese construction is identified in books so closely with the English passive. Our task, in explaining the difference between the English passive and the Japanese passive, does not lie in making the Japanese student of

English memorize rule (39): this will not help him at all. Our task, rather, is to help him understand *why* a speaker of Japanese will form a passive sentence rather than an active: what he presupposes when he does so, the circumstances under which he must, may, or must not apply the rule; then to show him the corresponding facts for English, and talk about where they differ, giving many examples. We will want to explain that *John was shot by Harry* is *not* a paraphrase, in English, of *Harry shot John, to my discomfiture*, as the translations of these sentences would be in Japanese. We must talk, particularly, about environment: in English, there are situations where the passive cannot be used without sounding odd, due to discourse phenomena, where the similarly-named construction might at times be quite acceptable in Japanese. We might give as an example the fragment of discourse in (40):

(40) Charlie is really terrible. He never forgives an insult.

We are talking here about Charlie: he is the topic of the paragraph, or the conversation. It is normal, when one continues to talk about the same general topic, to want to keep the topic in focus—to keep indicating that this is the crux of the matter, the thing the speaker is interested in talking about. But it might also be that a sentence will come up where someone else does something to Charlie: for example, the speaker, in giving an example of how Charlie never forgets an insult, might want to talk about something someone did to annoy Charlie. He can say (41), of course:

(41) Once someone bit Charlie on the arm, and Charlie never forgave him.

This is perfectly grammatical, and perfectly understandable. But it creates an abrupt break with the rest of the sentence which is stylistically odd. Here, a speaker may choose to use the passive, since it puts *Charlie* back in subject position, where the topic of a sentence usually is in English, as in (42):

(42) Once he was bitten on the arm by someone, and he never forgave him.

To explain to the non-native speaker this sort of delicate discrimination, we must refer to notions like "topic," "focus," and "discourse," which neither the sort of transformational treatment which stops at formal mechanisms, nor the very similar behavioral-structural approach can capture.

It should be noted that the ungrammaticality of *John was washed by himself* is universal. It follows from universal constraints noticed by Postal (1968) to the effect that in a wide variety of environments nouns cannot cross over nouns that are co-referential to them. Since this is universal, and has to be on the basis of the nature of the constraint, we know that we need not mention it in a grammar of English for speakers of Japanese. This is helpful in case the writer of the textbook is not thoroughly familiar with the native language of the users of the textbook—a circumstance that is necessarily and unfortunately frequent.

It isn't that we avoid stating rules. In discussing the passive, what we have done is to provide a non-formal explanation in English words, of what is done to an active sentence to produce the corresponding passive. It is, basically, a description in words of the oversimplified transformational rule, but its virtue is first that it is immediately accessible and second that it makes no claims to being the explanation for these facts, but merely a description. We use transformational grammar, of course; the rules themselves, wherever they appear to exist or can be guessed at as a model for our non-formal descriptions; and, more importantly, our own knowledge of transformational theory and practice keeps us from doing irresponsible things, and gives us a means of testing our findings, as well as a heuristic device that makes the deep structures more accessible to our investigation.

The theory of transformational grammar has built into it various self-policing mechanisms in the form of principles by which the linguist can judge whether an analysis is rigorous or *ad hoc*; whether it is a complete analysis, or only scratches the surface of the problem, whether a formulation is precise or vague. These principles will enable the linguist to know, for instance, whether to posit an analysis in which two superficially different sentences are identical at a deeper level; whether two superficially identical sentences are different at a deeper level. One, the principle of recoverability of deletion mentioned already, allows deletion to take place only in case there is an element identical to the element to be deleted, which will remain in the surface structure so that its meaning can be recovered, or there is an abstract element that has left behind it syntactic markers from which its original presence can be deduced. We allow two sentences to be derived from the same deep structure only in case the selectional restrictions in one are the same as those in the other: the same kinds of nouns can be subjects or objects, the same classes of verbs occur. We assume two superficially identical sentences are not really identical if it can be shown that, by substituting one word for another, one of the meanings is made impossible. Tests of this kind allow us to propose deep structures in a responsible way, and relate these deep structures to the proper surface structures. This is of use in language teaching in a number of ways, none direct in the sense that writing transformational rules is direct. First, we ourselves become more sensitive to language through applying these tests and demanding proof of every claim. This enables us, hopefully, to see better than someone who has not been trained the relationships among sentences in English, and their relationship to universal facts and language-particular rules of the learner's native language. Then, when we say that a sentence of a certain type in English is related to, or obeys some of the constraints of, a sentence of maybe a quite-different-looking type in the learner's language, we have a reasonable idea that we are basing our conclusions on more than personal caprice. The danger of the latter is that, if the relationship is not real, or is only partial, the speaker may wrongly generalize. So, for instance, let us say that we have taught the speaker sentence (43):

(43) John couldn't lift 500 lbs.

and we point out to him that it is ambiguous because it can be paraphrased either by (44) or (45):

(44) John was physically unable to lift 500 lbs.
(45) It is impossible that John lifted 500 lbs.

Now if we look only this far into the language, and don't do any testing, we may give the speaker a rule saying: *can* can have either of these two meanings. And, if, as is frequent, there are in the learner's language two verbs translatable as *can*, one with one sense and one with another, if we're not careful we may say that *can* will translate either of these, freely, and that the synonymy is total.

But now let us look at sentence (46). Here something surprising happens. Only the second interpretation, that of "is possible that," is found:

(46) John couldn't be as stupid as Harry!

The reason is that the verb following the modal in (43) is active, or voluntary, while that of (46) is stative, or involuntary. Physical inability is not a factor in the meaning of stative verbs. If we know this fact, we are better able to explain the use of the modal *can* to non-native speakers, and, having tested and looked at various facts, we can avoid overgeneralizations, such as assuming (since when there are two identical verbs conjoined in a sentence conjunction reduction is possible) that, if the verbs *can* underlying (43)'s two meanings are identical, we could get sentences like (47):

(47) John couldn't lift 500 lbs. or be as stupid as Harry.

with the interpretation of the first *can* as "be physically able." Knowing there is a distinction and pointing it out avoids this danger.

We can also use transformational analyses when two sentences that look quite different share similar deep structures. This can be shown to be true for (48) and (49):

(48) Bill cut the salami with a knife.
(49) Bill used a knife to slice the salami.

It would take too long to go through the proofs that these sentences do, in fact, come from similar or identical deep structures.[9] But if we can make that assumption, we can show that this similarity of underlying structure can be put to use in teaching English as a foreign language. Suppose we are dealing with a language in which either the analog of (48) or of (49) did not occur, or where one or both looked quite different from either (48) or (49), and we wanted to teach how both were used. We could point out that they shared a common meaning; and, further, that just as the ungrammaticality of (50) can be expressed in terms of selectional restrictions between a verb and its subject (*use* selects an animate

---

[9] Evidence for this view is given in Lakoff (1968).

subject) the analogous sentence with *with* (51), is ungrammatical in the same way. If one of these constructions exists in the learner's language, he can make the generalization and know at once which sentences will be grammatical, which will not, though no rule can be stated (since *with* occurs with other meanings and restrictions) in English.

(50) *The book used a knife to cut the salami.
(51) *The book cut the salami with a knife.

Using insights such as these, made possible by a knowledge of transformational grammar, but not its formal devices, we can, we hope, teach languages better.

This leads to the final question, with which I want to deal briefly. I said earlier that the structuralists resorted to rote learning and pattern practice in the belief that they would thus recapitulate in second-language learning the processes of first-language learning as seen by behavioral psychologists. I said that we were trying to teach students to use their reasoning ability to generalize, and that giving them ungrammatical sentences and detailed contexts enables them to do so. I also said that first-language learning clearly involved rule-formation, or generalization from raw data. Are we then trying to reproduce the process of first-language learning in second-language teaching? It should be noted that in the other transformational approaches, the answer would have to be 'no.' It is never assumed that the child memorizes rules such as have been given.

Despite numerous psycholinguistic experiments, which show the order in which rules are learned, and mistakes made in learning a few isolated syntactic phenomena, mostly in English, practically nothing is known about first-language learning. No one knows how the child sifts out the rules from the huge mass of data, how he decides what is grammatical from the semi-grammatical and ungrammatical strings he hears along with the fully-grammatical ones. Also unknown is how he tells what rules are universal, what are not. It is not likely that we will know the answers to these questions for a long time. The question of the nature of first-language acquisition is just as dark, in fact, as second-language acquisition.

We can say a little, and that little enables us to give the answer to our question: are we attempting to recapitulate first-language learning? The answer is both yes and no. No, first, because certain abilities the child has are lost, and we cannot hope to use them again after he is ten years old or so. We do not even know what these abilities are. We know the child can, given raw data, derive the rules with no help from anyone. He can learn and memorize astounding amounts of vocabulary, including lists of exceptions. And he does all this, or most of it, unconsciously. You never hear him muttering, 'Let's see—is there a variable in that relative-clause formation rule or not?' or 'Hmmm . . . I wonder if equi-NP-deletion is governed, and what the exceptions to it are?' But somehow he knows. We have tried to enable the second-language learner to recapture some of his old ability by providing him with lists of things to be memorized (as is usual) and with the generalizations that the child would make himself. We have not yet tested our grammar: it is not even written. We would hope that, provided artificially with what the child has naturally, the second-language learner would go about learning his second language rather in the way he learned his first. But we must remember that artificial devices are seldom as good as the real thing. Probably too the fact that the generalizations must be consciously articulated will make a difference in how they are learned. But the similarity lies in appealing to the learner's ability to reason, compare data, and generalize. In this way our second-language teaching is like the process of first-language learning as transformational theory views it.

Some interesting similarities and differences have been noticed between the two types of learning. First, some work of Carol Chomsky's seems to indicate, if we can give this interpretation to her findings, as she did not, that universals are learned in a different way and at a different time from language-particular facts, in first-language learning.[10] According to a universal constraint on pronominalization, in no language is it possible to say sentences like (52):

(52) *He$_i$ said that John$_i$ was here.

where *he* and *John* refer to the same person. But some pronominalization-related facts are dialectal, or at least not universal. Thus, for instance, in a sentence like (53):

(53) John asked Bill when to leave.

in most dialects of English, the understood subject of *leave* is John. But dialects have been found where it can also be *Bill*. So this is not universal. It has been found that, with facts that are universal, like those in sentence (52), a child learns not to make mistakes in them very quickly, over a short time. But with cases like (53), he goes through a period of fluctuation—from one interpretation to the other, it takes a good deal longer for him to master the rule completely, and he makes many more mistakes. This is of interest in teaching second languages, because, as I noted above, it gives us a bit of a clue as to how to integrate universals in our texts. We now have, perhaps, some evidence from transformational grammar, that universals are kept apart from language-specific facts by the child in learning a first language. Moreover, he keeps them apart: one never hears a question in a language class as to the grammaticality of (52), while one might get questions on the meaning of sentences like (53). Therefore, we can assume the speaker is probably unconsciously aware that the universals are universal, and we need not talk about them, unless they are of use in explaining language-specific facts.

And, lastly, there seems to be a difference in the way a rule is learned by first and second-language learners. There is some evidence that a child, given data,

---

[10] Unpublished doctoral dissertation. Harvard, 1968.

will try to extract from it the simplest possible rule: the simplest in terms of structural description, structural change, and exceptions if any. He will do this sometimes even if it means speaking sentences quite different from the sentences he actually hears. (This, again, could not be explained by behaviorists.) Thus, children are frequently faced with sentences involving the rules of negative-attachment and negative-incorporation, as when they hear (54) and (55):

(54) Nobody ever did that to anyone.
(55) I didn't see anybody.

In the first of these sentences, there is one negative word in the deep structure, and three indefinites, one of which happens to be the subject of the sentence. In (55), there is also one negative, and one non-subject indefinite. In the first case, the negative is obligatorily attached to the indefinite subject. In the second, it has not been attached to anything. The rule in standard English is that, once the negative is written out once, whether by attachment or not, it is not repeated anywhere. This is, of course, not true in many languages, including non-standard English dialects, where multiple negation is the rule. It can also be shown that a rule allowing multiple negation is simpler in formulation than one allowing only single negation. But standard English has the more complicated formulation. It has been observed[11] that children frequently will learn the rule as though it allowed multiple negation—the simpler way—even though they may never have heard such sentences. But in second-language learning, there seems to be no mislearning of this sort. Speakers of English do not learn the negation rules of Spanish particularly readily, or more easily than speakers of Spanish learn the corresponding rules of English. This shows that we cannot assume that second-language learners still have at their disposal the means to invent rules, no matter how much information they are given: if they did have these means, they would probably search for the simplest formulation. Instead, the only mistake they make with rule-learning is that they apply the rules of their own language in learning the other language—a sure sign they have not learned the new rule. So, the evidence, scanty as it is, from psycholinguistics shows that we cannot expect to recapitulate first-language learning. We are doing something different, something that utilizes the unique capacities of human beings to a fuller extent than other methods, which we hope will give learners more insight into other languages and enable them to use them more like native speakers. We do not know whether we will succeed, or whether our premises are even valid. But it seems like an interesting and promising experiment, and we have great hopes for it.

[11] This is discussed by Kiparsky (1968).

REFERENCES

Chomsky, N. (1965). *Aspects of the Theory of Syntax.* Cambridge, Mass., M.I.T. Press.

Jacobs, R. and P. S. Rosenbaum. (1968). *English Transformational Grammar.* Boston: Ginn-Blaisdell.

Kiparsky, P. (1968). "Universals of Change," in *Universals of Linguistic Theory*, edited by E. Bach and R. Harms, New York: Holt, Rinehart & Winston.

Lakoff, G. (1968). "Instrumental Adverbs and the Concept of Deep Structure," *Foundations of Language*, vol. 4, no. 1, pp. 4–29.

Morton, F. R. (1966). "The Behavioral Analysis of Spanish Syntax: Toward an Acoustic Grammar," *International Journal of American Linguistics*, vol. 32, no. 1 (Publication 40), pp. 170–184.

Postal, P. (1968). "The Cross-Over Principle." Ditto, Thomas J. Watson Research Center, Yorktown Heights, N.Y.

Roberts, P. (1966). *The Roberts English Series: A Linguistics Program.* New York: Harcourt, Brace & World.

Thomas, O. (1966). *Transformational Grammar and the Teacher of English.* New York: Holt, Rinehart & Winston.

Weir, R. H. (1963). *Language in the Crib.* The Hague: Mouton & Co.

Part
Two

Methods,
Techniques, and
Materials

Overview

*T*he contents of this Part may seem somewhat dispar-
ate, but they have a common focus in their attention
to what goes on in the ESL classroom or language
laboratory.

Clear evidence of how the long-time British professional teacher of English as a second language
could construct pragmatically successful classroom
methods from years of experience appears in Hornby's
down-to-earth article. Hornby, who in the introductory matter of the *Advanced Learners Dictionary of
Current English* (London: Oxford University Press,
2d ed., 1963) achieved an excellent structural analysis without benefit of American structuralism, here
calls attention to the simple fact that learners must
be motivated by bona fide opportunities to communicate in the target language, a fact conspicuously
ignored during most of the period of pattern drill
and mim-mem dominance in American ESL pedagogy.

With similar awareness of the value of communicative practice rather than of simple repetition drill,
Stevick uses an analytic framework, taken from the
linguist Kenneth Pike, in which to create an ordered
situation that motivates the injection of such drill.
Although Stevick's "etic" and "emic" vocabulary is
peculiarly Pike's, the principles adduced are applicable in any terminology.

Several writers are concerned with how ESL materials can induce in classes the kind of motivation
that an actual two-way communication situation automatically has. Mrs. Allen suggests that in preparing
natural dialogues writers should keep in mind both
the students and the teacher lest the latter feel reluc-
tant to accept them as natural. Newmark and Diller
apparently are doing just this as they outline steps

that lead toward listening during a guided free conversation, although their approach does not depart far from traditional pattern practice and comprehension drill based upon that practice.

In this second article Stevick believes that often the teacher should modify the standard exercises and dialogues of the textbook so as to accommodate a particular group of students. Such modification, he insists, must take into account the students' own environment and experience so that the revised materials can actually provide for them the nucleus for free conversation.

For the teacher unsure of the resources available in different types of structural drills, Cook provides a detailed and illustrated description. He cautions against the danger of confusing the student by a structurally required response that for him is meaningfully inappropriate. Mrs. Paulston also presents a detailed, but different, description of structural drills, but with awareness of the adverse criticism directed against them by transformation grammarians and also with cognizance of the need for simulating real-life communication as much as possible.

Next, Prator, disturbed by the inadequate attention given to the needs of intermediate and advanced students, strongly invokes the principle of motivation in maintaining that on these levels classroom activities should be far along a scale ranging from manipulation through drill to free composition in both speaking and writing. Even some manipulation, he thinks, can become communicative (as Stevick indicates in Art. 9) if responses draw upon, or stimulate the use of the students' own experience.

The concern with listening shown by Newmark and Diller in their proposals leading to free conversation had first been urgently expressed fourteen years earlier by Nida. Alarmed by the persistent emphasis upon oral production, Nida, in his 1950 paper, argues for greatly increased emphasis upon its obverse, listening. He especially asks the teacher to encourage listening to language details in a planned order of importance, an order itself varying according to the relative difficulty of the features of the target language compared with those of the native language.

In the final article in this section, Locke, whose leadership in the field has long been unquestioned, offers both a description of the functions of the language laboratory and a sober prediction for its future (one which has already been fulfilled).

8

THE SITUATIONAL APPROACH TO LANGUAGE TEACHING

A. S. HORNBY

Is Hornby's use of *approach* consistent with Anthony's? (Art. 1)

Select a picture or series of pictures that you believe would be suitable to teach a specific aspect of English to a specific group of ESL students known to you. Be ready to tell how you would use it.

What pedagogical function do Hornby's sample questions serve? Are they structured in the same manner as those discussed by Stevick? (Art. 9)

Classroom situations, as described in the first of these two articles, will take the teacher through two or even three terms' work. But, as has been pointed out, interest, one of the most important elements in teaching, cannot be maintained indefinitely in this way. Young learners like to use the new language for something more exciting than the kinds of action chain that can be performed in the classroom. They want to learn about life in the country whose language they are learning, they want adventure stories and tales from history. Above all, they want to use the new language in talking about the affairs of daily life.

The printed text is the traditional answer to this demand. But this means concentration on reading at a stage where the spoken language should still have priority. In this article, therefore, an attempt will be made to show how pictures may be used to supply situations which are outside the classroom, situations likely to arouse and hold the learner's interest, situations suitable for intensive oral work. There is nothing new in the use of pictures for this purpose. In Eckersley's *Essential English for Foreign Students*,[1] for example, pictures reproduced from *Punch* and other humorous periodicals are used as "Stories without Words." F. G. French's *First Year English for Africa, Part 1, Speaking*,[2] contains twenty-six pages of pictures without text, sixteen of these picture pages being available

Reprinted by permission from *English Language Teaching*, 4 (March, 1950), 150–156. Mr. Hornby officially retired in 1963 from a long professional career in the teaching of English as a second language, during which he edited several dictionaries, produced a variety of teaching materials, and held teacher-training positions in Asia and Africa.

[1] Longmans Green.

[2] Oxford University Press.

in a large size as wall pictures. But the number of picture books suitable for the kind of work to be described here is very small and the books available are not always suitable for general use. There is no reason why teachers should not design and prepare their own material, at any rate until a better supply of suitable material becomes commercially available.

"Every picture tells a story," but today it is more usually a picture strip, the kind of strip we are accustomed to see in our popular newspapers. The picture strip has great potential value in language teaching. Not the comic strip of the popular press, with balloons issuing from the mouths of the characters portrayed, balloons usually full of idiomatic and slangy language, but a series of panels or frames each showing a stage in a story or incident specially designed for story telling and question-and-answer work.

To illustrate the possibilities of this device, I shall take an incident from the Life and Labours of the Greek hero Hercules. Five drawings are needed. These may be provided, perhaps, by the art teacher, or even made by the older pupils in their art classes. They should be of a size large enough for display on the classroom wall or the teacher's desk, and made either on stiff cardboard or on paper stout enough to be tacked to a wooden frame. The drawings should be in clear outline, free from elaborate detail. The five pictures needed for the incident are:

1. The infant Hercules sleeping in a cradle; arms underneath the bed coverings.

2. Two snakes appearing at the foot of the cradle, only the heads shown; the infant Hercules with eyes open and arms outside the coverings.

3. Snakes with their heads reared, fangs showing; the infant Hercules sitting up and looking at them fearlessly.

4. Snakes being strangled, infant Hercules holding a snake in each hand.

5. Snakes lying dead across the cradle, heads touching floor; infant Hercules again sleeping peacefully.

These five pictures provide the situations. The story can be used at various levels and can be told using only the tenses and constructions with which the class is familiar. Here I am assuming that the tenses known are the Present Progressive, the Simple Present, the Present Perfect and the Future of Intention with *going to*, ...

The teacher should first tell the story, holding up or pointing to each picture in turn. (At a later stage the teacher may require members of the class to tell the same story in their own words, and, at a later stage still, to tell a story from pictures *without* a preliminary telling by the teacher.) In the text below words in italic type are assumed to be unknown to the class. These new words will be taught by reference to the pictures, or, if necessary, by contextual procedures. The teacher may occasionally ask for the translation of a word or phrase as a check on its correct identification.

"Look at this picture. This is a *baby*. It's a baby boy. The baby's name is *Hercules*. Say after me: [ˈhəːkjuliːz]. Again, please: [ˈh kujiliːz]. What's the baby doing? He's sleeping, isn't he? The baby isn't awake, he's asleep. The baby's sleeping. He's sleeping in his *cradle*. Look, this is the cradle. The baby's asleep in the cradle.

"Look at his eyes. Are they open or shut? They're shut. Are our eyes open or shut when we're asleep? They're shut, aren't they? Do we sleep with our eyes open? No, we don't, we sleep with our eyes shut.

"Can you see the baby's arms? No, you can't. Why can't you see them? Because they're under the *blanket*. This is the blanket. The blanket is over the baby's arms. You can't see his arms."

The teacher may now either go on to talk about the second picture or put questions to the class about the first. The choice will depend upon the time available. If he can devote a whole lesson to the story, it may be better to tell the story in full. If he is using the picture method for only ten or fifteen minutes of the period, he will be able to deal with only one picture in each lesson. Here are suggestions for question-and-answer work. Note the possibilities and advantages of getting away from the story situation and bringing in real situations.

"Is this a baby boy or a baby girl?"
"Is this baby awake or asleep?"
"Is he sleeping in a big bed or in a cradle?"
"Have you any baby brothers or baby sisters?" *or*
"How many baby brothers have you?"
"Look at the picture. Are the baby's eyes open or shut?"
"Can you see the baby's arms?"
"Why can't you see the baby's arms?"
"Are the baby's arms outside the blanket or under the blanket?" (etc.)

"Look at this picture. This is the second picture, picture number two. What are these? They're *snakes*. This is a snake and this is a snake. How many snakes are there in the picture? There are two. Look, I'm drawing a snake on the blackboard. This is its head, this is its body, this is its *tail*. Has a snake any legs? No, a snake has no legs. Look at this picture again. How many snakes can you see in the picture? Can you see their bodies and tails? No, you can't, you can see their heads but you can't see their bodies and tails.

"Look at the baby. Is Hercules sleeping now? No, he's not sleeping now. He's awake. Look, his eyes are open. Are his arms still under the blanket or are they outside the blanket? They're outside the blanket now, aren't they?"

The words *poison, bite, dangerous* and *die* are not essential for the story. It is possible to tell the story without bringing in the possibility of snake-bite and death. But there is no reason for avoiding a small number of extra words whose use helps to make the story vivid and exciting. The words may not occur again in the reading-texts for a year or more, perhaps, and will be forgotten. This is not a serious matter. They are immediately useful and this is sufficient justification for their use. The meanings may be given through translation. Rare words such as *fang* are, however, better avoided.

> "Is the baby still asleep?"
> "Are his eyes open or shut in this picture?"
> "Are his arms still under the blanket?"
> "Where are the baby's arms now?"
> "How many snakes can you see in this picture?"
> 'Are they on the cradle or on the floor (on the left-hand side or on the right-hand side)?"
> "Can you see their tails?"
> "Can you see their bodies or only their heads?"
> "How many legs has a snake?"
> "Are the snakes in this country dangerous (poisonous)?"
> "Do men sometimes die from snake-bite?"
> "Have you ever seen a snake in your bedroom?" (etc.)

The remaining three pictures should be treated in the same way—first a talk by the teacher, then a questioning of the class, or, with advanced learners, questions put by one half of the class and answered by the other. Having dealt with the story in this way, using the progressive form throughout, the teacher may then use the pictures for practice in other forms. Future of Intention and Present Perfect are obvious choices.

> "Look at this picture, the third picture. What are the snakes going to do?"
> "Look at picture number five. What has Hercules done?"
> "Who has killed the snakes? Have the snakes bitten Hercules?" (etc.)

The advantage of making one's own pictures for this type of lesson is that one can choose the kind of subject which one knows to have an appeal to the learner. The Greek legend used here may have little interest for pupils in Europe—it is almost certainly one with which they are already familiar. They may prefer something modern—riding a bicycle, making a journey by air, some sporting event. With a little ingenuity it is not difficult to design a series of pictures to illustrate a situation suitable for treatment of the kind discussed and exemplified here.

The essentials may be summarized thus:

1. The series should be designed so that a variety of questions is possible, especially of the types—

a. *What is he going to do?*
b. *What is he doing?*
c. *What has he just done?*
d. *What did he do next?*

This makes it possible to use the same set of pictures several times. With a class of beginners, the *b*-type question is used, Past Tense and Present Perfect Tense being as yet untaught. A year later, the pictures appear again, but this time the story, already familiar, is used with *a*-type and *c*-type questions.

Question-and-answer work based on a text-book story is usually, by its very nature, limited to Past Tense forms. One asks: "Who first *saw* the bear?" *Did* the guide kill it or *did* he only wound it?" "*Did* the wounded bear attack the guide or *did* it run away?" It is only with pictures, exhibited or pointed to one at a time, that one can ask: "What is the guide going to do?" "What has the guide just done?" and so on.

2. It is an advantage if the subject of the pictured story can be chosen so that it enables the teacher to deal not only with the situations in the picture but with real situations in real life—escape from the classroom into the outside world.

Here is an example of a series of pictures of this kind, suitable for a third or fourth-year class:

1. A bicycle left against a wall; boy walking towards it.
2. Boy with his hands on the handlebars of the bicycle.
3. Boy with left foot on left pedal, right leg raised over saddle.
4. Boy cycling along road, flat type.
5. Boy turning bicycle upside down.

6, 7, 8, etc. Illustrations showing removal of tyre, extraction of inner tube, finding and repair of puncture, etc.

A long series such as this is more suitable, perhaps, for a picture-strip in a book than for large-scale drawings on the classroom wall. There is the possibility of questions on intention, present activity and achievement.

> "What's the boy going to do?" ("He's going to get on his bicycle," etc.)
> "Where's the boy putting his left foot?" ("He's putting it on the left pedal.")
> "What has the boy just done?" ("He's just got on his bicycle—got off his bicycle—pulled out the inner tube," etc.)

There is the possibility of questions of a general nature, on real situations in the lives of the pupils:

> "Have you a bicycle?" "Do you come to school by bicycle?"
> "Do you often have punctures?" "What must we have if we want to repair a puncture?" "What's the pump used for?" (etc.)

There is the possibility of using the strip for written work:

> "Describe how a boy gets on a bicycle."
> "Explain how to repair a puncture."

There is the advantage of teaching practical everyday English—and this is a real advantage not possessed by the average text-book. The language text-books of the not very distant past usually gave far too much space to narrative—Aesop's Tales, Tales of Robin Hood, Shakespeare Retold—and very little to language useful in practical affairs. Language is needed for situations and should be taught with situations as the starting-point A knowledge of the English names of all the beasts in Aesop's Tales will help the learner to read Aesop's Tales—and very little else. The subject matter of arithmetic has been reformed. Children now make out shopping bills instead of doing problems about water running into and out of bath-tubs. We now need a reform in the subject-matter of language teaching. To those who say that the purpose of foreign-language study should be the study of literature, it may be answered that the study of literature should begin only when the learner has acquired a knowledge of the everyday language. He can rightly appreciate good literature only when he can distinguish between the language used for everyday affairs and the more elevated style used for poetry and fine prose.

9   "TECHNEMES" AND   EARL W. STEVICK
        THE RHYTHM OF
        CLASS ACTIVITY

What does Stevick see as the possible benefits of preparing certain lessons within the framework of *technemes*?

Prepare a set of questions on some English passage that would include all the technemes represented in Stevick's example (p. 90).

What technemes could be defined for *reading in class, doing substitution drills*?

This article[1] presents one principle of language teaching. It is a simple principle, yet in observing scores of teachers, I have seldom seen it followed. The teachers who have followed it have been successful ones. The principle applies, I believe,

Reprinted by permission from *Language Learning*, 9 (1959), 3.45-51. Professor Stevick is coordinator of the African Language Program at the Foreign Service Institute, U.S. Department of State.

[1]Based on a paper read before the EFL Section of the University of Kentucky Foreign Language Conference, April 24, 1959.

to all successful systems of language teaching, even to systems which seem to be mutually contradictory. What I shall describe is not a method; it is rather an "emic" approach to the devising of methods.[2]

There are two very broad conditions for language learning: "exposure to the language" to be learned, and morale. Morale in turn represents a combination of self-confidence and keen interest in the work at hand. But if morale and rate of exposure are to remain high over long periods of time, the student must feel a continuing sense of progress. Closely connected with the sense of progress is the rhythm of class activity.

With respect to the rhythm of activity, the teacher faces twin problems: the foot-shuffling of those for whom things are moving too slowly, and the head-hanging of those who are baffled. Often when we establish or break routines, we do so because we have recognized that one of these is taking place. Frequently, of course, they develop side by side in a single class.

Even in a homogeneous class, however, the problem of rhythm would remain. No matter what cycle of activity we establish, it will fail if we do not control the rate at which the student encounters difficulties. Too many difficulties per minute will overwhelm him, while too few will leave him restless.

What I am suggesting is that we may effect changes, and thus maintain in the class a sense of progress, with little or no change in the linguistic problems. We do this, obviously, by varying the type of activity. But successful manipulation of class activity is not always as easy as it sounds. To be effective, it must be flexible. And it can be flexible only if the teacher knows thoroughly, not only a few principal methods, but also dozens of partially similar techniques which may be substituted for one another.

That is to say, somewhere in the process of making a lesson plan, we select a sequence of broad and general types of activity in which we expect to engage. Too often, that is exactly where we stop: we select categories of activity that are broad and general. Then, when we get into class, we go ahead and engage in them—broadly and generally. I am recommending that we take a sharper look at these "categories of activity."

I would like to illustrate this approach by applying it to one of my own favorite teaching devices for advanced students, the anecdote. The general procedure is one which I first saw used in German, by Dr. Heinz von Schüching, but which I have also heard described with enthusiasm by teachers from various parts of the world.

Following this procedure, the teacher first reads an anecdote aloud several times, with the students relying entirely on their ears. The teacher then uses questions and paraphrases to insure comprehension and to make the students familiar with the language of the story. Finally, the students write the story in "their own words."

[2]The term "emic," like some of the key ideas of this article, is borrowed from Kenneth L. Pike.

One of the "categories of activity" which we have just mentioned is that of asking questions. But within this category we may make some further distinctions. We may differentiate first of all among various types of questions according to their grammatical structure. Writers commonly distinguish at least yes-no questions, alternative questions, and questions that begin with question words. Harold Palmer[3] and Faye Bumpass[4] are among those who make still more such distinctions. Professor Gurrey,[5] using a different principle, classifies questions according to their content. He speaks of "Stage I Questions" (questions whose answer is contained in the wording of the story), "Stage II Questions" (those with an answer implied in the content of the story), and "Stage III Questions" (questions pertaining to the students' own lives).

If we cross-classify according to both form and content, we find that there are at least nine different kinds of questions which we may ask about a story. See the diagram for a set of simple examples. Each of these kinds of question is the

Included in "story":

This little boy is holding a broom. . . . He has cleaned his room. . . . He has put the toys under the bed. . . . He is showing his room to his mother. . . .

Types of questions on this story:

	"Stage I"	*"Stage II"*	*"Stage III"*
Yes-no	Is the boy holding a broom?	Is the boy's mother angry?	Do you clean your own room?
Alternative	Is the boy holding a broom, or a toy?	Is the boy's mother pleased, or angry?	Do you clean your room, or does your mother?
Question Words	What is the boy holding?	How does the boy's mother feel?	Who cleans your room?

basis for what is potentially a separate "technique." That is, the teacher may ask a series of yes-no questions taken directly from the story. The example given is "Is the boy holding a broom?" At another time, he may ask a series of questions using interrogative words (*who, when, why*) taken from the same story. The example given is "What is the boy holding?" I would like, for the purposes of

[3] H. E. Palmer, *The Teaching of Oral English* (London, 1940).

[4] F. L. Bumpass, *The Teaching of English as a Foreign Language* (Ciudad Trujillo, 1950).

[5] P. Gurrey, *Teaching English as a Foreign Language* (London, 1955).

this article, to use the word "technique" in such a way that these two types of question are taken as exemplifying two different "techniques."

Now, it is doubtful that most teachers, as they stand (or sit) in a classroom "doing-questions-and-answers," are aware of these nine different techniques which they have at their disposal. All too often, we blur the distinctions by asking one kind of question after another, in random order. We may even fail to exploit the entire range, confining ourselves to one or two grammatical types of question, or to "Stage I Questions."

A crucial question, of course, is whether these nine kinds of question are of interest to anyone except the armchair pedagogue; are they relevant to the problems of teaching real students? How important, in other words, *is* the difference between a yes-no question whose answer is implied in a story, and a yes-no question whose answer comes from the lives of the students? Or, perhaps we should recognize *more* than nine categories! Would it be profitable to distinguish, for example, between what-questions and why-questions? Or between questions with a "true subject" and those in which "the place of the subject is filled by the word *there*"?

In answering questions such as these, we inevitably find ourselves driven toward the kind of attitude which Pike has called "emic."[6] An "emic" approach to a set of data

> is in essence valid for . . . only one minimum dialect at a time or for the relatively homogeneous and integrated behavior of one . . . culturally defined class of people; it is an attempt to discover . . . the pattern . . . of that particular . . . culture in reference to the way in which the various elements of that culture are related to each other in the functioning of that particular pattern. . . .[7]

By contrast, an "etic" approach "studies data in reference to [a] system"[8] which has *not* been created with reference to the particular set of data being studied.

In Pike's theory, an "emic behavior cycle," also called a "behavioreme," "[has] closure signalled by overt objective clues within the verbal or non-verbal behavior of the domestic participants. . . ."[9] I am here suggesting that the teacher consciously look for and deliberately exploit the clues which are present in the behavior of the domestic participants (the students) in a particular subsubculture (an individual class). That is, the answers to the questions that we

[6]Pike coins the terms *emic* and *etic* by utilizing the last parts of the words phonemic and *phonetic.*

[7]K. L. Pike, *Language in Relation to a Unified Theory of the Structure of Human Behavior* (Glendale, 1954), p. 8a. I wish to acknowledge the value of Pike's work in stimulating my own thinking: at the same time, he is in no way responsible for any mis-applications of his ideas which I may have introduced into this article.

[8]*Ibid.*

[9]*Ibid*, p. 58a.

asked above depend on the reactions of the students: does their behavior show those distinctions to be "emic?"

Specifically, how do the students respond to a change from one of those apparently different techniques to another? There are two criteria: (1) will a switch from one to the other dissipate restlessness among those students for whom things have been moving too slowly? (2) will a switch from one to the other cause trouble for the slower students? Any pair of techniques which, for a given teaching situation, satisfy either or both of these criteria are then significantly ("emically") distinct in *that situation*: we might call them separate technique-emes, or "technemes." In some situations, of course, these usable ("technemic") distinctions will be etically relatively narrow, and in others relatively broad. It has been my experience, however, that most teachers *fail to recognize how fine a distinction of technique is needed* either to dispel restlessness or to create difficulty.

Note that the same pair of techniques which proved to be "different technemes" in one situation might in some other situation fail to satisfy either of our two criteria. *In that situation*, no matter how great or small the "etic" difference between them, and notwithstanding the fact that in the first situation they were emically distinct, we could not say that the two techniques represented "different technemes."

Technemes in this sense are very numerous. Furthermore, they are related to one another systematically, much as the phonemes of a language are related to one another in an interlocking set of distinctive features. For that reason, we frequently find that transition from any one techneme, say Techneme A, to some other techneme, B, is easier than transition from A to C. For example, the shift from yes-no questions on a text to question-word questions on the same text should be smoother than a shift from the same yes-no questions to question-word questions based on the extracurricular interests of the students. The goal of the teacher as he works with a class is to select a series of technemes which will give the amount of drill needed, forestalling restlessness without causing trouble for the poorer students: frequent changes to satisfy the strong, but small ones to preserve the weak.

As a matter of fact, the nine techniques in the diagram are only a beginning. Some further "etic" differences which in many situations will prove "emic" are (1) type of answer (long or short), (2) type of response (unison or choral), (3) order of students giving individual answers (fixed or random), (4) order of questions (parallel to story or not), (5) tempo (slow or brisk). Combining these distinctions with those in the diagram, we arrive at a total of at least 108 workable combinations representing potential technemes, in place of the one broad and general activity "asking questions about a story." In a situation for which all 108 of these differences were "emic," a skillful teacher would select not two or three, and not all 108, but the two or three dozen which seemed most suitable for the class and the subject matter he was teaching.

A second illustration of this technemic approach to the devising of methods will help to put the first into perspective. One sort of class activity which is receiving wide discussion these days is the memorizing of dialogues. What are some of the etic differences of technique which will prove to be emic in some situations? Here are a few of the most obvious:

Listening	(3)	Books closed	(3)
vs.		*vs.*	
Repetition		Books open	
vs.		*vs.*	
Reprod. without direct imitation		Books open, but used as little as possible	
Choral repetition	(2)	Repeating each line two or more times	(2)
vs.			
Individual repetition		*vs.*	
		Going straight through the dialogue	
Calling on students in fixed order	(2)		
vs.			
Calling on them in random order			

(72 possible combinations)

I have found all of these differences to be "emic," using Paratore's *English Dialogues for Foreign Students*,[10] with a class of advanced university students in this country.

If space permitted, we could analyze other sorts of class activity from this point of view: reading in class, doing substitution drills, and so forth. Each type of activity would yield its own family of techniques (potential technemes). With any of these activities, by choosing an appropriate succession of tech*nemes*, and properly timing the switches from each one to the next, we can do much toward maintaining a firm and rapid rhythm in the drill session.

Unfortunately, when the teacher is planning a lesson, he cannot fully anticipate those choices and their timing. Many of the decisions must be made on the spot. For this reason, the application of a technemic point of view is as much a muscular skill as it is an intellectual exercise. Teachers in training (or in retraining) should derive benefit from practicing changes of this sort in a systematic way, just as they themselves drill their students in switching from one tense to another, or from direct to indirect questions. Ideally these changes should be overlearned. Even in a training situation which is not ideal, should not the trainees learn them, or at least become explicitly aware of their existence? We don't expect language *students* to pick up *phon*-emic contrasts out of the thin

---

[10] (Rinehart & Co., New York, 1956).

air as they study a language: should we ask teacher trainees to learn *techn*-emic contrasts haphazardly? True, some good teachers do instinctively what we have recommended but why make the new ones learn the hard way?

One final word: even if technemes are all that we have said they are, and even if teachers everywhere began to organize and conduct their classes with technemes in mind, good teaching would not have become a mechanical procedure. Technemes are only the pigments. It still takes the hand of an artist to blend them into a masterpiece.

10   PREPARATION OF   VIRGINIA F. ALLEN
DIALOGUE AND
NARRATIVE
MATERIAL FOR
STUDENTS OF
ENGLISH AS A
FOREIGN
LANGUAGE

For use in a specific class known to you, prepare two dialogues: one of which is an adaptation of a dialogue found in a play, novel, or story, and the other one of which you compose. Discuss the advantages each has in terms of preparation and usability.

Most programs in English now use dialogues or narratives, or both, to show how words work in "real-life" situations, and to help students become acquainted with the common life experiences that make English mean what it means to native speakers. Sometimes this material is written expressly for foreign students; sometimes passages from stories and novels are simplified or otherwise adapted for use with foreign students in this country or abroad.

These two operations (*adapting* materials and *composing* materials) have much in common, of course. But for convenience in discussion we might look at each of the two separately, beginning with problems met in rewriting something intended just for an English-speaking audience. Since I have recently been

Reprinted by permission from *Language Learning*, special issue, June, 1958, pp. 97–104, and originally presented as a paper at the Conference on Linguistics and the Teaching of English as a Foreign Language, University of Michigan, July 28–30, 1957. Dr. Allen is professor of English education at Temple University.

working for the USIA on an adaptation of A. B. Guthrie's *The Way West*, my examples for the first part of this discussion will be taken from that novel.

When people find that I am doing this sort of work, they usually say, "Oh, yes. You're putting the book into Basic English." Or, on a slightly more sophisticated level, they say, "Oh, yes. You're substituting high-frequency words for the vocabulary of the original." The following examples will show how much more is involved than that.

Problem 1. Stylistic deviations from the "normal" sentence patterns students have learned in class.

e.g. *"What lived inside herself* she had no . . . words for." (p. 411)
"Always in between would rise the past." (p. 433)

Problem II. Possibly misleading uses of dependent-clause constructions.

e.g. "He hadn't got around to asking Dick, feeling somehow backward, as if the asking would show a *doubt Dick hadn't earned."* (p. 377)

Problem III. Unfamiliar combinations of words which may be familiar words to the student.

e.g. "It was *bound* to come." (p. 343)
"An hour or so, and they would see." (p. 363)
"He hadn't *got around* to asking . . ." (p. 377)

Problem IV. Regional or non-standard items.

e.g. ". . . neither of them able to say anything but little, piddling things . . ." (p. 39)
"I'll camp 'em off a piece and *fix for palaver* . . ."* (p. 262)

Problem V. Social and cultural meanings of words probably known to the student only in the dictionary sense.

e.g. "He was a *slave man* himself, but still . . . he didn't know as one man had a right to own another, black or white." (p. 5)
". . . a better companion than . . . McBee, the *poor white."* (p. 19)
"Sometimes he felt like thanking God for *preachers."* (p. 231)

These few examples are perhaps enough to show that the adapting of material involves a great deal more than mere substitution of high-frequency synonyms for the word stock of the original story. It is necessary also to simplify syntax, to explain or change puzzling collocations, to provide clues to words and expressions fully understood only by people brought up in our culture.

When a person is writing dialogue and narratives of his own devising, his task is relatively easy so far as controlling vocabulary and syntax is concerned. The writer of original material gives his characters thoughts, and puts them into situations, that can be conveyed by words either frequent or useful or both. In assessing the frequency of usefulness of words that he plans to include, he does not rely on his own hunches or observation: he bases his selection on some standard list (such as the Thorndike's *Teacher's Word Book of 30,000 Words*[1] or the *General Service List of English Words*[2] which resulted from Michael West's recent substantial revision of the earlier *Interim Report*). In general, the writer of a dialogue or story for foreign students will assume that a word from the West list, or a word marked A or AA on the Thorndike list, will be understood by most students who know enough English to use dialogues and narratives. If the material is intended for beginners, the writer will introduce words from the standard lists in such a way as to help the student learn them.

A close look at any of the existing word lists, however, makes one wary of overdependence on such lists. Some very high frequency words are quite sure to baffle students. For example, *close* and *bound* are among the thousand most frequent words, according to the Thorndike count. That does not guarantee, however, that an intermediate-level student in Chile will understand such a sentence as " Sit *close* to your mother" or "It was *bound* to happen."

Conversely, many vocabulary items actually known by most foreign students are not found on standard lists of frequent or useful words. *Blackboard* is not on the West list, and Thorndike's word-counters rated *blackboard* as rarer than *bunny*.

Most writers of dialogues and narratives for foreign students have for some time recognized the importance of vocabulary controls, but there has been less recognition of the necessity for controlling sentence patterns. Many books labeled "Elementary" contain readings in which scant attention has been paid to syntax. Thus, we find this sentence in Lesson One of a reader for students in Japan: "It is thinking that makes what we read our own." One could hardly mention ten easier, more frequent, or more useful words than the words of that sentence. Yet structurally the sentence certainly does not belong in Book One.

Other guides to the writing of such material come to mind when one considers the *audience* for whom the dialogues and stories are intended. The writer needs to remember that many members of this audience are *not* undergraduates on American campuses. Many are mature men and women who never expect to have a date, or discuss a football game, or gripe about an examination (at least in English). Except when the material is written specifically for the use of college boys and girls, the writer needs to avoid "Joe college" themes and situations, and a language level represented by sentences like "Quit kidding" or "Brother, I've had it!" Furthermore, characters in stories and dialogues might well include some professional people, designated as Mr., Mrs., Dr., Miss, as well as characters called Betty, Jim and Jack.

As a matter of fact, many students and teachers around the world feel it is

[1] Edward Thorndike, *Teacher's Word Book of 30,000 Words*, New York: Columbia University Press, 1932.

[2] Michael P. West, *General Service List of English Words*, New York: Longmans, Green, 1953.

unfortunate that so much American textbook material is based on work with classes in American universities. The vast majority of English-learners in the world are not and never will be students on American campuses. The vast majority do not live in English-speaking areas and most of them will never have occasion to *speak* English at all. Looking at the material currently exported to foreign classes, one wonders how much of it offers really relevant help to this forgotten audience.

Writers of dialogues might note, too, that even in the United States, there are likely to be more *men* than *women* in a class of foreign students. And somehow women seem to feel more comfortable reading men's parts than men feel reading women's. I have often had a class in which two overworked women did more than their share of talking, because no man wanted to "be" Mrs. X or Miss Y.

Speaking of audiences, too, we ought not to overlook the fact that the material must be palatable to *two* important—and usually quite *different*—audiences: the foreign *student* and his *teacher*. If the teacher feels that the story or conversation sounds stilted or trivial, his lack of enthusiasm soon carries over to the class. On the other hand, the most sparkling material (from the teacher's point of view) soon falls flat if the students fail to understand it or feel that it is something they would never want to say.

On first trying his hand at this kind of writing, the American tends to forget one or the other of these audiences. Either he is so conscious of the student's limitations that he makes his characters talk like a poor translation of Esperanto, or—more commonly—he writes the way one would for a sophisticated American reader, and shuns clichés. Yet clichés are precisely what the student needs to learn. A first step, then, in learning to write such material is to resist the temptation to be clever and creative. A smart retort may give the *teacher* a flattering opinion of the writer's wit, but what the *student* needs is the banal response that eight out of ten Americans would utter in the situation portrayed.

When this much has been said, however, we need to add that the material should somehow manage not to seem dull—to the teacher or to the students. Somehow the banalities and the stock situations need to be made interesting, because, without interest—psychologists tell us—little learning takes place.

Perhaps such an emphasis on audience-analysis may seem more appropriate to a conference on public relations or creative writing than to a conference on linguistics. Yet people who learn languages are human beings. We need to consider who these human beings are, under what circumstances they are studying English, and what *they* want to learn.

11 EMPHASIZING THE AUDIO IN THE AUDIO-LINGUAL APPROACH

GERALD NEWMARK
and
EDWARD DILLER

Choose a dialogue from some ESL textbook and prepare the teaching steps for the development of the
listening skills suggested by the authors.

Are the steps you prepared equally appropriate for
elementary school children and adults? Be ready to
discuss this.

Does Nida (Art. 16) disagree with the authors of this
article in any substantial way?

Modern audio-lingual theory stresses a listening-speaking-reading-writing sequence
in foreign-language instruction. The importance of ear training in developing
speaking proficiency receives particular emphasis. There are strong arguments,
both physiological and psychological, for preceding speaking practice with training in listening comprehension. For example:

1. Ear training facilitates speaking. Articulation is dependent upon hearing
sounds accurately, discriminating among sounds, establishment—i.e., memorization or internalization—of proper auditory sound images, and development of a
feel for the new language.

2. Concentration on one skill at a time facilitates learning by reducing the
load on the student and by permitting the use of materials and techniques geared
to the specific objectives and requirements of each skill.

3. When students are required to speak from the outset, the likelihood of
errors is increased, apprehensiveness on the part of the student impedes learning,
and confidence develops slowly (if at all). When listening comprehension precedes speaking, the student's initial experience includes more correct responses
and more frequent positive reinforcement, less apprehension, and more rapid
development of confidence in his language learning ability.

4. Prematurely listening to his own unauthentic pronunciation, and to that
of other students, may interfere with the student's discrimination and retention
of correct sounds.

To date, there has been practically no experimentation to determine how

Reprinted by permission from *The Modern Language Journal*, 48 (January, 1964), 18–20.
Mr. Newmark is a human-factors scientist with the System Development Corporation and
also language consultant to the California State Department of Education. Professor Diller
is a member of the department of German at the University of Oregon.

much time should elapse between listening experiences and speaking practice. Systematic research is needed, not only on the relationship between listening and speaking in foreign language instruction, but also on how best to teach listening comprehension as a skill in its own right.

Most language programs neglect listening comprehension. It is generally treated as incidental to speaking, rather than as a foundation for it. Classroom exercises are mainly speaking exercises in which the student hears an audio stimulus and then immediately imitates it or makes some other oral response. When students listen to and participate in exercises with partial sentences, backward build-up, pattern practice, and pronunciation drills they are hearing unnatural speech. As important as these exercises may be for developing skill in speaking, the question may well be asked, "When do the students hear the language as it is actually spoken?"

Texts, guides, and courses of study frequently contain tests for evaluating progress in listening comprehension, but rarely do they contain specific learning materials designed for the systematic development of this skill. Until such materials become available, teachers who wish to do more with listening comprehension can adapt present materials for this purpose.

The present vogue in learning instruction is centered around memorized dialogues and pattern drills. Within the dialogue-pattern drill approach the teacher can take the following steps to emphasize listening comprehension:

1. Present the dialogue as a story, in the foreign language, using simple language. Explain the meaning of some of the new words and expressions that will appear in the dialogue through gestures, visual aids, use of synonyms, paraphrasing, etc. The idea, at this point, is not to teach the exact meaning of every new linguistic element in the dialogue, but rather to convey the general idea of the content in story form. Further, in order to provide additional listening comprehension practice, embellish the story by making up facts about the characters which are not in the dialogue, using only previously learned vocabulary.

2. Present the dialogue verbatim, acting out the various roles. Point to stick figures on the chalk board, drawings, or cut outs on a flannel board to make clear to students at all times which character is speaking. Stop to get across meanings of new words and expressions through gestures, visuals, paraphrasing, etc. As a last resort, provide an English equivalent. Time spent in paraphrasing and acting out meanings is not wasted as far as listening comprehension is concerned as long as the student is hearing authentic language.

3. Go through the dialogue again, without stopping, to give students a feel for how the entire conversation sounds at a normal rate of speed. If a recording of the dialogue is available, play it, using several voices for this presentation.

4. Have a "programmed" (in the sense of "programmed learning") true-false activity based on the dialogue in order to insure comprehension. The teacher presents one or two lines of the dialogue, followed by a question or a statement. The students make a written "yes" or "no" response. The teacher checks the students'

answers, by a show of hands, and then immediately provides the students with the correct response. Thus, the teacher is also receiving feedback regarding the students' comprehension. If a number of students have difficulty with the item, the teacher may wish to reread the line of the dialogue that illustrates the correct response or take other action to insure comprehension.

5. Repeat the entire dialogue again at normal rate of speed (live or tape recording) without interruption. This time have the students listen to it with their eyes closed. Having eyes closed helps eliminate distractions, increases listening concentration, and adds variety to the classroom activities.

6. Have a role-playing activity. Assign roles from the dialogue to individual students or rows of students. Phrase questions in the foreign language to which students will make "yes" or "no," or short responses, according to their assigned roles. Then have the students play themselves or other people, such as famous personalities, using the same technique, i.e., answering "yes" or "no" to the foreign-language questions used before. This provides further listening practice with the same linguistic elements. The change in roles and the corresponding changes in answers provide variety and prevent boredom.

7. Have students hear the entire dialogue again, with their eyes closed, without interruption, but this time at slightly faster than normal rate of speed. To make this presentation of the dialogue challenging, inform students that it will be at a faster speed and that it will be followed by a listening comprehension test. It will be even better if still another tape can be used of the same text but with voices unfamiliar to the students.

8. Give a listening comprehension test.

9. At this point, periodically, recombination listening comprehension practice can be given, using dialogues from other courses of study, motion pictures or any type of recorded materials which contain, for the most part, language elements previously learned by the students.

In the approach being suggested here, speaking practice would begin after item 8 above. It is expected that students would be anxious and ready to speak at this point. Following the outlined listening comprehension activities, speaking practice might proceed according to this sequence:

1. Pattern practice based on material taken from the dialogue.

2. Mimicry practice of the dialogue itself.

3. Memorization of the dialogue.

4. Performance of the dialogue in front of class and at seats with students changing roles and partners from time to time.

5. Dialogue adaptation.

6. Free (but guided) conversation closely paralleling the situations in the dialogues.

Memorization of dialogues and other such material for oral presentation is a difficult task even when it is to be done in a language which we completely understand and have been speaking all our lives. We believe, therefore, that the techniques and sequence suggested here represent an approach that will enable students to memorize larger segments at a time and to perform dialogues as a whole, more quickly, and with greater confidence, understanding, and enjoyment.

The suggestions made in this paper are aimed at having students spend more of their time listening to natural speech and authentic models of the foreign language. They underline the need for the systematic development of listening comprehension not only as a foundation for speaking but also as a skill in its own right. New materials will undoubtedly be produced in the future to facilitate this development. In the meantime, if teachers are willing to use their imagination and experiment with new techniques many ways can be found to emphasize the *audio* in the *audio*-lingual approach.

12 EVALUATING AND ADAPTING LANGUAGE MATERIALS EARL W. STEVICK

Select a textbook designed to teach English to a particular group of students known to you and evaluate all or any part of it in terms of *strength-weakness, lightness-heaviness*, and *transparency-opacity*.

Draw up a *socio-topical* matrix that would be appropriate for a group of students known to you and then consider the adequacy of some textbook in terms of your matrix.

Would you need to modify the *occasions for use* list offered in this article for university students? for elementary school students? for adult non-academic students?

Reprinted by permission. This article is a revised version of a report prepared under a contract from the U.S. Office of Education, printed for use by the Peace Corps, and intended in its present form as Chapter 3 of *Adapting and Writing Language Lessons*, to be published by the U.S. Government Printing Office, Washington. The author is professor of linguistics in the School of Languages, Foreign Service Institute, Department of State, Washington, D.C.

INTRODUCTION

With the growing shortage of time and money for writing new textbooks, particularly in the seldom-taught languages, there is a premium on making effective use of what already exists. We have sometimes acted as though, for any given set of materials, the choice was only between using them and rejecting them. Adaptation, as a third alternative, has received very little in terms of time or of money or of prestige. Rewriting, a fourth possibility, is often viewed both as unjustifiably troublesome for the rewriter, and as an affront to the original author.

Yet among the many dozens of language teachers who have been consulted in the preparation of this book, there has been scarcely one who does not claim that he or she makes some changes or additions to the printed textbook, even if it is supposedly of the programmed self-instructional variety. Many of those interviewed described major changes. A few operate with a minimum outline and a few props, and recreate the course every time they teach it. Under these circumstances, two points need emphasis: first, the various degrees of adaptation, augmentation, and rewriting form a continuum, at the far end of which stands the preparation of original materials; second, before one can begin to adapt or augment or write or rewrite, and before one can even decide which of these four to undertake, it is necessary to evaluate what is available. This chapter offers guidelines for evaluation, and outlines a general procedure for adaptation.

EVALUATION

More than courses in French, Spanish, German, or English, a course in a seldom-taught language is likely to be the brain child of one author, conceived in desperation, brought forth in obscurity, and destined to be despised and rejected by all other men. Sometimes rejection is inevitable, but often it is the result of hasty, or unperceptive, or unappreciative examination of the existing book. The following guidelines for evaluation may be applied to the efforts of others, but also to one's own handiwork both before and after it is completed. The guidelines are stated in terms of three qualities, three dimensions, and four components.

EVALUATION: THREE QUALITIES

Every lesson, every part of every lesson, and even every line may be judged on three qualities, which we shall call *strength*, *lightness*, and *transparency*. As we shall use these terms, their opposites *weakness, heaviness,* and *opacity* are usually undesirable. There are however situations in which a certain amount of heaviness and opacity can be useful, and the same may even be true for weakness. ... It would be a mistake, therefore, to assume that strength, lightness, and transparency are absolute virtues, or that an increase in one of these values necessarily means an improvement in the lesson. Nevertheless, weakness, heaviness, and opacity are in general warning signs, and their presence calls for special justification in terms of the lesson or the textbook as a whole.

STRENGTH

Does it carry its own weight by means of the rewards that it makes available? . . . Rewards may be of at least five different kinds; they *must* be valid in terms of the values of the learner, and not of the materials writer only.

In the evaluation of an entire course, concern about strength will lead to such questions as:

Is the content relevant to the present and likely future needs of the trainees?

Does the textbook provide for the tools, both in vocabulary and in structure, that students will need in order to reach whatever goal has been set?

Are the materials authentic both linguistically and culturally?

Looking at a single lesson from the same point of view, one may ask:

Will the students derive from this lesson satisfactions that go beyond the mere feeling of having mastered one more lesson, and being ready for the next? . . .

In particular, to what extent will the students be able to use the content of this lesson immediately, in a lifelike way?

On the smallest scale, a sentence like "Your horse had been old" (cited by Jespersen, 1904) is weak to the point of being feeble, because there is no situation in which anyone can use it. The cliché "The book is on the table" is stronger, because the situations in which it *can* be used are fairly frequent. But we must distinguish between the ease with which a situation can be created in the classroom, and the frequency with which it actually gets commented on in real life. In this latter respect, "The book is on the table" is still relatively weak. A sentence like "I need a taxi" (Taylor, p. 50) is potentially stronger because most people are more concerned about being able to verbalize this need than they are about being able to describe the most obvious location of a book. In the same way, "I need a taxi" is stronger for most students than "I need a hinge." But other things being equal, strength is always relative to the needs and interests of the students: some people talk about hinges every day and never see a taxi. For this reason, we cannot build strength as a permanent and absolute quality into any fixed set of materials.

It is impossible to give simple directions for determining what would make materials strong for any given class. Questionnaires may help, and being psychically 'with' one's students may help. Certainly it is necessary to be more than a purveyor of words and a master of drill techniques. (See pp. 108–109, following.)

LIGHTNESS

Is a single "unit" so long that the student wearies of it before it is finished, and loses any sense of its unity? Does an individual line weigh heavily on the student's tongue, either because of the number of difficult sounds or because of its sheer length? Insofar as new words or structures, by virtue of their newness alone, make a line or a lesson tiring, they may also be said to contribute to its weight, lightness is intended here to refer primarily to sheer physical characteristics. With respect to lightness, "Your horse had been old" and "I need a taxi" are approximately equal. Heaviness in this sense may vary with the language background of the learner: many would find "I need a hinge" to be noticeably heavier than "I need a label," depending on whether the native language has initial /h/ (German has, French and Spanish have not), or final voiced stops (French has, German and Spanish have not).

In general, of course, we try to make early lessons rather light. But Alex Lipson is one authority who advocates putting some heavy items into the very first sessions of a new class, while the students are in their freshest and most open state. This is one example of how none of the three qualities has absolute positive value and temporary lack of one of these qualities is not necessarily bad.

TRANSPARENCY

Transparency is primarily a cognitive problem: how readily can the user of the materials see the units and their relationships? Looking at a textbook as a whole, we may ask:

> Do these materials make clear at least one way in which the teacher may use them in class?
> Is it easy to find where a given point of grammar has been covered?

With regard to single lessons, we may ask:

> To what extent does the student know what he is doing and why?
> How easily can a teacher or adapter find places where he can make changes or additions without destroying the lesson?

With regard to single lines, we may ask:

> Can the meaning be put across without translation?
> Can the student see the structure of this sentence clearly enough so that he will be able to use it as a help in composing or comprehending new ones?

Once again, transparency is not an absolute value. One good aspect of inductive teaching of grammar, for example, is the fun of working one's way out of a temporary structural fog.

Needless to say, opacity is to be calculated from the point of view of the learner. If the writer or adapter knows the language too well, he may forget that what seems obvious to him may be perplexing for students from a very different language background. On the other hand, writers sometimes spend much effort in elaborate explanation of a point that really causes the students no trouble.

SUMMARY COMMENTS ON THE THREE QUALITIES

The differences among the three qualities may perhaps be clarified by looking at the following sentences:

Weak, light, transparent: The book is on the table.

Weak, heavy, transparent: The big red book is on the little table by the open window.

Weak, heavy, opaque: The seldom commented-upon but frequently observed location for a book is that in which we now find this one.

(Potentially) strong, heavy, opaque: The repast which the cook, for our enjoyment and his own self-satisfaction has (in a manner of speaking) prepared for our lunch today is pizza.

(Potentially) strong, light, opaque: I paid half the then going rate.

(Potentially) strong, heavy, transparent: We're going to have pizza with mushrooms, anchovies and pepperoni.

(Potentially) strong, light, transparent: We're going to have pizza for lunch!

Obviously, in even the best of lessons some lines will be stronger than others, every line has some heaviness, and many will be partly opaque. Furthermore, the three criteria will often conflict with one another: a line may be very strong but also heavy, or transparent but also weak. Even so, they may be worth the attention of anyone who is writing or evaluating language lessons. Lightness and transparency can conceivably be made permanent attributes of permanent lessons, but only constant adaptation will keep strength from deteriorating.

EVALUATION: THREE DIMENSIONS

The content of a textbook, or a lesson, or a drill, or a single line may be plotted in each of three dimensions: linguistic, social, and topical.

THE LINGUISTIC DIMENSION: *How well must they speak?*

In a course as a whole, the linguistic content that is needed is relatively independent of the age, occupation or special interests of the prospective students. This content consists mainly of phonological patterns and structural devices. Because this aspect of content is so dependable, text writers have too often accorded the linguistic dimension absolute primacy: social and topical content need not be absorbing, but only plausible and appropriate for illustrating a series of linguistic points. This is particularly likely to happen when the materials developer is also a trained linguist, intent on sharing with the readers his enjoyment of the intricacies and symmetries of linguistic structure. Even before the ascendancy of linguistic science, of course, one type of textbook subordinated everything else to the purpose of conveying patterns. (That must surely have been the purpose behind "Your horse had been old.") But in the absence of resolute and meticulous planning for other sources of reward, strength is drawn primarily from the social and topical dimensions. This is one reason why some linguistically brilliant text-books have been pedagogical flops.

THE SOCIAL DIMENSION: *Who is talking with whom?*
It is therefore a good idea, before starting to adapt existing lessons, to draw up a simple two-dimensional matrix. The social dimension lists the kinds of people with whom the student most urgently needs to interact, by occupation of course, but also according to their social status with reference to the communication event. The choice of interlocutors determines not only the content of what one says, but also the style in which one says it. If the training site is a junior high school in an entirely English-speaking town, the original list might include only the teacher and the other students. The reality to which the matrix refers may be prospective as well as immediate, however. Many teachers prefer to operate on the principle of 'now now and later later:' stick to present realities while the students are coping with the rudiments of the language, and begin to use more distant ones in the intermediate stage. Policemen, taxi drivers, landlords, and many others may thus be added to the matrix. But they may only be added if the prospect of encountering them is psychologically real to the students them-selves. To add them at the whim of the teacher *or for the convenience of the materials writer* would result in a spurious matrix, invalid from the point of view of the student, and *a source of weakness rather than strength*.

The same principle applies to the training of adults who expect to go immedi-ately to jobs where they will use the language. The roles that make up the social dimension will be more numerous, and the prospects will be more clearly de-fined, but care in selecting and defining the roles can still make the difference between strength and weakness.

Most writers give some attention to the social dimension when they are writ-ing dialog material, although there have been some exceptions. Drill materials, on the other hand, are usually treated as socially neutral. They are not always com-pletely so, of course. Any German, French, Russian, or Spanish sentence in the second person must necessarily imply choice as to level of respect, and the same is even more true for many other languages. Some drills may in fact concentrate on the contrast between *tu*-forms and *vous*-forms. This is fine as far as it goes, but it is not enough. Even the lowliest substitution drill can be checked for its social implications ("Who might say these things to whom?"). Thus, "Have you received an invitation?" and "Have you met the ambassador?" are compatible with each other, but not with "Have you brushed your teeth?" Any internal in-consistencies should have some clear justification.

THE TOPICAL DIMENSION: *What are they talking about?*
At right angles to the social dimension, the topical dimension lists the things that the trainee is most likely to want to talk about: greetings and general phrases for getting a conversation started, expressions needed in conducting a

class, street directions, diagnoses of poultry diseases, and so forth. Some topics are of interest to trainees of almost all kinds, while others are highly specialized. The problem, for the writer who wants to produce strong materials, is that the trainees' most specialized interests are often the very ones that are most vivid for them. Even for a generally useful topic like street and road directions, the actual locales that excite most interest will vary from one class to another.

THE SOCIO-TOPICAL MATRIX

The intersection of the social and topical dimensions produces a set of boxes. For some situations, the boxes might be labeled as follows:

	Greetings, etc.	Street directions	Food	Work schedule	etc.
Adult stranger					
Small child					
Policeman					
Colleague					
Host					
etc.					

Note that not all the boxes will be equally plausible: one will not expect to praise the policeman's cooking or ask directions of a four-year-old child.

This kind of matrix[1] is useful both for making an inventory of what is in an existing book, and also for plotting the needs of a particular group of students. With the addition of a linguistic dimension, . . . such a matrix may serve in planning entire courses. For the adapter's needs, however, this two-dimensional grid is easier to manage, and almost as effective.

Ted Plaister (private communication) has suggested how selected boxes from such a matrix might be placed on individual cards or sheets of paper and made into starting points for adaptations or for complete lessons.

[1] A matrix with a social dimension was suggested to me by Dr. Albert R. Wight (private communication).

EVALUATION: FOUR COMPONENTS

Earlier drafts of this chapter ventured the guess that a successful lesson needs components of four—and only four—kinds. Subsequent experiments, and discussions with many dozens of language teachers, have turned this hunch into a belief. The four essential components, whether for speech or for writing or for both, are: occasions for use, a sample of the language in use, exploration of vocabulary, and exploration of (phonetic, orthographic, or grammatical) form. To make this assertion is not, however, to prescribe a method or a format. Each of the four components may take any of countless shapes, and the student may meet them in any of several orders. It should also be pointed out that the order in which the components are written need not be that in which they are placed before the student.

COMPONENT 1: OCCASIONS FOR USE

Every lesson should contain a number of clear suggestions for using the language. Each of these suggestions should embody a purpose outside of the language itself, which is valid in terms of the student's needs and interests. Insofar as these purposes relate to the external world . . . , most of them will fall under one or more of the following rubrics:

1. Establishing or further developing real social relationships with real people, including classmates. Simple examples are greetings, introductions, autobiographical matters including personal anecdotes, participation in games, exploration of likes and dislikes.

2. Eliciting or imparting desired information. What is the climate like at various times of year in Sarkhan? How does the currency system work? How is a certain dish prepared? How does the electrical system of an automobile work?

3. Learning or imparting useful skills: sewing, dancing, playing soccer, thatching a roof.

4. Learning to make culturally relevant judgments: distinguishing ripe from unripe fruit, candling eggs, predicting the weather, estimating water depth.

5. Doing things for fun: humor, games, singing, relaxation.

Some of the occasions for use should involve muscular activity: playing, pointing, handling, writing, etc.

As many occasions for use as possible should be written in the form of behavioral objectives: what students are to do should be described so clearly that there can be no question as to whether any one student's performance meets the requirements. There should be some overt way in which each student can know (a) that he has performed, and (b) how well he has performed. For example:

"Tell your instructor the names of the people in the family with whom you are living, and how they are related to one another."

is better than:

> *"Find out* the names of the people in the family with whom you are living, and how they are related to one another."

Even the latter is better than:

> "Try to use this vocabulary (i.e., kinship terminology) outside of class."

Occasions for use, then, should be both *useful* and *specific*. But they should also be *stimulating* and *open-ended*. . . . . Rehg (private correspondence) comments on some of these examples as follows:

> An important aspect of Ponapean culture is the title system. Each adult, unless he is something of an outcast, is assigned a title, and is subsequently known by that title in all formal and many informal situations. However, most foreigners do not know these alternate 'names.' A student who has learned the relevant structures and vocabulary can be assigned a task of the following kind:
> (a) Elicit the titles of the adult members of the family you are staying with. Record this information, and bring it back to your instructor.
> (b) What are the literal meanings of these titles?
> (c) Within the Ponapean title system, how important are these titles?
> Completion of these tasks accomplishes a number of objectives. Part (a) gives the trainee an opportunity to use the language that he has learned in a manner that is *useful* following an assignment that is *specific*. Part (b) provides him with the basis for countless hours of interesting discussion on a topic that fascinates most Ponapeans; therefore, the task is *open-ended*. Part (c) brings the student to grips with the power structure of the community. Foreigners seem to be very curious about the matter of titles, and so the task is also *stimulating*. Students very quickly recognize busy work, so a useful, specific, open-ended but non-stimulating task will probably be non-productive.

We have discussed occasions for use before the other three components because writers and teachers so often slight them, or ignore them altogether. It is true that the student normally performs them at the end of a lesson, if at all, but a writer or adapter would be wise to begin thinking about them as soon as he has chosen a lesson. Even in the student's book, the planned occasions for use might be listed at the head of the lesson, so that the student can form a clearer idea of the potential strength of the rest of the lesson. Occasions for use should certainly affect the writing or revision of every other component.

COMPONENT 2: A SAMPLE OF LANGUAGE USE

Every lesson should contain a sample of how the language is used. The sample should be:

1. long enough to be viable. (Two-line dialogs, no matter how timely or realistic, have proved *not* to meet this requirement.)

2. short enough to be covered, with the rest of the lesson, in 1-4 hours of class time.

3. related to a socio-topical matrix that the students accept as expressing their needs and interests.

The sample may take any of several forms. Many courses in the past twenty-five years have used the *basic dialog* to fulfill this role, but other kinds of sample are more useful for some purposes. The most concrete is probably the *action chain* (or *action script*), which lists a series of activities that normally occur together. The most familiar example is "I get up. I bathe. I get dressed . . . ," but the same format may accommodate discussion of technical processes, negotiation with a landlord, public ceremonies, and many other topics. Another kind of sample, particularly suitable after the first fifty to one hundred hours of instruction, is a *short* passage of expository or narrative prose. . . .

Whatever form the sample takes, it should contain at least one or two lines that lend themselves to lexical and/or structural exploration of the kinds that will be discussed in the next two sections of this chapter. If the sample does not contain such lines, then it will become an isolated compartment within the lesson, rather than a productive part of it. . . .

Language in use of course implies *language as one part of a communication event*, and spoken language is always accompanied by other bodily activity, including gestures, facial expressions, posture, nearness to other people, and so forth. These aspects of communication ought to receive attention also. See Appendix B for examples.

COMPONENT 3: LEXICAL EXPLORATION

In this and the following section, we have made frequent use of the word *exploration*. This word is perhaps confusing, and hence ill-chosen. We have used it in order to emphasize the active, creative, partially unprescribed role of the learner, and to avoid an image of the learner as one whose every footstep is to be guided by a pedagogue. Exploration in this sense stands in contrast to *inculcation*.

Lexical exploration, then, refers to those aspects of a lesson through which the student expands his ability to come up with, or to recognize, the right word at the right time. The simplest kind of lexical exploration uses lists of words, sometimes with a sentence or two illustrating the use of each. In a well-constructed lesson, there may be a number of sub-lists, each related to some part of the basic sample. Thus, the basic dialog for Unit 2 of *French Basic Course* (Desberg et al., 1960) contains the line:

C'est ça, et reveillez-moi demain à sept heures.	Fine, and wake me tomorrow at seven.

and the section devoted to *Useful Words* provides the expressions for "one o'clock" through "eleven o'clock," plus "noon" and "midnight." The dialog for Unit 5 includes the words for "autumn" and "winter," and the *Useful Words* add "spring" and "summer."

For a more coherent lesson, it would be desirable to relate lexical exploration not only to the basic sample, but also to the projected occasions for use. One way of approaching this goal is through use of *Cummings devices*. . . . In a Cummings device, a question of some other line from the sample may be presented along with a number of sentences which are alternative answers or other rejoinders to it. The device may also include other questions that are very similar to the first. Both questions and answers should be chosen with careful attention to how the student can use them for more than mere linguistic drill. For example, in one set of lessons in Mauritian Creole . . . a narrative sample of the language describes a woman going to market. It contains the sentence:

| Zaklin aste rasyõ | Jacqueline buys groceries |
| komã too le semen. | as [she does] every week. |

A Cummings device that focuses on the lexical exploration of this sentence is:

Questions:

Lil Moris, eski zot aste dipẽ too le zoor?	In Mauritius, do they buy bread every day?
Lil Moris, eski zot aste doori too le zoor?	In Mauritius, do they buy rice every day?
etc.	etc.

Rejoinders:

Zot aste dipẽ too le zoor.	They buy bread every day.
Zot aste doori too le semen.	They buy rice every week.
etc;	etc;

Students first learn to pronounce, understand and manipulate these sentences, and then go on *immediately* to use them in the form of two-line conversations. Note that these conversations remain in touch with reality, for this Cummings device contains accurate information about the frequency with which various items are bought. Because of differences in marketing practices and refrigeration facilities, the student will find certain differences between Mauritius and his home. A factually inaccurate answer to one of these questions is just as wrong as a linguistically incorrect one. Thus, as the student practices a new construction ("too le zoor/semen"), he is also learning some down-to-earth facts about the place where he expects to live.

COMPONENT 4: EXPLORATION OF STRUCTURAL RELATIONSHIPS

The final essential component of a language lesson guides the student in exploring such matters as the relationship in both form and meaning between the third person singular present subjunctive of a verb and the corresponding third person singular present indicative; or between two different ways of embedding one sentence in another; or between the definite and the indefinite article. These relationships are the subject matter of what is usually called "the study of grammar." Bosco (1970) [Article no. 40 in this collection. Eds.] distinguishes among three *modes of representation*. Following his analysis, the exploration of structural relationships may take the form of drills (*enactive mode*), charts and diagrams (*iconic mode*), or grammar notes (*symbolic mode*). Much past and present controversy among language teachers turns on the relative prominence to be assigned to each of these modes, and the order in which they should occupy the student's attention. Learners' synopses . . . are principally symbolic presentations of major structural relationships.

Lado (1958) may have been right in speculating that "it is possible to learn a language without ever repeating the same sentence twice." To do so, however, would require extraordinary materials, extraordinary teachers, and probably extraordinary students as well. For some structural relationships, adequate exploration may require a certain amount of retracing one's steps, both within and between lessons. This may involve one, two, or all three of the modes. What we usually call drills may in this sense be regarded as *reiterated enactive exploration*, to use a phrase which is as monstrous as it is descriptive. Looking at them in this way is probably better than inflicting them as *necessary neuromuscular inculcation.*

Because the sentences in any one Cummings device are often grammatically similar to one another, the device has advantages in structural, as well as lexical, exploration.

A FINAL WORD ON EVALUATION

Instructional materials do not consist of qualities, dimensions, and components. Nor do the descriptions of the qualities, dimensions, and components provide a blueprint for writing or adapting. Rather, the three terms stand for ways of looking at materials, and these ways are not merely restatements of one another. We have said that strength is often derived from appropriate socio-topical resources in a lesson, but a socio-topically relevant lesson that is poorly organized may still be weak, and some teachers know how to make lessons amply rewarding and strong with almost no relation to external reality. Similarly, occasions for use contribute to but do not guarantee strength.

ADAPTATION

Throughout recorded history, and probably longer than that, language teachers have been reminding one another of the necessity for bridging the gap between manipulation and communication, or between the classroom and life. One of the ways in which they quite properly attempt to do so is through adapting old textbooks to fit new needs. Most, however, tend to place the center of gravity of their bridges on one side of the gap or another. To put the same thing in another way, they focus their attention either on the original textbook or on the rewards and relevancies of the project at hand, and slight the other. In the original sense of the word "focus," the first kind of adapter seems to be working his way out from the warmth and comfort of a hearth (the printed lesson) toward a perimeter (the end of the lesson) beyond which lies darkness. He sees his task as providing additional activities (dialogs, drills, games, or whatever) that lie not too far beyond the perimeter, and which may help to extend it. If this adapter were a plant, he would be a morning glory vine in the springtime, putting out its tendrils in search of anything at all to which it can attach itself. The second kind of adapter warms himself by a portable hearth wherever the interests of the students seem to lie, and may forget where home was; botanically he would be a dandelion whose seeds are scattered by the wind.

. . . we suggest that a prospective adapter begin by making a careful survey of both sides of the gap he is trying to bridge. Once he has done so, he can connect the two sides by using whatever devices he is most comfortable with. The point is that he is working with two basic documents and not just one. Certainly he must take account of the lessons that he has set out to adapt, but just as certainly he must exploit the socio-topical matrix that summarizes his students' interests. He must satisfy the demands of the textbook, but in ways that will be satisfying to those who learn from it. He works around two foci, and not just one. Depending on the nature of the original materials, he may find himself preparing Cummings devices to go with dialogs, or dialogs to go with Cummings devices, or drills to go with either or both, or all of these to flesh out an existing set of grammar notes. In all cases, his most creative contribution will probably lie in suggesting how the learners can make early and convincing use of what they have just learned to manipulate.

Obviously, in view of the great variety both of original textbooks and of student objectives, adaptation is and will remain an art. We cannot here offer a mechanical procedure for accomplishing it. Nevertheless, on the basis of the principles outlined earlier in this chapter, we may venture to suggest an overall strategy:

1. Predict what the students will need and respond to in each of the three dimensions: linguistic, social and topical.

2. Make an inventory of the material at hand, in the same three dimensions.

3. Compare the results of the first two steps, in order to form a clear picture of what you need to add or subtract.

4. Draw up a list of ways in which the students may use the material. This is the most delicate step in adaptation because the list should be as heterogeneous as possible, yet stated in terms of actual behavior that the students are to engage in. It is also the most important step, however, because it opens up such valuable sources of motive power.

5. Supply whatever is necessary (dialogs, drills, Cummings devices, etc.) in order to bring the students from mastery of the existing materials to the uses

which you have listed in Step 4. Politzer (1971) has pointed out that changes may be in rate of progress, or in the means employed, or in the goals themselves. Adaptation of rate may take the form of added materials to make more gradual the transition from one part of the existing materials and another. It may also take the form of more complete instructions for the teacher, or detailed check lists to show the student what he should get out of each part of the lesson. Changes in the means employed will depend on what the adapter and the prospective users find mutually congenial. Changes in goals should take account of one fact that some teachers seem not to be aware of: *any topic may be treated at any degree of linguistic difficulty*, from the simplicity of "What is this? It is a (papilla, colony, Petri dish, centrifuge, etc.)" to the complexity of "The never before published volume lying at an angle of approximately thirty-seven degrees to the edge of the table is wholly supported by it."

APPENDIX: ADAPTING A PATTERN-PRACTICE COURSE (ENGLISH)

One of the most pregnant sentences in history of language teaching was Fries's dictum that "a person has learned" a foreign language when he has. . .mastered the sound system. . .and. . .made the structural devices. . .matters of automatic habit." (1947, p. 3). Even though the person who has done these things may not be a fluent speaker, "he can have laid a good, accurate foundation upon which to build" through the acquisition of "content vocabulary" (*ibid.*). Since its publication, the last half of this formulation has determined the strategy of much "scientific" language teaching, just as the first half has determined the tactics. The priority, both logical and chronological, of the basic structural habits goes unchallenged in many circles, and we sometimes act as though we think the best way to internalize the structures is to concentrate on them to the virtual exclusion of everything else.

A relatively recent and sophisticated representative of this tradition is the series *Contemporary Spoken English*, by John Kane and Mary Kirkland (Thomas Y. Crowell, 1967). The first lesson of Volume 1 contains two short dialogs (total approximately 2 pages), pronunciation, rhythm and intonation drills (7 pages), and grammar drills (10 pages). The dialogs, which consist of simple introductions and greetings, have no integral relation to the drills, which concentrate on present affirmative statements with *be*. Most of the substitution drills may be summarized in three tables:

I	'm	in class
you	're	at church
he	's	in bed
she		etc.
Sue		
John		
we		
they		

| I
Dick | 'm
's | a farmer
a lawyer
etc. |

| I
we | 'm
're | hungry
married
tired
etc. |

In addition, the rhythm and intonation drills include:

| this
that
it | 's | a pen
a coat
etc. |

In keeping with one interpretation of the Friesian emphasis on structure, there is nowhere in the book any indication as to when or how the teacher is to put across the meanings. (Many would be easy to picture or dramatize, but "lawyer," and the difference between "in school" and "in class," might pose problems.) The nearest reference to meaning is a statement (p. viii) that the vocabulary has been drawn from "basic semantic fields." Echoing Fries, the authors state that their goal is to teach "with a limited vocabulary of high-frequency words, those features of English phonology and syntax which students should be able to comprehend and manipulate before proceeding beyond the intermediate level" (p. vii).

Teachers who are philosophically in communion with the authors will welcome their work and will probably adopt it. Those who reject the philosophy will also reject the book. In the field of English as a Second Language it makes little difference, for if one book is cast aside, there are still dozens of others waiting to be examined.

The same is not true for seldom-taught languages, where the available courses usually number between one and five. All too easily, a new teacher or language coordinator despairs of all that is in print and decides to set out on his own. But such a decision is expensive in money and time, and dubious in result. A Swahili proverb tells us that "there is no bad beginning," and so the newcomer, encouraged by the ease with which he has pleased himself with his first few lessons, launches yet another material-writing project.

This appendix, then, is *not* a review of Kane and Kirkland's *Contemporary Spoken English*. It is primarily addressed, not to practitioners of TESOL, but to prospective teachers and lesson writers in the so-called "neglected languages." Its purpose is to demonstrate how, by following a particular set of principles, one may adapt and supplement existing materials instead of rejecting them. English has been chosen for this illustration only because examples are easier to follow in a widely known language. To this end, we shall pretend that *Contemporary Spoken English* is one of only two or three ESOL courses in print.

The first step toward adaptation is to form a clear picture of the students, their needs and interests. This picture may take the form of a simple sociotopical matrix. Let us assume that we are adapting for an evening class of adults who live in one major part of a metropolitan area, and who speak a number of different languages but little or no English. In general, the matrix can be more specific and more accurate in smaller groups, but even the largest and most diverse class has in common its classroom or training site, and current events both local and worldwide. The matrix will also be more effective if the students feel that they have had a hand in designing it or at least adding to it. For the purposes of this illustration, however, we shall have to be content with guessing that a partial matrix might look something like this:

	getting from place to place	greetings and courtesy formulas	meetings and appointments	shopping	role as guest or host
neighbors	2	1			
clerks in stores					
English teacher		1			
fellow students		1			
people on street	2				

The next step is to analyze the existing lesson for its content in all three dimensions: linguistic, social, and topical.

LINGUISTIC CONTENT:
Dialogs: Eleven sentences, invariable except for substitution of personal names, suitable for use in introducing oneself and in exchanging morning greetings. Intonation contours are marked.

Pronunciation sections: Lists of monosyllabic words containing the diphthongs which the Trager-Smith transcription writes /iy, ey, oy, ay, aw, ow, uw/, and short phrases or sentences that include these words. (The authors do not assume that these words and phrases will be intelligible to beginning students.) Lists of phrases and sentences with the common 231⌐ statement intonation pattern, realized in short utterances that have various stress patterns. Stress and intonation are portrayed "iconically," with an effective system of lines and geometrical figures.

Grammar sections: The sentence patterns represented on pp. 114–115 above, requiring the student to produce person-number agreement between a subject and the present tense of "be," followed by three kinds of complements. Nouns standing for locations follow prepositions, with no intervening article; all other nouns have the indefinite article.

SOCIAL CONTENT:

Dialogs: Generally suitable for adults who don't know each other, or who are not close friends. May be used "for real" among members of the class.

Pronunciation sections: Strictly speaking, no social content at all, since they are intended only for practice in repetition.

Grammatical sections: Quite non-specific. Even the teacher and the student can hardly be said to be playing genuine social roles in a substitution drill of the type:

	Dick's in school.
in class	Dick's in class.
at home	Dick's at home.
at church	Dick's at church.
	etc.

TOPICAL CONTENT:

Dialogs: As stated above, introductions and morning greeting.

Pronunciation sections: None. (see above)

Grammatical sections: Statements about locations, occupations, states, classification (see substitution frames on pp. 114–115). The content words in the grammatical sections are either common nouns, personal names, or adjectives. Except for the personal names, none of the content words that appear in one type of statement ever appear in another. Each list of nouns refers to several different real-life contexts, e.g. class, church, bed.

In summary, the linguistic content of this lesson is delineated with unusual clarity; the topical content is clear enough, but is unified only in terms of a grammatical criterion; the social content is almost entirely concentrated in the dialogs, which have no close relationship to the rest of the lesson.

The third step in preparing to adapt a lesson is to check its components: Does it include 1) a convincing sample of language use? Does it provide for both 2) lexical and 3) grammatical exploration beyond the sample? Does it suggest 4) ways in which the students can put their new linguistic skills to work for non-linguistic purposes that they can accept as their own?

The lesson under consideration does contain two short samples of genuine use, in the form of the dialogs. The lists of words in the drills provide for lexical exploration, and the grammar drills themselves lead the student to explore a bit of English structure. The fourth component is not overtly represented in the lesson itself, and is only hinted at in the introduction.

Finally, one may look at the individual lines of the various components and judge them according to their lightness, transparency, and strength. (See pp. 102-105, above.)

The sentences of this lesson, with an average of three syllables apiece, show up very favorably with respect to the first of these three qualities. Most of the meanings could be put across easily without translation, and the structures are lucidly presented; accordingly, the lesson also rates well on average transparency of sentences.

Where this lesson leaves most to be desired is in what we have called strength. Here is a striking demonstration that high-frequency vocabulary may still produce sentences that are relatively weak. *As the lesson now stands*, the students can do very little at the end of Lesson 1 except introduce themselves, greet one another, and go on to Lesson 2.

As we have seen, the dominant dimension in this course and the one according to which the lessons are sequenced, is the linguistic. The goal of an adaptation will therefore be to enable the students, in relation to the existing linguistic framework as much as possible, to use the language in a connected and communicative way in one or more contexts that are meaningful to them. We shall aim at non-linguistic occasions for use that have the students getting acquainted with each other and with the immediate area in which they live.

The most obvious and also the simplest first step is to change "good morning" in the second dialog to "good evening," since our students go to night school. A much larger step, also in the lexical realm, is to introduce the names of local destinations: "grade school, high school, gas station, restaurant, parking lot" etc. alongside or instead of the non-specific "work, class, bed" etc. There are four advantages in doing so: 1) The destinations may be readily and cheaply brought into the classroom by means of locally produced color slides. At the same time, the slides themselves are stronger in our sense because they portray places that the students have actually seen and will be seeing in real life. 2) The same list of nouns can now appear in two different substitution frames: "This is a ____" and "We're at a ____." (pp. 114-115). This helps to unify the lesson in the topical dimension. 3) These words and slides will be useful in later lessons, and thus strengthen the continuity of the whole book. 4) They will help clarify the grammatical facts in Lesson 1. We have noted that as the lesson now stands, nouns that follow a preposition do not have an indefinite article, while all the other nouns do. In talking about local destinations, nouns have the article both without a preposition ("This is a _____.") and with it ("We're at a _____.")

The suggestion that an adaptation should introduce pictures and new vocabulary should not be taken as a criticism of the original lesson for lacking them. What will be most live and real in the night schools of Arlington County, Virginia, will necessarily fall flat everywhere else. On the other hand, expertly chosen vocabulary and technically excellent pictures would have been specific for nowhere, and would only have added to the cost of publication.

Having (as we hope) livened the lesson up topically by bringing in new words and color slides to illustrate them, we would like to do the same in the social dimension. The simplest way to do so is to convert at least three of the substitution frames (pp. 114–115) to Cummings devices. We can do so by teaching the questions "What is this? Where are (we)? What are (you)?" Where formerly we had only repetition and substitution drills, we now have some two-line embryonic conversations.

There is of course a price to be paid for the Cummings devices, because they introduce wh-questions. The authors of the original, who introduced yes-no questions only in Lesson 4 and wh-questions in Lesson 6, might object that this price is in fact prohibitive, since it disrupts their carefully planned sequence of structures. But each of the new question patterns is closely related to one of the statement patterns that are already in the lesson, and the mechanical aspect of changing from an interrogative sentence to its corresponding statement is the same throughout. This is then a much less serious change in the structural sequence than, say, the introduction of present tense of content verbs. The question is whether the extra weight of the new engine is more than compensated for by the gain in power. My guess is that it is.

Another slight addition in the linguistic dimension would open up further opportunities for interesting conversation. The construction with "this" plus a noun would enable the students to handle a Cummings device like:

Where is this (gas station)?
It's (near here, on Fairfax Drive, at Parkington, etc.).

Going still further, if one is willing to introduce yes-no questions at this stage, then the students could use questions like "Is this a parking lot? Are we at the library?" and also learn each other's marital status and inquire about such states as fatigue and hunger. But this too is a question of balancing new communicative potential against increased length and complexity of the lesson. Would such an extension be justifiable? The most important fact about this kind of question is not whether the answer is yes or no, but rather who is qualified to answer it. We sometimes forget that a worthwhile answer can only come from a classroom teacher who understands its implications, and that even he or she can answer it for only one class at a time. Someone writing a case study like this one can only guess at the answer, but *the same is true for the textbook writer himself.*

This is one reason why published textbooks are so often rejected by prospective users. It is also one reason why we must give to adaptation much more thought, time, and prestige than we have been accustomed to doing.

The final proof of the lessons, as we have said, is in what the students can now do that they recognize as immediately useful or enjoyable in its own right, or potentially so in the immediate future. Greetings and introductions, marked 1) in the matrix on p. 116, are certainly socio-topical behavioral objectives in this sense, and these were in the lesson from the beginning. New objectives relate to the boxes marked 2) in the matrix. Although the student is still unable to carry out sustained conversation with neighbors on the subject of getting around in Arlington, he at least has some of the most crucial sentence patterns and vocabulary items. In the meantime, he can demonstrate his new ability to ask and answer questions about (pictures of) places in his immediate vicinity. This activity may be varied by reducing the time each picture is on the screen, or by putting slides in backward, upside down, or sideways.

Referring once more to Fries's famous definition, we may question whether, in fact "to have learned a foreign language" is in itself a serious goal for any adults except a few professional linguists and other language nuts. Certainly in addition to extrinsic motivations like fulfilling a requirement or preparing for residence abroad, one needs the intrinsic rewards of esthetically agreeable activities with frequent rewards of various kinds. But the work of Lambert and others indicates that even the extrinsic motivations vary dramatically in their driving power, according to the breadth and depth of their integration with the total personality of the learner. That principle must be both the adapter's raison d'être and his guiding star.

13   SOME TYPES OF   V. J. COOK
                        ORAL STRUCTURE
                        DRILLS

Compare Cook's *four degrees of contextualization* with Prator's (Art. 15) *manipulation to communication* scale and Paulston's (Art. 14) three *classes of drills.*

Analyze a particular grammar lesson from some ESL textbook known to you to determine a) which of the

Reprinted by permission from *Language Learning*, 18 (1968), 155-64. Mr. Cook is a member of the staff of Ealing Technical College, London.

four degrees of contextualization are used and b) which of the basic operations (substitution, mutation, repetition, addition) are used.

Choose some grammatical structure that would be appropriate for some students known to you and develop drills that are sequenced from non-contextualized to situational.

If the *input* in a drill were "Do you want coffee, or tea?", and the expected *output* were "I don't want either, I want milk," what activities (cf. p. 122) are required of the students? Analyze a number of exercises in textbooks known to you in these same terms.

This article does not set out to evaluate the usefulness of the types of structure drill but solely to describe them. The present scheme was worked out to account for drills in English; there seems no reason why it cannot be adapted for use with other languages.

The question of medium will not be considered at length. Unless otherwise indicated, these are purely oral drills in which the learner hears something spoken and responds orally. For a classification of the ways in which the different media of reading, writing, vision, and gesture can be combined, readers are referred to the analysis by St. P. Kaczmarski.[1]

The basic premise behind this article is that, regardless of their differing linguistic or psychological justification, all structure drills have one objective in common: that the learner should produce a number of utterances consisting of the same grammatical structure. From this it follows that, in the terms of a particular drill, there is only one "right" grammatical answer. The information that directs the learner to produce this right answer must, then, be given in such a way that it is unambiguous and cannot lead to more than one answer. A drill has two parts: what the student hears and what he has to say. The usual terms for these two parts are *stimulus* and *response*. However, these terms are associated closely with one learning theory and it seems preferable to use more neutral terms. A convenient pair of substitutes are *input* and *output* and these terms will be used throughout this article. Input (I.P.) refers to the information supplied to the learner, whether orally or visually; output (O.P.) to what the learner has to produce himself.

There are, perhaps, two basically different ways of describing drills. In the first, one considers the grammatical or lexical relationship between the pairs of

[1]St. P. Kaczmarski, "Language Drills and Exercises—A Tentative Classification," *IRAL*, III/3 (1965).

input and output, as in the following drill.[2] (Like all drill examples, this is presumed to be part of a much longer drill consisting of examples followed by practice items.)

    I.P.   *Is Bill playing tennis tonight?*
    O.P. *No, he's not going to play.*
    I.P.   *Is Susan helping her mother this evening?*
    O.P. *No, she's not going to help.*
    I.P.   *Are Mr. and Mrs. Green paying the bill tomorrow?*
    O.P. . . . .

Here one could say that the learner has to perform six activities:

    i.   Change question to statement,
    ii. make the sentence negative,
    iii. change the present continuous to *going to*,
    iv. substitute a personal pronoun for a proper name,
    v. delete a prepositional phrase,
    vi. delete the object.

In the second approach, one considers not the input/output pairs, but the successive outputs. The same drill consists of a master output *No, he's not going to play* which is varied at three points: *No X Y not going to Z.* The learner has to do three things:

    i.   At X he selects a personal pronoun according to the sex and person of the input.
    ii. At Y he selects either *'s, 're, or 'm* according to his choice at X.
    iii. At Z he inserts the verb provided in the input.

This approach treats the output as a master sentence into which successive items are inserted according to information selected from the input, rather than as a process of changing the whole input into an output.

A crucial issue in drill design that has great bearing on one's teaching method is the extent to which *context* or *situation* plays a part in the drill. (Context is here used for the linguistic environment, situation for the non-linguistic environment.) One can recognise four broad divisions.

1. NON-CONTEXTUALISED

Here the structure drill does not pretend to be more than an artificial game similar to a pianist's practising of scales. The learner may hear inputs that are not possible utterances of the language; he may be asked to perform activities that have no relation to what speakers do in actual speech.

[2]Cf. F. L. Marty, "Language Laboratory Learning," (Wellesley, Massachusetts: Audiovisual Publications, 1960).

I.P.1. *John's going to Paris.*
O.P.1. *John's going to Paris.*
I.P.2. *He*
O.P.2. *He's going to Paris.*
I.P.3. *She*
O.P.3. *....*

II. SEMI-CONTEXTUALIZED

Here the relationship between input and output is always one possible in speech, and both input and output are natural utterances of the language.

I.P.1. *Fred's going to change his job.*
O.P.1. *Fred? Changing his job? I don't believe it!*
I.P.2. *Jane's going to clean the car.*
O.P.2. *Jane? Cleaning the car? I don't believe it!*
I.P.3. *Susan's going to paint the bedroom.*
O.P.3. *....*

III. CONTEXTUALISED

Not only does each pair of input and output have a conversational relationship but the consecutive pairs are linked together to form a conversation.

I.P.1. *Are you coming to the party?*
O.P.1. *No I'm not.*
I.P.2. *But Susan's coming, I'm sure.*
O.P.2. *No she's not.*
I.P.3. *Well I know Basil's going to be there.*
O.P.3. *....*

IV. SITUATIONAL

The drill is here integrated into a situation in the classroom and on the objects or activities available. For instance, the teacher or students may perform various actions; the teacher asks *What is he doing?* and the class has to reply using the right grammatical structure.

The degree of contextualisation is particularly important in English because of the problem of personal pronouns. If the learner does not know that the drill is contextualised, he will often produce an output that is perfectly acceptable grammatically but wrong in the terms of the drill. For instance, let us suppose the required output is *I'm French.* In a non-contextualised drill this output might be elicited thus:

I.P.1. *You.*
O.P.1. *You're French.*
I.P.2. *I*
O.P.2. *I'm French.*

In a semi-contextualised drill this output might be elicited thus:

I.P.1. *What am I?*
O.P.1. *You're French.*
I.P.2. *What are you?*
O.P.2. *I'm French.*

If the learner has confused the drill type, he will produce exactly the wrong answer and will become unnecessarily alarmed by his mistake. He must, then, always know whether he is practicing the structure mechanically or is engaged in a pseudo-conversation before he knows what to answer. Simple as this point may be, it is surprisingly easy to overlook and very confusing to the learner.

Closely connected with contextualisation is the question of whether the input and output have *frames*. A frame is a setting for the input or output that has nothing to do directly with the particular grammatical structure being taught. First an example of a drill without any frame:

I.P. *Tennis*
O.P. *She plays tennis.*
I.P. *Golf*
O.P. *She plays golf.*

Here the input is non-contextualised and there is nothing redundant: it has to be incorporated into the output in its entirety. Now the same drill with frames:

I.P. *Does she play tennis?*
O.P. *Oh yes, she plays tennis all right.*
I.P. *Does she play golf?*
O.P. *Oh yes, she plays golf all right.*

Both input and output are more contextualised, because of the redundant language now included: only a part of the input is incorporated in the output; only a part of the output now practices the relevant structure. The frame is an expansion of the minimal input and output necessary for a particular drill. They can be expanded either by including more deletable parts of the sentence (*Does she always play tennis in the park on Sundays?*) or by the use of conversational phrases (*What I mean to say is, does she play tennis?*). The frame, then, leads itself to contextualising the drill and to practising forms like *Good Heavens, I'm terribly sorry*, and *you know* that are difficult to teach in any other manner. As we shall see below, it can also be used to divert the learner's conscious attention away from the grammatical point he is practising.

Bearing in mind that the previous classifications will be operating at the same time, let us now consider the basic operations in a structure drill. These can be seen essentially as variations of substitution, mutation, repetition, and addition. In actual practice, a drill may utilise more than one of these techniques; it is, however, convenient to separate them theoretically.

A. Substitution

Under this heading come those drills that can most simply be described by the master sentence approach mentioned above. Inevitably there will be some overlap with mutation, where the other approach will be adopted. In most disputable cases the master sentence approach yields a simpler description. A substitution drill, then, has a master output into which items are inserted according to information supplied in the input; all the outputs are variations of the original master (or masters) if sufficient examples are given to the learner.

1. Plain

This is the basic type of substitution drill. A number of examples have already been given. It may or may not have frames and it can function in two ways. In the first the substituted item, which may consist of a word, phrase, or clause, always replaces the same grammatical constituent of the output.

 I.P. *Do you like whisky?*
 O.P. *I love whisky.*
 I.P. *Do you like tea?*
 O.P. *I love tea.*

In the second the substituted item replaces any constituent of the output.

 I.P. *Whisky*
 O.P. *I love whisky.*
 I.P. *Hate*
 O.P. *I hate whisky.*
 I.P. *He*
 O.P. *He loves whisky.*

It is also possible to change the master output cumulatively rather than returning to it each time. The last output would then read *He hates whisky*.

2. Sequence

Here the learner chooses the item to substitute because of its position in a list in the input. This type will invariably have a frame.

 I.P. *I can't decide whether I like swimming or skating best.*
 O.P. *Oh, I prefer skating.*
 I.P. *I can't decide whether I like dancing or walking best.*
 O.P. *Oh, I prefer walking.*

Another advantage of the frame is here apparent in that it elucidates and provides a synonym for *prefer*.

3. Lexical drills

Unlike the two preceding types, the item to be substituted is not present in the input. The learner has instead to select an item to fit the input according to the principle established in the input. It must not be thought that this type of drill is teaching vocabulary; rather it is using lexis to guide the learner's choice of the item to substitute.

There are a number of relationships within lexis that can be used in drills. The following are examples only.

(i) Lexical pairs.

These are pairs that occur naturally in the language (*tall/short, aunt/uncle, lend/ borrow*). The input has one member of the pair, the output the other. If the pairs are sufficiently common, then they need not all be illustrated to the learner; the rarer the pairs, the fewer there should be.

I.P. *Is Bill young?*
O.P. *No, he's old.*
I.P. *Is John rich?*
O.P. *No, he's poor.*

One should also mention here a type of drill similar to this, but in which the pairs are linked purely for the drill. Obviously these have to be much more limited than natural pairs, but they serve the same purpose of limiting the output to one particular utterance. In the following drill all women are fascinating, whereas all men are boring.

I.P. *Mike's a doctor.*
O.P. *Oh, I think doctors are boring.*
I.P. *Susan's an actress.*
O.P. *Oh, I think actresses are fascinating.*

(ii) Lexical sets

Some well defined lexical sets such as days of the week and months can be exploited by using a regular progression between input and output.

I.P. *I'm seeing him on Tuesday.*
O.P. *Couldn't you see him on Wednesday instead?*
I.P. *He's meeting her on Saturday.*
O.P. *Couldn't he meet her on Sunday instead?*

(iii) Collocation

The learner has to select the appropriate collocation to fit the input.

I.P. *When did you get to London?*
O.P. *I arrived in London about ten.*

(iv) Lexical meaning

Out of a limited number of choices, the learner has to select the right reaction according to the meaning of the input.

I.P. *It's raining!*
O.P. *How annoying!*
I.P. *The sun's come out!*
O.P. *How nice!*
I.P. *It's pouring!*
O.P. *How annoying!*

This type would probably most often occur as the frame of another drill rather than by itself.

4. Pronoun Substitution

Using the master output approach, we can regard this type as one of choosing an item to substitute from the limited set of pronouns in accordance with the input. This very common drill technique has already been used above without comment. As was mentioned, drills using pronouns must have their degree of contextualisation specified as the correct choice of person will depend on this. In English, also, confusion can arise from the inclusive and exclusive uses of *we*. The only way of making the student choose between *Yes, we can* and *Yes, you can* as answers to *Can we go?* is by a carefully framed input.

It is also possible to exploit this relationship in reverse.

I.P. *I suppose he was there.*
O.P. *Oh yes, John was there.*
I.P. *I suppose she was there.*
O.P. *Oh yes, Mary was there.*

5. Knowledge drills

In this case, as with lexical drills, the item to substitute is not in the input but has to be supplied by the student from his own knowledge.

I.P. *Who wrote "Hamlet"?*
O.P. *Shakespeare did.*
I.P. *Who was Queen Victoria's husband?*
O.P. *Albert was.*

These can be based either on information given to him in other parts of the course, or be pure general knowledge, arithmetic, and so on. The distinction between this type and a quiz is that the outputs always conform to a given grammatical structure and that the student merely inserts one item from his background knowledge into this structure.

B. Mutation

Mutation drills are those where the successive outputs have nothing in common apart from the grammatical structure being drilled. Substitution is, then, basically paradigmatic: the learner selects from a real or arbitrary set of items the one to use in the output. Mutation is basically syntagmatic: the learner changes the grammatical structure of the input to produce the output. In the majority of drills, the two operations happen simultaneously (as in the concord of subject and verb in pronoun substitution). In most cases of dispute, the master output approach describes the learner doing a lesser number of things; for this reason it has been used up to now.

The possible types of mutation are limited only by the possible grammatical relationships of the language. The following reported speech example is chosen because it shows a clear case where description by the master output approach would imply the learner was performing an impossibly large number of substitutions:

I.P. *Open the door!*
O.P. *He told me to open the door.*
I.P. *Would you like some tea?*
O.P. *He asked me if I'd like some tea.*

One other type of mutation drill that is common is the combination drill. Here the input has two distinct parts, sometimes said by different speakers, parts which the learner has to combine into one output. (This should be distinguished from Addition below, where the learner has to add successive outputs together, rather than two parts of one input.)

I.P. *I met Mr. Brown yesterday. What's he? A teacher?*
O.P. *Oh yes, it was the Mr. Brown who's a teacher.*
I.P. *I met Mr. and Mrs. Stevens yesterday. What are they? Teachers?*
O.P. *Oh yes, they're the Mr. and Mrs. Stevens who are teachers.*

C. Repetition

The learner merely repeats the input; input and output are identical. Though this may play an incidental part in other types of drill, it does not seem very useful as a drill technique by itself for drilling grammatical structure.

D. Addition

The successive inputs are added together, gradually building up to the required final output. This addition can take place either at the beginning or end of the output. The following drill is then an addition drill building up at the beginning.

I.P.1. *to the cinema*
O.P.1. *to the cinema*
I.P.2. *goes*
O.P.2. *goes to the cinema*
I.P.3. *Charles*
O.P.3. *Charles goes to the cinema.*

Like repetition, addition does not possess much variation but can be used as part of the frame.

The discussion so far has been restricted to drills with spoken inputs so the question of medium has not arisen. Most of the preceding types could have written or visual inputs just as well. There are, however, some features which are specific to a given medium that lend themselves to drills. In a spoken drill, for instance, the frame can depend on the sex, age, or role of the speaker as revealed by his voice (*Good morning madam/sir, Would you like a whisky/ice-cream?*) or use can be made of sound effects.

This article has dealt with some of the methods of drill design. It has left untouched such areas as the phases of a drill, the length of a drill, the number of examples, and recognition drills in which the student distinguishes between grammatical structures but does not use them. It attempts to provide a tentative conceptual framework for the discussion of drills.

One point that does emerge from this framework is the extremely limited number of operations that the learner has to perform in a structure drill. In previous discussions, there appeared to be a multitude of drill types, but, if one accepts the master output approach, this is shown to be an illusion due to considering the input-output pairs rather than the successive outputs. It does appear that what is happening in a drill is much more limited than had been previously thought. This limitation is particularly apparent when one applies the distinction between deep and surface structure to drills. All the operations we have described appear to deal solely with the manipulation of surface structure. Whether this is due to the inadequacy of the present treatment or to the inadequacy of structure drills for teaching deep structure is not yet clear.

14   STRUCTURAL   CHRISTINA BRATT
       PATTERN DRILLS: PAULSTON
       A CLASSIFICATION

Why does Paulston feel it necessary to classify drills?

To what degree do Paulston's three classes of drills correspond to Prator's (Art. 15) four steps from manipulation to communication?

What would Newmark's (Art. 4) reaction be to Paulston's *mechanical* drills?

Reprinted by permission from *Foreign Language Annals*, 4 (December, 1970), 187–193. The author is assistant professor of linguistics and director of the English Language Institute at the University of Pittsburgh.

> Choose several drills from a textbook available to you and try to identify each of them in terms of Paulston's three classes of drills.

The basic core of the audiolingual method of teaching foreign languages is drills: pronunciation drills, vocabulary drills, but most of all structural pattern drills. This emphasis on drills reflects the beliefs about the nature of language and of learning by the advocates of this method. Wilga Rivers has examined these assumptions and a quick glance at the table of contents tells us what they are:[1]

1. Foreign-language learning is basically a mechanical process of habit formation. Corollary 1: Habits are strengthened by reinforcement. Corollary 2: Foreign-language habits are formed most effectively by giving the right response, not by making mistakes. Corollary 3: Language is behavior and behavior can be learned only by inducing the student to behave.

2. Language skills are learned more effectively if items of the foreign language are presented in spoken form before written.

3. Analogy provides a better foundation for foreign language learning than analysis.

Small wonder then that drills are emphasized in the classroom. By what other method could one teach a set of spoken habits by inducing the students into active habit formation with a maximum opportunity for immediate reinforcement and with a minimum opportunity for making mistakes? Indeed, one might wonder how people learned languages before the audiolingual method.

The plethora of various types of drills is overwhelming. To give but a few examples, Brooks lists twelve types: repetition, inflection, replacement, restatement, completion, transposition, expansion, contraction, transformation, integration, rejoinder, and restoration.[2] Finocchiaro describes eleven pattern practice activities under their "commonly agreed upon names": substitution, replacement, paired sentences, transformation or conversion, expansion, reduction, directed practice, integration, progressive replacement, translation, and question-answer.[3] Dacanay claims that there are basically four kinds of drill activity: substitution, transformation, response, and translation, but with a variety of subtypes which are: simple substitution, correlative substitution, moving slot substitution, transposition, expansion, transposition with expansion,

---

[1] Wilga M. Rivers, *The Psychologist and the Foreign Language Teacher* (Chicago: Univ. of Chicago Press, 1964), pp. vii–viii.

[2] Nelson Brooks, *Language and Language Learning* (New York: Harcourt, 1964), p. 156.

[3] Mary Finocchiaro, *English as a Second Language: From Theory to Practice* (New York: Regents, 1964), pp. 60–65.

reduction, integration, integration with transposition and reduction, comprehension, check-up, short answer, short rejoinder, choice questions, patterned response and five types of translation drills.[4] The criteria in classifying drills into these typologies are primarily in terms of what Frank Johnson has named the "restructuring range" and the "amount range." The restructuring range indicates the type of restructuring of a cue and the complexity of this restructuring which a learner must go through to arrive at a response. The amount range indicates how much information a learner is expected to retain and reproduce in giving a response.[5] The major drawback with these typologies is that they do not provide a method of gradation of drills even though gradation of language teaching materials is considered one of the most important aspects of the audiolingual method.

Furthermore, these assumptions of language learning on which drills are based have been challenged by the transformational-generative grammarians[6] who believe that language learning involves internalizing a complex system of rules—by innate propensities for language acquisition—which will generate all and only the grammatical sentences of a language. T-G grammatical theory distinguishes between competence, the intuitive knowledge of this complex system of rules, and performance, the actual utterance. "Acceptable performance is not possible while competence is defective. Practice in performance in the classroom is practice in generating new utterances, not in parroting utterances produced by the teacher."[7]

At this point I would like to propose a theoretical classification of structural pattern drills which attempts to incorporate both the theories of Chomsky and Skinner.[8] The proposal does not contain any new data, but rather reinterprets old data in light of new theory in order to provide a more efficient working model for the classroom.[9]

[4] Fe R. Dacanay, *Techniques and Procedures in Second Language Teaching* (Dobbs Ferry, N. Y.: Oceana, 1963), pp. 107–51.

[5] Dr. Francis C. Johnson, Professor of English, Univ. of Papua and New Guinea. In personal communication, 31 July 1970. I am for once in complete concord with his observations and very grateful to him for having made them.

[6] For a succinct discussion, which reviews the literature and sums up the major points, see Wilga M. Rivers, *Teaching Foreign Language Skills* (Chicago: Univ. of Chicago Press, 1968), pp. 64–67.

[7] Rivers summarizing the implications for foreign language teaching based on T-G principles. *Teaching Foreign Language Skills*, p. 67.

[8] I want to express my gratitude to my students in "Techniques and Procedures in TESOL," especially Mary Newton Bruder, Walter Davison, and Frank Giannotta for their contribution to the development of the classification and the zeal with which they have tested it in their teaching. Whatever inadequacies remain are entirely my own.

[9] See, e.g., Brooks, *Language Learning.*

When one talks about language learning, one really is talking about the concatenation of two separate areas, the system of language and the process of learning. Rivers, reviewing the writings of Skinner, Osgood, Chomsky, Lashley and Miller, Galanter and Pribram, points out that they all seem to agree that there are probably at least two levels of language: mechanical skill and thought.[10] These levels seem to correlate with what Katona has found in his experiments on learning by two methods: a "direct practice" and a "method of understanding" or as Rivers rephrases "a mechanical level and a level which involves understanding of how one is learning and the essential elements of what is being learned."[11]

If language involves more than one level and there are two types of learning, then this should be reflected in the nature and use of drills. In fact, with the judicious use of drills, we should find the answer to the constant plaint of the language teacher: "How can I make my students express their own ideas, using those language patterns they have memorized so laboriously?"

My contention is this. Given the plethora of different kinds of drills, we could use these drills more efficiently in our teaching if we analyzed them in terms of 1) expected terminal behavior, 2) of response control, 3) of the type of learning process involved, and 4) of utterance response. I suggest that basically there are three classes of drills: mechanical, meaningful, and communicative. There is no such thing as a more meaningful drill; either a drill is meaningful or it is not. However, there are gray areas between the classes, and they are of two kinds. One is a mixed drill where the cue in a chain-drill or a three-step drill may be mechanical and the response meaningful, and the other where a knowledge of the structural class (as in a moving slot substitution drill) may be sufficient.

A mechanical drill is defined as a drill where there is complete control of the response, where there is only one correct way of responding. Because of the *complete* control, the student need not even understand the drill nor necessarily pay attention to what he is doing. The most extreme example of this type of drill is repetition and mim-mem. Substitution drills lend themselves particularly well to this:

	+	3	+
Example:	Pɔɔm:	nakrian	Pɔɔm
	+	3	+
	suuŋ:	nakrian	suuŋ
	2	3	2
	ʔuan:	nakrian	ʔuan

[10] *The Psychologist and the Foreign Language Teacher*, p. 47. Not to be confused with structural versus semantic meaning.

[11] *The Psychologist and the Foreign Language Teacher*, p. 50.

Continue the drill:

+

1. naaw
   3
2. rɔɔn
3. dii
   2
4. suay[12]

I don't know how many readers know Thai, but I do know that you could all successfully complete the drill. There is complete control of the response.

The expected terminal behavior of such drills is the automatic use of manipulative patterns and is commensurate with the assumption that language learning is habit formation. It involves the classical Skinnerian method of learning through instrumental conditioning by immediate reinforcement of the right response. This is clearly the mechanical level of learning, and this class of drills provides practice in mechanical associations such as adjective-noun agreement, verb endings, question-forms and the like. This is a very necessary step in language learning, and as long as the student is learning, he won't mind the mechanical nature of the drill. The teacher needs to remember that the student can drill without understanding and to make sure that in fact he does understand. Because of the response-control, it is eminently suited for choral drills.

However, much of the criticism against the audiolingual method is based on the mechanical drill or rather on the overuse to which it has been put. Drilled beyond mastery of the pattern, it induces tedium and a distaste for language learning.[13] Lambert points out that motivation is one of the prime factors in

---

[12] Edward M. Anthony et al., *Foundations of Thai—Book 1, Part 1* (Pittsburgh: Univ. of Pittsburgh, 1967), p. 31.

This drill in translation runs like this:

Example (by teacher):

Cue:	thin	Response:	the thin student
	tall		the tall student
	fat		the fat student

Continue the drill:

Cue (by teacher):	Response (by student):
cold	the cold student
hot	the hot student
good	the good student
pretty	the pretty student

[13] An operational definition of mastery of a pattern at this level might be when a student can run through a drill without paying attention to what he is saying. To illustrate, I remember sitting by the window watching the futile efforts of a policeman to control Lima traffic, thinking about the menu for tomorrow's party, all the while loudly and clearly running through Spanish verb endings. The dinner was a success, but I certainly was not learning any Spanish.

successful language learning, and we simply cannot afford student distaste.[14] Furthermore, "it has been demonstrated that there is a limit to the amount of repetition which is effective for language learning,"[15] i.e., overuse of mechanical drills is not efficient teaching.

While not denying the need for mechanical drills, we may note that on the mechanical level alone, the student certainly cannot yet express his own ideas fluently. He now needs to work through a set of meaningful drills:

Association/Fixed reply[16]

1. Teacher: for five years
   Student: How long did he (study)?
2. Teacher: during March
   Student: When did he (register)?
3. Teacher: until four o'clock
   Student:

In a meaningful drill there is still control of the response (although it may be correctly expressed in more than one way and as such is less suitable for choral drilling), but the student cannot complete the drill without fully understanding structurally and semantically what he is saying. You might say there is a built-in test design. There is a choice involved in his answer, and the criterion he uses in answering is often given to him; the class supplies him with the information. Comprehension-type questions and answers based on assigned readings fall in this class:

Teacher: What time did John come to school?
Student: John came to school at 9 o'clock.

as well as much "situational" teaching:

Where is the book?
It's on the table.
Where is the chalk?
It's in the box.

If the teacher is unsure of whether a drill is mechanical or meaningful (the borders are not completely clear), he can test it with a nonsense word.

Example:
  I walk to school every day.
Cue: run Response:
  I run to school every day.

[14] Wallace E. Lambert, "Psychological Approaches to the Study of Language," *Modern Language Journal*, 47 (1963), 51–62, 114–21.

[15] Rivers, *The Psychologist and the Foreign Language Teacher*, p. 151.

[16] William E. Rutherford, *Modern English: A Textbook for Foreign Students* (New York: Harcourt, 1968), p. 234.

Teacher: skip
 Student: I skip to school every day.

Teacher: summersault
 Student: I summersault to school every day.

Teacher: boing
 Student: I boing to school every day.

Now do the same drill in Thai.

+   3

Example: Can dəən pay roŋrian Tuk wan
Cue: wiŋ   Response:

+   2   3

Can wiŋ pay roŋrian Tuk wan

Teacher: kradoot

+ | | 3

Student: Can kradoot pay roŋrian Tuk wan

Teacher: tii laŋ kaa

+   3

Student: Can tii laŋ kaa pay roŋrian Tuk wan

Teacher: boing

+   3

Student: Can boing pay roŋrian Tuk wan[17]

Those are mechanical drills. But in the drill on prepositions above, no native speaker could ever answer "Where boings the book?" for the simple reason that he does not understand. It is a meaningful drill. Complexity of pattern is not an issue.

Example: John kicked the door.
           The door was kicked by John.

Cue: The dog bit the man.
           The boing boinged the boing.

Response: The man was bitten by the dog.
           The boing was boinged by the boing.

That is a mechanical drill. For the language teacher who is fluent in the target language, it is difficult to appreciate the enormous difference in difficulty by these two classes of drills. This is not to deny that a response like "The man was bitten by the dog," albeit in a mechanical drill, is much more difficult for the learner than a single lexeme substitution drill. Language learning is also the

---

[17] Miss Patamaka Patamapongse translated this drill.

ability to control increasing amounts of language in mechanical manipulation and we need to consider the difficulty level within the "amount range" as well.

A word of caution. Sometimes a drill will seem meaningful when it really isn't.

Teacher	Holds up a book
Student 1:	What is this?
Student 2:	It is a book.

Meaningful or mechanical? It depends on what you are teaching. If you are teaching the structural patterns: Question word/thing + be + demonstrative pronoun/thing and personal/thing + be + Np, it is one of the mixed class drills I mentioned earlier. Student 1 does not have to understand anything as long as he says "What's this?" Student 2 has to understand in order to answer. However, this may be a vocabulary drill (we surely don't teach structural patterns and vocabulary at the same time) and that easily confuses the classification of the drills. Vocabulary by definition has lexical meaning and so does not fit into this classification of structural pattern drills.

It will be noticed that in the meaningful Q-A drills above the long answers were given. The expected terminal behavior has not changed. We still want an automatic use of language manipulations; we are still working on habit formation. But the method is different. The drill should be preceded by analysis of the characteristics of the language pattern—be it inductively coaxed out of the students or explained by the teacher. Unless the student understands what he is doing, i.e., recognizes the characteristic features involved in the language manipulation, he cannot complete the drill. There still is a right response (we have supplied facts and information), but we allow a bit of trial-and-error process in finding it.

But there is still no real communication taking place. Students have a tendency to learn what they are taught rather than what we think we are teaching. If we want them to acquire fluency in expressing their own opinions, then we have to teach that. The expected terminal behavior in communicative drills is normal speech for communication or, if one prefers, the free transfer of learned language patterns to appropriate situations.

In a communicative drill there is no control of the response. The student has free choice of answer, and the criterion of selection here is his own opinion of the real world—whatever he wants to say. Whatever control there is lies in the stimulus. "What did you have for breakfast?" is likely to limit the topic to the edible world but not necessarily. "I overslept and skipped breakfast so I wouldn't miss the bus" is an answer I have heard more than once. It still remains a drill rather than free communication because we are still within the realm of the cue-response pattern. Communication "requires interpersonal responsiveness, rather than the mere production of language which is truthful, honest, accurate, stylistically pleasing, etc.—those characteristics which look at language as language rather than as behavior, which is the social purpose of language. Our end product is surely getting things done, easing social tensions, goading ourselves into doing this or that, and persuading others to do things. Communication arises when language is used as such inter-personal behaviour, which goes beyond meaningful and truthful manipulation of language symbols."[18] To recapitulate, the differences between a meaningful drill and a communicative drill lie in the expected terminal behavior (automatic use of language manipulation versus free transfer of learned language patterns to appropriate situations) and in response control. But the main difference between a meaningful drill and a communicative drill is that the latter adds *new* information about the *real* world. All of us have seen a meaningful drill turn communicative when the students suddenly took the question or cue personally and told us something about himself that we did not know from the classroom situation. "I have three sisters" is communicative, but "My shirt is red" is merely meaningful; that information is supplied by the situation, and I can see it as well as the student.

Language teachers have always used communicative drills in the classroom (where else is one asked such personal questions as "Did you brush your teeth this morning?"), but my point is that there should be an orderly progress from mechanical drilling through meaningful to communicative drills, that the teacher should know one from the other, and that one should not rely on chance that the students will turn a drill into communication.

Communicative drills are the most difficult to arrange within the classroom. They can of course never be drilled chorally. Still, if we want fluency in expressing personal opinion, we have to teach that. One way of working with communicative drills is to structure the classroom activity so that it simulates the outside world of the students and to work within this situation. Need I point out that running through a memorized dialogue with accompanying gestures and action is not communicative drill nor necessarily language learning: non-language teachers refer to such activity as acting. Another, simpler way of working with communicative drills is simply to instruct students to answer truthfully.

Example:
1. What is your responsibility?
   My responsibility is { to (learn English). (learning English).
2. What's your hobby?
   My hobby is { to (make models). (making models).
3. What's your favorite pastime?
4. What are your lab instructions?

[18] Johnson, personal communication, 31 July 1970.

5. What will your occupation be?

6. What are your interests?

7. What is your advice to (Ahmed)?[19]

Gone is the instrumental conditioning; there is no facilitating of the correct response. What we have is John Carroll's " 'problem-solving' situation in which the student must find . . . appropriate verbal responses for solving the problem, 'learning' by a trial-and-error process, to *communicate* rather than merely to utter the speech patterns in the lesson plan."[20] We are clearly working within a level of language that involves thought and opinion and teaching it in a way that necessitates an understanding of the essential elements of what is being learned. It is a very different experience from mechanical drilling. It is indeed practice in performance by practice in generating new utterances, and if it is indeed true that this is the only type of practice in performance, then it is also the only way of internalizing the rules of grammar so that competence will not be defective. I am not saying that language teaching should be concerned solely with communicative type drills, but I am suggesting that any amount of mechanical drills will not lead to competence in a language, i.e., fluency to express one's own opinions in appropriate situations.

To summarize, in language teaching we ought to classify the drills we use into three classes: mechanical, meaningful, and communicative in order to reach free communication. We then need to proceed systematically, not leaving out any one step. Mechanical drills are especially necessary in beginning courses and in learning languages markedly different from the native tongue, such as Thai is for me. I do not believe that this is the only way of teaching languages because it patently is not. Rather, given what we know about languages and learning today, this classification of drills will provide for more efficient language learning.

The limitation of this classification is that it only fits structural pattern drills. By definition, vocabulary involves meaning and thus cannot exist on a mechanical level only. Pronunciation drills are frequently carried out in nonsense syllables in order to concentrate the better on sounds; pronunciation of segmental phonemes does not involve meaningful utterances.

[19] Rutherford, *Modern English*, p. 175. The teaching point here is using the complement to $V_t + O$ (as in *to learn English*) in free variation with $V + ing + O$ (as in *learning English*). The teacher asks the questions and the students answer.

[20] John B. Carroll, *The Study of Language* (Cambridge, Mass.: Harvard Univ. Press, 1953), p. 188.

DEVELOPMENT   CLIFFORD H. PRATOR
OF A MANIPULATION-
COMMUNICATION
SCALE

To what extent does Prator's criticism of the influence of structural linguistics on second-language teaching parallel that of transformational linguists as
described by Bolinger (Art. 3)?

Do you agree with Prator's statement that *the recitation of freshly memorized dialogue . . . cannot be
said to involve any considerable element of communication as that term is defined in this article?*
Why?

Choose some discrete phonological, syntactic, or lexical problem, and develop a sequence of exercises
exemplifying each of Prator's four steps from manipulation to communication.

To judge by the topics of papers read at scholarly meetings, teachers have been
increasingly worried for a decade or more about the effectiveness of the instruction in English as a second language that goes on in the United States at the
intermediate and advanced levels. We are comparatively satisfied with our elementary classes and have produced a respectable number of successful texts for
beginners or near-beginners. But at more advanced levels we are bedeviled by
uncertainties as to our aims, lack of conviction in our choice of classroom
activities, and a persistent shortage of good teaching materials.

The purpose of this article is to investigate briefly the causes of this situation
and to suggest a theoretical guideline that may be of help in remedying our
deficiencies.

In the opening sentence of his *Gallic War*, Julius Caesar notes the fact that
"all Gaul is divided into three parts." The most notable fact about most language departments is somewhat similar. All, or almost all, are divided into two
quite distinct, often antagonistic, parts: language and literature. The language
courses, which are usually assigned to the youngest and most defenseless members of the staff, tend today to be devoted to drill work of a rather mechanical

Reprinted by permission from *NAFSA Studies and Papers*, English Language Series, No. 10,
March, 1965, 385–391. The author is professor of English and vice-chairman of the department of English, University of California, Los Angeles.

sort and are likely to have little intellectual content. On the other hand most courses in literature, typically reserved for senior personnel, are either taught largely in the mother tongue of the student or, if conducted in the second language, make no deliberate systematic attempt to help the student improve his practical command of that language. In the two sets of courses, aims, methods, and subject matter are utterly dissimilar. If another paraphrase is permissible, language is language, and literature is literature, and never the twain shall meet.

SOURCES OF DIFFICULTY

It is just such a meeting—of language and literature—that is called for in the intermediate or advanced class in English as a second language. The unfortunate dichotomy prevailing in our language departments means that we have little precedent for the kind of course that makes a gradual and orderly transition from activities that emphasize the development of basic linguistic skills to activities designed to encourage the free communication of thought. It is apparent, then, that some of the difficulty we experience in pushing on beyond the beginning level stems directly from the prevalent concept of departmental organization and the consequent separation of language and literature.

An even more important source of our difficulty may lie in our current excessive dependence on the structural linguists as the fountainhead of our attitudes toward language teaching. There is no gainsaying the fact that we teachers of English as a second language owe the linguists a tremendous debt. One can no more deny the idea that language teaching must be grounded on linguistics—that is to say, on the body of knowledge we possess about the nature of language and of specific languages—than one can deny virtue, home, and mother. But it should be equally obvious that our discipline should rest on other foundations as well, particularly on that branch of psychology that deals with the nature of the learner and of the language-learning process.

Furthermore, American linguists have been notably uninterested in certain aspects of language with which the teacher must concern himself, especially in advanced classes. Since Bloomfield, the focus of attention in linguistic research has been the spoken language, with little attention paid to writing above the level of graphemics. Grammatical analysis has developed almost exclusively within the limits of the individual sentence, and there has been little study of the relationships between sentences in larger units such as the paragraph. Yet, the advanced student of English as a second language must be taught composition.

THE IMPORTANCE OF MEANING

In their effort to develop more rigorous methods of linguistic analysis, the Bloomfieldians have tended to downgrade the importance of meaning as an element of language. However healthy this de-emphasis of meaning may have been in analytical work, it should never have been extended to the practical activities of the language classroom. In following the linguists too trustingly on this point, we language teachers have often fallen into grievous error: extended drills on nonsense syllables, failure to make sure that our students understand the sentences they are so assiduously repeating, the use of language that bears no relationship to the realities of the situation, exercises made up of totally disconnected sentences.

Perhaps most serious of all as a cause of the difficulties we are now experiencing in advanced instruction, we seem to have largely lost sight of the role of communication in language teaching. If meaning is not important, then neither is communication. Yet, even on the theoretical level, it should be easy to convince ourselves that communication is an essential component of language—that language bereft of its communicative function is not language at all but mere parroting.

The teacher who underestimates the importance of communication is likely to attach correspondingly greater weight to another element of language that has a clear methodological significance—its systematic nature. One of the greatest services the linguists have rendered is to insist that a language is basically a system of structural signals by means of which a speaker indicates the relationship between content words. It follows that a primary aim of instruction must be to practice these arrangements of signals, these structural patterns, until they can be handled automatically as a matter of habit. Hence, our fully justified fondness for pattern practice.

We must realize, however, that pattern practice and communication are to a considerable degree antithetical. If our students are to form correct speech habits through pattern practice, we must not allow them to practice errors. Therefore, we must exercise strict controls, and must supply the proper words and structures in the form of an external model that we require the students to imitate. On the other hand, the beginning and essence of communication is the presence of a thought that the speaker wishes to share with a hearer, followed by that mysterious process whereby he produces from within himself the words and patterns that express thought. True communication implies the absence of external controls.

TWO TYPES OF CLASSROOM ACTIVITIES

For the purposes of this article, then, we may define communicative classroom activities as those that allow the student himself to find the words and structures he uses. The other type of activity, in which he receives the words and structures from teacher, tape, or book, may be called—for want of a better word—a manipulative activity. In this sense, an example of pure manipulation would be a drill in which the students merely repeat sentences after the teacher. An example of pure communication would be a free conversation among the members of a class.

When we begin to analyze activities from this point of view, however, we soon discover that most of them do not fall entirely within either category but are mixtures of communication and manipulation in various proportions. Thus, a teacher can frame a question in such a way as to control the form of the student's answer to a considerable degree but still leave him some freedom in the choice of words: *Before you came to school this morning, what had you already done at home?* That one seems to involve a rather larger element of communication than of manipulation.

What all this has to do with the problems of advanced English instruction begins to become apparent when we reflect that the principal methodological change that should characterize the progression from the lower to the upper levels of language teaching is precisely the increased freedom of expression given students in the higher classes. In the beginning stages, the teacher exerts such rigorous control as to reduce the possibility of error to a minimum; at least, this is what happens in classes taught by the methods most widely approved today. At some later stage the time must inevitably come when these controls disappear, when oral pattern practice gives way to the discussion of ideas, and dictation is superseded by free composition. We may regard the whole process as a prolonged and gradual shift from manipulation to communication, accomplished through progressive decontrol. We determine the speed of the transition by allowing the student the possibility of making certain errors only when we are reasonably sure that he will no longer be likely to make them.

It is fortunate that the movement from manipulation to communication does not have to be made abruptly, and it is probable that the shift should never be total, even in the most advanced classes. Therein lies the importance of analyzing all the great range of possible language-teaching techniques from the point of view of their manipulation-communication content, and of arranging them in our minds along a sort of scale extending from the most manipulative to the most communicative types.

A FOUR-WAY SCALE

In the development of a manipulation-communication scale, it may be helpful to divide classroom activities into at least four major groups: 1) *completely manipulative,* 2) *predominantly manipulative,* 3) *predominantly communicative,* and 4) *completely communicative.* For ease of reference, we can label these as groups *one, two, three,* and *four.* Obviously, the dimensions of this article will not permit an attempt at a complete classification of this sort, but a number of specific examples may be useful.

One of the currently most popular activities in language classes is the single-slot substitution drill: The teacher gives a model sentence, such as *My father is a doctor,* and asks the students to construct similar sentences by substituting for *doctor* a series of nouns of profession—*salesman, farmer, fisherman,* etc.—which the teacher also supplies orally. In this form the exercise is certainly completely manipulative and hence belongs in our group one. But by any of a number of slight changes we can turn it into a group-two activity and thus—even in an elementary class—come slightly closer to our ultimate goal of using language for communication. For instance, the students could individually substitute the name of their father's real profession. Such a change would, incidentally, avoid the element of silliness inherent in having the son of a professor chorusing that his father is a janitor. Another change that would permit a short step toward communication would be to cue the exercise visually, by means of a series of pictures, instead of cuing it orally. In this situation, though the structure is determined by the teacher, the student supplies at least a single word in each sentence. (It is to be hoped that this argument may have some weight with those too numerous instructors who are deeply fearful of losing dignity if they use visual aids with adult students.)

As I have already pointed out, the most typical group-one activity is probably the repetition of sentences by the students in immediate imitation of the teacher. Yet, the teacher can introduce an element of communication into even this type of exercise by allowing a significant period of time to elapse between the hearing of the model and the attempt at imitation. In a beginning class, this might take the form of returning to a repetition drill after having moved on to some other type of exercise; except that, the second time around, the teacher would ask the students to reproduce such sentences as they could remember without benefit of model. Clearly, in this delayed repetition the possibility of error and the need for the student to draw upon his own inner linguistic resources would be greater than in the original version of the activity. In an advanced class the teacher could apply the same principle by asking students to retell an anecdote quite some time after he had told it to them.

This would seem to be a good place to consider memorization, especially the memorization of material in dialogue form. The recitation of freshly memorized dialogue, whether it be recited with full comprehension by both participants or not, whether it be in perfectly authentic conversational form or not, cannot be said to involve any considerable element of communication as that term is defined in this paper. It is almost pure manipulation, since the opportunity for the speakers to supply all or part of the language is practically nil. On the other hand, if the teacher encourages students to paraphrase all or portions of a dialogue, then they can certainly move into the area of communication. One wonders why our textbooks so seldom contain versions of dialogues that leave blank some portions of sentences, to be filled in by student improvisation.

READING AND WRITING

In advanced classes, though the teacher may occasionally need to use a group-one exercise, he should probably place greater emphasis on activities that fall into groups two and three. Since reading plays a prominent role in most advanced classes, it is interesting to apply our scale to various activities usually connected with reading. Following our definitions, we would be forced to classify silent reading, in which no overt linguistic activity of any sort is demanded of the student, as belonging to group one—completely manipulative, hence not often desirable for use in class at the advanced level. Reading aloud in direct imitation of a teacher would also, of course, fall into group one. But reading aloud without an immediate oral model to follow would require the student to supply the appropriate sounds and sound sequences, and would be classified as a group-two activity, and should therefore probably have a place in advanced instruction.

Various types of questioning ordinarily follow reading. In measuring different types against our manipulation-communication scale, we can make good use of Gurrey's well-known classification of questions as step-one, step-two, and step-three. He labels as step-one a question the answer to which can be found in the exact words of the text. Since the student has only to locate and read the appropriate words, questioning of this sort would appear to be a predominantly manipulative activity, suitable as a starting point in advanced classes provided that the teacher then moves on to questioning of a predominantly communicative type, such as step-two and step-three questions. In Gurrey's thinking, a step-two question is one the student can answer by remembering information supplied by the text but not by using the exact words of the text. A step-three question relates to the student's own experience, with its content merely suggested by the text.[1] Obviously, this latter type approaches pure communication; the only remaining control lies in the form of the question itself.

Students in advanced classes are usually asked to write compositions. If these are assigned without advance preparation of any kind, the writing of them is a group-four activity, completely communicative. It is surely preferable to lead up to composition through a series of related group-two or -three activities. Consulting our scale, we might decide to begin the series with a dictation dealing with the content of the eventual essay to be written, then to move on to another dictation on the same subject but one in which sentences are left incomplete, to be filled in by the student, before finally assigning the related composition. Or we might prefer to base the composition on a text that has been read, and to prepare for it through a graded series of questions of a progressively more communicative sort.

Perhaps I have said enough to permit us to judge whether or not the kind of manipulation-communication scale here described can serve effectively as a theoretical guideline in our organization of classes and textbooks. It seems to be a way of reconfirming, through a new logical approach, quite a few of our established ideas and convictions. On other points, however, it brings us to certain conclusions that we may find upsetting, and therefore challenging.

[1]Cf. Stevick, Art. 9, for further discussion of questions of these types. (Eds.)

From the point of view developed in this article, a typical class would be seen as made up of several cycles of activities, with each cycle related to the teaching of a corresponding small unit of subject matter. Within each cycle the activities would be so arranged as to constitute a gradual progression from manipulation to communication. The same progression would characterize the whole movement from elementary to advanced English courses—though at the point where manipulative activities disappear altogether it might be well to stop thinking of the work as teaching English as a second language.

One result of the application of the scale might be a blurring of the sharp line that now separates language courses from literature courses. We might be encouraged to push through more often to communication in elementary language courses. We might realize the naiveté we now frequently display in trusting that our beginners will somehow find adequate occasion outside the class for using communicatively the structures that we have taught them but that they have never so used in class. We might be helped to realize that we simply cannot be sure that our students have mastered a given structure until we have heard them produce it in a communication situation free of all controls. We might even come to consent to the supreme heresy of including in early literature courses a solid element of manipulation, so that they could make a more direct contribution to the development of language skills.

16	SELECTIVE LISTENING	EUGENE A. NIDA

Plan sample listening exercises, as described by Nida, for specific English sounds and for specific aspects of English grammar for a particular student group known to you.

Nida suggests the extension of *selected listening* to *selected reading*. What specific areas of reading might be appropriate for such exercises?

Everyone recognizes the importance of the auditory approach to learning a foreign language; and yet this procedure is not as easy as it seems. The average person simply does not know where to begin listening. Everything floods in upon us in such confusion that we have no idea of exactly what we are hearing, and

Reprinted by permission from *Language Learning*, 4 (1952–1953), 3 and 4.92–101. Dr. Nida is secretary for translations of the American Bible Society.

we are at a loss to be able to make any sense of the jumble of sounds. If we make any attempt at all to learn by listening, we try to pick out words, but this seems such a terribly slow procedure that we very often return to the exclusive use of the textbook approach and give up attempting to "educate" our ears. The result is that we generally gain a very imperfect command of the language, and frequently our mastering of grammatical details stops the day we cease studying grammar from the textbooks.

Another reason why we shun the auditory approach is our prejudice, built up largely by our own ideas about education, namely, that the "eye gate" is really much more effective as a means of learning. There is no denying the importance of visual symbolism, but language is essentially a motor-auditory phenomenon, and our auditory sensitiveness and assimilative capacity must be developed. Furthermore, it can be developed, and without too much trouble, if only we go about the task in the proper way. One of these techniques we may call "selective listening."

GENERAL PRINCIPLES OF SELECTIVE LISTENING

The technique of selective listening consists fundamentally in listening only to certain features at a time. We do not try to hear everything; in fact, we attempt to hear only a restricted number of things. If more filters through to our consciousness (and it certainly will), well and good; but selective listening means just what it implies, namely, selecting certain features and listening concentratedly for and to them. The general principles of selective listening may be enumerated as follows:

1. Selective listening should begin from the very moment that one first hears a language.
2. One should listen for only one feature (or set of features) at a time.
3. One should listen successively to all the features of a language.
4. The order of listening to different features should be systematic.
5. One should concentrate particularly on those features which cause the learner difficulty in understanding or speaking.

Everyone who has had much experience in language learning or teaching will recognize that these suggestions are not necessarily new or different. However, the value of selective listening, as a technique, consists in 1) its selectivity and 2) its systematic and comprehensive approach. The application of these general principles will be indicated as we consider in some detail the matter of systematic ordering of features to which one should listen.

It is quite impossible to make rules for precisely the order in which certain features of a language should be listened to, for languages differ widely in their structures and to an extent the order of features should be determined by the needs of the individual learner. However, in general the order of features should be 1) phonetic features (sounds), 2) vocabulary, and 3) grammar, i.e., morphology and syntax. Of course, features 2 and 3 cannot be rigidly separated, but the reasons for the suggested order will be evident as we proceed.

PHONETIC FEATURES

Phonetic features of a language should be listened to right from the beginning. However, many people object "But I can't understand anything!" In some ways this is an advantage, especially with the intonation, and it is the intonation which should first attract one's attention. Without knowing the words, one can nevertheless become familiar with the principal intonational characteristics: the typical rise and fall of the voice, the staccato effect of syllable sequences, types of pauses, rhythms of long and short vowels, and types of emphatic forms. All these features are of great importance and should be listened to at length. It is not without significance that children learn to mimic intonational patterns even before they can babble all of the sounds. While listening, it is helpful to have a pencil and pad, on which the gross intonational features may be drawn in terms of the predominant contours. Of course, one cannot know the "meaning" of all these intonational distinctions; but even without knowing the meanings of the words, one can discover quite a number of the more important intonational patterns and can often determine the principal situations in which they should be employed.

After intonation one should listen for particularly striking consonants. It is true that vowels have greater audibility; but they usually appear to be less contrastive, and hence more difficult to isolate. Accordingly, "strange" consonants (i.e., strange only from the standpoint of the learner's experience) offer the best point of attack on the system of sounds. Heavy explosive consonants, clicks (if one happens to be in South Africa), glottalized stops, or "harsh" sibilants usually offer the best possibilities. However, one should not begin by trying to isolate all the aspirated stops. This is a later step. At first, one must be content with hearing individual consonant sounds.

After isolating eight or ten easily distinguished consonants (this does not mean, of course, that all the allophones, i.e., submembers of the phonemes, have been identified), one should tackle the vowels. First of all, one should listen to the extremes, e.g., *i* and *u* (if such exist in the language), since they are both high and extremes of fronting and backing. Later on one adds the lower and more central vowels. On the other hand, there may be some "queer" vowel that attracts one's attention first. To listen to this vowel in numerous contexts is quite all right, but as soon as one can identify this vowel sound with relative ease, then another should be taken up. As in the case of consonants we are not to suppose that by listening to and identifying these vowel sounds we are automatically phonemicizing correctly. We are only becoming aware of certain allophones. Nevertheless, it is amazing how much relatively accurate phonemicizing one can do (i.e., determining the limits of similar sounds which are contrastive in meaning), even without understanding the words.

All this procedure may seem like a considerable waste of time, especially before one begins to speak the language. Many people believe that one should begin to talk "correctly" (i.e., with proper grammatical forms), and then gradually the pronunciation will be improved as one gains greater facility. However, one often acquires so many bad habits in the period of unnatural learning that it takes a very long time to unlearn these incorrect pronunciations. If we can learn anything from the manner in which children acquire a language, we should note that almost without exception, children can babble with considerable activity (i.e., reproduce all the sounds of the language in their proper sequences and with correct intonation) before they can speak to any great extent. In other words, they have largely mastered the sound structure of the language without having mastered the lexical and syntactic patterns. The adult learner must not count on a complete mastery of the phonetic structure before learning some vocabulary and grammar (i.e., being able to talk some), but we will do much to improve our speaking if only we will learn to hear correctly. One of the secrets to correct speaking is correct hearing.

After one has learned to distinguish various individual sounds, he should then begin to listen for types of sounds, e.g., aspirated consonants, voiced stops, nasalized vowels, palatalized consonants, voicing vs. voicelessness, and long vowels vs. short ones. One should learn to listen systematically to the sound system. This means noting the component features of related, but non-identical, sounds. It may be that an aspirated p is easily heard, but that aspirated t or k is much less readily recognizable. However, by noting the puffs of air with the p, and trying to detect a similar feature with t and k, one is able to quickly improve his listening capacities. This does not mean, of course, that one can neglect a t vs. d and a k vs. g series. These are just other systematic contrasts, namely, voiceless vs. voiced quality. Our listening should include 1) the isolating of similar features, e.g., aspiration, glottalization, and palatalization, and 2) the awareness of contrast, e.g., long vs. short vowels, voiced vs. voiceless consonants, and aspirated vs. nonaspirated consonants. In some instances it may be better to begin by listening for the contrasts, and in others one may learn to detect sounds more readily by noting similarities. It really does not matter which order is followed, provided one does both. In general, one mixes the two, and to good advantage.

One may legitimately ask the question, "But how much time should be given to the process of listening to sounds before trying to master some of the vocabulary and grammatical structure?" No hard and fast rule can be given, but if one is learning a foreign language in a field situation there will be many hours when one is exposed to hearing the language before one has any chance of knowing enough to be able to understand anything of what is going on. One should not waste this valuable time, but rather, concentrate on the phonetic features of the language. If one's circumstances do not provide many opportunities for listening to the language, the use of the radio or recordings in the language can help. For the person who is learning a language in the unnatural situation of the classroom or through a tutor (while still living in an English-speaking community), one should spend *at least* fifteen to twenty hours concentrating on hearing the sounds of a language through recordings before undertaking to begin speaking. Repetition of the same material is quite satisfactory, provided there is sufficient variety so as to illustrate enough contrasts.

Selective listening to the sounds of a language should not end when one begins to understand some of the vocabulary and grammar. Certain niceties of pronunciation often elude one for a long time, and only by careful and concentrated listening to and for such distinctions can one satisfactorily reproduce them. Even after having learned to understand a high percentage of the language in its spoken form, one may find it very important to try to blot out the "meaning" of what is said in order to concentrate on some intricate phonetic details. The speaker of a foreign language practically never outgrows the need of attention to phonetic features.

VOCABULARY

Vocabulary which is listened to always comes in some structural context. However, in the initial stages, vocabulary may be identified (i.e., isolated from the continuum of sound) without too much attention to the structure. By vocabulary we do not necessarily mean separate words. The identifiable units may be anything from morphemes to complete utterances. However, generally they are words (as understood in the popular sense), for they are units which are meaningful when uttered in isolation and which recur frequently and for the most part have the same order of constituent parts. The relative flexibility of phrase patterns and their generally greater length mean that they are usually acquired after individual words.

Some people have assumed that the only way to listen for vocabulary is to memorize lists of words and then to listen for such words in context. Of course, this can be helpful, but it is not the only way and in fact is not the most effective way of selective listening for vocabulary. One can begin to listen by trying to catch a frequently recurring sequence of sounds. Sometimes the very situation will give one the clue to the meaning. For instance, the equivalents to such phrases as "Good-bye!" "Hello!" "What is this?" and "How are you?" can often be learned from natural context. If one does do this, the form of the expression will be readily retained in the memory and its recall will be relatively easy, since it was learned in context. One may wish to write the phrase down in some rough phonetic script, but such writing is quite secondary to the more important matter of learning from spoken context.

Even apart from the more obvious words and phrases of greeting, one can learn many words by isolating them from context. However, if it is impossible to discover their meanings from the practical context, they may be written down and then later one may ask for their meanings (or look them up in a dictionary). By the process of having isolated these words in context, one has inevitably stimulated his own curiosity and interest; and once the meaning is discovered, there is practically no trouble in remembering.

Identifying in spoken context those words and phrases which have already been learned is of utmost importance for two reasons: 1) we learn the acoustic form of the word or phrase (there is relatively little connection between recognizing the visual written symbol and identifying the acoustic impression, even in so-called phonetically written languages; that is to say, we have to learn to "hear a language") and 2) we fix the acoustic impression in our memories by process of repetition.

It is not easy to ascertain the exact value of recordings in the process of language learning, but experience has shown that for a quick and thorough mastering of vocabulary the repetition of identical wording in the same phonetic form (as provided only by recordings) has great value. In listening to a foreign language we all have the experience of thinking that the language is spoken abnormally fast. We may be able to identify a single word or phrase, but by the time we have mentally "catalogued" it the speaker has gone on to something else and we have the impression of having blanked out. However, if we are able to listen to exactly the same data again, we quickly identify those words and phrases which have been isolated in the previous hearing, and we are able to add further expressions. By listening over and over to the same recording, we are able to build our vocabulary quickly, and much of this can be done with a minimum of dictionary usage, for we learn the meanings of words from association in the context, even though it may be only partially understood.

During the process of listening to recordings one can refer to the written text, but this should never be done at first. One should attempt to identify as much as possible without recourse to the printed text. After listening several times, one may read and listen at the same time and again return to the purely spoken form.

In some situations it is quite impossible to have recordings (either purchased ones, following some course of study, or ones which can be obtained from an informant), but in such instances one can usually get an informant 1) to read the same material over and over or 2) to retell stories which have a more or less fixed form. In the initial process of language study recordings are in many ways preferable to the ordinary conversation or discourse, since repetition is fundamental to identification and learning and since one can build on partially understood data, rather than having to pick forms from utterly diverse and unfamiliar contexts. However, after a few weeks or months (depending upon speed of learning and availability of proper material to listen to) the importance of recorded data for vocabulary acquisition diminishes rapidly. However, they are still very helpful in listening to linguistic structure, i.e., the grammar of the language.

One of the most important features of selective listening as a technique of mastering vocabulary is that words are learned in context. In the traditional text-book too much of the vocabulary is acquired from lists, but in listening to a continuum of speech in order to identify words and phrases one is inevitably concerned with what precedes and what follows. By listening to repetitions of the same data the vocabulary increases, but it is in context.

GRAMMAR

Almost everyone recognizes the value of listening as an aid to mastering sounds and vocabulary, but few persons have considered listening as a means of master-ing the grammar of a language. Too often we depend entirely upon textbooks for grammatical explanations. Such books are helpful, but even the best grammar is quite incomplete and no speaker of a language can afford to depend on the in-complete comments of the average grammar. Only by becoming acoustically aware of linguistic structure can one count on obtaining an adequate grasp of the language. One often hears a speaker say, "I don't know just what is wrong, but that simply doesn't sound right." Such an impression, or "feeling" for the language, is built up over many years of listening. This process can, however, be greatly speeded up by concentrating on certain phases of the linguistic structure, and in this way one may acquire facility in the correct handling of the structural details.

The order which one should employ in listening to the grammatical features of the language depends very largely upon the structure of the language in ques-tion. However, in order to grasp the larger patterns of the language one should begin by listening for the order of words. This can be done best by identifying various important recurring structures (or frames), e.g. subject-object-verb, adjective-noun, verb-adverb, and adverb-adjective. The order of clauses (e.g. dependent and independent) is also important. One should also become aware of special patterns which may exist for negations, questions, declarations, or commands (these being in general the four most common modes).

Despite the advantages of concentrating on the broader (i.e., more inclusive) patterns of the language, we often get involved in the more minor details of government, cross-reference, and grammatical agreement, involving such cate-gories as gender, case, person, number, and mode. Because of the multitude of details we become lost, especially in languages with so-called "heavy morpho-logies." The best solution to these problems is to listen selectively to each type of grammatical feature. For example, in a language like Spanish we could listen for several days with our attention directed primarily to gender. This would in-clude identifying the gender of each and every word which we hear. Listening for a few days will not teach us all we need to know, about gender, but it will develop in our listening an awareness to gender which we did not have before.

Furthermore, we will more or less unconsciously continue to listen for gender, even when we are no longer concentrating on it. Having constructed a pattern for identifying gender, our minds keep on classifying grammatical data in this way. After gender we may wish to consider number, which in Spanish is much simpler, but if we concentrate on number in nouns, attributives, pronouns, and verbs, we will soon become so aware of the patterns that we will find ourselves almost automatically employing the proper forms in our speech. Using Spanish as a further illustrative example, we can take up such features as the subjunctive mode, various tenses, irregular verbs, and reflexive verbs. The order will depend largely upon one's recognition of the need for such attention. Where, as in Spanish, the choice of certain forms is determined by other forms, one can develop an awareness of such relationships by trying to anticipate the speaker's use. For example, wherever *para que* "in order that" occurs in Spanish the verb must be in the subjunctive form. Every time *para que* or a similar conjunction occurs one can say to oneself, "Well, now there will be a subjunctive," and then one can listen for it. Furthermore, if the *para que* occurs after a past tense, the past subjunctive will be used and if after a present or future tense, a present subjunctive. By predicting to oneself the form which the speaker is to use, one will establish the grammatical pattern firmly in mind.

With the Spanish conjunction *aunque* "although" one may or may not use the subjunctive, depending upon the context. Again, by deciding in advance what the speaker is likely to use, one may develop an awareness of grammatical facts which no amount of memorizing of rules will ever equal.

Listening for grammatical data could be illustrated at length, but this is not necessary. What are important are the techniques of 1) identifying a grammatical pattern (whether broad or very limited in scope) and 2) trying to anticipate what forms the speaker is obliged to use, in accordance with the pattern which has been identified. This feature of anticipation parallels our own experience in speaking and is very valuable.

As supplementary to selective listening one may profitably use "selective reading." That is to say, during the process of reading one may concentrate on certain features and thus build up an awareness of these.

In general, one of our greatest problems in language learning is the abundance of strange data which is thrust at us more rapidly than we can assimilate it. We get nowhere if we attempt to take it all in at once. We must concentrate on certain features at a time, and in order to do this systematically and efficiently, we should employ selective listening.

THE FUTURE OF LANGUAGE LABORATORIES   WILLIAM N. LOCKE

Given the background offered by Locke's article, develop an argument in favor of the installation of a language laboratory for use by a class of students known to you.

What are some of the possible counter arguments against the installation of a language laboratory for the same group of students?

What are the implications of the research done by Keating? Lorge? Buka, Freeman, and Locke?

The use of films is mentioned by Locke as a potential contributor to language teaching. Try to design a language lesson that could be efficiently taught by film or videotape.

Modern man is the child of technology, which is influencing and shaping the progress of all his affairs. But though we be the children of technology, we must be its masters and not its slaves.[1]

I have chosen to start with this quotation for several reasons. It applies to language laboratories but has a broader purpose, to show the proper relationship of machines and man in general. In view of the extravagant claims that have been made for the language laboratory of the future, I wanted to set the reader's mind at rest immediately. There is no question but that machines of many kinds have an increasing role to play in education at all levels, but they are not going to take charge. They will upgrade the teacher, but not replace him.

Just as in commerce and industry machines have changed the nature of man's labor, so in intellectual activities machines are making themselves felt. Electronic computers, which can do routine arithmetical operations with the speed of light,

Reprinted by permission from *The Modern Language Journal*, 49 (1965), 294–303. This paper was presented at the public session, September 4, 1964, of the International Conference on Modern Foreign Language Teaching held under the auspices of the Pädagogisches Zentrum in the Kongresshalle, Berlin, Germany. The writer is professor of modern languages and director of libraries at the Massachusetts Institute of Technology.

[1] Julius A. Stratton, "Science and the Process of Management," *Proceedings of the International Management Congress, September 16–20, 1963*, New York: Council for International Progress and Management, 1963.

compress years of mathematical computations into hours, or minutes. This is well-known. But what of language? Language is a more personal part of the human being. The tongue is the mirror of the soul, if I may paraphrase a common saying.

Everyone knows that his native language is a most intimate expression of his inner being, not to be tampered with without risk. The mere thought of a computer processing human language seems to threaten a violation of privacy.

Nevertheless, computers are translating language, crudely, to be sure—no better than an elementary student—but the important point is that they are doing it as well as an elementary student. Computers are doing indexing, thousands of pages a year, with savings comparable to those from computation. Computer programs have also been written to make automatic abstracts of articles (not very satisfactorily). Others style text and compose pages by means of tape-operated photo-composing machines or typesetting machines.

As we witness these encroachments on the citadel of language, it is comforting to retreat behind the thought that all these applications deal only with the finished product, as it were, of someone's mind, and this is true. In all these cases words are treated just as though they were strings of mathematical symbols. The semantic part of language remains untouched by machines. Yet in each case, a machine has taken over part of a job that used to be done by a man. The quality of the output may not yet be very good, but it is improving; and as it improves, more and more of man's routine intellectual operations can and will be done by machines; machines are cheaper, faster, and their mistakes are usually more obvious. Teaching is not a routine operation, though drill is. Teaching machines are drilling machines, but the program represents a high degree of teaching skill.

HISTORICAL

Now I'd like to jump back in time fifty years or more, from modern computers to a simple apparatus for recording sound on a wax cylinder or disk, a triumph of engineering just as stimulating to the mind of those days as the computer is for us today. The first language laboratory was the first room in which some scientist used apparatus to study language. I may seem to be using the words "study language" ambiguously, but I don't think so. The person who studies wave forms on a kymograph or an oscilloscope is not bringing to bear any more sophisticated part of his mental equipment than the person who studies a foreign language in order to master it. Both are intellectual operations of a high order. Both involve analysis. In addition, learning a language involves a great deal of memorization.

The name "language laboratory" was coined for a room in which equipment was used to help study language long after *phonetics laboratory* and *experimental phonetics* were applied to the scientific study of speech sounds and intonation by Rousselot.[2]

Until the 1930's "phonetics laboratory" was used for the most part instead of "language laboratory," and that was quite proper because the laboratory often combined the scientific study of speech, speech correction, and foreign language instruction.[3]

As early as 1929 over 200 students a year at Middlebury College French Summer School in Middlebury, Vermont were taking phonetics courses which required five hours a week of class work, and one hour a week in the phonetics laboratory. Listening, repeating, and memorizing phrases was an integral part of the course. The phrases were chosen to exemplify the sounds of French.[4] Ten booths providing sound isolation were set up, each with a record player, earphones, and a mirror for watching lip movements. Moreover, there was a recording machine in the next room and the voice of each student was recorded as he read a selection in French at the beginning of the course and again at the end.

I mention this installation because although it was not the first, it probably came nearer to the modern conception of what a laboratory should do than any other of the period. Not only that, but the importance of records for drill exercises, and of recording the student's voice to let him hear himself and evaluate his own progress, was imparted to over 5,000 teachers of French who attended the Summer School between 1930 and 1950. Smaller numbers in the German, Italian, and Spanish Schools were also involved. The rapid acceptance of the language laboratory in the United States is in no small measure due to the laboratory experience of a whole generation of teachers at Middlebury. I am happy to have this opportunity to pay tribute to the farsighted work at Middlebury, where I was the laboratory technician for a few summers, since nothing has been published concerning this really seminal laboratory operation.

The story of the rapid spread of language laboratories is too well-known for me to detail it here. It began immediately after the end of the second World War, first with disks and wire recorders. Then the great revolution came with the importation into the United States of the concept of the Magnetophone, using a paper tape with an iron-oxide coating. This is a truly international invention. The oxide coating is a Swiss invention developed in Germany; mylar, the nearly unbreakable plastic base, is French; and the two were put together and mass-produced in the United States.

Labs in schools received further great impetus with the availability of funds from the U.S. government, paying half the cost of the equipment for any

[2]Pierre Jean Rousselot, *Principes de phonétique experimentale*, Paris: A. Welter, 1897.

[3]Ralph H. Waltz, "Language Laboratory Administration," *The Modern Language Journal*, Vol. XVI, No. 3 (December, 1931), pp. 217-227.

[4]Nicolette Pernot, *Exercises de Pronounciation Française à l'usage des étudiants anglo-saxons* (Editions Phonomatiques), Paris: Rouart, Lerolle et Cie, 1932. The book was accompanied by five records.

publicly-supported school. A current estimate which I owe to Dr. Alfred S. Hayes, Head of Research and Special Projects at the Center for Applied Linguistics in Washington, is that there are now between 6,000 and 7,000 installations in secondary schools and perhaps 1200 or more in colleges and universities in the U.S.[5]

As a matter of general interest I have collected estimates of the numbers of laboratories in as many other countries as possible. Like the figures above, these are subject to the reservation that no definition of "language laboratory" was furnished. The following estimates have been supplied to me, as of the summer of 1964, by those indicated, and I want to take this opportunity to thank them:

> *Australia*—16 (Miss Kathleen McPhee, University of Melbourne)
> *Belgium*—40 (my own guess)
> *Denmark*—5 (Dr. Max Gorosch, University of Stockholm)
> *England*—about 150 (Dr. J. A. Harrison, Director of the National Committee for Audio-Visual Aids in Education)
> *Finland*—3 perhaps (Dr. Gorosch)
> *France*—152 (The Cedamel Company, Paris)
> *Germany*—150 to 200 (Mr. I. A. Höfig, Arbeitskreis zur Förderung und Pflege wissenschaftlicher Methoden des Lehrens und Lernens)
> *Holland*—15 (Dr. M. Buning, Language Laboratory, Vrije Universiteit, Amsterdam)
> *Japan*—over 200 (Prof. Mitoji Mishimoto, kindness of Mr. Harald Gutschow of Berlin)
> *Norway*—4 (Dr. Gorosch)
> *Sweden*—1 (Dr. Gorosch)
> *United Kingdom*—250 to 300 (Mr. R. H. Milner of the British Council)

ELEMENTARY SCHOOLS

It is striking that there are practically no figures available for language laboratories in elementary schools. For the most part the question has simply been dismissed by saying that laboratories are too expensive to provide them for the very large number of children at the elementary level. This reasoning is suitable for a business manager, but it seems to me that language teachers should approach the matter from a more idealistic point of view. Little experimentation has been done, though excellent results have been obtained in a few places, l'Ecole Active Bilingue, in Paris, for instance.

[5] Several hundred of these laboratories are in private schools or universities, which are ineligible to receive government funds. In these cases the laboratories have often been financed through gifts of graduates or of parents of students. It is also true that, in spite of more difficult financing, many of the better installations are in private institutions. In the United States the quality of the teaching and of the student body is at least as high in many private institutions as in the public schools.

Pre-adolescent children learn to speak languages easily by imitation. There-fore, the best time to start one or more foreign languages is in elementary school. I doubt if anyone who has ever taught a foreign language at that level, as I have, would debate the correctness of those two statements.[6] In the United States we have considerable opposition from administrators who claim that the curriculum in elementary school is already too full to introduce language work. This they always say at all levels. We also have extensive opposition, which I would characterize as "disloyal," from secondary school teachers of foreign languages. As the reason for their objection they allege the shortage of experi-enced teachers for elementary language instruction. Secretly they feel that they, and only they, know how to teach beginning language. One suspects that another reason for their opposition is that they only know how to teach beginning language.

To continue my line of reasoning concerning elementary schools, the labora-tory is so effective at higher levels that it could be expected to be even more so here, and to further improve and accelerate the pre-adolescent's progress. Only when we know how effective the laboratory is, can we know whether it is worth trying to find the money to pay for it.

Perhaps I might mention briefly the very extensive teaching of French by television in elementary schools of the United States, England, Canada, and a number of other countries. It is relevant because research[7] conducted under a grant from the United States Office of Education, by Professor Ralph Garry of the School of Education of Boston University, clearly shows that television teaching is effective only if the lessons are followed up in the classroom, either by a teacher who knows French, or by a teacher who does not know French but who uses records or tapes containing supplementary review materials and drills. The latter situation obviously calls for a language laboratory.

With between 2 and 2½ million elementary school children taking French by television, some with excellent, some with deplorable results, the secondary schools have begun to receive many pupils who have had two or three years of French. It is the arrival of these pupils which has crystallized the opposition of secondary school teachers to elementary school language programs. Overtly and covertly they have carried on the battle against them and have succeeded in many cities in persuading administrators who had frequently adopted them as a result of pressure from parents, to drop them. One strategy has been to try to prove that pupils entering secondary school with previous French do no better, in the beginning courses, into which they are usually put, than pupils with no previous

---

[6]See, for example, Wilder Penfield, "The Uncommitted Cortex," *Atlantic Monthly*, Vol. CCXIV, No. 1 (July, 1964); also his earlier historic work, "The Learning of Languages," *Speech and Brain Mechanisms* (FL Bulletin No. 62), New York: Modern Language Associa-tion of America, 1959.

[7]Unpublished, but available in mimeographed form from the Modern Language Project, 16 Arlington Street, Boston, Massachusetts.

French. These courses tend to use a traditional grammar and reading approach. Examinations are based on these skills rather than on speaking ability. In spite of this, and not surprisingly, pupils with previous French often do better.

SECONDARY SCHOOLS

On the secondary level the large number of laboratories in the United States and the growing number in other countries attest to the interest of teachers and administrators. True, a certain number are "fad labs," installed because someone thought the school had to have one in order to be up to date, and sometimes over the objections of the language teachers. In one such case, a high school teacher told me, "Yes, we're going to have a lab next fall, and I don't know what I'm going to do with it. They might as well put an organ in my classroom and tell me to play it."

Any new development may have this unfortunate side effect, but young people do learn to speak and understand spoken language better with the aid of a laboratory, provided the teacher is interested. Let me quote from P. R. Léon's excellent book, *Laboratoire de langues et correction phonétique.*[8] Based on extensive research and personal observation he writes: "Aux Etats-Unis, le même phénomène a eu lieu, et continue souvent encore. Les professeurs décident que les élèves n'aiment pas les machines. Un jour enfin lorsque le professeur est convaincu de l'efficacité du laboratoire, les élèves se mettent a y croire également-ment." In the rest of what I have to say I will assume that we are dealing with a teacher who is eager, or at least willing, to use the means at his or her disposal to do the best possible job of teaching.

This job is defined by Elton Hocking in his fine book, *Language Laboratory and Language Learning,*[9] as follows: "The adoption of a technology is, of course, much more than the invention and development of equipment. It is, instead, the creation and improvement of a man-machine system for teaching languages." Of course, much of this "creation and improvement of the man-machine system" has been done and will be done for the individual teacher by others. Just as textbooks are written by those who combine the skills of teaching and textbook writing, so those who are gifted in language laboratory techniques will devise exercises and create materials. Complete courses of study which integrate classroom, laboratory, and homework into an intelligent whole have been badly needed and are beginning to appear.

It has probably been sufficiently stressed in the literature that buying tapes of the exercises of a conventional textbook, then having the student listen to them, repeat them, or respond to them in the laboratory is a poor imitation of

[8] Paris: Librairie Marcel Didier, 1962, p. 220.

[9] Monograph No. 2, Washington, D.C.: Department of Audiovisual Instruction, National Education Association of the United States, 1964, p. 19.

effective laboratory work. In fact, many of the shortcomings of laboratories in the past can be traced to the use of this type of material. Yet commercial tapes may have one advantage over those made by the average teacher. They have usually been prepared by native speakers of the language who are not suffering from mike fright. On the other hand, some of these native speakers use an artificial diction instead of normal conversational pronunciation and intonation, which is what our students should learn first.

Teaching materials including laboratory exercises need to be designed differently for different levels of instruction, then used at the levels for which they are designed. This may seem obvious, but in the desire for a wider market, authors and publishers often claim application of their materials at many levels. I remember my feeling of shock when, during the last war, I got a charming letter from a girls' secondary school saying that they were enjoying using a textbook on military French, which a colleague and I had designed for liaison officers.

Because of differences in the maturity of students and in their command of their native language, materials and methods have to be adapted. Also the amount of supervision and the discipline needed at different levels results in various language laboratory techniques. If, in general, secondary school teachers in the United States recommend working with an entire class simultaneously in the laboratory whereas university professors prefer the library system, where students go and do their work in the lab at their own convenience, this is based more on the different organization of the student's day at the two levels than on any different philosophy of teaching methods.

Teachers themselves often benefit from a laboratory in a way that is rarely listed among its advantages. This is the effect on their own facility in the language. To the extent that high-quality tapes are used, the teacher has an opportunity for repeated contact with a good model. Many teachers have no chance to use their foreign language outside the classroom; so recordings give them a refreshing opportunity to hear a native speaker. Too, in preparing tapes the teacher is impelled to adopt a high standard of performance by the fact that he will hear himself and that others will hear him. This exercise has beneficial results, as I know from personal experience. In other words, benefits to the teachers are not limited to secondary school but extend to the universities, where we have teachers who cannot speak the language they teach. The less said about them the better.

UNIVERSITIES

In universities as in the later years of secondary school, advanced work may be done in the laboratory. Literary masterpieces of prose, poetry, and the drama may be studied for the expressive features introduced by the speaker.[10] There has been an active group in the United States headed by Mrs. Jeanne Pleasants of Columbia University, a respected phonetician and a pioneer in language laboratory methodology, which has for a number of years been studying applications of the laboratory to the teaching of literature. Mrs. Pleasants publishes a *Newsletter* full of valuable suggestions for those interested.[11]

A major application of the university language laboratory is for training teachers not only in the language they will teach but also in the use of the language laboratory. Since most teachers teach the way they were taught, rather than the way they were taught to teach, it is doubly important that the laboratory be used and thoroughly integrated with classroom work in teacher-training institutions. The best practices and the most complete and flexible equipment must be used. This unfortunately is not generally the case in the United States. The majority of our teacher-training institutions have not had language laboratories at all. In fact, I suspect that the majority still do not. The teacher-training institutions in our country have been under strong attack for poor teaching, antiquated methods and philosophy.[12]

Fortunately, the summer institutes run by universities under contract with the United States Office of Education have given many beginning teachers a brief exposure to a language laboratory. From the answers to a questionnaire sent out by Dr. Elton Hocking of Purdue University in 1962,[13] it is evident that a shortage of adequately trained teachers is a major hindrance to effective operation of language laboratories. He writes: "by an overwhelming majority . . . the most serious handicap was identified as 'teachers' lack of special training" (p. 41).

At last materials are beginning to appear which are effective for the training of teachers as well as for students. Particularly good are a set of tapes and a book, *La Structure de la langue française; Pattern drills in French for the Language Laboratory*, by Theodore Mueller.[14] We can expect more contributions in this field soon, as its importance is now widely recognized.

[10]Only "the student who can pronounce a poem correctly can grasp its complete significance." Pierre Delattre, "Le Français et les laboratoires de langue," *Esprit* (November, 1962), p. 598.

[11]Available on subscription from *Newsletter*, General Editor, Language Laboratory, Columbia University, New York 27, New York.

[12]See Dr. James Bryant Conant, *The Education of American Teachers*, New York: McGraw-Hill, Inc., 1963.

[13]*Op cit.*, pp. 37–46.

[14]Available from the Wayne State University Modern Language Audio-Visual Research Project, Detroit, Michigan: book $5.00, tapes $154.50. Reviewed by Edward M. Stack in *The Modern Language Journal*, Vol. XLVI, No. 7 (November, 1962), p. 324, ". . . in these days of extreme lack of truly effective tapes for the lab it is a pleasure to be able to recommend this well-prepared set which is so adaptable to all texts. The students using these tapes will immediately be involved in an active and systematic learning experience, rewarding to student and teacher alike. Prof. Mueller and his colleagues in this project are to be congratulated."

EFFECT OF EQUIPMENT ON METHODS

Let us turn now to the effect that laboratory equipment may have on methods. The word laboratory implies the presence of equipment, which differentiates it from a classroom, but it is what is done with the equipment that is important. In most laboratories the teacher uses, or perhaps one should rather say the students use, tape-recording equipment to provide a model for their imitation, drills to which they are to respond, and facilities for testing.

Whatever the equipment, it should have two principal effects on teaching methods. The first is negative. It should not get in the way. It should be simple enough to operate and flexible enough to allow the teacher to do anything he needs to do in the teaching process. These are fairly difficult requirements. Simplicity of operation means a minimum of controls. The ideal would be to have none, so that the operation would be completely automatic; but this is in direct contradiction to my second requirement of flexibility. Flexibility means the possibility of recording the student's voice, both in order that he may evaluate his own performance and for testing. It means the possibility of monitoring, or two-way communication between teacher and student.[15] It means the student can stop his tape to give time to ponder a reply. It may mean facilities for immediate playback of the last few words.

Every added feature of flexibility means more complexity of equipment and may mean more knobs and buttons, more delays and errors which interrupt the learning process. Much has been done, more needs to be done, to rationalize equipment controls and make them as automatic as possible.

Flexibility entails not only complexity of equipment but also additional cost. This has to be justified on the same basis that one justifies equipment for other laboratories, physics, for instance. There are many instruments in a physics laboratory which are only used part of the time, for particular experiments, for students on a certain level, by the teachers who teach certain courses. The same must be true of a good language laboratory. Not all the possibilities of the equipment will be used all the time, but they must be there when they are needed.

The second effect of equipment on teaching is positive. It helps the teacher to do things which he could not do before. As has been pointed out ever since the introduction of the first recordings into language teaching, you can now have an unchanging model for the student's imitation. I like Hocking's analogy: the "teacher's repetitions can be only approximate and they are thus a moving target for the student; the machine presents a stationary bull's eye."[16]

The laboratory has made possible the evolution of a new rationale of drill: starting with the original recordings, without pauses, designed for memorization,

---

[15]"Il est pourtant très important que l'étudiant soit contrôlé. S'il répète cent fois la même erreur celle-ci va s'ancrer plus profondément au lieu de se corriger," Léon, *op. cit.*, p. 129.

[16]*Op. cit.*, p. 107.

then recordings with pauses to allow time for repetition or response, then various kinds of pattern drills, substitution, expansion, and recently programmed instruction. A first-rate treatment of drill procedures by Gustave Mathieu bears the misleading title, "A Brief Guide to Sound Labmanship."[17] Another good one is Paul Pimsleur's "Pattern Drills in French."[18]

EFFECT OF METHODS ON EQUIPMENT

The ideal relationship between teaching methods and equipment is that of the hen and the egg. You can't decide which one came first. They had to evolve together. The evolution of teaching methods, as mentioned above, has brought into being new types of equipment. Just entering the picture is programmed instruction, which requires a pause button to stop the master tape while the student reflects. When he releases the button, the tape advances and gives him the answer he should have found. In one application the student repeats the correct answer, then both the answer and his repetition are recorded and instantly played back to him to drive the point home. All the elements of this equipment are within the present technology; so, as research shows what elements of programmed instruction are valuable, the necessary facilities can be incorporated into all language laboratories. There has been rapid development in the last few years and there is every reason to believe that it will continue. It is a fortunate coincidence for the proponents of the teaching machine that the language laboratory offers a ready-made setting for the testing of their ideas.

Perhaps I might be excused if I mention one or two personal experiences with the effect of teaching methods on equipment. Five years ago, when we installed our first lab at Massachusetts Institute of Technology we bought 20-minute endless-loop cartridges—20 minutes was considered a good length; the students could go through the lesson twice in an hour. We decided on cartridges to eliminate waste of time in rewinding. Little by little we have found that shorter drills and exercises are more effective. All of our cartridges are now 10 minutes or less; that is, except for selections of prose or poetry for advanced students.

Another personal reminiscence concerns the value of recording the student's voice and letting him hear it. Having worked in the Middlebury College laboratory described above and having observed the rapid improvement in performance when a student recorded his voice and played it back on the Brush Mirrophone before the war, I became a firm proponent of the record-compare laboratory. I

[17] *The Modern Language Journal*, Vol. XLIV, No. 3 (March, 1960), pp. 123–126. Mathieu is also the editor of the invaluable *ML Abstracts*, available from Professor G. Mathieu, Chairman, Department of Foreign Languages and Literature, Orange State College, Fullerton, California.

[18] *The French Review*, Vol. XXXIII, No. 6 (May, 1960), pp. 568–576.

can't help relating a conversation with Professor André Malécot of the University of Pennsylvania, who visited us at Massachusetts Institute of Technology last year. As we walked back from lunch he was arguing that letting the student record his voice and then listen to it is a waste of time. He happened to be carrying a new moving-picture camera, and I asked him about it. He said he and his wife were going skiing and were going to take pictures of each other so that they could study their form and improve it.

This evidence and the evidence of musicians, actors, and public speakers who record their performance in order to study it, clearly indicates to me the desirability of providing for recording in the laboratory.

Hearing and speaking are closely related. Let us take two statements: "You can't hear yourself while you're talking,"[19] (obviously we do hear ourselves while talking but we don't perceive the detail), and "you can't pronounce anything that you can't hear."[20] If these statements are both true, as I have every reason to believe they are, then it follows that the student can hear how he says something only by recording his voice and playing it back. The audio-active laboratory is erroneously claimed by its proponents to help in this.[21] It cannot. All it does is to attenuate the voices of others; at best it gives one the illusion of being in a room alone. The physiological and psychological factors that prevent you from hearing your own voice objectively are still present.

The great advance provided by the complete language laboratory is that it can break the vicious circle described above. By interposing recordings in the cycle, hear model—speak, you get a new cycle which provides for self-improvement, hear model—speak—hear model again—hear own speech.

On the basis of my teaching experience I believe improvement in pronunciation is a stepwise process. You hear the model and you hear your own imitation. You estimate the difference. You try again and narrow the gap, each time setting your sights higher, so to speak. In time the individual reaches a plateau, his natural limit at the moment. This may be raised by further practice over a period

---

[19]"Elle énoncait d'abord le principe bien connu mais toujours oublié qu'on n'entend jamais ses propres fautes lorsqu'on parle une langue étrangère." Jeanne Vidon-Varney (Pleasants), *Pronunciation of French: Articulation and Intonation*, Ann Arbor, Michigan: Edwards Brothers, 1933, cited by Léon, *op. cit.*, p. 33.

[20]". . . la voix ne reproduit que ce que l'oreille entend. En d'autres termes un sujet ne sait réaliser avec certitude que ce qu'il est capable de contrôler." Alfred Tomatis, *L'Oreille et le langage*, Paris: Les Editions du Seuil, 1963, p. 104.

Léon, *op. cit.*, pp. 132–133, gives several other references on this point, summarizing as follows: "Mais une chose est certaine—quel que soit le moyen par lequel l'oreille est ameneé à entendre le son nouveau—*si ce son n'est pas perçu correctment il ne sera jamais reproduit correctement*, ou seulement par hasard. *Le role de l'audition est primordial.* La première fonction du laboratoire sera donc l'entrainement auditif, ce qui n'exclut nullement un entrainement à l'expression orale parallèle, bien au contraire."

[21]"To Record or Not," *The Modern Language Journal*, Vol. XLIV, No. 6 (October, 1960), pp. 278–279.

of time up to another plateau which seems the best he can do unaided. The laboratory introduces new possibilities. I have repeatedly seen students reach their individual plateau outside the lab, then go on to improve their performance in the laboratory. Again a plateau is reached, and it in turn may be raised with the aid of individual corrective work by a trained phonetician. The question of whether each adult has an individual plateau beyond which no amount of assistance will take him remains open, though it seems probable. In some way very young children seem to be able to attain native performance in a foreign language without these plateaus along the way. This ability drops off sharply at adolescence, hence the importance of starting a first foreign language young.

In view of the above, it is clear that I disagree strongly with those who would postpone recording until the later stages of instruction, for instance, James M. Watkins: "in a beginning course, though it may be chiefly based on pattern assimilation as it is here, student *recording* is actually of little real value. In the beginning course, therefore, our students use the master machine alone as just described and record only when taking a quiz. In the more advanced courses, however, and in phonetics particularly, facilities for individual recordings are indispensable."[22]

As to the statement that recording is indispensable in phonetics, this is true, but here the implication is that the work in phonetics takes place only in advanced courses. If this refers to phonetics theory and the teaching of corrective methods to teachers, these would indeed be in advanced courses, but the methods of phonetics must be used from the very beginning to establish a correct pronunciation. As everybody knows, once well rooted, wrong pronunciations are almost impossible to eradicate.

One of the debatable points in methodology is whether the student's native language shall be used or excluded at various levels. The audiolingual method, a lineal descendant of the direct method, has generally proscribed the native language. The student is to be given sequences of phonemes, the meaning of which he has to deduce from the context, verbal or visual or both and avoid all reference to his native tongue. At the same time the proponents of this method, pointing to the work of the structural linguists at the English Language Institute of the University of Michigan and elsewhere, are espousing the philosophy that a comparative analysis of the phonology and syntax of the native language and the foreign language should be made, then only the elements which differ in the two languages are to be taught. Implicit in this latter approach is the idea that the student will make a transfer of all the phonemes and grammatical constructions which the two languages have in common. Unless I am dreaming, this is a flat contradiction to the basic philosophy of the direct method.

A point which should be clarified is the question of whether one should start

---

[22]"The Library System and the Language Laboratory," *The French Review*, Vol. XXXIV, No. 1 (October, 1960), pp. 60-66.

pronunciation training with phonemics or phonetics. This argument is meaningless to me because I see the phoneme as a theoretical concept pertaining to *langue*, which is represented in *parole* by one or another of its allophones. So no one can pronounce a phoneme, only allophones. Nevertheless, a confusion does arise. For instance, P. Léon:[23] "La discrimination phonémique sur laquelle repose tout le système des oppositions significatives de la langue est évidemment l'essentiel, ainsi qu'il a été établi par le mouvement structuraliste. Il est donc entièrement justifié, au *stade élémentaire* de s'en tenir au système phonémique . . ." He does immediately contradict this statement: ". . . la distinction phonémique ne suffit pas à corriger un accent. La discrimination auditive doit, pour être efficace, sur le plan orthophonique, s'accompagner de jugements valeur du système phonique tout entier, en considérant l'aspect phonétique comme complémentaire de l'aspect phonémique." If Léon and Watkins are suggesting that correction of accent need not take place from the beginning, they are very wrong.

RESEARCH

Good research is the only sound basis for the language laboratory of the future. As Hocking says: "The language laboratory and the materials are too recent for us to know all the answers to the questions; indeed, we do not yet know all the questions."[24] Not enough research has been done and some of what has been done is woefully defective in design. When there are uncontrolled variables, concealed assumptions, or obvious bias in interpretation, the research can only do the profession more harm than good. Such is the case with the Keating report.[25] It was published after a campaign of publicity in the press announcing that Keating had shown language laboratories to be worthless, and with a large free mailing to school administrators; so a careful attempt has been made to determine exactly what the report proved and what it did not. What it proved was that Keating knew nothing about the language laboratories in the schools he studied, whether they were used, or how they were used. Apparently his principal purpose in publishing the report was to gain personal notoriety. In this he succeeded. In the April 1964 issue of *The Modern Language Journal* a symposium of four articles analyzes the Keating report in detail.

Quite the opposite is the case of the experimental work done by Sarah W. Lorge,[26] Bureau of Audio-Visual Instruction, New York City Board of Education.

---

[23] *Op. cit.*, p. 147.

[24] *Op. cit.*, p. 39.

[25] Raymond F. Keating, *A Study of the Effectiveness of Language Laboratories,* Institute of Administrative Research, Teachers College, Columbia University, New York, 1963.

[26] "Language Laboratory Research Studies in New York City High Schools: A Discussion of the Program and the Findings," *The Modern Language Journal,* Vol. XLVII, No. 7 (November, 1964), pp. 409–419.

This is carefully designed, well carried out, and completed by a thorough statistical analysis. For the first time the value of frequent laboratory sessions and the superiority of audio-active-record over audio-active labs is clearly shown. Another good job is that by Peter Doyé at the Pädagogische Hochschule, Berlin.[27] This is careful, thoughtful work which should be imitated. One would appreciate a few more details about the *modus operandi*. Were the students' voices recorded and played back to them? This is not clear.

A program of research of immediate application to language laboratory equipment is reported in two papers, "Language Learning and Frequency Response," by M. Buka, M. Z. Freeman, and W. N. Locke,[28] and a second now being prepared for publication. Studies were made of the ability of American students to distinguish phonemic contrasts in German and in French under different conditions of frequency response of the language laboratory equipment. To summarize the results: as to discrimination, a system frequency response of less than 7,300 cycles per second and especially below 5,000 cycles per second prevented a substantial number of high school students, who had never studied a foreign language, from perceiving phonemic contrasts in German and French. Low frequency limitation, when frequencies below 500 and 1,000 cycles per second respectively were filtered out, gave much the same picture; i.e., the difficulty of recognition of unfamiliar phonemic contrasts increased. Consonants are more affected than vowels by both high and low frequency limitation and German shows a much clearer picture than French. Evaluation of the students' pronunciation on the whole supported the conclusions of the discrimination tests.[29]

These results supply a small part of the answer to the puzzle as to what the specifications for language teaching equipment should be, confirming the conclusions of Alfred S. Hayes in his book, *Language Laboratory Facilities*, which is a major work of synthesis.[30] Among the most valuable parts of the book is the appendix: "A Sample Procurement Specification." This is the epitome of what one needs to know to buy a good laboratory, except that it envisages mainly

[27] Reported in his article, "Französischunterricht im Sprachlabor" in *Programmiertes Lernen und programmierter Unterricht*, Heft I, 1964, pp. 32–37.

[28] *International Journal of American Linguistics*, Part II, Vol. 28, No. 1 (January, 1962), pp. 62–79.

[29] The experiment was conducted as follows: Pair tests were used. Two words differing by a single phoneme were pronounced. Then one was repeated and the student indicated by a check mark in the proper column on a test sheet whether the first or the second member of the pair was repeated. This was for discrimination. As the student heard each member of the pair the first time, he repeated it. This was recorded and later evaluated by native speakers. This gave pronunciation scores.

[30] Alfred S. Hayes, "New Media for Instruction, 4," United States Office of Education Bulletin 20124, 1963, No. 37.

individual tape recorders at student positions, which is not the simplest to operate, the most flexible, or the most trouble-free equipment. The future of the laboratory belongs to automatic, remote-control equipment.

As one reads Hayes' book, that of Tomatis, and the other research which bears on language laboratory equipment, one is discouraged by how little of it there is and by the difficulty of drawing practical conclusions from it. Hayes admits that his specifications are incomplete.[31] Tomatis claims that the frequency response of all equipment used for the teaching of English should go up to 12,000 cycles per second.[32] He does not mention how low the frequency response must go nor how flat it must be.

One thing has been clear for a long time. It is that the best criterion for excellence of sound reproduction in the laboratory is naturalness. The engineers' criterion of intelligibility is worthless in the foreign language teaching context. But there is no scientific definition of naturalness. May I urgently recommend to any language teacher who is interested and able to work with engineers that we need far better sound quality than the average laboratory has, and that we will not get it until we can prove by further research what happens when we do not have it.

THE FUTURE

My title is *The Future of Language Laboratories* and it may seem that I have been a long time getting to it. Yet one can hardly talk of the future except in terms of the present. In talking about the laboratories of yesterday and today I have mentioned the directions in which they should develop. Moreover, in a very real sense the future is already here. Around us, unknown perhaps, are people doing outstanding work. The best methods and the best equipment will be imitated. Careful research with publication of the results is a major item for the future of the laboratory. It is needed on the part laboratories can play in elementary schools. It is needed to determine the best proportions of listening to tapes, repeating, recording, and comparing at different levels. This is an extremely difficult area and studies so far have been inconclusive. It is needed on the quality of tape, on the length of pauses, how many voices should be used, how many repetitions, what is really most effective in helping ability to learn, as opposed to motivation. The same is true of the contribution which a visual component can play. About the best that can be said so far is that it improves motivation. I agree with Howard Lee Nostrand of the University of Washington when he writes, "In my opinion, the sound film is a more effective medium than tape for

[31] *Op. cit.,* p. 60. "Some things are definitely known and others are disputed or imperfectly understood."

[32] *Op. cit.,* p. 125. "La linéarité qu'il faut exiger est absolument nécessaire jusqu'a 12,000 hz, par exemple, pour l'anglais."

modeling a foreign language and the accompanying behavior patterns. I hope that audio-visual models will become more usable in language labs, with 8-mm sound projectors and cartridges. Meanwhile the showing of a film can usefully be followed by audio exercises which use the sound track of the film and which prompt the recall of the visual component."[33]

As to the equipment of the future there seems no reason to believe that the sound system will be basically different from that of today. New facilities will be added, no doubt, but magnetic tape with its high-fidelity capabilities and its ease of recording, erasing, and re-recording will continue to be the heart of the language laboratory. The contribution of films, slides, and other pictorial material to enrich the auditory has been badly neglected, but it seems likely that within ten years video tape or some similar medium will be widely used. Then we shall have the same advantages of flexibility and reduced cost in the visual domain that we now have in the auditory.

Another area that should be explored is that of stereo or binaural sound. The remarkable results with music and drama should not be overlooked. Many shudder at the further expense, but again I say that it is our first duty to learn what is best for pedagogy, then worry about the cost afterward. Money for new experiments is relatively easier to get than money for day-to-day operation.

The introduction of programmed instruction will mean that the laboratory will play a larger part than it has previously. The shortage of qualified teachers and the success of experiments in the teaching of foreign languages by audio-visual media without experienced language teachers[34] probably indicates a large extension of this sort of teaching both in and out of the laboratory. The concept of independent learning in the laboratory makes one wonder if it might not come to be called the Language Learning Center, as someone has suggested.

At the same time, there is a real possibility that decentralization may change this picture. In residential colleges in the United States there is already a feeling on the part of administrators that too many separate spaces have to be provided for each student. He has the room in which he sleeps, a seat in a classroom, a seat in the library, and one or more places in various laboratories. The question is being asked whether the total amount of space required by the university cannot be radically reduced by giving the student remote access from his room or from an adjoining study area to the laboratories, to recorded lectures, and to the library. Under this plan each student would have a closed circuit television apparatus with which he would see and hear the lessons he needs, plus the possibility of interacting with a large program source and of calling upon a teacher

[33]Private communication to the author.

[34]See, for example, Charles E. Johnson, Joseph S. Flores, Fred P. Ellison, and Miguel Riestra, *The Development and Evaluation of Methods and Materials to Facilitate Foreign Language Instruction in Elementary Schools,* 805 W. Pennsylvania Avenue, Urbana, Illinois: University of Illinois Foreign Language Project, 1963.

for assistance. There is no reason at all why the language laboratory should not be decentralized also, with individual student positions in the library, in the students' living areas, or even in their homes.

A step in this direction is a new lab under construction for Ohio State University. At the other end of the spectrum is the design for the new laboratory for Middlebury College where individual rooms will be provided for the student.[35] This is not as much of an extravagance as it may seem because, if the rooms are properly designed with walls which are not parallel and adequate sound treatment on the floor and ceiling, a loud-speaker can be used instead of earphones, giving much better sound quality. Still, one wonders why the final logical step was not taken: why bring the students together in one building at all? Why not instead provide these rooms at strategic points in the dormitories, the library, and other buildings on the campus?

In non-resident universities we shall see in our lifetime students attending the university, doing laboratory work, and taking their examinations, all by means of a special television receiver and console which they can rent for the duration of their period of instruction. This is made possible by the mammoth computer as a public utility with service to subscribers at a distance over telephone lines, which is only a year or two away. It will profoundly affect education as well as business.

Over the years the original concept of the phonetics laboratory combining the work that now goes on in the language laboratory with research in phonetics has been lost. This is unfortunate, but inevitable with the multiplication of language laboratories; for many of the teachers who are now using laboratories know little of phonetics. Still, many of the devices used in phonetics research or their offspring should eventually be brought into the language laboratory to assist in corrective work—the sound spectrograph, the speech stretcher, and apparatus for measuring loudness, pitch, and syllable rate, for instance.

Translating machine research can also be counted on later for computer programs which will evaluate the correctness of sentences produced by a learner, since identification of syntactical construction is a prerequisite to translation. As to the spoken language, it is more resistant to machine processing, but eventually we should also have programs to evaluate the acceptability of pronunciation and intonation.

To conclude, the major changes that I see in teaching methods in the laboratory in the next decade involve the techniques of programmed instruction, thus making the student more independent of the teacher; a greater emphasis on the visual, to provide improved motivation and a better understanding of the cultural background of the language to be learned, and large-scale decentralization of the laboratory.

[35] Hocking, *op. cit.,* pp. 170–171.

As I see it, the teacher will do less "live" presentation of factual material to classes of students, less drill, but more advisory, consultative, and corrective work with individual students. He will be freed from the drudgery of repetition required to help the student build auditory discrimination, the mastery of the paradigms, and the rules of grammar. He will be deprived of the questionable joy of delivering the same lectures annually to captive audiences. In their place he will have to work harder than ever finding, organizing, and preparing audio and visual materials. The technological revolution of language teaching is upon us. Machines are willing slaves, cheaper and more reliable than human beings. We shall have to master them, for I am afraid that those who are not willing to make the effort to master the machines will be replaced by others who are.

Reading
and
Writing

Although the first two Parts deal with basic theory and with practice, that practice was in what modern theory holds as primary—speech, not writing. The subsequent development of the learner's competence in consecutive reading and of his skill in composition merits special consideration, which is given to it by the following writers.

Instruction in reading, even with an initial exclusively oral approach, begins within two or three months, and normally progresses until the student is able to read objective expository prose fairly easily. But literature presents new problems of interpretation—connotative and cultural. For years the teaching of English in non-Anglophone countries introduced students to literature through the work of such classical writers as Dickens, Thackeray, Defoe, and Shakespeare, with perhaps a daring inclusion of H. G. Wells. More recently, contemporary writers are appearing in textbooks. But even current literature, perhaps especially current literature, poses for foreign students a formidable task of comprehension across the barrier of cultural differences. The deeper the difference, the more formidable the task.

True, students in an English-speaking country, such as Spanish-speaking students in the United States, have already dealt with some of the competing values in two cultures, but even they require sympathetic help as they attempt to understand literature reflecting what English teachers often like to refer to as the "Anglo-Saxon heritage."

Elliott, a British specialist in ESL teacher preparation, suggests that an elementary consideration in the approach to literary reading must be rigorous attention to the meaning of words, especially as that meaning is determined by context.

What to read in introducing literature is a problem which was solved empirically by Carroll, a young British teacher in an African situation, through enlisting the cooperation of his students in an evaluation experiment. Carroll and Elliott hold different views, however, about the need for close reading.

Povey, an American who has taught in Africa, describes the aims of teaching literature in an ESL program but warns that these will not be achieved unless the teacher helps students to avoid miscomprehension due to their reading in terms of their own cultural values. How cultural difference produces serious misunderstanding is further exemplified by Gladstone.

Pattison, an institutional colleague of Elliott, advocates a planned procedure in teaching a literary assignment, a procedure in which he includes discussion to induce the student to apply his personal experience.

For years the ESL teacher, especially if he was trained in the United States, complained that although theorists and textbook writers gave him all kinds of ideas and materials for beginning writing they neglected the problem of moving the student toward free use of the target language in sustained written composition. Within the past half dozen years, however, several ESL composition textbooks have been published. In this Part, six writers variously tackle the problem and in Part 4 Kaplan (Art. 34) supplies another indispensable dimension.

For Mrs. Arapoff, teaching composition means helping the student to organize his own experience through actually thinking about it, to select his material according to his purpose, and to move progressively from simple dialogue presentation to carefully reasoned argument. She supports her position with clear examples.

Dykstra and Paulston report that through an experimental application they found success in a method they call "guided composition," in which the rewriting of a model passage involved a controlled series of steps, each of which required the student, on his own, to make certain modifications in the model.

What to do about grammatical and syntactic errors in composition, guided or otherwise, is a perpetual source of trouble for the ESL teacher. Correct everything? Mark only a certain kind of error in any one composition? Maintain a sequential list of errors to be attended to during a course? Ignore all errors and let freedom—and creativity—reign? Out of a wealth of experience Knapp tells about a specific method for developing correctness and, as a bonus, offers a detailed check list for use in the classroom.

Sawyer and Mrs. Silver's article could be equally well assigned to Part 2; it is here because, although their emphasis is not upon the whole composition, they treat a long-tried ESL device, dictation, as a way to reduce error. Their practice may be usefully compared with that proposed by Knapp.

What are Elliott's assumptions about the teaching of new vocabulary in the reading lesson? Do you agree with them?

Do the sample questions presented by Elliott correspond to the types of questions suggested by Stevick? (Art. 9)

What would a lesson on the use of English dictionaries include if it were based on Elliott's recommendations? Would you add anything? Why?

And so we return to the classroom where a class is waiting for its English reading lesson. But we are faced with one initial difficulty. This is, that each teacher is different from all other teachers; furthermore, each class is different from all other classes. The details of a lesson depend so much on the individual teacher and his individual class that no outside adviser can say exactly what is to happen. All he can do is to lay down, and illustrate, certain principles in the hope that teachers, and those who train the teachers, may find them useful.

Here is the classroom, then, and here is the teacher standing ready with a book in his hand. Facing him is his class and each pupil has (we hope) a book at the ready. This morning the books are open at the beginning of a story and the lesson begins with the teacher reading aloud a paragraph or two. (Stories often lend themselves to some reading aloud by the teacher. Provided this is carefully prepared and is done well, it can form a valuable introduction to the lesson.) Having finished his reading, the teacher says to the class: "Now read on to the end of the story. Put your hands up when you have finished." Silence falls on the classroom while the pupils read to themselves.

We will assume that the passage which is now being read is the following extract from an Irish folk tale. This is about a woman who had three sons and one daughter. The eldest son was weak in the head and so the second son set out in search of the Nuts of Knowledge which would cure his brother. But the second son did not return from his mission and so the third boy went off to find the nuts. When he too did not return the sister went to try her luck and

Reprinted by permission from *English Language Teaching*, 17 (1962-63), 2.67-72, where this article appeared as the second of a series. A. V. P. Elliott, M.A. (Cambridge), is senior lecturer in English, Institute of Education, University of London.

after many adventures she reached the place where the nuts grew. The story continues:

> . . . Fedelma ate her supper and lay down under her magic coat, because she was very tired. Soon she was asleep. While she was sleeping she heard distant voices and the voices called her sadly. Then she woke up and knew that they were the voices of her two lost brothers. She got up and walked to the magic well; there were waves on the surface of the water and a big fish was swimming there. The nut tree stood near the well and its branches were creaking although there was no wind. It was midnight, and Fedelma knew that the nuts would soon fall from the tree. So she stood there near the well and watched the branch with its great red bunch of nuts. There was no wind, but the branch creaked again, the nuts fell, and the fish opened its mouth; but Fedelma held out her hand and caught the nuts while they were falling. Immediately, she knew everything. She knew that her brothers lay under the two stones and she knew how to bring them to life again. She took some water out of the well and poured it on the stones. The stones rolled away and her brothers rose and greeted her gladly and they all returned to their mother's house.

The pupils have now put up their hands to show that they have finished reading; and the teacher is ready to ask questions and to set his class thinking about what they have read. Here, then, are some questions which the teacher might ask:

1. "Fedelma went to sleep, and while she was sleeping she heard her brothers' voices. Do you think these voices were real, or did Fedelma hear them in a dream?"

2. "What do you think the voices said to her?"

(There is no certain answer to either of these questions. Their object is to put the pupils' imaginations to work and to provide the occasion for a little discussion in the class.)

3. "What were Fedelma's feelings when she came to the well?"

(A little prompting may be necessary: "Well, did she feel glad, or frightened, or excited? What do you think, John? And you, Peter?")

4. "What does the story tell us about the well? Do you see the well, John? Tell us about it."

(The first question gets the pupils' eyes down to the text; the second asks for a mental picture. The teacher can help to form this picture if necessary; the well is probably about four feet in diameter with a low stone wall round it, and it is in a forest.)

5. "The word *creaked* means a kind of noise. What kind of noise do you think it is, William? The branch creaked, didn't it? Yes, what else creaks? The door of this room, that's right. What else, Peter?"

(The pupils must be quite sure of the meaning of this word. We remember that one of our principles is precise understanding.)

6. "Luke, show us how Fedelma took the water out of the well."

(Pupils are required to mime the actions—in front of the class where everyone can see them—until a representation is given as exactly as possible. Once again we require precision, this time not in language but in action.)

It is not essential to ask as many as six questions on a short passage. There are times when pupils should be allowed to forge ahead in their reading, provided the teacher is satisfied that they can understand the text. Above all, over-questioning is to be avoided; nothing is worse than to see a class battered by a stream of questions, most of them unnecessary and unhelpful. Like everything in teaching this matter depends on the teacher's common sense and on his judgement of his class and of the text they are reading. Good questioning is the result, and only the result, of careful thought about the lesson before it is given.

Two further remarks must be made here, about language and about vocabulary. The specimen passage given above is written at a certain level of language; it is assumed that the language it contains has been taught and practised before the pupils meet it again in their reading. Most of the vocabulary should also be familiar, though the words *nuts, bunch,* and *creaked* may be new. The time for the teacher to deal with these new words is *not* at the beginning of the lesson. Pupils must learn to face passages in which there are some unfamiliar words, and they must be trained in ways of discovering their meanings. Once *nuts* has been discovered, perhaps in the dictionary, it should be possible to arrive at *bunch*. As we have already seen, *creaked* was selected for rather longer treatment as part of the training in precise understanding. It should be clear to the teacher that at this stage of English (perhaps the third year) pupils should not be encouraged to memorize a large vocabulary, for they should be concentrating on learning to use the essential structures of the language.

Returning once again to our classroom, where the lesson is more than half over, the teacher may decide to set the pupils reading a further passage or he may occupy the remainder of the time with some practice in reading aloud. The fact that the greater emphasis must be put on silent reading need not entirely preclude reading aloud, for which fiction is especially appropriate. But reading aloud is a waste of time unless it is done really well. The teacher's own model is important; and if he is lucky enough to have such things, he may use a tape recorder or record player to let his class hear English read by a reputable native speaker. Pupils or groups of pupils who are reading aloud should preferably stand facing the class, with the teacher facing them at the back of the room. The teacher is like the producer of a play. His job is to see that the pupils read clearly, audibly, and intelligently—that is, that they express the meaning of the passage without any extravagant or unnatural variations of stress or intonation. They must express the meaning: and so reading aloud can only take place after the passage has been read silently and after the necessary questions have been asked and answered, and after the passage has been fully understood.

We now turn to a different kind of lesson with a different kind of text. It is clearly of great importance that pupils should be trained to read for information and that such reading should be geared to work that is expected of them now or later in scientific and technical subjects. And so a great number of texts are needed which give information of this kind and which are written in language which pupils of different stages of linguistic ability can read. The following is a short specimen of this kind of material. It is written at a certain linguistic level, and in a book it would, of course, be illustrated by a map, diagrams, and pictures.

> Look at a map of Europe and find Holland. It is in the north-west corner of the continent, opposite England. You will see in the middle of Holland a big lake—or is it a sea? If your map is a good one, you will find that this lake or sea is cut off from the North Sea by a thick black line. This line represents a great wall which the Dutch built to separate the Zuyder Zee or, as it is now called, the Ijssel Lake, from the North Sea. Why did they build this wall? Because they wanted to take away the water from the Ijssel Lake and to turn the lake into dry land. Holland is a small country and it has a big population, so the Dutch want more land to grow food for their people.
>
> But how do they turn the lake into dry land? First of all, they choose a corner of the lake and they build a wall in the water to cut it off from the rest of the lake. They have to build this wall from boats and they use cranes to lift up and set down the materials necessary for building the wall. When the wall has been built, the water inside it, between it and the land, is pumped out until only mud remains. Then they must wait until the water in the mud has evaporated; and then at last crops are sown and the land which was once water begins to produce food for the people.

This short passage represents a kind of material which provides information. We believe that there should be a great deal of such material available to pupils both in and outside the classroom, on all manner of subjects and at different levels of language. It would not only provide general knowledge, but also satisfy the pupils' curiosity about the world they live in and—perhaps most important of all—it would provide a foundation for scientific and technical studies later on.

So far as the class work is concerned, this kind of reading material is particularly useful for training pupils in precise understanding. To this end, the following are examples of the questions which might be asked on the above passage:

1. (If the pupils have atlases) "Find the map of Europe in your atlases. Now put your fingers on Holland. Hold your atlases up and show me where it is."

(Atlases are used in the geography lesson: there is no reason why they should not also be used in the English lesson.)

2. "Put your fingers on that big lake in the middle of Holland. . . . That's right."

3. "Why did the Dutch build the wall between the Ijssel Lake and the North Sea?"

4. "Holland has a big *population*. What does that mean? . . . Well, look at your books again and see if you can guess what it means. . . . Yes, that's right, it means *people*, or more exactly *a number of people*. The population of Holland is eleven million. That's a lot of people for a small country. What is the population of this country?"

5. "How do the Dutch turn the water into dry land? What is the first thing they do? . . . Yes, that's right, they choose a corner of the lake and then they build a wall to cut it off from the rest of the lake."

6. "What do they use to build this wall? . . . Boats? Quite right; and what else? . . . yes, cranes. What does a crane look like? . . . Well, can anyone draw a crane on the board? . . . That's not bad, you've drawn the shape of a crane, but you've left out some important details." (There follows some discussion on cranes and how they work, together with some more drawings, until the class has a reasonably accurate idea of a crane.)

7. "What happens when the wall has been built? . . . Yes, the water is taken out. But how? . . . Yes, with pumps. The water is pumped out." (There follows some discussion about pumps. The class should learn what these are, if they do not know, and have some idea as to how they work. The English teacher is not expected to have, or to teach, a scientific knowledge of such things, but should know enough to give his pupils a precise—though not technical—understanding of the text.)

8. (The last question might deal with the word *evaporated*, or else ask the pupils what crops they think the Dutch grow on their reclaimed land.)

The passage on which these questions are asked is written at a certain level of language; it will be seen that the passive voice is used in it five times. Pupils who go on eventually to scientific or technical subjects must get used to the passive in their reading since it is so widely used in the kind of books and journals they will have to use. It should be noted that reading material of this kind does not easily lend itself to being read aloud.

FROM SIMPLIFIED TO "FULL" ENGLISH

For much of the English course reading material must inevitably be simplified —that is to say, it must be within the linguistic range of pupils at different levels of the language. It must either be specially written within a precise range, or texts in "full"—that is, unlimited—English must be re-written in simplified versions. (It is not enough to write in a simplified vocabulary; there must also be limitation of structure.) But the time will come when at least some pupils, those who reach the top of the secondary school, for example, should be moving from simplified to "full" English reading. By this time, they should have achieved a command of the essential structural items of the language, and have acquired a useful, though not a large, vocabulary.

Now is the moment for three important pieces of work. First, the pupils should be initiated into the use of the English dictionary. "Not until now?" some teachers may ask. No, not until now, except to check spelling. Young people are all too fond of finding long and fine-sounding words in a dictionary and using them (wrongly, of course) in their compositions. Furthermore, it is not easy to use a dictionary until one has a certain knowledge of the language.

What is meant by initiating pupils into the use of an English dictionary? In the first place, they should have some practice in finding a word quickly. Secondly, where more than one definition or synonym is provided they need practice in discovering which is relevant to the context in question. Thirdly, they need some direct instruction in the use and misuse of the dictionary: its use, as an aid to reading and as an instrument for checking the words they use in writing; its misuse, as a quarry for long and impressive words to be learned by heart.

The second piece of work to be undertaken at this stage is intensive practice in discovering the meanings of words from the context. The ability to do this is most necessary since, in reading "full" English, the use of the dictionary for every unfamiliar word will make reading intolerably slow.

The third necessary activity at this stage and indeed, through much of the English course, is quite simply a great deal of practice in reading a wide variety of material both in and out of class. Any school in which English is taught after the very early stage should provide a plentiful supply of books and magazines for both class and library reading. If it does not do so, or if administrators do not provide it with the money to do so, a great deal of the time devoted to English teaching is wasted.

19   THE BATTLE FOR   GEORGE R. CARROLL
        BETTER READING

What is your evaluation of Carroll's experiment? Can you think of additional ways of choosing the reading material for a group of students known to you?

Do you agree with Carroll's assumptions regarding the learning of vocabulary?

This article might well be subtitled *"From* a Young Teacher," not only to distinguish it from the ELT's section entitled *"For* the Young Teacher," but because it is an account of a problem faced by myself as a young teacher in teaching English as a second language to secondary school pupils in Zambia. Since it is a common problem—finding which books are suitable for any given pupils and discovering how to make the pupils read them—other teachers may be interested in my attempts to solve it.

Reprinted from *English Language Teaching*, 22 (October 1967), 34–40. The writer teaches in the Mungwi Secondary School, Kasama, Zambia.

The size of the problem was shown by an initial examination of the pupils' reading habits, which revealed that

(i) in class, they each had a copy of a "class reader," chosen for them by the teacher, and this was read aloud paragraph by paragraph round the class. In this way they read two or three books a term (10–12 weeks);

(ii) out of class, despite the existence of a fairly good library, they read very few books indeed, but numerous comics and picture-story magazines;

(iii) what few books they did read were their own unguided choice and either cheap gangster/sex stories which they found exciting and which they could read without much mental effort, or classics, especially nineteenth-century classics such as Dickens. This latter choice was dictated by a feeling among the more conscientious that they ought to read the classics, since the classics would be good for them, even if very difficult;

(iv) they took great pains to note down or score under and mark for future attention any unfamiliar word. Thus the reading book was usually attended by a dictionary; the reading was considerably slowed down; and in the long run, despite all the effort, the meaning of the word was wrongly or ineffectively learnt!

In addition, it soon became clear that their reading, or lack of it, was reflected in both the form and the content of their composition work. Indeed, it was the poor quality of their composition work indicating in its turn a lack of imagination and experience and ideas, that first caused my anxiety about their reading habits. Composition, after all, carries fifty per cent of the marks in their Cambridge School Certificate English Language examination—a strong motivating factor.

The first offensive in the battle for better reading was, therefore, to demonstrate to the students that, although their favourite comics and gangster/sex stories were exciting and easy to read, they had a harmful influence on their compositions. I was able to show this harmful influence in many of their own compositions, and in one in particular, written by a student at the beginning of his pre-School-Certificate year and entitled *An Amusing Adventure*. The following extract is typical of the whole composition:

> The boss was seated on a comfortable chair. The house was well furnished. The windows were expensively curtained. The room was filled with a good scent from flowers.
>
> "Hello Alex," he said in a hard tone. "I hope you haven't forgotten what you're here for!"
>
> "No, I haven't. Never in my life do I forget or have forgotten anything. The only thing is I am not giving you the money because you're a liar, a blackmailer and a hoodlum. People who want money work for it not in the way you do. By the way where's my Kay? If you have already hurt her I'm wanna gush your head in with one blow and your face's gonna run with purple blood and prepare for interminable slumber."
>
> "Kill him men," shouted the boss, "he's mad."
>
> A blow on the head finished me to be out of the way.

The cheap gangster/sex story characteristics are, of course, obvious: the short simple sentences; the slang and the tough talk; the untruthfulness to life; the poverty of ideas. Fortunately, they were also obvious to the pupils. Even the dullest of them could see that the mind of their fellow-pupil had been influenced for the worse, unbeknown to him, by his reading.

On the other hand, I had to admit to the pupils that, although I could show them in the above way that bad books had a harmful influence, I was unable to show them in a similar way that good books had a good influence. This is a point which still intrigues me and which, I think, deserves the attention of research students. In 1960, Dr. K. Lovell wrote in *Educational Psychology and Children* (p. 180): "Surprisingly enough, little direct evidence has been reported of the desirable effects of good reading matter, although in the writer's opinion it is hardly possible to deny that good literature may be beneficial to children. There are, however, many who stress the evil effects of bad literature." Later in this article, I shall submit some evidence of what I consider to be the desirable effects of good reading matter, and shall suggest that such evidence is to be found chiefly in the reactions, attitudes, and experiences of the readers and is, therefore, less tangible than the glaringly obvious harmful effects of bad books.

Another line of attack in the battle for better reading was to persuade them to read as quickly as possible (at least two books a week) without stopping to look up unfamiliar words in a dictionary. Here it was helpful to point out to them the difference between intensive and extensive reading, between, for example, the comprehension passages in their textbooks, which they *should* read slowly and thoroughly, finding out the meaning of each word, and novels and other books which they *should not* read slowly, but rather, quickly for enjoyment. There was general agreement that stopping to look up words did spoil the enjoyment of a good story, but it was apparent that many seemed to suffer from a sense of guilt if they read merely for enjoyment. If they did not make a conscious effort to learn new words, they could not feel that they were working hard. It was helpful to explain how the meanings of words could be learned from the context, and how the mind, after meeting the same word often enough in different contexts, would unconsciously come to know the meaning of the word. A personal anecdote also helped. I recalled that in my own schooldays I was an avid reader of the Hornblower novels by C. S. Forester, and that I was able to enjoy them, and no doubt profit from them, even though I did not know (and still do not) the meaning of many of the technical terms about the sea and ships.

The pupils were by now quite eager to stop listening to me and to get on with the reading. It was clear that the high claims that I had made for reading good books quickly would stand or fall by the actual books that I was going to offer them. I had brought with me to the class forty different books that I thought would be suitable, although I was not too happy about my selection, since my choice had been confined to the local booksellers' stocks. It is important to note here that I had brought forty *different* books. When ordering books, the teacher of English has a choice between ordering forty copies of one particular book or forty different books. If the volumes cost five shillings each, there will be no difference in the total cost. The differences lies in the fact that if he orders forty different books, his pupils have the chance to read forty books, whereas if he orders *forty* copies of one book, his pupils have the chance to read only *one* book.

Anyway, the question now was: would the books that I had chosen be really suitable for these Form 3 students of English as a second language? Would they like the books or not? To help me find out the answers to these questions, I asked them to regard their reading as an experiment and to fill in an assessment form for each book they read. They seemed quite excited and flattered to be asked to take part in such an experiment, and therefore did not regard the filling-in of numerous forms as a chore which detracted from any enjoyment they might have had from a book.

The assessment form included the following questions and instructions (there were other questions to test whether or not the book was in fact read):

Put a tick after the answer you agree with.
1. Had you read this book before?   Yes . . . . . .   No . . . . . .
2. Did you finish reading it?   Yes . . . . . .   No . . . . . .
3. How did you like it?   Very much . . . . . .
                                   Quite well . . . . . .
                                   A little . . . . . .
                                   Not at all . . . . . .

4. (a) Did you think this book was suitable for
          Form 3 students?   Yes . . . . . .   No . . . . . .
   (b) If your answer is 'No,' which form, if any,
          do you think it would be suitable for?   Form 1 . . . . . .
                                   Form 2 . . . . . .
                                   Form 4 . . . . . .
                                   Form 5 . . . . . .

At the end of term, an analysis of pupils' opinions was made by grouping together all the assessment forms for a particular title and finding out how many readers had liked the book very much, quite well, a little, or not at all. Some of the results are shown in the following table:

Title (simplified edition in some cases)	Very much	Quite well	A little	Not at all	Suitable for Form 3	Un-suitable	More suitable for Higher/ Lower Forms
The Moonstone	4	2	6	—	8	4	Higher
Salifu the Detective	7	1	—	—	6	2	Lower
The Silver Sword	7	2	2	—	7	4	Lower
Born Free	4	4	1	—	8	1	Lower
The Insect Man	2	1	3	1	4	3	Lower
The New Noah	5	4	—	—	7	2	Higher
A Pattern of Islands	4	5	3	5	9	8	Higher
The Kraken Wakes	4	6	2	—	8	4	Higher
The Island of Adventure	6	2	—	—	4	4	Lower
Strangers at Snowfell	7	—	—	—	6	1	Lower
The Otterbury Incident	3	3	3	—	6	6	Lower
People of the City	10	2	—	—	12	—	—
Mine Boy	6	2	1	—	6	3	Lower
Doctor at Large	3	3	2	—	4	4	Higher
The Thirty-Nine Steps	13	2	2	—	9	8	Lower

The popularity of the two books published in Heinemann's African Writers Series is evident and significant, and all in all the results contain no surprises. Unfortunately this is as far as the experiment has gone at the moment, and one would like to base one's conclusions on several terms' reading with a greater number of pupils, but even on these results, one would, I think, be justified in stating that *People of the City, Strangers at Snowfell,* and *Born Free* are suitable books for extensive reading in, at least, Form 3 in Zambia. One's eventual aim would be to build up in this way a list of about forty books of *proven* suitability for each form from Form 1 to Form 5, so that the pupil can be encouraged to read at least two hundred books during his secondary school career.

With such a large number of different books being needed to enable pupils to read different books at their own individual pace, it was necessary to devise an efficient system for distributing and controlling the books. This was done by ruling a large piece of white cartridge paper as shown in the diagram, and displaying it in the classroom.

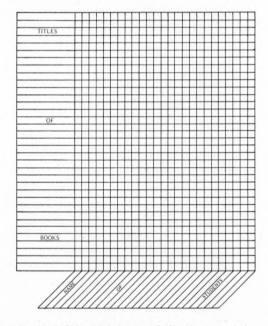

The titles of books were listed in the left-hand column of the chart, and the names of pupils at the bottom. When a pupil took out a particular book a diagonal line was placed in the appropriate square i.e. ◹ and when he returned it, this line was crossed by another diagonal i.e. ⊠ . It was thus easy to see at a glance who was reading what, and how many books any student had read. This chart can also be used as an assessment record by getting the pupils to put in the appropriate squares various symbols indicating whether the book was enjoyed or not.

In these ways the battle for better reading was largely won. The pupils were in general keen to read out of class and seemed to appreciate the efforts which were made to give them individual attention. To encourage the less keen and to keep up the impetus of the others, the one or two periods a week that had previously been used for reading one book aloud in class, were given over to silent reading with pupils reading their own particular books. In a nine-week term, a couple of pupils read as many as twenty-three books each. Pupils claimed that they would not have read as many books as they did read if there had been no reading experiment, and they wanted it to be continued in the following term.

As far as the desirable effects of good reading-matter are concerned, I *know* that were desirable effects, although, as I mentioned earlier, I find it difficult to prove. As evidence of some sort, however, I submit the following extracts taken from three compositions on 'What's the Use of Reading Novels?'

(i) The real advantages (of reading novels) are found in their conciseness on things which we vaguely learn through geography and history. In the case of history an extract from The Silver Sword explains vividly what happened to civilians in Europe . . . This story tells of the suffering of people in the Second World War.

By reading novels of exploration we learn geography. Before I read The Ascent of Everest I had thought of Mountain Everest simply. I had never realized that it was so high that the top of it was covered with ice. I had never come to my senses to imagine its height.

On the whole novels are the most thrilling books one can find. They are in other words great entertainers. Much more they widen our knowledge to a greater extent. One novel may deal with detectivity and one may learn something about that . . .

(ii) If the story is very interesting a reader imagines the story as a real one. By doing so he is increasing his power of imagination whereby he can write his own story using his imagination.

(iii) Foreigners get the idea of the way the English act or do things in their own country . . . By reading more novels one can choose which are good or bad novels to read. This can be achieved by looking at the model of English used in a particular novel. If the novel uses a colloquial type of English then that book can spoil your English [debatable of course!] . . . Novels refresh our brains when they are tired. They also entertain our minds when we are lonely without anyone to talk with.

I suggest that it is in such insights and reactions and attitudes and experiences that one can see the desirable effects of good reading-matter. This evidence would seem to support, and be supported by, "results of the Birmingham experiment in library-centred English, where two matched groups of children were systematically compared over a year, the one taught by traditional textbook methods and the other by library-centred reading, discussion, and writing. The results showed that there was little difference between the two groups when tested with exercises in vocabulary, grammar, and usage, but the library-centred group was significantly better in reading skill, in spelling, and in composition work."[1]

[1] Esmor Jones: 'New Trends in the Teaching of English,' *Teachers World*, 20 May 1966.

The reading experiment also gave me the opportunity to correct some very confused ideas about reading, which discussion and written work revealed and which I had never suspected existed. Some students were unaware of the difference between a book and a novel, and between fiction and fact—some refused to believe that James Bond was not a real person! Also, there was the idea that fiction is "lies" and, therefore, that to read novels is a rather undesirable activity. And again, the idea that "some novels contain good stories but in poor English—the American English. The American English is poor because it shows the signs of laziness by shortening words, for instance *because* written *'cos* in American English."

Several conclusions are worth drawing. Firstly, an effort should be made, certainly in Zambia and probably in other countries, to draw up lists of books of proven suitability for particular forms in secondary schools. It is important that these lists should consist of actual titles of specific books, and not be merely a list of publishers' series. Often, if one asks an outside agency to recommend books, one tends to get a list stating that books in Longmans' Bridge Series, the O.U.P. English-Reader's Library, Heinemann's New Windmill Series, etc., are suitable, the implication being that all the titles in a particular series are equally suitable. This is, unfortunately, not always the case. What is needed, therefore, is a list of titles, not a list of series. Some time ago, the Cambridge Conference on the Teaching of English Literature Overseas recommended that "the British Council should draw up comprehensive lists of texts suitable for use in schools where English literature is taught. These lists should include books in English by overseas writers. The lists should be annotated so as to indicate which books are suitable (and at what levels) for enjoyable reading and for dramatization, and which texts are also suitable for language teaching. The lists would need to be periodically revised with the help of teachers working overseas."[1] This recommendation was made some time ago, but the need is just as pressing today.

Secondly, once such lists have been drawn up, an effort should be made to persuade local booksellers to stock "package deals" of forty different titles, and also, of course, to persuade teachers to buy books in this way rather than a "set" of forty copies of the same title. Extensive reading out of class should become a more accepted and recognized part of the English teacher's responsibility than it is at present. If a school has a library, it should not be assumed that reading will take care of itself.

Finally, such experiments as Birmingham's library-centred English course and some of the new C.S.E. syllabuses involving extensive reading should be examined in order to evaluate their relevance to the teaching of English as a second language.

---

[1] *The Teaching of English Literature Overseas*, ed. John Press (Methuen), p. 165.

20

LITERATURE IN
TESL PROGRAMS:
THE LANGUAGE
AND THE
CULTURE

JOHN F. POVEY

In some piece of American literature available to you,
try to isolate concrete examples of material that might
satisfy the first two of Povey's aims in the teaching
of literature.

Do you agree with Povey's four general aims for
teaching literature in ESL classes? Would you wish
to extend them in any way?

An interesting study would be to analyze certain episodes in a piece of American literature in terms of
how they would be interpreted by people in other
cultures.

As we begin to plan a course which offers an introduction to English literature
to non-native speakers, we find that the need for a fresh approach makes
us first begin to reconsider our justifications for teaching literature at all.
Usually our presuppositions remain unquestioned because of the long tradition of such courses for native speakers. Even to pose the question of purpose may cause shocked responses, for is not the value of literature so self
evident as to be beyond discussion? Yet for ESL students we must at least
define our assumptions, the more so in that a sad amount of literature teaching
(and dare I add literary scholarship) seems to maintain only a remote connection with that enobling of the human spirit which is supposed to be the justification of our early assaults on the fortress of Chaucer's medieval style, for example.
  There is a basic dichotomy in English studies in this country (as in England).
We learn "grammar" until some ill-defined point of competence is reached.
(Freshman composition classes are certain to be the last formal English language
training a native speaker could receive.) Language studies are gradually phased
out in favor of literary studies which finally become the only "English" taught
at all. At any age level above about seven years, the division between language
and literature is deliberately engineered into the planning of the general syllabus.

Originally read at the TESOL convention, April, 1967, this paper is reprinted from the
TESOL Quarterly, 1 (June 1967), 40–46. The writer is professor of English as well as
associate director of the African Studies Center at the University of California, Los Angeles.

The fact that in the earliest levels of English learning educationalists perceive the advantage derived from the interaction of language and literature may be suggestive of the direction into which we should lead the ESL student, but this thought would make the theme of another paper and is only observed in passing here. The more significant point is that we have inherited from the format of English studies in this country a division from which we derive most of the extra difficulties which confront us as we plan English courses for the non-native speakers. In educational terms English has become two "subjects," and an "A" for grammar and a "C" for literature or vice versa does not strike us as extraordinary, so accustomed are we to the attitude it exemplifies. We have exported this system with lamentable results. Professor Donald Bowen's recent study visit to India confirmed my own African experience that students are being required to study English "classics" without the least attempt being paid to the inadequate language skills they bring to such a study. Even foreign teachers, forgetting their own student days of despair, have inherited much of this attitude about literature. As one student patiently explained in answer to a class enquiry I had assumed was merely rhetorical, "Why should we teach literature?": "If you didn't have literature what would you teach in the classes when you didn't teach grammar?" I was polite, but I mildly resented the not unique attitude that literature fills up the class programs when there isn't any more grammar to teach. We might recognize that this would give us a very long wait.

Where we have classes of native speakers, many of the difficulties that ought to intrude from the unsuitable division we are making in our classes are kept out of sight. There are signs of the problem in the whimpers that come from freshmen who spend their first class morning of the inevitable survey course approaching the mysteries of *Beowulf* because academics have only a spatial concept of time, even if such planning means that a student flounders into the deep end of the most difficult works first. (Such chronological order does have one advantage. In the face of some revolutionary protest from the dragooned engineering students who always demand, "Why do we have to read Chaucer?" you can always answer firmly, "Because it comes next.") Rapidly such students take refuge in "ponies" which are wretchedly written originally and gain little by being dimly comprehended and garbled in the transition through memory to the "D" blue-book. But these native speakers, for all their problems that we blinkered professors are refusing to see, do have the all important qualification that the English which they use suffuses all their learning. Homelife, play, school, all reinforce their English to such a degree that the fact that literature is an awkwardly isolated part of language learning for them may be overlooked.

The same cannot be said of the unfortunate foreign student struggling with inadequate English to handle the survey courses for freshmen. Hindered by language, denied the short cuts of common cultural assumptions, the non-native speaker flounders. What method can we devise that may help him to learn

English in that fullest sense which must surely include an acquaintance with the literature of our language?

This problem necessitates an examination of our defined aims even though they may in themselves contain contradictory elements. This need was brought home to me when I began planning the courses which I had been asked to initiate in the TESL section of the English Department at UCLA. Since I was given a completely free hand in planning such a course, I had to take considerable time in deciding my intentions. When you have only yourself to blame, you cannot indulge in that luxury of inertia that permits you to blame some externally imposed syllabus or text for the inadequacies of the result. I was dealing, I might explain, with advanced non-native speakers only. They usually had first degrees from universities in their own countries. Since most of them were destined to teach English when they left the States, I was the more determined to treat them to a first acquaintance with some of the major authors in the language. I felt that the following were a reasonable series of general aims in the teaching of literature.

1. Literature will increase all language skills because literature will extend linguistic knowledge by giving evidence of extensive and subtle vocabulary usage, and complex and exact syntax. It will often represent in a general way the style that can properly stand as a model for students. (One would have to qualify here what one assumed was a suitable model. Hemingway's would seem a safer style for a student's emulation than Faulkner's, though both may be admirable for the artists' purpose.)

2. Literature is a link towards that culture which sustains the expression of any language. American literature will open up the culture of this country to the foreign student in a manner analogous to the extension of the native speaker's own awareness of his own culture. We must consider, however, whether we wish in our choice of material to seek for the universal elements in order that the students will find familiarity with the human experience or whether we wish to select the most American of cultural incident. The latter will obviously be more difficult to comprehend but will be guiding the students towards the culture of their target language.

3. We must acknowledge the indefinable, though all-important, concept that literature gives one awareness and human insight. In this respect great literature can be justified as one could assert the value of listening to a major symphony.

4. Literature may guide a few more gifted students towards their own creativity by example derived from their reading of successful writers. There is already fascinating evidence of a second-language literature in English from several countries across the world, especially India and Nigeria.

Although each of these four elements is relevant to the foreign student, the first and second will be of most immediate and specific concern to the ESL teacher. This is because the issues listed as three and four have the clearest analogies with the students' first-language culture. Many of the foreign students in our universities come to us with an intelligent and broad perception of their own literatures, and some are no doubt beginning to experiment with writing in their own language.

We may ask ourselves despairingly whether it is possible for any piece of writing to combine a suitability for teaching the student all these elements appropriately. It is clear that we must, in fact, weigh the varied and sometimes conflicting elements in the function of literature in the classroom. My own concern has been that in our estimate of relevant importance of those aspects upon which we must base our selection of text material, we have, to date, placed far too heavy a premium upon the issue of language. Language has been so stressed that it has been elevated to the totality of expression, whereas it is rather the technique by which expression and ideas are conveyed. I wish to argue that language difficulty for the ESL student may have been exaggerated as a greater dragon than it really is. Obviously language must come first—there can be no other basis for comprehension at all. This is even more obvious in the case of the non-native speaker, for his limitation of comprehension will be more sharply defined since he will not be able to draw upon that common pool of instinctive language recognition which is available to the native speakers.

Yet if we have to accept the primacy of language, we cannot make this our only concern, otherwise the most effective ESL reading material would be those items we created ourselves to the specific linguistic architecture of levels of difficulty. Such works more often become readers without any element of literature in them. The simplified stories from the classics are justified by a similar appeal to language necessity, but they are usually only a thin reminder of what was once a significant book. My basic belief is that we have exaggerated the significance of the element of linguistic difficulty in ESL reading by assuming that reading requires that same total comprehension that comes with understanding speech in our aural/oral methods. The fact that the great impetus to TESL has come from linguistic science may also account for this attitude. The existence of a "recognition" vocabulary is well known, and there is, I believe (though I freely admit this to be an entirely unscientific and subjective impression), a similar partial perception of syntax and style. There can be a general comprehension even when there has not been a precise understanding of a certain syntactic structure. Perception may be general as well as literal. My students saw this when we found Rip Van Winkle sitting under a sycamore tree and one worried individual lamented that he could not understand because he did not know what a sycamore was. I discovered with some embarrassment that I didn't know what a sycamore was either—at least in any botanical sense. We then agreed that if we got as far as "tree," as the context dictated, we would have got as far towards comprehension as that detail needed.

One especial aspect of language difficulty we are inclined to exaggerate is the dialog parts. One is instinctively doubtful about the accents and colloquial idioms of such sections in a piece. I prepared very anxiously for the introduction of the regional accents in Willa Cather's story "The Sculptor's Funeral." In spite of the apparent lexical problems, I had wanted to use this story to initiate some discussion about the American attitude towards artists and intellectuals. To my surprise they had no difficulty at all in comprehending the dialog because they said (with some exaggeration surely) that it was "like the speech we hear every day on television." I am not always happy with the priority given to the TV experience. Introducing some ESL students to a section of *The Grapes of Wrath*, I elicited the following response: "I see a lot of TV, and this story reminds me of the Beverly Hillbillies, so the characters were stuck in my mind before I knew who John Steinbeck was." It is a clear comment on our newer language-teaching method, with its emphasis upon the heard rather than the read, that dialog appears to offer little difficulty. On the other hand when I tried the students on the introduction to USA by Dos Passos, I had a reaction opposite to my expectation. I had chosen this piece because I had wished to discuss the common vision of the American man, the lone hero, enviable in his aloofness. The language looked direct enough in its vocabulary and syntax so that I anticipated no serious difficulties. The students found it inordinately hard to appreciate because of its rhetorical and mannered style. As one student remarked indignantly, "I had to read the story twice in order to understand what Dos Passos meant." Where I had seen simple enough underlying structures, they saw the occasional inversions and repetitions, and their recognition broke down at once.

Clearly our assessment of the difficulty that will be encountered in reading needs rethinking in the light of the fact that our present students have not learned English as I learned French, through a reading of texts and translation. They have learned English through speech. The omnipresence of TV (shades of Marshall McLuhan) has "massaged" the areas of their easier comprehension. This argument was summed up unexpectedly by a Japanese girl who wrote modestly, "My English is poor. For instance when I hear President Johnson speaking, I don't understand well. But on TV shows I understand quite well in spite of my poor English. This is because most shows concern affairs which I experienced in Japan." (I should like to have pursued this assertion further, but unfortunately the section is culled from a terminal blue-book.)

It has been my experience that the whole area of cultural comprehension is more likely than language problems to cause difficulty. This is aggravated by the fact that confusion shows up in such unexpected ways. In preparing for the difficulties one will encounter it is necessary to strike a balance, as I observed earlier, between writing which stresses cultural universality, the generality of human emotions, and those cultural elements which are most specifically and individually American. Discovery of American attitudes through such a presentation will aid the student's awareness of this country and his adjustment to it.

As an example of my attempts in this direction I would like to describe my experiences in teaching that famous American story "Rip Van Winkle." This story proved very difficult in its language, but the readers persevered. We talked generally about folk tales and the reason that Washington Irving felt it necessary to initiate that form in the Eastern States. In subsequent discussion students told me several tales from their own traditions which concerned the same situation, the man who sleeps for a generation without recognizing the passing time. Several countries seem to have such a tale. Then with the similarities established it was time to stress the American element. "If this story were told in your country, would it come out roughly the same in its characters and motivation?" I questioned. "No," said the Latin Americans. "Our women are satisfied with their position at home, and we have no stories of this henpecking." (That last word caused great delight for its expressiveness.) The Japanese were in general agreement with this view, though they expressed it a little more cautiously. "There is a Japanese word for this. It is *kakadena* which means 'petticoat government,' but I have never read a story about it." There were several other responses from students in the same tone. "A Chinese wife is obedient to her husband. Wives in Taiwan don't take part in social activities at all." The Africans responded more firmly. "It is foolish to put the blame on the wife, for a man's friends would say 'Why don't you marry another one?' " "Our people would blame the wife's bad temper on the wrath of the unappeased spirit of his dead grandfather." (I admit by the time I got to that latter remark I began to wonder whether I was merely having my leg pulled as I sought for cultural anthropology.)

At this point with the differences clearly established I tried to lead them into the specifically American elements by appealing first to their personal experience here. "Is Rip a typical American man?" I asked. Opinion in the class divided in a way that revealingly exposed the accepted stereotypes. "Yes, Rip is typical because all men are henpecked by their wives in this country." One student felt so strongly about this that he went so unreasonably far as to insist, "And his dog is an American dog, for it too is frightened of a woman." Others thought that Rip was hardly the conventional American since by definition all Americans work hard to gain the material comforts of this society and Rip is indifferent to keeping up with the Joneses.

This division of attitude exposes the nature of the prejudice which is established when the American scene is observed from the viewpoint derived from films and magazines. The possibility of using such comments as the link into a more rational class discussion of American culture is clear. In every piece which we read, we make many cultural presuppositions with unthinking confidence, most of which are going to be quite literally foreign to the non-native speaker. This introduction to a nation's literary culture has got to be undertaken with some concessions to general interest, too. A half-term blue-book produced this disconsolate assessment: "Nothing happens, nothing changes. I think that these writings can be appreciated only by a certain group of people who are interested in things like this and understand them." Include me out, I detected there. But that remark did make me question whether my own "literary" standards had been pitched too high. I therefore fell back upon one of the Hyman Kaplan stories. I had considerable doubts about this. The language is difficult because of its errors and the attempt to record idiosyncratic pronunciation. I wondered, too, whether the tone did not indicate a certain kind of mockery in the characterization for all its general affection: "Foreigners speak funny." Surprisingly it was a great success. My concern that I was proving myself unable to estimate what was a suitable piece for the students' enjoyment was offset by my pleasure in the very warm response they had to Kaplan's predicament. "The characters are all foreign as we are, and so we see ourselves through the story. Kaplan could be one of us." "It shows students having the same problems that we had when we came to this country, and it gives us a good feeling that we can already laugh at them."

It is a common enough truism of linguistic studies that an accurate contrastive analysis between the language of the learner and the target language will facilitate the recognition of likely areas of difficulty. What an overwhelming task it is going to be if we are also going to require a similar contrastive analysis between the cultures. Perhaps this is too strong a view, yet the response of a particularly able Japanese student remains in my mind. We had been reading through Nathaniel Hawthorne's *Ethan Brand* in class. We had discussed the universality of certain human fears—of darkness and madness. "But how would Ethan have behaved if he had not had that puritanical conscience?" asked this student. "What can an unforgivable sin be to a Buddhist or a believer in Shinto?" Such an enquiry pierced my parochial outlook and opened up to me evidence of the yawning gulfs of misunderstanding of ideas and motivations that may make virtually all a foreign student's reactions distorted by the difference between his intellectual and cultural presuppositions and ours.

We know now roughly how to control difficulties so that items may be presented in an ascending hierarchy of difficulty. Can we begin to plan a similar control of the degree of cultural difficulty by leading the student more gently from the most familiar, the most readily comprehensible, ideas into those elements of our own culture which will be most foreign to him? Those beliefs most difficult for him to appreciate will be those which are in greatest contrast with his own national and racial assumptions.

If we cannot yet do this in a broad, theoretical way, we can only plead for more general and wider individual experiment with materials in the classrooms. Some pieces seem to have an immediate appeal; others unwarrantably seem a dreary flop. Which are which, and why? The linguists have established a very successful basis for the teaching of language at the elementary levels. Perhaps we can be equally successful at this more advanced level of language study in bringing to the foreign student the beginning steps in his acquaintance with our extensive range of literature. It seems a challenge to the humanist as teacher to show others successfully the delights of his own discipline.

21

LANGUAGE AND CULTURE   J. R. GLADSTONE

How does Gladstone account for *cultural accent*?

Give additional examples of *cultural accent* that you have observed.

List the examples you have collected in the order of most important to least important. On what basis did you decide their relative importance?

What vehicles are available to language teachers to reduce the amount of *cultural accent* a student might have?

Language and culture are inexorably intertwined. Language is at once an outcome or a result of the culture as a whole and also a vehicle by which the other facets of the culture are shaped and communicated. The language we learn as a child gives us not only a system for communication, but, more importantly, it dictates the type and the form of the communications we make. The universe is ordered in accordance with the way we name it. An Eskimo would think us extremely vague if we told him it was snowing. His language provides him with a universe that encompasses dozens of types of 'snowing.' In the same way we would consider the Eskimo vague if he made an appointment with us for 'some time later.' To the North American time is a real commodity. He can waste time, spend time, charge for time, kill time, pass time, sell time, and be on time or in time. Our language reflects and reinforces our cultural patterns and value system.

The sounds and patterns that we learn as our first language cause what have been described as linguistic blind spots. While learning our native language we are trained not only to produce certain sounds, which are rewarded, but we are also rewarded not to produce other sounds. We are trained to ignore and ultimately not to hear many sounds that naturally occur in other languages. The tones in the Chinese language are an excellent example of a linguistic blind spot for native English speakers. A Spanish speaker, on the other hand, when first learning English cannot usually hear the difference between the two English words *beat* and *bit*.

Since language and culture are intimately bound together, it is not surprising

Reprinted by permission from *English Language Teaching*, 23 (January, 1969), 114–117. The author is a member of the staff of Ealing Technical College, London.

that there are also cultural blind spots. As linguistic blind spots are developed as responses to our early language training, cultural blind spots are developed as responses to our environment. Our culture rewards us for producing certain behaviour patterns and for ignoring others. This training develops in us a cultural perspective by which we judge all acts: a cultural sieve through which we pour all we perceive. Usually, this cultural filter performs below the conscious level, producing in us cultural blind spots.

The South American who breaks into the middle of a line-up (queue) in an American city sees himself as an individual breaking the institution's hold over him. The Americans in the queue see an unmannered foreigner, breaking the "first come, first served" tradition. Rudeness or individuality? The same act seen through different cultural filters. We are taught that cleanliness is not only good, but that it is next to godliness. We accept this as a fundamental fact of life and are quite shocked to discover other cultures that do not. Bargaining in our culture is not an acceptable way of conducting business, except in very specific cases, such as buying a house or a car. It bewilders, amuses, or even repels us when we are exposed, in reality or vicariously, to a Persian market-place.

When a linguistic blind spot is revealed we gain insight into our own and the target language. We accept this as part of the learning process. When a cultural blind spot is revealed, we recoil. For most of us the cultural fabric of our lives is so binding that a break from ethnocentrism is extremely painful. It is the severity of the cultural change that causes many immigrants to experience cultural shock.

There is a stronger drive for the foreign student to superimpose his own cultural patterns on the new environment than his linguistic habits on the new culture's language. This causes a cultural accent.

Many of you will have experienced the feeling that a person you have only seen from a distance was a foreigner. If asked why, you would have been hard pressed to answer. Probably you would have replied in vague terms about his mannerisms, his way of standing, his hand motions, the distance he keeps from his listener, his head movements, his listening posture, and hundreds of other small details that you could not put your finger on, but which would produce an overall impression of strangeness. You would have been attempting to describe his cultural accent.

A culture and the language used by it are inseparable. Most of the cultural attitudes which a native speaker has built into him are reflected in his speech patterns. The reader is invited to consider the numerous expressions we have in North American English for talking about success. We even differentiate between material success, meaning money, and other forms of success, such as artistic or moral. The native speaker also brings with him to his language a background of knowledge that is culturally based. We approach the words 'raw flesh' with a built-in abhorrence. Expressions such as the 'revolution,' 'the Indian wars,' 'the Great Plains,' and 'New York City' all have a significance to the native American speaker that the foreign student will not automatically understand or appreciate.

Language and culture are connected in several other intricate and dynamic ways. The language is a product of the culture, but simultaneously the culture is shaped by how the language allows us to view it. In English we must view things in some time-oriented manner. Nothing can exist outside of time, no two activities can take place in the same place at the same time. The backgrounds of most inhabitants of a culture are similar. A majority of us hear similar stories when we are young. When we encounter such descriptions as "as capricious as the Queen of Hearts" or "like Long John Silver" we understand the intended character. The language and the culture reinforce each other. The culture begins by giving a viewpoint. Language gives this idea oral expression, which in turn gives validity and habit response to the viewpoint.

A cultural pattern is one of these forms that is extremely difficult to delineate. We have far less trouble in deciding whether or not a specific act belongs to our culture than we do in setting down the criteria that we use in making such a decision. Given the social context and the specific act, a native speaker seldom has difficulty in naming the cultural pattern. A man eating bacon and eggs at nine in the morning we would label as a man eating breakfast, but if asked to describe the cultural concept "breakfast" we would probably say "It depends."

That would be correct, it does depend. It depends upon the time of day, the type of food being eaten, how many meals had been eaten before, where the meal is being eaten, and many more cultural considerations built into the linguistic form. Certainly a wedding breakfast is not the same as a regular breakfast; a coffee grabbed on the way to the office is a different breakfast from steak and eggs eaten after one has worked from four a.m. to eight a.m.

The cultural concept is the underlying pattern, not the specific act, but the specific act usually contains and reflects all of the major elements of the basic pattern. By expanding a specific incident and drawing upon the pupils' experience, you will be able to bring into sharp focus many important areas of our society that often are only on the periphery of the students' understanding.

It would be futile to attempt to teach your class what breakfast consists of for a North American, but using some specific episode you can teach the class the important underlying assumptions. It is really not difficult to decide what aspects of an act are important and worth teaching and which are not. Ask yourself these two questions:

1. Is this information needed by the students for the proper understanding of the habit and/or concept?

2. Am I, as a native speaker, sure about this detail?

If the answer to either question is No, do not bother about teaching or discussing that aspect of the cultural pattern. In the second question, we are not assuming that you can judge every aspect of our culture. Rather we feel that the students have so many new things to learn, and that if you got on without that particular knowledge then surely your pupils will be able to also.

We feel that materials in a language programme should take cognisance of the relationship between culture and language. Using materials that do, the teacher will be able to effectively teach the linguistic items within their cultural context, thus providing not only the patterns of the language but also the trappings that make them meaningful.

22   THE LITERATURE   BRUCE PATTISON
LESSON

What materials comparable to the author's Little Red Riding Hood example would be appropriate for older students and yet would serve the same purposes?

What criteria does Pattison suggest for the selection of material which has a role to play in personal development and social adjustment? Would you modify these criteria in any way?

Learning to read literature must be carefully distinguished from studying it. This is not always done, and confusion of aim produces confused results.

Literature can be considered as a social force or a manifestation of "man's unconquerable mind." Its forms and modes of operation, its history, and its influence can be studied, either with the practical purpose of becoming a writer, or objectively as an aspect of a particular culture or as a universal human interest. But such study is not very profitable unless there has first been considerable direct experience of particular literary works. It is for a small minority, whereas reading literature with interest and pleasure should be within everybody's reach.

. . . literary forms can be used to provide material for language learning. There are thus three distinct teaching problems: (1) the treatment of specially written material in literary form for language teaching; (2) arranging direct experience of particular works produced originally for the authors' own speech community, trying to secure a fuller response to them, and so encouraging students to go on reading and to get more out of their reading in future;

Reprinted by permission from *English Language Teaching*, 18 (January, 1964), 59–62. Professor Pattison is head of the Division of Language Teaching in the University of London and a member of the editorial board of *English Language Teaching*. In 1968 he was president of the British Association of Teachers of English as a Foreign Language.

(3) the study of works in relation to each other and to their contexts, leading perhaps to generalizations about literature as an art and as a human activity.

The important requirement in specially written material to be used as an aid to language teaching is that each specimen should, in addition to including previously learned language, repeat several times a structure or other systematic feature of the language to be learned. This requirement is not always met by course books, which follow up reading passages with grammatical items scarcely represented in them.

Stories for young children can easily be constructed to provide the necessary repetition: repetition is a favourite device of fairy stories and nursery rimes. In "Goldilocks and the Three Bears," Goldilocks goes into the bears' house and sits in each bear's chair, tastes each bear's porridge, and finally tries each bear's bed, before settling down to sleep in the little bear's bed. When the bears return and find traces of their visitor, each in turn asks questions with the same form: *Who has been sitting in my chair? Who has been eating my porridge? Who has been sleeping in my bed?* We thus get nine sentences containing the present perfect continuous tense. Again, in "Little Red Riding Hood" the wolf impersonates the little girl's grandmother, and, when the little girl looks at her supposed grandmother closely, we get the dialogue:

"What big ears you have, grandmother!" "All the better to hear you with, my dear."

"What big eyes you have, grandmother!" "All the better to see you with, my dear."

"What big teeth you have, grandmother!" "All the better to eat you with, my dear."

Then in "Old Mother Hubbard" we have the repetition of the past continuous tense:

She went to the baker's to buy him some bread,
But when she came back the poor dog was dead.

She went to the hatter's to buy him a hat,
But when she came back he was feeding the cat.

She went to the fruiterer's to buy him some fruit,
But when she came back he was playing the flute, etc.

It is not so easy to arrange for this repetition in more sophisticated material, but it can be done. It is perhaps noteworthy that anecdotes tend to rely on it. The kind of story in which one person after another tries to do something and fails, or in which the main character consults one person after another or looks in one place after another, affords opportunities for repetition.

The literary material that is designed to assist language teaching will usually be preceded by presentation of the linguistic feature to be given special prominence and will be followed by further practice of the feature. Any discussion of the story or poem will be concerned only with the events and characters, making sure the context and the contents are fully understood and the significance of the repeated linguistic feature and its mode of operation appreciated. Any literary study or mention of literary terminology will be inappropriate. Otherwise the general treatment will be similar to that of genuine literary material of the second type mentioned above.

Securing an interest in, and encouraging voluntary reading of, literature are important aspects of education where English is a second language. When English is a foreign language the contribution of literature to general education must be made through the first language. In many countries of Asia and Africa the first language of students is inadequately equipped yet to deal with many functions necessary in the modern world, and imagination must be stimulated by English literature to help students to live in the new world emerging from contact with Europeans and the pressure for national development.

When literature has a role to play in personal development and social adjustment, interest in it, and ability to progress in reading it, must be helped by careful selection of material. What is offered to students must not only suit their linguistic capacities but be within their general experience. The reputation of a work is irrelevant: it is the possibility of securing a response that matters. Good, simple, but perhaps not first-rate, material may be an encouragement to further progress, if it arouses interest; but what is too difficult will only set up a distaste for literature and will fail to establish a reading habit, which is essential for self-teaching and should be the teacher's constant aim.

In presenting any material it must be remembered that a work of fiction is a structure, a unity, and the form is an essential feature of it. It should therefore be presented entire as quickly as possible with the minimum of preamble. The best way of doing this is to read it right through straight off. When it is too long for this, it should be divided into more or less self-contained episodes and each made the subject of a lesson. It will not all be clear to the uninitiated, but the general impression is important, and details can be dealt with later.

First impressions are very important. When a class needs help in reading a work, a good reading aloud is the best introduction. The only person who can give it is a person who knows the work. The exception is drama; it may be wise to plunge right into the dramatic situation by starting with a reading in parts. Otherwise the teacher should prepare his reading carefully and try to convey as much meaning as possible by it. If he doubts his own ability to read well, he may be well advised to play a good recording of a skilled reader performing the work.

After the presentation of the whole work comes discussion. The aim is to get the details clearer, but they must always be related to the total effect. The teacher is helping the class to read for itself. He asks questions to direct attention to the relevant parts of the text. The questions should work inwards from the whole impression. The first questions will be general, and there is no need at any time to work through the poem or story in the order in which it lies on the page. The discussion can get down to single words, but should always concern itself with what they are doing in that particular context and why they are chosen rather than other possibilities. The literature lesson should never degenerate into a language lesson: always the question is how each detail fits in with each other detail to minister to the general effect. The class is invited to think, to remember what the author is trying to do, and to draw on other experience to help it guess why he has chosen specific means of doing it. There is no place for dictated responses: the class is being trained to read for itself. Perhaps there is much it cannot yet appreciate. That has no reason to be mentioned at all. But the class should be pressed to use its imagination and to look closely and to get as much as it can out of the work.

Having looked at the work in detail, the final task is to look at it whole again. It will now be more fully appreciated because of the detailed examination to which it has been subjected. A final reading is the appropriate method of doing this. As the work is now known to the class, perhaps it can take part in this, but the last impression should not be a bad reading.

The amount and kind of discussion a work receives will depend on its characteristics. As each work is unique, literature lessons should never be stereotyped: they should vary. But the general principles of treatment are fairly constant, because they are derived from the nature of literature itself.

When a student has read a great deal of literature and developed a strong interest in it, he can go on to the third stage I mentioned at the beginning of this article, to the study of literature. I shall not deal with teaching at this stage, because it is reached only by a minority at universities. It cannot be attempted until students have gone through the second stage, with which I have been mainly concerned in this article. It is a great mistake to get involved with it prematurely. Only specialists in universities are fitted for the study of literature, and they are fitted only after they have attained a fairly high level of reading ability. Such ability is most likely to be developed by teaching of the kind I have discussed, though, of course, exceptional students often teach themselves. The teacher who encourages them to run before they can walk risks rote learning instead of the development of genuine capacity to deal with literature. He should forget his own college notes when he starts teaching students who have very little literary experience.

What is Arapoff's basis for insisting that *writing is a thinking process?*

Do you agree with Arapoff that reading is a passive process?

Restate briefly the explicit differences, as supplied by this article as well as from your own experience, between writing and speaking.

Choose a dialogue similar to the one Arapoff presents on page 203. Using her model, prepare samples of the various types of writing that follow her dialogue. What specific skills are required for each type that could constitute a problem in teaching writing?

WHY TEACHING WRITING IS DIFFERENT
FROM TEACHING OTHER LANGUAGE SKILLS

For some years linguists have been writing textbooks designed to teach foreign students spoken English. But only recently, as teachers have found that many students want and need to learn how to write English as well as to speak it, have linguistically-oriented textbooks designed to teach written English appeared. These textbooks have a number of approaches, from variations on the "copybook" method at one end of the spectrum to the "free composition" method at the other end. No doubt most of you have tried some of these approaches, and, I suspect, found all of them lacking in some way. In my experience, this lack has always been in efficiency. None of the textbooks so far published seems to teach anything that cannot be learned from other ESOL courses: from courses in oral production, grammar, or reading.

Obviously, grammar, aural comprehension, reading, and even oral production are to varying degrees involved in writing. Certainly we cannot teach a writing course which never touches on these areas. But at the same time teaching a writing course which covers *only* these areas is redundant. Given the limited time most of us have to teach students as much as we can about English, we ought to, if purely for efficiency's sake, use a method which teaches the students something they will not learn in their other courses; something they cannot

Reprinted by permission from the *TESOL Quarterly*, 1 (June, 1967), 33–39. This article was first read at the TESOL convention, April, 1967. The author is an instructor in the English Language Institute of the University of Hawaii.

learn from conscientiously translating vocal symbols into orthographic ones, from oral or written pattern practice, or from reading; i.e., a method which emphasizes that which is *unique* to writing.

Writing is much more than an orthographic symbolization of speech; it is, most importantly, *a purposeful selection and organization of experience.* By experience I mean all thoughts—facts, opinions, or ideas—whether acquired first-hand (through direct perceptions and/or actions) or second-hand (through reading or hearsay). This includes all kinds of writing from the poem to the scientific experiment, for all have a purpose and an organized body of selected facts, opinions, or ideas. How clear the purpose, and how relevant and well-organized the facts, determines the effectiveness of the writing.

Since, then, learning to write does not just involve learning to use ortho-graphic symbols, but primarily how to select and organize experience according to a certain purpose, it follows that teaching our students to write is different in a very important way from teaching them to speak or teaching them to use grammar. A purposeful selection and organization of experience requires active thought. When writing, the students must keep in mind their purpose, think about the facts they will need to select which are relevant to that purpose, and think about how to organize those facts in a coherent fashion. The process of learning to write is largely a process of learning to think more clearly.

On the other hand, learning to speak and learning grammar essentially in-volve learning *not* to think. The goal is to form habits; the procedure is to drill the students on pronunciation or grammar to the point where they will no longer have to think about what they are saying. It is more than likely that the habit-forming process which students of oral English and grammar must go through *interferes* with the process of learning to write well.

And the students don't learn to write via a reading course, either. Although, unlike pronunciation and grammatical production, the process of reading re-quires thought, it does not, as does writing, also require *activity*. Reading is a passive process while writing is active. Although they can learn through reading how various writers have selected and organized facts in order to carry out a specific purpose, the students themselves must ultimately be forced to undergo the intense mental activity involved in working out their own problems of selection and organization if they are ever really going to learn to write. This is why the copybook approach, which requires that the students copy or emulate certain writings, doesn't work very well, for while it does require that the students memorize structures, thereby increasing their grammatical ability, and perhaps even teaching them something about style, it does not require them to do much thinking.

Because the combination of thought and activity are unique to writing, we must in planning a writing curriculum devise exercises which necessitate intense concentration. While grammar and reading are both certainly indispensable to such a curriculum, they must be presented in such a way that students will learn to use them as tools. For example, one of the first things they will have to learn is that writing has certain structural differences from speech. One difference is that writing generally has longer sentences—what might be two or three sentences in speech is often only one sentence in writing. So the students should learn how to combine the short sentences of spoken English by modification, or by using sentence connectors of various kinds (conjunctions, words like *however, therefore*, phrases like *in the first place*, etc.). This involves learning grammar, but the students should learn to *consciously* select and use various grammatical devices with which to combine sentences as the problems arise in a writing situation: e.g., when they convert a dialog or narration into a paraphrase.

Of course, one of the biggest problems in teaching writing is that the students must have facts and ideas in order to write and that these must be manifested in the form of grammatical English sentences. But if we allow them to use the facts and ideas gained from their first-hand experiences, they will think of these in their own language and then try to translate them word-for-word into English, often with most ungrammatical results. This is why the free composition approach to teaching writing is just as unsatisfactory as the copybook method, but in a different way. The students make so many grammatical errors that their compositions lose much of the original meaning.

We can, however, avoid the problems caused by the students' limited knowledge of grammar and of the idioms of English by requiring that instead of using the facts of first-hand experience, they use second-hand facts gained through the vicarious experience of reading. Since what is unique in learning to write is not so much learning to *state* facts as it is to *use* them, we can *give* our students the facts they will be required to use in the form of reading assignments. By using sentences gleaned from reading they can avoid making grammatical errors and actively concentrate on the purposeful selection and organization of these sentences; i.e., they can concentrate on thinking.

A NEW METHOD FOR TEACHING WRITING

Contending, then, that learning to write is a process whereby students learn to use grammar and facts as tools in carrying out a particular purpose, we are confronted with the question of precisely how we are going to teach them to do this. Obviously, just as writing is a process, so too is the teaching of writing. We must proceed by stages from simple to complex. Because we cannot expect students to learn all there is to learn about writing at once, or even in a short time, we must in some way control the complexity of the writing they will be expected to do at various learning stages.

We can do this by controlling the *purpose* of the writing, for it is largely the purpose the writer must implement which determines the complexity of the selecting and organizing process. While a purpose of some sort is inherent in any kind of writing, it is the writing with an explicit rather than an implicit purpose that we should teach: i.e., expository prose. This kind of writing, because it "exposes" its purpose, lends itself much more easily to analysis than does writing with an implicit purpose (i.e., "fiction" or "literature" or "creative writing"), and therefore it is easier to teach. Too, expository prose is the only kind of writing that the students will need to use in their school work (except for assignments given in certain specialized English courses). Finally, the students will learn a great deal about *all* kinds of writing from learning to write good expository prose.

There are roughly three types of expository prose that students regularly use in school: these are lecture and reading notes, answers to examination questions, and research or critical papers. Each type has a different general purpose: note-taking is intended to *report* the facts, answering exam questions to *explain* them, and paper-writing to *evaluate* them. Each purpose—reporting, explaining, and evaluating—requires a selecting and organizing task of differing complexity.

For example, a student whose assignment is to summarize an essay has a purpose of the first type: reporting. His summary might begin with an assertion like: "The essay 'We Shall Overcome' says that the Negro is slowly making gains in status." This assertion tells us that the writer will use facts selected from the essay which exemplify the Negro's gain in status and that he will organize them in much the same order as they appeared in the essay.

But a student asked in an essay exam to write on, say, the types of gains in status the Negro has made must go through a more complicated process of selection and organization. His beginning statement might read: "The essay, 'We Shall Overcome' lists gains in status the Negro is making which can be classified as either material or spiritual," and he will have to explain the facts he selects by organizing them into two categories—a more complex process than reporting, requiring deeper thought.

An assignment which requires that the student write a paper giving his opinion of an essay necessitates a still more complicated selecting and organizing process. He will have to begin with an assertion like: "The essay 'We Shall Overcome' is a realistic appraisal of the Negro's gain in status," and then he will have to cite evidence making a case for his opinion; i.e., he will have to evaluate the facts.

The curriculum for writing, then, should be planned in accordance with the three general types of expository prose the students will need to use in school: prose which reports, prose which explains, and prose which evaluates. Of course, such a task isn't simple. Teaching beginners or near-beginners in English how to summarize, for example, is not a one-step process. Before they can do this successfully, they must learn to recognize structural and semantic clues which identify the important ideas within a given piece of prose. And the most efficient way for them to learn to do this (if we remember that writing involves the unique combination of thought and activity) is by having them use such clues in their own writing. Similarly, teaching reasonably sophisticated students how to write essays involves the complex process of teaching them how to find topics and sub-topics, how to recognize relevant similarities or differences between facts, and how to make assertions about their findings. Finally, teaching even advanced students how to judge various written pieces on a logical basis is a very involved process which includes teaching them to recognize the two parts of an argument, how to look for fallacies in these, and how to compose their own logically sound arguments.

So, although there may be only three general types of expository prose, teaching these is a long process which takes the students through several stages of writing, beginning with a form very close to speech—direct address—and ending with a form very different—a footnoted thesis. Naturally, as the purpose of the writing becomes more complex, the facts that the students are given to use must become more complex also. However, the teaching process can be most clearly illustrated by showing how the facts from one simple six-line dialog could be used in all stages of writing, from simple to complex:

Bill: Hi, Mary.
Mary: Hi.
Bill: Where are you going?
Mary: To the beach. Why don't you come along?
Bill: I think it's going to rain. Look at those clouds.
Mary: It *can't* rain again today! It's rained every day this week.

Direct address
"Hi, Mary," said Bill.
"Hi," the girl answered.
"Where are you going?" he asked.
"To the beach," Mary replied. "Why don't you come along?"
"I think it's going to rain." Bill pointed. "Look at those clouds."
"It can't rain again today!" his friend exclaimed. "It's rained every day this week."

Narration
Bill greeted Mary.
Mary greeted Bill.
He asked her where she was going.
She said that she was going to the beach. She asked Bill to go along.
He answered that he thought it was going to rain. He told Mary to look at the clouds.
Mary said that it couldn't rain again that day. It had rained every day that week.

Paraphrase
Exchanging greetings with Mary, Bill asked her where she was going. She said that she was going to the beach, and asked Bill to go along; however,

he said that he thought it was going to rain, and told Mary to look at the clouds. But Mary said that it couldn't rain again that day because it had rained every day that week.

Summary

When Mary asked Bill to go to the beach with her, he said that he thought it was going to rain, and told her to look at the clouds. However, she said that it couldn't rain again that day since it had rained every day that week.

Factual analysis

Topic #1: Mary

1. Mary asked Bill to go to the beach with her.
2. She said that it couldn't rain again that day since it had rained every day that week.

Topic #2: Bill

1. Bill thought it was going to rain.
2. He told Mary to look at the clouds.

Assertion

Bill and Mary had opposite ideas about the weather: he was a pessimist and she was an optimist.

Essay

"The Pessimist vs. The Optimist"

Bill and Mary had opposite ideas about the weather: he was a pessimist and she was an optimist.

When Mary asked Bill to go to the beach with her one day, he was very pessimistic, telling her that he thought it was going to rain, and to look at the clouds. On the other hand, Mary was optimistic. She said that it couldn't rain again that day since it had rained every day that week.

People like Bill, who notice clouds in the sky, are pessimists, while people like Mary, who don't notice them, are optimists.

Argumentative analysis

Argument #1: premise—there are clouds in the sky; conclusion—it is going to rain.

Argument #2: premise—it has rained every day this week; conclusion—it can't rain again today.

Evaluation of the arguments

Argument #1 is reasonably sound: the evidence is both verifiable and relevant although the conclusion may be somewhat hasty. Argument #2 is fallacious: the evidence is verifiable but irrelevant, or, if relevant, leads to an opposite conclusion.

Critical review

In the essay "The Pessimist vs. The Optimist" by _____ in _____, Bill argued that it was going to rain because there were clouds in the sky, while Mary disagreed saying that it couldn't rain again that day because it had rained every day that week. Bill's argument was stronger than Mary's.

Bill's evidence was both verifiable and relevant. He said that there were clouds, which anyone could immediately verify by looking toward the sky. Since rain occurs only when there are clouds, certainly the evidence—clouds in the sky—was relevant to the conclusion that it was going to rain. However, the conclusion may have been somewhat hasty; it does not always rain when there are clouds. But Bill's argument was reasonably sound.

On the other hand, Mary's argument was fallacious. Her evidence, like Bill's was verifiable: one could check with the Weather Bureau. But from the fact that it had rained every day that week it did not follow that it therefore could not rain again that day; the evidence was irrelevant. In fact, a stronger logical case could have been made for the opposite conclusion: that because it had rained every other day that week, it would also rain that day, since in some areas there is a rainy season during which it rains almost every day.

Therefore, Bill's argument was sounder than Mary's, and from the evidence given in the essay, the chances for rain that day were higher than the chances for a good beach day.

Term paper

Contrasting Opinions About Weather

People are often either pessimists or optimists about the weather. Evidence of this is widespread. One example is the case of Bill and Mary in the essay "The Pessimist vs. the Optimist"[1] . . .

Each of the above samples of writing is, of course, the product of several lessons and "practices." Even learning to convert a dialog into what appears to be a simple form—direct address—involves learning a number of concepts about punctuation, about speaker identification, about stylistic variety. Learning to write a narration involves learning to change verbs to other tenses, to change first and second person pronouns to third person, to change words like *now* and *here* to *then* and *there*, and so forth. A given lesson, then, is designed to teach just a few of many concepts that the students need to learn at a certain stage of the writing process.

The following two lessons appear in the mimeographed text—REPORTING THE FACTS—which we are now using at the University of Hawaii, and they illustrate how learning to write can be a step-by-step process, but at the same

LESSON 10

---

1. Compare the two models below.

Narration:

Liz called Mary. She told her that it was almost nine o'clock. They had better drive to school.

Mary told Liz that her car had a flat tire. They would have to walk. They would probably be late.

Liz said that she didn't mind being late. They needed the exercise. It would be good for them to walk.

Paraphrase:

Liz called Mary, and told her that it was almost nine o'clock, so they had better drive to school. Mary told Liz that her car had a flat tire; therefore they would have to walk. They would probably be late as a result. Liz said that she didn't mind being late; besides, they needed the exercise, so it would be good for them to walk.

---

2. In what ways are *so, therefore,* and *as a result* similar in grammatical usage to *and, in addition,* and *besides*?

3. *Therefore* and *as a result* occur in the same position and have the same punctuation. How does *so* compare with them in this?

4. What are some other sentences that can be connected by *so, therefore,* and *as a result*?

5. Make a paraphrase out of the narration below. Use *so/therefore/as a result* as well as *and/in addition/besides* where appropriate.

Liz asked Mary how she liked French I. She asked her if she was planning to take French II the following semester.

Mary said that the teacher gave them a lot of homework. She had to stay up late doing it. It was difficult. They also had to memorize a long list of words for each lesson. She didn't like French I. She wasn't going to take French II.

Liz said that she had been thinking of taking French. She was glad Mary had warned her about it. She thought she would take Spanish instead.

LESSON II

---

1. Compare the two models below:

Paraphrase #1:

Liz called Mary, and told her that it was almost nine o'clock, so they had better drive to school. Mary told Liz that her car had a flat tire; therefore they would have to walk. They would probably be late as a result. Liz said that she didn't mind being late; besides, they needed the exercise, so it would be good for them to walk.

Paraphrase #2:

Liz called Mary, and told her that they had better drive to school, for it was almost nine o'clock. Mary told Liz that because her car had a flat tire, and since they would have to walk, they would probably be late. Liz said that she didn't mind being late; besides, it would be good for them to walk because they needed the exercise.

---

2. What are the differences in the grammatical usage of *therefore/as a result* and *because/since*?

3. In what ways are *and*, *so*, and *for* similar?

4. *For/because/since* and *so/therefore/as a result* indicate a cause-effect relationship between two sentences or clauses. Which words occur within a sentence stating the cause? The effect?

5. What is the *time* relationship of a cause to an effect?

6. Which of the following three sentences states a cause? An effect? Both a cause and an effect? *Mary told Liz that her car had a flat tire. They would have to walk. They would probably be late.*

7. What are some ways of writing the above three sentences using one or more of the six cause-effect sentence connectors?

8. *For/because/since* and *so/therefore/as a result* do not occur in the same cause-effect relationship, but they can occur in the same sentence. Why? Give an example.

9. Rewrite the paraphrase you did for Lesson 10. Use *for/because/since* instead of *so/therefore/as a result*. Make all of the necessary changes in punctuation and word order.

Lessons like these, then, are designed to teach only a small amount of the writing process at a time, but to teach it in such a way that the students learn to think more and more actively as they progress. They learn to read more carefully than they have in the past, for they must compare two similar but slightly different models, noting the grammatical and semantic differences between them. And they learn to discover reasons for these differences as they answer the questions following the readings. They learn to review constantly in order to compare and contrast previous lessons with the current one. Finally, they learn to make analogies as they work with an entirely different model, deciding whether their changes in the new model are justifiable on the basis of changes made in the old model.

As they go through the lessons, then, the students learn that grammar and semantics are interrelated, and that they are important tools for them to use consciously in order to make coherent pieces of prose out of different sets of English sentences. In short, they learn, first and foremost, that writing is a thinking process.

GUIDED
COMPOSITION

GERALD DYKSTRA
and
CHRISTINA BRATT
PAULSTON

What advantages for the teacher and for the students are claimed by the authors if the composition techniques described in this article are used?

Choose a reading passage that would be suitable for a group of students known to you; then, draw up a number of steps similar to the samples given on page 210 and rewrite the passage following your steps. What difficulties do you encounter? How may these be eliminated?

Where would the composition techniques suggested in this article fit on Prator's manipulation-communication scale?

Teachers of English as a foreign language make extensive use of control in the oral-aural reading aspects of language learning. The claim is being made that there is far too much use of control. But this claim does not extend to the writing aspect, simply because control has been minimal in this area. Without directly entering the dispute about the value of control, we suggest it would be nice if the profession had available a range of tools which permitted control in writing, so that teachers would have available to them the choice of use or rejection.

In teaching written English, the concept of control has taken longer to become established. Recently, however, several articles and texts have appeared dealing with this topic. In the texts, the control is regularly of the kind which employs several composition exercises to cover one grammatical feature, the first composition rigidly controlled while the last is almost a free composition. The next grammatical feature to be covered is again highlighted in several composition exercises, the first of which is rigidly controlled and the last almost free writing. There is thus in this type of control a constant change in the rigidity of the language control.

Ideally it would seem that the nature of the language control should be

Reprinted by permission from *English Language Teaching*, 21, January, 1967, 135–141. Professor Dykstra is a member of the department of speech, University of Hawaii; Professor Paulston directs the English Language Institute at the University of Pittsburgh.

such that it would permit a gradual relaxation throughout the programme, without returning at all to closer control.

We have experimented with such a programme and think we have found what promises to be a solution to some of the ills that befall the composition class for foreign students.

By the application of graded and structured language manipulations to model passages, the students' compositions can be taken from nearly full control to free composition with steadily diminishing controls. The programme allows enforcement of correct writing procedures; it gives the students a sense of progress and improvement which (*a*) builds confidence in their own ability to write, and (*b*) motivates them to further improve their writing ability. This improvement can be plotted graphically. The programme provides the students with maximum writing opportunity; they learn writing by writing, not primarily by discussing writing, nor by learning the old or the new grammar, nor primarily by reading the products of others' successful writing (watching the process would probably be more helpful anyway), nor by being taught to think. It is quite possible, however, that some, possibly all of these factors, are present to some degree in the programme. Each student is able to proceed at his own rate of speed at his own level of ability, and in so doing he covers the main grammatical features of the language. The language the student is asked to deal with is always correct; he is not asked to correct deliberate errors. The writing consists of language in context, not isolated sentences. And for overburdened teachers, one of the more notable features of the programme is that the compositions take no more than seconds to correct; rarel/ do they take more than a minute.

This approach is being applied to materials for grade 2 up through college composition. So far a text for grades 8–10 and one for the college level are in existence, with the others under preparation.

The texts consist of model passages, written especially for the purpose or adapted from existing literature or selected from the writings of American and British authors. The higher the level, the longer and less controlled the passages; in the text for the college level they run to about 150 words in general. With the models there are a series of steps or instructions for the student to follow in rewriting the models. Each step covers a specific language pattern. The composition, i.e. the modification of the model which the student produces, is controlled and graduated through the application of the steps. A student is never asked to proceed beyond any step or level on which he is making mistakes nor need he repeat a step he can execute correctly. Each student is thus able to proceed at his own pace, independently of his classmates.

The following is a sample of a model passage from the college text. It will give an idea of the format and may serve to suggest something of the scope of the steps. Note, however, that a student is never asked to rewrite a model after the first time; the teacher will have selected only one step for him to apply to the model.

Edmund Wilson, *The Wound and The Bow*.

(1) In *Bleak House*, the masterpiece of this middle period, Dickens discovers a new use of plot, which makes possible a tighter organization. (2) (And we must remember that he is always working against the difficulties, of which he often complains, of writing for monthly installments, where everything has to be planned beforehand and it is impossible, as he says, to 'try back' and change anything, once it has been printed.) (3) He creates the detective story which is also a social fable. It is a *genre* which has lapsed since Dickens. The detective story has dropped out the Dickensian social content; and the continuators of the social novel have dropped the detective story.

14-15.	Situation:	Most of the present tenses here are what is called historical present. You could just as well tell about Dickens's new use of plot in the past.
	Assignment:	Rewrite the entire passage in the past tense, beginning *In Bleak House, Dickens discovered* . . . See directions for rewriting the tenses.
18.	Situation:	Retell about Dickens's new use of plot.
	Assignment:	Rewrite the entire passage in the present perfect tense, beginning *In 'Bleak House,' Dickens has discovered. . .'* See directions for rewriting the tenses.
35-38.	Situation:	Write and describe Dickens's literary innovations.
	Assignment:	Sentence No. 2 contains two verb clusters in passive voice. Change them to active voice, supplying a subject for each, and rewrite the entire passage.
102.	Situation:	Pretend that you are Dickens himself, reminiscing about his writing.
	Assignment:	Rewrite the entire passage as if Dickens himself were writing. Begin *In 'Bleak House,' I discovered* . . . You will have to make changes in the original sentence structure. Omit the last two sentences.[1]

The procedure for using the texts in this programme is the following. First, the teacher estimates the number of compositions to be written during the course. For instance, during a fifteen-week course, sixty compositions will provide four a week, two as homework and two written in class. The instructor then selects from the catalogue of steps—a list of all the steps, the grammatical features they cover, and the passages they appear in—those to be covered by the class.

All students are then assigned the first step on the instructor's selected list.

[1] From Christina Bratt Paulston and Gerald Dykstra, *Controlled Composition* (New York: Simon Schuster, 1971).

Each student rewrites the model in his notebook, incorporating the assigned changes, which he may be asked to underline. As soon as a student has finished, he brings his composition to the instructor who, familiar with the materials and the assignment, need only glance at the underlined changes to correct the composition, a procedure which should take no more than a minute. It may be added here in parentheses that if a possible copying error should escape the teacher's attention, this does not result in any serious loss of the effectiveness of the materials. A dropped article, a forgotten third person *-s*, soon reoccurs correctly and repeatedly in subsequent work.

If the student's composition is correct, he proceeds to the next step on the teacher's list. If the composition is not correct, the student is asked to repeat the step but with another model, after the teacher has either explained his error or directed him to a reference grammar. The instructor does not make his list of selected steps available to the students, since each step a student writes depends on his mastery of the preceding step and, if allowed, the students tend to charge ahead on their own, defeating to some extent the control.

After some weeks there is a noticeable range in the steps the students are working on, and the slower students are encouraged to spend some extra time in writing compositions. This is accomplished through extra homework assignments or through special conference hours or through informal 'tutorials' with a friendly neighbour, usually a native speaker of English.

The common first objection to this type of writing is that it is too mechanical to have any meaning to the student. The fact is that most of the language manipulations result in an incorrect response if the student is not fully aware and cognizant of what he is doing. The passage quoted from *The Wound and The Bow*, for instance, is written in the narrative present except for the last sentences. Step 14 asks the student to rewrite the passage in the past. Unless he understands what he is writing, that is, unless the writing is meaningful to him, he will also rewrite the general present by substituting the past, and this will result in an incorrect composition. In classroom use, however, with ten groups of students, their continued satisfaction with their work and their sense of achievement and purpose give us the best answer so far to this objection. Evidently the satisfaction in producing correct even though intricate compositions[2] compensates for the loss of freedom and it results in a class morale which has surprised the teacher accustomed to the frustration of so many of the composition classes for foreign students. The discussion of morale by a biased investigator may seem a tenuous undertaking, but even though morale may be an unmeasurable quantity, many of its symptoms are less so, and some anecdotal evidence may not be out of place.

During a recent experiment a composition class was divided into two groups,

[2] At a spot check in one class, out of 280 compositions written during the semester 231 were without error.

A and B, with only Group A using the approach suggested here. Both groups were taught by the same instructor.

Group A, after the first two weeks, handed in their assignments on time; they never omitted an assignment. Group B had considerable difficulty with their essays—they wrote only free compositions. One or two essays were always late each week and a variety of excuses was offered, including frequently the protestation that the student just could not write anything correct that day and had given it up. Group B, especially in the first half of the term, often expressed feelings of discouragement, something Group A rarely did. Group B could not be said to be eager for extra assignments, while Group A throughout the term hurried to complete a composition during class so they could be assigned another for homework. There developed a sense of competition among some members of the class. On their own initiative several students in Group A made intricate charts to plot their progress, and establishing their progress graphically seemed to lend further encouragement.

Probably the clearest difference in behaviour between Group A and Group B lay in their attendance at the extra conference hour, presided over by student teachers. In the control group (Group B) only one student attended regularly while three-fourths of the students in Group A regularly attended.

There seemed to be less hesitation in asking questions in Group A. There are probably several reasons for this. The students could ask the questions privately, while the rest of the class was writing. Furthermore, they were *forced* to ask questions as well, since without the correct answer they could not proceed to the next step, and this seemed to develop the habit of asking questions. Probably the most important reason was that by the nature of the control, the students knew what questions to ask before making mistakes. These students became accustomed to writing good and correct compositions and did all possible to avoid a slowing of their steady progress; the control group never expected to write a perfect essay and the members passively accepted the red markings as their meet due.

Another conclusion from the same experiment emerged from the teaching of the student teachers assigned to the classes. Within a week, these teachers were perfectly capable of managing an extra hour of class completely on their own, using the controlled composition texts, although in oral classroom teaching they showed all the signs of the inexperienced teacher. The conclusion seems to be that the control extends both ways, toward the teacher as well as the student. The significance of this in a time of shortage of fully qualified teachers could be important. It could allow the integration of voluntary workers, student teachers, or another category of insufficiently trained teachers into a programme under a master teacher, where larger numbers of students might be efficiently taught.

Guided composition is not a panacea for all the problems of teaching composition to foreign students. There is still much that needs further exploration and experimentation. In the meantime, it will provide the profession with a substantial step toward the goal of developing a teaching tool which will permit frequent assignment of writing exercises even in large classes, at the same time assuring that the work will be substantially acceptable while permitting the student to work at a level commensurate with his ability, whether that be at a very low level or a very high one.

25 A FOCUSED, EFFICIENT METHOD TO RELATE COMPOSITION CORRECTION TO TEACHING AIMS

DONALD KNAPP

What are the advantages of Knapp's *Method* for the teacher? For the student?

Which items on the composition check-list would you modify or delete? What additions would you make? Why?

I think you will agree that the title of this paper sounds formal and safe enough, but I start reading it to you with some uneasiness. The check-list system I am going to recommend rests on at least four assumptions that most of you have probably already rejected in your composition teaching, and I don't expect that you will be easily won over. The assumptions are:

1. That composition teachers aren't proofreaders and shouldn't be.

2. That it is a mistake in itself to mark all the mistakes in a student composition.

3. That the correction of grammatical errors is only a subsidiary aim in teaching composition.

4. That giving a composition a grade is unnecessary and undesirable.

I expect to begin rather formally in setting out what we might agree on as desirable qualities in a system of composition correction, looking at the subject both from the point of view of the student and of the teacher. Then I hope

Printed by permission of the author, who read this paper at the Conference on the Teaching of English to Speakers of Other Languages, Tucson, Ariz., May 9, 1964. Professor Knapp is a member of the department of the teaching of English, Teachers College, Columbia University.

to show how the check-list you have in your hands can be used to meet a good many of these requirements in an effective system of composition correction. I hope you will agree that a perfect system is too much to expect, so in the last part of the paper I will try to suggest additional techniques that will compensate for its imperfections and blend with the check-list to make a workable system, one that can be recommended to you as "a focused, efficient method to relate composition correction to teaching aims."

THE SYSTEM WE SEARCH FOR

The value of any new system for teaching or correcting composition has to be determined in the last analysis by how well it does what we want done, and at what cost. A method that achieves amazing results but demands a half-hour a day per pupil in corrections would have to be reluctantly set aside until we could retire from classroom teaching and tutor in some ignore-the-cost crash program. Even spending 15 minutes per student per week amounts to 25 hours a week of teacher corrections if the teacher has four classes of 25 students each; no wonder early-in-the-semester hopes of a composition a week come to naught. Likewise, a method that could do wonders in stimulating expressive, imaginative writing with great sentence variety and wide-ranging vocabulary is not much use to us unless we are teaching very advanced students in a creative writing section. The problem is to find a system that recognizes the time limits within which we teachers work, but that clearly helps the students expand the use of their present patterns in clear expository writing. It has to be a system that teaches the kind of writing which satisfies the student that he is expressing what he means and which satisfies his readers and instructors that his ideas are written in academically acceptable English.

QUALITIES OF A DESIRABLE SYSTEM OF COMPOSITION CORRECTION

Allow me to suggest some teaching aims and assumptions that may fit the kind of composition teaching we have been called on to do. Later I will try to relate them as far as I can to the check-list system of composition correction this paper proposes.

First, looking at composition, especially composition correction, from the student's point of view, the corrections and grades ought to be fair; they ought to represent what the student has achieved in *this* course, based on the material taught by *this* teacher, rather than be a penalty for what the student didn't learn or wasn't taught in previous classes. There ought to be a feeling that the course is going somewhere, that there is a body of knowledge or a set of skills that can reasonably be learned with the syllabus (as outlined in the check-list) in the time allowed. The teacher and the student should both be able to state quite definitely at any particular time what more is to be done in order to reach the course goals. There ought to be no chance for the student to feel that the writing he is expected to do represents an art, something demanding a mysterious quality that non-authors couldn't be expected to have. In a creative writing class this transmutation of writing into art might be a reasonable expectation, but not in a required basic course in composition for the non-native speaker.

Corrections ought to set reasonable tasks that the student can perform without much chance of error and with the expectation of learning something. The student, when he is making an attempt at rewriting a section marked "awkward," changing the tense in a "condition contrary to fact" clause, changing a comma to a period in a "comma splice," or changing the preposition in an idiom—whether these changes are indicated by a correction symbol or by the teacher supplying the correct form—cannot in most instances be considered to be learning, even if the student knows why the old form was wrong and why the new one is necessary. We only have to think back to the repetition necessary in teaching pronunciation and patterns to realize that recopying a sentence or correcting a word as a student response to teacher proofreading is only a single feeble step toward real learning.

To the teacher, there are additional considerations that a desirable system of composition teaching and correcting should reflect. Let's assume that programmers are right and that learning is done in discrete units; if that is so, then a good system for composition teaching and correction ought to help break the complex of composition skills down into learnable units. At very least, a good system of composition correction should isolate specific skills as units for focus so they can be taught efficiently. This is what we do when we teach one structure at a time in pattern drill or when we isolate one phoneme or contrast of phonemes in teaching pronunciation; the same kind of focus ought to be used in teaching topic sentences, specific transitional devices, kinds of parallel structure, and other aspects of good composition.

Related to this is another assumption supported by recent research in the psychology of learning, namely that people are more apt to learn from their successes than their failures, that positive reinforcement of right choices is most apt to increase learning efficiency. Would you agree, then, that this suggests that composition assignments ought to be structured so as to insure right choices in what is being taught, and correction should involve the teacher's search for successes rather than proofreading for mistakes? "Fine improvement" on a composition covered with red marks is not very likely to reinforce those right choices the student did make, and the considerable effort of the teacher to find all the mistakes in the composition may be almost totally wasted considering how efficient people are in forgetting or ignoring what they don't want to recognize. An almost ideal system would be one in which the teacher was free of the alienating role of the error-hunter or penalizing judge and instead was able to assume a cooperating, praising role, especially with those weaker students who need reassurance and encouragement most.

At the same time, though, a desirable system should be honest; it should not mislead a student into thinking that he had mastered more than in fact he had.

Grades should reflect achievement against some absolute standard; they shouldn't be mixed up with encouragement and thus be rendered meaningless. Ideally each returned composition should show what the student had done well against a background of what he still needed to learn in order to complete the course satisfactorily.

There are clearly more criteria that we could set up for a desirable system of composition correction—and I am sure you are aware that I have chosen for mention some of those criteria I feel a check-list is most successful in fulfilling—but allow me, if you will, to go on directly to an explanation of the use of the check-list you have in front of you, one that has grown out of previous work with check-lists at Teachers College by Gerald Dykstra, Emma Rutherford, and others.

THE CHECK-LIST AS USED IN TEACHING

This check-list has been used with intermediate and advanced students, most of whom had written few compositions before taking a course in composition in this country. They had mastered most of the basic structures of English, but almost all of these students retained serious troublespots that reflected their native language backgrounds: articles for Orientals, perfect tenses for Middle-Easterners, and statement-word-order clauses introduced by question words (for example, I don't know when did he go), for almost everybody. Most were not aware of topic sentences, supporting statements focusing on the central idea of the paragraph, transitional elements, and the like, even in their own languages; in their introductory compositions they generally paid little attention to formal requirements or mechanics.

This composition check-list acts as the syllabus for the course; were you to adopt it for your own course, it would certainly need revision to fit your own particular teaching aims. In operation copies of it are distributed to each of the students at the beginning of the course with an explanation that the final evaluation of the student's work at the end of the course will be based on how well he is able to show evidence in class compositions of having mastered all the items. It is made clear, though, that the first compositions will focus on only a few of the items, with the other items added cumulatively as they are treated in class. For example, the first week of class work might center on only the four following items on the check-list: "A clear thesis statement that can be supported or proved" which is the first item under *Rough Outline*, and the items that deal with margins, indentation, and clear writing that come under the heading *Mechanics give a clean, orderly impression.* In class the students would be shown examples of well-done thesis statements and compositions with adequate margins, clear paragraph indentation and easy-to-read handwriting or clean typing; then they could practice recognizing the items—or the lack of them—in written work supplied to the class for examination (perhaps from last year's compositions). And finally, before they were assigned thesis statements and paragraphs for homework the students would practice writing and criticizing thesis statements and copying paragraphs with good mechanics until they were clear as to what was expected of them. They would be asked to make checks on the Composition Check-List next to those items which had been taught in that class session (in this case the thesis statement and the margins, indentation and neatness) to remind themselves that those were the items they would be expected to show mastery in when they turned in their homework at the next class session.

THE CHECK-LIST AS USED BY THE TEACHER IN CORRECTION

In correcting the composition, the teacher has three goals. The first is to see that the student has been able to use successfully those items which were singled out in the classroom teaching (and in later corrections, also those items which the teacher had previously covered in class). If the student has done well—and the teacher is probably trying to go too fast or is giving inadequate preparation if almost all the students don't do well on those items taught—the teacher marks a red plus in front of the item on the Composition Check-List to indicate that it was well done. A particularly fine job might rate a double plus, but there are no negative marks and there is no general grade given the paper. In each succeeding class session, more items are taught, and since the process is cumulative, by mid-term probably all the items on the top half of the check-list, together with those listed under *Corrections* and a few under *Imaginative, precise use of language* should regularly be receiving red pluses. Usually the student—and the teacher—enjoy a solid sense of achievement as the number of red pluses grows from week to week. Besides this, the student is always conscious of how much of the syllabus has been covered and thus how much he has achieved, over against how much is expected of him.

I am sure it will surprise most teachers that never in my experience with the use of these check-lists, even with students with very grade-conscious backgrounds, has there been a request for a letter grade. Something more meaningful has been substituted in its stead. Another gratifying result is frequent student initiative in asking for help on a specific point if one of the items the student is responsible for remains without a red plus after two or three tries. You can imagine how much more fruitful this makes the student-teacher conference than when a student, anxious to defend his work and worried about his poor grades, comes to ask if there is any chance of getting a "C" in the course.

When asking the students to use some of the aspects of composition listed under the heading *Imaginative, precise use of language* in their homework compositions, I have found it helpful to have them use the numbers in parentheses following the items on the Composition Check-List, placing the corresponding number in their composition where they feel they have shown mastery of the item. Artful phrasing or parallel structure, for example, can hardly be expected in every sentence, but if parallel structure were the concern of that lesson, the student would be asked to put a (6) next to his uses of parallel constructions in his composition. The teacher then can identify what the student hoped he was doing, and with no uncertain, time-consuming search through the composition.

PROCEDURES FOR REMEDYING MISTAKES ON ITEMS NOT ON THE CHECK-LIST

I am sure some teachers will want to ask, What is done about mistakes? Are they just left unmarked and uncorrected with no indication to the student that there may be serious flaws in his writing? No, this would hardly be fair or honest. Often it is not the strictly compositional aspects of writing such as those listed on the check-list that make foreign student writing unacceptable; it is errors in patterns or spelling or punctuation. Together with the check-list and perhaps some short note or comment on what the composition communicated —something to acknowledge the writer's personality and his ideas as well as to establish a communicating relationship between the teacher and the student— there are two other procedures which have been helpful, both of them concerned with outright mistakes.

CARELESS, "RED-MARK" MISTAKES

The first is a "Red-mark List" of items which the class, during the first few sessions, agrees could only be careless mistakes indicating sloppy work rather than lack of knowledge or practice. Forgotten terminal punctuation, capitals, or -*s* endings for present tense third person singular verbs are the kind of mistakes I mean. For most intermediate or advanced students they are akin to mis-speaking. The teacher underlines them as a reminder of carelessness and no further issue is made of them except in extreme cases when the student may be asked to count the number of red-mark mistakes and put it in the upper right-hand corner as a confession of sloppiness. Probably you will agree that continued stringent punishment on these irritating and detracting details, although it may be intended to make the student proofread more carefully, seldom does more than add to teacher and student frustration, and deflect attention away from more important things that really merit attention. A caution is necessary, though: the teacher needs to be sure that red-mark items are on a level that truly reflect carelessness only. If the same error is made consistently, it may be that elementary as this mistake is, it has been overlooked or unlearned at an earlier state of English language learning and will have to be treated now as a new pattern to be learned.

FOCUSED DRILL ON PATTERN MISTAKES

A second procedure for dealing with pattern mistakes and others of a non-compositional nature is to revert to individual written pattern drill. Here it is important that the teacher mark only as many mistaken patterns as the student can truly master independently in the interval between compositions; then the teacher needs to set up the kind of written drill that could be effective in helping the student remove this mistake from his writing. (What value would more red marks have, except to discourage the student and remind him how bad his writing is?) In most cases this focused correction would involve underlining a mistaken pattern—perhaps with the mistaken word or ending crossed out—and then writing the correct pattern in the margin with a star to identify it.

In practice, two or three of these starred correction items are about as much as most students can master by themselves in a week. Often in the case of a confusion between two patterns, or in something as confusing as the use of definite articles, it is most helpful to single out only one pattern or one of the uses to be mastered before drilling the two as contrasts. Thus, when a student mistakenly uses *few* for *a few*, there might be a note to describe the particular use and patterning of *few* and then some example sentences to use as models, but not yet a conscious contrasting with *a few*. Teaching through contrasts seems to work best when one of the contrasted items is firmly in hand, and that cannot be assumed in this case. The student is expected to write an additional 10 to perhaps 30 or 40 *true* sentences using the corrected "starred" pattern until he feels sure that he has mastered it. To make this drill homework easier for the teacher to check, the sentences are written on a separate sheet of paper headed with the correct pattern. In this way the checking can be done quickly, but it should be done only to see that *that* pattern is used correctly, not to check on all the other possibilities for mistakes.

This practice in writing meaningful sentences using the now-correct pattern is admittedly only a single, beginning pattern drill, so the student is also asked to copy the correct pattern on a patterns-to-be-learned list. Each week he can be asked to write sentences, each of which uses a pattern from the patterns-to-be-learned list. A requirement that each sentence be meaningful and verifiable will make the sentences more interesting both in the writing and in the correcting, and will help avoid useless nonsense like "I have few lions; I have few tigers," etc. This course-long review is essential for intermediate students; without it, a student often sinks back into the original mistake in just a few weeks.

That only two or three mistakes are treated this way in each composition means, however, that there are still many mistakes that are not corrected. Because of this, it is made clear to the students from the start that even their corrected compositions cannot be thought of as models; instead, the compositions have been focused exercises in writing with perhaps the added interests of communicating with the teacher and practicing the use of English in the form in which they ultimately will need to use it.

There is an additional important advantage to the teacher in being able to focus on only a few mistakes rather than cataloging them all: he can choose his own ground when teaching the use of difficult constructions. In cases where the use of the construction is only questionable, or where the pattern itself is not wrong but it probably doesn't communicate what the student intended, or where the pattern mistake seems almost impossible to unravel from a whole confused paragraph, the mistake can be passed over until it appears in a context that makes it a clear teaching example. Rather unhelpful comments like "awkward" or "rewrite" can be abandoned, also the long explanatory notes we sometimes feel we need to write in order to help the student understand our corrections. This focus on what is best teachable in its most self-evident context in a composition, not only makes for better teaching, but speeds correction. I think you will agree that, besides the agonizing time we spend trying to settle on an honest but not too discouraging grade, it is in the marking of questionable, unclear passages that the teacher invests a disproportionate amount of time—and gets very little return from it.

SUMMARY

To sum up, this check-list method of composition correction tries for efficiency and focus in the following ways:

1. It eliminates proofreading, in favor of marking only those items that have teaching significance.

2. It provides for sufficient teaching and drill on the points to be learned so that they *are* learned, not just introduced or acknowledged.

3. It means that even grammar points and punctuation can be taught *when the teacher is ready to teach them*, and in the clearest, most favorable contexts.

4. It is structured to reinforce what the students *want* to remember and practice—their successes—instead of trying to force them to remember and learn from their failures. (And what do we usually learn from our failures but to give the attempt up entirely?)

5. It makes basic composition into a course with knowable, achievable goals; it takes it out of the art mystique.

6. It offers both the student and the teacher specific evidence that progress is being made—and how much.

7. It lets the student feel he is being judged on his present achievement, not on his misspent past.

8. It eliminates the need for grading, and in its stead gives more precise evaluation of achievement in the separate composition skills.

9. The evaluation is direct and honest in terms of composition skills; it can be easily supported by the teacher, and accepted and respected by the students.

10. It changes the teacher's correction attitude from one of looking for errors and failures to one of looking for successes—and the students feel it.

There may be more advantages that could be claimed, but I will leave them up to those of you whose interest has been won and who look forward to experimenting in your own classrooms with composition check-lists revised and tailored to your own particular needs. If your experience parallels mine, this system will not save you much time in the first year—perhaps never—but the difference in student response and in what your time accomplishes will be astonishing.

Date _____

Name _____ Subject _____

COMPOSITION CHECK-LIST

Rough Outline
    A clear thesis statement that can be supported or proved
    Three or more useful supporting points

Rough Draft
    Shows examples of thoughtful editing

Final Draft
  Mechanics give a clean, orderly impression
    The title—is correctly capitalized
      shows imagination in phrasing
      indicates the subject clearly
    Adequate margins—sides, top, bottom
    Clear indentation for paragraphs
    Clear, easy-to-read handwriting or typing
  Logical development of one idea in a paragraph
    A topic sentence that gives the idea of the paragraph
    A clear controlling idea in the topic sentence
    Supporting statements that focus on the controlling idea
    Clear relationship or transition between sentences
  Imaginative, precise use of language
    Connectives used with precision to show relationship (1)
    Careful, correct use of expanded vocabulary (2)
    Examples of artful phrasing (3)
    Correct spelling and hyphenating (4)
    Correct punctuation to develop the meaning of sentences (5)
    Good use of parallel structure in series (6)
    Good use of phrases or clauses to modify or to tighten the expression of an idea (7)
    Good selection of detail to suggest larger meaning (8)
    A good conclusion that draws the paragraph together (9)
  Good idea content
    A clearly expressed idea, easy for the reader to understand
    An interesting idea, worthy of adult communication
    Challenging, original thinking

Corrections—with adequate practice to insure mastery
    Corrections under all "Red Marks"
    Spelling: 5 times + used in five sentences. Listed.
    Focus items used in at least 10 true sentences. Listed.

26

DICTATION IN
LANGUAGE
LEARNING

JESSE O. SAWYER
and
SHIRLEY KLING
SILVER

What are the most compelling reasons for a teacher to use *text dictations*?

Do you agree that *text dictations* are reasonable first steps toward writing compositions? Why?

To what degree is *note taking* similar to *text dictation*?

In the somewhat sweeping changes that have taken place in language teaching during the last twenty years, dictation as an effective teaching device has been neglected because it has appeared, on the surface, to run counter to the approach to language learning and teaching which strongly emphasizes the spoken languages as the model.[1] Because dictation involves orthographic forms in at least the student's reaction to a language stimulus, and because the introduction of orthography is delayed in some elementary language instruction today, refinements in the uses of dictation do not seem to have been made.[2] It is the purpose of this paper to suggest some possible functions of dictated speech and to recommend these uses to teachers and students of spoken languages.

The objection most likely to be raised to dictation is that the student should not be introduced to a writing system until the sounds of the language and

Reprinted by permission from *Language Learning*, 11, 1961, 1 and 2, 33–42. Mr. Sawyer is director of the language laboratory and lecturer in linguistics at the University of California, Berkeley. Mrs. Silver is coordinator of linguistic analysis, Mechano-linguistics Project, University of California, Berkeley.

Parts of this article were presented at the meeting of the American Speech and Hearing Association in Los Angeles on November 4, 1960.

[1] "Modern linguists are inclined to take the view that Language is the spoken language and that presentation of its visual form too soon is likely to be confusing and ineffective. There is at least one empirical study, by Richards and Appel ("The Effects of Written Words in Beginning Spanish," *Modern Language Journal*, 1956), with the finding that delaying the introduction of orthography resulted in superior pronunciation. But again there is lack of complete agreement." Don E. Dulany, Jr., "Notes for an Investigation of Second Language Learning," (Mimeographed paper), p. 13.

[2] For examples of the types of treatment given see the following discussions: Earl W. Stevick, *Helping People Learn English*, (Nashville, Tenn., 1957), p. 73; Edwin T. Cornelius, Jr., *Teaching English*, (Washington, D.C., 1955), pp. 54–56; Edward S. Joynes, "Dictation and Composition in Modern Language Teaching," *Modern Language Association Publications*, Vol. XV, App. I, 1900, pp. xxv–xxx.

their patterns have been thoroughly learned. This argument is probably valid if a teacher is lucky enough to have a class of students who have never seen the orthographic forms of the language they are learning. However, in American schools and colleges, the more usual situation is that the student has learned the foreign language more from textbooks than from speech, and often has studied under teachers whose assumption is that spelling is the central symbolization of the language.

In many language learning situations the student has not only begun his study of the second language with exposure to an orthographic system, but intermixed with the confusions resulting from the phonological and grammatical impositions which his native language places on the language he is learning are those recognition and production problems which arise out of an automatic set of reactions to the written symbols of his own language. Such problems can occur, for example, in situations in which a Roman alphabet is employed as a source for symbols and the student's native language uses some other system. The student will almost certainly have set up a one to one relation of the Roman symbols to symbols he uses for his own language. A Russian learning English may have some difficulty refraining from substituting /d/ for /g/, since the Cyrillic representation for Russian /d/ looks like the Roman "g." A similar but more extreme example occurs in Indian schools in elementary primers of English using a Devanagari transcription of English. The persistent retroflection of English /t/ and /d/ by many Indian speakers may be blamed in part on the fact that the Devanagari symbols used are traditionally taken from the retroflex series, although a series of symbols for dentals is available. The fact that his native language does not use a Roman alphabet will only rarely prevent a student from making sound-symbol associations based on his own or possibly even a third language.

For the student who has learned a writing system together with some greater or smaller part of the second language, the teacher has no real choice. It would be unrealistic to pretend that the student knows nothing of the new writing system. It would be uneconomical to force the student to act as if he knows nothing of the language and to pretend that he is a child learning a language as a child learns one. Indeed the teacher of English as a foreign language in America almost always finds that many of the errors made by students are due to confusion about the orthographic system. We suggest that dictation is one very effective way of correcting such errors. For the student who has learned the sounds before going on to the writing system, it will form a logical next step.

Dictation can be divided into four types: phonemic items, phonemic text, and orthographic items or orthographic text dictations. In languages such as English, where a phonemic transcription of a fairly long passage presents a problem too difficult for elementary or intermediate students, *phonemic* text dictation would be impractical; in languages having near-phonemic writing systems such a text dictation would be unnecessary. Because item dictations are most useful when teaching pronunciation, *orthographic* item dictation would be pedagogically useless in languages having non-phonemic writing systems; such an item dictation would best be used for teaching spelling after a correlation has been made between the spelling system and the sound system. The following discussion centers around the remaining possibilities, phonemic item and orthographic text dictations.

Phonemic item dictation can be extremely useful in increasing the student's ability to recognize sounds and the contrast in sounds, facilitating his production of those sounds and contrasts. However, its usefulness is primarily limited to encouraging him to stop imposing the sound system of his native language upon the system of the second language. The usefulness of orthographic text dictation is wider and offers the student and the teacher a multiplicity of advantages, both in techniques used and materials presented. We will discuss phonemic item dictation first, as it is the more modest in scope.

One aim of an item dictation is to present the allophonic distributions of phonemes and the contrasts between phonemes in such a fashion that the student will learn, by means of the visual symbols, to associate sounds he already knows with the appropriate sound units and symbols of the second language. He will also correct previously established unsatisfactory patterns, no matter what their origin. Since some languages have writing systems which are near-phonemic, it is practical to use a special system of notation only for those where the orthography does not accurately represent the sound system. Although the importance of the use of a special notation system varies according to the language being learned, the item dictation patterning which emphasizes the contrast in sound is always of importance.

Because in item dictation the attention is centered in the structuring of the sound system, and the effort is to correct those points at which the student introduces unsatisfactory phonemic or subphonemic variations into the system he is learning, the dictation exercises for these problems should be short and consist of single items or brief phrasal items. The student should have already been introduced to the sounds of the language he is studying. Material should not be used for dictation until after pronunciation drill on the problem at hand and oral exercises in production and recognition. A form may be used that did not occur in the pronunciation drill, but that form should consist of an arrangement of sounds already drilled orally.

The dictations should be presented systematically so that they lead from recognition of contrasts to recognition of predictable variants. In presenting English to Hungarians, the contrast between /e/ and /æ/ before voiceless stops, and then before voiced stops, would be dictated before presenting the predictable variation in length of /e/ and /æ/ before the voiceless and voiced stops taken together. This arrangement is followed because Hungarians tend to use vowel length, which is non-phonemic and predictable in English but phonemic and not predictable in Hungarian, as the distinguishing feature when trying to produce the contrast between such words as "met" and "mat." There is no phonemic contrast between /e/ and /ae/ in Hungarian.

The dictations should be structured in the most efficient way possible, according to the distinctive features which mark the contrasts, the similarity in points of articulation and differences in manner of articulation, or the reverse. One or another combination of distinctive features may be used depending upon the problem being dealt with. The environments of the sounds to be recognized should be as rigorously controlled as possible. The reasons for this are obvious. If a student has difficulty recognizing a certain contrast, the fewer non-relevant contrasts he has to listen to the better. As he becomes aware of the pairs of sounds with which he has difficulty, the environments may be elaborated and the dictation may be constructed so that he is simultaneously recognizing two, three, four, or more contrasts in as many different environments. The basic idea of the item dictation may be used in many different ways,[3] but it should be kept in mind that we are talking about dictation as a learning exercise and that the visual symbols used are only aids to help the student achieve adequate production.

The amount of phonological material which can be treated in dictation and the order in which phonological problems should be treated depend, of course, on the language being taught. For English, it might be best to concentrate on segmental phonemic problems before suprasegmental ones. Then too, since we are dealing with items, probably only primary stress should be introduced. As the pitch and juncture phenomena and the stresses other than primary have more significance over longer stretches of speech than the single word, and since it is not practical from the point of view of effective instruction to have students transcribing long utterances, it may be that in English the item dictation could be limited to the segmental phonemes and their arrangements and to primary stress. However, in a language such as Thai, where the tone phenomena serve as the only contrast in many monosyllabic forms, it would obviously be necessary to introduce the learning of tones from the beginning.

For the foreign student of a language who must become skillful enough to follow lectures and live in a new language, orthographic text dictation, in sharp contrast with item dictation, is crucially important, although greater emphasis on phonemic dictation might be desirable in other situations.

A text dictation is a dictation of about 100–150 words taken from contemporary sources that offer reasonable models of the written or spoken varieties

---

[3] R. Rackley has suggested an interesting format for brief phonemic dictations. Ten items are printed on a sheet of paper alongside of two columns of ten blanks each. The paper is folded so that the student does not see the correct forms. After the dictation the student scores his own performance by unfolding the sheet and comparing his own answers with the ten printed items. He then folds the sheet so that he can see neither the answers nor his first effort as the teacher repeats the dictation. The completed papers are then collected by the instructor for grading.

of the language being learned. Like item dictation, the text dictation, which is usually from written rather than spoken sources, should be used as a learning exercise and only secondarily as a testing exercise. Its most important function is providing drill in understanding connected speech. It may consist of a series of isolated sentences or a paragraph, a unified group of sentences. Since speech does not occur as isolated items and context can help the student correct the structural difficulties he has, paragraph dictations that are self-contained contextual units are best for most drills.

The dictations may be selected from materials the student has already read and studied. If this is done, the pattern of presentation would be entirely changed. The strong reason for using material not previously studied is that the student must learn what he hears and what he does not hear. This can only be accomplished by making his experience of hearing the primary and first aspect of the dictation, as indeed it should be.

The materials for dictations must be selected according to the students' abilities and the levels of usage and style for which there will be the most need. If one is teaching high school or college students who must become familiar with a prose style that commonly appears in textbooks and lectures, students who must learn to use such a prose style in examinations and term papers, it is preferable to select dictations that are examples of expository prose, covering a variety of subjects with which the students may have contact. For an elementary class one should select dictations which do not employ stylistic variations that are too different from the grammatical norms the students are learning, (e.g. the uses of the English adverbs of frequency[4]). One should also try in selecting dictations to choose paragraphs containing good examples of problems the class may be dealing with in another area of instruction: features of grammar, vocabulary, spelling, or punctuation.

Although careful consideration must be given to the dictation as a model, it is even more important that the teacher devise a method of graphically distinguishing the difference between the comprehension errors and the spelling errors made when the dictation is taken.[5] A student's "misspelling" of a form may be due to mistaken substitutions (phonological and/or grammatical), e.g., "he thought it wise" > "he has ⟨started⟩ wise"; "Louis XIV was an aristocrat"

---

[4] "never," "often," "always," etc., because of the unusual positions in which they can occur, are confusing to the student who has learned only the most frequent patterns.

[5] In marking student text dictation it is convenient to circle comprehension errors, underline spelling errors, and mark punctuation errors with a caret. A further refinement uses a slant to separate items which should not be joined and a subscript breve to show items which should be joined. The symbols used in marking should be held to a very small number. Examples: "not is" for "is not" would be marked "⟨not is⟩"; "hability" for "ability," " ⟨h⟩ ability"; "triumph" for "triumphs," "triumph◯ "; "be held" for "beheld," "⟨be_held⟩"; "maybe" for "may be," "⟨may be⟩"; "wroar" for "roar," "⟨w⟩ roar"; "triumpht" for "triumphed," "triumpht."

> "Louis XIV was an a (l) istoc (l) at"; "the art of reading is not a virtue" >
"the art of (grad)ing is not a (vulture)"; "he robs no one" > "he r (u) bs no
one," "he (rope)s no one," "he (love) no one," "he (laughs) no one"; "she
is giving a party tonight" > "she is giv (en) a party tonight." However, an
error may be just a spelling error of the sort a native speaker of the language
in question might make, e.g., "receive" > "recieve." Having defined the difference between these two kinds of errors, the absence of forms which were dictated and the presence of forms which were not dictated must also be included
as comprehension errors.

For maximum effectiveness, in order that the student can become acutely
aware of the kinds of errors he makes and begin to correct them, the dictation
is presented three times. When the student first took down the dictation, it
was collected, the errors were marked but not corrected, and it was handed
back to him before the second presentation. Before the preliminary reading
through takes place the second time the dictation is presented, the student
looks at his marked first effort, paying particular attention to the comprehension
errors, and prepares to listen carefully for the forms as they are actually uttered,
so that he can try to supply correct forms when the dictation is repeated at the
rate of speed at which he can write. After the reading through, the teacher
dictates in natural speech-phrase units, repeating each unit and allowing enough
time in the pauses for the student to write. Throughout this repetition the
student has been concentrating on comprehension. At the end the teacher
repeats the dictation for a third time, this time sentence by sentence, and it is
now that the student tries to supply the correct spellings and the appropriate
punctuation, which may or may not be marked phonologically. During all repetitions the person dictating should approximate as closely as possible an appropriate speaking style and a normal speech speed. When the dictation is collected for the second time, the teacher gives the student a typed or dittoed copy
of what he has heard, and he is told to study that copy, if necessary memorize
it. When he hears the same dictation at the next class meeting he should be able
to write it perfectly.

Since a dictation is presented three times and during each presentation is
repeated three times, the student is exposed to the same stream of speech,
divided into units consisting of the paragraph, the spoken phrase unit, and
the sentence, a total of nine times, three times on each of three days. He is
forced into an awareness of his comprehension errors, phonological or grammatical or both. Along with the comprehension problems, his attention is drawn
to the kinds of spelling errors he is prone to make and to the phonological
cues to punctuation. Most important of all, he is forced to correct the errors
he makes.

Another important function of the orthographic text dictation is the practice
it gives the students in simply putting pen to paper in response to a spoken
stimulus. When a student writes a grammar exercise or drills a grammar exercise

orally, especially one which is not properly controlled, or when he writes a free composition, he is often likely to produce grammatically correct sentences that are meaningless, or sentences of "the pen of my aunt is in the garden" variety, which are never either spoken or written. In the paragraph dictation situation he is not responsible for the construction of grammatical patterns, he does not have to make vocabulary choices, he is not forced to make decisions concerning stylistic patterns he may not be aware of, and yet he is writing meaningfully in this second language in a manner approximating the way a native speaker would write.[6]

The text dictation, then, correlates the stream of speech and its written manifestation and presents glimpses of the language in its entirety—the system and the spoken and written variations of a lexical and syntactic nature occurring within the system, and the orthographic conventions used to represent the system and its variations.

Text dictation serves the teacher and the student variously and efficiently. The advantages to the teacher include:

1. Dictation can be used with a class of any size. During the time the dictation is given all of the students are working, not just one or two.

2. If the dictation is presented as the first item in the proceedings of the class, it will effectively quiet the class down. It will also discourage tardiness.

3. The teacher is able to identify and correct a maximum number of different problems in a minimum time. One dictation may take no more than a total of thirty minutes out of three class meetings, but if correctly chosen, it will uncover and correct as many as fifty different errors in a class of ten students.

4. If the class consists of students whose native languages are not the same, the dictation will uncover and force the correction of different types of errors for students with different language backgrounds.

5. Once the dictations are selected and reproduced, no preparation is necessary before going to class except a brief preliminary reading.

6. Dictations are very easy to correct and grade. The teacher will have memorized the dictation by the time he is done presenting it for the first time, and when he has marked the first few papers he will be conscious of the most frequent patterns of mistakes. It takes longer to correct a 150-word essay than

[6]It is worthwhile to quote some comments of Edward S. Joynes', op. cit.: ". . . In dictation we have the most perfect combination of faculties and functions. There is the accurate tongue, speaking to the listening and discriminating ear; there is the reproductive hand, bringing back to the intelligent and critical eye that which the mind has heard by ear—all the faculties of perception, conception, and expression are alert and in harmonious co-operation. As an aid to accurate pronunciation, as a stimulus to alert attention, and as conducive to the sprachgefühl which rests so largely upon the quick apprehension of the spoken language, it presents distinct advantages which no form of written composition can possibly secure.

. . . dictation should be substituted for composition, largely if not wholly, during the earlier stages of instruction."

it does to mark a dictation of the same length. Moreover, because marking is simple, the chore can be more easily delegated than can the reading and marking of compositions.

The advantages to the student are these:

1. He is guaranteed at least ten minutes of work during the class hour. In a class of ten students meeting for fifty minutes, an individual cannot ordinarily expect to recite more than four minutes at best.

2. The student gets practice in the sort of note-taking that many courses require.

3. He gets practice in writing. For some students, particularly those whose native language uses a radically different written symbolization, practice in penmanship is actually necessary. The student is forced to correct writing errors and confusions.

4. He discovers the things he doesn't hear. Many students never fully realize their problems in incorrectly identifying what they hear. They may be able to read and spell a word, but they don't recognize it when it is spoken, or they confuse different words or phrases with the ones they are hearing. They may never realize that they never hear certain elements at all. For instance, a foreign student of English tends not to hear articles when they occur in unstressed position. The dictation, if the marking adequately emphasizes comprehension errors, serves as visual proof of the mistakes a student is making in hearing.

5. Dictation forces the student to be aware that, if he is making errors, only he can correct them. The teacher or the dictation can make him aware of his errors, but he has to correct them himself.

The mechanics for text dictation are these: each dictation is presented at three separate class meetings; after the first day the papers are marked but not corrected; on the second day the student has his first, marked effort in front of him as he writes; at the end of the second presentation the class papers are picked up by the teacher and a copy of the dictation is given to each student; on the third day, the third presentation, the teacher can reasonably insist that all students turn in perfect work.

For the teacher who is tempted to try this device it can be forecast from our own experience that the average student at the end of one semester will have decreased the number of errors he makes in dictations of comparable difficulty by from one third to one half. It is true that such a dramatic change does not mean that the student's control of his new language is proportionately that great. He has, however, learned to listen, to concentrate, to write from dictation; he has become familiar with the teacher's particular voice quality; but these abilities are also part of learning a language. In acquiring them he has learned some part of his second language.

Part Four

Contrastive
Studies

*T*he mere knowledge that another language exists besides one's own implies at least an elementary notion of difference. Teaching a foreign language must always have occurred with at least a tacit awareness of specific differences. It remained for Charles Fries, in founding the University of Michigan's English Language Institute, to deduce from linguistic theory that a sound ESL program should rest upon a detailed structural contrastive analysis of the first and second languages. A denial of this principle later came from universal grammar proponents among transformational linguists on the ground that since the deep structure rules are universal, any describable contrasts are superficial and hence not essential in language teaching. Recently, however, transformational grammar is seen as providing a more substantial basis for contrastive analysis than structural grammar. Ronald Wardhaugh treats this development at length in "The Contrastive Analysis Hypothesis" (*TESOL Quarterly*, 4 (1970), 123-129).

In the meantime the contrastive (or comparative) approach has been extended to a broad range of language matters as found in two languages—or even in two dialects of the same language.

The latter concerns Marckwardt, who dispassionately discusses the overblown differences between British English and American English. He quite effectively reduces them to relatively inconsequential proportions and in effect says, "Let's get on with the job, honorably or honourably, as we wish." A lively and more comprehensive presentation is found in *A Common Language*, a series of dialogues between Marckwardt and Randolph Quirk of University College, University of London, prepared for world broadcast by the British Broadcasting Corporation and the Voice of America. (It is available from the National Council of Teachers of English, Urbana, Ill.)

Bowen examines the contrasts found between the formal and the informal ranges in the regional varieties of American English and advocates a policy of teaching for versatility in receptive control and consistency in productive control. He says nothing, however, about what a teacher whose dialect is Northern American English should do when he gets students whose first year of English has been provided by a teacher from Alabama or East Texas. At this point Marckwardt's guiding principle may well be applicable.

Lee, a British professional in the field, drawing upon his own experience in Czechoslovakia, concludes that teaching bilingualism necessitates the construction, whenever possible, of a systematic contrastive study of the native language and the target language. He arrived empirically at the same position that Fries had taken on theoretical grounds.

Quite a different kind of contrast is the object of Abercrombie's attention. He deals with the language contrasts that occur because of the many relationships of man as a social being to the language that he uses. These relationships, he says, cannot be ignored in helping students gain native-speaker control of English.

The kind of significant contrastive study permitted by generative theory is described and illustrated by Shachter, with a demonstration of relativization in different languages that could not be effectively provided by structural comparison of surface features. Shachter's examples enable a teacher who has been introduced to transformational grammar to develop other useful studies with languages relevant to his teaching.

One effect of this concern with contrastive analysis has been a revival of interest in problems of second-language vocabulary acquisition. Lado, known for his pioneer monograph on cross-cultural problems (*Linguistics Across Cultures*, University of Michigan Press, 1957), discusses the need to treat such acquisition in terms of cultural differences that, for instance, make cognates rather deceptive equivalents. Prator, sympathetic to this point of view, is even more specific in showing how dangerous it is to attempt to equate the complex semantics of English temperature terminology with ostensibly analogous terms in other languages.

Cultural contrasts in the ordering and selecting of ideas and their linguistic representation have long been left ignored, if not unrecognized. Students who advance to the stage where they are asked to write compositions are often criticized adversely for what the teacher calls faults but what are actually the customary characteristics of prose structure in their own language.

When Kaplan came to the ESL field, his personal background in rhetorical studies allowed him to identify the problem as one caused by cultural interference: two rhetorical systems were in conflict. The nature of this quite different kind of interference appears clearly in the results of Kaplan's analysis of compositions written by students coming from different language cultures. His evidence affirms the need for the composition teacher to be as aware of the relevant contrastive rhetorical analysis as the language teacher is of the relevant contrastive linguistic analysis.

27

AMERICAN AND BRITISH ENGLISH

ALBERT H. MARCKWARDT

Which aspects of British and American English differ most? Vocabulary? Pronunciation? Grammar? What additional examples can you provide in each category?

How difficult do you think it would be for an American to teach British English or vice versa?

What arguments might you use to defend teaching your particular variety of English rather than some other?

Most teachers of English as a foreign language in various countries throughout the world are aware of differences between the forms of the language which may be encountered in the United States and that which prevails in England. At one time this caused relatively little difficulty. British English was accepted as the form to be taught, and that put an end to the matter.

Over the past fifteen or twenty years the situation has changed. The greater involvement of the United States in the international scene, the presence of larger numbers of Americans in foreign countries, the improved ease and speed of travel have made for a much wider dissemination of American English than was formerly the case. More residents of foreign countries are hearing American English; more of them find it necessary to communicate with Americans. As a consequence, the previously held assumption that the British variety of English is necessarily the one to be taught in the schools has been challenged upon more than one occasion. Some teachers have recommended a shift from British to American English; others, feeling that the form of the language as it occurs in the country of its origin is somehow more correct or more eloquent, have resisted change.

There is no single easy answer to this question, nor will the answer necessarily be the same for all of the countries in which it is now an issue. Certainly the geographic factor must be given serious consideration. In Mexico, for example, the people are much more likely to come into contact with Americans than with speakers of British English. It would seem eminently reasonable, therefore, to teach the American variety of the language in Mexico. On the other hand, in such countries as Holland or Sweden our conclusion might be exactly the

Reprinted by permission from *ELEC Publications*, 6 (December, 1963), 12-20, the English Language Education Council, Tokyo. The author is professor of English at Princeton University and former director of the English Language Institute at the University of Michigan.

opposite. The situation in a country like Italy permits no easy conclusion. Although closer to England than to the United States in sheer number of miles, the amount of contact with speakers of American English is surprisingly great.

Another factor enters in as well. If English is employed as the language of instruction either wholly or in part from some point in the curriculum onward, one must then consider whether the students will hear American or British English, will read English or American books. In short, the use which is to be made of the language will inevitably have a bearing upon the variety of the language which may be most helpful to those who are learning it.

We must be careful, however, not to fall into the error of exaggerating the differences between American and British English. If we are to consider the question which has been raised, let us by all means do so in the light of as much accurate information as we can assemble. To what extent do British and American English differ? How much alike are they? Where do they differ? Where are they similar? It is only in the light of factually accurate and emotionally neutral answers to these questions that the question should be approached at all. Neither chauvinism nor cultural snobbery is at all helpful in setting the stage for an informed and useful consideration of this problem.

What is so very frequently overlooked is the amount of similarity between these two forms of English, and indeed throughout the English-speaking world in its entirety. It is nothing short of astonishing that in a language spoken as a native tongue by at least 270,000,000 people distributed over five continents of the globe the common element should be so great and the differences so few.

The unity of English is particularly evident in its inflectional system and its syntax. Where they do occur, differences in these grammatical features of the language reflect social or class rather than regional or geographic differences. The inflections of the verb or the uses of the genitive case do not differ perceptibly in the standard language, whether it be that of San Francisco, Canterbury, or Sydney, Australia. It is true, of course, that the speaker of British English may surprise an American by his pronunciation of the past tense form *shone* with the vowel of *fawn* rather than that of *phone* which the latter habitually employs. Likewise, the American's use of the singular verb in *The committee has adjourned* would sound strange to the Briton, who normally uses the plural form in a situation such as this.

But these, after all, are minor matters. The framework or skeleton of the standard language is basically the same on both sides of the Atlantic. Few Americans would hesitate even for a minute to use an English grammar written in the United Kingdom for their classes in the United States. Conversely, I feel safe in assuming that a teacher in England would not be likely to question the applicability of a grammar written in the United States to his teaching situation. The subject precedes the verb in statements, and the adjective comes before the noun no matter where English is spoken. The differences between American and

British English are to be found principally in a few features of pronunciation and in certain sectors of the vocabulary.

Let us consider first some of the differences in pronunciation. Without question there are two characteristic features of the segmental phonemes of American English which are immediately apparent to speakers of British English as well as to non-native speakers. The first of these is the American use of the /æ/ phoneme in words like *calf, bath, pass,* and *aunt,* where British English employs a retracted vowel of the /a/ type, often lengthened. It should be noted, however, that this difference occurs principally when the vowel in question is followed by a voiceless fricative continuant and on occasion by the nasal /n/. It is to be found, so John S. Kenyon once estimated, in approximately 150 commonly used words.

However, when the vowel in question is followed by consonants other than those which have been mentioned, as in *cap, cab, cat, bad, back, bag, sand, hang,* both British and American English employ /æ/. There are approximately 450 commonly used words which behave in this fashion, roughly three times as many as those in which the two varieties of English differ. Even here, therefore, the points of similarity significantly outweigh the points of difference.

The other principal difference between British and American in the segmental phonemes is to be found in words like *learn, core, fork, brother.* In most varieties of American English, specifically all except coastal New England and the tidewater South, the tongue has an upward glide in pronouncing the /r/, producing a type of sound which phoneticians classify as retroflex. In British English the tongue remains flat in the mouth, resulting in the so-called *r*-less type of speech. But again we should not permit our awareness of the differences to obscure the similarities. Both American and British English pronounce initial /r/, in such words as *real, race, rat, roll,* and *run* with a downward movement of the tongue. In both varieties of English an /r/ between vowels, in words like *carry, forest, mural,* consists of an upward and a downward tongue glide. Again the story is not entirely one of difference; there are similarities as well.

In words like *secretary, dictionary, stationery,* and *territory,* amounting to several hundred all told, American English places a distinct secondary stress upon the next to the last syllable. In British English the stress is weak. In this instance American English preserves a feature of the language which has become archaic in England. Shakespeare's line from Hamlet, "Nor customary suits of solemn black," can be scanned only with a pronunciation similar to that of present-day American English, and the same is true of Spenser's "Forsaken, woeful solitary maid."

In fact, all three of the differences between British and American pronunciation which have been dealt with thus far are alike in one respect: they represent older stages of the language, features which were originally a part of British English, which have been replaced in England by innovations but which have remained characteristic of the speech of the United States.

No discussion of British and American pronunciation would be complete without reference to the differences in intonation pattern. The following pairs of sentences will serve as illustrations:

British	*American*
My name is John	My name is John.
Are you quite sure?	Are you quite sure?
Will you pass the salt, please?	Will you pass the salt please?

Note that there are several rather striking differences in the tonal melody of these two varieties of English. For one thing, the range of the British sentence, the distance from the highest to the lowest tone, is generally greater. Moreover, the British sentence reaches a high tone either at the very beginning or soon after, and then the tone descends gradually until the final terminal juncture, with its accompanying intonation turn, is reached. In contrast, the American sentence maintains a fairly level tone until just before the termination.

These differences in intonation, and what has been illustrated here is by no means comprehensive, make it difficult for Americans to understand speakers of British English when they first hear them, and *vice versa*. In fact, they are in all probability primarily responsible for whatever difficulties in mutual comprehension do exist. The reason for this is evident. Any departure from the intonation pattern to which the listener is accustomed will so absorb his attention that he does not cut or separate the continuum of speech into its component elements.

Thus far the comparison between British and American English with respect to pronunciation has brought to our attention distributional differences in two segmental phonemes, the retention of secondary stress in American English in certain plurisyllables, and certain features of intonation characteristic of each of the varieties of the language. Although this is by no means a complete inventory, it does include the principal points of difference. Certainly the list is not a large one.

Vocabulary differences between British and American English occur in certain well-defined and predictable situations, namely when they reflect differences in physical objects or features characteristic of the two countries, when they reflect different practices or ways of dealing with things, and when they are the product of institutional differences.

We may begin most conveniently with differences in physical features and objects. That the plant and animal life in England and America should differ to some degree is easily understandable. The United States is a large country with a far greater range of climate and topography than England. There are trees and plants which flourish in America which occur rarely if at all in England. Such words as *hickory*, *tamarack*, and *squash* are all borrowings from American

Indian languages. This is true also of such animal names as *moose, raccoon,* and *caribou.*

In general the landscape of much of England may be described as neatly tailored. Though it may possess grandeur in its own way, it lacks the immense variety and some of the extreme features of American topography. It is not surprising, therefore, that the United States has built up its own set of topographical terms, some of which were taken over from the vocabularies of those European nations which were displaced in America by the aggressive English-speaking colonials. Words like *mesa* and *savannah* have been taken over from Spanish; *butte* and *bayou* came into American English from the French. In addition such terms as *water gap, bluff,* and *hog back* represent peculiarly American developments of native English elements.

To select just one other aspect of life, we must recognize that there is little correspondence between farms and farming in England and America. The crops are by no means identical; land use differs, and so do the very buildings. In fact, farms throughout the United States are by no means the same. Thus, such words as *ranch* and *corral* occur only in parts of the United States. What is a *hay loft* in an American barn in one part of the country may be a *hay mow* in another. Hay in the field may be temporarily stacked in *doodles.*

American domestic architecture has, on the whole, been somewhat more experimental than its English counterpart. An Englishman might be puzzled by an American's reference to a *tri-level house,* a *ranch house,* a *family room,* or a *recreation room.* There would be little in his experience with homes that would explain such terms. At the same time the American reading an English classified advertisement would be bewildered by the terminology of land tenure: *entailed* and *free hold* are entirely out of his experience, and although he could upon reflection understand what was meant by *hire-purchase plan,* it is not a term that he habitually uses.

Even when the material or physical objects are quite alike in the two countries, they are not always dealt with in precisely the same manner, and again this leads to some differences in terminology. This is particularly true with respect to food. Meat is cut quite differently. No American ever speaks of a *joint,* a *hunch,* or a *collop.* He rarely eats mutton, and if he did it would be likely to call it lamb. He *broils* a steak; he does not *grill* it. The American housewife is much more inventive in the way in which she prepares chicken for the table; consequently in purchasing one she is likely to request a *broiler,* a *stewer,* a *roaster,* or a *fryer.*

Although the sandwich was invented in England, it is the Americans who have shown an amazing degree of versatility in developing it in all its variety. Combinations and the resulting terminology range all the way from the *cheeseburger* to peanut butter and jelly, or bacon, lettuce, and tomato. Indeed, the American vocabulary of the sandwich and the soda fountain, the latter with its innumerable combinations of ice-cream sodas and sundaes, constitutes a unique development in the language.

A totally different type of difference is to be found in the vocabulary of musical notation, as it is employed in the two countries. The American uses a mathematical terminology for the length of time that a note is held: he speaks of full notes, half notes, quarter notes, eighth, sixteenth, and so on. The British terms are wholly different. Note such terms as breve, semibreve, crotchet, quaver, semi-quaver, semidemiquaver, hemisemidemiquaver. The British terminology is similar to that employed in the various Latin countries of Europe, whereas the Americans appear to follow a pattern current in Germany.

Strangely enough, the American propensity for a mathematically graded terminology appears again in the vocabulary of type sizes; he speaks of eight point, ten point, twelve point type, whereas the corresponding English terms are based upon jewel names: ruby, agate, pearl, etc.

Another type of situation likely to result in terminological differences occurs when a new invention strikes both countries at the same time, facing each with the necessity of developing a new terminology almost immediately. This was the case, for example with the *railroad*, as it is called in America, or the *railway*, as it is much more likely to be called in England. The Englishman rides in a coach; the American takes his seat in a car. Merchandise transported by rail is called *freight* in America. In England, a depot would be a depository for such merchandise only at a railway terminal. An American may purchase a ticket at a depot, wait in it for a train to arrive, or pick up some merchandise which has been stored there. In America merchandise is conveyed by rail in a *freight car*, in Britain in a *goods van*. The last car on an American freight train is a *caboose*; its English counterpart is a *braking van*.

Differences as extensive as this could be found in the vocabulary of the automobile, the radio or wireless, and television. The American's *TV* is the Englishman's *telly*, just to mention a random instance. The important thing is not so much the items themselves as a recognition of the situations in which differences are likely to occur.

Finally we come to the third type of situation likely to produce varying terminologies in the two countries, namely institutional differences. We may as well begin with the object of our immediate concern, namely education. What is called a *public school* in England is known as a *private school* in the United States. The English university *staff* (American *faculty*) lacks the academic hierarchy of instructor, assistant professor, associate professor, and professor, which is characteristic of the United States. The Americans have no dons, nor do they employ the title *reader*. The American student's concern with credits, semester hours, honor points, and grade-point average would be so much Greek to the Oxonian, who has his own terminology equally incomprehensible to the American.

As soon as the United States gained its independence, it was faced with the necessity of devising its own governmental system. In some ways this followed the English pattern, but in other important respects it differed. The United States constitution refers to a written document; the English constitution is an un-written body of doctrine and precedent. The term *cabinet* is used differently in the two countries; moreover, American cabinet members are *secretaries* of one executive department or another; their English counterparts are *ministers*. An English candidate for office is *named* by his party, and he *stands* for election. The American is *nominated* and he *runs* for office. Actually, the differences here are considerable enough so that an entire dictionary of American political terms has been compiled.

It would be possible to dwell at equal length upon differences in the ter-minologies of religion, of law, of medicine, even of sports, but I believe that the point has been made with sufficient clarity that institutional differences produce differences in terminology. We may, however, note briefly that England has a state religion; the United States has not. Thus there are no *dissenters* in the United States, since there is no established church to dissent from. Moreover, the proliferation of minor sects in the United States has given rise to a long list of names which has no English counterpart, terms such as Holy Rollers, Hardshell Baptists, Dunkards, and Amish.

The English distinction between *barrister* and *solicitor* goes back ultimately to a division between common law and equity which does not exist in the same form in the United States, hence the terminological difference has disappeared. In England the title *Doctor* is confined primarily to physicians, and is extended even to surgeons only under special circumstances. In the United States, not only are all physicians and surgeons called *Doctor*, but the title is extended to dentists, veterinarians, osteopaths, and chiropractors. This constitutes one illus-tration of a practice widely prevalent in America, the much wider extension of honorific titles in almost all areas of life.

Another way of looking at these lexical differences is to consider them as illustrative of certain cultural themes or processes which have served to differ-entiate life in America from that in the United Kingdom. To begin with, it is widely recognized that American culture is an amalgam of the many foreign cultures which have been fused with an Anglo-Saxon base. The United States has been called the melting pot of the world, a term first applied by Israel Zangwill. The millions of immigrants from Scandinavia to the Balkans, from the Indies, the Orient, and Africa, though in the main conforming to the new ways of life which they found in their adopted home, could not help leaving some im-press upon the heterogeneous mixture of which they formed a part. In the realm of language, in precisely the same fashion, the acquisitiveness of the American vocabulary in drawing upon these many component elements of the culture, makes of American English a linguistic melting pot in miniature.

At the same time, both the culture and the language in America tend to pre-serve certain traits which were originally English but which have since been dis-continued in the mother country. We have already seen how this has operated in connection with pronunciation. Similarly, the American vocabulary frequently preserves words and meanings of words which have been discontinued in England. American English, for example, retains the term *druggist*, which has been replaced by *chemist* in England. Andirons, still in common use in America, died out in England at the end of the eighteenth century. The verb *guess* in the sense of "suppose" or "estimate" is now recognized as an Americanism, although it was used in this way by Chaucer. *Cabin*, now confined to nautical use in England, means "a poor dwelling" in the United States; it did so in England up until about 1832. In short, these post-colonial survivals of earlier phases of mother-country culture, in language as well as in other phases of culture, appear to constitute what might be appropriately called a colonial lag.

We have already mentioned certain developments in American English which reflected the peculiar growth of American ways and institutions. Many of these were connected with life on the frontier of European civilization in this new continent, a way of life which led to the development of native ingenuity and impatience with tradition. This is illustrated in the language as well, in such practices as the ready conversion of nouns into verbs, nouns to adjectives, and so on. Impatience with tradition condones the clipping of words: as a consequence we have shortened *telephone* to *phone*, *cablegram* to *cable*, *turnpike* to *pike*, and so on. Inventiveness accounts for our constant creation of new compounds and blends. The results are not always pleasing to those with conservative taste; they are frequently striking and apt.

Again, this is by no means a complete inventory of the culture or of the linguistic developments which occurred as a consequence of the culture traits. It serves to show, nevertheless, that what happens in a language does not occur by accident but is a concomitant of the life of a people. The same factors account for such regional differences which are to be found within America as well as the differences between American and British English.

This brings us back to the question which was posed at the outset of this discussion—what type of English is to be taught as a foreign or second language in various countries throughout the world. Although this discussion has dealt with the differences between American and British English rather than the similarities, the point that the similarities outweigh the differences, both in number and proportion, has constantly been emphasized. We have seen that differences in pronunciation were confined to relatively minor matters, particularly if one keeps his eye upon the entire phonological system of the language. The fact that differences in vocabulary permit the kind of organization that I have given them is in itself evidence that they occur only in certain sectors and do not pervade the entire lexicon. As we have seen, inflections and syntax are generally uniform throughout the entire English-speaking world.

All of this means, perhaps, that the question causes more concern than is really justified. The differences which do exist have been presented in terms of the historical and cultural background of these two great English-speaking nations. It is evident, therefore, that any notion of the supposed superiority of one type of English over the other is quite beside the point, since we cannot with any pretense at reason say that one kind of life, or one chain of historical development is superior to the other. The two varieties of the language differ simply because the speakers of each of these major divisions of the English language reflect a different total environment and a different set of historical events as a background.

This leaves only one criterion for approaching the question of which kind of English to teach, namely the cultural aspects of British and American life which the students in question are likely to encounter. In some instances the solution will be easy; in others it will be much more difficult. Nevertheless, if this is taken as a guiding principle in dealing with the problem, it places social utility in the foreground. This is precisely where it should be in any consideration of language and language teaching.

28   LINGUISTIC   J. DONALD BOWEN
VARIATION AS A
PROBLEM IN
SECOND-LANGUAGE
TEACHING

> Can justification be found for teaching ESL students more than one of each of the five linguistic variations of *time, space, level, form,* and *intention* discussed in this article?

> Compare prescriptivism as it applies to the study of the first language and to the study of a second or foreign language.

> What skills must be taught to make a student a proficient writer of English over and beyond those that would make him a proficient speaker of English?

Modern linguistic studies have contributed in a number of important ways to our understanding of language. Perhaps the most basic contribution has been a definition which states that language is speech, the speech of its users, and the implied corollary that a course in a language should describe the sounds, the

Printed by permission. This paper was read at the convention of the National Council of Teachers of English, San Francisco, Calif., Nov. 29, 1963. Dr. Bowen is professor of English at the University of California, Los Angeles.

grammatical structures, and the lexicon which speakers employ when they use the language.

This view of language was proposed at a time when most people thought of language teaching as a means of presenting an ideal. Classes typically presented what the teacher thought the language ought to be, and the teacher followed a tradition which was formed by men who thought that a written grammar would give the same stability to English usage that it seemed to give classical Latin and Greek. The eighteenth century grammarians did not appreciate the enormous difference that exists between living and dead languages.

When the new, linguistically-oriented scholars became vocal, they characterized their approach as *descriptive*, and rather impiously tagged the tradition as *prescriptive*. The implication for teaching was made specific: we should teach what people actually say when they communicate, not what someone thinks they should say. Otherwise we lose touch with reality, and the most important purpose of teaching is frustrated.

But we need not flog a dead horse. The attitudes of the descriptive approach have by now found fairly general acceptance, and it is no longer fashionable to berate Miss Fittich as the symbol of weaknesses in traditional language classes. Sufficient time has passed to allow us to look back with the advantage of perspective.

Miss Fittich was undoubtedly a sincere teacher who was able to observe and see that among her acquaintances some were able to use the language more effectively than others. Why not copy the best? The natural standard to follow was the not then successfully challenged tradition of the prescriptive grammarians.

Those of us who teach English as a second language today are faced with essentially the same problem. We are aware of variety in language usage, and we want to teach the most effective or most useful variants to our students. We have mostly abandoned the prescriptive tradition, but—we cannot renounce the prescriptive approach. Why? Because this is the most important function of the teacher in a second-language classroom: to supply a model and to provide guidance for the students. Every time a student utters a sentence or asks for a confirmation of his efforts the teacher must check the performance against the established standard for the class. If necessary she must prescribe corrections, modifications, additional attempts, etc.

If there have to be standards, as of course there must be, how are these standards to be determined? Miss Fittich had it easy in this respect. She just referred to the textbook or to the handbooks and followed the advice given. We who have forsaken traditional answers in order to follow actual usage have the unhappy responsibility of determining just what usage we will follow.

One apparent solution is to say, "I'll follow my usage," but will any one person's usage be typical of the whole language? And even if we follow the speech of one individual—our own—how can we reconcile the fact that our own usage changes in different situations, on different occasions, and for different purposes? This is a dilemma that is not easy to resolve.

We should approach an attempt at a solution by first trying to understand as much as possible about linguistic variation in general and then determine how it applies to English in particular. Then we will perhaps be better able to handle the thorny question of classroom standards.

There are at least five concepts of variation that can be described.[1] The first is the dimension of time. As time passes, language changes. We notice these changes when we try to read something that was written several hundred years ago. Though there are changes in grammar and usage, the most noticeable changes are in the lexicon. Even words which we readily recognize and occasionally use may have an archaic flavor. Examples of such words are *whence, thither, raiment, betake, gladsome, pleasance, foregather, milady, goodwife, quoth.* Some words have become obsolescent because the items they name are no longer in common use, such as *rumble seat, celluloid, corset, gramophone, penny postcard.*

One area of our experience maintains the systematic use of archaic language: religious services and ceremonies. As a tie with the past, religion places a high value on traditional language. Thus religious sermons, and especially prayers, preserve older forms, such as the pronouns *thee, thou, thy, thine* and the verb forms that are associated with them: *art, sayest, preparest,* as well as the older third person singular verb forms: *maketh, leadeth, restoreth.* Certain of the formulas for marriage, a traditionally religious ceremony, preserve archaic usage, "With this ring I thee wed." All of these are acceptable to speakers of English, if they are used in the right context.

Of course over a period of time there are considerable changes in pronunciation, many of which are reflected in older spellings that have been retained, such as in *Knight Templar, Wednesday, Worcestershire sauce, colonel, gnash,* and many others. Pronunciation changes, while they are historically very interesting, create no problem for contemporary English beyond the incorrect productions which are suggested to students by archaic spellings, when the word is seen before it is learned orally.

A second concept of linguistic variation is in space. This is perhaps the most widely recognized form of variation. People in one place do not speak like people in another, even when both are using the same language. We speak of these differences in terms of dialects, and we recognize numerous dialect regions throughout the English-speaking world.

---

[1] The underlying analysis of linguistic variation presented in this paper was developed at the Philippine Center for Language Study for inclusion in a textbook tentatively titled *Freshman English—A Textbook for Filipino College Students.* The analysis was prepared by Tommy R. Anderson with criticisms and revisions by other members of the writing team including Roderick J. Hemphill, Anne Newton, Bonifacio Sibayan, and the present author.

Dialect differences are a result of changes in language where people in one area have not had the opportunity of easy and continuous communication with people in another area. Probably all languages have dialects, with the possible exception of languages which have only a very small number of speakers all of whom know and communicate with each other.

Dialect differences may be very limited, with hardly any notice of variations made by speakers, or they may be considerable, with variations that are quite obvious. If dialect divergency continues without intercommunication, new languages emerge, which are mutually unintelligible, and these languages may then begin to develop dialects of their own.

Dialect differences stem from changes in the spoken language which usually are not immediately reflected in the writing system. As a result there is a time lag in the awareness of differences when the written form of the language is used. Where the Englishman says *zed*, for example, the American says *zee*, but both use the same symbol to represent the twenty-sixth letter of the alphabet.

A third type of linguistic variation is in level. In almost any society there are occasions which differ from one another in the amount of formality necessary. The relationships between people may vary from intimate and familiar to highly formal. Two speakers may consider each other equals in rank or position or they may recognize a considerable difference. The relative ages of speakers will affect the level of formality they observe when they communicate. Even the same two people may feel a difference in the level of formality on two different occasions; a bull session in the dormitory might discuss the same issues as a formal debate, but the level of the discussions would certainly be different.

Formality levels must be appropriate to the situations they are used in. Otherwise the language becomes conspicuous and the situation incongruous. One may not say to his professor, "Hi, Pete. Howsa kid?" And it is equally inappropriate to say to one's classmate, "How do you do, Joseph. I trust you are enjoying this magnificent morning."

There are likewise formality contrasts in the written form of the language. A personal letter to a close friend would certainly be more informal than a research paper. In a letter one can use contractions, abbreviated spellings like *thru* and *tho*, and use an appropriately informal vocabulary. In a research paper for publication the writer will probably observe all the traditional rules, avoiding split infinitives and sentence-final prepositions, since this display of erudition will inspire more confidence in the educated reader.

The fourth type of linguistic variation is in form: the consistent differences one finds between the spoken and written forms of language. Oral and written communication are different in several ways. The speaker usually has the advantage of personalized human contact and interaction. The hearer participates in an immediate manner, signaling by his confirmations, his gestures, and his comments and questions that the ideas expressed are indeed being understood. But the writer can't model his message to the particular situation as he goes along. He must anticipate the reader's reaction, provide careful transitions from one idea to another, avoid any possible ambiguities. Speech is unilinear and uni-directional, and usually cannot be relistened to, but a reader can reread any part of a message he chooses. Furthermore a writer can use charts and tables to show more than one dimension, and these are comprehended much more readily from paper than from oral explanation.

These differences are important to expression. Speech must be reasonably simple, but the speaker can model his sentences as he speaks, adapting his presentation to the comprehension level of his hearers. The writer must judge his most probable audience in advance and write for them. In his writing he may employ much more complicated structures, but at the same time he must develop his ideas much more explicitly. He cannot utter a parenthetical "You know what I mean?" to insure the success of his communication efforts.

Speech and writing are, then, quite different skills. A person who speaks well can be a poor writer, and vice versa. Almost everybody has experienced the college professor who may have written brilliant books, but who is incapable of an articulate presentation before a class.

The final type of linguistic variation is in intention, which may be charac-terized as straightforward language, designed for basic communication, versus artistic language, designed not only to inform, but also to impress, to amuse, or to convince. Straightforward language is effective if it communicates accurately, with a minimum of distraction from errors, from inappropriately matched levels, or from extraneous ideas. Artistic language is effective if it communicates beautifully, amusingly, or persuasively. We can refer to these three intentions of artistic language as poetry, humor, and propaganda. In each case the speaker or writer attempts to do more than just inform; he tries to influence.

This kind of variation is visible in literature, and literature has been used to clothe the most important ideas that man has conceived. Indeed one way to in-sure attention and survival for an idea is to express it skillfully in artistic lan-guage so it will become part of the world's great literature.

Variation for intention can be thought of in terms of the difference between prose and poetry, though the comparison is not always formally applicable. Some prose is highly poetic, and some poetry is completely prosaic. Either form must be judged by the intention of the author and by the degree to which he suc-ceeded in expressing his intention effectively.

This is probably the most difficult kind of language production. It is not easy to communicate clearly and at the same time beautifully. Our great writers have succeeded, and that is why they are great. We enjoy reading a recognized work of literature because it is a worthy art form.

What are the implications of the five kinds of linguistic variation discussed above to teaching English as a second language? Two of these variations, in time and in intention, are usually met for the first time in school by first *or* second-language students. The main handicap imposed on the learner of a second language is the need to know which words are archaic and which are literary, so these can be avoided in situations which are contemporary and nonliterary.

Variations in space are something of a problem, especially in learning a language that is spoken over a wide area and has many recognized dialect differences. Native speakers usually prefer dialect consistency, and an indiscriminate mixing will call attention to the speech rather than the message of the speaker. It would be disturbing to hear: "Well now, I don't want to ask for any more candy" pronounced as: /wǽel ǀ nǽew ↓ áh dō͞w wân ậ < sk ǀ fir êniy mǭh kéhndiy ↓ /. Actually, however, dialect consistency is not a serious pedagogical problem, since a student who can approximate *any* native English dialect will usually be found doing satisfactory work.

The other two types of variation, in level and in form, are the most troublesome in second-language teaching. In most typical situations, native speakers get their experience in informal and in spoken language outside of school. They have mastered the spoken language (appropriately for their age level) when they enter school, and almost all their linguistic experience has been relatively informal. Hence the job of the school is to teach them the written language, and, in the relatively formal context of the schoolroom, to instill an appreciation for various degrees of formality and a recognition of the situations in which these are appropriate. It is quite a satisfactory arrangement for the student to get most of his oral, informal English outside of school and his contact with written, formal English in school. One means supplements the other, and the student has a well rounded linguistic and social development.

But the situation is quite different in the case of a student who studies a foreign language. Usually he must depend upon the classroom for his total experience in his new language, and any imbalance in the class presentation will be reflected by a comparable imbalance in his total control of the language. Yet traditionally our second-language classrooms have been modeled on first-language teaching situations. Students are taught the formal forms of the language, and a major attention is given to writing from the very first meetings of the class. The result has been an inadequate control of the language for even the best students, generations of whom have been told "If you really want to learn to speak French, you've got to go live in Paris."

An important responsibility of the second-language classroom that is not shared by first-language teaching is to adequately present oral, informal language. This is not to say there is no room for written or formal English. These too must be presented, and the student must be given the experience that will enable him to match the appropriate linguistic resources to the needs of a variety of situations. It is not too difficult to teach a child to say "Hi, Gloria," but "Hello, Mrs. Williams" and even "Good morning, ma'am" to an adult stranger. I once witnessed a class of American children studying French. They were taught a greeting formula for use with their peer group which consisted of saying "Bonjour, Monsieur (or Mademoiselle)," shaking hands, and bowing stiffly from the waist. French children in France do not greet each other in this way, and to require this unnatural procedure of American students violates every canon of linguistic and cultural reality, with no corresponding pedagogical gain.

Perhaps it can be said that students will need formal more often than informal forms, or that if they must err, formality in an informal situation is less of a social breach than informality in a formal situation. But why must we be satisfied with only one level of formality when more can be presented so easily?

Even if the students will use the language mostly in formal situations one can still justify teaching informal patterns. It is still desirable to learn both, and experience has shown that a student who can handle informal forms will have almost no difficulty recognizing the language used in formal situations. A student who can easily understand the spoken form "Whaddaya wanna know?" will have relatively little difficulty with the pronunciation "What do you want to know?" If he can handle the elisions and reductions of informal speech he will be able to understand the precise pronunciations of formal style. But the opposite is not true. A student familiar only with the formal language is likely to be lost when the situation is authentically informal.

The discussion up to this point suggests that the teacher of a second language has a difficult assignment. She is forced by the situation she is placed in to be a prescriptivist, though modern descriptive grammarians have told her prescription is bad. Nevertheless, she is the most important and very often the only source of language models and linguistic guidance available to the students, and she must make decisions every minute of the class hour on the acceptability of pronunciation, forms, and structures used by students groping their way toward effective fluency.

But unlike the traditional prescriptivist in a first-language class, there is no clear authority she may appeal to for decisions in various situations. There is no uniformity but rather a multiplicity of standards, with different usage requirements for different purposes on different occasions, and there is no supporting context of out-of-school experience to supplement and reinforce the students' classroom learning.

To fulfill this rather large order, to accommodate to the needs of multiple standards and heavy demands on flexibility, the teacher needs help and cooperation from others involved in the educational process. She is, in effect, being asked to provide vicarious experiences which will be a satisfactory substitute for growing up in a linguistic and cultural community. She needs to know as much as possible about language usage at different levels, for different purposes, and in different forms. She needs to have a set of text materials that incorporates this knowledge into meaningful and appropriate situations. And she needs a set of workable pedagogical guidelines that will help her interpret and present these materials to her students.

This set of guidelines for teaching English as a second language should possibly include some of the following ideas: 1) The teacher should master the language as well as she can. This is relatively simple for an American teaching English, but is often quite difficult for a second-language teacher. Perhaps more important, any teacher should present the language as naturally as possible, with variations that reflect the different areas of experience the student must become familiar with. Validity of selection should be matched by naturalness of presentation. 2) An adequate variety of forms should be presented, with special attention to the needs of informal, oral English, which has been neglected in much of the teaching of the past. 3) Minimum contrasts should be presented to students. Differences in form which are not essential to a working control of the language, such as the pronunciation contrasts between *merry, marry, Mary,* (or /mériy, mǽriy, méhriy/) can perhaps be omitted from active presentation in the interest of simplicity, though students should probably have an opportunity to hear such variants. 4) Structural simplicity may be encouraged where it does not conflict with basic patterns of English, and especially where the background language of the students lacks some feature or pattern. If consonant clusters are a difficult problem, certain clusters such as /ty, dy, ny/, etc. in words like *tune, dew, news* can be eliminated since /túwn, dúw, núws/, are quite acceptable alternates. 5) In selecting forms or pronunciations, the text and the teacher should probably follow the majority rule within the dialect area being represented in the text. A teacher might not use certain items or might lack certain contrasts, but if they are generally present in the speech of most people, they should probably be taught actively. The /ɔ/ of *taught* is not distinguished from the /a/ of *tot* by some speakers, but most people do make the distinction, so the second-language student should learn it. 6) Perhaps the most important guideline is a recommendation that the student be exposed to linguistic variety, to all the variations of dialect, form, level, or intention that he should be in control of or familiar with as an educated and articulate second-language speaker of English.

From very early in the language-learning process, when this is an academic experience, a student should begin to develop receptive versatility by hearing different speakers (in person or recorded) in a variety of linguistic situations. It is my belief that this will not significantly affect a student's chance of developing consistent dialect habits, but in developing a tolerance for differences in individual speakers a student will have an opportunity to extend his tolerance to an acceptance of patterned varieties in the language. This is highly desirable in view of the necessity of developing multiple standards. The chance of confusion is a much smaller risk than the alternative likelihood of limited adaptability to varied situations.

This recommendation is based on an analysis of the different roles all of us play as speakers and as hearers of the language we use, that is, on an analysis of the differences in our performance on the productive and the receptive levels of language. In both roles we operate with linguistic systems. In pronunciation we are involved in the phonemic system. An individual speaker will utter the sounds of his language with an amazing consistency of pronunciation detail. In linguistic terms we say he has a limited number of allophones and these are distributed in a pattern that gives minimum scope to free variation. But as a listener the same person must be capable of distinguishing a wide variety of pronunciations since different people speak differently—even within a limited speech community. We are conscious of certain common variants, such as /íyðir ~ áyðir/, /ráwt ~ rúwt/, /rúf ~ rúwf/, /grísiy ~ gríyziy/, /ráeðir ~ ráðir/, and /énvilòwp ~ ánvilòwp/, but there are others that are less obvious to many native speakers of English, such as /árnj ~ɔ́rnj ~ ówrnj ~ árinj ~ɔ́rinj ~ ówrinj/. A well-taught student of English should recognize any of these for the famous Sunkist product and should be able to identify the oral expression of mirth when pronounced /láef ~ léhf ~ láehf ~ lá f ~ láf/ or láef/. He must be prepared to interpret the varied allophones of numerous idiolects and to gather the speakers' meanings by a correct phonemic analysis of what he hears.

The second-language speaker, like the native speaker, needs more flexibility and more versatility as a listener than as a speaker. This is even more likely to be true in his case because he may have to interpret the speech of other second-language speakers who produce the language with a variety of more or less closely modeled approximations to native phonemic systems.

A similar increased demand is made on versatility in sentence structures. All of us hear a greater variety and complexity of sentence patterns than we commonly use ourselves, and the problem of interpretation is correspondingly greater. The same difference can be noted even more readily in vocabulary. Our active vocabulary constitutes only a small proportion of the number of words we must be prepared to understand, and our passive vocabulary is therefore very much greater in size.

The second-language speaker needs this extra flexibility as a listener (or as a reader) of the language just as much as a native speaker does. In some cases he may need it more. It is my contention that the second-language classroom should be specifically geared to provide for this need, and that the way to do this is to provide multiple standards for all the legitimate variations of the language and to present these in a context of situations that is sufficiently varied to develop the kinds of adaptability and versatility that the student must achieve. The prescriptive guidance of the teacher should always be directed toward this end.

THE LINGUISTIC   W. R. LEE
        CONTEXT OF
        LANGUAGE
        TEACHING

Explain the *mountain-molehill* analogy Lee uses with examples from various languages.

What advantages does Lee believe can be derived from *mistakes analysis?*

Why is a single *analysis of mistakes* for speakers of a given language not sufficient?

In what way is knowledge of the students' language useful?

No language is ever studied in a linguistic vacuum. The environment of learning includes at least that same language or another, and may include several languages, audible and perhaps visible on every side. When a second language is attempted, it is usually in an environment of the learner's first language, acquired as a child, so that all around him are linguistic patterns whose tyranny he is struggling to escape. And even in a community using the second language he needs, a learner has his home-language habits to combat.

D. Y. Morgan, in a recent article (*E.L.T.*, X, 3), divided English language teaching into the three categories of presentation, practice, and remedial work, and argued that the last of these can be well planned only by basing it on an inquiry into pupils' mistakes. He is undoubtedly right on the latter point, and has shown too that diagnosis of this kind can be readily made. The merit of such an approach is that we get down to the pupils' level and see some of the difficulties through their eyes. So doing, we are constantly reminded that it is not simple English we teach, but English to Spaniards, English to Chinese, English to Poles, to Nigerians, to Pakistanis, to Brazilians, to Finns, as well, of course, as to pupils of various ages, attitudes, and capacities. It is clear that English, quite apart from the local features which characterize it in different parts of the English-speaking world, appears variously against various linguistic backgrounds. Certain characteristics are thrown into

Reprinted by permission from *English Language Teaching*, 11 (April-June, 1957), 77–85. Dr. Lee is the editor of *English Language Teaching*, and former lecturer in the teaching of English as a foreign language, Institute of Education, University of London.

relief in some countries, and other characteristics in others, and this because of contrast with the first language, that which the pupils speak at home. For speakers of Serbo-Croat or Czech, English is a language of several past tenses and puzzling article usage; but these are not a headache to Spanish or Hungarian pupils. Among the problems facing Turkish learners are the English word-order patterns, so different from their own; yet word-order is much less of a stumbling-block to the Italians or Dutch. Speakers of tone-languages, such as Chinese, have to pay special attention to the very different English use of voice-pitch, while some nationalities lose sleep over rhythmic patterns. And although certain features of English are no doubt everywhere fairly easy or fairly hard to acquire, the difficulty of each of these also has, in accordance with the pupils' home language, its varying degrees. In fact, one country's linguistic mountain, to be patiently climbed, is another's molehill, to be lightly skipped over. Mistakes analyses based on adequate material show clearly what is most troublesome for the learners concerned and thus where they most need support.

However, it is not only remedial work which can be guided thus, but the whole of a language course, and at every stage. Writing is the obvious basis for analysis, but mistakes in speaking can be noted too, especially by a trained phonetician and with the help of a tape-recorder. A broadly based and representative collection of spoken and written errors, sufficiently classified, may help to determine several things—the scope and nature of pronunciation teaching, the time given to practice with certain structures, the time given to practice with certain expressions and words, and even the order in which these structures, expressions, and words are introduced.

Let us look first at the problem of pronunciation teaching.

It is important during early language lessons not to let the temperature of interest drop too low. "More haste, less speed" is a good enough motto up to a point, but we must also remember that a snail's pace can lead to boredom. Interest is a strong driving-force at any stage: its value at the beginning is enormous. It is necessary to push on, to get somewhere and to let the pupils see they have got somewhere. They should be able to answer and ask simple questions, using the present continuous tense, and deal with simple requests and commands, before the initial impetus is exhausted. A new current will then carry them along, arising from interest and pride in their linguistic acquirement. To begin with, however, there is or should be an orderly presentation of commonly used words in commonly used structures. But if an oral method is used, the majority of the basic sounds of the language will occur within the first two or three lessons. Progress in the meaningful use of sentences in situations real or contrived cannot safely be delayed for a high polish to be put on pronunciation. It will necessarily be a little awkward and rough in places, and the risk of minor faults becoming a habit has courageously to be taken. This does not at all mean that pronunciation cannot methodically be dealt with.[1] Words and structures which have already been in-troduced furnish the material for short, regular, and intensive practices involving isolation and comparison not only of sounds, but of rhythmic and intonation patterns, juncture-patterns, and in fact of any devices capable of changing the meaning of what is said. At least five minutes of a forty-minute period can be regularly spared for speech-work of this kind, over and above incidental correc-tion. A comprehensive review of the phonetic material is unnecessary and in-deed digressive. Attention should be focused on the difficult points, and those which cause little bother may be left, more or less, to look after themselves. And this is where mistakes analyses come in. For if these analyses are based on the speech of enough learners, and of a sufficient variety of learners, of the same linguistic background, they enable a teacher to prophesy. Forewarned is forearmed. Mistakes can, of course, be dealt with as a course proceeds, with-out the prior help of any analysis; but it is preferable to know beforehand what is likely to happen and so to be prepared for the necessity of coping with it. If English [ɔː] is going to be made too much like English [ou], for instance, as when *George saw Nora at the ball* resembles [dʒoudʒ sou nourə ət ðə boul] (a common mispronunciation among Russians), the obvious thing is to be ready to make it more like [aː], and to make in advance its occurrence in texts used. If learners are likely to want to put the stress and pitch-fall too early in sen-tences demanding a stressed pitch-fall near their end, such as *I shan't go oftener than ↘necessary* (where ↘*oftener than necessary* would be an unusual pattern), the error can be held at arm's length if the teacher is aware of this tendency and prepared to impose the suitable pattern, perhaps by exaggerating it in some way, on the learners' melodic ear. If, again, it is known that glottal stops may be added to syllables which should begin smoothly with a vowel sound, more trouble can be taken to demonstrate the fact of "linking," and additional phrases to impress the point can be prepared. There are many ways in which a teacher's knowledge of the language strains under which his pupils labour and of the kind of mistakes they are liable to make during a course or even a single lesson can influence his attitude and teaching plans. It is chiefly a matter of knowing the pupils better beforehand, at least in one respect, so that less time and energy have to be spent on getting to know them at the moment of instruc-tion. Instead of discovering at the last minute their tendencies to err, and so in a sense following in the pupils' tracks, we are ahead of the pupils and thus able to lead them better.

Teaching Prague University students English just after the war, and having then an elementary acquaintance with Czech, I noted down and grouped over

---

[1]Nor does it mean that attempts at grading the course phonetically are valueless. Cer-tainly some of the more awkward successions of sounds can be postponed, and intona-tions other than the simplest can also wait (as they do in A. S. Hornby's "Oxford Progressive English," for example.) However. it is primarily words and structures which are graded.

twenty-five typical errors in their pronunciation.[2] Weekly contact with about three hundred students enabled me to make this collection at odd moments as we went along. The grouping was somewhat rough-and-ready too, yet it could form the basis of a programme of ear and speech-organ training, one essential means to the improvement of language-hearing and language-speaking skill.[3]

As with pronunciation, so with other aspects of the language. Once an adequate analysis of errors has been made, this can and indeed must influence the whole course. About eleven years ago I compiled a record of two thousand mistakes occurring in Czechoslovak students' essays. The essay themes were various and of thier own choosing, the students (about seventy on this occasion) from whose work the mistakes were gathered were picked out haphazard, and all the mistakes they made were included. Wishing to apply the result of this inquiry at once, I hurriedly grouped them into a few categories, e.g. wrong punctuation (14.4 percent of all errors), misuse or omission of articles (13.6 percent), mis-spellings (13.5 percent), non-English constructions and wrong word-order (11 percent), wrong use of tenses (3.4 percent), and so on. In the light of further language study, I should probably make a somewhat different analysis of this material today and enlarge the collection of mistakes, basing it on a greater number of learners. Nevertheless the immediate purpose was served: I was in a better position to decide how teaching time should be spent. There is no need, of course, to act upon the results of such investigation slavishly. Many would treat punctuation and spelling mistakes in the way I did, as on the whole less serious than mistakes with, for instance, articles and prepositions. But at least one gets a fairly clear picture of what the major difficulties are. It may be that with some classes of (say) French or German pupils, literal translations from the home language, such as *We are here since two hours* (= We have been here since two o'clock) are not one of the commonest types of mistake: there is no need, therefore, to prepare for extensive demonstrations or repeated practice of the correct pattern. An analysis of mistakes made by some West African learners would probably show a need for ample practice of word-order in direct and indirect speech, while Turkish learners' mistakes reveal that word-order in general required particular attention. Slavonic pupils, weaknesses on the articles and some relative clauses, as well as on comma usage, would all be shown up

[2]This sounds a large number but, even so, little enough account was taken of rhythm and intonation, perhaps more important for intelligibility than "sounds." On the other hand, several minor mistakes were included.

[3]To classify many of the vowel mispronunciations I made use of Prof. Jones's cardinal vowel diagram. It can easily be carried in the mind's eye, and the relationship between the tongue-positions of the vowels one is concerned with, i.e., the vowel one is trying to teach, the nearest vowel in the learner's language, and the learner's attempt, can be readily pictured. It seems to me a most serviceable tool in an English-teacher's equipment. However, a good tool calls for a trained user. (Lip position is also important for some vowel sounds, but can easily be observed.)

in their degree of importance by mistakes analyses, and so the teacher is the better prepared for teaching the points involved to other pupils speaking the same first language.

The behaviour of words, and of invariable or slightly variable expressions, in so far as it can be separated from the behaviour involved in the chief syntactic patterns, is still another aspect of language. What has been said about the analysis of other types of error applies here too. The frequency with which a word occurs in English is not the only thing of importance about it: there may be no word in the learners' language more than roughly corresponding, or this word may associate with others in a manner quite different from the English word. Choice of vocabulary with which to "operate" the basic patterns, however, is commonly determined more by frequency or by thoughts of its immediate use in classroom situations than by considerations such as these, at least in a printed course meant for use anywhere. Study of the mistakes made by speakers of any other language in using common English words will suggest the inclinations they have to fight against. To take a simple instance, Czechs are liable to say *The news are good and Christmas are coming*—the Czech words for "news" and "Christmas" go with a verbal form commonly felt to be plural. Knowing this, a teacher of English to Czechs will be ready to give these words special treatment, and may perhaps postpone using them.[4] Word-mistake study helps a teacher to see which English words are best suited for the "operation" of patterns: possibly those which give difficulty may be avoided for a time.

Thus mistakes analyses may influence the order in which vocabulary is introduced. Can they also help to determine the similar ordering of structures? This may seem unlikely. It is mainly a question of the usefulness of those structures, dependent in part on their frequency of occurrence in English and in part on their capacity for accretion.[5] It is necessary to keep dissimilar structures apart: that is to say, not to introduce them to the pupils simultaneously nor until those already taught have had a chance to establish themselves in the learner's newly acquired speech habits. The word-order patterns of *This is a chair, Is this a chair?*, and *What is this?* are an example.[6] If we teach these question-types too soon, there is a risk of muddle, resulting perhaps in *What this is?*, a pattern which may be hard to get rid of. Nevertheless the risk is slight where in the learner's language there are similar very commonly used patterns, with the equivalents of *This is* and *Is this* interchangeable in the same

---

[4] D. Abercrombie (E.L.T. III. 7, p. 171) points out the undesirability of introducing *head* and *hand* very early in a course intended for Greeks: "the words sound to him identical— and his resentment is increased by discovering an unexpected problem of meaning in the word *hand*." [Mr. Abercrombie's article is no. 30 in this collection. Eds.]

[5] See W. F. Mackey's "What to Look for in a Method: (II) Grading," p. 48, in E.L.T., VIII. 2.

[6] The same intonation pattern *can*, of course, be used in each.

way. This change in English is then no problem. In German, for instance, there is *Das ist ein Stuhl, Ist das ein Stuhl?*, and *Was ist das?*, and in Spanish *(Esto) es una silla, ¿Es esto una silla?*, and *¿Qué es esto?*. On the other hand, in Czech there is *To je stůl* and *Je to stůl?*, but commonly *Co to je?*. Czech learners of English thus tend to say *What it is?*, but this mistake is much less usual among Spanish and German learners. With the latter we need not, therefore, so carefully space out these patterns to avoid confusion. Again, learners from some countries will readily take to the tense change in converting direct to indirect speech (He said, *"I am coming"—He said he was coming*), while elsewhere this will call for cautiously graded treatment. Nevertheless, on the whole it is not so much the sequence in which structures are taught that mistake analyses are likely to influence as the speed with which some of them are taught.

Mistakes in the use of sounds, words, and structures may thus be usefully collected and examined, and mistakes analyses at each of these levels can be applied to language teaching. We are also concerned, however, with stages of achievement in learning the language. On what stage should a mistake analysis be based? Do we require to know only the errors which the class we are teaching is likely to make? Or is it helpful to have an analysis of more advanced learners' errors as well?

It is plain that a whole series of analyses, based on various stages of achievement from elementary to advanced, is desirable. Light shed on the immediate task in hand is of prime interest, and the teacher will look firstly for an analysis of errors made by pupils like his own. Analyses made at more advanced stages, however, can also help, showing as they do what types of error tend to persist and which therefore demand skillful avoiding action or remedial treatment.

Such analyses are of use to both inexperienced and experienced teachers. Previous experience with similar pupils may have given a teacher some of the knowledge a particular analysis yields; but few have had experience so broad as to be able to forecast the errors of any type of class, even in a single language area. Mistakes analyses, especially valuable to the inexperienced, can also be a great help to those faced with a grade of pupil they have not taught before, or pupils speaking a different first language. Even a teacher of great experience, or one to whom a particular type of class is not new, may welcome a systematic statement of difficulties, well illustrated by examples. It is a valuable guide when planning a course of lessons. Without it a teacher is less aware of the task which confronts him, and so plans less effectively.

Through an examination of learners' mistakes a teacher may enter more fully into the environment of teaching and put on, as it were, his pupils' linguistic spectacles. This should enable him to see his way more clearly. An obvious question to ask, however, is whether there is not a more effective manner of looking at things from the learners' viewpoint. As we have already noticed, many learners' difficulties reflect features of the home language. Would a knowledge of this language not be a better pair of spectacles to put on? Are we perhaps not doing things by halves in examining mistakes only? The question can at once be re-stated, since in most parts of the world the majority of those teaching English will already speak the home language of their pupils. The problem for them, on the contrary, is whether to bother about mistakes analyses. However, a substantial minority of teachers do not speak the learners' language, and have to ask themselves if they can manage well enough without it.

At first sight it would appear that they can. What concerns us chiefly, after all, is the encounter between the two languages. Attention should be focused, it seems, on the struggle of second-language usages against those of the first. If knowledge of the learners' language enables one only to forecast mistakes, why bother to acquire it? Those who speak it, on the other hand, would seem to gain something from a study of mistakes, for this involves direct concentration on what is relevant and the reduction of guesswork to a minimum.

To guess at probable types of error from a knowledge of the first language only is, without doubt, to take a somewhat far-off view of teaching problems. Thus if a first language has no final [ŋ], as in *laughing*, it is a good guess that another nasal may be substituted, as in ['la:fin]. But this is not at all the same thing as seeing that it *is* substituted, and in what positions. If a language has no vowel sound close to that in *bet* or that in *bat*, but only a sound lying somewhere between the two, it is likely that [e] will often be pronounced too open and [a] too close. Yet it is surely more helpful to see what happens in practice, for other factors may be influential too, such as frequency of occurrence and the nature of the other first-language vowels. All such factors could perhaps, in forecasting error types, be taken into consideration, but the forecaster's task would be extremely complicated if they were. Study of the mistakes themselves seems to be a short cut.

There is much to be said on the other side, however. Learners' mistakes must inevitably mean more to those who know something of the learners' language than to those who are ignorant of it. Using mistakes analyses, the latter have a good close-in view of what may go wrong, but can only guess at the underlying causes. Unless these are understood, the teacher is less aware of the connection between one mistake and another, and is thus less well equipped for systematic treatment. Without some knowledge of the learners' language, moreover, it is sometimes hard to see what is meant. Take, for instance, "They have arrived there are three days," a sentence that would never be perpetrated by anyone properly taught. Could it mean "They have arrived and are staying three days"? Nobody would think so who knew a little French, although an extensive context alone might suffice to give the meaning: "They arrived three days ago." Or take a Czech learner's "I don't know already," almost incomprehensible without a knowledge of Czech, which makes it clear that the speaker wanted to say, "I no longer know." Lastly, a teacher ignorant of the home language cannot use features of it as starting-points in instruction. It is an advantage to be proficient at making the sounds, for some of them may be modifiable into English sounds.

At other levels too it is desirable to know what there is or is not to work from. Teaching English tense usage to learners whose language has only one past tense form is apt to perplex a teacher unaware of the fact, but errors in several tenses are seen to be linked by one who is so aware. Translation may be excluded from the teaching method: nevertheless it is wise to look closely at the use of single past tense forms in varying contexts, if only to discover that there is little support in the learners' language for what one is trying to teach. Again, at word level there can be a chance similarity between the English and a first-language word of different meaning, as with *cigar* and Turkish *sigara* (cigarette), *clinic* and Czech *klinika* (teaching hospital), *station* and Spanish *estación* (season); if the teacher knows such things he can guard the better against misunderstanding.

Knowledge of the learners' language is of practical teaching use in many ways, of which a few only have been illustrated. Yet there is a broader and possibly more powerful argument in favour of acquiring such knowledge, for the evident possession of it awakens the pupils' sympathies and reassures them that the teacher is "on their side." Few learners are not pleased at the accurate, if occasional, use of the teacher of their own tongue; and a little goes a long way. It suggests at least that he is trying to see things from their viewpoint. It makes clear that the learners' language is not looked down upon or regarded as an irrelevant nuisance.

Both procedures are thus to be recommended, a study of the first language and also of characteristic mistakes in learning the second. Advanced knowledge of a language is not necessarily accompanied, of course, by the ability to analyze it. Unfortunately there are many English-speaking teachers who assume that because they speak English they are well qualified to teach it: their ideas on the phonetic and grammatical make-up of English are sometimes extremely naïve. Non-English-speaking teachers may have similarly crude notions of their own language. They in particular, since most of them are permanently occupied with English teaching in one language area, should make as careful an analytical study of that language as of the one they teach. Otherwise the comparisons they try to draw between the two languages will be hesitant and often invalid.

What co-operation can there be between the "local" teacher, possibly born and brought up among the kind of pupils he teaches, and the teacher from an English-speaking country, born and brought up among those who speak English alone? Each has his strong suit—the former an expert acquaintance with the first language, the latter, a special knowledge of the second. The most obvious form of mutual assistance they can give is to improve each other's grasp of their own language. If both have had a measure of linguistic training, they can usefully co-operate also in the collection and analysis of learners' mistakes. By referring the learners' speech or writing to his own ideas on acceptable English, the one discovers and describes these mistakes. The other looks at the mistakes and, referring them to his experience of the learners' home language, describes them, if possible, in terms of failure to resist the attraction of its phonetic, lexical, syntactic, or other forms. Every mistake is thus seen from two angles, and the resulting account of major types of mistake will show clearly, in the context of any language area, what is most difficult in English for the learners and what in the home language for the teachers. An English-speaking teacher can himself, of course, excavate in the home language to uncover the causes of mistakes; but the "local" teacher seems the better qualified to do so. Similarly the "local" teacher may be able adequately to list and describe the mistakes themselves; but on the whole this appears to be the Englishman's job. Overlapping of the two activities is nevertheless essential if both parties are to get the maximum benefit from this work. Such a project for joint research is likely to have a practical outcome and to be worth doing anywhere, but especially where the rivalry between "local" and "English" teachers is more obvious than the co-operation.

30   THE SOCIAL BASIS   DAVID ABERCROMBIE
OF LANGUAGE

In what way, if any, should language courses include instruction in *phatic communion*?

If an individual's language is an *index* to his personality, as Abercrombie suggests, in what way is that a concern of the language teacher?

Prepare yourself to discuss whether language teachers should include *slang, jargon,* and *cant* as part of a language course.

Can you give additional examples of differences in *semantic structures* found in two languages? What are the implications of *different semantic structures* for the teaching of vocabulary? (Also, see Lado's and Prator's articles (32 and 33) for additional discussion of vocabulary).

Under what circumstances, if any, should a language course teach only literary language?

Reprinted by permission from *English Language Teaching*, 3 (September, 1948), 1–11 and from the author's *Problems and Principles in Language Study* (Longmans, Green & Co., Ltd., London, 1956), where this article appeared as chap. 1 under the title "Linguistics and the Teacher." The author is head of the phonetics department at the University of Edinburgh.

Detailed knowledge of particular languages is a necessity for the language teacher; he must have full command of the language he is teaching, and at least a descriptive acquaintance with the language of those being taught. Knowledge of the nature of language in general is not a necessity, but it is certainly a very useful adjunct to his equipment. Although general linguistics is a highly theoretical study, important practical consequences for teaching can follow from its speculations.

General linguistics is partly concerned with the problem of *what language does*, that is, with the *functions* of any and every language. It is also concerned with *what languages are*, how they may best be analysed, described, and classified; in other words, with the *form of different* languages. It is what language does, however, that the teacher would do well to consider first. An exhaustive survey would be well beyond the scope of this article, but I should like to suggest five aspects from which language, in its relation to man, society, and the world, can be considered.

i

First, language makes it possible for individuals to live in a society. It is characteristic of, indeed fundamental to, the modern point of view in linguistics to regard language as a *social* activity rather than as a means of *individual* self-expression. "Speech is the instrument of society," as Ben Jonson said; there is a very close connection between the two facts that man is a speaking animal, and that he is the social animal *par excellence*. The definition of language as "a means of communicating thoughts" is nowadays commonly held to be, as a partial truth, more misleading than illuminating; a more fruitful definition is that language is *a means of social control*.

It is true, of course, that language does communicate thoughts, but many—perhaps most—of its uses cannot really be said to involve this. When an order is given to a squad of soldiers by an officer, no thought has first to be interpreted and then acted upon; the response is as automatic as the appearance of light when a switch is pressed. This is a simple example of a normally more complicated process: the use of language to co-ordinate activities. Any cooperative effort carried out by a number of people skilled in that operation depends entirely for its unity and success on language, though that language will not be communicating thoughts. Anybody who, with this aspect of language in mind, has watched a team of piano movers negotiating a tricky staircase with a grand piano, has received an object lesson on speech-in-action.

There are other uses of language which are not concerned with the communication of thoughts. The conversations which English people hold about the weather, for example, do not as a rule leave the participants any the wiser; only on rare occasions can information be said to have been exchanged. As far as communicating thought is concerned, they get nowhere; are they then quite pointless? No; a little reflection will show that this kind of use of language also has great social value.

Most peoples have a feeling that a silent man is a dangerous man. Even if there is nothing to say, one must talk, and conversation puts people at their ease and in harmony with one another. This sociable use of language has been given the name *phatic communion*. The anthropologist Bronislaw Malinowski invented the term, "actuated" he said, "by the demon of terminological invention"; and although he was half in joke, the name has stuck. Malinowski defined it as "a type of speech in which ties of union are created by a mere exchange of words." It enters the everyday experience of everybody, from the most highly civilised to the most primitive, and, far from being useless, this small-talk is essential to human beings getting along together at all.

The actual sense of the words used in phatic communion matters little; it is facial expression and intonation that are probably the important things. It is said that Dorothy Parker, alone and rather bored at a party, was asked "How are you? What have you been doing?" by a succession of distant acquaintances. To each she replied, "I've just killed my husband with an axe, and I feel fine." Her intonation and expression were appropriate to party small-talk, and with a smile and a nod each acquaintance, unastonished, drifted on.

Although the sense matters little, however, certain subjects only are reserved for use in phatic communion, and these chosen subjects differ widely among different peoples. Each of the following questions is, in some part of the world, good form when meeting a person:

How are you?
Where are you from?
How much money do you earn?
What is your name?
What do you know?

Some of them, however, would cause deep offence when used in other parts of the world, though in each case the replies required, and expected, are purely formal.

A knowledge of the spoken form of any language must include knowledge of its conventions of phatic communion. Conversation is impossible unless one is equipped with meaningless phrases for use when there is nothing to say, and the teacher dealing with advanced students will take care to give them command of the necessary formulas and the rules governing their use.

Grace de Laguna, in her excellent book *Speech: Its Function and Development*, said, "men do not speak simply to relieve their feelings or to air their views, but to awaken a response in their fellows and to influence their attitudes and acts." The profoundly social character of language should constantly be borne in mind by the language teacher.

ii

But language has a very individual side also: "language" (to quote Ben Jonson once again) "most shows a man; speak, that I may see thee."

When a person speaks, a listener interprets what he says as, simultaneously, two quite different and separate systems of signs. An utterance consists of *symbols* referring to whatever is being talked about; but it is also at the same time an *index* to various things about the speaker, particularly his personality. These two systems of signs are quite independent of each other. In a similar way things such as gait, or the wearing of clothes, can, in addition to their main function, reveal personality; but probably no aspect of human behaviour does this so constantly or so subtly as speech. It is especially the least conscious parts of talking—pronunciation, general handling of the voice, gesture—which are the vehicle of these clues to personality. Almost everyone, when meeting a stranger, bases an immediate judgment on the way he or she talks, and we can often infer from their speech, when meeting people known to us, whether they are in a bad temper, or feeling well-disposed.

It is not always easy to say how present to consciousness these interpretations are. Sometimes it is only on careful reflection that an attitude taken up towards someone can be traced to his voice and pronunciation; at other times, we are fully conscious of the effect of someone's voice on us. It is not always easy to say, either, to what extent the speaker intends that certain judgments should be made. There may be completely conscious control, as when an Egyptian hopes to arouse feelings of respect towards himself by introducing into his speech consonants such as [q, θ], which do not normally occur in the spoken Arabic of Egypt. At the other extreme is the epileptic who betrays this fact to the skilled ear by his intonation, but is as unable to get rid of the features which give him away as the malingerer is to assume them.

Judgments concerning a person made on the basis of his speech may, or may not, of course, be correct. Wrong judgments are particularly apt to be made on foreigners. It is likely, for example, that English assertions concerning the excitability of Frenchmen are founded on the fact that certain features of the speech of normal Frenchmen are closely similar to features of excitable Englishmen's speech. Americans, again, often accuse Englishmen of superciliousness: normal English intonation closely resembles the intonation adopted by supercilious Americans. However, speech is often an astonishingly sure guide to personality, and one, moreover, which requires very remarkable delicacy of perception, of which most people seem to be capable.

Not only are certain features of speech an index to personality; they may sometimes be very strongly felt as a *part* of personality, and the language teacher should be prepared to encounter this. The inability of an intelligent pupil to acquire a reasonable pronunciation may not be due to a bad ear; the pupil may be resisting the attack on his personality which he (unconsciously) feels is involved in any attempt to change his pronunciation habits. The wise teacher will handle such a situation with care.

Possibly something similar lies behind the conviction in some countries that the presence of foreign words in the language is a menace to the national consciousness. Such a feeling has never, fortunately, been effective in this country, but elsewhere it has on more than one occasion given rise to legislation. There is little chance that the English will ever substitute "folkwain" for "omnibus," but the Germans have been persuaded to say *Fernsprecher* for "telephone." "Man lebt in seiner Sprache," said a Nazi poet.

iii

Thirdly, forms of speech delimit social groupings, or classes, within a language community. When people congregate in a group they tend to behave in a similar way, and this similarity in behaviour, in so far as it is different from the behaviours of others, then becomes one of the factors which characterize, and so preserve, the group. Speech behaviour is deeply affected in this way: "one may wonder" wrote Edward Sapir, "if there is any set of social habits that is more cohesive or more disrupting than language habits."

Pronunciation is perhaps the most obvious point where speech behaviour is influenced by social groupings, but any feature of language may be involved. We have probably all been misleadingly taught in school that the French word *tu* is distinguished from *vous* by being employed only when the person addressed is intimately known, or is decidedly inferior—a dog or child. *Tu* is, certainly, employed on these occasions; but that is not the real clue to its use, and does not explain how, for example, one Frenchman could say to another on being introduced "Enchanté de faire *ta* connaissance." The fact is that *tu* is regularly used, not as a sign of *personal* familiarity, but between members of certain social groups, political parties, and so on; and may often be used, therefore, between complete strangers.

The role of language in social differentiation helps to explain an otherwise puzzling phenomenon—the existence of slang. Slang is a matter almost entirely of vocabulary. It is to be distinguished from *jargon*, the technical terminology of occupations and sports: the cricketer's *inswinger, yorker, wrong 'un, late cut;* the B.B.C. engineer's *mike, top, level, fade.* These are practically necessities, which it would be most awkward to do without. Slang is to be distinguished also from *cant*, concealed or secret language. Used mainly by the cardsharp, the confidence trickster, the pickpocket, to escape conflict with the law, cant too is a necessity. But slang is puzzling because it merely duplicates the conventional vocabulary, does not seem to be in any way necessary, and can cover almost any topic.

One powerful impulse to the creation of slang is boredom with outworn locutions, and the desire to be expressive and vivid; which is why it is nearly always picturesque and sometimes in doubtful taste. But its real explanation lies in the fact that it is always the property of a group; its use proclaims membership of that group and distinction from other groups. As a competitor in a *New Statesman and Nation* competition put it:

> The chief use of slang
> Is to show that you're one of the gang.

Slang is fascinating to foreigners, and acquirement of it seems to promise admission to the real intimacies of communication. As a learner of languages I have felt the fascination myself, and have often observed it in my students. Learning how, or rather *when*, to use slang is, however, a tricky business. Foreign students have on several occasions confided to me that they have met with signs of discomfort—even hostility—when they have introduced their proudly acquired slang into their conversation with English students. The reaction seemed inexplicable to them. The explanation, however, probably was that they had unwittingly claimed a social intimacy to which they were not entitled, producing an effect like that of misplaced *tutoyage*; or possibly they had given the appearance of flaunting the slang of a hostile group. It may, moreover, be the case that no type of slang is compatible with a foreign accent.

A certain amount of slang usually appears in courses of "colloquial" English, and some people have recommended teaching, even in the early stages of a language, a few chosen expressions. These are, of course, gratifying to learners— "they use them with roguish aptness" says one author—and therefore useful pedagogically. Nevertheless, it is a dubious expedient. Not only are complex social problems involved, but there is another difficulty: slang is ephemeral. The very impulses which give rise to it ensure that it will be short-lived. The new vivid expression will itself become as worn out and boring as those it has replaced. It may also spread outside the group and cease therefore to be a badge of membership, particularly if the group has considerable prestige (a common fate of R.A.F. slang). A very few slang words attain respectability, as have English *mob, queer*, French *tête*, German *Kopf*, but most old slang is distasteful:

> When it dates,
> It grates,

as the *New Statesman and Nation* competitor continued. Nothing can be more embarassing than roguish inaptness.

Language not only brings human beings into relationship with each other, it also brings them into relationship with the external world. Language mediates between man and his environment.

The naïve, or common-sense, view is that language reflects the world and our thinking about it, that to the categories of language correspond categories of the real world. Modern linguistics, however, inclines to the view that language is not a passive reflection of, but rather an active practical approach to, the world—a sorting out of it for the purpose of acting on it. Experience is dissected, split up, along lines laid down by language, not necessarily along lines laid down by nature.

The way in which the vocabulary of a language is organised to deal with the outside world may conveniently be called its *semantic structure*. If it is not imposed by nature, there is no reason to expect that languages will be identical in semantic structure. We are all inclined to look on the categories of our own language as inevitable, but a comparison of even closely related languages reveals surprising differences, and wide divergencies appear between languages of very distant families.

For example, the words of a language can be arranged at various levels of generality. The difference between *table, chair, cushion* is not the same as the difference between *table, furniture, object:* the first three are clearly at the same level, the second three at different levels. Perhaps the most obvious variations in semantic structure occur here. An urban Englishman is content with the fairly general word *weed*; there are tribes of American Indians, however, for whom the medicinal properties of all plants are most important, who possess no such general term but will always refer to any specimen by its specific name. The English word *snow* does not seem to us very general, but it is more so than the several (unrelated) words which an Eskimo uses in its place, and by which he specifies snow in various states which are, to him, sensuously and operationally different.

It is often thought that the possession of words at the specific level enables a language to be more precise, but this is not necessarily so. Since we have in English the word *tail*, we gain nothing in precision from the word *scut*. *Scut* may be more *concise* than *tail of a rabbit*, but it is not more *precise*.

The distribution at different levels of the vocabulary of a given language has to some extent, probably, been governed by chance; it is difficult to think of any reason why the English *finger, thumb, toe* can all be called δάκτυλος in Greek. A considerable influence, however, is exercised by the practical interest of a people in the elements of their environment. The more necessary it is, for their way of life, to make distinctions within a range of phenomena, the less likely they are to possess a general term covering the range as a whole; the more indifferent culturally the range, the more probably an all-embracing term. A highly developed language such as English, used all over the world by peoples of widely different cultural interests, can provide if *necessary* both general and specific terms on most subjects: if the urban Englishman wishes to be more specific than *weed*, he has only to look the word up. Similarly a Greek, if he must specify *thumb*, can resort to the literary ἀντίχειρ. Nevertheless, the semantic structure of the highly developed languages of the world is capricious in certain places. English lacks an equivalent for the German *Geschwister* (though the recently introduced *sibling* will now fill the gap when it is necessary to do so). We can talk about our *cousins* without specifying their sex, though the French can not.

In addition to differences in the organisation of vocabulary into levels, languages may vary in the isolation, or delimitation of the elements of environment. Colour names provide a striking example of this. Every language, apparently, divides the spectrum differently, however close superficial correspondence may seem. There are dialects of English in which the word *foot* includes all of the leg below the knee. The Greek word χέρι covers the arm from elbow to finger-tips, though it is usually translated "hand."

Language enables man to live in society, but the *kind* of society in which he lives will profoundly affect his language. Semantic structure and social structure are intimately connected, and it is here that the most serious difficulties for the language learner are probably to be found. A language is not only part of the cultural achievement of a people, it also transmits the rest of their culture system, and English words such as *gentleman, respectable, genteel, shy, whimsical, sophisticated, self-conscious, lowbrow* are only intelligible in their social setting. They must be explained, if this is unfamiliar, by long and involved descriptions of social facts; apparent equivalents in other languages are almost always misleading.

Here again it may be noted that semantic structure does not merely *reflect* the psychological environment resulting from social structure. "In acquiring the vocabulary of his day," writes Grace de Laguna, "each adolescent youth is being fitted with a set of variously coloured spectacles, through which he is to look at the world about him, and with whose tints it must inevitably be coloured." Heinz Paechter, in his book *Nazi-Deutsch*, points out how the new and extensive terminology introduced by the Nazis provided people with a stock of accepted ways of talking, and eventually transformed the categories of Nazi moral, social, and political thought into the folklore of the community.

The late B. L. Whorf, an American student of linguistics, coined the expression "linguistic relativity" to express the view that the same physical evidence will not lead people to the same picture of the universe unless their linguistic backgrounds are similar. Investigation of American Indian languages has revealed that even the grand generalisations of the Western world—time, velocity, matter— are not essential to the construction of a consistent picture of the universe. This does not mean that the psychic experiences classed under these headings are destroyed, but that in certain languages categories derived from other kinds of experiences become the grand generalisations, and seem to function just as well. Hopi is an example of a language which lacks expression, grammatical or other, for concepts of time. Whorf has indulged in a fascinating speculation concerning how, within this linguistic structure, it would be possible to construct a science of physics; he has demonstrated that, by using for example the concepts *intensity* and *variation* in place of *time*, such a feat could have been accomplished, supposing the Hopi had ever reached a stage of development where it became necessary.

The dependence of thought on language has not been generally recognised owing perhaps to exclusive preoccupation of scholars with languages of the Indo-European and Semitic families. Growing knowledge of very different language families in Africa and America is now making clear how great this dependence is, and the popular "semantics" is now being put forward by many people as the panacea for all the ills of the world.

v

Fifthly, language is the medium of literature, and its use in artistic creation is nearly always associated with a "literary language," more or less different from the language of everyday life. A literary language is not necessarily a written language, neither is it a prerogative of civilised peoples. It is reported that the Saramaccaner Bush Negroes of Dutch Guiana, descended from escaped slaves and normally speaking the *lingua franca* known as Talkee-Talkee, have a special noble language appropriately called Deepee-Talkee. This is reserved for their religious ceremonies and songs, and is unintelligible to other inhabitants of the country.

A literary language, however, is usually a written language, and usually derived from some particular dialect, to which chance has given prestige, of the spoken language of the people (only rarely is it, like Deepee-Talkee or Latin, a foreign language). It requires to be learnt, to at least some extent, by the native, since in the course of time all literary languages diverge from their spoken origins; the differences may be small, as in the case of English, or very considerable, as the case of Greek, Arabic, or Chinese. A literary language, though primarily the language of literature, usually becomes the accepted norm for written communication for any purpose; and moreover always exercises some degree of influence over the spoken language. Its standards of correctness become the standards for all uses of the language, spoken or written, and departures from the accepted literary norm—"solecisms"—are strongly reprobated.

In the teaching of foreign languages the literary language has, until recently, been supreme. Even today books are published which purport to deal with spoken English, but which inform the learner that English nouns have three cases. Examination papers in "English for foreigners" show how strong is the tendency to concentrate on those mistakes which are "solecisms" for the native speaker, but which the foreigner would seldom be tempted to commit. However, the efforts of Viëtor, Jespersen, Passy, and others have not been in vain, and a sane approach to the spoken language is becoming more and more widespread. In fact reaction from the old tradition may, in some quarters, be going too far, and the claim is sometimes heard that the spoken form is the only possible first step to learning a language in any form for any purpose.

It is not, of course, the use of a special language, but a special way of using language, that produces the highest forms of literature. Many writers, and most notably Ogden and Richards in *The Meaning of Meaning*, have drawn the distinction between the *referential* or *scientific*, and the *emotive* or *lyrical* uses of language. The first is not, of course, confined to science, nor the second to poetry. Even though certain words are commoner in one than the other, the difference between them does not depend on vocabulary; the use of scientific terminology is no guarantee of a scientific use of language.

Language in its "lyrical" use is characterised by the fact that it cannot be paraphrased, or translated into another language, without loss; it cannot be summarised; and phonetic features, particularly rhythm, are of the greatest importance to it. The opposite of each of these points is true of the scientific use (which, therefore, is all that an international auxiliary language can hope to cover). Moreover, a phrase from the scientific use has one single fixed sense, which if not clear can be made so; that this is not true of the lyrical use has been well demonstrated by William Empson in his *Seven Types of Ambiguity*.

Misunderstandings often arise through one use of language being taken for the other. When D. H. Lawrence insisted that "whatever the sun may be, it is certainly not a ball of burning gas," he was interpreting a scientific statement as if it was a lyrical one. H. L. Mencken, on the other hand, does the opposite when he maintains that all poetry consists in the flouting of what every reflective adult knows to be the truth. Shelley certainly said "bird thou never wert"; but he was not denying that the skylark belongs to the class *aves*.

31   TRANSFORMA-   PAUL SCHACHTER
         TIONAL GRAMMAR
         AND CONTRASTIVE
         ANALYSIS

How would Schachter's approach differ from earlier approaches to contrastive analysis?

What would be examples of aspects of English that a student *already knows* simply because he has already mastered his own language?

Can you compare the rules to form relative clauses in English with those for some other language not discussed by Schachter? Are the *linking, alteration,* and *subordinating* rules the same?

Reprinted by permission from *Workpapers in English as a Second Language*, University of California, Los Angeles, April, 1967, pp. 1–7. The author is professor of Linguistics, University of California, Los Angeles.

INTRODUCTION

The purpose of this paper is to examine briefly the implications of some recent developments in the theory of transformational generative grammar for the contrastive analysis of languages. By contrastive analysis is meant the analysis of the similarities and differences between two or more languages. The value of such analysis to the foreign-language teacher, including the teacher of English as a second language, has long been recognized. This value stems from the fact that students tend to transfer the features of their native language to the language they are learning. From this it follows that features of the foreign language that are similar to features of the native language will present little difficulty, while features of the foreign language that are different from those of the native language will require some amount of attention on the teacher's part. A contrastive analysis, by specifying just which features the two languages have in common and which they do not, can thus alert the teacher to what in the foreign language really needs to be taught.

Until fairly recently, structural linguists have tended to emphasize the respects in which languages differ from one another. This emphasis upon the idiosyncratic characteristics of languages originated in an essentially healthy rejection of an earlier grammatical tradition in which it had been assumed that all languages were more or less reasonable facsimiles of Latin, and could be analyzed in terms of Latin-like case systems, Latin-like verbal conjugations, etc. Reacting to this obviously incorrect assumption, twentieth-century linguists proposed—to quote one of them—"that languages could differ from each other without limit and in unpredictable ways." (Martin Joos, *Readings in Linguistics*, p. 96.)

But it has recently been suggested that this reaction was something of an over-reaction, in which one incorrect assumption was replaced by another. And the experience of those who have successfully taught English to students with a wide variety of language backgrounds would seem to confirm that this is the case. For if it were true that the native languages of some of these students were limitlessly different from English, how could we explain the fact that the students do after all learn English when they have really been taught rather little? That is, when we consider the enormous complexity of English, and, indeed, of languages in general, and the relatively short time that it takes to learn such a complex system, mustn't we conclude that much of what the student knows when he has learned a new language he has not been taught at all? Must it not, rather, be the case that, for example, the Japanese student of English already knows, in a sense, a good deal of the structure of English before he has heard or uttered his first English word, that the mastery one has of the structure of one's native language automatically involves mastery of a substantial part of the structure of any other language?

Now I have perhaps been a little unfair to those linguists who have claimed that languages could differ from one another without limit; for these linguists would probably not claim that there are any two languages whose grammatical systems have absolutely nothing in common. They would, however, certainly claim that there is no reason to expect that two unrelated languages should share any *particular* set of grammatical or other features, so that they would not, for example, expect to find any substantial overlap between the grammatical features shared by Japanese and English, on the one hand, and those shared by, say, Chinese and English on the other. And it is just this claim that has lately been challenged by Noam Chomsky and others concerned with developing the theory of transformational generative grammar.

"DEEP" AND "SURFACE" STRUCTURE

In his *Aspects of the Theory of Syntax*, Chomsky proposes certain major revisions in the theory of transformational grammar. Of particular interest here is the distinction Chomsky now makes between "deep structure" and "surface structure." According to Chomsky, all sentences have both a deep structure and a surface structure. The deep structure is specified by a set of "base rules." It includes all of the syntactic features—constituency relations and so forth—that are relevant to the meaning of sentences. The surface structure of sentences results from the operation of another set of rules, the "transformational rules," upon deep structures, and includes all of the syntactic features—order relations, and so forth—that are relevant to the way sentences are pronounced.

Now Chomsky has suggested that a substantial part of the base rules of the grammar of any language may not be specific to that language, but may, instead, be rules of human language in general. This is not at all to deny the obviously considerable differences between languages that may be found in even the simplest types of sentences, but it is, rather, to account for these differences on the basis of the effect of diverse sets of transformational rules operating upon essentially similar deep structures. To quote Chomsky on this subject:

> It is commonly held that modern linguistic and anthropological investigations have conclusively refuted the doctrines of classical universal grammar, but this claim seems to me very much exaggerated. Modern work has, indeed, shown a great diversity in the surface structures of languages. However, since the study of deep structures has not been its concern, it has not attempted to show a corresponding diversity of underlying structures, and, in fact, the evidence that has been accumulated in modern study of language does not appear to suggest anything of this sort (*Aspects*, p. 118).

Obviously the claim that languages are highly similar in their deep structures, if true, has important implications for the contrastive analysis of grammatical systems. For it means, in effect, that the contrastive analyst can concentrate most of his attention upon the transformational rules of the languages he is comparing, investigating the ways in which these rules operate to change similar deep structures into possibly very different surface structures.

But Chomsky's current model of transformational grammar goes beyond this in its potential for simplifying the task of the contrastive analyst. For not only does the model direct the analyst's attention primarily to the comparison of transformational rules. It even tells him, in many cases, just what transformational rules to compare. In this connection, it is important to note that, in the new model of transformational grammar (as opposed to earlier models), transformational rules are, in general, obligatory. That is, the deep structures specified by the base rules, in general, *must* undergo transformation. Now from the hypothesis of the non-language-specificity or universality of base rules it follows that if, in any one language, there is a certain deep structure that must undergo transformation, there will be corresponding deep structures in other languages that must also undergo transformation. In such cases, then, the contrastive analyst knows precisely which transformational rules to compare: namely, those rules that apply to the corresponding deep structures in the several languages.

RELATIVE CLAUSES

I would like to turn now to a case in point: a programmatic contrastive analysis of relative clauses in English and some languages unrelated to it and to one another. In the sketch of the grammar of English that he provides in *Aspects*, Chomsky proposes that all English relative clauses represent transformations of deep-structure sentences that are embedded in noun phrases. That is, the basic rules of English include a rule to the effect that a noun phrase may consist (among other things) of a noun plus a sentence, and the transformational rules of English include rules that, under specified circumstances, transform a sentence that is part of a noun phrase into a relative clause. Thus the base rules might specify a noun phrase that includes the noun *people* and the sentence *I saw people,* and the transformational rules might operate to transform this into the noun-plus-relative-clause structure, *people whom I saw*.

Let us assume—as, I think, we have some reason to—that relative clauses in all languages represent transformations of deep structure sentences that are embedded in noun phrases. Let us assume, in other words, that the English base rule that specifies that a noun phrase may include a noun plus a sentence is, in fact, not a rule specific to English, but, instead, a rule of human language in general. Our task as contrastive analysts then becomes that of comparing the transformational rules that operate, in the languages in which we are interested, to convert deep structures that include a noun plus a sentence (as parts of a noun phrase) into surface structures that include a noun plus a relative clause.

Transformational rules have two parts: a *structural description* and a *structural change.* The structural description specifies the domain or scope of the transformation: that is, the structures to which it applies. The structural change specifies the form of the transformation: that is, the ways in which the transformed structures differ from the structures specified in the structural description. In comparing the relative-clause transformations of two or more languages, then, differences in the structural descriptions will correspond to differences in the scope of relativization in the languages—that is, differences in the types of deep structures that can be relativized. Differences in the structural changes, on the other hand, will correspond to differences in the surface structures of the relative-clause constructions themselves.

SCOPE OF RELATIVIZATION

If we compare the structural descriptions of the transformational rules of relativization in English and Tagalog (a Malayo-Polynesian language of the Philippines), we find that they have both striking similarities and striking differences. In both languages, of course, we find that the structural description specifies certain noun-phrase structures that include a noun (which we shall hereafter call the *head noun*) and a sentence (which we shall hereafter call the *embedded sentence*). In both, furthermore, we find that the structural description specifies that the embedded sentence must include a noun that is identical with the head noun (we shall call this noun the *identical noun*). To take an English example, a deep-structure noun phrase with the head noun *people* and the embedded sentence *I saw people* is relativizable. But if the base rules should produce a deep-structure noun phrase with the head noun *people* and the embedded sentence *I saw animals* or *John loves Mary*, relativization transformations fail to operate, and no surface structure, and hence no pronounceable utterance, results. Tagalog relativization transformations—and, presumably, those of all other languages—include a similar restriction. There are, in addition, certain other shared restrictions on the structure of the embedded sentence. For example, it may not be a question; nor may it be an imperative.

The most important *difference* between the structural descriptions of English and Tagalog relativization rules has to do with restrictions upon the syntactic role of the identical noun within the embedded sentence. English, in general, does not impose restrictions. The identical noun may be the object, as in the deep structure underlying *people whom I saw*, the subject, as in *the flowers which are on the table*, a prepositional object, as in *the table which the flowers are on*, etc. In Tagalog, on the other hand, the identical noun—with a few minor exceptions—always has the same syntactic role within the embedded sentence, that of *topic*. The Tagalog topic has no precise counterpart in English. It will be sufficient for present purposes to say that in simple sentences of Tagalog there is in general only one topic, that this topic has certain distinguishing formal characteristics in the surface structure (e.g., if it is a common noun, it is preceded by the function word *ang*), and that in some cases (but by no means always, or even generally) it corresponds to the subject in English.

The most important point to be noted, with respect to relativization transformations, is that in Tagalog simple sentences generally include only one noun functioning as topic and that only this noun may serve as the identical noun specified in the structural description of the relativization transformation. Thus in the Tagalog equivalent of the embedded sentence *The flowers are on the table* (*Nasa mesa ang bulaklak*), the noun *bulaklak* "flowers" is the topic and so may serve as the identical noun for purposes of relativization, but the noun *mesa* "table" is not the topic, and may not serve as the identical noun. That is, if there is a deep-structure noun phrase consisting of the noun *bulaklak* "flowers" and the embedded sentence *Nasa mesa ang bulaklak* "The flowers are on the table," the relativization transformation operates to produce the noun-plus-relative-clause construction *bulaklak na nasa mesa* "(the) flowers which are on the table." But if there is a deep-structure noun phrase consisting of the noun *mesa* "table" and this same embedded sentence, the conditions imposed on the structural description of the relative-clause transformation are not met, and no noun-plus-relative-clause transformation can result. This is to say that Tagalog has no structure precisely paralleling the structure of English *the table which the flowers are on* or *the table on which the flowers are*. Tagalog can, of course, express the approximate *semantic* equivalent of these English structures. This it does with the structure *mesang may bulaklak*, literally "table having flowers." This structure results from the application of the relativization transformation to a deep-structure noun phrase consisting of the noun *mesa* and the embedded sentence *May bulaklak any mesa* "The table has flowers." Note that in this embedded sentence *mesa* is the topic, so that both the universal conditions and the specific Tagalog conditions for relativization are met. This, then, is one example of differences in the scope of relativization in different languages that would, in a transformational generative grammar of these languages, be expressed by differences in the structural descriptions of transformational rules.

FORM OF RELATIVIZATION

Let us turn now to differences in the form of relativization in different languages. In generative grammars such differences would be expressed by differences in the structural-change portion of those transformational rules that convert deep structures in which there is a noun phrase that includes a head noun and an embedded sentence into surface structures that include a head noun and a relative clause.

Since relativization transformations serve in all cases to transform sentences into relative clauses, there are certain types of structural changes that one can reasonably expect to find present in the relativization transformations of all languages. In the first place one can expect some kind of *linking*, that is, some kind of explicit marking of the fact that the clause is syntactically connected to the head noun. Secondly, one can expect some kind of *alteration of the identical noun*, that is, alteration of the noun within the embedded sentence that is identical with the head noun. This alteration is to be expected because languages tend to be economical, and it would be obviously uneconomical simply to repeat the head noun within the relative clause. Finally, one may encounter various other changes that can be grouped together under the rubric, *other subordinating devices*.

Comparing the structural changes involved in the relative clause transformations of English, Tagalog, and two African languages unrelated to one another, Twi (a Niger-Congo language of Ghana) and Hausa (an Afro-Asiatic language of Nigeria), we find that all do, in fact, involve linking and alteration of the identical noun. In the case of all four languages, linking is accomplished by the insertion of a linking element at or near the beginning of the relative clause. In English this element is the *wh-* of *who, whom*, or *which*; in Tagalog it has the form *-ng* or *na*; in Twi it is *a* and in Hausa *da*. Except for the fact that the linking element is in some cases just part of a word (English *wh-* or Tagalog *-ng*) while in others it is a more-or-less independent word (as in Twi and Hausa), all four languages are substantially similar with respect to the way in which they achieve linking.

Alteration of the identical noun shows more diversity. In Twi the identical noun is replaced by its personal-pronoun counterpart. Thus the Twi equivalent of *people whom I saw* may be literally glossed "people-linker-I saw them." In Tagalog, on the other hand, the identical noun is deleted, so that the equivalent of *people whom I saw* may be glossed "people-linker-I saw." Hausa shows pronominalization of the identical noun in most cases, but in some cases allows either deletion or pronominalization. Thus Hausa has two freely alternating equivalents of *people whom I saw*, which may be glossed, respectively, as "people-linker-I saw them" and "people-linker-I saw." English is like Twi in using pronominalization consistently, but whereas Twi replaces the identical noun with an appropriate personal pronoun, English uses a special set of forms, the relative pronouns, in which the pronominal replacement of the identical noun is combined with the linking element *wh-*.

It is with respect to the use of other subordinating devices that the four languages being examined show the most idiosyncratic characteristics. In English we have the front-shifting of the pronominal replacement of the identical noun, i.e., the occurrence of the relative pronoun at or near the beginning of the relative clause, regardless of its syntactic role within this clause. There is nothing at all like this in any of the other languages. Twi and Hausa also have subordinating devices without counterparts in the other languages: in Twi, the use of a special set of tone patterns that occur only in subordinate structures; in Hausa, the use of a special set of verb tense markers that occur only in subordinate structures. Tagalog differs from all of the others in that, apart from linking and deletion of the identical noun, no other subordinating devices are used at all.

The above, then, are some examples of similarities and differences involved in the forms of relative-clause structures in different languages, similarities and differences of the kind that, in generative grammars of these languages, would be reflected in the structural-change portion of pertinent transformational rules.

CONCLUSIONS

I believe that, were the structural-change portion of the relativization transformations of English, Twi, Hausa, and Tagalog compared in a more systematic way than I have attempted to do, the comparison would provide a very clear statement of the major formal differences among the relative-clause structures of these languages. Similarly, I think that a very clear statement of differences in the scope of relativization would emerge from a systematic comparison of the structural-description portion of the pertinent transformations. I hope, at any rate, that I have demonstrated that such statements may be of considerable interest and value to language teachers.

32   PATTERNS OF   ROBERT LADO
                                  DIFFICULTY IN
                                    VOCABULARY

What priority should endings such as *-ation, -al, -er,* as in imagin*ation,* arri*val,* and hunt*er,* be given in the teaching of vocabulary?

Evaluate Lado's seven patterns of difficulty in terms of your own teaching/learning experience (past, present, or projected). Are they all equally relevant to all students?

Can you find additional examples for each pattern?

1. *Words*

1.1 Undue emphasis on words as words to the neglect of pronunciation and grammatical structure is not in keeping with modern linguistic thinking. Sapir says bluntly in talking about linguistic study, "The linguistic student should never make the mistake of identifying a language with its dictionary."[1] On the other hand, one cannot deny or ignore the existence of the word as a tangible unit of language. Sapir again, with characteristic insight, puts it thus:

> No more convincing test could be desired than this, that the naïve Indian, quite unaccustomed to the concept of the written word, has nevertheless no serious difficulty in

Reprinted by permission from *Language Learning,* 6 (1955), 23–41. Dr. Lado is dean of the Institute of Languages and Linguistics, Georgetown University.

[1] Edward Sapir, *Language,* (New York, 1921), p. 234.

dictating a text to a linguistic student word by word; he tends, of course, to run his words together as in actual speech, but if he is called to a halt and is made to understand what is desired, he can readily isolate the words as such, repeating them as units. He regularly refuses, on the other hand, to isolate the radical or grammatical element, on the ground that it "makes no sense."[2]

1.2   The word has been defined for scientific linguistic study by Bloomfield:

A free form which consists entirely of two or more lesser free forms, as, for instance, *poor John* or *John ran away* or *yes, sir* is a *phrase*. A free form which is not a phrase, is a *word*. A word, then, is a free form which does not consist entirely of (two or more) lesser free forms; in brief, a word is a *minimum free form*.[3]

1.3   A clear insight into the way words are used by the speakers of a language is given by Fries. He says,

For us, a *word* is a combination of sounds acting as a stimulus to bring into attention the experience to which it has become attached by use. . . .[4]

More than that, while the experience that is stimulated by the sound combination is a whole with a variety of contacts, usually only one aspect of this experience is dominant in attention—a particular aspect determined by the whole context of the linguistic situation. When one uses *head* in such a context as "a *head* of cabbage," it is the shape which is the dominant aspect of the experience that has made a connection with the material unit, a cabbage. When one uses head in such a context as "the *head* of a department," it is the head as the chief or dominating part of the body. When it is used in "the head of the river," another aspect of the relation of head to the body is important in attention. From a practical point of view, the various separate dictionary meanings of a word are the particular aspects of the experience stimulated by a word that have been dominant in the attention of users of the word as these aspects may be inferred from the context of a large number of quotations in which the word appears. For the native user of a language, the symbol, with the wide range of experience it stimulates, is so much a part of the very texture of his thought that he exercises great freedom in turning upon any aspect of this experience in line with the pressing needs of his thinking. The "meanings" of words are, therefore, more fluid than we realize. For the foreign speaker of a language who learns this new language as an adult, the words as stimuli probably never function with anything like the same fullness and freedom as they do for a native.[5]

1.4   Three aspects of words concern us here: 1) their form, 2) their meaning, and 3) their distribution.

[2] *Ibid.,* pp. 34–35.

[3] Leonard Bloomfield, *Language,* (New York, 1933), pp. 177–178. For a more complete discussion of the word see also pp. 178–183 and 207–246. For a mechanical procedure that shows word and morpheme boundaries see the recent article by Zellig S. Harris, "From Phoneme to Morpheme," *Language,* XXXI (1955), pp. 190–222.

[4] Charles C. Fries, with the cooperation of A. Aileen Traver, *English Word Lists, A Study of Their Adaptability for Instruction,* Washington, D.C., American Council on Education. Reprinted Ann Arbor, 1950, p. 87.

[5] *Ibid.,* p. 88.

1.41   Form. In most languages the form of words consists of sound segments, stress, and, in tone languages such as Chinese and Thai, pitch. The form of the Spanish word *jugo* "juice" is made up of four significant sound segments (phonemes) /xúgo/ and stress—primary stress on the first syllable. If we change one of the sound segments, *j*, to *y*, a new word results, *yugo* "yoke." If we change the position of the primary stress, a new word results, *jugó* "he played." The Thai word ม้า [ma:ʔ] "horse" is made up of certain sound segments and a high, level pitch. The same segments with a rising pitch would mean "dog."

The form of words varies according to the formality of the situation, speed of talk, position in the sentence, position as to stress, etc. For example, the English word *and* varies from three segmental phonemes /ænd/ through intermediate degrees of reduction, /ənd/, /æn/, /ən/, to one segmental phoneme, /n/. The word *not* occurs as /nat/ and /nt/; *will* as /wil/ and as /l/; *is* as /iz/ and /s/ or /z/. Naïve speakers of a language find it difficult to believe that the words they use vary so much in form.

Another relevant feature of form is that of the parts of words. English *observational* is made up of a stem *observ-* (compare *observe*),[6] a suffix -(a)*tion*, and another suffix -*al*. Other languages, on the other hand, permit more complex combinations than those of English. As something of a linguistic curiosity, but definitely a form of the language, Sapir mentions the example from Paiute, *wii-to-kuchum-punku rũgani-yugwi-vantü-m(ü)*, meaning "they who are going to sit and cut up with a knife a black cow (or bull)."[7]

The frequency of the parts of words may counteract the lack of frequency of the total word. If we use the word *observational*, it will probably be understood by elementary students of English as a foreign language even though it appears among the 1,358 least frequent words in Thorndike's list.[8] The parts *observe* + (a)*tion* + *al* are much more frequent than the word itself. The word *observe* is listed by Thorndike among the 2,000 most frequent words in English. The suffix -*tion* is used in so many words in English that its total frequency must be very high. I found examples of -*tion* in every page of a random ten page sample of Bloomfield's *Language* and in a similar spot-check of ten random pages of the lighter style of *The Art of Plain Talk* by Rudolf Flesch.[9] The suffix -*al* is less frequent than -*tion*, but it is still frequent enough to occur on practically every page of text.

English has lexical forms made up of patterns of separate words, for example *call up* "to phone." Many languages do not permit such units or do not permit

[6] It is doubtful that native speakers break this form further into *ob* + *serve*.

[7] Edward Sapir, *Language*, p. 31.

[8] Edward L. Thorndike and Irving Lorge, *The Teacher's Word Book of 30,000 Words*, (New York, 1944).

[9] Rudolf Flesch, *The Art of Plain Talk*, (New York, 1946).

the same types of formal patterns. Compare for example Spanish *telefonear* "to telephone" or *llamar por teléfono* "call by telephone" but nothing like the construction *call up*.

1.42 Meaning. It is quite an illusion to think as even literate people sometimes do that meanings are the same in all languages, that languages differ only in the forms used for those meanings. As a matter of fact the meanings into which we classify our experience are culturally determined or modified and they vary considerably from culture to culture. Some meanings found in one culture may not exist in another. The meaning "horse" did not exist in American Indian languages until the Spanish conquest and colonization brought horses to America. Similarly, the meanings "corn" (in the sense of maize) and "potatoes" did not exist in Europe until the same people took those products from America to Europe in their ships. But even when the reality is available to the culture, the meanings will differ, or not exist in some cases. The Eskimos have many meaning distinctions correlating with different types of snow and use separate words to express those distinctions, whereas other cultures that have considerable experience with snow simply do not have as many meaning distinctions. These meaning differences are seldom as forcefully noticeable as when one attempts to translate accurately a text from one language to another.

Meanings can be classified according to the forms they attach to. Meanings that attach to words as words are lexical meanings; for example the meaning, "a building for human habitation," that attaches to the form *house* is a lexical meaning in English. The meaning "two or more; plural" that attaches to the bound form -s [s] in *books, cats, maps,* can be called a morphological meaning, while the same meaning "plural" that attaches to the word form *plural* is a lexical meaning. The meaning "question" attached to the word arrangement in the sentence, *Is he a farmer,* is a syntactic meaning, but the meaning "question" attached to the word form *question* is a lexical one.

At the moment, we are primarily concerned with lexical meanings, but different languages classify their meanings differently; that is, what is habitually a lexical meaning in one language may be a morphological meaning in another. Speakers of one language who have not come in meaningful contact with other languages assume not only that the meanings are the same but that they will be classified the same way. Speakers of English find it difficult to imagine a language in which the singular-plural distinction in *book:books* is not made morphologically. "How else can you communicate that idea?" they are apt to ask. In Chinese, for example, that distinction is not made, that is, it is not made morphologically, by a bound form such as -s in English. In Chinese, the meanings "two" "three" "more than one" etc. are lexical meanings; those meanings attach to words. When the meaning is relevant to the message, the words are included, and when the meaning is not relevant, the words are left out. Greek had the meanings "singular," "dual," and "plural" as morphological meanings. We can assume that Greek speakers wondered how languages that have only singular and plural could express the meaning "dual; two." That distinction is a lexical one in English.

The matter of the frequency of the various meanings of a word is relevant to us. If one uses the word *get,* which appears among the 500 most frequent ones in Thorndike's list, in the context, *We did not want to overdo the thing and get six months,* meaning "suffer imprisonment by way of punishment," we would find that some fairly advanced students of English as a foreign language would not "know" the word. Yet we could not convincingly assume that they did not really know one of the 500 most frequent words in English. That particular meaning of *get* is so infrequent that it was not reported as having occurred at all in a sample of over half a million running words.[10] The *Oxford English Dictionary* lists 234 meanings for the word *get* and obviously one can know a good many of those meanings and still miss the word in the particular context used as an example above.

The meanings discussed are usually part of the intended message in communication. These meanings are more or less consciously intended by the speaker and may be called primary meanings. In actual use, however, other meanings are conveyed by words, for example, if a word is restricted in use to a given social class, its use by a speaker may give the listener the meaning of social class identification. Similarly if a word is restricted to a geographical area, its use by a speaker will convey a locality meaning, also.

1.43 The distribution of words is important to us because at any given moment in the history of a language the speakers of that language carry with them the habits of the restrictions in distribution and because different languages have different restrictions. There are grammatical restrictions so that in English, *water* may be a noun as in *a glass of water,* a verb as in *water the garden,* a noun adjunct as in *water meter,* but not an adjective without some change in form, e.g., *watery substance.* In other languages the restrictions may be greater; for example in Spanish, *agua* "water" as a word may only be a noun unless its form is changed.

The fact that words may show different geographic distribution, falling in or out of this or that dialect area of a language, is important. And, as already indicated, distribution in the various social class levels also has to be considered because of the secondary meanings such distribution conveys. Statements of raw frequency alone leave these matters unresolved. Thorndike's list gives *ain't* among the 2,000 most frequent words in English, but the list does not say if *ain't* is typical of Standard English or of the speech representing certain other dialects.

Words are not only restricted geographically and socially; they are often restricted as to styles of speaking and writing. For example, many words found in poetry will not be found in ordinary conversation or in ordinary

[10] Estimated from data supplied in Irving Lorge.

prose; and vice versa, some words used in prose will not be found in poetry.

1.5 Classifications. It should be abundantly clear from the above brief discussion, if not previously so, that the words of a language are more than merely a list of lexical items. The words of a language are a highly complex system of classes of items—interlocking classes as to meaning, form, grammatical function, distribution, etc.

1.51 Fries[11] classifies English words into four groups that seem relevant to us. They are 1) function words, 2) substitute words, 3) grammatically distributed words, and 4) content words. The function words primarily perform grammatical functions, for example, *do* signalling questions. The substitute words, *he, she, they, so,* etc., replace a class of words and several sub-classes. Grammatically distributed words, *some, any,* etc., show unusual grammatical restrictions in distribution. The number of words in the first three groups is rather small, say 200 in round numbers in English.[12] The fourth group, content words, constitutes the bulk of the vocabulary of the language. In English and in many other languages the content words are subdivided into items treated as things, as processes, as qualities, etc.

1.52 Two further distinctions in vocabulary are required to complete our model. We need to distinguish between a common core vocabulary known to all the members of a language community, and specialized vocabularies, known only to special groups. We are of course primarily interested in the common core vocabulary, because specialized vocabularies have to be learned by native as well as non-native speakers. We are interested primarily in the special problems of the latter.

1.53 The other distinction is that between vocabulary for production and vocabulary for recognition. As a rule our recognition vocabulary is much larger than our production vocabulary. Various estimates have been made of the minimum necessary vocabulary for a student to be able to communicate in ordinary situations. Basic English uses approximately 1,000 words for that purpose.[13] Michael West considers a vocabulary of 2,000 words "good enough for anything, and more than enough for most things."[14] Obviously these are minimum production vocabularies. For recognition, larger minimum vocabularies are necessary.

2. *The Native Language Factor*

2.1 Ease and difficulty. Given the above model and making use of available vocabulary studies one might attempt to select a sample vocabulary for teaching

[11]Charles C. Fries, *Teaching and Learning English as a Foreign Language,* (Ann Arbor, 1945), pp. 44–50.

[12]Estimated from data supplied in Fries, *The Structure of English,* (New York, 1954), Ch. VI.

[13]C. K. Ogden, *The System of Basic English,* (New York, 1934).

[14]Michael West, "Simplified and Abridged," *English Language Teaching,* V, No. 2, p. 48.

or for testing. Such attempts have been made and have received wide circulation. C. K. Ogden's Basic English list and West's *A General Service List of English Words*[15] are well known examples in an active field. Nevertheless, in spite of the care and experience that have gone into the preparation of such lists, they cannot give us a vocabulary sample graded as to difficulty because by their very nature they fail to take into account the most powerful factor in acquiring the vocabulary of a foreign language, namely, the vocabulary of the native language.

If in a test of English vocabulary for Spanish speakers one uses the words *machete, suppuration,* and *calumniator* which appear among the 1,358 least frequent words in Thorndike's 30,000 word list, one would find that practically all the students knew them. Could we then assume that those students possessed a vocabulary of over 28,642 words in English? Obviously not. Spanish has the words *machete, superación,* and *calumniador,* similar in form and meaning to the English words, and Spanish-speaking students will know those words by the mere fact of knowing Spanish. We simply cannot ignore the native language of the student as a factor of primary importance in vocabulary, just as we cannot ignore it in pronunciation and grammatical structure.

Another example arguing for the importance of the native language has to do with grammatical distribution of two very simple words. The words *fire* and *man* will probably be more difficult for Spanish speakers in the contexts, *Fire the furnace,* and *Man the guns,* than in *Open fire* "start shooting" and *A man broke his leg.* The difference is more subtle than in the previous example, but it is there nevertheless. Spanish has a noun, *fuego,* "fire" used in *Abran fuego,* "Open fire" but not used as a verb as in *Fire the furnace.* Similarly, a Spanish noun, *hombre,* "man," is used in *Un hombre se rompió una pierna,* "A man broke his leg," but is not used as a verb as in *Man the guns.* There are other elements involved in these examples to be sure, but grammatical distribution is definitely a factor.

2.2 Difficulty patterns. Similarity and difference to the native language in form, meaning, and distribution will result in ease or difficulty in acquiring the vocabulary of a foreign language. Comparing the foreign language vocabulary with that of the native language we will find words that are 1) similar in form and in meaning, 2) similar in form but different in meaning, 3) similar in meaning but different in form, 4) different in form and in meaning, 5) different in their type of construction, 6) similar in primary meaning but different in connotation, and 7) similar in meaning but with restrictions in geographical distribution.

Since some of these groups overlap, with the result that some words will fall into more than one group at the same time, the difficulty will vary somewhat.

---

[15] Michael West, *A General Service List of English Words with Semantic Frequencies and a Supplementary Word-List for the Writing of Popular Science and Technology,* (New York, 1953).

Nevertheless, we can predict general level of difficulty on the basis of these groupings, and will classify each group into one of three levels of difficulty: 1) easy, 2) normal, and 3) difficult.

The term *similar* is restricted here to items that would function as "same" in the other language in ordinary use. We know that complete sameness is not to be expected in language behavior. The actual behavioral boundaries of similarity depend on the items that persons of one language "identify" or "translate" as same from and into the other language. References to form are to the sounds of the words, not to the spelling, even though spelling is used to represent the words in this paper.

Pattern 1, *Cognates:*[16] Words that are similar in form and in meaning. English and Spanish have thousands of words that are reasonably similar in form and in meaning, for example *hotel, hospital, calendar.*[17] Some of these were kept in Spanish as it evolved from Latin and were borrowed into English from Latin or French. Some go back to earlier forms presumably found in Indo-European, the common ancestor of English and Spanish in what is known as the Indo-European family of languages. Whatever the cause of the similarity, these words usually constitute the lowest difficulty group—they are *easy*. In fact, if they are similar enough, even students who have never studied English at all will recognize them. These words are of value at the very elementary level.

Even though there are thousands of words that are similar in English and Spanish, these similarities can be classified into a relatively small number of sub-patterns, for example, English *-tion* is similar to Spanish *-ción*, and hundreds of words can be classified as similar under that sub-pattern.[18] When using such words in teaching and testing beginning students we will do well to sample them as sub-patterns rather than as independent items.

Vigorous discussion often results when cognate words are mentioned in connection with teaching. We do not need to get involved in such discussions since cognates are presented here for recognition rather than for production. There can be little quarrel with having the student recognize them when they are used by others.

It is sometimes falsely assumed that cognates are to be found only between

[16]Cognates here mean words that are similar in form and meaning regardless of origin. The usual meaning of cognate is "related in origin." For us even if two words are not related in origin they will be called cognates if they are similar in form and meaning. Similarly, if two words have the same origin but are now so different that speakers do not identify them as similar, they will not be considered cognates for our purpose.

[17]For a list of Spanish-English cognates see Marshall E. Nunn and Herbert A. Van Scroy, *Glossary of Related Spanish-English Words*, University of Alabama Studies, Number 5.

[18]For a brief account of nine patterns of Spanish-English cognates see *Lessons in Vocabulary*, from *An Intensive Course in English* by the Research Staff of the English Language Institute, Charles C. Fries, Director, (Ann Arbor, 1954). Compare also E. M. Anthony, "The Teaching of Cognates," *Language Learning*, IV (1952–53), pp. 79–82.

two related languages such as English and Spanish, not between unrelated languages such as English and Japanese, Chinese and English. In actual fact, numerous cognates can be found between English and Japanese and between English and Chinese, and many other languages which are quite unrelated to each other. There are many words which have circled the globe, and many more that have extended far beyond the boundaries of any one language or any one culture.

Pattern 2, *Deceptive Cognates:*[19] Words that are similar in form but represent meanings that are different. Words that are similar in form in two languages may be only partly similar in meaning, they may be altogether different in meaning but still represent meanings that exist in the native language, or they may be different in meaning and represent meanings that are not grasped as such in the native language. Japanese borrowed the word *milk* from English but restricted its meaning to "canned milk." The form of the word in Japanese is similar to English but the meaning is only partly similar since it does not include fresh milk, for example. Spanish has a word, *asistir,* which is similar in form to English *assist,* but the meaning is practically always different. Spanish *asistir* is similar in meaning to English *attend,* while English *assist* carries with it the feature of helping, of supporting. As a result of this difference in meaning, Spanish speakers learning English say they *assisted a class* when meaning they *attended,* "were present." English *in the table* and *on the table* are similar in meaning to Spanish *en la mesa* in ordinary conversation. Only under very special circumstances will a Spanish speaker make a meaning distinction between *in* and *on* the table, and then it will not be only an *in:on* contrast but a *table* vs. *drawer* contrast as well. Spanish speakers will say *en el cajón* "in the drawer" and *sobre la mesa* "on the table." The problem here is not simply attaching a familiar meaning to a new form but also grasping a new meaning distinction, a different way of classifying reality.

These words that are similar in form but different in meaning constitute a special group very high on a scale of difficulty. We will label them *difficult.* They are not adequately sampled on frequency criteria alone because their similarity in form to words in the native language raises their frequency in student usage above normal for the language. In other words, they are more important than their frequency rating might indicate. They are sure-fire traps.

Pattern 3, *Different Forms:* Words that are similar in some of their frequent meanings but different in form. Difficulty level: normal. Example. English *tree* in the context, *The leaves of that tree are falling* is similar in its primary meaning to Spanish *árbol* in a comparable context. The learning burden in this case is chiefly that of learning a new form, *tree,* for a meaning of *árbol* already

---

[19]"Deceptive cognates" as used here refers only to similarity in form and difference in meaning; it does not refer to the origin of the words. In usual linguistic terminology deceptive cognates would refer to words in two languages that because of their form would seem to be related by origin but are not so related. For us such a case would be classed as a cognate provided the meanings are also similar.

habitually grasped by Spanish-speaking students. This kind of vocabulary learning is naïvely taken by many to represent all vocabulary learning. Such an oversimplification fails to account for the various vocabulary groups which appear
when we have looked closer and have considered the native language.

It is also important to note that although certain meanings of a word in one
language are sometimes translatable into a word in another language there are
very few if any words in two languages that are the same in all their meanings.
It is difficult for example to realize that the words *tree* and *árbol* of our example
are similar in only about four out of their twenty or more meanings and uses.
Only the poorest two-language dictionaries will show numbers of words in a
one-to-one meaning correspondence in the two languages. Only words such as
penicillin, which are borrowed into many languages simultaneously, can be considered equivalent in all their meanings, and even then if such words gain any
currency at all they soon develop new meanings that are not parallel in different
languages.

It is in these content words that are different in form but similar in some
meanings, however, that decisions can and should be made as to vocabulary size
on the basis of frequency lists for recognition and adequacy for expression on a
production level.

Pattern 4, *"Strange" Meanings:* Words that are different in form and represent
meanings that are "strange" to speakers of a particular native language, that is,
meanings that represent a different grasp of reality. Difficult. In American
English, *first floor* is different in form from Spanish *primer piso* and different
in its grasp of what constitutes "first." Spanish *primer* "first" in this case does
not mean number one at ground level but number one above ground level, and
so *primer piso* refers to what in American English is called *second floor* and
not *first floor,* which would be the literal translation.

These cases constitute special problems in the vocabulary of a foreign language. Obviously it is not enough merely to teach a new form; the strange meaning must be made familiar. Some of the instances covered by this pattern—the
instance in which the form in the two languages is similar—fall also under Pattern
2, *deceptive cognates*. Pattern 4, however, includes all those in which there is
no particular similarity in the form of the words in the two languages.

There is every reason to believe that the same kind of distortion that we can
observe in the sounds of the speech of a non-native speaker also occurs in the
meanings he is trying to convey. In both cases he is substituting sounds and
meanings of his native language and culture. In the case of sounds the untrained
person hears a vague "foreign" accent and the trained person hears specific distortions. In the case of meanings the distortions go largely undetected by the
observer or listener because the native meanings stimulated in him by the speech
forms may not be accompanied by outwardly observable behavior. It is only
when a word form is used in an "unusual" way that our attention is drawn to possible meaning differences. Similarly, when the non-native speaker of a language

listens to the language as spoken by natives, the meanings that he grasps are not those that the native speakers attempt to convey, but those of the system of the language of the listener.

Pattern 5, *New Form Types:* Words that are different in their morphological construction. Difficult. When the speakers of various Romance languages and of Japanese, Chinese and other languages learn English they have great trouble learning such lexical items as *call up* "to telephone," *call on* "to visit," and *run out of* "to exhaust the supply of." If in the native language of the student there are no lexical items made up of two otherwise separate words in patterns like the one illustrated, he will not easily grasp these "two-word verbs" in the foreign language. The difficulty is increased when the elements can be separated by other words as in the example, *Did you call the boy up?* These two-word verbs constitute a difficulty group all its own for speakers of various languages.

"Idioms"—expressions peculiar to a language—are identifiable as we compare two languages rather than within the language itself. An expression which may seem peculiar to native speakers may be quite natural to speakers of another language and would therefore not be an "idiom" to them. On the other hand, an expression which seems quite natural to native speakers may be strange to foreign speakers of a particular language background. If we should find on comparing the expression with a variety of languages that it is strange to all or nearly all of them, we would be justified in calling it an idiom in general, but even then the statement would be meaningless in those cases in which the other language had a parallel expression. As a matter of fact, the idiom counts made in the wake of the Modern Foreign Language Study were two-language studies. *The Spanish Idiom List* by Keniston[20] lists expressions in Spanish that are strange to English speakers. In all of the counts the compilers looked at expressions in the foreign language with English as their frame of reference.

Pattern 6, *Different Connotation:* Words that have widely different connotations in two languages. Difficult. A special difficulty group is represented by words that are harmless in connotation in the native language but offensive or taboo in the foreign language, or vice versa. When they are harmless in the native language the student will use them in the foreign language without realizing their effect. When they are harmless in the foreign language the student will avoid using them for fear of setting off the same reactions they produce in his native language. In either case they are important on the level of social acceptability of words. A few examples will show how important these connotation differences can be.

In Spanish the expression *Dios mío* meaning literally "My God" is often used as an appeal to the Almighty in matter-of-fact conversation. Even those Spanish

---

[20]Hayward Keniston, *Spanish Idiom List Selected on the Basis of Range and Frequency of Occurrence*, Publications of the American and Canadian Committees on Modern Languages. XI (New York, 1929).

speakers who have progressed considerably in their control of English will sometimes use the expression with the same feeling and intent in English, but the effect on English listeners is of course different. The name *Jesús* is often used as a given name in Spanish. Parents who thus name their children may actually feel they are honoring Christ, or at least do not feel any lack of respect. In English, however, people find it difficult to call a person by that name. It seems to smack of irreverence to English speakers to use the name for a human being, a radically different connotation from that in Spanish. In whistling at sports events or political rallies the difference is in the opposite direction: Spanish speakers may be shocked to hear a speaker whistled at and applauded at the same time. They believe the whistles indicate disapproval and they wonder why disapproval is expressed so openly as it appears to them. In Spanish the applause indicates approval, and whistling, a vulgar form of disapproval. Some youthful students of foreign languages delight in learning certain unprintable expressions not approved in polite company. When they ask for translations they get colorless rendering which when uttered leave us wondering why they are uttered at all.

These differences in connotation sometimes develop between dialects of the same language. In Cuba the familiar form of the second person pronoun, *tú*, is more widely used than in Mexico for example. A Cuban young man was rebuked by two Mexican young ladies because he used the familiar *tú*, which sounded a bit too bold to them. No amount of explaining was enough to completely convince the girls that the young man actually meant no disrespect. The word *grueso* "fat" is used as a compliment, at least in some dialects of present day Spanish. On a visit to Spain I was greeted repeatedly with "flattering" expressions of how "fat" I was. Being aware of the favorable connotation I appreciated the remark, but many an American young girl may not have felt flattered.

These have been obvious, even coarse examples of wide differences in connotation. More subtle differences exist and remain in the speech of speakers of foreign languages through the advanced stages of control of the language. We cannot do much to teach or to test these subtle differences specifically and completely, but it is possible to sample the more frequent and obvious cases of wide discrepancy in connotation.

Pattern 7, *Geographically Restricted:* Words that are restricted as to the geographic areas in which they are used in the foreign language. Difficult, because the restrictions must be learned also. Restrictions in geographic distribution of words are important to the selection of words for teaching and for testing. Unless we are interested in teaching or testing a particular geographic dialect of a language we will choose forms that are part of the standard language if there is one, and words that are common to the major dialects if there is not a standard language. If we are interested in English without regard to whether it is Standard British or Standard American English we would avoid such words as *petrol* and *gasoline* in testing because they are typical of British and American usage respectively. If on the other hand we are interested in Standard American English as distinct from British English, we would use *gasoline*. Within American English, if we are not interested in any one dialect, we would use *dragonfly* for the insect known by that name, because that term is more general than Northern *darning needle* and Midland *snake feeder* for the same insect.[21]

Although part of what has been said about Pattern 7 seems not to apply directly to the definition of a pattern of difficulty, it is an important consideration. The matter of geographic distribution fits more neatly into a difficulty pattern when we consider that a student who has learned a geographically restricted form must learn another for the same meaning if he is to communicate with speakers from geographic areas where the form he learned has no currency. Hence, the label "difficult" we have given to the pattern.

* * *

There has been on the whole much superficial oversimplified thinking about the vocabulary of languages, and a great deal of vocabulary research such as word frequency lists and simplified vocabularies suffers from that oversimplification. In dealing with vocabulary we should take into account three important aspects of words—their form, their meaning, their distribution—, and we should consider the various kinds or classes of words in the operation of the language. If these things are important in understanding the vocabulary system of a language, they become even more important when one learns the vocabulary of a foreign language since the forms, meanings, distribution, and classifications of words are different in different languages. Out of these differences arise vocabulary problems and difficulty levels that constitute teaching and learning problems and are telltale matters for vocabulary tests. The patterns of difficulty described above are an attempt to clarify and classify the problems involved.

REFERENCES

Bloomfield, Leonard. *Language.* New York: Henry Holt and Company, 1933.

Bongers, Herman. *The History and Principles of Vocabulary Control.* Woerden, Holland: Wocopi. Three volumes in two, 1947.

Flesch, Rudolf. *The Art of Plain Talk.* New York and London: Harper & Brothers Publishers, 1946.

Fries, Charles C., with the cooperation of A. Aileen Traver. *English Word Lists.* A Study of Their Adaptability for Instruction. Washington, D.C.: American Council on Education, 1940. Reprinted 1950 by The George Wahr Publishing Co., Ann Arbor.

Fries, Charles C.
Teaching and Learning English as a Foreign Language. Ann Arbor: University of Michigan Press, 1945.
The Structure of English. New York: Harcourt, Brace and Co., Chapt. VI, 1954.

Keniston, Hayward. *Spanish Idiom List,* Selected on the Basis of Range and Frequency of Occurrence. New York: Publications of the American and Canadian Committees on Modern Languages. Vol. XI, 1929.

[21] Hans Kurath, *A Word Geography of the Eastern United States.* (Ann Arbor, 1949), p. 14.

Kurath, Hans. *A Word Geography of the Eastern United States,* Ann Arbor: University of Michigan Press, 1949.

Lorge, Irving. *The Semantic Count of 570 Commonest English Words.* New York: Bureau of Publications, Teachers College, Columbia University, 1949.

Nunn, Marshall E., and Van Scroy, Herbert A. *Glossary of Related Spanish-English Words.* University, Alabama: University of Alabama Studies, Number 5, 1949.

Ogden, C. K. *The System of Basic English.* New York: Harcourt, Brace and Company, 1934.

The Oxford English Dictionary. Vols. I–XII and Supplement (Corrected Reissue). Oxford University Press, 1933.

Rodríguez, Bou, I. *Recuento de vocabulario español.* Rio Piedras, Puerto Rico: Universidad de Puerto Rico. Two volumes in Three, 1952.

Sapir, Edward. *Language.* New York: Harcourt, Brace and Co., 1921.

Thorndike, Edward L., and Lorge, Irving. *The Teacher's Word Book of 30,000 Words.* New York: Bureau of Publications, Teachers College, Columbia University, 1944.

West, Michael. "Simplified and Abridged," *English Language Teaching,* V, no. 2 (Nov.): 48–52, 1950.

A General Service List of English Words, with Semantic Frequencies and a Supplementary Word-List for the Writing of Popular Science and Technology. London; New York; Toronto: Longmans, Green and Co., 1953.

33   ADJECTIVES OF   CLIFFORD H. PRATOR
TEMPERATURE

What support does this article give to proponents of the use of contrastive analysis in developing language courses?

To what extent are grammatical questions involved in contrasting adjectives of temperature in two or more languages?

What would optimally be included in a lesson (or lessons) to teach French speakers the use of English *cold, cool, warm,* and *hot*?

Can you think of other lexical sets which could be analyzed and contrasted with the same interesting results?

In which of Lado's (Art. 32) seven patterns of difficulty do these adjectives of temperature fall?

Reprinted by permission from *English Language Teaching,* 17 (July, 1963), 158–164. Dr. Prator is professor and vice-chairman of the department of English, University of California, Los Angeles.

A fuller title for this study would be "Some Temperature Words in English and in Several Other Languages." It deals with the four adjectives which we ordinarily use to describe temperature, their relationships to one another, and the way in which their meanings combine to cover a given area of experience. It then points out that certain other languages cover the same area of experience in quite different ways. Even so limited an exercise in contrastive linguistic analysis gives evidence in support of certain conclusions regarding language instruction, conclusions which have often been formulated but which have by no means been universally accepted.

The four adjectives in question are *cold, cool, warm,* and *hot.* In an article recently published in *Language Learning,*[1] Yao Shen argues that the meanings of all four are essentially parallel, that in any particular season and locality *cool* represents a higher range of temperature than *cold, warm* a higher one than *cool,* and *hot* one still higher. "In Ann Arbor, *warm* can be said to have a higher temperature than *cool.* Between the two poles of *hot* and *cold, warm* is closer to *hot* and *cool* is closer to *cold,* regardless of . . . whether the temperature is moving from *hot* toward *cold* (getting cooler or colder) or from *cold* toward *hot* (getting warm)."[2]

She contrasts the use of the four items in English with that of the four terms which cover the same total area of meaning in Chinese: *rè, nwǎnhwo, lyǎngkwai,* and *lěng.* When one speaks of the weather in Chinese, the two intermediate terms are experienced differently. "From *rè* (hot) to *lěng* (cold), the state of warm = cooler is *lyǎngkwai.* From *lěng* (cold) to *rè* (hot), the state of cool = warmer is *nwǎnhwo.*"[3] If we are to accept this analysis, then, the four English terms are simply successive points in a reversible sequence, whereas in Chinese there are two separate sequences, one for rising temperatures and one for falling, each of which includes only three of the four terms.

When a large number of examples are studied, little evidence can be found to support this classification of English temperature words, whether the speaker is referring to the weather, to inanimate objects, or to living creatures. We might state on a day when the thermometer stood high, "It's *hot.*" As the temperature fell, however, we would hardly say: "Now it's *warm,*" "Now it's *cool,*" "Now it's *cold.*" Conversely, on a winter day, though we might declare that we ourselves were cold, we would surely not consider it a logical progression to say as the thermometer rose: "I'm *cold,*" "I'm *cool,*" "I'm *warm,*" "I'm *hot.*" Instead, a normal falling sequence would be: "It's (or I'm) *hot,*" "It's getting *cool,*" "It's *cold*"—omitting *warm.* And a natural rising progression would be: "I'm (or it's) *cold,*" "I'm *warming* up," "I'm *hot*"—leaving out *cool.*

[1] Vol. X, Nos. 1 and 2, 1960, pp. 1–13.

[2] Ibid. p. 2.

[3] Ibid. pp. 2–3.

It would seem, then, that Yao Shen's arrangement of the four Chinese words into two separate sequences of three words each applies equally well to English. *Warm* is a term that we use on the way from *cold* to *hot*, and *cool* fits into a series which begins with *hot* and moves toward *cold*. "It's getting *warm*" always indicates a rising temperature, and "It's getting *cool*" always means that the thermometer is falling. *Warm* and *cool* are alike in that they indicate a change from a generally opposite temperature. The two-word verbs we use to describe a rise or fall in temperature are *warm up* and *cool off*, and no comparable verbs are formed with *hot* and *cold*.

The entire picture, however, is certainly much more complicated than that. Each of the four English adjectives of temperature may be used with the verb *to be* to describe the weather, an inanimate object, or a living creature. We can say "It's *cold* today," "The iron is *cold*," or "I'm *cold*"; and *cool, warm*, or *hot* can be substituted for *cold* in any of the three sentences. But in describing living creatures English is ambiguous. Even if we leave aside possible figurative meanings, "You're *cold*" may signify either that you are externally cold when someone else touches you—cold in the sense that an inanimate object is cold—or that you feel cold to yourself internally. There appears to be no way to remove the ambiguity short of using an explanatory phrase; "You *feel cold*" still has two possible literal meanings. As we shall see, some other languages are not ambiguous on this point.

Under most circumstances *cold* and *hot* have disagreeable connotations in English, but *cool* and *warm* are agreeable. In so far as *cold* is a disagreeable term, then, its antonym is *warm*, not *hot*. And in a situation where *hot* is disagreeable its opposite is *cool* rather than *cold*. Looking out through the window on a wintry day, we would never turn to our companion in the room and say: "My, it's *cold* outside! Are you *cool* enough?", or "Are you *hot* enough?" It would always be, "Are you *warm* enough?" After strenuous exercise outside on a hot summer's day, we might declare: "It's too *hot* out here; let's go inside where it's *cool*," but never, "Let's go inside where it's *cold*," or "Let's go inside where it's *warm*." *Warm* means pleasantly comfortable against a *cold* background, whereas *cool* means pleasantly comfortable against a *hot* background.

This partial analysis omits consideration of the various figurative and idiomatic uses of *hot, warm, cool, cold* (for example, "a *hot*-blooded man" but a "*warm*-blooded animal"). Even so, it is obvious that the problem of a foreign student of English is much more complex than merely to learn to use the four adjectives to indicate appropriate ranges in a single temperature scale.

Our insight into the nature of that student's difficulties can, of course, be increased by a knowledge of the way in which his mother tongue expresses the area of meaning covered by *cold, cool*, etc., in English.

Even a language as closely related to English as French provides a very substantial amount of interference in this area. In French there appear to be only three commonly used adjectives whose central meaning has to do with temperature: *froid, frais,* and *chaud*—two words for the lower temperatures, one for the higher. One is inevitably tempted, in passing, to wonder if there is any connection between the rather cool French climate and the fact that the vocabulary, when compared with that of English, seems unbalanced in the direction of coolness. To be sure, there is another word, *doux*, which might be equated with the English *warm*, but *doux* is used much less frequently to describe temperature than the other three terms and refers most often to qualities of mildness, softness, or gentleness. To some extent *chaud* must carry alone the burden which in English is divided between *hot* and *warm*. Therefore the native speaker of French will have difficulty learning to distinguish between *hot* and *warm*.

We have already noted that the four English adjectives may be used in the same construction, with the verb *to be*, in referring to either the weather, inanimate objects, or living creatures. French requires an entirely different construction for each of the three types of reference.

In speaking of the weather, *froid, frais, doux,* and *chaud* are all used with the verb *faire* (*to make* or *to do*): "Il fait *froid*" (It's *cold*), etc. In this construction the four words are invariable in form and would traditionally be labelled as nouns rather than adjectives. To indicate a rising temperature, the progression would be from *froid*, through *doux* (or perhaps more commonly *moins froid* [less cold]), to *chaud*, omitting *frais*. In the opposite direction the series would be *chaud, frais, froid,* with *doux* omitted.

Referring to inanimate objects, *doux* is never employed to indicate temperature, but only *froid, chaud,* and—with certain nouns—*frais*. In this type of reference the verb *être*, equivalent to the English *to be*, is used, and the three descriptive terms are certainly adjectives marked by appropriate endings for gender and number: "Le fer est *froid*" (The iron is *cold*), "Les assiettes sont *froides*" (The plates are *cold*).

The same construction is occasionally heard in reference to living creatures: "Vous êtes *chaud*" (You are hot). In this case the meaning would be that you are externally hot to the touch rather than that you feel hot to yourself internally. In order to express the latter meaning, it would be necessary to use the verb *avoir* (*to have*) and the nominal form of the descriptive term: "Vous avez *chaud*" (You are *hot*). French can thus avoid the ambiguity of the English "You are *hot*." Neither *doux* nor *frais* is applicable to living creatures as an indication of temperature, which leaves only *froid* and *chaud*, the terms at the two ends of the scale. The student of English with a French background will thus have to learn, in speaking of persons, to split his single concept, *chaud*, into two concepts, *warm* and *hot*, and the same will be true of *froid* in relation to *cool* and *cold*.

As we might expect, the agreeable or disagreeable connotation of the French temperature word depends on the general background and on what is being described. *Chaud* in particular may be unlike its nearest English counterpart, *hot*, in connotation. On a cold day it may be pleasant for a person to be *chaud*, though it is certainly not agreeable for him to be *hot*. On the other hand, weather described as *chaud* or *hot* is always unpleasant.

It is perhaps worthy of note, in passing, that there is another fairly common French word which would usually be translated as *warm*: *chaleureux*. The latter, however, seems to be restricted to figurative uses: *une recommendation chaleureuse* (a warm recommendation). The learner's difficulty here would be in moving from English to French, splitting a meaning, rather than in moving from French to English, in which case the two meanings are coalesced.

The native speaker of Spanish would share most of the Frenchman's problems in learning to describe temperature reactions in English, since the two Romance languages use mostly cognate terms and constructions in covering this particular area of meaning. Spanish even has a special word, *caluroso*, which corresponds to *chaleureux* in that it is employed only in cases when the warmth is figurative. There is one quite striking difference, however. From the point of view of the Spanish speaker, both French and English are ambiguous in describing inanimate objects. By his choice of verb, *ser* or *estar*, the speaker of Spanish indicates whether the coldness or warmth is an inherent, permanent quality of the object or merely a temporary state: *"El hielo es frío"* (Ice is cold), *"El agua está fría"* (The water is cold). In French or English this type of distinction would often necessitate a periphrasis.

In order to round out this brief analysis of temperature terms, it is instructive to examine a non-Indo-European language. Yao Shen mentions the national language of the Philippines, Tagalog, in her study. However, she merely lists the two terms *maginaw* and *mainit*, equating the former with *cold* and *cool*, the latter with *warm* and *hot*.[4] The implication is that Tagalog covers this area of meaning in a very simple fashion, without complications of the sort noted in English and Chinese. As might be expected, upon closer examination such does not turn out to be the case.

There are in Tagalog at least three temperature terms which one very commonly employs in speaking of the weather: *maginaw, mainit*, and also *malamig*. Like *maginaw, malamig* means cold, and both indicate coolness to approximately the same degree. The only difference in meaning between the two appears to be that *malamig* is somewhat more objective, a word which one might use upon reading the thermometer. On the other hand, *maginaw*, even when used in reference to the weather, indicates that the speaker is also feeling the coldness. *Maginaw* is not used in describing inanimate objects, but only *malamig* and *mainit*. In the Philippines, then, in a climate which is distinctly and characteristically hot, we find the vocabulary unbalanced in the direction of coldness, just as was the case in France; the temptation to try to associate climate with the way in which temperature words are used vanishes.

In Tagalog the temperature words enter into constructions which differ greatly

[4] Ibid. p. 3, fn.

from those of English or French, and the interference which thus arises is certainly a major source of difficulty for the Filipino student of either Indo-European language. The construction used in speaking of the weather includes neither verb nor subject pronoun: *"Mainit ngayon"* (literally, *"Hot* now"). To describe an inanimate object, one can place either adjective or noun first, but the two must be linked by a particle which varies in shape: *"Mainit* na palantsa" or "Palantsang *mainit"* (hot iron). People may be described as though they were inanimate objects: *"Mainit* ka" (You are *hot).* The meaning is then that the person is externally hot to the touch. To indicate that the person feels internally hot, a verbal affix is substituted for the adjectival affix *ma-*: *"Naiinitan* ka" (You are *hot).*

In Tagalog the matter of pleasant and unpleasant connotations is handled by the use of very typical Malayo-Polynesian linguistic devices, repetition and reduplication. If the temperature adjective is repeated and the particle *na* is interposed, the connotation is generally unpleasant: *"mainit na mainit"* (very, very hot). If the root is reduplicated, the connotation is pleasant: *"mainit-init"* (nicely warm).

By using these derivative forms of the adjectives, one can obtain two separate sequences of expressions, similar to those in English, for indicating temperature changes. The rising sequence is *malamig, mainit-init, mainit, mainit na mainit.* The falling sequence is *mainit, malamig-lamig, malamig, malamig na malamig.*

The writer realizes that in the course of these comments he has mixed linguistic levels—lexical and grammatical—in a manner which would be inexcusable in a serious analytical study of a single language. The fact seems to be, however, that what is vocabulary in one language may be grammar in another. As linguists try to extend their contrastive analyses into the lexical area—something which has rarely been attempted up to now—they will almost certainly find that it is impossible to treat vocabulary and grammar as discrete entities, just as it is usually impossible to compare the grammatical structures of two languages while keeping morphology and syntax in strictly separate compartments.

It is hoped that this study will serve to underscore and to illustrate once again certain facts about the teaching of English as a second language. The latter is a job which can be done with full effectiveness only by one who has a considerable analytical knowledge of English and insights into the way the student's native tongue interferes with his learning of the new language. The usual freshman composition instructor is simply not equipped to do the work, to say nothing of the person whose only qualification is that he speaks English as his mother tongue.

The teaching of English as a second language is a perfectly respectable academic field which offers immense opportunities for serious research. It is a discipline which desperately needs more practitioners who will devote their entire career to it and not regard it as a mere temporary way of winning one's bread while preparing to teach courses in linguistics or literature. It is definitely not a job which some university departments of English can continue with impunity to wish off on the most recently hired and most defenseless members of the teaching staff.

34

CULTURAL
THOUGHT
PATTERNS IN
INTER-CULTURAL
EDUCATION

ROBERT B. KAPLAN

What definition of *rhetoric* do you derive from this article?

How does Kaplan account for a student's inability to compose adequate English compositions even though he has mastered syntactic structures?

On the basis of this article, how would you characterize the structure of a typical expository English paragraph?

If you were now teaching English in a non-Anglophone culture, what might you do to ascertain its expository rhetorical principles?

An interesting exercise would be to "scramble" such a paragraph, as suggested by Kaplan (page 306), and ask a number of students, both English and non-English speakers, to arrange the sentences in a normal order. How much agreement is there among the English speakers? In what ways do the non-English speakers disagree among themselves and with the English speakers?

The teaching of reading and composition to foreign students does differ from the teaching of reading and composition to American students, and cultural differences in the nature of rhetoric supply the key to the difference in teaching approach.

. . . Rhetoric is a mode of thinking or a mode of "finding all available means" for the achievement of a designated end. Accordingly, rhetoric concerns itself basically with what goes on in the mind rather than with what comes out of the mouth. . . . Rhetoric is concerned with factors of analysis, data gathering, interpretation, and synthesis. . . . What we notice in the environment and how we notice it are both predetermined to a significant degree by how we are prepared to notice this particular type of object. . . . Cultural anthropologists point out that given acts and objects appear vastly different

Reprinted by permission from *Language Learning*, 16 (1966), 1–20. Professor Kaplan directs the communication program for foreign students at the University of Southern California.

in different cultures, depending on the values attached to them. Psychologists investigating perception are increasingly insistent that what is perceived depends upon the observer's perceptual frame of reference.[1]

Language teachers, particularly teachers of English as a second language, are latecomers in the area of international education. For years, and until quite recently, most languages were taught in what might be called a mechanistic way, stressing the prescriptive function of such teaching. In recent years the swing has been in the other direction, and the prescriptive has practically disappeared from language teaching. Descriptive approaches have seemed to provide the answer. At the present moment, there seems to be some question about the purely descriptive technique, and a new compromise between description and prescription seems to be emerging. Such a compromise appears necessary to the adequate achievement of results in second-language teaching. Unfortunately, although both the prescriptivists and the descriptivists have recognized the existence of cultural variation as a factor in second-language teaching, the recognition has so far been limited to the level of the sentence—that is, to the level of grammar, vocabulary, and sentence structure. On the other hand, it has long been known among sociologists and anthropologists that logic per se is a cultural phenomenon as well.

> Even if we take into account the lexical and grammatical similarities that exist between languages proceeding from a common hypothetical ancestor, the fact remains that the verbal universe is divided into multiple sectors. Sapir, Whorf, and many others, comparing the Indian languages with the Occidental languages, have underlined this diversity very forcefully. It seems, indeed, as if the arbitrary character of language, having been shown to be of comparatively little significance at the level of the elements of a language, reasserts itself quite definitely at the level of the language taken as a whole. And if one admits that a language represents a kind of destiny, so far as human thought is concerned, this diversity of language leads to a radical realitivism. As Peirce said, if Aristotle had been Mexican, his logic would have been different; and perhaps, by the same token, the whole of our philosophy and our science would have been different.
>
> The fact is that this diversity affects not only the languages, but also the cultures, that is to say the whole system of institutions that are tied to the language. . . [and] language in its turn is the effect and the expression of a certain world view that is manifested in the culture. If there is causality, it is a reciprocal causality. . . .
>
> The types of structures characteristic of a given culture would then, in each case, be particular modes of universal laws. They would define the Volksgeist. . . .[2]

Logic (in the popular, rather than the logician's sense of the word) which is the basis of rhetoric, is evolved out of a culture; it is not universal. Rhetoric, then, is not universal either, but varies from culture to culture and even from time to

---

[1] Robert T. Oliver, "Foreword," *Philosophy, Rhetoric and Argumentation*, ed. Maurice Nathanson and Henry W. Johnstone, Jr. (University Park, Pennsylvania, 1965), pp. x-xi.

[2] Mikel Dufrenne, *Language and Philosophy*, trans. Henry B. Veatch (Bloomington, 1963), pp. 35-37.

time within a given culture. It is affected by canons of taste within a given culture at a given time.

> Every language offers to its speakers a ready-made *interpretation* of the world, truly a Weltanschauung, a metaphysical word-picture which, after having originated in the thinking of our ancestors, tends to impose itself ever anew on posterity. Take for instance a simple sentence such as 'I see him. . . .' This means that English and, I might say, Indo-European, presents the impressions made on our senses predominantly as human *activities,* brought about by our *will.* But the Eskimos in Greenland say not 'I see him' but 'he appears to me. . . .' Thus, the Indo-European speaker conceives as workings of his activities what the fatalistic Eskimo sees as events that happen to him.[3]

The English language and its related thought patterns have evolved out of the Anglo-European cultural pattern. The expected sequence of thought in English is essentially a Platonic-Aristotelian sequence, descended from the philosophers of ancient Greece and shaped subsequently by Roman, Medieval European, and later Western thinkers. It is not a better nor a worse system than any other, but it is different.

> . . . As human beings, we must inevitably see the universe from a centre lying within ourselves and speak about it in terms of a human language by the exigencies of human intercourse. Any attempt rigorously to eliminate our human perspective from our picture of the world must lead to absurdity.[4]

A fallacy of some repute and some duration is the one which assumes that because a student can write an adequate essay in his native language, he can necessarily write an adequate essay in a second language. That this assumption is fallacious has become more and more apparent as English-as-a-second-language courses have proliferated at American colleges and universities in recent years. Foreign students who have mastered syntactic structures have still demonstrated inability to compose adequate themes, term papers, theses, and dissertations. Instructors have written on foreign-student papers such comments as "The material is all here, but it seems somehow out of focus," or: "Lacks organization," or: "Lacks cohesion." And these comments are essentially accurate. The foreign-student paper is out of focus because the foreign student is employing a rhetoric and a sequence of thought which violate the expectations of the native reader.

> A personality is carved out by the whole subtle interaction of these systems of ideas which are characteristic of the culture as a whole, as well as of those systems of ideas which get established for the individual through more special types of participation.[5]

[3] Leo Spitzer, "Language—The Basis of Science, Philosophy and Poetry," *Studies in Intellectual History,* ed. George Boas et al. (Baltimore, 1953), pp. 83–84.

[4] Michael Polanyi, *Personal Knowledge: Towards a Post-Critical Philosophy* (Chicago, 1958), p. 9.

[5] Edward Sapir, "Anthropology and Psychiatry," *Culture, Language and Personality* (Los Angeles, 1964), p. 157.

The fact that sequence of thought and grammar are related in a given language has already been demonstrated adequately by Paul Lorenzen. His brief paper proposes that certain linguistic structures are best comprehended as embodiments of logical structures.[6] Beyond that, every rhetorician from Cicero to Brooks and Warren has indicated the relationship between thought sequence and rhetoric.

> A paragraph, mechanically considered, is a division of the composition, set off by an indentation of its first sentence or by some other conventional device, such as extra space between paragraphs. . . . Paragraph divisions signal to the reader that the material so set off constitutes a unit of thought.
>
> For the reader this marking off of the whole composition into segments is a convenience, though not a strict necessity. . . . Since communication of one's thought is at best a difficult business, it is the part of common sense (not to mention good manners) to mark for the reader the divisions of one's thought and thus make the thought structure visible upon the page. . . .
>
> Paragraphing, obviously, can be of help to the reader only if the indicated paragraphs are genuine units of thought. . . . For a paragraph undertakes to discuss one topic or one aspect of a topic.[7]

The thought patterns which speakers and readers of English appear to expect as an integral part of their communication is a sequence that is dominantly linear in its development. An English expository paragraph usually begins with a topic statement, and then, by a series of subdivisions of that topic statement, each supported by example and illustrations, proceeds to develop that central idea and relate that idea to all the other ideas in the whole essay, and to employ that idea in its proper relationship with the other ideas, to prove something, or perhaps to argue something.

> A piece of writing may be considered unified when it contains *nothing* superfluous and it omits nothing essential to the achievement of its purpose. . . . A work is considered coherent when the sequence of its parts. . . . is controlled by some principle which is meaningful to the reader. Unity is the quality attributed to writing which has all its necessary and sufficient parts. Coherence is the quality attributed to the presentation of material in a sequence which is intelligible to its reader.[8]

Contrarily, the English paragraph may use just the reverse procedure; that is, it may state a whole series of examples and then relate those examples into a single statement at the end of the paragraph. These two types of development represent the common *inductive* and *deductive* reasoning which the English reader expects to be an integral part of any formal communication.

For example, the following paragraph written by Macaulay demonstrates normal paragraph development:

> Whitehall, when [Charles the Second] dwelt there, was the focus of political intrigue and of fashionable gaiety. Half the jobbing and half the flirting of the metropolis went

[6]*Logik und Grammatik* (Mannheim, Germany, 1965).

[7]Cleanth Brooks and Robert Penn Warren, *Modern Rhetoric*, 2nd ed. (New York, 1958). pp. 267-68.

[8]Richard E. Hughes and P. Albert Duhamel, *Rhetoric: Principles and Usage* (Englewood Cliffs, New Jersey, 1962), pp. 19-20.

on under his roof. Whoever could make himself agreeable to the prince or could secure the good offices of his mistress might hope to rise in the world without rendering any service to the government, without even being known by sight to any minister of state. This courtier got a frigate and that a company, a third the pardon of a rich offender, a fourth a lease of crown-land on easy terms. If the king notified his pleasure that a brief-less lawyer should be made a judge or that a libertine baronet should be made a peer, the gravest counsellors, after a little murmuring, submitted. Interest, therefore, drew a constant press of suitors to the gates of the palace, and those gates always stood wide. The King kept open house every day and all day long for the good society of London, the extreme Whigs only excepted. Hardly any gentleman had any difficulty in making his way to the royal presence. The levee was exactly what the word imports. Some men of quality came every morning to stand round their master, to chat with him while his wig was combed and his cravat tied, and to accompany him in his early walk through the Park. All persons who had been properly introduced might, without any special invitation, go to see him dine, sup, dance, and play at hazard and might have the pleasure of hearing him tell stories, which indeed, he told remarkably well, about his flight from Worcester and about the misery which he had endured when he was a state prisoner in the hands of the canting meddling preachers of Scotland.[9]

The paragraph begins with a general statement of its content, and then carefully develops that statement by a long series of rather specific illustrations. While it is discursive, the paragraph is never digressive. There is nothing in this paragraph that does not belong here; nothing that does not contribute significantly to the central idea. The flow of ideas occurs in a straight line from the opening sentence to the last sentence.

Without doing too much damage to other ways of thinking, perhaps it might be possible to contrast the English paragraph development with paragraph development in other linguistic systems.

For the purposes of the following brief analysis, some seven hundred foreign student compositions were carefully analyzed. Approximately one hundred of these were discarded from the study on the basis that they represent linguistic groups too small within the present sample to be significant.[10] But approximately six hundred examples, representing three basic language groups, were examined.[11]

[9] From *The History of England from the Accession of James the Second* (London, 1849–61).

[10] The following examples were discarded: Afghan-3, African-4, Danish-1, Finn-1, German-3, Hindi-8, Persian-46, Russian-1, Greek-1, Tagalog-10, Turk-16, Urdu-5, Total-99.

[11] The papers examined may be linguistically broken down as follows: Group I—Arabic-126, Hebrew-3; Group II—Chinese (Mandarin)-110, Cambodian-40, Indochinese-7, Japanese-135, Korean-57, Laotian-3, Malasian-1, Thai-27, Vietnamese-1; Group III—(Spanish-Portugese) Brazilian-19, Central American-10, South American-42, Cuban-4, Spanish-8, (French) French-2, African-2, (Italian) Swiss-1. Group I total-129; Group II total-381; Group III total-88; TOTAL-598. These papers were accumulated and examined over a two year period, from the beginning of the fall 1963 semester through the fall 1965 academic semester.

In the Arabic language, for example (and this generalization would be more or less true for all Semitic languages), paragraph development is based on a complex series of parallel constructions, both positive and negative. This kind of parallelism may most clearly be demonstrated in English by reference to the King James version of the Old Testament. Several types of parallelism typical of Semitic languages are apparent there because that book, of course, is a translation accomplished at a time when English was in a state of development suitable to the imitation of those forms.

1. Synonymous Parallelism: The balancing of the thought and phrasing of the first part of a statement or idea by the second part. In such cases, the two parts are often connected by a coordinate conjunction.

    Example: His descendants will be mighty in the land
    and
    the generation of the upright will be blessed.

2. Synthetic Parallelism: The completion of the idea or thought of the first part in the second part. A conjunctive adverb is often stated or implied.

    Example: Because he inclined his ear to me
    therefore
    I will call on him as long as I live.

3. Antithetic Parallelism: The idea stated in the first part is emphasized by the expression of a contrasting idea in the second part. The contrast is expressed not only in thought but often in phrasing as well.

    Example: For the Lord knoweth the way of the righteous:
    But the way of the wicked shall perish.

4. Climactic Parallelism: The idea of the passage is not completed until the very end of the passage. This form is similar to the modern periodic sentence in which the subject is postponed to the very end of the sentence.

    Example: Give unto the Lord, O ye sons of the mighty,
    Give unto the Lord glory and strength.[12]

The type of parallel construction here illustrated in single sentences also forms the core of paragraphs in some Arabic writing. Obviously, such a development in a modern English paragraph would strike the modern English reader as archaic

[12] I am indebted to Dr. Ben Siegel for this analysis.

or awkward, and more importantly it would stand in the way of clear communication. It is important to note that in English, maturity of style is often gauged by degree of subordination rather than by coordination.

The following paper was written as a class exercise by an Arabic-speaking student in an English-as-a-second-language class at an American university:

> The contemporary Bedouins, who live in the deserts of Saudi Arabia, are the successors of the old bedouin tribes, the tribes that was fascinated with Mohammad's massage, and on their shoulders Islam built it's empire. I had lived among those contemporary Bedouins for a short period of time, and I have learned lots of things about them. I found out that they have retained most of their ancestor's characteristics, inspite of the hundreds of years that separate them.
>
> They are famous of many praiseworthy characteristics, but they are considered to be the symbol of generosity; bravery; and self-esteem. Like most of the wandering peoples, a stranger is an undesirable person among them. But, once they trust him as a friend, he will be most welcome. Hoever, their trust is a hard thing to gain. And the heroism of many famous figures, who ventured in the Arabian deserts like T. E. Lawrence, is based on their ability to acquire this dear trust!
>
> Romance is an important part in their life. And "love" is an important subject in their verses and their tales.
>
> Nevertheless, they are criticized of many things. The worst of all is that they are extremists in all the ways of their lives. It is there extremism that changes sometimes their generosity into squandering, their bravery into brutality, and their self-esteem into naughtiness. But in any case, I have been, and will continue to be greatly interested in this old, fascinating group of people.

Disregarding for the moment the grammatical errors in this student composition, it becomes apparent that the characteristics of parallelism do occur. The next-to-last element in the first sentence, for example, is appositive to the preceding one, while the last element is an example of synonymous parallelism. The two clauses of the second sentence illustrate synonymous parallelism. In the second "paragraph" the first sentence contains both an example of antithetic parallelism and a list of parallel nouns. The next two sentences form an antithetic pair, and so on. It is perhaps not necessary to point out further examples in the selection. It is important, however, to observe that in the first sentence, for example, the grammatical complexity is caused by the attempt to achieve an intricate parallelism. While this extensive parallel construction is linguistically possible in Arabic, the English language lacks the necessary flexibility. Eight conjunctions and four sentence connectors are employed in a matter of only fourteen "sentences." In addition, there are five "lists" of units connected by commas and conjunctions.

Another paper, also written by an Arabic-speaking student under comparable circumstances, further demonstrates the same tendencies:

> At that time of the year I was not studying enough to pass my courses in school. *And* all the time I was asking my cousin to let me ride the bicycle, *but* he wouldn't let me. *But* after two weeks, noticing that I was so much interested in the bicycle, he promised me that if I pass my courses in school for that year he would give it to

me as a present. *So* I began to study hard. *And* I studying eight hours a day instead of two.

My cousin seeing me studying that much he was sure that I was going to succeed in school. *So* he decided to give me some lessons in riding the bicycle. After four or five weeks of teaching me and ten or twelve times hurting myself as I used to go out of balance, I finally knew how to ride it. And the finals in school came *and* I was very good prepared for them *so* I passed them. My cousin kept his promise *and* gave me the bicycle in a safe place, *and* everytime I see it, It reminds me how it helped to pass my courses for that year.

In the first paragraph of this example, four of the five sentences, or 80 percent of the sentences, begin with a coordinating element. In the second paragraph, three of the six sentences, or 50 percent of the total, also begin with a coordinating element. In the whole passage, seven of the eleven sentences, or roughly 65 percent, conform to this pattern. In addition, the first paragraph contains one internal coordinator, and the second contains five internal coordinators; thus the brief passage (210 words) contains a total of thirteen coordinates. It is important to notice that almost all of the ideas in the passage are coordinately linked, that there is very little subordination, and that the parallel units exemplify the types of parallelism already noted.

Some Oriental[13] writing, on the other hand, is marked by what may be called an approach by indirection. In this kind of writing, the development of the paragraph may be said to be "turning and turning in a widening gyre." The circles or gyres turn around the subject and show it from a variety of tangential views, but the subject is never looked at directly. Things are developed in terms of what they are not, rather than in terms of what they are. Again, such a development in a modern English paragraph would strike the English reader as awkward and unnecessarily indirect.

The following composition was written, as a class exercise, by a native speaker of Korean, under the same circumstances which produced the two previous examples. Obviously, this student is weaker in general English proficiency than the students who produced the two prior examples.

Definition of college education

College is an institution of an higher learning that gives degrees. All of us needed culture and education in life, if no education to us, we should to go living hell.

One of the greatest causes that while other animals have remained as they first man along has made such rapid progress is has learned about civilization.

The improvement of the highest civilization is in order to education up-to-date. So college education is very important thing which we don't need mention about it.

Again, disregarding the typically Oriental grammar and the misconception of the function of "parts of speech," the first sentence defines college, not college education. This may conceivably be a problem based upon the student's misunderstanding of the assignment. But the second sentence appears to shoot off

[13] *Oriental* here is intended to mean specifically Chinese and Korean but not Japanese.

in a totally different direction. It makes a general statement about culture and education, perhaps as *results* of a college education. The third sentence, presented as a separate "paragraph," moves still further away from definition by expanding the topic to "man" in a generic sense, as opposed to "non-man." This unit is tied to the next, also presented as a separate paragraph, by the connecting idea of "civilization" as an aspect of education. The concluding paragraph-sentence presents, in the guise of a summary logically derived from previously posited ideas, a conclusion which is in fact partially a topic sentence and partially a statement that the whole basic concept of the assignment is so obvious that it does not need discussion. The paper arrives where it should have started, with the added statement that it really had no place to go to begin with.

The poorer proficiency of this student, however, introduces two other considerations. It is possible that this student, as an individual rather than as a representative native speaker of Korean, lacks the ability to abstract sufficiently for extended definition. In the case under discussion, however, the student was majoring in mathematics and did have the ability to abstract in mathematical terms. While the demands of mathematics are somewhat different from the demands of language in a conventional sense, it is possible to assume that a student who can handle abstraction in one area can also probably handle it at least to some extent in the other. It is also possible that the ability to abstract is absent from the Korean culture. This appears quite unlikely in view of the abundance of Korean art available and in view of the fact that other native speakers of Korean have not demonstrated that shortcoming.

The examples cited so far have been student themes. The following example is from a professional translation. Essentially, the same variations can be observed in it. In this case, the translation is from French.

> The first point to which I would like to call your attention is that nothing exists outside the boundary of what is strictly human. A landscape may be beautiful, graceful, sublime, insignificant, or ugly; it will never be ludicrous. We may laugh at an animal, but only because we have detected in it some human expression or attitude. We may laugh at a hat, but we are not laughing at the piece of felt or straw. We are laughing at the shape that men have given to it, the human whim whose mold it has assumed. *I wonder why a fact so important has not attracted the attention of philosophers to a greater degree. Some have defined man as an animal that knows how to laugh. They could equally well have defined him as an animal which provokes laughter;* for if any other animal or some lifeless object, achieves the same effect, it is always because of some similarity to man.[14]

In this paragraph, the italicized portion constitutes a digression. It is an interesting digression, but it really does not seem to contribute significant structural material to the basic thought of the paragraph. While the author of the paragraph is a philosopher, and a philosopher is often forgiven digressions, the more important fact is that the example is a typical one for writers of French as well as for

[14]From *Laughter, An Assay on the Meaning of the Comic,* Trans. Marcel Bolomet (Paris, 1900).

writers of philosophy. Much greater freedom to digress or to introduce extraneous material is available in French, or in Spanish, than in English.

Similar characteristics can be demonstrated in the writing of native French-speaking students in English. In the interests of keeping this report within some bounds, such illustrations will be inserted without comment. The first example was written under circumstances similar to those described for the preceding student samples. The writer is a native speaker of French.

American Traffic Law as compared with
Traffic law in Switzerland

At first glance the traffic law in United States appeared to me simpler than in Switzerland.

The American towns in general have the disposition of a cross, and for a driver who knows how to situate himself between the four cardinal points, there is no problem to find his way. Each street has numbers going crecendo from the center of the town to the outside.

There are many accidents in Switzerland, as everywhere else, and the average of mortality comparatively to the proportion of the countries is not better than in United States. We have the problem of straight streets, not enough surveillance by policemen on the national roads, and alcohol. The country of delicious wines has made too many damages.

The following illustration, drawn from the work of a native speaker of Latin American Spanish, was produced under conditions parallel to those already cited:

The American Children

In America, the American children are brought differently from the rest of the children in other countries. In their childhood, from the first day they are born, the parents give their children the love and attention they need. They teach their children the meaning of Religion among the family and to have respect and obedience for their parents.

I am Spanish, and I was brought up differently than the children in America. My parents are stricter and they taught me discipline and not to interrupt when someone was talking.

The next and last example is again not a piece of student writing, but a translation. The original was written in Russian, and the translation attempts to capture the structure of the original as much as possible, but without sacrificing meaning completely.

On the 14th of October, Kruschev left the stage of history. Was it a plot the result of which was that Kruschev was out of business remains not clear. It is very probable that even if it were anything resembling a plot it would not be for the complete removal of Kruschev from political guidance, but rather a pressure exerted to obtain some changes in his policies: for continuations of his policies of peaceful co-existence in international relations or making it as far as possible a situation to avoid formal rupture with the Chinese communist party and at any rate not to go unobstructed to such a rupture—and in the area of internal politics, especially in the section of economics, to continue efforts of a certain softening of "dogmatism," but without the hurried and not sufficiently reasoned experimentation, which became the characteristic traits of Kruschev's politics in recent years.[15]

Some of the difficulty in this paragraph is linguistic rather than rhetorical. The structure of the Russian sentence is entirely different from the structure of the English sentence. But some of the linguistic difficulty is closely related to the rhetorical difficulty. The above paragraph is composed of three sentences. The first two are very short, while the last is extremely long, constituting about three quarters of the paragraph. It is made up of a series of presumably parallel constructions and a number of subordinate structures. At least half of these are irrelevant to the central idea of the paragraph in the sense that they are parenthetical amplifications of structurally related subordinate elements.

There are, of course, other examples that might be discussed as well, but these paragraphs may suffice to show that each language and each culture has a paragraph order unique to itself, and that part of the learning of a particular language is the mastering of its logical system

> . . .One should join to any logic of the language a phenomenology of the spoken word. Moreover, this phenomenology will, in its turn, rediscover the idea of a logos immanent in the language; but it will seek the justification for this in a more general philosophy of the relations between man and the world. . . . From one culture to another it is possible to establish communication. The Rorschach test has been successfully applied to the natives of the island of Alor.[16]

This discussion is not intended to offer any criticism of other existing paragraph developments; rather it is intended only to demonstrate that paragraph developments other than those normally regarded as desirable in English do exist. In the teaching of paragraph structure to foreign students, whether in terms of reading or in terms of composition, the teacher must be himself aware of these differences, and he must make these differences overtly apparent to his students. In short, contrastive rhetoric must be taught in the same sense that contrastive grammar is presently taught. Now not much has been done in the area of contrastive rhetoric. It is first necessary to arrive at accurate descriptions of existing paragraph orders other than those common to English. Furthermore, it is necessary to understand that these categories are in no sense meant to be mutually exclusive. Patterns may be derived for *typical* English paragraphs, but paragraphs like those described above as being atypical in English do exist in English. By way of obvious example, Ezra Pound writes paragraphs which are circular in their structure, and William Faulkner writes paragraphs which are wildly digressive. The paragraph being discussed here is not the "literary" paragraph, however, but the expository paragraph. The necessities of art impose structures on any

[15]From S. Schwartz, "After Kruschev," trans. E. B. Kaplan, *The Socialist Courier* (April, 1964), p. 3

[16]Dufrenne, pp. 39-40.

language, while the requirements of communication can often be best solved by relatively close adhesion to established patterns.

Superficially, the movement of the various paragraphs discussed above may be graphically represented in the following manner:

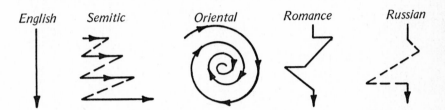

English   Semitic   Oriental   Romance   Russian

Much more detailed and more accurate descriptions are required before any meaningful contrastive system can be elaborated. Nonetheless, an important problem exists immediately. In the teaching of English as a second language, what does one do with the student who is reasonably proficient in the use of syntactic structure but who needs to learn to write themes, theses, essay examinations, and dissertations? The "advanced" student has long constituted a problem for teachers of English as a second language. This approach, the contrastive analysis of rhetoric, is offered as one possible answer to the existing need. Such an approach has the advantage that it may help the foreign student to form standards of judgement consistent with the demands made upon him by the educational system of which he has become a part. At the same time, by accounting for the cultural aspects of logic which underlie the rhetorical structure, this approach may bring the student not only to an understanding of contrastive grammar and a new vocabulary, which are parts of any reading task, but also to a grasp of idea and structure in units larger than the sentence. A sentence, after all, rarely exists outside a context. Applied linguistics teaches the student to deal with the sentence, but it is necessary to bring the student beyond that to a comprehension of the whole context. He can only understand the whole context if he recognizes the logic on which the context is based. The foreign student who has mastered the syntax of English may still write a bad paragraph or a bad paper unless he also masters the logic of English. *"In serious expository prose, the paragraph tends to be a logical, rather than a typographical, unit."*[17] The understanding of paragraph patterns can allow the student to relate syntactic elements within a paragraph and perhaps even to relate paragraphs within a total context.

Finally, it is necessary to recognize the fact that a paragraph is an artificial thought unit employed in the written language to suggest a cohesion which commonly may not exist in oral language. "Paragraphing, like punctuation, is a

[17] Hans P. Guth, *A Short New Rhetoric* (Belmont, California, 1964), p. 205.

feature only of the written language."[18] As an artificial unit of thought, it lends itself to patterning quite readily. In fact, since it is imposed from without, and since it is a frame for the structuring of thought into patterns, it is by its very nature patterned. The rhetorical structures of English paragraphs may be found in any good composition text.[19] The patterns of paragraphs in other languages are not so well established, or perhaps only not so well known to speakers of English. These patterns need to be discovered or uncovered and compared with the patterns of English in order to arrive at a practical means for the teaching of such structures to non-native users of the language.

In the interim, while research is directed at the rhetorics of other languages, certain practical pedagogical devices have been developed to expedite the teaching of rhetorical structures to non-native speakers of English. An elementary device consists simply of supplying to the students a scrambled paragraph. A normal paragraph, such as the one cited from Macaulay above, may be arbitrarily scrambled, the sentences numbered, and the students asked to rearrange the sentences in what appears to them to be a normal order. Frequently, the results of such an assignment will demonstrate the diversity of views or cultures represented in the classroom. The exercise can be used effectively to point out the very disparity. The students must then be presented with the original version of the paragraph, and the instructor must be able to explain and justify the order of the original.

[INSTRUCTIONS: Arrange the sentences below into some normal order.]

[This is the order in which the author arranged his sentences. Can you detect his reason?]

Scrambled Order

Normal Order

1. A jackass brays; a turkey cock gobbles; a dog yelps; a church bell clangs.
2. The narrow streets and lanes leading into the market are crammed with Indians, their dark skins glistening like copper or bronze in the bright sun, their varicolored cloaks looking like a mass of palette colors smeared together.
3. There is the smell of animal dung mingled with the odor of carnations

The narrow streets and lanes leading into the market are crammed with Indians, their dark skins glistening like copper or bronze in the bright sun, their varicolored cloaks looking like a mass of palette colors smeared together. In the open plaza outside the market the crowd mills about. A kind of blending of Indian talk in various dialects creates a strange droning noise. A jackass brays; a turkey cock gobbles; a dog

---

[18]Edward P. J. Corbett, *Classical Rhetoric for the Modern Student* (New York, 1965), p. 416.

[19]Important work in the rhetoric of the paragraph is being done by Francis Christensen, among others. See especially "A Generative Rhetoric of the Paragraph," *College Composition and Communication* (October, 1965), pp. 144–156.

and heliotrope from the flower stalls.

4. In the open plaza outside the market the crowd mills about.

5. Mothers sit on the curb nursing their babies.

6. A kind of blending of Indian talk in various dialects creates a strange droning noise.

7. On the narrow sidewalks, merchandise is spread so haphazardly that in order to pass, pedestrians have to press against the wall or leap the displays.

8. Wrinkled old women squat over charcoal braziers cooking corn cakes, or black beans, or pink coconut candy.

yelps; a church bell clangs. On the narrow sidewalks, merchandise is spread so haphazardly that in order to pass, pedestrians have to press against the wall or leap the displays. Wrinkled old women squat over charcoal braziers cooking corn cakes, or black beans, or pink coconut candy. Mothers sit on the curb nursing their babies. There is the smell of animal dung mingled with the odor of carnations and heliotrope from the flower stalls.[20]

[This paragraph is descriptive, presented in the present tense, and arranged perceptually in the order of sight, hearing, and smell.]

A second device consists of giving the students carefully written topic sentences, arranged in some convenient way such as that suggested below, and then asking the students to fill out the subdivisions of the topic sentence with examples and illustrations chosen to support the point. Depending upon the relative difficulty of the topic, the examples may be supplied by the instructor in scrambled order.

American television

American commercial television appears to consist of three principal classes of material; programs of serious interest, such as news broadcasts and special features; programs intended primarily as entertainment, such as variety shows, situation comedies, and adventure tales; and the advertisements which link all of these.

    I. Programs of serious interest:
      A. News broadcasts:
          1._____
          2._____
      B. Special Features:
          1._____
          2._____

[20]Hudson Strode, "The Market at Toluca," *Now in Mexico* (New York, 1947).

II. Programs intended primarily as entertainment:
   A. Variety shows:
      1._____
      2._____
   B. Situational comedies:
      1._____
      2._____
   C. Adventure tales:
      1._____
      2._____

III. Advertising:
   A. _____
      1._____
      2._____
   B. _____
      1._____
      2._____

IV. [Conclusion:]

[INSTRUCTIONS: The student is to supply contrasting examples for each of the spaces provided under items I and II. In item III the student must also supply the main subdivisions, and in item IV the point of the whole essay must also be supplied by the student. Obviously, item IV will vary considerably depending upon the kinds of illustrations selected to fill the blanks.]

The illustration constitutes a very simple exercise. Greater sophistication may be employed as the student becomes more familiar with the techniques. Obviously, too, the outline must be introduced and taught simultaneously. A simple technique for teaching the outline may be found illustrated in a number of texts for both American and foreign students.[21]

It is important to impress upon the student that "A paragraph is *clear* when each sentence contributes to the central thought. . . [and that] clarity also demands coherence, that is, an orderly flow of sentences marked by repetition of key ideas."[22]

While it is necessary for the non-native speaker learning English to master the rhetoric of the English paragraph, it must be remembered that the foreign student, ideally, will be returning to his home country, and that his stay in the United States is a brief one. Under these circumstances, English is a

---

[21] At the risk of being accused of immodesty, I would recommend in particular the section entitled "Outlining" in Robert B. Kaplan, *Reading and Rhetoric* (New York, 1963), pp. 69-80.

[22] Francis Connolly, *A Rhetoric Casebook* (New York, 1953), p. 304.

means to an end for him; it is not an end in itself. Edward Sapir has written:

> An oft-noted peculiarity of the development of culture is the fact that it reaches its greatest heights in comparatively small, autonomous groups. In fact, it is doubtful if a genuine culture ever properly belongs to more than such a restricted group, a group between the members of which there can be said to be something like direct intensive spirtual contact. This direct contact is enriched by the common cultural heritage on which the minds of all are fed. . . . A narrowly localized culture may, and often does, spread its influence far beyond its properly restricted sphere. Sometimes it sets the pace for a whole nationality, for a far flung empire. It can do so, however, only at the expense of diluting the spirit as it moves away from its home, of degenerating into an imitative attitudinizing.[23]

He is absolutely correct in pointing out the dangers of spreading a culture too thin and too far from home. However, in the special case of the foreign student learning English, under the conditions stipulated above, the imitation which would be an error in most cases is the sought aim. The classes which undertake the training of the "advanced" student can aim for no more. The creativity and imagination which make the difference between competent writing and excellent writing are things which, at least in these circumstances, cannot be taught. The foreign student is an adult in most cases. If these things are teachable, they will already have been taught to him. The English class must not aim too high. Its function is to provide the student with a form within which he may operate, a form acceptable in this time and in this place. It is hoped that the method described above may facilitate the achievement of that goal.

---

[23]Sapir, "Culture, Genuine and Spurious," *Culture, Language and Personality* (Los Angeles, 1964), pp. 113–14.

O<i>nly</i> recently have journals accorded more than meager attention to the specific subject of ESL testing. The American concern surfaced conspicuously in the testing program developed by the English Language Institute at the University of Michigan, out of which there grew the book *Language Testing* (1961), by Robert Lado, the Institute's director at that time. In that same year a report emerged from a conference sponsored in Washington by the Center for Applied Linguistics which was published as *Testing the Proficiency of Foreign Students*. A significant outcome of the conference was a meeting in January, 1962, that led to the formation of the Advisory Council on the Testing of English as a Foreign Language and hence to the TOEFL tests and testing program, now operated on a world basis by the Educational Testing Service and the College Entrance Examination Board. His experience there and elsewhere led David Harris, TOEFL's first director, to write *Testing English as a Second Language* (McGraw-Hill, 1969), the second major book in the field. Recently, with the mounting concern over the inadequacy of tests for the Indians and the Spanish-speaking children now in or entering American schools, the emphasis on testing has shifted to research that would yield reliable tests for these groups.

Carroll, whose article first appeared in the report of the 1961 conference, gives here in substantial outline the psychologically sound principles and practices fundamental to language testing. What further research must do is then critically suggested by Brière, who is currently directing a research project intended to prepare culturally adjusted ESL tests for American Indians.

311

Cooper calls attention to the first prerequisite of test construction, i.e., the determination of precisely what a given test is presumed to test, and why the information is sought. Only then, he says, can the test maker safely proceed to follow the five basic steps in construction, which are as necessary for the teacher who seeks only to assess a class's progress toward a week's objective as they are for the person preparing a test for multiple use via commercial publication.

That dictation itself can be soundly utilized for testing is the contention of Oller, who supports his view by data derived from his own experiments, one of which employed the recently-devised cloze technique.

Finally, in this Part, the principle that teaching English as a second language also involves awareness of the cultural patterns of native English speakers is the basis for Upshur's article. He proposes a special kind of testing for cross-cultural understanding. Although Upshur recognizes that much is yet to be achieved in cross-cultural test preparation, his perspicacious observations yield valuable suggestions for both the test maker and the classroom teacher.

35

FUNDAMENTAL   JOHN B. CARROLL
CONSIDERATIONS
IN TESTING FOR
ENGLISH LANGUAGE
PROFICIENCY OF
FOREIGN STUDENTS

Discuss possible answers to the questions posed by Carroll on page 315, beginning with . . . what kinds of English mastery are required for the foreign student to comprehend reading matter and lectures in the several academic disciplines? (continue)

Compare the matrix presented by Carroll (page 316) with the one presented by Cooper (page 337). How do they differ?

What advantages does Carroll see in the integrative approach to the testing of language proficiency?

How else might integrative testing be accomplished? Is dictation, as discussed by Oller (Art. 38), an integrative test?

This is not the first conference ever called on language testing, nor will it be the last one. Language testing has a long history, and much experience and wisdom have accumulated. Most test constructors are aware of the various kinds of tests that can be built; they are knowledgeable about such matters as item construction, item analysis, reliability, validity, standardization, norms, and so forth. Most testers can recite all the arguments pro and con the use of objective tests, the use of "translation" in testing, and the use of incorrect linguistic forms. Language testing has reached such a stage of professionalization that a whole book on the subject is about to appear—or perhaps has already appeared. A speaker who is asked to talk about the "theory of language testing" is surely not expected to go back to elementary principles, as if the audience were not already adequately indoctrinated. The work papers which you have already had a chance to see are impressively sophisticated on many aspects of testing. All I can expect to do, therefore, is to readdress the attention of the audience to certain basic and fundamental problems and points of view, some of which may have been lost sight of in the heat of enthusiasm for technical detail.

Reprinted by permission from *Testing*, pp. 31–40, Center for Applied Linguistics, 1961. Dr. Carroll, former professor of educational psychology at Harvard University, is now with the Center for Psychological Studies, Educational Testing Service, Princeton, N.J.

Let us speak first of the *purpose of testing*. The purpose of testing is always to render information to aid in making intelligent decisions about possible courses of action. Sometimes these decisions affect only the future design or use of the tests themselves, in which case we are dealing with solely experimental uses of tests. Sometimes the decisions have to do with the retention or alteration of courses of training, as when one decides that poor test results are due to ineffective training. Most often, the decisions have to do with the management of the educational careers of individuals. Different stages of the training cycle call for different kinds of tests. Before training begins, one may wish to predict learning rate or ultimate success in training—and a test which will do this validly is called an aptitude test. At the start of training we may also wish to give *pretests* to ascertain the status of the individual's skill or knowledge before training, and as a basis for measuring the true effects of training when pretest scores are eventually compared with posttest scores. Educators make all too little use of pretests, although foreign language teachers are probably frequently right in their assumption that their students start at a virtual zero point. At various points in a particular training course, and especially at the end, achievement tests are given to ascertain progress and to diagnose learning difficulties. The content and design of such tests can be tailored to suit the purposes of the designers of the course. Somewhat different problems arise when there is a problem of assessing achievements of learners in a variety of courses which ostensibly have the same subject-matter but which actually vary considerably in content and rationale. Such examinations are often called *external examinations* and are exemplified by the College Entrance Examination Board Achievement tests in a number of secondary school subjects, including several foreign languages. Note that although the construction of the College Board examinations is supervised by a nationally representative committee of teachers and subject-matter authorities who come to agreement on a common content on which the examination is to be built, there is still much discrepancy, in some cases, between what a student has been exposed to and what the examiners assume he has been exposed to. It is small wonder that a proposed external examination on English proficiency, designed for the testing of candidates from many countries and courses, will have to face the fact of profound differences in the kinds of preparation that these candidates will have had. Of course, after a program of external examinations has been conducted over a sufficient number of years, the nature of the test program gets to be known to the teachers, who may actually begin to shape their teaching in the direction of the examination. But if an external examination in English is to be held on a world-wide basis, natural forces will hardly be sufficient for insuring a modicum of uniformity in course content. A sensible step, it seems to me, would be for the universities who are to use the results of a world-wide test to announce the kind of product they seek and the kind of training course content they would expect candidates to have mastered at a minimum. American universities should try to get together to specify what kinds and levels of English language proficiencies they desire in foreign students. If this were done, it would undoubtedly have a beneficial influence upon English training courses abroad and hence upon the preparation of students. Incidentally, the development of specifications for the desired product would be a necessary step in the design of the examination or examinations.

Nevertheless, there is a further step that should be taken. The mere announcement of desired standards could all too easily be done without adequate forethought and without taking stock of the actual experiences of foreign students. There is need for surveys of the kinds of linguistic situations faced by these students and the success or failure of students at various levels of English proficiency in meeting these situations. For example, what kinds of English mastery are required for the foreign student to comprehend reading matter and lectures in the several academic disciplines? What standard of proficiency in English pronunciation is the minimum required for foreign students to be understood by American students and teachers? What are typical social situations in which foreign students must engage? In which language skills is there most deficiency in failing or dropout cases? Perhaps these analyses have all been undertaken, but if so, I am unaware of them.

In the present case, the external examination in English proficiency takes on some of the characteristics of an aptitude test, at least in the sense that it would be designed to help predict success in collegiate subject-matter courses. After a preliminary test has been designed and administered, its scores should be kept on file and carefully compared with students' performance in their subject-matter courses in American universities. Only on the basis of such information will it be possible to establish rules and guides for using examination results to make decisions concerning the admissibility of foreign students to American universities. This requirement may entail selection and placement of a few foreign students who are below standard. But because the external examination is so largely an *aptitude test*, it should be designed and constructed like an aptitude test; i.e., it should be subjected to external validation. External validation in this case, would be solely against the criterion of *having sufficient English to operate in given situations*. Thus, measurements would be taken of students' ability to comprehend lectures and reading material, and ability to be understood in specified social settings. Obviously, all these procedures would ideally entail a not inconsiderable program of validation research, but I believe the outcome would be worth the effort.

The kinds of performance that should be tested on the proposed external proficiency examination should, then, be dictated by, and flow from, the specifications of the performance abilities desired in candidates to be selected by the examination. These specifications may be divided up into several levels. For example, there is already the suggestion that students entering engineering schools do not have to be as proficient in English as those entering liberal arts colleges and majoring in literature and the humanities. Some students may not have to be as proficient in speaking as others.

The specification will refer, then, to a series of at least logically independent kinds of performances. For example, speaking ability and reading ability are logically quite different kinds of performances, because one can exist without the other; this is true even though they may be rather highly correlated in a given group of people simply because this group of learners had common training experiences which led them to perform equally well, on the average, on both types of performance. Logically different kinds of language performances have sometimes been identified by using a grid in which different kinds of mastery are displayed against different aspects of the language structure which one is testing. Thus, one could theoretically obtain measures of ability in each cell of the following grid:

	Language Aspect			
Skill	*Phonology or orthography*	*Morphology*	*Syntax*	*Lexicon*
Auditory comprehension				
Oral production				
Reading				
Writing				

In practice, however, it would be foolish to attempt to obtain these sixteen different measures, for this would be carrying the process of analysis too far. It is unlikely that ability varies in precisely these sixteen independent ways. As far as morphology, syntax, and lexicon are concerned, the important aspect of ability which should be tested is the individual's knowledge of the "facts" of the language itself. Since language is recognized as primarily a vocal phenomenon, one would prefer to test these in spoken form, but in the case of English as a second language for foreign students, we can agree to use the expedient of written testing because use of written language is taught to these students and is expected of them in American colleges. One can assume that all the "facts" of the language, such as the constancies of its grammar and the meanings of its words and grammatical structures, form a more or less continuous spectrum of frequency and utility—from the most frequent and useful items to the rarer and only occasionally useful items. One of the main jobs of the language test is to determine how far towards the end of this spectrum the examinee can demonstrate a substantial and useful degree of knowledge. It is a matter of convenience, however, to separate structural and lexical aspects, partly because structural and lexical items may be learned in somewhat different ways or in different contexts. Further, it can be argued that mastery of structure is more essential than, and in a sense prerequisite to, mastery of lexicon.

For the sake of clarity let us list the separate aspects of language competence which might be considered in drawing up specifications for a proficiency test. Let us begin with a large category which we will call:

1. *Knowledge of structure* (morphology and syntax). The *knowledge* aspect is emphasized here because we will first be concerned with what the individual has learned, not with how rapidly or facilely he can use it. This aspect will therefore be measured by a "power" test, with a liberal time-limit. Many types of test items exist for testing knowledge of structure. The items would be chosen so that each one focuses on a single "structure point," but there would be a sufficient sampling of such structure-points, with a range from some of the more frequent of them to some of the less frequent, to yield a reliable score and a suitable score distribution. Specification of level of knowledge would if possible be based upon the level of difficulty reached. We will next list:

2. *Knowledge of general-usage lexicon* (vocabulary and "idiomatic phrases"). Here again, *knowledge* would be emphasized, rather than speed, and the test would be composed in such a way as to give reliability and a wide-ranged score distribution. If possible, specification of level of knowledge could depend upon level of word rarity attained, rarity being measured with reference to such compilations as the Thorndike frequency tables.

It might be desirable, however, to draw up separate specifications for vocabulary knowledge in certain semantic areas. Thus, let us list:

2a. *Knowledge of lexicon in designated specialized areas.* The subtests of the Michigan Vocabulary Profile Test, a commercially available vocabulary test, might be used as a guide. (These are: human relations, commerce, government, physical sciences, biological sciences, mathematics, fine arts, and sports. Obviously not all of these categories would be suitable for drawing up specifications for foreign students' vocabulary knowledge.)

Only in matters of phonology and orthography does it make sense to use the separate cells under "phonology or orthography" in our grid; the resulting categories may be labeled as follows:

3. *Auditory discrimination* (of phonemes, allophones, and suprasegmentals)

4. *Oral production* (of phonemes, allophones, and suprasegmentals)

5. *Reading* (in the sense of converting printed symbols to sound, i.e., mastery of word pronunciation and stress patterns)

6. *Writing* (in the sense of converting sounds to printed symbols, i.e., spelling)

The four skills of listening, speaking, reading, and writing must also be regarded as integrated performances which call upon the candidate's mastery of the language as a whole, i.e., its phonology, structure, and lexicon. It is worthwhile to specify the level of competence desired in each of them, independently of essential "language fact" mastery, because each involves elements of quickness of response. In fact, the specification could well be partly in terms of rates, i.e., rate at which material of some set standard of difficulty could be heard and understood, rate of speaking in a standard interview situation, speed of silent reading attained under conditions where comprehension was to be tested, and speed of written composition. Hence we have:

7. *Rate and accuracy of listening comprehension*
8. *Rate and quality of speaking, as in an interview situation*
9. *Rate and accuracy of reading comprehension*
10. *Rate and accuracy of written composition*

The work of Lado and other language testing specialists has correctly pointed to the desirability of testing for very specific items of language knowledge and skill judiciously sampled from the usually enormous pool of possible items. This makes for highly reliable and valid testing. It is the type of approach which is needed and recommended in the first six categories of language proficiency specification listed above—that is, where knowledge of structure and lexicon, auditory discrimination and oral production of sounds, and reading and writing of individual symbols and words are to be tested. I do not think, however, that language testing (or the specification of language proficiency) is complete without the use of the approach recommended for categories 7 through 10, that is, an approach requiring an integrated, facile performance on the part of the examinee. It is conceivable that knowledge could exist without facility. If we limit ourselves to testing only one point at a time, more time is ordinarily allowed for reflection than would occur in a normal communication situation, no matter how rapidly the discrete items are presented. For this reason I recommend tests in which there is less attention paid to specific structure points or lexicon than to the total communicative effect of an utterance. For example, I have had excellent success in ascertaining levels of audio-lingual training by a listening comprehension test in which auditorily-presented sentences of increasing length and rapidity are to be matched with an appropriate picture out of four presented. The examinee is not concerned with specific structure-points or lexicon, but with the total meaning of the sentence, however he is able to grasp it.

Indeed, this "integrative" approach has several advantages over the "discrete structure point" approach. It entails a broader and more diffuse sampling over the total field of linguistic items and thus depends less upon the specifics of a particular course of training. It thus may lend itself somewhat more effectively to the problem of an external examination in which the examiner does not ordinarily know, in detail, what was covered in any particular course of training. Furthermore, the difficulty of a task is subjectively more obvious than in the case of a "discrete structure point" item. Thus, when the tasks of an "integrative" approach test are arranged in the order of their difficulty for a typical class of examinees, the interpretation of performance relative to a subjective standard may be easier. Finally, the "integrative" approach makes less necessary the kind of comparison of language systems upon which much current language test is premised. The important question is to ascertain how well the examinee is functioning in the target language, regardless of what his native language happens to be. Indeed, the overconscientious use of the bilingual comparison axiom could lead to different tests of English proficiency for each native language group, and a virtual impossibility of establishing common standards of English language proficiency across native language groups.

I should like to summarize the major point of this paper up to this point. It is this: that an ideal English language proficiency test should make it possible to differentiate, to the greatest possible extent, levels of performance in those dimensions of performance which are relevant to the kinds of situations in which the examinees will find themselves after being selected on the basis of the test. The validity of the test can be established not solely on the basis of whether it appears to involve a good sample of the English language but more on the basis of whether it predicts success in the learning tasks and social situations to which the examinees will be exposed. I have attempted to suggest what might be the relevant dimensions of test performance, although I have not attempted to link them with collegiate learning and social situations—that is a task for college foreign student advisers and others who are familiar with the matrix of foreign student experiences.

Having made my major point, I wish to devote a little space to certain subsidiary issues which I consider important to testing.

THE CONTROL OF EXTRANEOUS VARIABLES OR INFLUENCES

In some ways, a good test is like an experiment, in the sense that it must eliminate or at least keep constant all extraneous sources of variation. We want our tests to reflect only the particular kind of variation in knowledge or skill that we are interested in at the moment. Suppose that we have an auditory comprehension test in which the examinee hears a question, and then has to select one of four *printed* answers. Is this a test of auditory comprehension? Not necessarily: it could be a test of reading skill for an individual who understands the question but cannot read the answer. Again, suppose that we have a written test of grammar: the printed instructions tell the examinee to "convert" a positive statement to a negative question. Is it a test of grammar? Not necessarily: It can be a test of vocabulary for the individual who knows the grammatical facts but who does not know such words as "convert," "positive," and "negative." Or suppose we have an oral production test in which the individual must make his response into a microphone: for many examinees, this might be a test of experience with a microphone, or even a personality test. Some of these examples are familiar and obvious; nevertheless, if one scrutinizes the tests currently being used for assessing English proficiency abroad, one finds many instances where the test response may depend, for many people, on some quite incidental fact or circumstance, such as failure to understand instructions through lack of a sufficient number of sample items. It is true, of course, that one cannot control *all* extraneous sources of variation, and there are situations in which it is actually desirable or necessary to test two or more things simultaneously. Nevertheless, the problem needs constant attention from test constructors. Otherwise we tend too often to put our examinees in double jeopardy or multiple jeopardy, and to reduce our chances of making useful diagnoses of learning difficulties of areas of ignorance on the part of the examinees.

THE PROBLEM OF SAMPLING

If one happens to be dealing with a test of some very well circumscribed area of knowledge or skill, such as knowledge of the order of an alphabet, one can test for the presence of the total range of that knowledge. In most cases, however, the items that can be tested in any reasonable amount of time constitute only a small sample of all those that might be tested. It is important to be conscious of this fact, and to define as carefully as possible the total area from which one is sampling. Ideally, one should have a list of all the possible items which one might cover, and draw a sample by random sampling techniques, but this is rarely possible. Some makeshift approaches are available, however, and should be used whenever feasible. One of these, for example, is to sample from actual texts—e.g., to construct items deliberately on the grammatical structures found at the top of every fifth page of a text. Ingenuity will suggest other methods to help avoid the biases to which one is subject if the materials of a test are gathered solely on the basis of one's free associations.

THE DISJUNCTIVE FALLACY

This is the fallacy that one must do either one thing, or the other. Some writings on testing seem to assume that because a certain technique, e.g., the objective test time, will not do what one desires it to do at a given moment, e.g., test skill in constructing sentences, it is totally to be abandoned for all purposes. Different objectives may require different techniques, and there is no reason why a variety of techniques should not be used in one examination.

THE PROBLEM OF SCORE INTERPRETATION

Nothing is more frustrating in the area of testing than to be given a test score, even in percentage or percentile terms, without a ready means of interpreting this score in terms of some immediately practical consequence. Unfortunately, such scores are the customary way of reporting performance on objective tests, and considerable effort is required to establish proper interpretations. *Percentage* scores are frequently misleading because their interpretation depends upon the intrinsic difficulty levels of the items on which they are based; *percentile* scores cannot be properly interpreted unless one is thoroughly familiar with the nature of the norming or comparison group. Contemporary test makers are turning to two types of score interpretation. One is to make use of the fact that test tasks can be arranged in difficulty level, and to report the difficulty level which the examinee can pass some set percentage of the time, say 75 percent. Thus, one might report that a given examinee has a vocabulary knowledge such that he knows 75 percent of the words near the rank of 10,000 in order of frequency, and one might then proceed to list sample words at this difficulty level. The other is to make greater use of what have been called expectancy tables. These are tables showing, for any given score level, the chances that an examinee has of succeeding in a variety of possible future courses of action. For example, the table might show that the chances are only three out of ten that an examinee with a given score level would be able to pass the freshman year in a college. Obviously, both types of score interpretation require considerable research in order to establish them on a firm basis, but even so, careful consideration should be given to these possibilities in developing a worldwide testing program in English.

36   ARE WE REALLY   EUGÈNE J. BRIÈRE
MEASURING
PROFICIENCY
WITH OUR FOREIGN
LANGUAGE TESTS?

On the basis of this article, what is your conclusion as to the *state of the art* of measuring foreign language proficiency?

Which of the studies reported on by Brière correspond most closely to the development of *integrative* tests as discussed by Carroll (Art. 35)?

An interesting project would be to take a natural dialogue from some source and try to determine the aspects of *communicative competence* required to understand the dialogue fully, over and beyond knowledge of the phonology and grammar involved.

Reprinted by permission from *Foreign Language Annals*, 4 (May, 1971), 385-391. The author is associate professor of linguistics at the University of Southern California.

"Achievement" and "proficiency" in foreign languages mean different things to different people. In order to provide a common denominator, for discussion, I would like to start by giving operational definitions for both terms.[1]

We will define "achievement" in language performance as the extent to which an individual student has mastered the specific skills or body of information which have been presented in a formal classroom situation. For example, an achievement test may be given to a class after the students have finished studying chapter X in book Y. Such a test may be designed to measure the degree of achievement acquired by the students of all, or part of, the phonological, morpho-syntactic and lexical categories which were first presented in chapter X. Presumably the teacher would be interested only in the degree of achievement of the information presented in chapter X and would not try to measure achievement of the material contained in chapter W until this chapter was presented to the students in class.

"Proficiency" in a language is much more difficult to define and, obviously, much more difficult to measure in a testing situation. Proficiency is frequently defined as the degree of competence or the capability in a given language demonstrated by an individual at a given point in time independent of a specific text book, chapter in the book or pedagogical method. In other words, as defined by Harris (1969)[2], "a general proficiency test indicates what an individual is capable of doing now (as the result of his cumulative learning experiences)."

One of the reasons that the term "proficiency" is much more difficult to define than the term "achievement" is the inherent notion of "degree of competence" in defining "proficiency." Are we talking about "linguistic competence," "communicative competence," or both? Furthermore, since language testing measures behavior, where can we find a model of behavior which we could use as a guide in designing a general proficiency test?

Perhaps a quick review of the development of language pedagogy and the subsequent testing instruments involved would be useful in understanding the problems in testing language proficiency and serve as a useful introduction to the current testing techniques reported here.

Over the past several years, different methods of teaching foreign languages or second languages have been used.

In the beginning, language was considered synonymous with literature. Put differently, language was thought to consist of the printed words contained in books—preferably in books which had been written by prestigious authors. Consequently, classroom teaching consisted primarily of learning the writing system of the target language and then reading literary passages in the target

---

[1] A portion of this paper was given at the seminar sponsored by the South East Asian Ministers of Education Organization in Bangkok, Thailand, in May, 1970.

[2] David P. Harris, *Testing English as a Second Language*. New York: McGraw-Hill Book Co., 1969.

language or translating these passages into the native language. When any attention was paid to anything other than translated prose, school programs were designed to provide memorization of verb paradigms or parsing of written sentences.

The tests or evaluation procedures developed from these literary-grammar-translation methods of teaching consisted of compositions and dictations in the target language or grammar translation exercises. Clearly, the scoring, evaluation and grading used in the three techniques were subjective and made it difficult, or sometimes impossible, to assess the students' resulting performances in any systematic objective manner. Stylistics, spelling and the examiner's personal prejudices frequently interfered with objective evaluation of achieved results and with reasonable predictions of success or failure in future learning in the target language. Since the variables of interest were not defined precisely, each examiner could use a different set of criteria for grading a composition or a translated passage. Some teachers placed more emphasis on grammatical precision (based of course on some literary style) while others were more concerned with imaginative, complex performances or stylistic considerations which showed "creativity" rather than simple-minded, grammatically precise inanities such as the "Look-Jane-look", "See-the-ball" variety. Frequently, the net result was that fifteen, or more, different teachers could evaluate the same composition in fifteen, or more, different ways.

If any attention at all was given to developing oral proficiency in the target language, the ensuing "tests" frequently consisted of unstructured interviews or "oral compositions" which lead to the same chaotic conditions in evaluation as those described for the written tests.

After the structural linguists such as Fries[3] and Lado[4] began to emphasize the primacy of proficiency in oral language, teaching methods and testing procedures changed considerably.

For one thing, oral, structural pattern practice replaced the previous literary methods. "Discrete point" teaching and testing become the order of the day. What I mean by "discrete point" is the assumption that there are a number of specific things, the knowledge of which constitutes "knowing" a particular language and that these things could be precisely identified at the different levels of syntax, morphology, and phonology. Lado,[5] for example, using a paradigm developed by psychologists in paired associate learning to identify proactive interferences, assumed that a contrastive analysis of the native language with the target language could precisely identify those learning problems which would

[3] Charles C. Fries, *The Structure of English*. New York: Harcourt, Brace & Company, 1952.

[4] Robert Lado, *Linguistics Across Cultures*. Ann Arbor: The University of Michigan Press, 1957.

[5] *Ibid.*

be encountered by native speakers of L_1 attempting to learn a specific target language. Moreover, the learning problems identified through the procedure of contrastive analysis could be developed into discrete point teaching materials or tests by simply writing patterns or test items for each of the learning problems involved. In actual practice, however, the things which are thought to constitute a language are not frequently defined through contrastive analysis but more often through a structural analysis of the target language only. The ensuing identification of the phonemic contrasts, the morphemic privilege of occurrence in certain pattern slots, the vocabulary items and the contrasting sentence patterns which are to be taught and then tested are frequently chosen in a very arbitrary manner. TOEFL[6] is an example of a discrete item test which was definitely not based on contrastive analysis.

Perhaps the largest gain made in turning to discrete point testing was a specific identification of the categories to be tested and an objectivity in scoring which was impossible with the translation or composition type of tests. Multiple choice items can be statistically analyzed for difficulty scores, discrimination scores, and correlations with external or internal criteria. We now have a method of reducing reliability and validity to a number which we can readily and easily understand. However, there is a growing concern among certain language test designers over the *actual* validity of this discrete point approach because of the very difficult problem of identifying precisely many of the complex variables which define the competence of a speaker or listener in any act of communication.

There is a growing agreement among psycholinguists and sociolinguists that traditional linguistic definitions of the notion of competence in a language are too narrow and are inadequate in identifying all of the skills involved when two people communicate. Consequently, discrete item language tests based on the narrow definition of linguistic competence will be inadequate. At best, such tests only give us some kind of measure of behavior which I will call "surface" behavior based on the analogy of a floating iceberg. The part of the iceberg which is seen floating on top of the water is but a small fraction of what lies underneath the water. So it is with communicative competence. We suggest that the language tests being used today are limited to measuring that which is on the "surface" and can give us no information about what is "underneath." However, probably it is precisely these unidentified and unmeasured variables "underneath" which constitute the "bulk" of communicative competence. What is needed is a serious attempt to develop a model which will identify and measure those variables which, at the moment, are "underneath the surface." I'd like to spend the remainder of this paper briefly summarizing some of the serious and sophisticated attempts which are currently being conducted in the United States.

[6]Test of English as a Foreign Language produced by the Educational Testing Service, Princeton, New Jersey.

Bernard Spolsky,[7] University of New Mexico, suggested in a recent paper that although Fries rejected the layman's notion that knowing a certain number of words in a language constituted the criterion for knowing that language, he still maintained the related notion that knowing a language involves knowing a set of items. Spolsky suggests that testing of individual elements such as sound segments, sentence patterns, or lexical items, is still inadequate.

He points out that the layman's criterion for *knowing* a language is usually expressed in some type of *functional* statement. For example, "He knows enough French to read a newspaper and ask simple questions for directions." Statements such as these refer to language *use* and not to grammar or phonology. The question then arises, how does one go about deciding when someone knows enough language to carry out a specified function? One approach would be to give someone a language-using test to perform, such as having a physics major listen to a lecture on thermodynamics and then test the comprehension. Another approach would be to characterize the linguistic knowledge which correlates with the functional ability. However, one of the fundamental reasons that this approach has not proved successful is that it fails to take into account the fact that language is redundant and that it is creative.

Redundance (part of the statistical theory of communication) is present in all natural languages since more units are used to convey a message than are theoretically needed. Spolsky has experimented with redundancy as a testing technique.

In his experiments, noise was added to messages on tapes and the tapes were played to native and non-native speakers. The non-native's inability to function with reduced redundancy suggested that the key thing missing was the richness of knowledge of probability on all levels phonological, grammatical, lexical and semantic. At least two implications follow from these experiments. The first is that knowing a language involves the ability to understand a message with reduced redundancy. A model of understanding speech must then include the ability to make valid guesses about a certain percentage of omitted elements. The second implication is to raise some serious theoretical questions about the value of deciding a person knows a language because he knows certain items in the language. The principle of redundancy suggests that it will not be possible to demonstrate that any given language item is essential to successful communication, nor to establish the functional load of any given item in communication. He makes the distinction between language-like behavior, for example, the utterance of a parrot, and knowing a language on the basis of creativeness, that is, the ability to produce and understand a sentence which may never have been heard before. One fundamental factor involved in the speaker-hearer's per-

---

[7] Bernard Spolsky, "What Does it Mean to Know a Language or How Do You Get Someone to Perform His Competence?" Paper delivered to the University of Southern California Testing Conference, 1968.

formance is his knowledge of the grammar that determines an intrinsic connection of sound and meaning for each sentence. We refer to this knowledge (for the most part, obviously, unconscious knowledge) as the speaker-hearer's "competence." Therefore, in searching for a test of overall proficiency, we must try to find some way to get beyond the limitation of testing a sample of surface features, and seek rather to tap underlying linguistic competence. Testing selected items can only give us a measure of surface behavior or performance.

Richard B. Noss,[8] with the Ford Foundation in Bangkok, Thailand, used an interesting technique which involved the students' own speech as interference and lack of redundancy factors. Noss instructed 24 Thai students (in Thailand) to read three typewritten pages arranged in order of difficulty from easy to hard. The students' responses were recorded. One week later, the students were asked to return and transcribe their own tapes. Not only was the hierarchy of difficulty of the stimuli confirmed by their scores, but also it was clear that many of the students were unable to transcribe their own recordings perfectly. I suggest that not only did the students' recordings provide interference, (even though they were listening to their own voices), but also that the factor of redundancy was lacking in their understanding of the target language.

John Upshur,[9] University of Michigan, feels that attempts to measure a "general proficiency factor" have been essentially unsuccessful primarily because of the lack of any performance theory generally available to, and useful for, those who might prepare production tests. He has suggested a simplified model which would specify some of the variables needed in a performance theory.

Upshur suggests that in the act of communication a Speaker's Meaning (SM) be distinguished from Utterance Meaning (UM) or Word Meaning (WM). In communication it is the task of the producer (a task certainly shared by the receiver or audience) to "induce" in, or transmit to, the audience a meaning (AM) which has as a part an equivalent of SM.

Because communication requires that AM contain SM, because UM is a medium through which this is accomplished, and because SM need not be equivalent, more is required than that S (and A) have competence in some language. For S to get his meaning across to A (i.e., to communicate, to have AM contain SM), it is necessary 1) for A to get the word meaning, 2) for A to know the case relations for each W (this seems to be a part of UM), and 3) for A to get the relations between a proposition and other concepts.

Upshur then develops a model for A which could account for the processing of SM in A. The kinds of "components" in A which he suggests are such things as: perceptions of the outer world (PO); a store of concepts (AMs) resulting

[8] Richard B. Noss, English Language Center, Bangkok, Thailand. Personal communication.

[9] John A. Upshur, "Measurement of Oral Communication," in Heinrich Schrand (ed.), *Leistungfmessung Im Sprachunterricht*. Marburg/Lahn: Informationszentrum fur Fremd-strachenforschung, 1969.

from the current communication transaction (CCS); a semantic net (NET); a linguistic competence (COMP) and several others.

From S's point of view, he must have a concept to communicate (SM), and some reason for doing so. S has the belief that A lacks the concept SM, and cares to have it. His communication ability is then a function of 1) his success in determining the constraints imposed by the contents of A's components, 2) his success in altering the contents of those components, and 3) his success (in language communication) in adapting his own competence.

The model suggests that oral production testing, viewed as one of the four skill components of the 1961 Carroll[10] model, is but one part of speaker communication testing. Communication measurement involves a matching of SM and AM, therefore "precise" measurement is not likely without comparable measures of both.

One experimental form to test one kind of communication situation has been and is being investigated by Upshur. In this technique, a set of thirty-six four-picture items was prepared. The S's specific task was to communicate to a remote A which one of the four pictures was identical to a single picture shown to him by an examiner. Students of English as a foreign language took the initial thirty-six-item test and the utterances were recorded. Four naive A's listened to the tapes. The inter-judge reliability for correct items was .87. Uniformly high coefficients were found between raw scores, total response and communication rate scores with composition and achievement tests scores. (Incidentally, we are currently using a modification of this technique to elicit oral responses on our project to develop ESL proficiency tests for North American Indian elementary school children).[11]

Leslie Palmer,[12] Georgetown University, has been experimenting with the evaluation of oral responses in English made by foreign students through the use of different elicitation techniques. He has his students read a story, paraphrase the story they have read and tell a story about a holiday or festival in their own words. The responses elicited by the three different techniques are judged by trained members of his staff. The variation of degree of proficiency depending upon the *method* used for elicitation is unbelievably and discouragingly large.

Leon Jakobovits[13] from the Center for Comparative Psycholinguistics at the

---

[10] John B. Carroll, *Fundamental Considerations in Testing for English Language Proficiency of Foreign Students*, Washington, D.C.: Center for Applied Linguistics, 1961.

[11] English Language Testing Project sponsored by the Bureau of Indian Affairs, Washington, D.C.

[12] Leslie A. Palmer, Georgetown University. Personal communication.

[13] Leon Jakobovits, "A Fundamental Approach to the Assessment of Language Skills," in Jakobovits, *Foreign Language Learning: A Psycholinguistic Analysis of the Issues.* Rowley, Massachusetts: Newbury House Publishers, 1970.

University of Illinois points out that there is an obvious difference between linguistic competence as it is traditionally defined and communicative competence. The latter involves wider considerations of the communication act itself; considerations which the linguists have dismissed in their definitions of linguistic competence as being primarily the concern of paralinguistics, exolinguistics, sociolinguistics and psycholinguistics. Since the authors of language tests are aware that the study of language *use* must necessarily encompass the wider competencies in communication competence, the development of language tests must move from the present position of measuring merely linguistic competence to the position of measuring communicative competence.

Jakobovits points out that speakers of a language have a command of various codes that can be defined as a set of restriction rules that determine the choice of phonological, syntactic and lexical items in sentences. For example, the choice of address form in English, "using the title Mr. followed by the last name versus first name," is determined by the social variable which relates the status relation between the speaker and the listener. These selection rules and others of this type are as necessary a part of the linguistic competence of the speaker as those with which we are more familiar in syntax, such as accord in gender, number and tense; and it would seem to be entirely arbitrary to exclude them from a description that deals with linguistic competence.

In order to be able to account for the minimum range of linguistic phenomena in communicative competence, it will be necessary to incorporate in the analysis three levels of meaning, namely linguistic, implicit and implicative.

By "linguistic meaning" Jakobovits refers to the traditional concerns of linguists such as Chomsky and Katz. This includes a dictionary of lexical meanings and their projection rules, syntactic relations and phonological actualization rules.

By "implicit meaning" he refers to the elliptically derived conceptual event which an utterance represents. By this is meant that particular implications for homonymous utterances are a function of the situational contents in which the utterance is used.

In order to recover the particular meanings of the word intended by the speaker, the listener must engage in an inferential process which makes use of his knowledge of the dictionary meaning of words as *well* as his knowledge of the overall situation to which the sentence as a whole refers.

"Implicative meaning" refers to the information in an utterance about the speaker himself, e.g. his intention, his psychological state, his definition of the interaction, etc. In some cases these implications are necessary to recover the intended meaning of the utterance. For example, "Do you have a match?" is not a question to be answered verbally, but a request for fire to light a cigarette.

The problem, then, of assessing language skills becomes the problem of describing the specific manner in which an individual functions at the three levels of meaning just identified. Language tests, then, must take into account the full range of phenomena in communicative competence if language *use* is to be tested.

Jakobovits makes some tentative suggestions with respect to some methodological approaches which may be used in connection with his classification scheme. Some of the methods suggested are as follows:

1. *Judgments of Acceptability:* ask a subject to judge the acceptability of an utterance or pick the most appropriate of two similar utterances.

2. *Semantic differential techniques:* subjects rate a word on a seven point bi-polar adjectival scale according to the Osgood method.

3. *Acting out situations:* ask a subject how he would say something under specified conditions in order to assess his encoding skills in terms of the different kinds of meaning just described.

Even scholars in the field of neuro-physiological speech are beginning to question discrete point teaching, and presumably, discrete point testing. In a paper entitled "Physiological Responses to Different Modes of Feedback in Pronunciation Training," Richard Lee,[14] Florida State University, reported some exciting experimental results to the TESOL conference in San Francisco in March 1970.

Working on the premise that pattern drill and phonemic discrimination drill is not genuine language behavior, has *no counterpart* in natural language behavior and produces boredom, lack of motivation and little learning among the students, he performed the following experiment.

It has been established that some physiological arousal is necessary for learning to occur. Arousal is most often measured by heart rate, galvanic skin response and breath rate. Of these measures, heart rate is the most robust.

Ten women and eight men, all foreign students taking ESL courses, were measured on an E and M Physiograph Six. This machine is similar to the polygraph used in lie detector tests but free from connecting wires to a central recording machine, thus allowing the student complete mobility.

The heart rates of the students were measured at seven different points in time under two basic conditions: one was during normal conversation and the second was during pattern practice.

The peaks of arousal which are expected during normal conversations did occur. Unfortunately, the measurements during pattern practice showed such little arousal in heart rate that Professor Lee was led to believe that no learning was occurring at all. In fact, the lines during pattern practice were almost flat with a slight drop at the seventh or last reading in time.

Admittedly, this is a small population from which to extrapolate to the universe, but I certainly hope he continues with this rather unusual technique

[14] Richard Lee, "Psychological Responses to Different Modes of Feedback in Pronunciation Training." Paper delivered to the TESOL conference in March, 1970.

for measuring learning in hopes that we can gain some insight into language teaching methods we are currently using.

The sociolinguistic works of Robert Cooper and Joshua Fishman at Yeshiva University, Charles Ferguson at Stanford and William Labov at Columbia (to name but a few) are providing language teachers, language testers and linguists with data which could lead to that "breakthrough" which is now needed if we are to move ahead into an era of sophisticated understanding of what to teach and what to test in order to provide psychologically sound understanding of the complex variables involved in communicative competence.

Furthermore, I would like to conclude with my personal bias which is that any *real* "breakthroughs" and new insights *must* be the results of an inter-disciplinary team of teachers, testers, psychologists, sociologists, linguists and many others. I can't think of any one single discipline (let alone a single person) which can provide all of the answers we now realize we need in order to provide new and exciting teaching materials and methods and truly valid test instruments to evaluate communicative competence.

37   TESTING   ROBERT L. COOPER

Which of the various types of tests discussed by Cooper are most likely to be needed by classroom teachers?

How does the classroom teacher determine what to test (a) at the end of a given lesson, (b) at the end of some term?

Does Cooper's discussion of varieties of language correspond to Bowen's (Art. 28) discussion of the same topic?

Examine some language test(s) available to you to determine which of the cells are tested in Fig. 1 of this article.

Incorporate the recommendations made by Cooper in the construction of a test for some group of students known to you. The sample test could be limited to testing the variable included in just one or two of the cells of Fig. 1.

Printed by permission from *Preparing the EFL Teacher: a Projection for the '70's*, where it appears as Chapter 3, pp. 75–97. Philadelphia: Center for Curriculum Development, Inc., 1971. The author is assistant professor of English, San Diego State College.

There are many users and uses of second-language tests. Admissions officers at American universities, for example, rely on scores obtained from tests of English as a second language to help evaluate the qualifications of foreign applicants. Directors of programs which teach English as a second language employ tests to help place students in classes at an appropriate level of instruction. Teachers of these classes use tests to help them to determine whether or not students have mastered a given unit of instruction or to identify students' strengths and weaknesses or to rank students for purposes of assigning grades. Teacher trainers use tests to help evaluate the effectiveness of alternative methods of instruction. Language tests, in short, are used at all stages of second-language instruction: for the admission and placement of students, for the evaluation of the success with which instructional objectives are met, and for the prediction of the success with which language learners can use the second language both inside and outside the classroom.

It is the purpose of this chapter to provide a brief introductory guide to the construction, selection, and use of second-language tests, with particular reference to tests of English as a second language. For more detailed treatments, the reader is referred to Lado (1961) and to Valette (1967) for second-language testing generally, and to Harris (1969) for the testing of English as a second-language specifically. Useful discussions of the problems involved in second language testing may also be found in Pimsleur (1966), Davies (1968), and Upshur and Fata (1968). For an exposition of testing issues more generally, the reader is referred to Thorndike and Hagen (1969). Reviews of published tests of English as a second language may be found in Buros (1965).

PHILOSOPHICAL PRELIMINARIES

For our purposes, we may define a test as a task or set of tasks which can be assigned under uniform conditions for purposes of assessment or evaluation. When we ask a student to respond to a question, for example, we have assigned him a task. If we can ask the same question in the same way to other students (or to the same student at a later time), then we are able to assign the task under uniform conditions. And if the task is assigned primarily to collect information about the people who perform it, then the task may be considered a test. We are not concerned here with the informal evaluations which language teachers make in response to their students' performance on relatively uniform tasks such as pattern-practice exercises or written assignments. We are concerned instead with those tasks which are assigned primarily for information-gathering purposes and which are relatively formal in nature, i.e., they are customarily viewed as tests both by those who administer them and by those who take them.

There is little point in asking people to take our tests if the resulting test scores are not put to use. Therefore, before we seek, construct, or administer a test, we must ask ourselves what use we expect to make of the test scores. Before we use a test, in other words, we must ask ourselves if the information which it provides is relevant to any decision we must make about the individuals who take the test. All too often tests are administered routinely, the original purpose of testing forgotten, and the scores serving no purpose beyond that of employing test makers, examiners, scorers, and file clerks. Are we to give a test of English listening comprehension, for example? Then we must ask why we need to know about the examinees' English listening comprehension ability. We would be more justified in trying to obtain this information if we were to use the test scores to evaluate our success in teaching English listening comprehension, or to decide whether the examinees are likely to be able to understand lectures in English, than if we planned to use the scores to decide whether they could read technical material in English well enough to pursue graduate study. We would certainly not be justified in administering the test, however, if the scores were not consulted at all. Testing, in short, is not justified unless decisions are made on the basis of test scores and unless the information provided by the test scores is relevant to these decisions.

Not only must we ask if the test scores provide relevant information which will be used, we must also ask if the information we seek cannot be obtained in other ways. Testing is only one way to gather information about people. If we wanted to make judgments about a student's ability to understand spoken English, for example, we could play a taped conversation to him and then ask him to answer questions designed to assess his comprehension of the passage. But we could also gather information about his listening comprehension in English by asking him to tell us how well he can understand English. Or we could ask people who have had an opportunity to observe him, in situations where English is spoken, to rate his ability. Or we could rate him ourselves on the basis of our own past observations of him. Or we could, perhaps, make inferences about his ability from the grades he has received in courses in which English was the medium or the subject of instruction. Each of these means of gathering information about the student has certain advantages and disadvantages, and the test does not necessarily have more advantages on balance than the others. Tests do offer certain advantages: they facilitate ranking the performances of individuals, since the individuals are presented with identical tasks, and they usually offer greater precision of measurement. On the other hand, they are often expensive to develop, and they require time and money to administer and score, and they typically elicit only a tiny sample of the behavior that we want to evaluate. Thus, the decision to use a test ought to be made in terms of the usefulness and cost of the information which it yields in comparison to the usefulness and cost of information available from other sources.

THE CONTENT OF LANGUAGE TESTS

Once we have decided to gather information by testing, we must specify the content of the test. That is to say, we must describe the kinds of behavior to be elicited by the test. What kinds of performances should a test elicit, for example, if we want to make valid inferences about a student's control of

English grammar? What kinds of test behaviors will allow us to make valid inferences about a student's ability to read university-level textbooks written in English? What should a test contain if it is to yield scores which are maximally predictive of an elementary-school student's ability to speak English in a classroom setting? We are unlikely to obtain tests which will permit sound inferences unless we first specify the tests' content.

There are some skills for which it is relatively simple to specify test content. For example, if we want to know if a person can ride a bicycle, we can give him a bicycle and ask him to ride it. Similarly, if we want to know if a person can swim twenty yards, we can bring him to a pool twenty yards long and ask him to swim its length. In these examples, the skill in which we are interested and the test which allows us to measure it are identical. When we wish to test proficiency in English, however, our task is not so simple. Unlike bicycle riding or swimming, English proficiency is not identical to any task which is used to assess it. We can learn whether or not a man can ride a bicycle or swim twenty yards by giving him a test. We can, it is true, learn something about a man's English proficiency by means of test scores, but the conclusions we draw from them are far more tentative, since we can only observe a small fraction of all the behaviors which English proficiency makes possible.

There are really two problems involved in specifying the content of a language test. First, we must determine what it is we wish to measure. Second, we must specify the tasks which will allow us to make valid inferences about what we want to measure. Do we want to measure English proficiency? Then first we must decide what we mean by English proficiency. Do we mean implicit knowledge of English syntax? Do we mean knowledge of a basic vocabulary? Do we mean the ability to read English at a given level of difficulty? Once we have decided *what* we want to measure, then we can decide *how* to go about measuring it.

We have identified two steps in the specification of test content: 1) determining *what* it is we want to test and 2) determining *how* to test it. Let us consider each of these steps in turn.

DETERMINING WHAT TO TEST

The determination of what it is we want to test involves making specifications along each of three dimensions: language variety, knowledge, and skill. "Language variety" refers to the dialect, register, style, or level of formality in which proficiency is to be tested. "Knowledge" refers to linguistic competence in the selected variety or varieties; and "skill" refers to the behaviors through which this knowledge or competence is realized, specifically listening, speaking, reading, or writing.

VARIETY

Recent work in sociolinguistics has emphasized the systematic variation which appears to exist in the use of different language varieties by members of a given speech community. Systematic alternation between varieties is more obvious where the varieties are viewed as separate languages and where the speech community is thought of as "bilingual" (e.g., the use of Spanish and English by the Puerto Rican speech community in New York City) than where the varieties are viewed as different styles or levels of formality of the same language and where the speech community is thought of as "monolingual." Even "monolingual" speakers, however, have more than one style of speech. Consider, for example, an American university professor's use of English. His style of speech will not be the same when he talks to his wife at home as when he talks to the president of his university in the latter's office; similarly, the way he delivers a paper before a plenary session of a learned society will differ from the way he talks to a close friend when both are seated at a prizefight. The variations in his speech which are systematically associated with the different social contexts in which he enters can be described explicitly in terms of specific phonological, morphophonemic, syntactic, and lexical variants, and it is one of the tasks of sociolinguists to do this. Even if we were unable to describe explicitly the nature of the variation, however, we recognize implicitly, on the basis of our everyday experience, the existence of such variation.

Thus, when we define the content of an English proficiency test we must identify the variety or varieties of English that the test should represent. The content of a test designed to assess the ability of a student to understand the kind of English used in formal university lectures, for example, ought to differ from the content of a test designed to assess the ability of a student to understand the informal conversation of fellow students outside of class. The varieties to be tested could be identified in terms of relatively intuitive notions such as "formal standard," "casual standard," or "intimate standard," or in terms of the contexts in which English is to be used, e.g., university seminar, professional consultation, relaxed peer-group conversation, etc. In either case, recognition should be given to the code switching which typically occurs among so-called "monolingual" speakers of English. It would be appropriate to frame test content in terms of the speaker's knowledge of only a single code if, and only if, we are interested in measuring his knowledge of one code only.

KNOWLEDGE

Once we have identified the variety or varieties of English that we wish to cover, we must select the particular aspect or aspects of competence that we wish to test. If we accept the generative transformational grammarians' view of a language (or variety) as an infinite set of sentences, then linguistic competence is the ability to produce and understand this infinite set (Chomsky 1965). The speaker-hearer's competence can be viewed as that knowledge which enables him to produce any and all the sentences in this set. It is the task of grammarians to specify or make explicit this knowledge. According to the formulations of the generative transformational grammarians, there appear to be three components of this knowledge: 1) syntactic, 2) phonological, and 3) semantic.

SYNTAX

The syntactic component enables speakers to assign structural descriptions to sentences. That is, knowledge of the syntactic component enables speakers to distinguish grammatical English sentences, e.g., *the boy is hitting the ball*, from nongrammatical ones, e.g., **The is ball hitting by the*. Knowledge of the syntactic component also enables speakers to identify two sentences with identical structures, e.g., speakers would agree that the sentences *The boy is here* and *The girl is here* are structurally identical (although lexically different), whereas they would also agree that the sentence *The boy is here* and *Is the boy here* are not structurally identical. Knowledge of syntax also enables speakers to identify syntactically ambiguous sentences, so that speakers would agree, for example, that the sentence *He likes entertaining girls* has two syntactic interpretations.

PHONOLOGY

Knowledge of the phonological component enables speakers to assign phonetic interpretations to sentences. That is, phonological competence allows speakers to produce and attend to those phonetic features of the stream of speech which are semantically empty but criterial. So for example in the sentence *The ship is here*, speakers of English will interpret the vowel in *ship* as /I/. Let us imagine, however, a speaker who has perfect command of English syntax but no knowledge of English phonology (e.g., a speaker of Spanish who has learned English from reading but has never heard it spoken). He would be able to assign a syntactic description to this sentence, e.g., he would know the sentences *The ship is here* and *The sheep is here* were structurally identical. However, he would not be able to distinguish the two sentences without contextual clues because he would not attend to the difference between /I/ and /i/ which is critical for speakers of English but not for speakers of Spanish.

SEMANTICS

The semantic system enables speakers to interpret sentences. If a speaker knew only the syntax of English he would know that the two sentences *The boy is here* and *The girl is here* were structurally identical. However, he would not know that the two sentences differed in meaning. Knowledge of the semantic component enables speakers to give different semantic interpretations to sentences which are structurally identical. Conversely, knowledge of semantics enables speakers to assign the same interpretation to sentences which are structurally different, e.g., *The boy hit the ball* and *The ball was hit by the boy*. Also, knowledge of the semantic component enables speakers to identify anomalies. For example, speakers of English would identify as anomalous Chomsky's (1957) famous sentence *Colorless green ideas sleep furiously*, or such sequences as *The table laughed* or *The dainty elephant*. In addition, knowledge of semantics enables the speaker to identify semantically ambiguous sentences. Thus, for example, he could assign two meanings to the sentence *We saw the late Mr. Smith*.

We may be interested in assessing the examinee's knowledge of one or more of the three components individually. For example, we may want to assess the degree to which he understands a given technical vocabulary, or we may want to measure the degree to which he is able to interpret syntactically complex spoken sentences. We may wish to make assessments in terms of individual components of competence because they represent specific goals of instruction or for other reasons. Thus, test content can be specified in terms of the degree to which each of the components of linguistic competence—phonological, syntactic, or semantic—should be covered specifically.

We may not, however, be particularly interested in the degree to which the examinee has mastered a given component of linguistic competence. We may, instead, be interested in the degree to which the examinee can combine all of these components into an integrated performance (Carroll 1961). If, for example, our purpose is to rank the examinees with respect to their ability to understand spoken English, we need not concern ourselves with their knowledge of any specific component comprising that skill. Instead, we can ask them to interpret recorded conversations, for example, a task which requires the simultaneous operation of phonological, syntactic, and semantic knowledge. Thus, in addition to specifying the various components of competence which we may want to test, we must indicate whether or not we wish to assess the ability to combine all of these components simultaneously.

SKILL

In principle, a speaker-hearer's knowledge of his language is the same for encoding as for decoding sentences. That is, the grammars which are written to account for his ability to produce the sentences of his language are also considered to account for his ability to understand the sentences of his language. However, his knowledge is realized through the application of different skills: speaking, listening, reading, and writing. People who speak the same first language differ with respect to their abilities as speakers, or as listeners, or as readers, or as writers of that language, even if they can all be presumed to have the same underlying linguistic competence. Just as there are interpersonal differences, there are intrapersonal differences. One person may be better at reading, for example, than at writing. Similarly, second-language learners may exhibit interpersonal as well as intrapersonal differences in the skills through which their knowledge of the second language is manifested. Thus, in addition to specifying the variety of English and the aspects of knowledge which are to be tested, we must specify which skills we want to assess—listening, speaking, reading, or writing.

LANGUAGE TESTING FRAMEWORK

The content of a language test, therefore, can be specified in terms of a three-dimensional framework. For illustrative purposes, let us assume that we have identified two varieties of English, knowledge of which we want to assess, and that we have labelled these varieties as A and B which may, for example, correspond to "formal" and "informal" standard English respectively. Our frame-work will then appear as in figure 1. In this figure we have specified four skills (listening, speaking, reading, and writing) on the vertical axis, four aspects of knowledge (phonology, syntax, and semantics, plus a combination of all three aspects or "total") on the horizontal axis, and two varieties (A and B) on the diagonal axis. The framework yields 4 X 4 X 2 = 32 theoretically distinct "cubes," each cube formed by the intersection of a particular skill, aspect of knowledge, and variety of English. For example, the cube formed by the inter-section of listening, semantics, and variety A would represent the ability of the examinee to assign semantic interpretation to spoken sentences in variety A; the cube formed by the intersection of writing, phonology, and variety A would represent his ability to spell in variety A; and the cube formed by the intersection of speaking, total, and variety B would represent his ability to speak in variety B, employing simultaneously his knowledge of the phonological, syntactic, and semantic features of that variety. Note that in this framework the phonological aspect represents orthographic skills when viewed in terms of reading and writing.

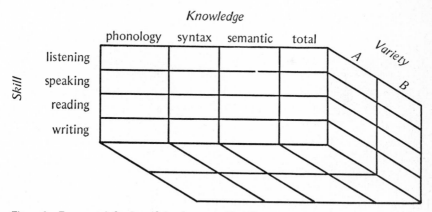

Figure 1: Framework for Specifying Language Test Content

The 32 cubes formed by our three-dimensional framework represent logical possibilities only. It is unlikely that we would want to find subtests or items to test each of these individually. We may, for example, be interested in only one skill. Or we may be interested only in knowledge when all aspects are manifested simultaneously in an integrated (total) performance. Furthermore, the ability represented by any given cube is likely to covary with the ability represented by any other. Thus, for example, although interpersonal differences exist in the ability to speak or to listen or to read or to write a given variety, in general those who attain high scores on a test of speaking that variety are likely to have relatively high scores on a listening comprehension test of that variety. Similarly, for a given variety, knowledge of phonology is likely to vary with knowledge of syntax and semantics since each is an interrelated component of the same system. Similarly, knowledge of one variety is likely to vary with knowledge of the other, since their systems or grammars are related.

The decision as to which of the 32 cubes should be assessed depends upon the use which we plan to make of the test scores. For example, if our instructional objectives have been stated in terms of auditory and spoken control of variety B's syntax, and if we want to assess the degree to which these objectives have been met, we will assess the abilities represented by the two cubes (listening-syntax-variety B and speaking-syntax-variety B). If, on the other hand, we want to predict the degree to which students will be able to understand spoken variety A, we will test the abilities represented by only one cube (listening-total-variety A). In general, when we want to measure an integrated skill (the cubes involving "total" knowledge), we get at least as good results when we assess complex performances directly, i.e., performances involving the simultaneous operation of phonological, syntactic, and semantic knowledge, as we do when we combine the results obtained from subtests or items testing each of these components separately (Carroll 1968).

DETERMINING THE TASKS

Once we have decided what we want to assess in terms of particular language varieties, skills, and aspects of competence, we are faced with the problem of specifying the tasks to be included in the test. The problem of specifying the tasks is essentially a problem of sampling, since there are many more items through which it is possible to assess the abilities represented by a given cube than can be used in a single test. For example, let us suppose we want to assess the ability to make syntactic interpretations of sentences spoken in variety A (the cube represented by the intersection of listening comprehension, syntax, and variety A). There are several types of operation which could be employed to test this. For example, the examinee could be asked to listen to a series of utterances and to 1) identify those utterances which were well formed or, conversely, those which were structurally deviant, 2) correct those utterances which were structurally deviant, 3) identify pairs of utterances with identical structures, 4) identify a unit in one sentence which had a given analogous function in another, 5) identify utterances which were syntactically ambiguous, 6) supply alternative interpretations to syntactically ambiguous utterances, or 7) supply items which had been randomly deleted from utterances. No doubt other operations could also be specified to test the ability to assign syntactic interpretations to spoken sentences. The particular operations which are chosen for the test will depend in part on their suitability for examinees at a given age and at a given level of English proficiency, in part on the difficulty of writing items to embody such operations, and in part on the limitations imposed by time and money.

Not only do we have to determine the operations to be embodied in the tasks to be included, we also have to determine the linguistic or contextual content of the tasks. In the example of testing the ability to assign syntactic interpretations to spoken sentences, what sentences are we to choose? Since the number of possible sentences is in principle infinite, we can present the examinee with only an infinitesimally small sample of these sentences. Clearly, we must choose sentences which exemplify certain structural relationships. But here again the number of possible types is very large. We are faced with a similar problem when we want to test the integrated or "total" skills. Here we must select not individual sentences or sentence types exemplifying specified syntactic relationships, or individual lexical items, or particular phonological contrasts. Instead, we must choose passages of connected discourse. And the passages must be representative of specified communicative contexts. Thus, for example, if we wanted to assess a person's ability to understand variety B when spoken, we must choose passages representative of the kinds of situations in which he is likely to hear variety B. If, for example, we wanted to assess the ability of foreign graduate students to read English-medium texts in their field of study, we would choose one type of passage. On the other hand, if we wanted to assess the ability of Mexican-American primary-school children to read third-grade English-medium primers, we would choose another. The particular structural or contextual content chosen for the test will be selected in terms of the same considerations involved in choosing the operations to be included: suitability for the examinees, ease of writing, and cost of administration.

Once we have specified the content of the test in terms of particular cubes of the test specification framework, and once we have decided the type of operations to be elicited and the kinds of linguistic and contextual content to be covered, we are ready to write the items for the test, or, if we are to select tests from published ones, to determine the extent to which the content of alternative tests is similar to the test content we have specified.

STEPS IN TEST CONSTRUCTION

The degree of care employed and the amount of time and money spent to construct a test can vary greatly, depending upon the purpose of the test. A classroom teacher, for example, who wishes to assess the degree to which the objectives of a one-week unit of instruction have been met with ten students will clearly need to expend less time and effort in constructing a test than the publishers of a test which will be widely used by university admissions officers to evaluate the English proficiency of foreign applicants. In general, the more people who take the test and the more important the decisions which are based on text scores, the more care should be devoted to the construction of the test.

The following steps in test construction can be identified: 1) planning, 2) writing, 3) item selection, 4) test tryout, and 5) standardization. The first two steps, planning and writing the test, are common to the construction of all tests. The additional steps would be followed for the construction of relatively more "important" tests.

PLANNING THE TEST

Planning the test, which includes the specification of test content, is the single most important and in some ways the most difficult aspect of test construction. We have already identified the steps involved in specifying test content: 1) determining *what* it is we want to test and 2) determining *how* to test it. The second part of content specification, determining the types of task to be required, involves the determination of 1) the particular operations to be required of the examinee and 2) the structure or context embedded in these operations. The content of the test should be determined according to the purposes for which the test scores are to be used.

In addition to determining the content of the test, planning involves specifying the time available for the administration of the test and the number of items to be included. If we are assessing more than a single cube of the test specification framework, the number of items to be allocated to each cube should be specified. The number of items allocated to each cube should be determined in accordance with the importance or weight we wish to assign each cube. Thus, for example, if we are preparing a 100-item test covering four cubes, and if we wish to assign equal weight to each cube, then each cube should be represented by twenty-five items.

We should also specify the degree of difficulty which we want the test to have for the examinees, i.e., the percentage of examinees which we expect to answer each item correctly. The fewer the examinees who answer an item correctly, the greater the "difficulty" of the item. Conversely, the more who answer it correctly, the easier the item. Sometimes, we expect that most of the items contained by a test will be passed by most of the examinees. If we want to assess the degree to which our students have mastered material presented in class, for example, and if the material has in fact been mastered, then we can expect the test items to be very "easy", that is, most of the examinees will answer most of the items correctly. On the other hand, sometimes we want tests which are moderately difficult—tests whose items are passed, on the average, by approximately fifty to sixty percent of the examinees. We would want such tests if we were interested in identifying differences among examinees in their English proficiency, so that we could reliably say that one examinee's performance was better than that of a second or worse than that of a third. We would want to be able to rank the performances of our examinees if, for example, we were assigning grades. We cannot identify individual differences by means of test items which are passed by all the examinees or, conversely, by items which are failed by all of the examinees because if all the examinees perform in the same way, no differences can be observed. However, items which are passed by about half the examinees will maximize the identification of individual differences.

We have described two types of test in terms of item difficulty: one in which almost all of the examinees will pass each item and one in which about half will pass each item. Sometimes other distributions of item difficulty will be desired, depending on the purpose of the test. For a detailed discussion of the planning of item difficulty, the reader is referred to Thorndike (1949).

In summary, the steps involved in planning the test include the specification of 1) test content, 2) time for test administration, 3) number of items and their allocation to the different content areas, and 4) item difficulty.

WRITING THE TEST

Once the test has been planned, items can be written to meet the specifications of the test plan. Item writing has been termed an art as well as a science. The novice item writer can avoid some of the more common pitfalls, however, by following the maxims for item writing offered by Thorndike and Hagen (1961). In addition, examples of foreign-language test items can be found in Lado (1961), Valette (1967), and Harris (1969). No matter how skilled the item writer, however, it is good practice to have the items reviewed by others. It is often difficult for an author to see faults in the items he has written, even though blemishes may appear obvious to a colleague. For tests which are to be standardized, it is a good rule of thumb to write twice as many items as are to appear in the final edition of the test.

Particular care should be expended on the preparation of the examinees' directions or instructions for taking the test. The preparation of unambiguous directions—instructions which will be uniformly and correctly interpreted—is a time consuming but vital task. Care also should be taken in the preparation of directions to examiners.

ITEM SELECTION

By administering our items to a group of examinees who are representative of the people for whom the test is designed, it becomes possible to select, for a final edition of the test, items which have been found to be at the desired levels of difficulty. For example, if we have specified that our items should range in difficulty from forty to fifty percent, with an average value of fifty percent, we can throw out all items passed by more than sixty percent of the examinees and all items passed by fewer than forty percent of the examinees. We can then select from the remaining items those which will yield an average value of fifty percent. We can do this, of course, only if we have written enough "extra" items. If we find that we have not written enough items conforming to the desired statistical characteristics, we will have to choose those items which come closest to meeting our specifications in terms of percentage passing.

We can select each item not only on the basis of the percentage of examinees passing it but also in terms of the degree to which the item meets certain other criteria. For example, we would tend to reject an item which was passed by the poorer students (defined in terms of their score on the rest of the test or in terms of performance on some other criterion) but was failed by the better students.

We may also wish to select items in terms of the ease with which they are passed by native speakers of English who are otherwise similar to the examinees for whom the test is designed. If the item cannot be passed by native speakers of English who are otherwise similar to those for whom the test is written, it is likely that the item is badly written or is testing something in addition to, or instead of,. English proficiency.

TEST TRYOUT

Once the items have been selected for the test, a "dress rehearsal" of the final edition can be made with examinees who are similar to those for whom the test has been written and with examiners who are similar to those who will usually be administering the test. In the test tryout, we have a final opportunity to learn whether the directions to examiners and examinees are clear, whether the time limits are adequate, and whether the format of the test (the printing, arrangement of items on the page, etc.) and scoring arrangements are satisfactory.

STANDARDIZATION

Standardization of the test enables users and prospective users of the test to determine the meaning and evaluate the usefulness of test scores. The steps involved in standardization include the collection of normative data and the gathering of evidence with respect to the reliability and validity of test scores.

Normative data enables the test user to interpret a test score in terms of the performance of one or more reference groups. A raw score—the actual number of items answered correctly—takes on meaning when we can compare it to the scores obtained by others. We would interpret a score differently if, for example, it represented the highest score obtained in a group of 100 students than if it represented the lowest. When we collect normative data, we attempt to describe the performance of various reference groups on the test so that such interpretations are possible. The reference groups we select should be chosen so as to be representative of the various groups who are likely to take the test, whether defined in terms of age, level of proficiency, first-language background, educational background, or type of prior language training.

The existence of data on reliability and validity enable us to judge the accuracy and the relevance of test scores. Reliability refers to the accuracy or stability of measurement. No language test can yield perfectly reliable scores. That is, examinees' scores (and their ranks in a group) would tend to change from one administration of the test to another if repeated measurements were possible. The data reported on reliability give us a means of estimating the stability of our scores—the extent to which an examinee's obtained (observed) score is close to his "true" score (the score which he would obtain on the average if it were possible to give him the same test repeatedly) or the extent to which the examinee would maintain his rank in the group if the test were given again. In general, the longer the test (the more items it contains), the more reliable it is. Thus the issue of reliability becomes more acute when we are dealing with short tests, particularly the relatively short subtest of a battery.

Validity refers to the relevance of the test scores to the purpose for which we plan to use the test. A test may be accurate without being relevant to our purposes. To take an extreme example, we may have a paper-and-pencil test containing 100 items requiring simple arithmetical operations, e.g., $4 + 3 =$, $4 - 2 =$, $5 \times 3 =$, etc. Such a test may be quite reliable. It would also be valid if our purpose was to use it to assess the ability to perform simple arithmetical calculations. However, it would not be a valid measure of reading comprehension in English. Thus, validity must be judged in terms of the purpose of the test. Test publishers, as part of the standardization procedure, can provide data which will allow us to judge the test's relevance for our purpose. Such data are of varying types. A test of English language proficiency could offer data such as the correlation of test scores with other tests of English that are considered valid or correlation of test scores with other relevant variables, such as grades in English language classes, number of years in which English has been studied, number of years in an English speaking environment, or ratings by competent observers. Sometimes, test publishers offer, as evidence of validity, the degree to which the specifications of test content and the correspondence of test items to the specifications are judged by authorities to be reasonable in view of the stated purposes for which the test was constructed.

SELECTING A TEST

In some cases, it may be possible to use a test which has already been developed. If a test has been developed for the same purpose and for the same or similar populations as ours, we can consider the possibilities of employing it. In part, we can judge the degree to which an existing test meets our purposes by evaluating its items. Do the items appear to tap the abilities that we wish to test? Do the items appear to be at the appropriate level of difficulty? Secondly, we can judge the test in terms of whatever data are available concerning reliability and validity. Third, we can judge the usefulness of the test in terms of the existence of norms. The test will be more useful to us if relevant normative data have been obtained. Finally, the usefulness of the prospective test can be judged in terms of such important practical considerations as the time required for administration, ease of scoring, cost per test, and the ease with which test security (preventing examinees from obtaining copies of the test) can be maintained.

USING THE TEST

No matter how good our tests, they can never be completely without error. All measurement involves some error, including the measurement of attributes such as second-language proficiency. Part of the difficulty in obtaining accurate measurement is due to the difficulty faced in adequately defining what is meant by second-language proficiency: hence, the importance placed upon specifying test content. Even with explicit specifications of content, however, language tests are by no means error free, and this fact should be constantly kept in mind when interpreting test scores or making decisions based on test scores. We should view test scores as hypotheses, not facts. We should view *differences* between test scores with even more wariness than we view a single test score, since the error contained by the difference between two scores is proportionately greater than the error contained by either of the scores alone. Thus, we should be quite cautious in hazarding the hypothesis that the difference between two scores is not due to chance. This is particularly true when we compare an individual's scores obtained on two subtests—for example between subtests of vocabulary and syntax—inasmuch as subtests are shorter and thus typically less reliable than scores based on the battery as a whole. Differences between foreign-language proficiency subtest scores should be viewed cautiously also because these scores tend to be related. In general, the greater the relationship between two scores, the greater the difference that must be observed between them before the difference can be considered real or not due to chance.

Whether we construct our own test or employ one which has been constructed by others, it is usually helpful to gather information about the test as we use it. Information can be collected about the individual test items—how many examinees pass each item and how well each item distinguishes the more proficient from the less proficient examinees. Such information can be useful when it comes time to revise the test or when other forms of the test are built. Information can also be gathered about the scores (on the test as a whole or on component subtests) of the various groups which take the test. Local norms—normative data based on the groups which we actually test—are ultimately the most useful ones and can be obtained by keeping records of the scores of those who take our tests. We should also keep records, if possible, of the degree to which decisions based on test scores have been found to be sound ones. For example, what proportion of the students admitted to a given program on the basis of test scores actually succeed in the program? Information about the way the test "works" can help us to 1) build better tests in the future, 2) interpret test scores more adequately, and 3) make better decisions based on test scores. We should not, in other words, unequivocally embrace a test once it has been constructed or selected. Tests can be improved, tests often should be improved, and the way we use them can be improved.

SUMMARY

We can summarize the present chapter by restating the following points:

1. The use of foreign-language tests can be justified if decisions are made on the basis of test scores and if the information provided by the tests is relevant to such decisions.

2. The specification of test content is the single most important step in test construction.

3. Foreign-language test content should be specified in terms of (a) a three-dimensional framework comprised of the intersection of language variety, knowledge, and skill, and (b) specific tasks identified by the particular operations required and their structural or contextual representation.

4. The steps followed in the construction of a standardized second-language test include (a) planning, (b) writing, (c) item selection, (d) test tryout, and (e) standardization, which in turn involves the collection of normative data and data with respect to reliability and validity.

5. Selection (as contrasted to construction) of a test can be made in terms of (a) the degree to which the test user's objectives appear to be met by the test's items, (b) evidence on reliability and validity, and (c) certain practical considerations.

6. Test scores should be viewed tentatively, as hypotheses, not facts, about an individual.

7. Records should be kept with respect to the way the test functions in the setting for which it was selected or designed.

REFERENCES

Buros, O. K. 1965. *The sixth mental measurements yearbook*. Highland Park, New Jersey: Gryphon Press.

Carroll, John B. 1961. Fundamental considerations in testing for English language proficiency of foreign students. In *Testing the English proficiency of foreign students*. Washington, D.C.: Center for Applied Linguistics. Pp. 30–40.

Carroll, John B. 1968. The psychology of language testing. In Alan Davies (ed.), *Language testing symposium*. London: Oxford University Press. Pp. 46–69.

Chomsky, Noam. 1957. *Syntactic structures*. 's-Gravenhage: Mouton.

Chomsky, Noam. 1965. *Aspects of the theory of syntax*. Cambridge: M.I.T. Press.

Davies, Alan (ed.). 1968. *Language testing symposium*. London: Oxford University Press.

Harris, David P. 1969. *Testing English as a second language*. New York: McGraw-Hill.

Pimsleur, Paul. 1966. Testing foreign language learning. In Albert Valdman (ed.), *Trends in language teaching*. New York: McGraw-Hill. Pp. 175–214.

Thorndike, Robert L. 1949. *Personnel selection*. New York: Wiley.

Thorndike, Robert L. and Elizabeth Hagen. 1969. *Measurement and evaluation in psychology and education* (third edition). New York: Wiley.

Upshur, John A. and Julia Fata (eds.). 1968. Problems in foreign language testing. *Language Learning*, special issue number 3, 1968.

Valette, Rebecca M. 1967. *Modern language testing: a handbook*. Harcourt.

38   DICTATION AS A   JOHN W. OLLER, JR.
 TEST OF ESL
 PROFICIENCY

For what purpose might an ESL proficiency test be given?

What are some of the implications of Oller's conclusions regarding the use of dictation as a test of proficiency in English?

What kinds of information about a student's ESL proficiency could be gained by judging his performance on a dictation test? What kinds of information could not be gained?

Although dictation is highly favored as a testing technique by many language teachers, it has not been blessed with the approval of many of the professionals in the business of language proficiency testing.[1] The present paper reports results from two experimental studies supporting the use of dictation as a device for testing ESL proficiency. The data from the first study were gathered as part of an evaluation and revision of the ESL Placement Examination (*ESLPE*) for the University of California at Los Angeles. The second study was actually an experimental investigation of the cloze technique as a test of ESL proficiency which incidentally yielded interesting data in support of dictation. First we will consider the experimental results and their implications. Then we will discuss some conflicting conclusions of language testing experts.

Reprinted by permission from *English Language Teaching*, 25 (June, 1971), 254–9. The writer is assistant professor of English at the University of California, Los Angeles.

[1]This is a revised and expanded version of an earlier paper, "Dictation as a Device for Testing FL Skills," which appeared in *English Language Teaching* (1971). It is reprinted here by permission of the publishers of that journal.

STUDY I

The format of the UCLA *ESLPE* which had been in use for about ten years as of 1969 (henceforth referred to as Form 1) consisted of five parts. Each part was intended to test one or more linguistic skills believed essential to the use of the English language by foreign students in the successful performance of required academic tasks. The five parts of the *ESLPE* Form 1 were: 1) a multiple-choice vocabulary test where students selected an appropriate synonym for a word underlined in a context; 2) a composition on one of three given topics for which students were allowed forty-five minutes; 3) a phonological discrimination task of the minimal-pair type; 4) a section on grammar in which students selected the most acceptable sentence from three alternatives; and 5) a dictation of about 200 words in length.

In an attempt to determine the amount of overlap in skills measured by the various parts of the *ESLPE* Form 1, Pearson product-moment correlations were computed for each part of the test with each other part and with the total score. A random sampling of 100 students from among 350 who took the exam in the fall of 1968 was used. The surprising result was that the dictation correlated more highly with each section of the test than did any other section. In other words, when the correlations between parts were rank ordered, the dictation came out first in every possible category (Table 1).[2] On the basis of

Table 1. Intercorrelation of part scores and total score on the UCLA ESLPE *Form 1*

ESLPE Form 1 / ESLPE Form 1	Grammar	Composition	Phonology	Total	Dictation
Vocabulary	.65	.56	.49	.81	.72
Grammar		.62	.55	.83	.69
Composition			.56	.88	.72
Phonology				.71	.60
Total					.88

[2] I would like to thank George Allen, now at the University of North Carolina at Chapel Hill, for help with the statistics of computer programming for Study I.

these data, the dictation clearly seems to be the best single measure of the totality of the language skills tested by the *ESLPE* Form 1.[3]

STUDY II

Partly on the basis of the data discussed in Study I, in 1969, the UCLA *ESLPE* was put into a new format (Form 2). In the new version, the phonological discrimination task was eliminated along with the composition. The vocabulary section was expanded from twenty items with three alternatives each to forty items with four choices each. The grammar section was revised to include a section of twenty items in which the students had to arrange words, phrases, or clauses in an appropriate sequence, along with twenty items in which the student had to choose from four alternatives the most appropriate word, phrase, or clause to fill a blank. A reading test in two parts was added. The first task, consisting of twenty-five items, required the student to select from four possible alternatives the best paraphrase for a given sentence. The second part, containing fifteen items, required students to select from four alternatives the sentence that best stated the central idea of a given paragraph. The final section was a dictation.

The *ESLPE* Form 2A was used in the fall of 1969, and on the basis of a test item analysis was revised. Form 2A Revised served as the touchstone for an extensive experimental investigation of the cloze procedure as a test of ESL proficiency (Oller, 1971).[4] The data from the latter study are particularly revealing. Table 2 gives the Pearson product-moment correlations for three cloze tests of differing levels of difficulty with the various parts on the UCLA *ESLPE* Form 2A Revised. It is interesting that in all three cases, the cloze tests correlate best with dictation. The more difficult cloze passages (II and III) yield correlations as high as .84 and .85 respectively with dictation. Another notable fact in Table 2 is that as we proceed from less "integrative" (see Carroll, Art. 35, for a definition) to more integrative tasks, the correlations increase. That is, in general, the correlation between cloze scores and vocabulary is less than

[3] Rebecca Valette (1967) reports that she also found a high correlation (.90) between scores on a dictation and combined listening, reading, and writing scores on a German examination. On the basis of another study, Valette (1964) had reported: "For students possessing minimal experience with dictée, the dictée can validly be substituted for the traditional final examination in first-semester French" (p. 434). Others who have argued in favor of the use of dictation as a testing and/or teaching device are Fe Dacanay (1963), Mary Finocchiaro (1958), and J. Sawyer and Shirley Silver (1961).

[4] A cloze test is constructed by deleting words from a selection of prose on a systematic basis. Usually, every fifth, sixth, seventh, eighth, ninth, or tenth word is deleted from a passage. The student must then fill in the blanks with the missing words. In order to do so he utilizes the context surrounding the blanks to make inferences concerning the missing items.

Table 2. Pearson product-moment correlation coefficients for three cloze tests with parts and total score on the UCLA ESLPE Form 2A revised

Cloze tests UCLA ESLPE 2A Revised	Cloze I Easy	Cloze II Medium	Cloze III Difficult
Vocabulary	.63	.75	.71
Grammar	.73	.76	.80
Reading	.71	.78	.82
Dictation	.76	.84	.85
Total	.80	.89	.89

for grammar, which in turn is less than that for reading, which is less than that for dictation. Moreover, this is true for all tests in all cases save one. The correlation between Cloze I and grammar (.73) is slightly higher than for Cloze I and reading (.71).

Statistically it is possible to specify more clearly the relations between the various test types by using a partial-correlation technique. By this method, the relation between two variables can be measured while controlling for one or more other variables. To illustrate, it is certain that vocabulary skill (as measured by the *ESLPE*) is a part of reading skill (as measured by the *ESLPE*). By correlating vocabulary with cloze scores while controlling for reading, and vice versa, we may get a much clearer picture of the actual extent of the relation between the cloze task and reading, and the cloze task and vocabulary. When only one control-variable is used, the correlation is referred to as a first-order partial; when two are used it is called a second-order partial, etc. Table 3 gives the first-, second-, and third-order partial correlations between cloze scores and each of the parts of the UCLA *ESLPE* Form 2A Revised.

There is an unmistakable progressive increase in correlations as the tasks required become more integrative in nature. Furthermore, we can scarcely fail to note that, of the part scores on the UCLA *ESLPE*, dictation is again first in every single category.

Table 3. First-, second-, and third-order partial correlations for three Cloze-tests-combined with part scores on the UCLA ESLPE 2A Revised

UCLA ESLPE Parts	First-order Partials	First-order Control variable	Second-order Partials	Second-order Control variables	Third-order Partials	Third-order Control variables
I. Vocabulary	.27*	II	.09	II, III		
	.25*	III	.10	II, IV	.00	II, III, IV
	.20*	IV	.05	III, IV		
II. Grammar	.41*	I	.33*	I, III		
	.40*	III	.23*	I, IV	.19*	I, III, IV
	.29*	IV	.20*	III, IV		
III. Reading	.42*	I	.34*	I, II		
	.41*	II	.29*	I, IV	.26*	I, II, IV
	.34*	IV	.28*	II, IV		
IV. Dictation	.53*	I	.43*	I, II		
	.48*	II	.45*	I, III	.37*	I, II, III
	.50*	III	.38*	II, III		

*$p < .001$

DISCUSSION

All of the above results raise grave doubts concerning the conclusions of certain authorities who have argued that dictation as a testing device is quite inferior to other techniques. For example, Robert Lado has stated:

> Dictation . . . on critical inspection . . . appears to measure very little of language. Since the word order is given . . . it does not test word order. Since the words are given . . . it does not test vocabulary. It hardly tests the aural perception of the examiner's pronunciation, because the words can in many cases be identified by context . . . . The student is less likely to hear the sounds incorrectly in the slow reading of the words which is necessary for dictation (1961: 34).

David Harris has remarked:

> As a testing device . . . dictation must be regarded as generally both uneconomical and imprecise (1969: 5).

D. F. Anderson says:

> Some teachers argue that dictation is a test of auditory comprehension, but surely this is a very indirect and inadequate test of such an important skill (1953: 43).

W. R. P. Somaratne states:

> Dictation is primarily a test of spelling (1957: 48).

Certainly, the data presented above tend to refute these statements. Even in the absence of such data, however, there is a great deal to be said from a theoretical point of view in support of dictation as a testing technique. For example, Lado's statement that in dictation "the word order is given by the examiner" is credible only from the vantage point of the speaker (examiner)—since he knows the words and word-order. For the listener (the student in this case), as Saussure observed many years ago:

> . . . the main characteristic of the sound chain is that it is linear. Considered by itself it is only a line, a continuous ribbon along which the ear perceives no self-sufficient and clear-cut division . . . (1959: 103-4).

In order to segment the chain an active process of analysis is necessary. This analysis is no simple matter as anyone who has attempted to accomplish speech perception by machine will attest.[5]

While the words and word-order may be "given" from the viewpoint of the speaker (who knows what message he has encoded), they are not in the same sense "given" from the vantage point of the hearer. The listener must discover them. A cursory look at errors common in dictations reveals order inversions: e.g., "as change to continues" for "as change continues to"; "some by an even" for "by something even"; "barely have a chance" for "has barely a chance."[6] Moreover, words and phrases are often understood incorrectly: e.g., "scientists examinations" and "scientists imaginations" which are foreign-student renderings of "scientists from many nations." Also extra words may be inserted: e.g., "for at least five hundred thousand years" instead of "for at least five thousand years"; "of our life" for "of life"; "of the time" for "of time"; "they are never made" for "they never made." These examples, which could be multiplied indefinitely, clearly illustrate the fact that neither words nor word orders are supplied to the student in a clear and unambiguous form. Rather, the student is given a sequence of sounds from which an intended set of words in sequence must be extracted.

Even in briefly glancing at the errors students make in taking dictation, it becomes quite clear that the student does not merely hear words in a particular

---

[5] For some discussion of the complexity of the speech recognition process and the mechanical simulation of it, see W. B. Newcomb (1967).

[6] These examples were taken from three students' renderings of the dictation given in September, 1969, as part of UCLA's *ESLPE*.

order and write them down. Rather, he hears sound sequences, bounded occasionally by silence or pauses, but which are otherwise strung together without obvious boundaries between them; he actively segments these sequences into words, phrases, and sentences that make sense to him. Clearly, common errors suggest a dynamic process of analysis-by-syntheses.[7] The student not only receives auditory information, but he processes this information in order to generate a sentence (or a sequence of them) that has meaning. This is by no means the simple activity that Lado's statement implies. It is in fact one of the most complex processes known to man—a process which to date is not fully understood. In fact, all attempts to simulate it have failed in important respects.[8]

Harris's statement that dictation is "uneconomical" and "imprecise" may have more in its favor. However, the economy of administering a test is largely to be determined in terms of the amount of information that the test ultimately provides. The fact that dictation tests a broad range of integrative skills may outweigh the difficulties involved in administration and correction. Moreover, the effectiveness of dictation as a diagnostic device may even be superior to tests involving multiple choice, short answers, fill-in blanks, etc., which are sometimes thought to be more accurate. The reason for this is that a dictation is apt to provide a more comprehensive sampling of the integrative skills involved in the understanding of a language.

Anderson's statement that dictation is an inadequate test of auditory comprehension is contradicted by our data, and seems to have no substantial arguments in its favor. Somaratne's interpretation of dictation as a "test of spelling" seems to indicate a serious lack of understanding of the process of speech perception. While dictation does measure control of a language's graphological system, this is certainly not all that it reveals.

Perhaps there is a still more basic error in arguments against dictation as a testing device. Lado's statement, quoted above, seems to imply that the "discrete point" (see Carroll, Art. 35) objective tests are superior to tests which require the integrative use of language competence. This is probably a reflection of the still current tendency of many linguists to treat the elements of language analytically. Bloomfieldian linguists attempted to deal with linguistic utterances as purely objective phenomena apart from the settings in which they occurred. They attempted to deal with language as much as was possible without considering meaning. The now prominent school of Chomskyan transformationalists also employs an analytical technique which treats language as a self-contained system apart from its use in communication. Both of these procedures have been seriously challenged,[9] and it would seem that the arguments employed

---

[7]Such models of human information processing are not at all uncommon. See Miller, Galanter, and Pribram (1960) and their references.

[8]See Chomsky's discussion of this process in *Language and Mind*, 1968.

[9]See Oller (1970) and the references listed there.

against them are to a certain extent applicable here. If it is indeed true that language cannot be successfully explained apart from its use as a medium of communication,[10] it would follow that analytical tests of language competence which remove linguistic units from the meaningful contexts in which they normally occur are apt to be less valid than integrative tests which are more relevant to communication skills. Certainly dictation, which requires the perception of meaningful speech, falls into the latter category.

The processes involved in taking a dictation may be represented as shown in Figure 1.

Figure 1. A Representation of the Processes Involved in Taking Dictation

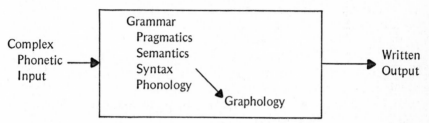

While the interactions between phonology, lexicon, grammar, and graphology are bound to be very complex, at least as many systems as those suggested in the diagram are required for writing a dictation. The student is tested for his ability to a) discriminate phonological units, b) make decisions concerning word boundaries in order to discover sequences of words and phrases that make sense, i.e., that are grammatical and meaningful, and c) translate this analysis into a graphemic representation.

In conclusion, though a good deal more experimentation needs to be done in evaluating second-language testing techniques, it seems safe to conclude that dictation is an extremely valuable tool for measuring language proficiency. It has, however, been the intent of this paper, not merely to support the use of these procedures, but also to encourage an experimental attitude toward problems related to language testing in general. While the statements of experts may be essential in the beginning stages of a science, for a field of study to progress, there must be an increasing reliance on tested hypotheses, and a decreasing dependence on the pronouncements of authorities.

---

[10] Incidentally, this argument finds an interesting application in theories of language teaching. Clifford Prator (1965) has given an excellent statement of the need for treating language as a medium of communication in teaching. Oller (1969) discusses experimental evidence supporting the need for presenting a foreign language through meaningful communicative activity (see also references listed there).

REFERENCES

Anderson, D. F. (1953). "Tests of Achievement in the English Language," *English Language Teaching*, vol. 7, no. 2, pp. 37-69.

Dacanay, Fe R. (1963). *Techniques and Procedures in Second Language Teaching.* Quezon City, Philippines: Phoenix Publishing House.

Finocchiaro, Mary M. (1958). *Teaching English as a Second Language.* New York: Harper Bros.

Harris, D. (1969). *Testing English as a Second Language.* New York: McGraw-Hill.

Lado, R. (1961). *Language Testing.* London: Longmans, Green and Co.

Miller, G. A., E. Galanter, and K. H. Pribram (1960). *Plans and the Structure of Behavior.* New York: Holt, Rinehart and Winston.

Newcomb, W. B. (1968). "A Dictionary Program for Speech Recognition," Mimeographed, General Dynamics, Rochester, New York.

Oller, J. (1969). "Language Communication and Second Language Learning." Paper presented at the Second International Congress of Applied Linguistics, Cambridge, England. Reprinted in *IRAL* (in press).

Oller, J. (1971). "Levels of Difficulty and Scoring Methods for Cloze Tests of ESL Proficiency." Unpublished paper, UCLA.

Oller, J. (1970). "Transformational Grammar and Pragmatics." *Modern Language Journal*, 54, 504-507.

Prator, C. H. (1964). "English as a Second Language: Teaching," *Overseas*, vol. 3, pp. 18-21. Reprinted in Harold B. Allen (ed.), *Teaching English as a Second Language.* New York: McGraw-Hill, 1965. pp. 87-92.

Saussure, F. (1959). *Course in General Linguistics.* Charles Bally and Albert Sechehaye (eds.), Wade Baskin (tr.), New York: The Philosophical Library.

Sawyer, Jesse, and Shirley K. Silver (1961). "Dictation in Language Learning," Language Learning, vol. 11, pp. 233-242. [Article no. 26 in this collection, Eds.]

Somaratne, W. (1957). *Aids and Tests in the Teaching of English.* London: Oxford University Press.

Valette, Rebecca M. (1964). "The Use of the Dictée in the French Language Classroom," *Modern Language Journal*, vol. 48, pp. 431-434.

Valette, Rebecca M. (1967). *Modern Language Testing: a Handbook.* New York: Harcourt, Brace, and World.

39

CROSS-CULTURAL TESTING: WHAT TO TEST   JOHN A. UPSHUR

What are some of the possible needs for *cross-cultural tests*?

According to Upshur's first simplifying assumption, which cultural patterns would not have to be tested?

Why is a second *simplifying assumption* needed?

Give real examples from two cultures known to you for each of the branches in the diagrams in Figures 2 and 3.

What problems in the construction of cross-cultural tests remain to be solved?

With ever increasing numbers of people crossing national, linguistic, and cultural boundaries in order to study and to work, it becomes more crucial to provide instruction and orientation so that they can function effectively in their new locations. A corollary need is to identify those people most in need of instruction, or orientation, to determine what the content of instructional and orientation programs should be.

Considerable work has already been done in devising techniques and tests for the identification of those persons who intend to cross linguistic borders but who haven't sufficient language ability for their new undertakings. Applied linguists and language teachers have done much to determine what the content of foreign language instruction properly should be. Experience, especially that with foreign students in the United States, has shown, however, that measures of language ability alone have limited power to predict who will be able to function effectively in the new linguistic and cultural environment. This is no longer surprising, if indeed it ever was. It has become a cliché to observe that some foreign student is performing poorly because he is "suffering from culture shock."

Such cultural orientation programs as are administered by universities, fellowship sponsoring agencies, professional societies, etc. are handicapped to the extent that participants cannot be "graded" on their lack of cultural understanding before these (usually brief) orientation programs are well under way. They likewise suffer from too little information that specifies which aspects of the new culture are not understood by the participants.

Reprinted by permission from *Language Learning*, 16 (1966), 183–196. The author is a member of the staff of the English Language Institute at the University of Michigan.

There exists, therefore, a clear need for test instruments and procedures which can supply reliable and valid measures of cultural understanding. As a stimulus to further attempts, as a guide for test construction, and because it is a by-product of an instrument which may soon be in use, Seelye's "Field Notes on Cross-Cultural Testing" is a welcome beginning.[1] And precisely because his article is a beginning (as Seelye emphasizes[2]), it is an invitation to another step. The purpose of this reply is twofold: to examine in some detail the direction of Seelye's beginning in order to ascertain the direction of a next step, and to anticipate the limitations of tests of cross-cultural understanding which would be produced by test writers continuing in that direction.

The purpose of cross-cultural testing which was implied above should foster the development of tests which are formally the same as foreign language tests. That is, the skills, the abilities and the knowledge to be tested are most relevant to communication. In language testing one is most concerned with whether the "linguistic stranger" can speak or write in such a manner that his intended meanings are understood by the members of the foreign language community, and whether he understands their intended meanings when he hears or reads what they have produced in their language. In cross-cultural testing one is concerned with whether the "cultural stranger" can behave (non-linguistically) in such a manner that his intended meanings are understood by members of the foreign culture community, and whether he understands their intended meanings when he observes their behavior or the products of their behavior. Obviously, cross-cultural testing is not restricted to directly observable behavior and behavioral products. It is perhaps equally important that the "cultural stranger" should understand the intended meanings of behavior which is verbally reported to him, and that the intended meanings of behavior which he reports are understood. This point is simply that a school teacher from Cleveland, for example, should not only be able to understand the intentions of two gentlemen whom she sees embracing on the platform of the Rome railway station, but should also understand if the incident is reported to her.

It should be pointed out that the purpose of Seelye's article was not to present a test description or a program for test construction, but to suggest some of the problems encountered during the preparation of cross-cultural tests. He succeeded remarkably well. After reading the paper no one could remain unaware of the amount of work involved in preparing such a test. Considerable effort is required in deciding what the content of the test should be, in writing items to reflect the decisions about content, in locating samples for pretesting

[1] H. Ned Seelye, "Field Notes on Cross-Cultural Testing," *Language Learning*, XVI, 1–2 (1966), 77–85.

[2] ". . . any conclusions insinuated in this paper should be regarded as tentative; here we are simply presenting field notes which might be helpful to those engaged in cross-cultural testing." *Ibid.*, p. 77.

items, in administering pretests, in analyzing pretest results, and in rewriting items and pretesting again. One can also appreciate the decisions which must be made about statistical criteria for acceptable items; the decision is necessary because no item will be answered one way by everyone who knows the target culture and another way by everyone who is naïve. One might wish that Seelye had written more about the intriguing problem of "cultural dialect" or "cultural style." Some of his examples of rejected items illustrate sex differences and differences according to the respondents' social class. Seelye also mentions age and urban or rural residence as factors which might affect responses on cross-cultural test items, but he does not address directly the central problem which these examples and factors imply—the problem of determining a "core" or "standard culture" shared by all members of a cultural community. It is certainly arguable that men and women, children and adults live in "separate worlds," that the peasant can never understand the ways of high society, and that a man from the country is always a "hick" when he comes to town. But the acceptance of such assumptions will not relieve one of discovering the "cultural dialect" in which rural, female, middle-class children (for example) communicate and interact with one another.

One might also wish that Seelye had been more explicit in telling why he wanted a cross-cultural test in the first place, in stating the nature of the information he hoped to derive from his test. A test which is wanted for ranking people who have lived in a new cultural community according to how much their preconceptions have changed will very likely differ from a test which is wanted for ranking people according to their abilities to use and interpret the patterns of the foreign culture[3] accurately and unambiguously. Seelye states only that he wants a test which will "determine approximately the level of cross-cultural awareness attained after residence in (a new cultural community)."[4] Despite this statement Seelye excludes certain items which would indicate cross-cultural awareness: those items which may accurately describe target culture patterns but which natives of that target culture do not recognize. He makes the aim of his test even more obscure by posing the rhetorical question, "Would (Americans) survive exposure to [the Guatemalan culture]?"[5] Because his testing aims are unclear, it is not possible to evaluate Seelye's item selection, test construction and validation procedures. There is no other sound basis for such evaluation. One may, however, assume the broadest possible aims for cross-

---

[3]The term, cultural pattern, is used here in the same sense as by Robert Lado in *Language Testing* (London: Longmans, 1961), pp. 275-289.

[4]Seelye, p. 77.

[5]*Ibid*, p. 78. Although this question was posed in a somewhat different context, it indicates that Seelye did have in mind a need for cross-cultural understanding which is consistent with (if not actually identical to) the need outlined in the first paragraphs above. Hence, one could conclude that he should accept the same testing purpose as that stated earlier in this paper.

cultural testing and note what procedures they would imply. Then it will become possible to determine which purposes may be satisfied by Seelye's procedures (insofar as they have been reported), and what different or additional procedures would have to be followed by someone who wishes to satisfy other aims.

Four aims of testing are generally recognized:

1. The test user wishes to determine how an individual would perform at present in a given universe of situations of which the test situation constitutes a sample.

2. The test user wishes to predict an individual's future performance (on the text or some external variable).

3. The test user wishes to estimate an individual's present status on some variable external to the test.

4. The test user wishes to infer the degree to which the individual possesses some trait or quality presumed to be reflected in the test performance.[6]

With respect to any one instrument these four aims are not mutually exclusive. That is, users may put the same test to each of these uses, and may have varying degrees of success according to their different purposes.

These relatively abstract statements of testing aims can be translated into aims for cross-cultural testing, and implied prescriptions for test construction can be deduced:

5. The test user wishes to determine how an individual would behave and what he would understand in a new culture by noting his understanding and behavior in a sample of situations from that culture. The test maker would collect a representative sample of situations to present to the individual so that the individual's understanding and behavior could be observed.

6. The test user wishes to estimate from a test score how well an individual will be able in the future to understand and behave appropriately in a target culture community. The test maker will assemble test items (of any sort) which he can demonstrate to predict such future understanding and behavior.

7. The test user wishes to estimate from a test score how well an individual is able at the time of testing to understand and behave appropriately in a target culture community. The test maker will assemble items which he can demonstrate to indicate such current understanding and behavior.

8. The test user believes that there is some trait or quality called "cultural awareness" (any other name will do) which underlies an individual's ability to communicate and interact in a foreign culture community, and he wishes to estimate the amount of this trait an individual possesses. The task of the test maker is especially complex; he must not only determine what the trait

[6]"Technical Recommendations for Psychological Tests and Diagnostic Techniques." Supplement to the *Psychological Bulletin*, LI, 2 (1954), p. 13.

called "cultural awareness" is, but must also demonstrate its relevance to effective communication and interaction.[7]

In three cases (5, 6, and 7 above), the test user is concerned with the ability of an individual to function effectively in a large universe of cultural situations. In the fourth case (8 above), the user is additionally interested in the trait which underlies, or is necessary to, that ability.

Neither Lado nor Seelye presents a theory of a trait or process underlying the ability to function in a foreign culture. They do not suggest, for example, that "rigidity" is a human trait which underlies this and other abilities, i.e., that the rigid personality cannot adapt to new cultural ways; and they do not suggest then developing tests of rigidity, which would include items with no apparent relevance to communicating through the use of foreign culture patterns.[8] Both Lado and Seelye seem to assume that, in the absence of such a theory of underlying traits or processes, the best place to look for test items is in the universe of situations one is ultimately (although not exclusively nor necessarily even predominantly) concerned with. This appears to be a most reasonable assumption to make.

Before describing the universe of situations—item sources—from which a cross-cultural test might sample, it is convenient to make one simplifying assumption; and it becomes necessary then to make at least one more. Without these assumptions it is necessary to include all cultural patterns in the universe of items. The first simplifying assumption is consistent with the view taken by Lado and Seelye, *viz.*, in some instances the "cultural stranger" will understand and behave correctly in the foreign culture community by virtue of similarities and identities between his own and the target cultures. But if this assumption about generalizations of cultural patterns is to reduce the universe of items (and, therefore, to be truly simplifying), it becomes necessary also to assume that the "cultural stranger" will not *learn* to do anything wrong or to misunderstand anything in the target culture.[9] The meaning of these assumptions can perhaps

[7] An example in a different domain may be useful here. Teachers are often interested in estimating the intelligence of their students because they believe that intelligence is one trait underlying academic achievement. They do not, however, think that intelligence is the same thing as academic achievement (or even of learning ability). They suppose instead that intelligence underlies many behavioral abilities, and that other traits (e.g., motivation, ego-strength, social adjustment, etc.) are significant to academic achievement. The psychologists who construct intelligence tests are constantly striving to refine their concept of intelligence, and at the same time they are obliged to demonstrate the relevance of intelligence for behavior—such as academic achievement.

[8] Such an apparently irrelevant item might be to require the examinees to recite their alphabet backwards in, say, five seconds. The item could be scored according to the number of letters which were recited in the correct reverse order within the time allowed.

[9] Arguments against making this assumption with respect to foreign language testing may be found in: J. A. Upshur, "Language Proficiency Testing and the Contrastive Analysis Dilemma," *Language Learning*, XII, 2 (1962), 123–127.

be best clarified by a hypothetical example which illustrates something which they would preclude. In both culture A and culture B (the target culture) it is customary first to present gentlemen to ladies when making introductions. In culture A gentlemen follow ladies through doors, and in culture B they precede them. The first simplifying assumption says that the pattern of introduction in the target culture need not be tested because it is identical in form to that of culture A but that the pattern of "who-goes-first" should be. The second simplifying assumption says that even if someone from culture A sees men preceding ladies in culture B, he will not generalize this to a concept of "men-and-women-are-treated-differently" which would lead him to alter his customary pattern of introductions—he could not change his native pattern and present ladies to gentlemen first.[10]

Because a cross-cultural test should provide information on an individual's ability both to understand the foreign cultural patterns and to behave so that his intended meanings are understood, a description of the universe of test items must include: 1) the set of observed behaviors (or behavioral products) to be understood, and 2) the set of behavioral patterns to be appropriately performed. In order to apply the simplifying assumptions it is necessary also that the description show which observed cultural patterns will be understood and which will be appropriately performed. The form of a description which satisfies these conditions (identifying the understanding and performance domains, and distinguishing between what must be and what need not be learned) can be shown.

The universe of test items is divided into two categories, the understanding and performance domains, as in Figure 1. The same patterns which must be understood are those which are used to communicate meaning. This is a necessary division because it cannot be taken for granted that an individual's understanding and performance of cultural behavior will be identical—just as it cannot be taken for granted that an individual will have the same difficulties in comprehension and production of foreign language behavior.

In order to apply the two simplifying assumptions, the formal description of the item universe must be extended. Figure 2 presents the subcategorization

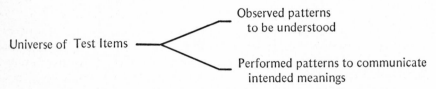

Figure 1. Universe of Items for Cross-Cultural Testing

[10]This assumption could be weaker than is stated here. It might be of the form: cultural mislearning is so infrequent and the results so inconsequential that it is an unimportant consideration in test construction.

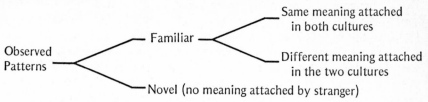

Figure 2. Subcategorization of Observed Cultural Behavior

of patterns which an individual will observe in the foreign culture and which he must understand. Figure 3 presents the subcategorization of the patterns an individual must perform appropriately in order to be understood.

"Familiar" patterns include not only those patterns which are so similar to his own that the cultural stranger would conclude that they are "just like we do it at home," but also those which are similar enough that most cultural strangers (from a single culture) would identify them with patterns of their own culture. "Novel" patterns are those which are different or ambiguous enough that cultural strangers cannot attach any meaning or would not agree upon which patterns of their own culture the observed patterns correspond to. There is probably no *a priori* way of telling whether any given behavior will seem "familiar" or "novel." It is more likely the case that this will have to be an empirical determination.

Figure 3. Subcategorization of Performed Behavior Patterns

Performed patterns with the same meaning in both cultures are those which would be appropriate in the foreign culture, i.e., the intended meanings of the cultural stranger would be communicated. Performed patterns with different meanings consist of patterns common to both the individual's native culture and the target culture, but for which each culture has a different meaning, and consists also of patterns from the native culture which are not interpretable by members of the foreign culture community. It is likely true that, similar to the case of novel observed patterns, there is no *a priori* way of determining what native patterns will prove uninterpretable to members of the target culture.

The two simplifying assumptions can now be applied to the description of the universe of cross-culture items. Observed patterns which are familiar to the cultural stranger and which have the same meanings in both cultures do not have to be tested; patterns performed by the cultural stranger which have the same meaning in both cultures do not have to be tested.[11]

Seelye has pointed out that Guatemalans are not always able to give accurate reports of cultural patterns. They might not be able to say what a particular pattern means or to say what pattern would be exhibited in a given situation. Presumably Seelye would agree that the Americans, for whom his test was written, share this inability; he would agree with Lado's general statement that "we are rather helpless to interpret ourselves accurately and to describe what we do."[12] This fact must be taken into account when preparing a cross-cultural test based upon people's reports. Seelye has taken this into account, and the results of the particular way in which he has chosen to handle the problem will be pointed out later.

The description of the universe of cross-cultural items can be extended to account for the inability of Guatemalans (G) and Americans (A) to give accurate reports of cultural meaning and behavior. Figure 4 shows the additional sub-categorization of target culture patterns which accounts for the fact that Guatemalans and Americans are sometimes able and sometimes unable to give accurate reports of the meanings of behavior. Figure 5 illustrates the ability or inability of Guatemalans and Americans to give accurate reports of what patterns are appropriate to communicate given intended meanings. According to this complete formal description there are eighteen classes of items in the cross-cultural item universe. For convenience of reference they are labeled: (A), (B), (C), . . ., (Q), (R). The simplifying assumptions provide that eight of these classes need not be tested: (A), (B), (C), (D), (K), (L), (M), and (N). Items from the other ten classes should be sampled if one takes the broadest purposes for cross-cultural testing. It should be noted at this point, however, that these classes are not of equal size, and that in actual test construction one should, *ceteris paribus*, select items to test from each class proportionally to class size.

In the construction of his test for Americans in Guatemala, Seelye began by trying to discover examples of cultural contrasts.[13] In that way he attempted to exclude from his test items which would be properly included in classes (A) - (D) and (K) - (N). The criterion which he adopts for a cultural contrast is, however, a Guatemalan pattern "which contrasts . . . to the pattern which Americans *recognize as their own*."[14] This criterion causes the invalid inclusion

---

[11] It should not be misinterpreted that this formal description accounts for differences in "form" and "meaning" but ignores differences in "distribution." The same overt behavior segment might be an item in more than one subcategory depending upon its larger context or upon the meaning intended by the performer in the context in which he finds himself.

[12] Lado, p. 278.

[13] Seelye, p. 78.

[14] Seelye, p. 77, emphasis added.

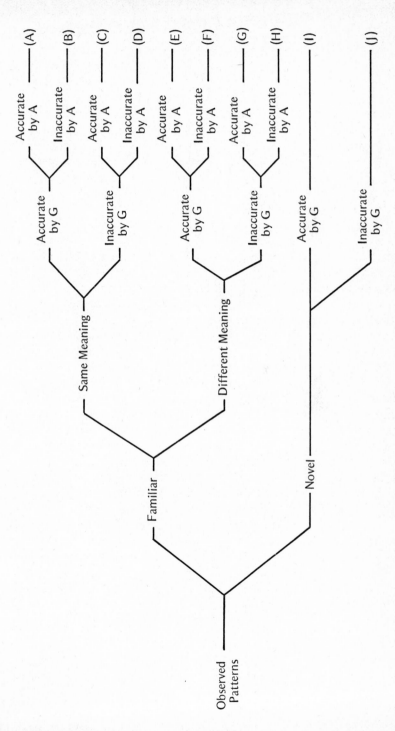

Figure 4. Description of Observed Pattern Domain for Guatemalan Culture Test Items

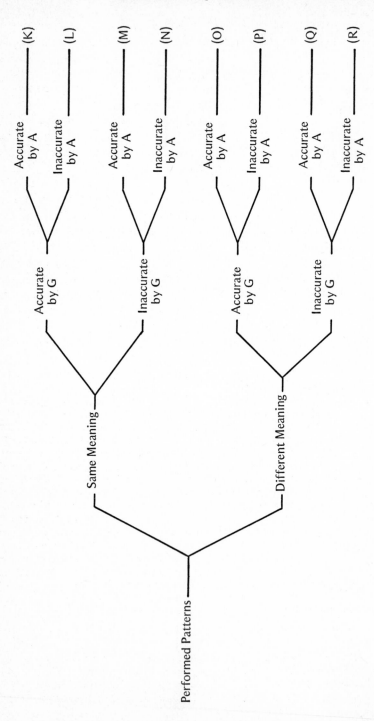

Figure 5. Description of Performed Pattern Domain for Guatemalan Culture Test

of the items of classes (B) and (L). It further causes the invalid exclusion of any items in the classes (F) and (P) for which the American "ideal" report coincides with the Guatemalan accurate report. Seelye further restricted the items which he would test by excluding those classes in which Guatemalans do not give accurate reports of meanings or appropriate behavior: the additional classes (G), (H), (J), (Q), and (R).[15] His resulting test includes all items in two of the eight classes which should have been excluded; it includes all of the items in only three of the ten classes which should have been included; it includes a portion of the items in two of the seven other classes which should have been included. The content of the test as compared with the theoretically ideal cross-culture test is shown in Table I.

It is now apparent that a cross-culture test constructed along the same lines as Seelye's has limited usefulness. Less than half of the desired item classes are sampled,[16] and almost half as many unwanted classes of items are sampled for inclusion in the test.[17] The test might in fact be quite useful for purposes 6 and 7 above. This cannot, however, be taken for granted; it must be demonstrated by comparing test scores with measures of the effectiveness of functioning in the foreign culture. And although such a test might be useful for these purposes, it is highly likely that a less restricted set of items would yield a more valid, and therefore more useful, test.

Seelye's paper described a number of problems encountered in cross-cultural

---

[15]The only reason he states for making this restriction is that it would be "ironic" for Americans to be able to report accurately items of Guatemalan culture which Guatemalans do not (p. 77). Whether or not irony is a sufficiently good reason for making such an exclusion, it is difficult to find anything ironic in such a state of affairs. It doesn't defy credulity or propriety to imagine that an American can learn the meaning of a Guatemalan pattern rather than its Guatemalan stereotype, and can behave in accordance with what he knows. Actually the Guatemalan knows the "real meaning" despite his stereotyped inventory response; otherwise he would not behave as he does behave, and it would be nonsense to talk about an "ideal" as different from a "real" meaning. The problem can be extrapolated to the field of foreign language testing, and one would have to conclude, for example, that if native speakers cannot accurately *describe* some fact of their language, it should not appear in a foreign language test. In an *ad hoc* "experiment," which is more illustrative than conclusive, four native speakers of English were asked how they could tell the difference between *can* and *can't* in speech. All answered that the presence of /t/ makes the difference. This was an obviously incorrect report, yet all can distinguish between "I can take it," and "I can't take it." It is also important for learners of English to be able to hear the difference. And it is not unthinkable that an English teacher would tell his students what to listen for. If Seelye's argument leads to any significant conclusion, it is probably that a different type of item is sometimes needed.

[16]Actually half (5) of the classes are sampled, but only a part of two of these five are sampled.

[17]In fact, there will also be included some items which properly belong in (M) and (N), classes which should not be included. As pointed out above, it is not always possible to predict when patterns of one culture will be generalized to patterns of another. Pretesting would not demonstrate that (M) and (N) items are not in fact items from (O) and (P).

Table 1. Makeup of American-Guatemalan Cross-cultural Test

Classes of items to be included	Classes of items to be excluded	Classes actually included	Classes included in part
E		E	
F			F
G			
H			
I		I	
J			
O		O	
P			P
Q			
R			
	A		
	B	B	
	C		
	D		
	K		
	L	L	
	M		
	N		

testing, and as a "case study" it has pointed towards other problems for which solutions should be found. One is the problem of testing methods; techniques which remove limitations upon the classes of cross-cultural items which can be tested must be developed. Seelye's paper illustrated what the limitations of the testing method which he chose may be. A second problem is that of determining (preferably by empirical means) whether the second simplifying assumption made by Seelye and Lado, and accepted in this paper, is indeed a valid one. If it should turn out not to be, the universe of cross-cultural items to be tested is radically altered. If, however, it proves valid, another problem arises—that of determining, for pairs of cultures, those patterns which are viewed by members of both cultures as the same. Another problem must be solved before it is possible to learn how well a cross-cultural test measures the ability of cultural strangers to function effectively in a foreign culture environment. This problem is to develop measures of non-linguistic communication and interaction. The final problem alluded to is that of developing a theory, which can be used by test writers, of the processes or traits underlying effective communication and interaction in a foreign language culture.

Seelye's paper raised a number of questions, and answered many of them. This paper has only raised more questions. Perhaps the next writer will supply some more answers.

Although several articles in earlier Parts have dealt with new and sometimes controversial changes and developments in accepted aspects of TESL, such as the application of transformational grammar, it seems appropriate to group in the last Part several papers about issues that are both relevant and new to teachers of English as a second language. All except the first relate to the general subject of bilingualism.

Stevick, in Article 12, referred to Bosco's psychological interpretation of TESL procedures as different modes, each subject to varying emphasis in the classroom. Here Bosco describes those modes in the setting of psychological theory, as they relate to the problem of getting students to actualize their language knowledge into functional behavior patterns.

The social psychologist has recently manifested his own interest in the language–learning field through study of the many effects of becoming a bilingual in various social situations. Lambert here reports several specific observations and studies of group behavior toward bilinguals and of the varying reactions of the bilinguals themselves to the social pressures upon them.

The bilingual student's reaction to group pressures may relate to his attitude toward his own group, toward a reference group he wants to enter, or toward his teacher and fellow-students. Spolsky discusses studies of this attitudinal effect upon language learning and then reports that a study of his own demonstrated the beneficial motivation provided by the student's desire to belong to the group speaking the target language.

The extraordinary attention which is currently being given to bilingual education, especially in the

United States and Canada, and the considerable and costly confusion about what is intended by the expression itself, make invaluable the meticulous typology developed by Mackey. Rather than imposing a definition as some current projects attempt to do, Mackey describes and classifies in descriptive detail the entire range of school situations and accompanying non-school situations in which two languages and two cultures come into conflict. Teachers may find it easier, however, to work with the simpler typology offered by Fishman and Lovas, who exemplify their four divisions by citing current programs. They, too, consider bilingual education of great value but likewise insist that societal information is imperative if a bilingual educational program is to be successful.

40

THE RELEVANCE OF RECENT PSYCHOLOGICAL STUDIES TO TESOL

FREDERICK J. BOSCO

What is meant by *the stimulus-free nature of language*?

What are the implications for language teaching of Bosco's statement (p. 370) that *a problem should be so structured that the significant features are brought into focus, and that non-significant elements are subordinated*? Give examples.

Inspect some foreign-language textbooks and try to identify samples of *enactive, iconic*, and *symbolic representations*.

In the same textbooks, determine the degree to which each of the six major functions defined by Jakobson (p. 379) is emphasized.

Take some instructional objective and develop a lesson to teach it following the steps suggested in Bosco's model (p. 382).

The problem of language acquisition has been the subject of increasing examination by linguists and psychologists alike. The task of assessing the relevance of recent psycholinguistic studies to the teaching of English to speakers of other languages (TESOL) is not an easy one in view of the necessarily restricted nature of experimental work and the vastly more complex problems confronting the classroom teacher. Nevertheless, it is important to reflect upon the growing body of psychological studies in order to come to a better understanding of what is entailed in a theory of second-language instruction.

This paper considers three recurring themes in psychological theory and research which bear on the pressing problems of classroom instruction. The relevance of these themes to TESOL is discussed, and concrete examples are offered. The paper concludes with suggestions for the teaching of a given aspect of grammatical structure in the form of a schema in which there is a convergence of the multiple factors considered earlier in the discussion.

Reprinted by permission from the *TESOL Quarterly*, 4 (March, 1970), 73–88. The author is assistant professor of linguistics and Italian at Georgetown University.

The first theme concerns the classic problem of transfer—the manner in which knowledge gained in one context is transferred to others. The student's exposure to formal language training is necessarily limited. The problem of making this limited exposure productive in situations encountered outside the classroom is critically important. The matter can be put in somewhat different terms. The language user is required to produce sentences in a more or less logical sequence in response to multiple demands and different social settings. The specific sentences which a speaker needs in any given situation cannot be anticipated. Instructional strategies cannot therefore limit themselves to matching specific linguistic responses to specific sets of stimuli. Rather, serious attention must be given to the "creative aspect of language use," that is, to the stimulus-free nature of language and to the virtually limitless possibilities of expression (Chomsky, 1966, 3–31). The speaker's internalized system of rules enables him to produce and understand sentences that he has not previously encountered. These new utterences are "similar to those previously produced or encountered only in that they are formed by the same grammar, the same internalized system of rules" (Chomsky and Halle, 1968, 3). The notion of transfer is therefore crucial to any theory of language acquisition. It is widely held by psychologists and educators alike that the student's understanding of the basic principles underlying a discipline is central to the problem of transfer and that transfer can be maximized by bringing out the underlying structure and generative propositions of a field of knowledge.

The second theme concerns the mode of representation of the subject matter, the way in which the subject matter is exposed to the learner. The student's perception of the critical elements of a problem is determined in large measure by the way in which the problem is displayed. Different facets of a problem are emphasized by different representations. Specific surface features of language, for example, can be displayed via iconic, or configural, representation while operations and internal relationships may require more abstract modes of representation. Cognitive theorists, particularly those of the Gestalt school, stress the importance of perception in learning, and consider the perceptual features according to which a problem is displayed to be an important condition of learning (Hilgard and Bower, 1966, 563). Therefore, a problem should be so structured that the significant features are brought into focus, and that non-significant elements are subordinated.

The third theme has to do with the establishment of experience-grounded and goal-directed learning tasks which focus on language from the standpoint of its essential functions. Language serves many purposes. It functions to maintain contact, to command, to describe, to point things out, and to express the internal feelings of a speaker; and it can itself become the focal point of discourse as, for example, in discussions of dialectal variations and grammaticality. Language programs must take into account the many concrete functions served by speech as well as the creative aspect of language use. [See also Stevick, article 12 of this collection. Eds.]

It is well at this point to ask precisely what the teaching of English to speakers of other languages entails. I should like to suggest that there are various tasks involved, each requiring different strategies.

I. Instruction in the language.

   A. Association of linguistic units with the cultural matrix in which they function. To initiate the process of expression, the learner requires raw material in the form of lexicon, basic sentences, and short verbal exchanges. These units must be learned in association with the cultural matrix in which they function if any degree of understanding and expression is to be achieved. The student can acquire the basic language data and associations in any number of ways, such as the imitation of models, the memorization of basic sentences and short dialogues, and the building of response patterns to verbal and situational stimuli.

   B. Internalization of the grammar of the language, the rules of competence. The student must master the rules that determine sound-meaning connections and characterize the structure of the language. Competence is achieved by way of performance. However, performance should not be blind and peripheral in its reference, but rational and motivated. Performance must be grounded on understanding if it is to build competence.

   C. Internalization of the relationships between language and its concrete functions. This task has to do with mastery of the basic functions of language for the purpose of effective operation in the language community. Communication is fundamentally directed toward the achievement of goals. It is the emphasis on communicative goals which characterizes this aspect of language instruction. Instructional strategies should treat language in all the variety of its functions.

II. Orientation into the life patterns of the members of the speech community with whom one is to deal.

   Language has a social, cultural, and historical dimension. If a person is to function effectively in a speech community, he must be acquainted with the life style of the members of the community. Such an orientation includes an understanding of what the speakers consider to be important and what they talk about.

TRANSFER OF LEARNING

Transfer of learning occurs when principles, skills, and patterns of experience gained in one situation are applied or transposed to new situations which share perceptual features with it. Psychologists speak of two kinds of transfer: specific and non-specific. Specific transfer refers to the application of skills from one task to another, while non-specific transfer refers not to the transfer of specific skills, but rather to the extension of general principles, methods of operation, and patterns of relationships from one situation to another. It involves the recognition that a given problem represents a specific instance of a more general class of problems that one has already encountered. A further distinction is made between positive and negative transfer. Positive transfer is achieved when learning in one situation favorably influences learning in subsequent situations. One might expect, for example, some positive transfer from the skill of reading Italian to that of reading Spanish. Negative transfer arises when learning acquired in one context has a detrimental effect on subsequent learning. Interference phenomena in language acquisition attest to the reality of negative transfer. For example, the learner gives evidence of negative transfer when he produces the utterance "Can you tell me where does Captain Walsh live?" based on the rules underlying the question "Where does Captain Walsh live?"

There has been extensive experimental work on the problem of transfer, particularly in the area of perceptual-motor skills and verbal learning. I shall not attempt to survey the literature, but only to note certain general trends. Conditioning theorists prefer to speak of generalization or induction rather than of transfer. Skinner (1957) uses the term *induction* to refer to the tendency for stimuli with similar properties to arouse similar behavior. Transfer is explained in terms of elements in the new situation which are "identical" with elements in the original situation. Cognitive theories expect a high degree of transfer in those situations in which the essential elements and patterns of relationship inherent in the situation are open to the inspection of the learner. The gestalt concept of transposition, for example, is based on the notion that the learner transfers patterns of dynamic relationships from one situation to another. Tolman (1932), whose "purposive behaviorism" is at one and the same time gestalt and behaviorist, considers transfer the result of the carry-over of a sign-gestalt from one context to another. The animal in a maze builds up a "cognitive map" of the maze by learning the significance of signs along the route, not by the building of motor habits. Bruner (1960) suggests that the acquisition of structure, rather than the mastery of facts and techniques, is central to the problem of transfer. In his view, the unifying concepts and ideas of a subject-matter field should receive priority in curriculum development to assure form and continuity to the program. In order to foster the transfer of general concepts, Bruner favors a *spiral* curriculum. Spiraling involves designing the instructional program in such a way that the basic principles and concepts underlying the subject matter are revisited at regular intervals, each time in more elaborate and complex forms. Thus, the systems of knowledge are constantly strengthened and deepened by a repeated return to the basic concepts of the systems. This emphasis on the structure of knowledge also appears in the work of Gagné (1965), whose hierarchical model of learning encompasses signal learning, stimulus-response learning, chaining, verbal association, multiple discrimination, concept learning, principle learning, and problem solving. Stephens (1960) suggests that for transfer to be maximized the feature to be transferred should be brought into focus, that meaningful generalizations should be developed, and that a variety of experiences should be provided to develop the generalizations that are to be transferred.

The problem of establishing the conditions for effective transfer of learning in an ESOL program should not be ignored. A number of strategies can be developed to maximize positive transfer and to minimize negative transfer. Negative transfer can be reduced in the initial stages of instruction by making available to the learner a significant amount of language without recourse to translation and analysis. In this way, a wide range of expression can be developed in a "molar," or functional, manner with transfer playing a minor role. Following the initial stages, the student can be introduced systematically to the rules of sentence formation. At this point, it is imperative that the underlying rules of sentence formation be converted into patterns of experience. Another strategy to promote positive transfer is the spiraling of the instructional program to assure that the major grammatical processes and integrative patterns are revisited at regular intervals.

Specific tasks designed to promote transfer should be utilized. Such tasks can be formulated in such a way that the learner is called upon to use familiar material in a new way. Once the learner has successfully carried out a series of introductory tasks to assure familiarization with the relevant grammatical features, he is given a series of transfer tasks in which he must apply the principles to new situations. To illustrate, let us assume that the student has been introduced to the rule that frequency words like *usually*, *always*, etc., normally precede verbs like *drive*, *feel*, etc., but follow *is* and other auxiliaries such as *can*, *might*, etc. To foster transfer, one might pose a series of questions which elicit meaningful responses, such as:

How do you usually feel after a hard day?
  I'm usually tired.
What do you usually do when you are hungry?
  I usually eat.
What do you usually do after your 9:00 class?
  I usually go to the '89 for coffee.

In an experiment concerning the development of language skill via pattern drills, Oller and Obrecht (1968) conclude that the effectiveness of a drill is increased if the language of the drill is related to communicative activity. Kolers (1968) and his assistants at M.I.T. and at the Center for Cognitive Studies at Harvard have reported on the series of experiments conducted with bilingual subjects concerning the acquisition, storage, and retrieval of information. Their studies demonstrate the importance of meaning in the storage of words. The work of Oller and Obrecht, as well as that of Kolers and his assistants, suggests that for the acquisition and storage of linguistic units, an informative context is vital.

How can an informative content be maintained in language drill without obscuring the critical features of grammatical structure? The answer to this question lies in utilizing tasks of a transfer type which embody an informative and cultural content, but which are carefully designed to reinforce specific grammatical features. To illustrate, the following contexts, though thematically diverse, can prompt structurally similar sets of sentences:

Context A: Changes of States

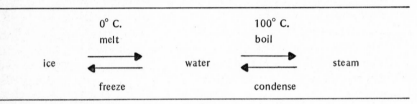

Water freezes at 0° Centigrade.
The freezing point of water is 0° Centigrade.
At what temperature does water freeze?
What is the freezing point of water? etc.

Context B: Cruising Altitude

Boeing 707	cruise	30,000 to 40,000 ft.

The Boeing 707 cruises at a typical altitude of thirty to forty thousand feet.
The typical cruising altitude of the Boeing 707 is thirty to forty thousand feet.
At what altitude does the Boeing 707 typically cruise?
What is the typical cruising altitude of the Boeing 707?

Other strategies can be utilized to reinforce grammatical structures while providing meaningful choices. Freedom of expression cannot be attained unless scope is allowed for choice and for personal comment. Consider the following examples, which permit some measure of choice and comment:

I can't decide whether to go skiing this weekend or spend the time at home. What do you think?
(I think you should go skiing. It'll do you good to get away for the weekend.)
I can't decide whether to take political science or economics next semester. What do you suggest?
(I suggest that you take political science. You should learn more about the American system of government.)

In summary, the major point that has been developed in this paper thus far is that transfer depends in large measure on the perception and generalization of the principles and relationships inherent in the subject-matter field that one is studying. The discussion now turns to the question of precisely how this understanding can be developed, how the subject matter can be represented in order to assist the learner in perceiving and understanding relevant principles and relationships.

MODES OF REPRESENTATION

In a number of research projects under way in the instructional areas of mathematics, natural and social sciences, reading, and foreign languages, particular attention is being given to the way of thinking which characterizes the subject-matter fields. The way of thinking which underlies a discipline involves the particular set of assumptions, generative propositions, and typical problems of the special field.[1] The problem of finding ways of expressing the ideas which are central to a discipline is sometimes referred to as the "psychology of a subject matter." The question of the psychology of a subject matter is of great importance in instruction. Specifically, it is the question of how the underlying ideas and generative rules which give form and unity to a discipline can be represented to fit the developmental level and needs of the learner; or again, how the specialized subject fields can be converted to a form suitable to the learner.

In a paper delivered to the American Psychological Association in 1964, Bruner outlined the means or instrumentalities which lead to cognitive development. These instrumentalities are described as modes of internal representation and are called enactive, iconic, and symbolic representation. Enactive refers to psychomotor response patterns, iconic to visual images, and symbolic to logical propositions and internalized language. It is interesting to note that enactive, iconic, and symbolic representation are manifested in that order in the developing child. Bruner develops these ideas in greater detail in *Toward a Theory of Instruction*, in which he states that the "problem of finding embodiments of ideas in enactive, iconic, and symbolic modes is central to the 'psychology of a subject matter' " (Bruner, 1966, 155).

The first type of representation, enactive representation, depends on action. It is based on the learning of response patterns and forms of habituation. The following concrete example will serve to illustrate this. In making the change from a tricycle to a bicycle, a child faces a number of new problems, among which is that of keeping his balance. After several trials and some injury, the youngster generally learns to maneuver the bicycle successfully, and maintain his balance while moving forward. Should he start falling to the right, he turns the handlebars to the right in order to deflect the course of the bicycle along a curve to the right. This throws him out of balance to the left, which he counteracts by turning the handlebars to the left. He continues to maintain

---

[1] One such project, known as Project Literacy, coordinates research in the area of the acquisition of reading skills. The project is directed by Dr. Harry Levin of Cornell University.

his balance by thus adjusting the curvature of the bicycle's path (Polanyi, 1958, 49, 50). The child "learns" the relevant principles via experience. He feels his way to success. That is, he achieves success by following certain procedures, though he may not be explicitly aware of the procedures.

Audiolingual strategies of instruction have long stressed the importance of enactive representation. The emphasis on active practice and the building of verbal response patterns to situational and verbal cues has support from contemporary learning theories, especially of the behaviorist type. There is, however, some disagreement among theorists as to the relative merits of drill and explanation in second language instruction. It is the classic problem of "doing" versus "understanding." While the two can be distinguished, they need not be opposed. Performance is an index of competence. It is only by observing the student's performance that one can assess his level of understanding. The need for understanding, then, does not suggest a de-emphasizing of drill in second language instruction in favor of explanation; rather, it shows the necessity of finding types of exercises which give the student an intelligent control of the language. It leads to such questions as what types of exercises are the most productive in language instruction, what types of exercises enable the student to achieve control of the underlying structure of the language, and what types of exercises lead to understanding.

Iconic representation has to do with perceptual organization. This mode of representation makes use of diagrammatic devices, summary images, and graphics. A thing may be represented in a configurative sense, in which there is an inherent correspondence between the representation and the thing itself (Furth, 1968, 144). For example, the map of a city represents the layout of the city; an architect's blueprint of a house represents the configuration of the house; and so on. The map and the blueprint are mediating instruments which represent the thing itself. Configurative representations can be utilized in instruction to highlight relevant semantic, syntactic, and phonological features of language. Spatial relationships, for example, can be brought out by means of line drawings:

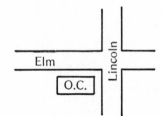

Where is the Officer's Club?
It's at Elm and Lincoln.

Grammatical features, particularly those relating to linear order, concord, and the like, can be displayed by means of spacing, arrows, and columns. In the following illustration of question patterns, grammatically similar words are arranged in columns:

The Bell X-1 Research Airplane[2]
    Designed and constructed: 1944–1946
    Purpose: research on problems of transonic and supersonic flight
    First piloted flight: October 14, 1947
    Pilot: Captain Charles Yeager
    Results of flight: demonstrated feasibility of piloted supersonic flight
    Number of X-1 aircraft originally constructed: three

wh-word	*aux.*	*subject*	*verb*	
When	did	the first piloted flight	take place?	
What	did	the flight	demonstrate?	
Where	can	I	get	more data?
When	will	we	see	the flight plans?
When	was	the aircraft	designed?	
When	was	the first supersonic piloted flight?		

			aux	*verb*	
		Who	was		at the controls?
		How many X-1 planes	were	constructed?	

It should be noted that in the above display of question patterns, there is a continuity of theme. The understanding of a situation is important in the acquisition of a second language and critical to the proper use of the patterns.

The third mode or instrumentality is that of symbolic representation. A thing can be represented in a broad significative sense. For example, the letter *S* may be used to represent any sentence of English. Unlike the example of the map, the symbol *S* has no inherent configurative correspondence with the thing for which it stands.

Let us consider certain aspects of relative-clause structures in English and Italian via symbolic representation to illustrate this mode of representation. A relative clause derives from an embedded sentence. These are symbolized in Figure 1 on the following page.

The utterances "paintings which are well-known" and "quadri che sono famosi" are generated by the application of the following rules:

1. $NP_1 \longrightarrow \phi$, where $NP_1 = NP$, that is, where the embedded noun phrase is identical to the noun phrase of the matrix sentence.
2. Insert Relative between NP and VP_1
3. $REL \longrightarrow \begin{Bmatrix} \text{which} \\ \text{che} \end{Bmatrix}$

---

[2]The data are taken from E. Seckel, *Stability and Control of Airplanes and Helicopters* (New York: Academic Press, 1964), 443.

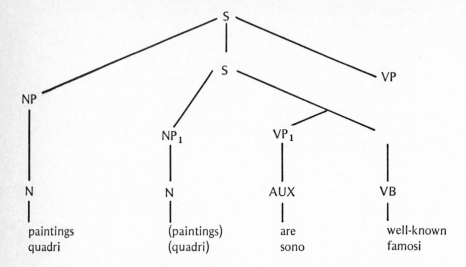

Figure 1. Relative-clause structures in English and Italian

For either language, this structure can be the input for further transformations. Both English and Italian have a transformation that reduces the relative
clause to a noun-verbal construction (Figure 2):

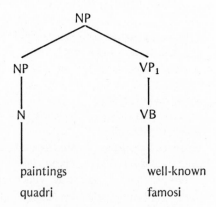

Figure 2. Transformation

Contrasting sharply with Italian is the English requirement of a final transformation affecting the word order in the noun-verbal construction, yielding
well-known paintings. Except for a few adjectives of high frequency, this further
transformation is generally blocked in Italian.

Let us consider another example of symbolic representation in which lines
are used to represent time relationships.

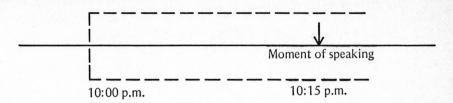

10:00 p.m.   10:15 p.m.

The above representation can be used to bring out the time relationship inherent in the sentences: "How long have you been waiting for the bus?" "I've been waiting for fifteen minutes."

The neglect of any one mode of representation for the adult learner of language impedes the instructional process. Enactive representation remains the principal avenue of instruction. Nonetheless, language practice must be firmly grounded on understanding. This understanding can be mediated most directly by iconic and symbolic representation. It is essential in the teaching of English to utilize multiple embodiments of language phenomena via enactive, iconic, and symbolic representation. Furthermore, the mode of representation should be adjusted to fit the developmental level of the learner. Younger students benefit most from both enactive and iconic representation; adults require more abstract modes of representation as well as enactive and iconic representation.

INTERNALIZATION OF THE RELATIONSHIP
BETWEEN LANGUAGE AND ITS FUNCTIONS

The third theme concerns the establishment of meaningful, experience-grounded learning tasks which respond to the basic functions of language. Two factors are important in giving direction to learning: the establishment of goals and the utilization of learning tasks which are relevant to the goals. For a learning task to have direction, the objectives must be anticipated in some fashion. The establishment of small, meaningful communication goals for each task helps provide the learner with the needed motivation for continued exploration and learning.

There is considerable evidence to support the thesis that a knowledge of expected results promotes learning. In reporting some studies of pilot training, Fitts (1962) indicates that the understanding of flight problems via knowledge of results and appropriate cognitive expectancy had a dramatic effect on promoting skill development. Tolman (1959) emphasizes that effective performance is motivated by cognitive expectancy.

It will be useful here to examine precisely what the essential functions of language are toward which instructional tasks should be directed. Communication is fundamentally directed toward the achievement of goals. Speech serves many purposes, pursues many ends. Roman Jakobson (1960) distinguishes six major functions of language: referential, emotive, conative, phatic, poetic, and metalingual. These functions are derived from the constitutive factors involved in discourse. The speech act consists, in its essentials, of an addresser, an addressee, a contact, a message, a context, and a code. The addresser directs a message to the addressee. The message requires a context or referent to which the message refers; a linguistic code, shared by the addresser and the addressee; and a contact, a physical channel and psychological connection between the addresser and the addressee.

Jakobson views each of the six factors as accounting for a different function of language. Verbal messages, however, seldom fulfill only a single function. Each message has a set of functions and the verbal structure of the message is determined primarily by its predominant function.

The emotive function, focused on the addresser, has as its object the expression of the speaker's attitude toward what he is saying. The emotive or expressive stratum in language is represented most directly by interjections, although phonological, lexical, and other grammatical devices are utilized for expressive purposes. Such utterances as "Oh hell, the flight plans have changed—" and "Damn, it looks like rain!" exemplify the emotive function. The conative function, focused on the addressee, seeks to evoke behavior on his part. It finds its best expression in vocatives and imperatives, such as "Captain, get your crew together!" and "Call S-1 for your final orders!" The referential or "denotative" function, oriented toward the context, is the most pervasive function. It concerns the manner in which the language identifies or points to things. "This is the flight plan." and "Captain Walsh returned to New York on a TWA flight." are examples of the referential function. Certain messages serve to establish, prolong or to discontinue communication. Jakobson employs Malinowski's term "phatic" to label this function of language, focused on the contact. This psychological set toward contact is illustrated by the expression "Hello, can you hear me?" uttered over a telephone to get attention and to check the proper functioning of the channel. Formulas spoken at the outset of a dialogue or to prolong a dialogue are profuse. The expression "Well . . .", for example, is a common device to sustain communication. Whenever the addresser or the addressee focus their attention on the linguistic code as such, discourse performs a metalingual function. The expressions "Do you understand what I mean?" and "Will you define that term?" concern information about the lexical code of English; consequently, their function is metalingual. Finally the poetic function is a turning to the message for its own sake; that is, to the sign aspect of the message. Though the poetic function is a determining function of poetry, it enters in a subsidiary fashion in normal discourse.

In the context of teaching English to speakers of other languages, it is imperative that the instructor focus on the relationship between linguistic structure and the multiple functions which it serves, and that instruction seek to simulate concrete communication situations in order to emphasize the functioning aspects of language. One illustration may serve to demonstrate the use of precise communication problems in instruction—problems which are goal-oriented and which highlight the functional aspects of language. The problem of how things are identified in English is posed. The student is shown a series of pictures of various types of aircraft and given the following information:

Aircraft	Purpose
Grumman AO-1 "Mohawk"	tactical observations and surveillance
Bell X-1 Research Airplane	research on transonic and supersonic flight
Sikorsky S-58 Helicopter	personnel and cargo transportation service

The student is asked to formulate statements on the model of:

This is a Grumman AO-1 Mohawk turboprop. It was designed for tactical observation and surveillance.

This is the Bell X-1 Research Airplane. It was designed for research on transonic and supersonic flight.

A SCHEMA FOR TEACHING A POINT OF GRAMMAR

To recapitulate, I have suggested that instructional strategists concern themselves with the problem of maximizing positive transfer, of representing language in all its modes, and of stressing the purposive character of language behavior. In considering the design of an instructional program which is sensitive to these aims, I should like to propose the following schema for the teaching of a given point of language structure. The process can be mapped out in successive stages, beginning with the initial presentation of a point and concluding with its mapping into a cohesive system.

As the first stage unfolds, the syntactic pattern is brought into focus by means of contrasting examples, syntactic analogies, problem solving, explanations, and so on. Through such devices, the learner is made aware of the critical features of the pattern—semantic, syntactic, and phonological. Emphasis throughout is on the *critical* features.

The critical features of a problem are those which identify it and serve to distinguish it from other problems. Since the learner is already in possession of complex skills, "critical" applies primarily to those aspects of a new skill which are different from, or in contrast to, the total set of skill-features already in his possession. It would be inefficient to concentrate learning efforts on those features of a skill which are not critical, that is, those which do not contrast in some way with the learner's already existing total set of skill-features. For example, a person who can ride a bicycle and who is learning to drive a car does not need to be told that the direction of the car must be guided, that he must apply the brakes if he is to stop, and that he must stop when there is an obstacle in his direct line of travel, or that he must watch where he is heading. All these features have been acquired in the skill of bicycle riding. For the bicycle rider, the contrasting or critical features of driving a car are steering

Stage	Purpose	Typical Procedures
1. Focusing on the linguistic feature in question and developing appropriate generalizations	–to develop an awareness of the problem –to develop an understanding of underlying principles	–Iconic and symbolic representation (syntactic analogies and contrast, problem solving, etc.)
2. Guiding language performance	–to familiarize the learner with relevant lexicon, sound units, etc. –to crystalize psychomotor response patterns –to guide the internalization of the rules of the language	–Enactive representation (dialogue development, pattern drills, etc.)
3. Developing communicative skill	–to train the learner to function in diverse communicative situations –to convert abstract principles into patterns of experience	–Enactive, iconic, and symbolic representation (transfer-type tasks, role-playing, specific communication problems, etc.)
4. Relating the point to previously taught points	–to map out the relevant systems of the language and to show interrelationships –to develop the basis for evaluation of performance –to give cohesiveness to the program via general orientation schemata –to develop more generalized patterns of experience	–Iconic, symbolic, and enactive representation ("testing" procedures which develop the learner's ability to handle a variety of communication problems, etc.)

with a wheel instead of with handlebars, controlling a great deal more power and potential speed, and so on.

The second stage in the instructional schema is concerned with the shaping of psychomotor responses via the imitation of fixed models and other restricted language experiences. The major instrumentality used at this stage is that of enactive representation, that is, the habituation of motor response patterns and the shaping of "grooves of expression." The student is trained to seek out the relevant mechanisms, to respond to them, and to use them accurately and consistently.

The third stage highlights the communicative aspects of the point in question. It involves the simulation of concrete communication situations and the articulation of precise functional goals toward which the learner is oriented. Emphasis at this level of instruction is not on the molecular character of the structure, but rather on its "molar" or "functional" aspects. There is an increasing internalization of the point in question as the learner begins to experience the multiple possibilities of the language structure to meet his specific communication needs.

In the fourth stage, the syntactic pattern is related to points which have been taken up previously. There is an enlargement of focus from specific, restricted points (molecular perceptions) to more comprehensive, integrating patterns (molar perceptions). The learner is confronted with schemata with a more general orientation which serve as a guide in subsequent performance. Thus a piecemeal approach to language structure is avoided in favor of one which stresses the integrative and generative aspects of language. This final stage assures the learner of a constantly more comprehensive understanding of the ways in which sentences are built.

The model outlined above is recursive in nature in that each point reappears regularly in contrast to other points. The first and fourth stages are designed to develop cognitive awareness of the point in question. The fourth stage is expressly designed to provide cognitive feedback. The third stage stresses divergent solutions to problems; that is, the learner is put in the position of creating novel sentences according to the demands of the situation and his own intentions. In essence, every point is embedded in every other point to assure spiraling and unity.

Instruction at its best has a quality of reciprocity, involving a response to the learner and his situation and the participation in a common enterprise toward clearly established objectives. Tasks of a routine nature stifle curiosity and the will to learn. Instruction is vitalized not simply by involving the student in activity or relating everything to the familiar; but rather, by initiating the process of dialogue. The language classroom should be a place in which there is genuine concern for expression and dialogue. Bruner (1966) underlines the importance of reciprocity in the following passage:

> I would like to suggest that what the teacher must be, to be an effective competence model, is a day-to-day working model with whom to interact. It is not so much that the teacher provides a model to *imitate*. Rather, it is that the teacher can become a part of the student's internal dialogue—somebody whose respect he wants, someone whose standards he wishes to make his own. It is like becoming a speaker of a language one shares with somebody. The language of that interaction becomes a part of oneself, and the standards of style and clarity that one adopts for that interaction become a part of one's own standards (124).

In short, what I have suggested throughout this paper is that the student has to know what he is doing at every stage in the instructional process and that he has to imagine that what he is doing is worth doing. Furthermore, the learner must be regarded as a center of consciousness and feeling, and not as a machine to be programmed.

REFERENCES

Bruner, J. S. *The Process of Education*. Cambridge: Harvard University Press, 1960.

Bruner, J. S. "The Course of Cognitive Growth." *American Psychologist*, 19 (1964), 1–15.

Bruner, J. S. *Toward a Theory of Instruction*. Cambridge: Harvard University Press, 1966.

Chomsky, N. *Cartesian Linguistics*. New York: Harper and Row, 1966.

Chomsky, N. and M. Halle. *The Sound Pattern of English*. New York: Harper & Row, 1968.

Fitts, P. M. "Factors in Complex Skill Training." In R. Glaser (ed.) *Training Research and Education*, pp. 177–197. Pittsburgh: University of Pittsburgh Press, 1962.

Furth, H. G. "Piaget's Theory of Knowledge: The Nature of Representation and Interiorization," *Psychological Review*, 75, 2 (1968), 143–154.

Gagné, R. M. *The Conditions of Learning*. New York: Holt, Rinehart and Winston, 1965.

Hilgard, E. R. and G. H. Bower. *Theories of Learning*. New York: Appleton-Century-Crofts, 1966.

Jakobson, R. "Linguistics and Poetics." In T. A. Sebeok (ed.) *Style in Language*, pp. 350–374. New York: John Wiley & Sons, 1960.

Kolers, P. A. "Bilingualism and Information Theory." *Scientific American*, 218 (March, 1968), 78–86.

Oller, J. W. and D. H. Obrecht. "Pattern Drill and Communicative Activity: A Psycholinguistic Experiment." *IRAL*, VI, 2 (1968), 165–174.

Polanyi, M. *Personal Knowledge, Towards a Post-Critical Philosophy*. Chicago: University of Chicago Press, 1958.

Seckel, E. *Stability and Control of Airplanes and Helicopters*. New York: Academic Press, 1964.

Skinner, B. F. *Verbal Behavior*. New York: Appleton-Century-Crofts, 1957.

Stephens, J. M. "Transfer of Learning." In C. W. Harris and M. R. Liba (eds.) *Encyclopedia of Educational Research*, pp. 1535–1543. New York: Macmillan, 1960.

Tolman, E. C. *Purposive Behavior in Animals and Man*. New York: Appleton-Century-Crofts, 1932. (Reprinted, University of California Press, 1949).

Tolman, E. C. "Principles of Purposive Behavior." In S. Koch (ed.) *Psychology: A Study of a Science*, Vol. 2. *General Systematic Formulations, Learning and Special Processes*, pp. 92–157. New York: McGraw-Hill, 1959.

Are there two groups with whom you are acquainted
that would be appropriate subjects for the *matched-guise* technique described by Lambert? For what
reasons might you wish to use this technique? What
human and material resources would be required to
carry out such a study?

Lambert reports that a student's degree of *integrative
orientation* toward a particular cultural group may reflect his parents' attitudes. What are other possible
determiners of a student's attitudes?

Are there inherent intellectual disadvantages in being
a bilingual?

Other contributions in this series have drawn attention to various aspects of
bilingualism, each of great importance for behavioral scientists. For instance, we
have been introduced to the psychologist's interest in the bilingual switching
process with its attendant mental and neurological implications, and his interest
in the development of bilingual skill; to the linguist's interest in the bilingual's
competence with his two linguistic systems and the way the systems interact;
and to the social anthropologist's concern with the socio-cultural settings of bilingualism and the role expectations involved. The purpose of the present paper
is to extend and integrate certain of these interests by approaching bilingualism
from a social-psychological perspective, one characterized not only by its interest
in the reactions of the bilingual as an individual but also by the attention given
to the social influences that affect the bilingual's behavior and to the social
repercussions that follow from his behavior. From this perspective, a process
such as language switching takes on a broader significance when its likely social
and psychological consequences are contemplated, as, for example, when a
language switch brings into play contrasting sets of stereotyped images of
people who habitually use each of the languages involved in the switch. Similarly, the development of bilingual skill very likely involves something more
than a special set of aptitudes because one would expect that various social
attitudes and motifs are intimately involved in learning a foreign language.
Furthermore, the whole process of becoming bilingual can be expected to in-

Reprinted by permission from the *Journal of Social Issues*, 23 (April, 1967), 91–109. The
author is professor of psychology at McGill University.

volve major conflicts of values and allegiances, and bilinguals could make various types of adjustments to the bicultural demands made on them. It is to these matters that I would like to direct attention.

LINGUISTIC STYLE AND INTERGROUP IMPRESSIONS

What are some of the social psychological consequences of language switching? Certain bilinguals have an amazing capacity to pass smoothly and automatically from one linguistic community to another as they change languages of discourse or as they turn from one conversational group to another at multilingual gatherings. The capacity is something more than Charles Boyer's ability to switch from Franco-American speech to Continental-style French when he turns from the eyes of a woman to those of a waiter who wants to know if the wine is of the expected vintage. In a sense, Boyer seems to be always almost speaking French. Nor is it the tourist guide's ability to use different languages to explain certain events in different languages. In most cases they are not fluent enough to pass and even when their command is good, their recitals seem to be memorized. Here is an example of what I do mean: a friend of mine, the American linguist, John Martin, is so talented in his command of various regional dialects of Spanish, I am told, that he can fool most Puerto Ricans into taking him for a Puerto Rican and most Colombians into taking him for a native of Bogota. His skill can be disturbing to the natives in these different settings because he is a potential linguistic spy in the sense that he can get along too well with the intimacies and subtleties of their dialects.

The social psychologist wants to know how this degree of bilingual skill is developed, what reactions a man like Martin has as he switches languages, and what social effects the switching initiates—not only the suspicion or respect generated by an unexpected switch but also the intricate role adjustments that usually accompany such changes. Research has not yet gone far enough to answer satisfactorily all the questions the social psychologist might ask, but a start has been made, and judging from the general confidence of psycho-linguists and sociolinguists, comprehensive answers to such questions can be expected in a short time.

I will draw on work conducted by a rotating group of students and myself at McGill University in Montreal, a fascinating city where two major ethnic-linguistic groups are constantly struggling to maintain their separate identities and where bilinguals as skilled as John Martin are not at all uncommon. Two incidents will provide an appropriate introduction to our work. One involves a bus ride where I was seated behind two English–Canadian ladies and in front of two French–Canadian ladies as the bus moved through an English-Canadian region of the city. My attention was suddenly drawn to the conversation in front wherein one lady said something like: "If I couldn't speak English I certainly wouldn't shout about it," referring to the French conversation going on behind them. Her friend replied: "Oh, well, you can't expect much else from them." Then one of the ladies mentioned that she was bothered when French people laughed among themselves in her presence because she felt they might be making fun of her. This was followed by a nasty interchange of pejorative stereotypes about French Canadians, the whole discussion prompted, it seemed, by what struck me as a humorous conversation of the two attractive, middle class French–Canadian women seated behind them. The English ladies couldn't understand the French conversation, nor did they look back to see what the people they seemed to know so much about even looked like.

The second incident involved my daughter when she was about twelve years old. She, too, has amazing skill with English and two dialects of French, the Canadian style and the European style. One day while driving her to school, a lycée run by teachers from France, I stopped to pick up one of her friends and they were immediately involved in conversation, *French-Canadian* French style. A block or two farther I slowed down to pick up a second girlfriend when my daughter excitedly told me, in English, to drive on. At school I asked what the trouble was and she explained that there actually was no trouble although there might have been if the second girl, who was from France, and who spoke another dialect of French, had got in the car because then my daughter would have been forced to show a linguistic preference for one girl or the other. Normally she could escape this conflict by interacting with each girl separately, and, inadvertently, I had almost put her on the spot. Incidents of this sort prompted us to commence a systematic analysis of the effects of language and dialect changes on impression formation and social interaction.

DIALECT VARIATIONS ELICIT STEREOTYPED IMPRESSIONS

Over the past eight years, we have developed a research technique that makes use of language and dialect variations to elicit the stereotyped impressions or biased views which members of one social group hold of representative members of a contrasting group. Briefly, the procedure involves the reactions of listeners (referred to as judges) to the taped recordings of a number of perfectly bilingual speakers reading a two-minute passage at one time in one of their languages (e.g., French) and, later a translation equivalent of the same passage in their second language (e.g., English). Groups of judges are asked to listen to this series of recordings and evaluate the personality characteristics of each speaker as well as possible, using voice cues only. They are reminded of the common tendency to attempt to gauge the personalities of unfamiliar speakers heard over the phone or radio. Thus they are kept unaware that they will actually hear two readings by each of several bilinguals. In our experience no subjects have become aware of this fact. The judges are given practice trials, making them well acquainted with both versions of the message, copies of which are supplied in advance. They usually find the enterprise interesting, especially if they are promised, and receive, some feedback on how well they have done, for example, if the profiles for one or two speakers, based on the ratings of friends who know them well, are presented at the end of the series.

This procedure, referred to as the *matched-guise* technique, appears to reveal judges' more private reactions to the contrasting group than direct attitude questionnaires do (see Lambert, Anisfeld and Yeni-Komshian, 1965), but much more research is needed to adequately assess its power in this regard. The technique is particularly valuable as a measure of *group* biases in evaluating reactions; it has very good reliability in the sense that essentially the same profile of traits for a particular group appear when different samples of judges, drawn from a particular subpopulation, are used. Differences between subpopulations are very marked, however, as will become apparent. On the other hand, the technique apparently has little reliability when measured by test-retest ratings produced by the same group of judges; we believe this type of unreliability is due in large part to the main statistic used, the difference between an individual's rating of a pair of guises on a single trait. Difference scores give notoriously low test-retest reliability coefficients although their use for comparing means is perfectly appropriate (Bereiter, 1963; and Ferguson, 1959, 285f).

Several of our studies have been conducted since 1958 in greater Montreal, a setting that has a long history of tensions between English- and French-speaking Canadians. The conflict is currently so sharp that some French-Canadian (*FC*) political leaders in the Province of Quebec talk seriously about separating the Province from the rest of Canada, comprising a majority of English Canadians (*ECs*). In 1958–59, (Lambert, Hodgson, Gardner and Fillenbaum, 1960) we asked a sizeable group of *EC* university students to evaluate the personalities of a series of speakers, actually the matched guises of male bilinguals speaking in Canadian-style French and English. When their judgements were analyzed it was found that their evaluations were strongly biased against the *FC* and in favor of the matched *EC* guises. They rated the speakers in their *EC* guises as being better looking, taller, more intelligent, more dependable, kinder, more ambitious and as having more character. This evaluational bias was just as apparent among judges who were bilingual as among monolinguals.

We presented the same set of taped voices to a group of *FC* students of equivalent age, social class and educational level. Here we were in for a surprise for they showed the same bias, evaluating the *EC* guises significantly more favorably than the *FC* guises on a whole series of traits, indicating, for example, that they viewed the *EC* guises as being more intelligent, dependable, likeable and as having more character! Only on two traits did they rate the *FC* guises more favorably, namely kindness and religiousness, and, considering the whole pattern of ratings, it could be that they interpreted too much religion as a questionable quality. Not only did the *FC* judges generally downgrade representatives of their own ethnic-linguistic group, they also rated the *FC* guises much more negatively than the *EC* judges had. We consider this pattern of results as a reflection of a community-wide stereotype of *FC*s as being relatively second-rate people, a view apparently fully shared by certain subgroups of *FC*s. Similar tendencies to downgrade one's own group have been reported in research with minority groups conducted in other parts of North America.

EXTENSIONS OF THE BASIC STUDY

The follow-up study

Some of the questions left unanswered in the first study have been examined recently by Malcolm Preston (Preston, 1963). Using the same basic techniques, the following questions were asked: (a) Will female and male judges react similarly to language and accent variations of speakers? (b) Will judges react similarly to male and female speakers who change their pronunciation style or the language they speak? (c) Will there be systematic differences in reactions to *FC* and Continental French (*CF*) speakers?

For this study, eighty English–Canadian and ninety-two French–Canadian first–year–college age students from Montreal served as judges. The *EC* judges in this study were all Catholics since we wanted to determine if *EC* Catholics would be less biased in their views of *FC*s than the non-Catholic *EC* judges had been in the original study. Approximately the same number of males and females from both language groups were tested, making four groups of judges in all: an *EC* male group, an *EC* female, a *FC* male and a *FC* female group.

The 18 personality traits used by the judges for expressing their reactions were grouped, for the purposes of interpretation, into three logically distinct categories of personality: (a) *competence* which included intelligence, ambition, self-confidence, leadership and courage; (b) *personal integrity* which included dependability, sincerity, character, conscientiousness and kindness; (c) *social attractiveness* which included sociability, likeability, entertainingness, sense of humor and affectionateness. Religiousness, good looks and height were not included in the above categories since they did not logically fit.

Results: evaluative reactions of English-Canadian listeners

In general it was found that the *EC* listeners viewed the female speakers more favorably in their French guises while they viewed the male speakers more favorably in their English guises. In particular, the *EC* men saw the *FC* lady speakers as more intelligent, ambitious, self-confident, dependable, courageous and sincere than their English counterparts. The *EC* ladies were not quite so gracious although they, too, rated the *FC* ladies as more intelligent, ambitious, self-confident (but shorter) than the *EC* women guises. Thus, *EC*s generally view *FC* females as more competent and the *EC* men see them as possessing more integrity and competence.

Several notions came to mind at this point. It may be that the increased attractiveness of the *FC* woman in the eyes of the *EC* male is partly a result of her inaccessibility. Perhaps also the *EC* women are cognizant of the *EC* men's latent preference for *FC* women and accordingly are themselves prompted to upgrade the *FC* female, even to the point of adopting the *FC* woman as a model of what a woman should be.

However, the thought that another group is better than their own should not be a comfortable one for members of any group, especially a group of young ladies! The realization, however latent, that men of their own cultural group prefer another type of woman might well be a very tender issue for the *EC* woman, one that could be easily exacerbated.

To examine this idea, we carried out a separate experiment. The Ss for the experiment were two groups of *EC* young women, one group serving as controls, the other as an experimental group. Both groups were asked to give their impressions of the personalities of a group of speakers, some using English, some Canadian-style French. They were, of course, actually presented with female bilingual speakers using Canadian-French and English guises. Just before they evaluated the speakers, the experimental group was given false information about *FC* women, information that was designed to upset them. They heard a tape recording of a man reading supposedly authentic statistical information about the increase in marriages between *FC* women and *EC* men. They were asked to listen to this loaded passage twice, for practice only, disregarding the content of the message and attending only to the personality of the speaker. We presumed, however, that they would not likely be able to disregard the content since it dealt with a matter that might well bother them—*FC* women, they were told, were competing for *EC* men, men who already had a tendency to prefer *FC* women, a preference that they possibly shared themselves. In contrast, the control group received quite neutral information which would not affect their ratings of *FC*s in any way. The results supported the prediction: The experimental Ss judged the *FC* women to be reliably more attractive but reliably less dependable and sincere than did the control Ss. That is, the favorable reactions toward *FC* women found previously were evident in the judgments of the control group, while the experimental Ss, who had been given false information designed to highlight the threat posed by the presumed greater competence and integrity of *FC* women, saw the *FC* women as men stealers—attractive but undependable and insincere. These findings support the general hypothesis we had developed and they serve as a first step in a series of experiments we are now planning to determine how judgments of personalities affect various types of social interaction.

Let us return again to the main investigation. It was found that *FC* men were not as favorably received as the women were by their *EC* judges. *EC* ladies liked *EC* men, rating them as taller, more likeable, affectionate, sincere, and conscientious, and as possessing more character and a greater sense of humor than the *FC* versions of the same speakers. Furthermore, the *EC* male judges also favored *EC* male speakers, rating them as taller, more kind, dependable and entertaining. Thus, *FC* male speakers are viewed as lacking integrity and as being less socially attractive by both *EC* female, and, to a less marked extent, *EC* male judges. This tendency to downgrade the *FC* male, already noted in the basic study, may well be the expression of an unfavorable stereotyped and prejudiced attitude toward *FC*s, but, apparently, this prejudice is selectively directed toward *FC* males, possibly because they are better known than females as power figures who control local and regional governments and who thereby can be viewed as sources of threat or frustration, (or as the guardians of *FC* women, keeping them all to themselves).

The reactions to Continental-French (*CF*) speakers are generally more favorable although less marked. The *EC* male listeners viewed *CF* women as slightly more competent and *CF* men as equivalent to their *EC* controls except for height and religiousness. The *EC* female listeners upgraded *CF* women on sociability and self-confidence, but downgraded *CF* men on height, likeability and sincerity. Thus, *EC* judges appear to be less concerned about European-French people in general than they are about the local French people; the European-French are neither downgraded nor taken as potential social models to any great extent.

Evaluative reactions of French-Canadian Listeners

Summarizing briefly, the *FC* listeners showed more significant guise differences than did their *EC* counterparts. *FC*s generally rated European-French guises *more* favorably and Canadian-French guises *less* favorably than they did their matched *EC* guises. One important exception was the *FC* women who viewed *FC* men as more competent and as more socially attractive than *EC* men.

The general pattern of evaluations presented by the *FC* judges, however, indicates that they view their own linguistic cultural group as *inferior* to both the English-Canadian and the European-French groups, suggesting that *FC*s are prone to take either of these other groups as models for changes in their own manners of behaving (including speech) and possibly in basic values. This tendency is more marked among *FC* men who definitely prefered male and female representatives of the *EC* and *CF* groups to those of their own group. The *FC* women, in contrast, appear to be guardians of *FC* culture at least in the sense that they favored male representatives of their own cultural group. We presume this reaction reflects something more than a preference for *FC* marriage partners. *FC* women may be particularly anxious to preserve *FC* values and to pass these on in their own families through language, religion and tradition.

Nevertheless, *FC* women apparently face a conflict of their own in that they favor characteristics of both *CF* and *EC* women. Thus, the *FC* female may be safe-guarding the *FC* culture through a preference for *FC* values seen in *FC* men; at the same time as she is prone to change her own behavior and values in the direction of one of two foreign cultural models, those that the men in her group apparently favor. It is of interest that *EC* women are confronted with a similar conflict since they appear envious of *FC* women.

The developmental studies

Recently, we have been looking into the background of the inferiority reaction among *FC* youngsters, trying to determine at what age it starts and how it develops through the years. Elizabeth Anisfeld and I (1964) started by studying the reactions of ten year old *FC* children to the matched guises of bilingual youngsters of their own age reading French and English versions of Little Red Riding Hood, once in Canadian-style French and once in standard English. In this instance, half of the judges were bilingual in English and half were essentially monolingual in French. Stated briefly, it was found that *FC* guises were rated significantly more favorable on nearly all traits. (One exception was height; the *EC* speakers were judged as taller.) However, these favorable evaluations of the *FC* in contrast to the *EC* guises were due almost entirely to the reactions of the monolingual children. The bilingual children saw very little difference between the two sets of guises, that is, on nearly all traits their ratings of the *FC* guises were essentially the same as their ratings of *EC* guises. The results, therefore, made it clear that, unlike college-age judges, *FC* children at the ten-year age level do not have a negative bias against their own group.

The question then arises as to where the bias starts after age ten. A recent study (Lambert, Frankel and Tucker, 1966) was addressed to solving this puzzle. The investigation was conducted with 375 *FC* girls ranging in age from nine to eighteen, who gave their evaluations of three groups of matched guises, (a) of some girls about their own age, (b) of some adult women, and (c) of some adult men. Passages that were appropriate for each age level were read by the bilingual speakers once in English and once in Canadian-style French. In this study attention was given to the social class background of the judges (some were chosen from private schools, some from public schools, and to their knowledge of English (some were bilingual and some monolingual in French). It was found that definite preferences for *EC* guises appeared at about age twelve and were maintained through the late teen years. There was, however, a marked difference between the private and public school judges: the upper middle class girls were especially biased after age twelve, whereas the pattern for the working class girls was less pronounced and less durable, suggesting that for them the bias is short-lived and fades out by the late teens. Note that we probably did not encounter girls from lower class homes in our earlier studies using girls at *FC* colleges or universités.

The major implication of these findings is that the tendency for certain subgroups of college-age *FC*s to downgrade representatives of their own ethnic-linguistic group, noted in our earlier studies, seems to have its origin, at least with girls, at about age twelve, but the ultimate fate of this attitude depends to a great extent on social-class background. Girls who come from upper middle class FC homes, and especially those who have become bilingual in English, are particularly likely to maintain this view, at least into the young adult years.

The pattern of results of these developmental studies can also be examined from a more psychodynamic perspective. If we assume that the adult female and male speakers in their FC guises represent parents or people like their own parents to the FC adolescent judges, just as the same-age speakers represent someone like themselves, then the findings suggest several possibilities that could be studied in more detail. First, the results are consistent with the notion that teen-age girls have a closer psychological relation with their fathers than with their mothers in the sense that the girls in the study rated FC female guises markedly inferior to EC ones, but generally favored or at least showed much less disfavor for the FC guises of male speakers. Considered in this light, social-class differences and bilingual skill apparently influence the degree of same-sex rejection and cross-sex identification: by the mid-teens the public school girls, both monolinguals and bilinguals, show essentially no rejection of either the FC female or male guises, whereas the private school girls, especially the bilinguals, show a rejection of both female and male FC guises through the late teens. These bilinguals might, because of their skill in English and their possible encouragement from home, be able to come in contact with the mothers of their EC associates and therefore may have developed stronger reasons to be envious of EC mothers and fathers than the monolingual girls would have.

Similarly, the reactions to same-age speakers might reflect a tendency to accept or reject one's peer group or one's self, at least for the monolinguals. From this point of view, the findings suggest that the public school monolinguals are generally satisfied with their FC image since they favor the FC guises of the same-age speakers at the sixteen-year level. In contrast, the private school monolinguals may be expressing a marked rejection of themselves in the sense that they favor the EC guises. The bilinguals, of course, can consider themselves as being potential or actual members of both ethnic-linguistic groups represented by the guises. It is of interest, therefore, to note that both the public and particularly the private school bilinguals apparently favor the EC versions of themselves.

TWO GENERALIZATIONS

This program of research, still far from complete, does permit us to make two important generalizations, both relevant to the main argument of this paper. First, a technique has been developed that rather effectively calls out the stereotyped impressions that members of one ethnic-linguistic group hold of another contrasting group. The type and strength of impression depends on characteristics of the speakers—their sex, age, the dialect they use, and, very likely, the social-class background as this is revealed in speech style. The impression also seems to depend on characteristics of the audience of *judges*—their age, sex, socio-economic background, their bilinguality and their own speech style. The type of reactions and adjustments listeners must make to those who reveal, through their speech style, their likely ethnic group allegiance is suggested by the traits that listeners use to indicate their impressions. Thus, *EC* male and female college students tend to look down on the *FC* male speaker, seeing him as less intelligent, less dependable, and less interesting than he would be seen if he had presented himself in an *EC* guise. Imagine the types of role adjust-ment that would follow if the same person were first seen in the *FC* guise and then suddenly switched to a perfect *EC* guise. A group of *EC* listeners would probably be forced to perk up their ears, reconsider their original classification of the person and then either view him as becoming too intimate in "their" language or decide otherwise and be pleasantly amazed that one of their own could manage the other group's language so well. Furthermore, since these comparative impressions are widespread throughout certain strata of each ethnic-linguistic community, they will probably have an enormous impact on young people who are either forced to learn the other group's language or who choose to do so.

The research findings outlined here have a second important message about the reactions of the bilingual who is able to convincingly switch languages or dialects. The bilingual can study the reactions of his audiences as he adopts one guise in certain settings and another in different settings, and receive a good deal of social feedback, permitting him to realize that he can be perceived in quite different ways, depending on how he presents himself. It could well be that his own self-concept takes two distinctive forms in the light of such feedback. He may also observe, with amusement or alarm, the role adjustments that follow when he suddenly switches guises with the same group of interlocutors. How-ever, research is needed to document and examine these likely consequences of language or dialect switching from the perspective of the bilingual making the switches.

Although we have concentrated on a Canadian setting in these investiga-tions, there is really nothing special about the Canadian scene with regard to the social effects of language or dialect switching. Equally instructive effects have been noted when the switch involves a change from standard American English to Jewish-accented English (Anisfeld, Bogo and Lambert, 1962); when the switch involves changing from Hebrew to Arabic for Israeli and Arab judges, or when the change is from Sephardic to Ashkenazic-style Hebrew for Jewish listeners in Israel (Lambert, Anisfeld and Yeni-Komshian, 1965). Our most recent research, using a modified approach, has been conducted with American Negro speakers and listeners (Tucker and Lambert, 1967). The same type of social effects are inherent in this instance, too: Southern Negroes have more favorable impressions of people who use what the linguists call *Standard Network Style* English than they do of those who speak with their own style, but they are more impressed with their own style than they are with the speech of educated, Southern whites, or of Negroes who become too "white" in their speech by exaggerating the non-Negro features and over-correcting their verbal output.

SOCIAL-PSYCHOLOGICAL ASPECTS OF SECOND-LANGUAGE LEARNING

How might these intergroup impressions and feelings affect young people living in the Montreal area who are expected by educators to learn the other group's language? One would expect that both French-Canadian youngsters and their parents would be more willing, for purely social–psychological reasons, to learn English than *EC*s to learn French. Although we haven't investigated the French Canadians' attitudes toward the learning of English, still it is very apparent that bilingualism in Canada and in Quebec has long been a one-way affair, with *FC*s much more likely to learn English than the converse. Typically, this trend to English is explained on economic grounds and on the attraction of the United States, but I would like to suggest another possible reason for equally serious consideration. *FC*s may be drawn away from Canadian–style French to English, or to bilingualism, or to European-style French, as a psychological reaction to the contrast in stereotyped images which English and French Canadians have of one another. On the other hand, we would expect *EC* students and their parents in Quebec, at least, to be drawn away from French for the same basic reasons. It is, of course, short-sighted to talk about groups in this way because there are certain to be wide individual differences of reaction, as was the case in the impression studies, and as will be apparent in the research to be discussed, but one fact turned up in an unpublished study Robert Gardner and I conducted that looks like a group-wide difference. Several samples of Montreal *EC*, high school students who had studied French for periods of up to seven years scored no better on standard tests of French achievement than did Connecticut high schoolers who had only two or three years of French training.

INSTRUMENTAL AND INTEGRATIVE MOTIVATION

When viewed from a social-psychological perspective, the process of learning a second language itself also takes on a special significance. From this viewpoint, one would expect that if the student is to be successful in his attempts to learn another social group's language he must be both able and willing to adopt various aspects of behavior, including verbal behavior, which characterize members of the other linguistic-cultural group. The learner's ethnocentric tendencies and his attitudes toward the other group are believed to determine his success in learning the new language. His motivation to learn is thought to be determined by both his attitudes and by the type of orientation he has toward learning a second language. The orientation is *instrumental* in form if, for example, the purposes of language study reflect the more utilitarian value of linguistic achievement, such as getting ahead in one's occupation, and is integrative if, for example, the student is oriented to learn more about the other cultural community, as if he desired to become a potential member of the other group. It is also argued that some may be anxious to learn another language as a means of being accepted in another cultural group because of dissatisfactions experienced in their own culture while other individuals may be as much interested in another culture as they are in their own. In either case, the more proficient one becomes in a second language the more he may find that his place in his original membership group is modified at the same time as the other linguistic-cultural group becomes something more than a reference group for him. It may, in fact, become a second membership group for him. Depending upon the compatibility of the two cultures, he may experience feelings of chagrin or regret as he loses ties in one group, mixed with the fearful anticipation of entering a relatively new group. The concept of *anomie* first proposed by Durkheim (1897) and more recently extended by Srole (1951) and Williams (1952), refers to such feelings of social uncertainty or dissatisfaction.

My studies with Gardner (1959) were carried out with English-speaking Montreal high school students studying French who were evaluated for their language–learning aptitude and verbal intelligence, as well as their attitudes and stereotypes toward members of the French community, and the intensity of their motivation to learn French. Our measure of motivation is conceptually similar to Jones' (1949 and 1950) index of interest in learning a language which he found to be important for successful learning among Welsh students. A factor analysis of scores on these various measures indicated that aptitude and intelligence formed a common factor which was independent of a second one comprising indices of motivation, type of orientation toward language, and social attitudes toward *FC*s. Furthermore, a measure of achievement in French taken at the end of a year's study was reflected equally prominently in both factors. This statistical pattern meant that French achievement was dependent upon both aptitude and verbal intelligence as well as a sympathetic orientation toward the other group. This orientation was much less common among these students than was the instrumental one, as would be expected from the results of the matched-guise experiments. However, when sympathetic orientation was present it apparently sustained a strong motivation to learn the other group's language. Furthermore, it was clear that students with an integrative orientation were more successful in learning French than were those with instrumental orientations.

A follow-up study (Gardner, 1960) confirmed and extended these findings. Using a larger sample of *EC* students and incorporating various measures of French achievement, the same two independent factors were revealed, and again

both were related to French achievement. But whereas aptitude and achievement were especially important for those French skills stressed in school training, such as grammar, the development of such skills, skills that call for the
active use of the language in communicational settings, such as pronunciation
accuracy and auditory comprehension, was determined in major part by measures
of an integrative motivation to learn French. The aptitude variables were in-
significant in this case. Further evidence from the intercorrelations indicated
that this integrative motive was the converse of an authoritarian ideological
syndrome, opening the possibility that basic personality dispositions may be
involved in language–learning efficiency.

In the same study information had been gathered from the parents of
the students about their own orientations toward the French community.
These data suggested that integrative or instrumental orientations toward the
other group are developed within the family. That is, the minority of students with an integrative disposition to learn French had parents who also
were integrative and sympathetic to the French community. However, students' orientations were not related to parents' skill in French nor to the
number of French acquaintances the parents had, indicating that the integrative motive is not due to having more experience with French at home.
Instead the integrative outlook more likely stems from a family-wide attitudinal disposition.

LANGUAGE LEARNING AND ANOMIE

Another feature of the language–learning process came to light in an investigation of college and postgraduate students undergoing an intensive course in
advanced French at McGill's French Summer School. We were interested here,
among other matters, in changes in attitudes and feelings that might take place
during the six-week study period (Lambert, Gardner, Barik and Tunstall, 1961).
The majority of the students were Americans who oriented themselves mainly
to the European-French rather than the American-French community. We adjusted our attitude scales to make them appropriate for those learning European
French. Certain results were of special interest. As the students progressed in
French skill to the point that they said they "thought" in French, and even
dreamed in French, their feelings of anomie also increased markedly. At the
same time, they began to seek out occasions to use English even though they
had solemnly pledged to use only French for the six-week period. This pattern of
results suggests to us that these already advanced students experienced a strong
dose of anomie when they commenced to *really* master a second language.
That is, when advanced students became so skilled that they begin to think
and feel like Frenchmen, they then became so annoyed with feelings of anomie
that they were prompted to develop strategies to minimize or control the annoy-
ance. Reverting to English could be such a strategy. It should be emphasized,

however, that the chain of events just listed needs to be much more carefully explored.

Elizabeth Anisfeld and I took another look at this problem, experimenting with ten-year old monolingual and bilingual students (Peal and Lambert, 1962). We found that the bilingual children (attending French schools in Montreal) were markedly more favorable towards the "other" language group (i.e., the *EC*s) than the monolingual children were. Furthermore, the bilingual children reported that their parents held the same strongly sympathetic attitudes toward *EC*s, in contrast to the pro-*FC* attitudes reported for the parents of the monolingual children. Apparently, then, the development of second–language skill to the point of balanced bilingualism is conditioned by family-shared attitudes toward the other linguistic-cultural group.

These findings are consistent and reliable enough to be of general interest. For example, methods of language training could possibly be modified and strengthened by giving consideration to the social-psychological implications of language learning. Because of the possible practical as well as theoretical significance of this approach, it seemed appropriate to test its applicability in a cultural setting other than the bicultural Quebec scene. With measures of attitude and motivation modified for American students learning French, a large scale study, very similar in nature to those conducted in Montreal, was carried out in various settings in the United States with very similar general outcomes (Lambert & Gardner, 1962).

One further investigation indicated that these suggested social–psychological principles are not restricted to English and French speakers in Canada. Moshe Anisfeld and I (1961) extended the same experimental procedure to samples of Jewish high school students studying Hebrew at various parochial schools in different sectors of Montreal. They were questioned about their orientations toward learning Hebrew and their attitudes toward the Jewish culture and community, and tested for their verbal intelligence, language aptitude and achievement in the Hebrew language at the end of the school year. The results support the generalization that both intellectual capacity and attitudinal orientation affect success in learning Hebrew. However, whereas intelligence and linguistic aptitude were relatively stable predictors of success, the attitudinal measures varied from one Jewish community to another. For instance, the measure of a Jewish student's desire to become more acculturated in the Jewish tradition and culture was a sensitive indicator of progress in Hebrew for children from a particular district of Montreal, one where members of the Jewish subcommunity were actually concerned with problems of integrating into the Jewish culture. In another district, made up mainly of Jews who recently arrived from central Europe and who were clearly of a lower socio-economic level, the measure of desire for Jewish acculturation did not correlate with achievement in Hebrew, whereas measures of pro-Semitic attitudes or pride in being Jewish did.

BILINGUAL ADJUSTMENTS TO CONFLICTING DEMANDS

The final issue I want to discuss concerns the socio-cultural tugs and pulls that the bilingual or potential bilingual encounters and how he adjusts to these often conflicting demands made on him. We have seen how particular social atmospheres can affect the bilingual. For example, the French-English bilingual in the Montreal setting may be pulled toward greater use of English, and yet be urged by certain others in the FC community not to move too far in that direction, just as EC's may be discouraged from moving toward the French community. (In a similar fashion, dialects would be expected to change because of the social consequences they engender, so that Jewish accented speech should drop away, especially with those of the younger generation in American settings, as should Sephardic forms of Hebrew in Israel or certain forms of Negro speech in America.) In other words, the bilingual encounters social pressure of various sorts: he can enjoy the fun of linguistic spying but must pay the price of suspicion from those who don't want him to enter too intimately into their cultural domains and from others who don't want him to leave his "own" domain. He also comes to realize that most people are suspicious of a person who is in any sense two-faced. If he is progressing toward bilingualism, he encounters similar pressures that may affect his self-concept, his sense of belonging and his relations to two cultural-linguistic groups, the one he is slowly *leaving*, and the one he is entering. The conflict exists because so many of us think in terms of in-groups and out-groups, or of the need of showing an allegiance to one group or another, so that terms such as own language, other's language, *leaving* and *entering* one cultural group for another seem to be appropriate, even natural, descriptive choices.

BILINGUALS AND ETHNOCENTRISM

Although this type of thought may characterize most people in our world, it is nonetheless a subtle form of group cleavage and ethnocentrism, and in time it may be challenged by bilinguals who, I feel, are in an excellent position to develop a totally new outlook on the social world. My argument is that bilinguals, especially those with bicultural experiences, enjoy certain fundamental advantages which, if capitalized on, can easily offset the annoying social tugs and pulls they are normally prone to. Let me mention one of these advantages that I feel is a tremendous asset.[1] Recently, Otto Klineberg and I conducted a rather

---

[1]For present purposes, discussion is limited to a more *social* advantage associated with bilingualism. In other writings there has been a stress on potential intellectual and *cognitive* advantages; see Peal and Lambert (1962) and Anisfeld (1964); see also Macnamara (1964) as well as Lambert and Anisfeld (1966). The bilingual's potential utility has also been discussed as a linguistic mediator between monolingual groups because of his comprehension of the subtle meaning differences characterizing each of the languages involved; see Lambert and Moore (1966).

comprehensive international study of the development of stereotyped thinking in children (Lambert and Klineberg, 1967). We found that rigid and stereotyped thinking about in-groups and out-groups, or about own groups in contrast to foreigners, starts during the pre-school period when children are trying to form a conception of themselves and their place in the world. Parents and other socializers attempt to help the child at this stage by highlighting differences and contrasts among groups, thereby making his own group as distinctive as possible. This tendency, incidentally, was noted among parents from various parts of the world. Rather than helping, however, they may actually be setting the stage for ethnocentrism with permanent consequences. The more contrasts are stressed, the more deep-seated the stereotyping process and its impact on ethnocentric thought appear to be. Of relevance here is the notion that the child brought up bilingually and biculturally will be less likely to have good versus bad contrasts impressed on him when he starts wondering about himself, his own group, and others. Instead he will probably be taught something more truthful, although more complex: that differences among national or cultural groups of peoples are actually not clear-cut and that basic similarities among peoples are more prominent than differences. The bilingual child in other words may well start life with the enormous advantage of having a more open, receptive mind about himself and other people. Furthermore, as he matures, the bilingual has many opportunities to learn, from observing changes in other people's reactions to him, how two-faced and ethnocentric *others* can be. That is, he is likely to become especially sensitive to and leery of ethnocentrism.

BILINGUALS AND SOCIAL CONFLICTS

This is not to say that bilinguals have an easy time of it. In fact, the final investigation I want to present demonstrates the social conflicts bilinguals typically face, but, and this is the major point, it also demonstrates one particular type of adjustment that is particularly encouraging.

In 1943, Irving Child (1943) investigated a matter that disturbed many second-generation Italians living in New England: what were they, Italian or American? Through early experiences they had learned that their relations with other youngsters in their community were strained whenever they displayed signs of their Italian background, that is, whenever they behaved as their parents wanted them to. In contrast, if they rejected their Italian background, they realized they could be deprived of many satisfactions stemming from belonging to an Italian family and an Italian community. Child uncovered three contrasting modes of adjusting to these pressures. One subgroup rebelled against their Italian background, making themselves as American as possible. Another subgroup rebelled the other way, rejecting things American as much as possible while proudly associating themselves with things Italian. The third form of adjustment was an apathetic withdrawal and a refusal to think of themselves in ethnic terms at all. This group tried, unsuccessfully, to escape the conflict by avoiding situations where the matter of cultural background might come up. Stated in other terms, some tried to belong to one of their own groups or the other, and some, because of strong pulls from both sides, were unable to belong to either.

Child's study illustrates nicely the difficulties faced by people with dual allegiances, but there is no evidence presented of second-generation Italians who actually feel themselves as belonging to both groups. When in 1962, Robert Gardner and I (1962) studied another ethnic minority group in New England, the French Americans, we observed the same types of reactions as Child had noted among Italian Americans. But in our study there was an important difference.

We used a series of attitude scales to assess the allegiances of French-American adolescents to both their French and American heritages. Their relative degree of skill in French and in English were used as an index of their mode of adjustment to the bicultural conflict they faced. In their homes, schools and community, they all had ample opportunities to learn both languages well, but subgroups turned up who had quite different patterns of linguistic skill, and each pattern was consonant with each subgroup's allegiances. Those who expressed a definite preference for the American over the French culture and who negated the value of knowing French were more proficient in English than French. They also expressed anxiety about how well they actually knew English. This subgroup, characterized by a general rejection of their French background, resembles in many respects the rebel reaction noted by Child. A second subgroup expressed a strong desire to be identified as French, and they showed a greater skill in French than English, especially in comprehension of spoken French. A third group apparently faced a conflict of cultural allegiances since they were ambivalent about their identity, favoring certain features of the American culture. Presumably because they had not resolved the conflict, they were retarded in their command of both languages when compared to the other groups. This relatively unsuccessful mode of adjustment is very similar to the apathetic reaction noted in one subgroup or Italian Americans.

A fourth subgroup is of special interest. French–American youngsters who have an open-minded, nonethnocentric view of people in general, coupled with a strong aptitude for language learning are the ones who profited fully from their language–learning opportunities and became skilled in *both* languages. These young people had apparently circumvented the conflicts and developed means of becoming members of both cultural groups. They had, in other terms, achieved a comfortable bicultural identity.

It is not clear why this type of adjustment did not appear in Child's study. There could, for example, be important differences in the social pressures encountered by second-generation Italians and French in New England. My guess, however, is that the difference in findings reflects a new social movement that has started in America in the interval between 1943 and 1962, a movement which the American linguist Charles Hockett humorously refers to as a "reduction of the heat under the American melting pot." I believe that bicultural bilinguals will be particularly helpful in perpetuating this movement. They and their children are also the ones most likely to work out a new, non-ethnocentric mode of social intercourse which could be of universal significance.

REFERENCES

Anisfeld, Elizabeth. A comparison of the cognitick functioning of monolinguals and bilinguals. Unpublished Ph.D. thesis, Redpath Library, McGill University, 1964.

Anisfeld, Elizabeth, and Lambert, W. E. Evaluational reactions of bilingual and monolingual children to spoken language. *Journal of Abnormal and Social Psychology*, 1964, 69, 89–97.

Anisfeld, M., Bogo, N., and Lambert, W. E. Evaluational reactions to accented English speech. *Journal of Abnormal and Social Psychology*, 1962, 65, 223–231.

Anisfeld, M., and Lambert, W. E. Social and psychological variables in learning Hebrew. *Journal of Abnormal and Social Psychology*, 1961, 63, 524–529.

Bereiter, C. Some persisting dilemmas in the measurement of change. In Harris, C. W. (Ed.), *Problems in measuring change*. Madison: The University of Wisconsin Press, 1963.

Child, I. L. *Italian or American? The second generation in conflict*. New Haven: Yale University Press, 1943.

Durkheim, E. *Le suicide*. Paris: G. Alcan, 1897.

Ferguson, G. A. *Statistical analysis in psychology and education*. New York: McGraw-Hill, 1959.

Gardner, R. C. and Lambert, W. E. Motivational variables in second-language acquisition. *Canadian Journal of Psychology*, 1959, 13, 266–272.

Gardner, R. C. Motivational variables in second-language acquisition. Unpublished Ph.D. thesis, McGill University, 1960.

Jones, W. R. Attitude towards Welsh as a second language. A preliminary investigation. *British Journal of Educational Psychology*, 1949, 19, 44–52.

Jones, W. R. Attitude towards Welsh as a second language, a further investigation. *British Journal of Educational Psychology*, 1950, 20, 117–132.

Labov, W. Hypercorrection by the lower middle class as a factor in linguistic change. Columbia University, 1964. (Mimeo)

Lambert, W. E., Hodgson, R. C., Gardner, R. C., and Fillenbaum, S. Evaluational reactions to spoken languages. *Journal of Abnormal and Social Psychology*, 1960, 60, 44–51.

Lambert, W. E., Gardner, R. C., Olton, R., and Tunstall, K. A study of the roles of attitudes and motivation in second-language learning. McGill University, 1962. (Mimeo)

Lambert, W. E., Gardner, R. C., Barik, H. C., and Tunstall, K. Attitudinal and cognitive aspects of intensive study of a second language. *Journal of Abnormal and Social Psychology*, 1963, 66, 358–368.

Lambert, W. E., Anisfeld, M., and Yeni-Komshian, Grace. Evaluational reactions of Jewish and Arab adolescents to dialect and language variations. *Journal of Personality and Social Psychology*, 1965, 2, 84–90.

Lambert, W. E., Frankel, Hannah, and Tucker, G. R. Judging personality through speech: A French-Canadian example. *The Journal of Communication*, 1966, 16, 305–321.

Lambert, W. E., and Anisfeld, Elizabeth. A reply to John Macnamara. Mimeographed and submitted to *Studies*, 1966.

Lambert, W. E., and Moore, Nancy. Word-association responses: Comparison of American and French monolinguals with Canadian monolinguals and bilinguals. *Journal of Personality and Social Psychology*, 1966, 3, 313–320.

Lambert, W. E., and Klineberg, O. *Children's views of foreign peoples: A cross-national study*. New York: Appleton, 1967.

Macnamara, J. The Commission on Irish: Psychological aspects. *Studies*, 1964, 164–173.

McDavid, R. I. The dialects of American English. In Francis, W. N. (Ed.), *The structure of American English*, New York: Ronald, 1958.

Peal, Elizabeth, and Lambert, W. E. The relation of bilingualism to intelligence. *Psychological Monographs*, 1962, 76, Whole No. 546.

Preston, M. S. Evaluational reactions to English, Canadian French and European French voices. Unpublished M.A. thesis, McGill University, Redpath Library, 1963.

Srole, L. Social dysfunction, personality and social distance attitudes. Paper read before American Sociological Society, 1951, National Meeting, Chicago, Ill. (Mimeo)

Tucker, G. R., and Lambert, W. E., White and Negro listeners' reactions to various American-English dialects. McGill University, 1967. (Mimeo)

Williams, R. N. *American society*. New York: Knopf, 1952.

42 ATTITUDINAL ASPECTS OF SECOND-LANGUAGE LEARNING

BERNARD SPOLSKY

Restate briefly the objectives and the conclusions of the study carried out by Spolsky and reported in this article.

In addition to *attitude* what are the other three factors discussed in this article that are determiners of success in foreign-language acquisition? On the basis of this article, how would you rank these four factors in importance? Are there others you feel should be considered?

A major difference between first and second-language acquisition is in the degree of variation in the levels of proficiency attained by learners.[1] While some speakers have a better control of their first or native language than do others, all normal

Reprinted by permission from *Language Learning*, 19 (December, 1969), 272–283. The writer is professor of linguistics and education at the University of New Mexico.

[1] An earlier version of this paper was read at the Annual Meeting of the Modern Language Association, New York, December 28–31, 1969. The research reported in it was partially supported by a grant from the Ford Foundation to the Human Resources Development Committee of Indiana University. I am grateful for the assistance of Ernest Migliazza and Faith Morse.

human beings reach a minimal standard in at least one language and are capable of communication using it. In the case of second languages, however, there is variation in proficiency ranging from no knowledge at all to native-like ability. A central problem in the development of a theory of second–language acquisition is to account for this.

Among the factors that have been proposed as significant are method, age, aptitude, and attitude. Of these, teaching method has generally been considered the most easily controllable (it has been considered a sufficient provision for a program in applied linguistics or language pedagogy to offer courses in methodology), but results of research into the effectiveness of various methodologies have generally proved to be disappointing.

The major two–year study by Scherer and Wertheimer (1964), for instance, looked into the relative effectiveness of an audiolingual approach and a traditional approach to teaching German in college. The study brought out many interesting points, but basically it showed that there was no real difference between the two except that the audiolingual students were better at speaking, and the traditional students were better at writing and translation. More recent studies by Smith and Berger (1968) and Smith and Baranyi (1968) of French and German teaching in over one hundred Pennsylvania secondary school classes showed traditional students doing better on all measures than audiolingual students, and showed also that language laboratories as they were used had no effect.

Several other studies have gone even further and questioned the effectiveness of language teaching at all. John Upshur (1968) studied the English learning of foreign student participants in the seven week 1966 Orientation Program in American law. These participants either received no instruction in English as a foreign language, or one or two hours of formal teaching daily. Analysis failed to produce any evidence that the amount of formal language instruction had any effect on the learning, a result which supports the notion that the adult, as well as the child, learns a language better in a natural environment than in a classroom.

This notion is borne out by another major study recently reported, John Carroll's investigation of the foreign language proficiency achieved by college language majors. Carroll (1967) found that the students were generally poor at speaking and understanding the language they had been studying for four years at college. Of all the factors he considered, the one that he found to correlate most highly with achievement was time spent overseas.

It would be a serious mistake, then, to consider teaching method to be the only variable that can be controlled; a more serious mistake to measure *its* influence when the other factors concerned have not also been measured. For this reason, a great number of methodological experiments have proved to be of little value (see Spolsky, 1968).

The importance of age as a factor is widely recognized. In general, evidence suggests the idea that up to puberty, children can acquire more than one language at once, going through a stage of confusion, but usually separating the two ultimately. Beyond puberty, there is more difficulty, and a much greater degree of variation in the speed and level of acquisition. The arguments put forward for foreign language teaching in elementary schools are generally based on this, although in actual practice the tendency to treat languages in elementary schools as just another subject has tended to minimize the effectiveness of an early start. But it is still there, as Carroll (1967) has shown.

Studies of language aptitude by Carroll (1962, 1967) and by Pimsleur (1962, 1963, 1966) have attempted to isolate abilities which are predictive of success in learning. With extraneous variables controlled as much as possible, it has been found that aptitude can be measured to some degree as a learner's ability to remember foreign language material, his ability to handle phonetic aspects of foreign language mastery, and his ability to make grammatical analysis of sentences and to find elements with analogous functions in English sentences. On the basis of this, it has been possible to build language aptitude tests that have a fair degree of validity. In all studies, however, the correlation of measured aptitude and success in language learning has been quite low.

Attitude is the fourth factor that has been proposed to account for variation in the level of achievement in second-language acquisition. In a typical language-learning situation, there are a number of people whose attitudes to each other can be significant: the learner, the teacher, the learner's peers and parents, and the speakers of the language. Each relationship might well be shown to be a factor controlling the learner's motivation to acquire the language. John Carroll for instance has suggested the importance of the attitude of parents. In his study of foreign language majors, he found

> the greater the parents' use of the foreign language in the home, the higher were the mean scores of the students. Thus, one reason why some students reach high levels of attainment in a foreign language is that they have home environments that are favorable to this, either because the students are better motivated to learn, or because they have better opportunities to learn. (Carroll 1967: 138)

This finding supports Gardner (1960) who showed that Montreal English-speaking students were apparently reflecting their parents' attitudes to French speakers; in a later study, Feenstra (1967) has shown clear relationship between Montreal English speakers' attitudes to the French–Canadian community and their children's achievements in learning French.

A number of recent studies (though not in language learning) have pointed up the importance of the attitude of the teacher to the learner for the latter's achievement. Teacher expectations have been shown to make a great deal of difference to student success. In one experiment, for instance, teachers of re-tarded children attempted to present a much greater number of new words to students they were erroneously informed to be faster learners, and these students learned more words than the students randomly labelled "slow."

Peer groups too are of great importance in language acquisition. Shuy's study of social dialects in Detroit, for example, shows how various dialect patterns cluster according to age, sex, and socio-economic status (Shuy, 1967); and a study of certain phonological features in the speech of people in a Piedmont community has shown clustering of these features among friends (Crockett and Levine, 1967).

One of the most important attitudinal factors is the attitude of the learner to the language and to its speakers. In a number of basic studies, Wallace Lambert and his colleagues (Lambert, 1963; Lambert and Gardner, 1959; Lambert et al., 1963; Anisfeld and Lambert, 1961) have drawn attention to the major importance of what they call integrative motivation to the learning of foreign languages. They suggest that there are two classes of motivation for language learning, instrumental and integrative, and that the presence of the latter is necessary to successful mastery of the higher levels of proficiency, signalled by the development of a native-like accent and the ability to "think like a native speaker." In general, the studies referring to this construct have established the presence or absence of integrative motivation by using an open-ended or multiple-choice questionnaire asking for the reasons for which someone is learning the language in question. Reasons are considered instrumental if they suggest the language is being used for such a purpose as to fulfill an educational requirement, to get a better position, or to read material in the language, and are considered integrative when they suggest the desire to become a member of the community speaking the language. In Lambert and Gardner (1959) for instance, which was a study of English-speaking Montreal high school students and their learning of French, the orientation index was considered integrative if students chose as their reason for learning French that it would be helpful in understanding the French–Canadian people and their life or that it would permit meeting and conversing with more and varied people, and instrumental if they chose the reason that it would be useful in obtaining a job or that it could make one a better-educated person. In Lambert et al. (1963), eight reasons were given, four classified as integrative and four as instrumental, with a ninth open-ended possibility being left to the judgment of the experimenters. Some difficulties of the interpretation of such questionnaires were reported by Anisfeld and Lambert (1961).

There are clear advantages in being able to handle this notion of integrative motivation precisely. From the point of view of the development of a theory of second–language acquisition, it is necessary to be able to specify each of the factors that are considered to account for variations in proficiency. Second, for studies of socialization, it would be very valuable to have precise data on the degree to which an individual's proficiency in a language serves as a measure of his attitude towards a social group. In this connection Lambert's work with the matched-guise technique (Lambert et al., 1960; Anisfeld et al., 1962; Lambert et al., 1963; Peal and Lambert, n.d.) has made clear the value of getting at social attitudes through the use of speech samples. A clearer understanding of integrative motivation will also be of great use in a study of ways to develop control of the standard dialect in speakers of substandard.

In our study, we were concerned with finding out more about integrative motivation by developing an instrument that would compare a subject's attitude to speakers of a foreign language in which he already has some degree of proficiency. In social–psychological theory, a distinction has been established between an individual's membership groups (the groups to which he belongs) and his reference groups (the groups in which he desires to attain or maintain membership). An individual is a member of the group speaking his native language: when he is placed in a second–language learning situation, he may choose the speakers of his own language or the speakers of the second language as his reference group. Integrative motivation is related to a choice of the second–language group. Our instrument was designed to show the learner's choice.

METHOD

We worked with four groups of subjects. Group I was composed of seventy-nine foreign students who had just arrived in the United States to attend American universities, had been judged by the sponsoring agency to be quite proficient in English, and were attending an orientation seminar at Indiana University. Group II was composed of seventy-one similar students attending a seminar at the University of Minnesota. Group III was made up of 135 foreign students enrolling for the first time at Indiana University; it was much more varied both in English proficiency and time spent in the United States. The fourth group was made up of thirty Japanese students at Indiana University. All told, students were included from eighty different countries.

The instrument we prepared consisted of a direct questionnaire on which students were asked to rate the importance of fourteen possible reasons for their having come to the United States and an indirect questionnaire (see appendices). The indirect questionnaire consisted of four lists of thirty adjectives such as 'busy,' 'stubborn,' and 'sincere.'[2] In list 1, the student was asked to say how well each adjective described him; in list 2, how well it described the way he would like to be; in list 3, how well it described people whose native language was the same as his; and in list 4, how well it described native speakers of English.

For each student, we also had available a score on an English proficiency test.[3]

The reasons on the direct questionnaire were classified as integrative (e.g., having a chance to be away from home, getting to know Americans, finding

[2]The use of this instrument, based on Robert E. Bills' Index of Adjustment and Values, was suggested to us by Dr. Alan P. Bell.

[3]For Group I and III, this was the overall Test of English Proficiency (Spolsky et al., 1968).

out more about what I am like) or as instrumental (getting a degree, finding out how people in my profession work here), and a score calculated according to the relative importance given each reason by the subject.

The responses to the indirect questionnaire were coded for computer handling, and similarity of responses to the various lists were calculated as a coefficient of correlation.

RESULTS

Using the criterion of the Direct Questionnaire, no more than twenty percent of the students could be considered integratively motivated, the remaining giving instrumental reasons for study in the U.S. A comparison of the relationship of this motivation with proficiency in English shows, however, no significant correlation (see Table 1). This result, contrary to those reported by Lambert and

Table 1. The Direct Questionnaire and English Proficiency

Group I		A	B
+		5	8
−		34	50

Group II		A	B
+		7	8
−		24	30

Group III		A	B
+		21	10
−		48	49

All Groups		A	B
+		33	26
−		116	109

A = upper group in English proficiency
B = lower group
+ = positive motivation
− = negative motivation

his colleagues, can be explained by the fact that foreign students when questioned directly, will not, so soon after their arrival, admit to motives which suggest they wish to leave their own country permanently, but will tend to insist on instrumental motives ("I'm here to get training, to get a degree").

The Indirect Questionnaire, on the other hand, shows a third of the students to be classifiable as considering speakers of English to be a more desirable reference group. The two questionnaires are clearly related (see Table 2), but there is good reason to suspect that the Indirect Questionnaire has been more sensitive, its results less disguised by student inhibition.

To explore in more detail what the nature of integrative motivation might be, we examined the correlation of various parts of the indirect questionnaire with English proficiency scores.

1. The correlation of scores on lists 1 and 2 (see Table 3) gives a measure of the difference between self-image and desired self-image; in other words, a measure of the student's self-satisfaction. This showed no significant correlation with proficiency in English.

Table 2. The Two Questionnaires

Group I

	Direct +	Direct −
Indirect +	2	24
Indirect −	11	40

Group II

	Direct +	Direct −
Indirect +	3	15
Indirect −	12	39

Group III

	Direct +	Direct −
Indirect +	20	25
Indirect −	22	71

All Groups

	Direct +	Direct −
Indirect +	25	64
Indirect −	45	150

Table 3. Self-satisfaction

Group I		A	B
	.5 or more	25	21
	less than .5	15	18

Group III		A	B
	.5 or more	35	44
	less than 5	29	20

2. The correlation of scores on lists 1 and 4 (see Table 4) gives a measure of the degree to which a subject perceives himself as already being like speakers of English. There was a significant correlation of this perception with proficiency in English.

3. The correlation of scores on lists 1 and 3 (see Table 5) gives a measure of the degree to which a subject perceives himself as being like speakers of his own language. This showed no significant correlation with proficiency in English.

4. When the correlation of lists 1 and 3 is subtracted from the correlation of lists 1 and 4, a positive remainder indicates that the subject perceived himself as being more like speakers of English than he is like speakers of his own language. This correlated slightly (chi-square = 2.8, significant at the .1 percent level) with proficiency in English (see Table 6).

5. When the correlation of lists 2 and 3 is subtracted from the correlation of lists 2 and 4, a positive remainder is a measure of a greater desire to be like speakers of English than to be like speakers of the native language: in other words, a sign that for the subject, speakers of English constitute his reference group. This measure appears to be the closest to integrative motivation. A comparison of it and English proficiency shows a clear relationship. For all groups, the correlation is highly significant (chi-square = 8.71, significant at the .01 level) (see Table 7).

The relationship holds in each of the groups taken individually, although the degree of statistical significance varies. In this respect, the correlation is better in Groups I and II, groups relatively homogeneous with respect to English proficiency, than in Group III.

6. Even better results are obtained if certain national groups are excluded. Japanese subjects, for instance, in Groups I and II, were almost all "positively" motivated but in the lower half in proficiency; similarly, results in Group IV did not show a significant correlation.[4]

[4]For a more detailed analysis of the Japanese group, see Cowan (1968).

Table 4. Similarity to speakers of English

Group I	A	B
.2 or more	21	15
less than .2	19	24

Group I	A	B
.5 or more	13	5
less than .5	22	34

Group III	A	B
.2 or more	42	26
less than .2	24	35

Group I and III combined	A	B
.2 or more	63	41
less than 2	43	59

Table 5. Similarity to own group

Group III	A	B
.5 or more	22	24
less than .5	42	39

Table 6. Relative similarity to speakers of English

Group III	A	B
+	24	15
-	40	48

Table 7. Integrative Motivation

Group I

	A	B
+	29	21
-	11	18

Group II

	A	B
+	20	15
-	12	24

Group III

	A	B
+	37	28
-	32	36

Group IV

	A	B
+	10	5
-	7	8

All Groups combined

	A	B
+	96	69
-	62	86

7. To shed some light on the relative importance to be attached to the factor of integrative motivation, a fourth analysis (limited by availability of subjects) was made of fifty-one students in Group III by adding another factor, the number of years they had studied English before coming to the United States. There was no correlation between length of study and integrative motivation, but clear correlation between each of these and proficiency in English. The correlation of integrative motivation and English proficiency (chi-square = 7.42, significant at the .01 percent level) was clearer than that of length of study and English proficiency (chi-square = 3.85, significant at the .05 percent level), but the possibility of bias in the sample cannot be ignored.

CONCLUSION

This study, then, has reaffirmed the importance of attitude as one of the factors explaining degree of proficiency a student achieves in learning a second language. His attitude to speakers of the language will have a great effect on how well he learns. A person learns a language better when he wants to be a member of the group speaking that language.

We are led to note the significance of sociolinguistics to second-language pedagogy, for while psycholinguistics will continue to contribute vital data on how second languages are acquired, it is only when we look at the social dimensions that we start to understand why. Learning a second language is a key to possible membership of a secondary society: the desire to join that group is a major factor in language learning.

REFERENCES

Anisfeld, Moshe, Norman Bogo, and Wallace E. Lambert. 1962. Evaluational reactions to accented English speech. Journal of Abnormal and Social Psychology 65.223-231.

Anisfeld, Moshe and W. E. Lambert. 1961. Social and psychological variables in learning Hebrew. Journal of Abnormal and Social Psychology 63.524-529.

Bills, Robert E. Index of adjustment and values. (Unpublished manual.) College of Education, University of Alabama.

Carroll, John B. 1962. The prediction of success in intensive foreign language training. Training Research and Education, ed. by Robert Glazer, 87-136. Pittsburgh: The University of Pittsburgh Press.

Carroll, John B. 1967. Foreign language proficiency levels attained by language majors near graduation from college. Foreign Language Annals 1.2.131-151.

Crockett, Harry J., Jr. and Lewis Levine. 1967. Friends' influence in speech. Sociological Inquiry 37.109-28.

Cowan, Susie. 1968. English proficiency and bicultural attitudes of Japanese students. The English Teachers' Magazine 17.9.38-44.

Feenstra, H. J. 1967. Aptitude, attitude, and motivation in second-language acquisitions. Dissertation, University of Western Ontario.

Gardner, R. C. 1960. Motivational variables in second-language acquisition. Dissertation, McGill University.

Gardner, R. C. 1968. Attitudes and motivation: Their role in second-language acquisition. TESOL Quarterly 2.141-50.

Lambert, Wallace E. and R. C. Gardner. 1959. Motivational variables in second-language learning. Canadian Journal of Psychology 13.

Lambert, Wallace E., R. C. Hodgson, R. C. Gardner, and S. Fillenbaum. 1960. Evaluational reactions to spoken languages. Journal of Abnormal and Social Psychology 60.1.

Lambert, Wallace E. 1963. Psychological approaches to the study of language, Part I: On second-language learning and bilingualism. The Modern Language Journal 47.3.51-62.

Lambert, Wallace E., R. C. Gardner, H. C. Barik, and K. Tunstall. 1963. Attitudinal and cognitive aspects of intensive study of a second language. Journal of Abnormal and Social Psychology 66.358-369.

Lambert, Wallace E., Moshe Anisfeld, and Grace Yeni-Komshian. 1963. Evaluational reactions of Jewish and Arabic adolescents to dialect and language variations. Mimeo, McGill University.

Peal, Elizabeth and W. E. Lambert. Evaluational reactions of bilingual and monolingual children to spoken languages. Mimeo, McGill University.

Pimsleur, Paul. 1962. Predicting achievement in foreign-language learning. International Linguistics 29.2.129–136.

Pimsleur, Paul. 1963. Predicting success in high school foreign-language courses. Educational and Psychological Measurements 33.2.

Pimsleur, Paul. 1966. Testing foreign-language learning. Trends in language teaching, ed. by A. Valdman. New York: McGraw-Hill Book Company.

Scherer, George A. C. and Michael Wertheimer. 1964. A psycholinguistic experiment in foreign-language teaching. New York: McGraw Hill Book Company.

Shuy, Robert W., Walter A. Wolfram, and William K. Riley. 1967. Linguistic correlates of social stratification in Detroit speech. East Lansing: Michigan State University.

Smith, Philip D., Jr. and Emanuel Berger. 1968. An assessment of three foreign-language teaching strategies utilizing three language laboratory systems. Final Report, USOE Project 5-0683, Grant OE-7-48-9013-273.

Smith, Philip D., Jr. and Helmut A. Baranyi. 1968. A comparison study of the effectiveness of the traditional and audiolingual approaches to foreign-language instruction utilizing laboratory equipment. Final Report, USOE Project 7-0133, Grant OEC-1-7-070-33-0445.

Spolsky, Bernard, Bengt Sigurd, Masahito Sato, Edward Walker, and Catherine Arterburn. 1968. Preliminary studies in the development of techniques for testing overall second-language proficiency. Problems in foreign-language testing, ed. by John A. Upshur. Language Learning Special Issue 3.79–101.

Spolsky, Bernard. 1968. Recent research in TESOL. TESOL Quarterly 2.304–7.

Upshur, John A. 1968. Four experiments on the relation between foreign-language teaching and learning. Language Learning 18.111–24.

43 A TYPOLOGY OF BILINGUAL EDUCATION WILLIAM F. MACKEY

What was Mackey's overall objective in writing this paper? Describe home-school situations known to you in terms of U+S, U–S, B+S, B–S, and B+SS.

Describe curriculum patterns in bilingual schools known to you in terms of the five patterns introduced on pages 417–418.

Reprinted by permission from *Foreign Language Annals*, 3 (May, 1970), 596–608, where it was slightly revised by the author after its original appearance in Theodore Andersson and M. Boyer, *Bilingual Schooling in the U.S.*, vol. 2, pp. 63–68 (Washington, D.C.: U.S. Government Printing Office, 1969). The author wishes the reader to note an application and adaptation of his typology by Andersson and Boyer in volume 1, pp. 69–112. Professor Mackey is director of the International Center for Research on Bilingualism, Université Laval, Québec.

> Describe the function of some non-official language in
> your country in terms of its use and domain in the
> home, in the school, and in the community at large
> by comparing it with the use of the official language.

There are few countries where one cannot find some instances of bilingual education. In the past decade the demand for bilingual education has been increasing in most parts of the world. In the developing or emerging nations the demand is caused by the rise in the status of one or more of the vernacular languages combined with the need to maintain an international language for purposes of secondary and higher education. In other nations, where the official language has already attained international status, a changing climate of tolerance toward minorities has often made it possible for ethnic groups speaking a language other than that of the national majority to organize, with official approval, their own schools in their own language.

Some of these changes have been the results of regional necessity; others are the fruits of local accommodations based on purely political motives. It is important that the pressures of politics be distinguished from local linguistic needs. And linguistic needs must not be confused with linguistic desires. Language minorities have often been the victims of emotional exploitation from within by the few who can use it as a lever to personal political power.

One of the pawns in the politics of local minorities has been the question of bilingual schooling. This is a question which often arouses bitter conflicts which are rarely resolved by the sort of objective analysis and impartial study needed. The situation is aggravated by the lack of knowledge on the advantages and disadvantages of bilingual education and on the conditions under which it is useful or harmful.

What has made it difficult to obtain such knowledge is the lack of stable references to the many sorts of bilingual education and the lack of standard measures for the numerous variables.

Schools in the United Kingdom where half the school subjects are taught in English are called bilingual schools. Schools in Canada in which all subjects are taught in English to French-Canadian children are called bilingual schools. Schools in the Soviet Union in which all subjects except Russian are taught in English are bilingual schools, as are schools in which some of the subjects are taught in Georgian and the rest in Russian. Schools in the United States where English is taught as a second language are called bilingual schools, as are parochial schools and even weekend ethnic schools.

Bilingual situations of entirely different patterns have unwittingly been grouped together under bilingual schools and used as a basis for research on bilingual education. This is partly because the concept of "bilingual school" has been used without qualification to cover such a wide range of uses of two languages in education. The term "bilingual school" means many things, even within the same country, and in any discussion is likely to mean different things to different persons. It cannot, therefore, in its present denotation, be taken as an object for research.

Since we are faced with various combinations of various factors, any single definition of bilingual schooling would be either too wide or too narrow to be of any use in planning and research, for what is true for one combination of factors may be untrue for another. And since the causes and effects of bilingual schooling are to be found outside the school, it is important to take these into consideration. What is needed, therefore, is not another definition of bilingual schooling or bilingual education but a classification of the field to account for all possible types—in other words, a typology.

Since bilingual education contains so many variables, a systematic classification of them in the form of a typology could be of help in designing experiments and in talking about bilingual education; it could contribute to the systematization of bilingual school programs and suggest ways of coordinating research and development in this expanding area of inquiry. As a preliminary to any typology, it is necessary to determine how much it will take into account.

Since the terms "bilingual education" and "bilingual school" are used to cover a wide range of different cases, it will be advantageous to have the widest possible inclusion. Otherwise we would have more use for definitions than for a typology. Instead of trying to change any current usage, we shall simply adopt the most inclusive. This will enable us to classify cases ranging from the unilingual education of bilingual children in unilingual communities to the bilingual education of unilingual children in bilingual communities. It will make it possible to include schools where some or all subjects are taught in the other language. It is necessary to isolate and classify all types of bilingual education before measuring their components. This is preliminary to any research.

In order to be of use to researchers, such a typology has to be entirely objective and based on criteria that are observable and quantifiable. Such criteria may be found in the pattern of distribution of languages in 1) the behavior of the bilingual at home, 2) the curriculum in the school, 3) the community of the immediate area within the nation, and 4) in the status of the languages themselves. In other words, bilingual education is a phenomenon in four dimensions. Let us take a look at the first.

1. If we study the language behavior of the learner at home, in relation to the language requirements of his school, we find that, classified according to language usage, there are five types of learners.

A learner who speaks only one language at home and the same language in school, even though it may not be the language of the community, is in quite a different position from that of the learner who uses two languages at home and the same two at school.

Without going into the degree of language proficiency, which will be accounted for below, we may divide our five types into two categories: those covering learners from unilingual homes (U) and those from bilingual homes

(B). In each category, there are the cases where one home language is used as a school language (+S) and those where no home language is used as a school language (-S); in the bilingual category there are the cases where both home languages are used as school languages (+SS). This gives us our five types of learner:

1) Unilingual home: language is school language (U+S).
2) Unilingual home: language is not school language (U-S).
3) Bilingual home: languages include one school language (B+S).
4) Bilingual home: languages exclude school languages (B-S).
5) Bilingual home: languages include both school languages (B+SS).

If we use a small square for the home, a larger one for the school, and shading for the languages, we may visualize the types thus:

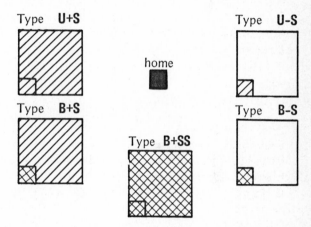

2. Belonging to any one of these five types, each learner, with his acquired language habits, ranging anywhere from complete unilingualism in one language to a complete unilingualism in the other, enters a school where the importance and uses of the languages may not correspond to what they are at home. His place on the scale of bilingual usage—the ratio of his use of his two languages— is likely to be different from that of the school. Only at the extreme ends of the scale, the unilingual school for the corresponding unilingual learner (U+S), are the two points likely to correspond exactly. In all other cases there is no guarantee that the ratio of bilingualism in the entering language behavior of the learner will correspond to the linguistic assumptions of a bilingual curriculum. For the curriculum patterns of bilingual schools vary as to 1) medium of instruction, 2) development, 3) distribution, 4) direction, and 5) change.

1) The medium of instruction may be one language, two languages, or more; in other words, the school may have a single medium (S) or a dual-medium (D) curriculum.

2) The development pattern may be one of maintenance (M) of two or more languages, or of transfer (T) from one medium of instruction to another.
3) The distribution of the languages may be different (D) or equal and the same (E).
4) The direction may be toward assimilation into a dominant culture, toward acculturation (A) or toward integration into a resurgent one, that is, toward irredentism (I). Or it may be neither one nor the other, but simply the maintenance of the language at an equal level. In this case, the languages may be equal but different (D) or equal and equivalent (E).
5) Finally, the change from one medium to another may be complete (C) or gradual (G).

2.1 Medium: single or dual

Schools may be classified according to the languages used to convey knowledge, in contradistinction to the languages taught as subjects. Knowledge may be conveyed in one language, in two, or more.

2.1.1 Single-medium schools (S)

Single-medium schools are bilingual insofar as they serve children whose home language is different from the school language, the area language, or the national language. This may be the only language used for all subjects at all times

2.1.2 Dual-medium schools (D)

In contradistinction to the type of school using a single medium of instruction are those which use two media—both the home and the second language, as the case may be, to convey knowledge. These are the dual-medium schools. Some subjects are taught in one language, some in the other language. In parts of Wales, history, geography, literature, and the fine arts are taught in Welsh; mathematics, social studies, biology, and other sciences are taught in English. Dual-medium schools vary not only in what is taught but also in how much. It is thus that they may be distinguished and classified. They can be compared quantitatively by measuring the amount of time devoted to the use of each language.

So far, we have made only a static or synchronic distinction between bilingual schools—single-medium and dual-medium schools. But, since education is progressive by its nature, these distinctions must also be viewed developmentally, that is, on a time scale.

2.2 Development: transfer or maintenance

If we examine bilingual schools on the time scale, that is, from the point of view of the distribution of the languages from the first to the last year of the school's program—or a section of it—we find two patterns: the transfer pattern and the maintenance pattern, both applying to single and dual-medium schools.

	Development	Transfer	Maintenance
Medium			
Single			
Dual			

2.2.1 Transfer (T)

The transfer pattern has been used to convert from one medium of instruction to another. For example, in some nationality schools in the Soviet Union a child may start all his instruction in his home language, perhaps that of an autonomous Soviet republic, and gradually end up taking all his instruction in the language of the Soviet Union. In schools of this type the transfer may be gradual or abrupt, regular or irregular, the degree of regularity and gradualness being available to distinguish one school from another.

2.2.2 Maintenance (M)

Contrariwise, the object of the bilingual school may be to maintain both languages at an equal level. This is often the pattern when both are languages of wider communication or are subject to legal provisions in the constitution which oblige schools to put both languages on an equal footing. The maintenance may be done by differentiation or by equalization.

2.3 Direction: acculturation or irredentism (A-I)

The direction taken by the curriculum may be toward the language of wider culture—toward acculturation; or toward that of the regional, national, or neo-national culture—the direction of irredentism.

2.4 Distribution: different or equal (D-E)

The subjects in the curriculum may be distributed differently, using different subjects for each, or equally alternating or repeating the instruction from one language to the other.

2.5 Change: complete or gradual (C-G)

The change in direction or distribution may be complete and abrupt—using, for instance, one language one year and the other language the next—or gradual—adding more and more instruction in the other language.

2.6 Curriculum patterns

The interplay of these basic distinctions generates a limited number of possible patterns, as illustrated in the following figure:

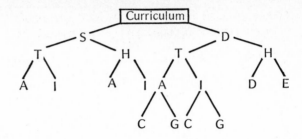

The distinctions between single (S) and dual (D) medium schools; accultural (A) and irredental (I) transfer (T) and maintenance (M); and complete (C) and gradual (G) change generate ten possible types of curriculum patterns. These are: SAT, SAM, SIT, SIM, DAT(C), DAT(G), DIT(C), DIT(G), DDM, and DEM. Let us see what each of these involves.

What is patterned in bilingual schooling is the use of two or more languages; one, all, or neither of which may be native to the learner and have a certain degree of dominance in his home environment. Any of the five types of home-school language relationship described above may enter the curriculum patterns described below. To represent these we shall take the home where the language used may or may not be the school language or one of the school languages.

The curriculum, made up of subjects (vertical columns) and time units in which they are taught (horizontal columns), will be symbolized in a grid:

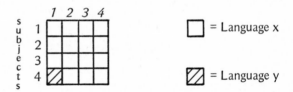

The home is placed beside the school, covering the lower left corner of the grid.

2.6.1 Type SAT (single-medium accultural transfer)

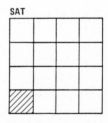

SAT

This type may transfer the language of learning from that of the home to that of the school. It may be completely accultural in that it takes no account of the language of the home. This type of single-medium acculturation is common among schools attended by the children of immigrants; for example, the English medium schools of Italian immigrants in the United States.

2.6.2 *Type SAM (single-medium accultural maintenance)*

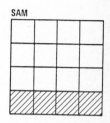

In some cases, as in the bilingual schools of certain parts of Canada, the home language or dominant home language is taught as a subject without, however, being used as a medium of instruction. The maintenance of the home language as a subject may be the avowed purpose, as in the English-medium schools for French Canadians in Western Canada.

2.6.3 *Type SIT (single-medium irredental transfer)*

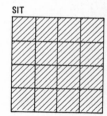

The converse also goes by the name of bilingual schooling. Here the home or dominant home language is used as a medium. Examples of this may be found in the multiple cases of language transfer along the borderlands of Europe, resulting from the reconquest of territory. Witness, for example, the history of transfer of languages of instruction along the frontiers of the former Austro-Hungarian Empires.

2.6.4 *Type SIM (single-medium irredental maintenance)*

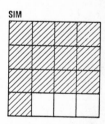

In some schools the dominant or formerly dominant national language is maintained as a school subject, as is the case of English in certain Gaelic schools of the West of Ireland.

The common characteristic of all these single-medium schools is that only one language is used to transmit knowledge—a single language is used as a medium of instruction in all school subjects, although another language may be taught as a school subject, as it is in unilingual schools. For this reason we call these bilingual schools single-medium schools.

2.6.5 Type DAT (dual-medium accultural transfer)

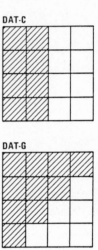

This type, which for obvious reasons of power and prestige is a common type, prepares children to take the rest of their education in a language or a dialect which is not dominant in the home—often a language of wider communication. Many of the schools in the emerging nations were, before they emerged, of this type. English in Africa was sometimes used after the third year. In other parts of Africa it was gradually introduced from the first year.

2.6.6 Type DIT (dual-medium irredental transfer)

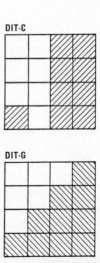

Conversely, in areas long dominated by a foreign language, the medium of instruction may revert to the language of the home, the foreign language being kept as a subject. Early Arabization of schooling in the Sudan illustrates this type.

2.6.7 Type DDM (dual-medium differential maintenance)

In maintaining two languages for different purposes, the difference may be established by subject matter, according to the likely contribution of each

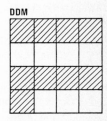

culture. Often the culture-based subjects like art, history, literature, and geography are in the dominant home language. Bilingual schools in certain parts of Wales are of this type.

2.6.8 Type DEM (dual-medium equal maintenance)

In some schools, as those found in certain parts of Belgium, South Africa, and Canada, it has been necessary—often for political reasons—not to distinguish

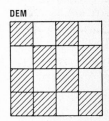

between languages and to give an equal chance to both languages in all domains. This is done by alternating on the time scale—day, week, month, or year—from one language to the other.

* * *

We have seen that, from the point of view of patterning, the curriculum of bilingual schools can be distinguished between single- and dual-medium schools, each following transfer or maintenance patterns—transfer being accultural or irredental, maintenance based on differentiation or equalization.

These patterns may remain stable or evolve, slowly or rapidly, along with changes in pressures and policies. If, for example, one studies the changes in the laws of Louisiana during the past century, one notices several changes in approved patterns of bilingual schooling. The law of 1839 assumes the existence of both French and English single-medium schools. The constitution of 1879 authorizes that all subjects be given in both languages (Article 226), whereas the 1898 constitution authorizes the teaching of French only as a subject (Article 251). In the constitution of 1921 all allusion to French disappears. Recent cultural accords between Louisiana and Quebec again encourage the use of French in instruction.

It is necessary, however, to distinguish between the patterns of language education used in a community and their avowed purposes. For example, a community may have language maintenance as its purpose, but be saddled with a transfer-type curriculum.

Any one of these ten types of curriculum patterns (SAT, SAM, SIT, SIM, DAT-C, DAT-G, DIT-C, DIT-G, DDM, DEM) may function in a number of different types of language areas and national states.

It makes a great difference whether one of the languages used in school is that of the surrounding community, or that of the wider community. The home and community contexts in which the language is used must be taken into consideration if the language is to be used in school, since it is on the assumption of usage and consequent knowledge that the teaching is based. There is a difference, for example, in using English as a medium of instruction in one of the special language schools of Kiev and using it as a medium of instruction in the Ukrainian bilingual schools outside Edmonton.

The following are the possibilities of area and national contextual settings in which the above curriculum patterns may appear.

1. The school may be located in a place where the language of neither the area nor the national language is that of the home.

1

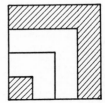

2. It may be in a country where the language of the home but not that of the area is the national tongue.

2

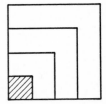

3. Conversely, the language of the area and not of the nation may be that of the home.

3

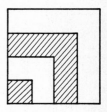

4. Both area and national language may be that of the home.

4

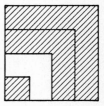

5. The national language may not be that of the home but the area may be bilingual, with both the home and national languages being used.

5

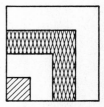

6. Conversely, the country may be bilingual and the area unilingual.

6

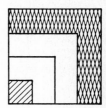

7. Both the area and the country may be bilingual.

7

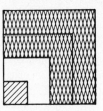

8. The area may be bilingual and the national language may be that of the home.

8

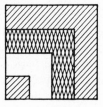

9. Finally, the country may be bilingual and the area language that of the home.

9

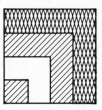

The typology so far elaborated has been based on variations in language patterning in the usage of the nation, the area, and the school. But much depends on which languages are used and what sort.

Certain languages may be worth maintaining regardless of the community. If Spanish and French, for example, are regarded as legitimate specialties for the unilingual, why should they not also be for the bilingual whose other language is one of these? On the other hand, the language may not lead far, even though the probability of community maintenance may be high.

If each of these nine contexts can absorb each of the ten types of curriculum patterns, then there are ninety basically different patterns of bilingual schooling, giving us the typology which appears in the appended figure. Each of these ninety patterns may absorb one or more of the five home-school categories.

If we eliminate mutually exclusive combinations, this leaves some 250 integrated types, ranging from (U-S) SAT 1 to (B+SS) DEM 9.

This should permit us to plan for the elaboration of objective distinctions between bilingual education and bilingual schooling. For example, a bilingual classroom with a DAT curriculum pattern may contain learners with different patterns of bilingual education, depending on the category of relationship with the home language. All five types may find themselves in the same classroom, all doing the same thing. Whether it is wise to put them in the same class is another question; but it cannot be answered until something is known about the different home language behavior patterns of the learners. What type of curriculum pattern is suitable for which type of bilingual is a question yet to be resolved.

A number of these curriculum patterns may be in operation within the same school system, in the same area, or in the same country. Which type of curriculum is most appropriate for which type of area is another question.

Before any of these questions can be answered with any degree of certainty some means must be found of quantifying the variables within each type. All that the typology can do at present is to enable us to distinguish one bilingual educational situation from another in order to observe both of them systematically. But within each type there may be quantitative variations. The DAT type, for example, indicates that some school subjects are taught in one language and some in another; it does not tell us which ones or how many. It is only by using the typology to obtain a more detailed profile of each program of bilingual schooling that it will be possible to find out exactly what is going on in any area in the field of bilingual education as compared with what may be going on someplace else. This is what has been attempted in the appended questionnaire, designed as it is to pattern descriptions of bilingual schooling into the typology for purposes of study and comparison.

The greatest problem of pattern quantification, however, remains in the area of contact between the languages themselves.

The component common to all types at all levels is language. In fact, the entire typology may be viewed as a series of patterns of distribution of two or more languages in the education of the learner, within the home, the school, the area, and the nation.

This common component is itself a variable so that each language appears in each pattern at a certain degree of intensity. Any planning or research design has to take this into account in trying to fit persons into the right patterns. For it makes a difference whether or not a child's proficiency in one or more languages is on a par with that of the rest of the class, and whether the level of proficiency is sufficient for the language to be used as a medium of instruction.

In order to understand the nature of the language variable in bilingual education it is important to make a distinction between the function of the languages, their status, and the linguistic and cultural differences between them.

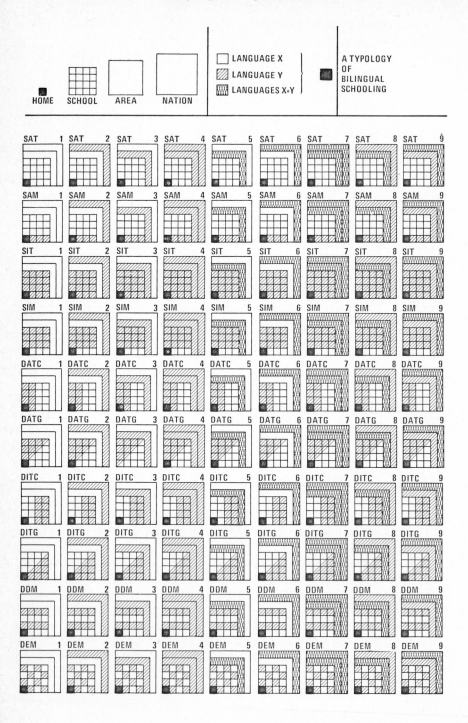

4.1 The functions of the languages

The languages involved in bilingual education may have different functions in the home, in the school, and in the country.

4.1.1 Languages in the home

The learner brings to the school a pattern of language behavior and a configuration of language dominance. It is not only a question of which language is involved, but to what extent.

There is a wide range of possible variation in the competence of the learner in each of his languages. Each language may be of a standard acceptable for unilingual education, or only one may be acceptable to a unilingual teacher, or neither may be comparable in degree to the language proficiency of unilingual speakers.

To study what happens to this entering behavior under the influence of bilingual schooling, standardized screening instruments are needed—both wide-mesh and fine-mesh. We need easily-used and validated wide-mesh screens for quantitative analysis of bilingual population samples. We need fine-mesh screens for small laboratory-type studies and depth analysis of individual cases. There is need for the application of language proficiency measures suitable for bilingual children.

But the child's proficiency may be limited in some domains and extensive in others, depending on his pattern of language behavior outside the school; he may, for instance, speak about certain things in one language to his father and about others in another language to his mother and her relatives. There is need, therefore, for simple scales to measure the degree of dominance in each of the child's domains.

If the child comes from a home where two or more languages are used, he may find it difficult to separate them. The extent and degree of language mixture may vary considerably from one bilingual child to the next, and from one domain to another. Tests will be needed to show how well a bilingual child keeps his languages apart.

4.1.2 Languages in the school

The language component also varies within the school—in the curriculum and in inter-pupil communication.

It is first important to determine the sort and amount of both languages used in the classroom. Two identical curriculum patterns may vary in the proportion of time devoted to each language; this is measurable by simple computation. But they may also vary in the domains in which each language is used. In one curriculum the second language may be used for history and geography; in the other, it may be used for science and mathematics. In practice, each curriculum pattern would have to be quantified for each language in terms of proportion and domain of use. (See appended questionnaire.)

What is the language of the playground and of the street? In inter-pupil communication, it makes a difference how many of the other learners speak the language or languages of the child, and to what extent. It also makes a difference whether or not the child uses the same language at play as he does in school or at home. Some simple measure of the use of the language or languages in the immediate context of the learner's activity would be a help in planning for bilingual education.

4.1.3 Languages in the community

The extent to which the language or languages of the school may be used in the area in which it is located is an important variable in the language education of the child. Some measurement of this is prerequisite to any planning or research into bilingual education.

The role that each language plays in the nation is also of importance. It makes a difference whether both or only one of the languages is rated as official or national. The legal status of a language may be limited to a juridical subdivision of the nation. Both the proportion of the population using each language and its distribution throughout the nation may have some influence on the curriculum pattern selected. So will the international status of the languages and the distance between them.

4.2 The status of the languages

If the languages involved are languages of wider communication, like Spanish and French, the bilingual situation is bound to be different from those involving local languages like Navajo. It is also important to find out the extent to which each language is dynamic or recessive, concentrated or diffuse, at the international, national, and regional levels.

4.2.1 International status

In order to determine the international status of a modern language as one factor in planning the curriculum, languages in a bilingual school may be rated according to five indices:

1) Degree of standardization.
2) Demographic Index: Population figures.
3) Economic Index: Population/Gross national product.
4) Distributional Index: Number and spread of areas in which the language is spoken.
5) Cultural Index: Annual production of printed matter/Cumulative production.

4.2.2 National and regional status

The dialects of the languages used may differ in the extent to which each deviates from the norm or norms that may have been established for them. If two international languages are used as instructional media, the dialect version of one may differ little from the standard speech comprehensible anywhere the language is used. The other language, however, may be available in the area only in a local substandard variety. And this variety may not be the same, either as the one used in the home, the school, or the nation. The Alemanic home dialects of German Switzerland, for example, are far removed from the sort of Standard German taught in Swiss schools.

4.3 *The difference between the languages*

The rapidity with which a learner is likely to understand another language which is used to teach him school subjects depends on the degree of difference or distance between both languages. Because of the close relationship between Portuguese and Spanish, a learner whose mother tongue is Portuguese may take less time to learn to understand instruction given in Spanish than instruction given in more distant languages like English or Chinese.

This same similarity, which facilitates understanding (listening and reading), may be the cause of multiple mistakes in speaking and writing—due to the interference caused by the closeness of both languages. We need measures of the closeness and mutual intelligibility of the languages involved in bilingual instruction and means of predicting the effects of these languages on the comprehension and expression of the bilingual learner.

Regardless of similarities and differences in structure and vocabulary, the two languages may differ considerably in available cultural concepts. For example, Hungarian is genetically as distant from English as is Eskimo; but it is culturally closer, since both English and Hungarian embody many common European cultural concepts, which can be assumed as a basis for bilingual education. Before making use of this variable in research into bilingual education, however, it would be most useful to determine some ways of quantifying it.

Once we have reduced our language variables to appropriate measures within the various types of bilingual education, it will be easier to analyze and classify specific cases.

It is only after we have taken all the variables into account and applied appropriate measures of them that we can achieve any degree of certainty in our planning in this important and complex field. Toward this end it is hoped that this preliminary typology may be of some help. [1]

[1] Earlier versions of this paper were presented to the ESC Conference Planning Committee on Bilingual Education (Univ. of Chicago, 3-5 March 1969) and to the Conference on Bilingual Education (Univ. of Maryland, 27-28 June 1969)—both under the auspices of the Bureau of Research of the United States Office of Education. The sincere gratitude of the author is here extended to those participants whose remarks helped improve the typology, the text, and the questionnaire.

<table>
<tr><td>

Name of institution or school system:

_____

Address: _____

_____

Name of person responding to questionnaire:

_____

</td><td>

CURRICULUM
PATTERNS
IN
BILINGUAL
EDUCATION

</td></tr>
</table>

1. Home language(s) of pupils: _____

2. Language(s) used in teaching: _____

3. Number of months of instruction a year: _____

4. For how many years has program presently described been operating? _____
   Is it experimental ☐ or operational ☐ ?

5. How many schools are included? _____

6. How many learners are involved? _____

7. How many teachers are involved? _____

8. Are there any teachers for special subjects? _____
   Which subjects? _____

9. How long is the subject or class period? (in minutes) _____
   If it varies, please explain. _____

10. Do you select pupils for the bilingual program? _____
    How do you select them? _____

11. Approximately what proportion of learners
    a) understand only the national language? _____
    b) do not understand the national language? _____

12. Does the learner do his written work in a language other than the national
    language? _____ Which language? _____
    At what level? _____ What proportion? _____

13. At the end of the program here described, what type of school or program
    do the students enter? _____

14. Outside the class, how often do your pupils use the national language to
    communicate?

    never   seldom   sometimes   often   always
    ☐   ☐   ☐   ☐   ☐

15. What are some of the main problems you have noticed in operating this
    program? Please feel free to comment at length. _____
    _____   _____

SUBJECTS

	2-year-olds	3-year-olds	4-year-olds	5-year-olds	6-year-olds	Grade 1	Grade 2	Grade 3	Grade 4	Grade 5	Grade 6	Grade 7	Grade 8	Grade 9	Grade 10	Grade 11	Grade 12	Other

° Footnotes and comments: _____

_____

° Most usual language of inter-pupil communication outside of class is: _____

ONE sheet per school

Name of school : _____

_____

INSTRUCTIONS

1. List in left-hand column under *subjects* name of subjects taught in the school. For example:
   English _____
   History _____
   Geography _____

2. Starting with the first year described in your program (horizontal list), indicate by grade the language in which the subject is being taught. Use first letter of language in appropriate square: French (F), Spanish (S), English (E), Navajo (N), etc. For example:
   ENGLISH   E E E E
   HISTORY   S S E E
   GEOGRAPHY S S S S

3. If both languages are systematically used in alternation (e.g. English +Spanish), indicate thus | E/S | and explain system in footnote. Do not include casual use of other language by the teacher.

4. If class teaching is in one language (e.g. Spanish) and pupils schoolbooks in the other, indicate thus: | E |
   | S |

Kindly photocopy questionnaire (p. 432) and above grid, complete both, and send to: Dr. William F. Mackey, CIRB–Laval, 4530 Bibliothèque générale, Cité universitaire, Québec 10, Canada. All completed forms will be gratefully acknowledged. Questionnaire and grid may be used for local surveys; copies of returns or results sent to the above address would be greatly appreciated.

BILINGUAL
EDUCATION IN
SOCIOLINGUISTIC
PERSPECTIVE

JOSHUA A. FISHMAN
and
JOHN LOVAS

How would you define for a lay audience the difference between *bilingual education* programs and *teaching-English-as-a-second-language* programs?

Briefly restate the implicit objective of each of the four categories of bilingual education programs defined by the authors.

What personnel and material resources would be required to establish a program which had *full bilingualism* as its goal?

What attitudes on the part of the parents, teachers, and students would be required to develop a successful *full bilingualism* program?

Bilingual education in the United States currently suffers from three serious lacks: a lack of funds (Title VII is pitifully starved), a lack of personnel (there is almost no optimally trained personnel in this field), and a lack of evaluated programs (curricula, material, methods). However, all in all, we are not discouraged. We live in an age of miracles. If we have reached the stage where even Teachers of English as a Second Language are becoming genuinely interested in bilingual education then, truly, the remaining hurdles should soon fall away and the millenium arrive in our own days!

As public educational agencies finally begin to develop programs in bilingual education for the 'other-than-English-speaking' communities in the United States, those who are committed to the notion that cultural diversity is a natural and valuable asset to this country (and the world) might be expected to simply set up a cheer of approval and to urge that we get on with this shamefully delayed task without further delay. Though I number myself among those who value the maintenance and development of cultural and linguistic diversity in the United States, it is not entirely clear to me that *that* is what most of the existing and proposed bilingual education programs have as their goal. Further,

Reprinted by permission from the *TESOL Quarterly*, 4 (September, 1970) 215–222. This article was first read as a paper at the TESOL convention, March, 1970. Dr. Fishman is dean and university research professor at Yeshiva University; Mr. Lovas is assistant professor in the language arts division at Foothill College, Los Altos, Calif.

even those programs that do explicitly state goals of language and culture maintenance often seem to overlook an important dimension in planning their efforts, an oversight which could seriously limit the success of these bilingual programs per se.

NEEDED: REALISTIC SOCIETAL INFORMATION
FOR REALISTIC EDUCATIONAL GOALS

Since most existing bilingual education programs in the United States provide only educational, psychological or linguistic rationales for their efforts, the insights into societal bilingualism recently advanced by sociolinguists have not yet been incorporated into their designs. Thus, many programs are attempting language shift or language maintenance with little or no conscious awareness of the complexity of such an effort when viewed from a societal perspective.

Let us try to be more explicit about the kinds of difficulties that may develop for bilingual education programs if school planners are not aware of the language situations in the communities to which these programs are directed:

1. The school may attempt a program aimed at language maintenance (e.g., developing high performance in all skill areas of mother tongue and second language, and promoting use of both languages in all major societal domains) in a community actually in the process of language shift. Thus, the school's efforts could be cancelled out because it did not take account of community values or preferences.

2. Conversely, the school may attempt a program aimed at language shift (e.g., developing competence in the second language only and extending its use to all major domains) for a community determined to maintain its own language in many (or all) social domains. Again, the school could fail (or achieve very limited success) because it ignored the sociolinguistic dimension of the problem.

3. Even if the school program and community objectives are fortuitously congruent, the school program may not take account of important characteristics of the speech community, e.g., (a) the existence of one or more nonstandard varieties (in one or more languages) whose school appropriateness as a medium or as a subject must be ascertained from the speech community itself; (b) differential use of these varieties by members of the speech community from one societal domain to another and from one speech network to another.

Schools often adopt simplistic notions, e.g., that there is only one "real" kind of Spanish and one "real" kind of English and that everyone everywhere uses (or should use) this "one kind." Such notions are obviously untrue.

FOUR BROAD CATEGORIES OF BILINGUAL EDUCATION PROGRAMS

It may be instructive to propose a tentative typology of bilingual education programs based on differing kinds of community and school objectives. Each of these types will be briefly illustrated by an existing or proposed bilingual education program for some Spanish-speaking community. In presenting this typology of bilingual education programs, I would like to distinguish clearly between them and English-as-a-second-language programs. The latter are programs which include no instruction in the student's mother tongue as part of the program. Andersson (1968) makes this point quite clear:

> Bilingual education in a Spanish-speaking area may be defined quite simply as that form of schooling which uses both Spanish and English as media of instruction. Bilingual schooling has often been confused with the teaching of English as a second language (ESL).

Another point about this typology is that it is not based on student and schedule characteristics such as proportion of students speaking a certain language and proportion of time devoted to each language (Gaarder, 1967; Michel, 1967; Andersson, 1968). Rather it looks to the kinds of sociolinguistic development implied in the program objectives, and suggests that various kinds of programs assume and lead to particular societal roles for the languages taught.

Type I. Transitional bilingualism

In such a program Spanish is used in the early grades to the extent necessary to allow pupils to "adjust to school" and/or to "master subject matter" until their skill in Englisn is developed to the point that it alone can be used as the medium of instruction. Such programs do not strive toward goals of fluency and literacy in both languages with opportunity throughout the curriculum for the continued improved mastery of each. Rather, they state goals such as "increasing overall achievement of Spanish-speaking students by using both Spanish and English as media of instruction in the primary grades." Such programs (consciously or unconsciously) correspond to a societal objective of language shift and give no consideration to long–range institutional development and support of the mother tongue. An example of such a program can be found in the grant proposal of the Los Cruces (N.M.) School District No. 2 for support of their Sustained Primary Program for Bilingual Students. Perhaps the best way to characterize this program would be to cite the three primary objectives against which the program is to be evaluated:

> 1. To increase the achievement level of Spanish-speaking youngsters through the use of a sustained K-3 program.
> 2. To determine whether Spanish-speaking youngsters achieve more in a program that utilizes instruction in both Spanish and English or in a program that is taught in Spanish only.
> 3. To involve the parents of the Spanish-speaking students in the educational program as advisors and learners, thus enriching the home environment of the child.

The entire proposal makes no mention of measuring performance in Spanish, or continuing Spanish in the curriculum past grade 3, or of making any survey of the language situation in the community.[1] Such programs are basically interested only in transitional bilingualism, i.e., in arriving at the stage of English monolingual educational normality just as soon as is feasible without injuring the pupil or arousing the community.

Type II. Monoliterate bilingualism
Programs of this type indicate goals of development in both languages for aural-oral skills, but do not concern themselves with literacy skills in the mother tongue. Thus, such programs emphasize developing fluency in Spanish as a link between home and school, with the school providing recognition and support for the language in the domains of home and neighborhood. but it does not concern itself with the development of literacy skills in the non-English mother tongue which would increase the formal domains in which the child could use the language. This type of program is intermediate in orientation between language shift and language maintenance. The likely societal effect of such a program might be one of language maintenance in the short run, but, given the exposure of students to American urban society which stresses and rewards literacy, it might well lead to shift. One example of such a program can be found in Christine McDonald's proposal for the El Rancho Unified School District in Pico Rivera, California. The program is designed for pre-school children and their parents, and would focus particularly on reading-readiness activities. The proposal envisions a teacher fluent in Spanish and acceptance of the parents' and children's home language. However, the focus of the program would be on ultimately developing literacy in English with no reference to similar development in Spanish. Bilingual programs for American Indians frequently fall into this category, because, in many instances, there is no body of written literature for the child to learn in his mother tongue. Obviously the intellectual imbalance between English literacy and mother tongue illiteracy poses a difficult situation for any maintenance-oriented community, particularly if it is exposed to occupational mobility through English.

Type III. Partial bilingualism
This kind of program seeks fluency and literacy in both languages, but literacy in the mother tongue is restricted to certain subject matter, most generally that related to the ethnic group and its cultural heritage. In such a program, reading and writing skills in the mother tongue are commonly developed in relation to the social sciences, literature, and the arts, but not in science and mathematics.[2]

[1] Other transitional programs, as mentioned by John and Horner (1970), are the Follow-Through Project at Corpus Christi, Texas, and the various informal programs for Puerto Rican students in New York City and elsewhere which depend on the use of "community aides" in the classroom.

[2] The Rough Rock Demonstration School (Navajo) initially tended to follow a program of this kind (John and Horner, 1970).

This kind of program is clearly one of language maintenance coupled with a certain effort at culture maintenance (perhaps even cultural development should the program result in the production of poetry and other literary art forms). In general, the program in the Dade County (Florida) Public Schools (as described in its administrative guidelines and also in Rojas, 1966) exemplifies this type of bilingual education. The program provides special instruction in English in all skills for all Spanish-speaking students who need it. Additionally, the program provides formal instruction in reading and writing Spanish with emphasis on Spanish literature and civilization as subject matter. Other areas of the curriculum do not utilize Spanish as a medium of instruction. Other programs of this type are conducted by numerous American ethnic groups in their own supplementary or parochial schools (Fishman, 1966). Such programs imply that while the non-English mother tongues are serious vehicles of modern literate thought, they are not related to control of the technological and economic spheres. The latter are considered to be the preserve of the majority whose language must be mastered if these spheres are to be entered. Nationalist protest movements since the mid-nineteenth century have consistently rejected any such limiting implication.[3]

Type IV. Full bilingualism

In this kind of program, students are to develop all skills in both languages in all domains. Typically, both languages are used as media of instruction for all subjects (except in teaching the languages themselves). Clearly this program is directed at language maintenance and development of the minority language. From the viewpoint of much of the linguistically and psychologically oriented literature, this is the ideal type of program, as illustrated by these comments:

> Since one of our purposes is as nearly as possible to form and educate balanced, co-ordinate bilinguals—children capable of thinking and feeling in either of two languages independently—instruction should, we believe, be given in both languages . . . (Michel, 1967).

> An education, both in and out of school, which respects these basic principles [to gain "progressive control of both languages" and "a sympathetic understanding of both cultures"] should hopefully produce after us a generation of bilinguals who really are fully bilingual as well as bicultural. (Andersson, 1967).

Programs such as these enable us to examine the difference between developing *balanced competency in individuals* and producing a *balanced bilingual* society. Though bilingual societies might find individuals with highly developed competency in all skills and domains very useful in a variety of interlocutor roles (teachers, translators, business representatives), a fully balanced bilingual speech community seems to be a theoretical impossibility because balanced

---

[3]Mackey (1969) refers to such limited bilingual programs as being of the 'Dual-Medium Differential Maintenance' Type.

competence implies languages that are functionally equivalent and no society can be motivated to maintain two languages if they are really functionally redundant. Thus, this type of program does not seem to have a clearly articulated goal with respect to *societal* reality.

Several examples of this type of program exist, but all of them are small pilot or experimental programs. The Coral Way Elementary School (Dade County, Florida) and the Laredo Unified Consolidated Independent School District (Texas) are two frequently cited instances which exemplify this kind of program (Gaarder, 1967; Michel, 1967; Andersson, 1968). In the Coral Way School, students receive instruction in all subjects in both languages, English in the morning from one teacher, Spanish in the afternoon from another teacher. At Laredo Unified, students receive all instruction from the same teacher who uses English half the day and Spanish the other half. The evidence so far suggests that these programs are quite successful, but looking at them from the view of the functional needs of the community, there is serious question whether they should serve as ideal models for large-scale programs. As social policy they may well be self-defeating in that they require and often lead to significant social separation for their maintenance rather than merely for their origin.[4]

NEEDED: SOCIETAL INFORMATION IN ESTABLISHING A BILINGUAL EDUCATION PROGRAM

Various types of bilingual education programs make implicit assumptions about the kind of language situation that exists in a given community and about the kind of language situation that ought to exist in that community. Program developers should make their assumptions explicit and attempt to test the validity of these assumptions by gathering various kinds of data regarding the societal functions of community languages and existing attitudes toward them, both before and during the development of bilingual education programs.

Gaarder (1967) suggests that the way in which a school or community goes about establishing a bilingual program will largely define the structure the program will take. That assumption underlies the suggestions here for gathering information beyond that normally available in school records and county census data as part of the process of deciding whether to establish a bilingual program and what kind of program to establish, if the first decision is affirmative. In this early stage of development the following information seems minimal, if the school and community are going to make conscious, explicit decisions about an appropriate bilingual program:

1. A survey that would establish the languages and varieties employed by both parents and children, by societal domain or function.

[4]Mackey (1969) has dubbed such programs as being 'Dual-Medium Equal Maintenance' in type. The Rough Rock Demonstration School currently tends in this direction.

2. Some rough estimate of their relative performance level in each language, by societal domain.

3. Some indication of community (and school staff) attitudes toward the existing languages and varieties, and toward their present allocation to domains.

4. Some indication of community (and school staff) attitudes toward changing the existing language situation.[5]

This information would allow citizens, board members, administrators, and teachers to decide which type of program (or combination of program types) would be most appropriate to the community, both in terms of the *existing* language situation and in terms of the *direction and extent of change* in that situation.

Once a decision to develop a program is made, more detailed information would be required, particularly for determining the materials and methods most appropriate to achieving the program's objectives. Such information might include the following:

1. A contrastive analysis of the major languages and/or varieties used in the community and any languages or varieties being introduced in the school.

2. An analysis of the phonological, grammatical, and lexical variables that most clearly distinguish varieties.

3. More detailed measures of student performance by language and domain.

Data of this sort would allow curriculum specialists and in-service training instructors to choose and/or develop instructional materials and methods appropriate to the students in the community, ideally avoiding the traps of (a) teaching them what they *already* know or (b) teaching them what they don't want at the expense of *developing greater skill in the domains which the community recognizes and wants developed.*

CONCLUSIONS

After a hiatus of more than half a century (Fishman, 1968a) we are just now re-entering the first stages of genuine bilingual education at public expense. We are just overcoming the deceptive and self-deluding view that teaching English as a second language is, in itself, all there is to bilingual education. We are just beginning to seriously ponder different curricular models of real bilingual education. This paper stresses that such models have societal implications, make societal assumptions, and require societal data for their implementation and evaluation.

We are just beginning to realize that public schools should belong to parents, to pupils, to communities. We are just beginning to suspect that these may be legitimately interested in more than learning English and affording better and

---

[5] For an introduction to domain-related applied sociolinguistic description see Fishman, Cooper, and Ma (1968b). For the theory underlying such description see Fishman (1967).

bigger TV sets. We may soon arrive at the disturbing conclusion that it is not necessarily treasonous for pupils, teachers, parents, and principals to speak to each other in languages other than English, even when they *are* in school, even when they *know* English too, and even when the languages involved are their *own mother tongues*!

However, we still have a very long way to go. We still do not realize that the need for bilingual education must not be viewed as merely a disease of the poor and the disadvantaged. We still do not realize that alternative curricular approaches to bilingual education make tacit assumptions and reach tacit decisions concerning the social roles of the languages (or language varieties) to be taught. We still do not realize that these assumptions and decisions can be empirically confirmed or disconfirmed by sociolinguistic data pertaining to the communities that our programs claim to serve. By and large, we still do not know how to collect the societal data we need for enlightened decision-making in the field of bilingual education.

We are learning all of these things the hard way—which may be the only way important lessons are learned in the world of public education—but we are learning! Thank God for poor Mexican-American parents and their increasingly short tempers. Because of their number and their growing organization our grandchildren have a chance of getting a bilingual public education in the United States without necessarily being either poor or even Hispanic.

REFERENCES

Andersson, Theodore. "The Bilingual in the Southwest." *Florida FL Reporter,* 5:2 (1967), 3.
——. "Bilingual Elementary Schooling: A Report to Texas Educators." *Florida FL Reporter,* 6:2 (1968), 3–4 ff.
——, and Mildred Boyer. *Bilingual Schooling in the United States.* Washington, USGPO, 1970.
Fishman, J. A. *Language Loyalty in the United States,* Chapter 5: "The Ethnic Group School and Mother Tongue Maintenance," pp. 92–126. The Hague: Mouton, 1966.
——. "Bilingualism With and Without Diglossia; Diglossia With and Without Bilingualism." *Journal of Social Issues,* 23 (1967), 29–38.
——. "The Breadth and Depth of English in the United States," in *Language and Language Learning,* Albert H. Marckwardt, ed., pp. 43–53. National Council of Teachers of English, 1968.
——, R. L. Cooper, Roxana Ma, et al. *Bilingualism in the Barrio.* New York, Yeshiva University, Report to USOE under contract OEC-1-7-062817-0297, 1968.
Gaarder, A. B. "Organization of the Bilingual School." *Journal of Social Issues,* 23 (1967), 110–120.
John, Vera, and Vivian Horner. Early Childhood Bilingual Education. New York, Modern Language Association, 1970.
Las Cruces School District No. 2, Las Cruces, New Mexico: *Sustained Primary Program for Bilingual Students,* ERIC No. ED 001 869.
Mackey, William F. *A Typology of Bilingual Education* [Article 43 in this collection. Eds.]

McDonald, Christina. *A Tentative Program for Combining the Education of Preschool Mexican-American Children with Parent Education.* Pico Rivera, Calif. El Rancho Unified School District, 1964.

Michel, Joseph. "Tentative Guidelines for a Bilingual Curriculum." *Florida FL Reporter,* 5:3 (1967), 13–16.

Planning for Non-English Speaking Pupils. Miami: Dade County Public Schools, 1963. ERIC No. 002 529.

Preschool Instructional Program for Non-English Speaking Children. Austin: Texas Educational Agency, 1964. ERIC No. ED 001 091.

Pryor, G. C. *Evaluation of the Bilingual Project of Harlandale Independent School District, San Antonio, Texas in the First and Second Grades of Four Elementary Schools During 1967–68 School Year.* San Antonio: Our Lady of the Lake College, 1968.

Rojas, Pauline. "The Miami Experience in Bilingual Education." *On Teaching English to Speakers of Other Languages,* Series II, Virginia F. Allen, ed., pp. 43–45. National Council of Teachers of English, 1966.

Name and Subject Index

(Italic numerals indicate the page limits of an article by the author whose name appears as the entry.)

A

Abercrombie, David, 255*n.*, *259-268*
Adaptation, 95
  sample of, 114-119
Age as a factor in second-language learning, 404-405
Allen, George, 347*n.*
Allen, Virginia French, *94-97*
American English and British English, 234-242
Anderson, D. F., 351, 352
Andersson, Theodore, 414*n.*, 436, 438, 439
Anisfeld, Elizabeth, 380, 394, 399*n.*, 406
Anisfeld, Moshe, 398
Anomie, 396-398
Anthony, Edward M., *4-8*, 8, 98, 133*n.*, 282*n.*
Any/some distribution, 68-69
Approach, 18
  audiolingual, 5, 23-24, 145-152, 404
  defined, 5-6
Aptitude test, 315, 405
Arabic, 299-301
Arapoff, Nancy, *199-207*
Army Specialized Training Program, 24
Arnauld, Antoine, 62*n.*
Attitudes:
  of listener, 386ff
  of second-language learner, 406
  in second-language learning, 403ff
Audiolingual approach (*see* Approach)
Audiolingualism, 35-36, 98-101, 133
    (*See also* Method, audiolingual)
Aural-oral (*see* Audiolingual)
Ausubel, David P., 53

B

Bandura, Albert, 42*n.*
Baranyi, Helmut A., 404
Barik, H. C., 397
Behavioreme, 91
Bell, Alan P., 407*n.*
Bereiter, Carl, 388
Berger, Emanual, 404
Bilingual, reactions of a, 399
Bilingual education, 414-433
  curriculum patterns in, 424ff
  defined, 436
  goals of, 434ff
  and sociolinguistics, 434-441
  typology of, 414-433, 435-439
Bilingualism, 385-403
Bills, Robert E., 407*n.*
Bloomfield, Leonard, 24, 276
Bogo, N., 394
Bolinger, Dwight M., *20-36*, 39*n.*
Bosco, Frederick J., 112, *369-384*
Bowen, J. Donald, 186, *242-250*
Boyer, M., 414*n.*
Brière, Eugène J., *321-330*
Brooks, Cleanth, 297*n.*
Brooks, Nelson, 130, 131*n.*
Buka, M., 166
Bull, William E., 55
Bumpass, Faye L., 90
Buros, O. K., 331
Burrows, Elaine, 51

C

Cannon, Garland, 32*n.*
Carroll, George R., *178-184*